D0208668

Library of Congress Cataloging-in-Publication Data

Cunningham, Steve.
Computer graphics : programming in OpenGL for visual communication / Steve Cunningham.
p. cm.
Includes bibliographical references and index.
ISBN 0-13-145254-1
1. Computer graphics. 2. OpenGL. 3. Three-dimensional display systems. I. Title.
T385.C854 2006
006.6'6—dc22 2006034153

Vice President and Editorial Director, ECS: *Marcia J. Horton*
Executive Editor: *Tracy Dunkelberger*
Associate Editor: *Carole Snyder*
Editorial Assistant: *Christianna Lee*
Executive Managing Editor: *Vince O'Brien*
Managing Editor: *Camille Trentacoste*
Production Editor: *Karen Ettinger*
Director of Creative Services: *Paul Belfanti*
Creative Director: *Juan Lopez*
Managing Editor, AV Management and Production: *Patricia Burns*
Art Editor: *Gregory Dulles*
Cover Art Director: *Jayne Conte*
Cover Designer: *Bruce Kenselaar*
Cover Photo: *Steve Cunningham*
Manufacturing Manager, ESM: *Alexis Heydt-Long*
Manufacturing Buyer: *Lisa McDowell*
Executive Marketing Manager: *Robin O'Brien*
Marketing Assistant: *Mack Patterson*

Pearson Prentice Hall
Pearson Education, Inc.
Upper Saddle River, New Jersey 07458

10 9 8 7 6 5 4 3 2 1
ISBN 0-13-145254-1

Pearson Education Ltd., *London*
Pearson Education Singapore, Pte. Ltd.
Pearson Education Canada, Inc., *Toronto*
Pearson Education—Japan, *Tokyo*
Pearson Education, Inc., *Upper Saddle River, New Jersey*
Pearson Education Australia Pty. Ltd., *Sydney*
Pearson Education North Asia Ltd., *Hong Kong*
Pearson Educación de Mexico, S.A. de C.V.
Pearson Education Malaysia, Pte. Ltd.

Computer Graphics

Programming in OpenGL® for Visual Communication

STEVE CUNNINGHAM

California State University, Stanislaus
and
Grinnell College

Upper Saddle River, New Jersey

To Mike Bailey for his outstanding example in computer graphics education and his help with many of the ideas that led to this book

The cover is a photograph of the formation "Stone Monkey Gazing over the Sea of Clouds" in the Yellow Mountains in Anhui Province, China. The photograph was taken by the author shortly before sunrise, the traditional time to view the sea of clouds in these mountains, in June, 2006. Below is a photograph (in black and white) of a plaque marking the best view of this formation.

The author chose this cover to honor Prof. Jiaoying Shi of Zhejiang University, a longtime leader in computer graphics in China, and because it looks like a student who is deeply contemplating a project (in computer graphics, of course!)

Contents

Preface

Computer graphics is one of the most exciting ways that computing has made an impact on the world. From the simple ways that spreadsheets allow you to create charts to see data, to the ways graphics has enhanced entertainment by providing new kinds of cartoons and special effects, to the ways graphics has enabled us to see and understand scientific principles, computer graphics is everywhere we turn. This important presence has come from the greatly improved graphics hardware and software that is found in current computing systems. With these advances, computer graphics has emerged from being a highly technical field needing very expensive computers and frame buffers and requiring programmers to master all the mathematics and algorithms needed to create an image. It has become a field that allows the graphics programmer to think and work at a much higher level of modeling and to create effective images that communicate effectively with the user. We believe that the beginning computer graphics course should focus on how the student can learn to create effective communications with computer graphics, including motion and interaction, and that the more technical details of algorithms and mathematics for graphics should be saved for more advanced courses.

What Is Computer Graphics?

Computer graphics is involved in any work that uses computation to create images, whether those images are still or moving; interactive or fixed; on film, video, screen, or print. This makes it a very broad field, encompassing many kinds of uses in the creative, commercial, and scientific worlds. The breadth of the field has led to the development of many kinds of tools to create and manipulate images for all these different areas. And finally, the large number of tools and applications means that one could learn many different things about computer graphics.

Most of the books on computer graphics fall into one of two groups. The first is the traditional academic textbook on graphics, emphasizing the algorithms and techniques used for modeling, rendering, and viewing. These are important concepts, but an emphasis on how images are made can take time away from considering what images mean. The second kind of book focuses on the applications used to create images, particularly in the commercial and entertainment areas. Here the capabilities and limitations of the applications shape the coursework, and you can do little that is not designed into the application. Basic concepts can be included in studies of applications, but they often take second place to a focus on learning how the application works.

This book takes something of a middle road between algorithms and applications. We do not give a major emphasis to the details of the algorithms and techniques involved in computer graphics, and we do not deal with applications for creating images. Rather, we view computer graphics as the art and science of creating synthetic images by programming the geometry, appearance, and presentation of the contents of the images, and by displaying the results of that programming on appropriate devices that support graphical output and interaction. This focus on creating images by programming means that we must understand something of basic concepts as we learn about representing graphical and interaction concepts in ways that can be used by the computer. This focus on programming to create images both empowers and limits the graphics student, because it places the student in control of the whole process of image making.

But the process of creating images is not the end in itself; the images are important because they communicate information to the viewer, and so our study must also include a consideration of effective visual communication. So the work of the graphics professional in creating images is to understand the content the images are to communicate, to develop appropriate representations for the geometric objects that are to make up the images, to assemble these objects into an appropriate geometric space where they can have the proper relationships with one as needed for the image, to define and present the look of each of the objects as part of that scene, to specify how the scene is to be viewed, and to specify how the scene as viewed is to be displayed on the graphic device. The programming may be done in many ways, but in current practice it typically uses a graphics API that supports the necessary modeling and does most of the detailed work of rendering the scene that is defined through the programming. A number of graphics APIs are available, but the OpenGL API is probably most commonly used currently and gives us a good platform to learn how to create effective images.

In addition to the creation of the modeling, viewing, and look of the scene, the graphics professional has two other important tasks. Because a static image does not present as much information as a moving image, it may be important to design some motion into the scene—that is, to define some animation for the image. And because the viewer may want or need to be able to control the content of the image, the way the image is seen, or the kind of computation that is done for the image, it may be important to design ways for the user to interact with the scene as it is presented. These additional tasks are also supported by the graphics API.

What Is a Graphics API?

An API is an *Application Programming Interface*—a set of tools that allow a programmer to work in an application area. The API's tools are oriented to the tasks of the application area and allow a programmer to design applications using the concepts of the area without having to deal with the details of the computer system. Among the advantages of an API is that it hides the details of any one computer system and allows the programmer to develop applications that will work on any of a wide range of systems. So a **graphics** API is a set of tools that allow a programmer to write applications that include interactive computer graphics operations without dealing with the details of graphics operations or with system details for tasks such as window handling and interactions.

Besides covering the basic ideas of interactive computer graphics, this book will introduce you to the OpenGL graphics API and to give you a number of examples that will help you understand the capabilities that OpenGL provides and will allow you to learn how to integrate graphics programming into your other work. Like most APIs, OpenGL supports quite advanced work that goes beyond the level we will use in a text for a beginning course; resources at `http://www.opengl.org/` will be useful if you want to look at the API in more depth.

Why Do Computer Graphics?

Computer graphics has many faces, so there are many reasons why one might want to use computer graphics in his or her work. Many of the most prominent uses of computer graphics are to create images for the sciences (scientific visualization, explanations to the public) and entertainment (movies, video games, special effects), for creative or aesthetic work (art, interactive installations), for commercial purposes (advertising, communication, product design), or for general communication (animated weather displays, information graphics). The processes described in this book are all fundamental to each of these applications, although some of the applications will require the kinds of sophistication or realism in images that are not possible through simple API programming.

In all of these application areas, and more, there is a fundamental role for computer graphics in solving problems. Problem solving is a basic process in all human activity, so computer graphics can play a fundamental role in almost any area, as shown in Figure 1. This figure describes what occurs as someone:

- identifies a problem
- addresses the problem by building a model that represents it and allows it to be considered more abstractly
- identifies a way to represent the problem geometrically
- creates an image from that geometry so that the problem can be seen
- uses the image to understand the problem or the model and to try to understand a possible solution

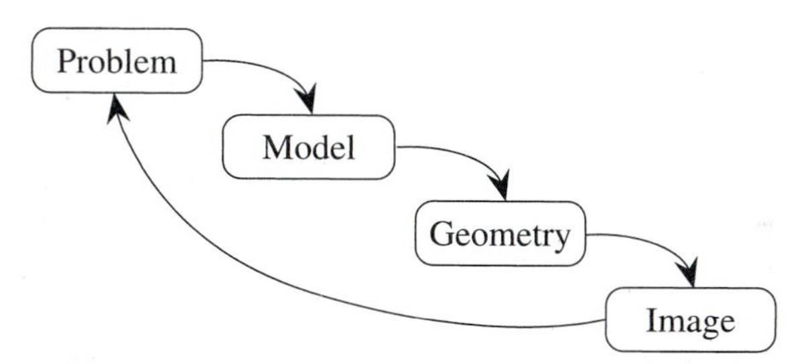

Figure 1 Computer graphics in the problem-solving process.

The image that represents a problem can be made in many ways. One of the classic uses of images in problem solving is simply to sketch an image—a diagram or picture—to communicate the problem to a colleague so it can be discussed informally. (It is folk wisdom that restaurants are not happy to see a group of scientists or mathematicians come to dinner because they write diagrams on the tablecloth!) But an image can also be made with computer graphics, and this is especially useful when it is important to share the idea with a larger audience. If the model permits it, this image may be an animation or an interactive display so that the problem can be examined more generally than a single image would permit. That image, then, can be used by the problem solver or the audience to gain a deeper understanding of the model and hence of the problem, and the problem can be refined iteratively and a more sophisticated model created, and the process can continue.

This process is the basis for all of the discussions in Chapter 9 on graphical problem solving in the sciences, but it may be applied to more general application areas. In allowing us to bring the visual parts of our brain and our intelligence to a problem, computer graphics gives us a powerful tool to think about the world. In the words of Mike Bailey of Oregon State University, computer graphics gives us a "brain wrench" that magnifies the power of our mind, just as a physical wrench magnifies the power of our hands.

Overview of the Book

This book is a textbook for a beginning computer graphics course for students who have a good programming background, equivalent to a full year of programming courses. We use C as the programming language in our examples because it is the most common language for developing applications with OpenGL, though the course could use C++ and extend some of the processes here into an object-oriented approach. The book can be used by students with no previous computer graphics experience and with less mathematics experience and advanced computer science studies than the traditional computer graphics course. Because we focus on graphics programming rather than on algorithms and techniques, we have fewer instances of data structures and other computer science techniques. This means that this text can be used for a computer graphics course that can be taken earlier in a student's computer science studies than the traditional graphics course, or for self-study by anyone with a sound programming background. In particular, this book can be used as a text for a computer graphics course at the community college level.

Many, if not most, of the examples in this book are taken from sources in the sciences, and we include a chapter that discusses several kinds of scientific and mathematical applications of computer graphics. This emphasis makes this book appropriate for courses in computational science or for computer science programs that want to develop ties with other science programs on campus, particularly programs that want to provide science students with a background that will support development of computational science or scientific visualization work. It has been tempting to use the word *visualization* somewhere in the title of this book, but we would reserve that word for material that is primarily focused on the science with only a sidelight on the graphics; because we reverse that emphasis, the role of scientific visualization is in the application of the computer graphics.

The book is organized along fairly traditional lines, treating projection, viewing, modeling, rendering, lighting, shading, and many other aspects of the field. These are all structured into the scene graph, a construct that is extremely useful to help the programmer organize scenes. There is also an emphasis on the graphics pipeline to produce images. Besides the basic techniques of creating images, the book has an emphasis on using computer graphics to address real problems and to communicate results effectively to the viewer. As we move through this material, we describe a full range of general concepts and techniques in computer graphics and show how the OpenGL API provides the graphics programming tools that implement these principles and techniques. Our goal is to give the student both an understanding of graphics concepts and skill in using a graphics API (application programming interface) to implement graphics operations and create effective images for communicating with a viewer. We are mindful of the limitations of a single course, so while we also outline or sketch the algorithms and principles that lie behind the way the techniques are implemented, we do not develop these as fully as a more theoretical text would. Your instructor will provide these in more detail if he or she finds it useful to do so.

We have tried to match the sequence of chapters in the book to the sequence we would expect to be used in a beginning computer graphics course, and in some cases the presentation of one chapter will depend on your knowing the content of an earlier chapter. However, in other cases it will not be critical that earlier chapters have been covered. It should be pretty obvious if other chapters are assumed, and we may make that assumption explicit in some chapters. Assuming that the course will want to cover interactive graphics, we believe that all the chapters through Chapter 7 on interaction should be covered (though the mathematics chapter, Chapter 4, may be treated as a reference), as well as Chapter 10 on the graphics pipeline. Beyond that, the chapters are relatively independent, and you may choose them as you will.

The book focuses on computer graphics programming with a graphics API and in particular uses the OpenGL API to implement the basic concepts that it presents. Each chapter includes a general discussion of a topic in graphics as well as a discussion of the way the topic is handled in OpenGL. However, another graphics API might also be used, with the OpenGL discussion serving as an example of the way an API could work. Many of the fundamental algorithms and techniques that are at the root of computer graphics are covered only at the level they are needed to understand questions of graphics programming. This differs from most computer graphics textbooks that place a great deal of emphasis on understanding these algorithms and techniques. We recognize the importance of these for persons who want to develop a deep knowledge of the subject and suggest that a second graphics course can provide that knowledge. We believe that the experience provided by API-based graphics programming will help you understand the importance of these algorithms and techniques as they are developed and will equip you to work with them more fluently than if you met them with no previous background.

This book includes several features that are not found in most beginning textbooks. These features support a course that fits the current programming practice in computer graphics. The discussions in this book focus on 3D graphics and almost completely omit uniquely 2D techniques. It has been traditional for computer graphics courses to start with 2D graphics and move up to 3D because some of the algorithms and techniques have been easier to grasp at the 2D level, but without that concern it is easier to begin by covering 3D concepts and discuss 2D graphics as the special case where all the modeling happens in the *X-Y* plane.

Modeling is a very fundamental topic in computer graphics, and there are many different ways that one can model objects for graphical display. This book uses the standard beginning approach of focusing on polygon-based modeling because that approach is supported by OpenGL and most other graphics APIs. The discussion on modeling in this book places an important emphasis on the scene graph as a fundamental tool in organizing the work needed to create a graphics scene. The concept of the scene graph allows the student to design the transformations, geometry, and appearance of a number of complex components such that they can be implemented quite readily in code, even if the graphics API itself does not support the scene graph directly. This is particularly important for hierarchical modeling, but it also provides a unified design approach to modeling and has some very useful applications for placing the eyepoint in the scene and for managing motion and animation.

A key feature of this book is an emphasis on using computer graphics to create effective visual communication. This recognizes the key role that computer graphics has taken in developing an understanding of complex problems and in communicating this understanding to others, from small groups of working scientists to the general public. This emphasis is usually missing from computer graphics textbooks, although we expect that most instructors include this somehow in their courses. The discussion of effective communication is integrated throughout several of the basic chapters in the book, because it is an important consideration in graphics modeling, viewing, color, and interaction. We believe that a systematic discussion of this subject will help prepare students for more effective use of computer graphics in their future professional lives, whether this is in technical areas in computing or is in areas where there are significant applications of computer graphics.

This book also places a good deal of emphasis on creating interactive displays. Most computer graphics textbooks cover interaction and the creation of interactive graphics. Historically this was a difficult area to implement because it involved writing or using specialized device drivers, but with the growing importance of OpenGL and other graphics APIs this area has become much more common. Because we are concerned with effective communication, we believe it is critically important to understand the role of interaction in communicating information with graphics. Our discussion of interaction includes a general treatment of event-driven programming and covers the events and callbacks used in OpenGL, but it also discusses the role of interaction in creating effective communications. This views interaction in the context of the task that is to be supported, not just the technology being studied, and thus integrates it into the overall context of the book.

You will probably notice that the figures in this book are not as sophisticated as those in most computer graphics texts. This is deliberate. We believe that if we are talking about creating graphical communications with the level of OpenGL that the book presents, we should make the figures with this same level. We hope that you will find these "homemade" figures effective and that perhaps you may be challenged to create illustrations of your own that may well be better than ours.

This book's approach, discussing computer graphics principles without covering the details of the algorithms and mathematics that implement them, differs from those of most computer graphics textbooks that place a much larger emphasis on understanding these graphics algorithms and techniques. We recognize the importance of these ideas for persons who want to develop a deep knowledge of the subject and suggest that a second graphics course can provide that knowledge. We believe that the experience provided by API-based graphics programming will help the student understand the importance of these algorithms and techniques as they are developed and will equip someone to work with them more fluently than if they were covered with no computer graphics background.

Outcomes

When you have finished with a computer graphics course based on this book, we believe that you should have the following knowledge or skills:

- An understanding of how graphical information is represented to a graphics system and encoded by the system to create images
- An understanding of how to organize graphical information in a program in order to create images with a graphics API
- An understanding of how to use events in a graphics system to create interactive graphics displays

- An understanding of the issues involved in making images that communicate effectively to a viewer
- Skill at using the OpenGL graphics API to create effective images

We hope that you will have applied the principles and skills you are learning to an area where computer graphics makes an important contribution, and that you will understand what that contribution is. We support this for the sciences but recognize that there are many other areas where this is also the case. If a course uses this text with an application area other than the sciences, the author would like to hear of it.

Credits

The initial development of this project was supported by National Science Foundation grant DUE-9950121. All opinions, findings, conclusions, and recommendations in this work are those of the author and do not necessarily reflect the views of the National Science Foundation. The author also gratefully acknowledges sabbatical support from California State University Stanislaus and thanks the San Diego Supercomputer Center (SDSC), most particularly Mike Bailey (now at Oregon State University) for hosting the sabbatical where this work was started and for providing significant assistance with both visualization and science content. Kris Stewart of San Diego State University, Angela Shiflet of Wofford College, Rozeanne Steckler and Kim Baldridge of SDSC, and Ian Littlewood of CSU Stanislaus provided helpful contributions to the chapter on graphics in the sciences. Sam Rebelsky of Grinnell College provided helpful comments. Sampson Asare of the University of Botswana, Petros Mashwama of the University of Swaziland, and Marcelo Zuffo of the University of São Paolo gave the author opportunities to use early versions of the manuscript in workshops. Several of the author's students at CSU Stanislaus and San Diego State University provided important examples and insight for this project. Ken Brown was particulary helpful with several figures and concepts in this manuscript. The author also thanks his students Mike Dibley, Ben Eadington, Jordan Maynard, and Virginia Muncy for their contributions through examples.

The author also wishes to thank the many reviewers who have looked at early stages of the book. They gave help at many levels, from general concepts to very detailed suggestions and corrections. To the extent that this book is successful, my students and colleagues and the reviewers get much of the credit; if anything in the book is not successful, that comes back to the author.

Steve Cunningham
Coralville, Iowa

0 Getting Started

This chapter provides a basic overview of the concepts of computer graphics so that you can have a frame of reference as you read the rest of the book. It focuses on three key content areas that give you the background for the work in this book.

The first key area is looking at visual communication through computer graphics. Throughout the book are sections discussing how most chapter topics support visual communication, because we believe that communication is the most important reason for working with computer graphics. In fact, in a later chapter on computer graphics in the sciences (Chapter 9), the main idea is creating effective communications on science. As we get started in our study of computer graphics, we lay out some general communication principles to keep in mind as we create computer graphics displays.

The second key area is the discussion of three-dimensional geometry, managed by the 3D geometry pipeline, and the concept of appearance for computer graphics objects, managed by the rendering pipeline. The geometry pipeline shows you the key information you must specify in order to create an image and the kind of computation a graphics system must perform in order to present that image. We discuss some of the ways appearance can be specified, but we will wait until a later chapter (Chapter 10) to present the rendering pipeline.

The third key area is a presentation of the way a graphics program is laid out for the OpenGL graphics API, the key API we use in this book. Here you will see both the general structure of an OpenGL program and a complete example of a program that models a particular problem and produces a particular animated image. In that example you will see how the information for the geometry pipeline and the appearance information are defined for the program. In the chapter exercises, you will be able to try out a number of changes to the program and see how these changes affect its operation.

Visual Communications and Computer Graphics

Computer graphics has achieved remarkable things in communicating information to specialists, to informed communities, and to the public at large. This is different from the entertainment field, where computer graphics gets a lot of attention, because we communicate information in order to help people get a deeper understanding of complex topics. In this book we focus on communicating information in the sciences, so our subjects can include cosmology, in showing how fundamental structures in the universe work; archaeology and anthropology, in showing the ways earlier human groups laid out their structures and cultures; biology and chemistry, in seeing the way electrostatic forces and molecular structures lead to molecular bonding; mathematics, in understanding the behavior of highly unstable differential equations; or meteorology, in examining the way global forces such as the temperatures of ocean currents or the depth of the ozone layer affect the weather.

While the importance of visual communication and its associated visual vocabularies has been known by artists, designers, and film directors for a long time, its role in the use of computing in the sciences was highlighted in the 1987 report on Visualization in Scientific Computing [ViSC]. That report noted the importance of computer graphics in engaging the human brain's extraordinary ability to create insight from images. The report noted that Richard Hamming's classic quote from 1962, "The purpose of computing is insight, not numbers," is particularly applicable when the computing can create images that lead to a deeper and more subtle insight into complex subjects than is possible with numeric data alone. We could paraphrase Hamming for computer graphics and say that our reason for using computer graphics is information, not images.

The process of making images—in particular, of making attractive and interesting images with computer graphics using powerful machines and a capable graphics API—is relatively straightforward, as you will see as you progress through this book. The difficult parts of effective computer graphics are understanding your problem and developing ways to present the information that describes your problem so you can make accurate images that communicate with your audience. This short section talks about this task and discusses some principles and examples that we hope can start you thinking about this question. This is just a taste of the topic, though; it is a significant task to develop real skill in communicating through images. We discuss this early to remind you that the main reason we use graphics is to communicate with others, and to help you keep that communication in mind as you learn about making images with computing. Some of the techniques we talk about will not be covered until later in the book but are not terribly complex, so you should be able to make sense of what the techniques mean even before you have learned how to make them work.

Throughout the book, as we discuss several techniques we consider their effect on communication, but this is only an introduction to the topic. Highly skilled communicators are constantly inventing new ways to present specific information to specific audiences, creating new visual vocabularies for these audiences. We have not tried to make this a complete textbook on visual communication. Instead, we want you to think about the information content of your images and about how you can make them communicate that content to your audience.

Visual communication also includes designing interactions so they provide effective support for the visual effects controlled by the interactions. Motion, selection, and control of graphical processes are all reflected in the images presented to the user, so in later chapters (Chapters 7 and 11) we discuss some ways you can design the way a user interacts with your programs to support effective and comfortable work. Again, our goal is not to make you an expert at designing interactions but to help you understand and implement them.

General Concepts in Visual Communication

Several points in communicating with your audience are so important that we want to highlight them before we begin looking at the details, and discuss some of the issues that are involved in carrying them out.

Use Appropriate Representation for Your Information

Using appropriate representation lets your audience get the most meaning from your images. There are many ways to represent any information. Sometimes you may use color, or sometimes you may use geometry or shapes. Sometimes you may need to use highly symbolic or synthetic images while at other times you may need to use highly naturalistic images. Sometimes you may present the relationships between things instead of the things themselves. Perhaps you may use purely two dimensions, or possibly three dimensions with the third dimension used only for impact; other times you may use three dimensions with the third dimension a critical part of the presentation. The best way to know what works for your audience is to observe the way they are used to seeing things and to ask what makes sense for them. This may involve showing them many examples of options and alternatives, and some of the options you devise may be new to your audience. Do not assume that you know what they should use, however, because you probably think differently from people in their field and are probably not the one who needs to get the information from the images.

Keep Your Images Focused

Your images should focus on just the information that is needed for your audience to understand the things you are trying to communicate. Remember that simple images create focus by eliminating extraneous or distracting content. Don't create images that are "eye candy" and simply look good; don't create images that suggest relationships or information that are not supported by the data. For example, consider whether to choose flat shading (each polygon in the display is a single color) or smooth shading (the color can vary smoothly across each polygon). When you represent experimental sample data with geometric figures, you can use flat shading with only the resolution your data supports because smooth shading suggests that you know more than your data says. On the other hand, if you represent theoretical information with your figures, it is reasonable to use smooth shading if you know that the quantity you are representing is continuous. The fundamental principle is not to distort the truth of your information in order to create a more attractive image.

Use Appropriate Presentation Levels for Your Information

A very useful concept that may help you determine how much effort you put into polishing your images suggests that there are three levels of information presentation: for yourself (personal), for your colleagues or collaborators (peer), and for an audience on whom you want to make an impression (presentation). When you're trying to understand something yourself, you might use very simple images because you know what you are trying to show with them; you can include only essential material and need not polish the images. When you share your work with colleagues who have an idea of what you're working on but who don't have a deep knowledge of your problem, you might want higher quality or perhaps a legend to help them see your point, but you don't need to spend a lot of time polishing your work. But when you are creating a public presentation such as a scientific paper or a grant proposal (think of how you would get a point across to a congressional committee, for example, or to a community zoning commission), you will need to make your work as highly polished as you can. When you understand this principle, you will find that sometimes your work will be simple or low resolution, with very sketchy images; sometimes smoother and with a little thought as to how you look at things, perhaps with a little simple animation or with some interaction to let people play with your ideas; and sometimes fully developed, with very smooth animation and high-resolution images, with great care taken to make the maximum impact in the minimum time.

Use Appropriate Forms for Your Information

It is very useful to categorize information (or data) into *interval* data, *ordinal* data, and *nominal* data. Interval data is that which is associated with a meaningful number such as speed, weight, or count. It involves measured data in individual cases and has a natural representation in real numbers that you can use for your graphical presentation. Ordinal data is that which can be compared with other similar data but that is not necessarily meaningful in itself. Thus the educational level of one person can be compared with that of another, but the most you can say is that one person has more (or less) education than another. Ordinal data can be represented by size (larger, smaller) or by color (brighter, darker; more red, more blue) in color ramps that are discussed in the chapter on color (Chapter 5). Note that with a color ramp, a viewer can tell which color is higher or lower than another on a color legend but cannot usually discern a precise numeric value from the color. Thus color ramps are more useful for ordinal data than for interval data, and when they are used for interval data it is rarely possible to discern actual numerical values from the color. Nominal data is that which describes something with no ordering or numerical meaning; an example might be hair color, with descriptions "red," "brown," "blonde," or "gray." Nominal data can be shown by shapes, patterns, or individual distinct colors.

Be Very Careful to be Accurate with Your Display

If you have only scattered data for a topic, show only the data you have; do not use techniques such as smooth geometry or smooth coloring to suggest that information is known between the data points. Recognize that a simpler, more accurate representation is going to give your users better information for understanding the situation than a fancier representation. If you use simple numerical techniques, such as difference equations, to model a behavior or to determine the motions in your geometry, note this in a legend or title instead of implying that a more exact solution is presented, so that the modeling you present is not taken as exact. In general, try very hard not to introduce misunderstandings in your presentation.

As an example of these points, let's consider a display of a function surface such as we will see several times in Chapter 9. We will often work with real-valued functions defined on a domain in 2D space, and we will devise ways to visualize these functions. Let's look at the way a function $f(x,y)$ defines a surface in 3D space and think about how we might present that surface. Let's also think about how we can show the value of $f(x,y)$ by using an artificial color on the 2D domain region. We see that there are different ways to examine and understand the function, as we see in the three parts of Figure 0.1; the dual goals of this book are to show you how you can create displays such as these and to help you understand when you would want to use one or another representation to communicate the function to your audience.

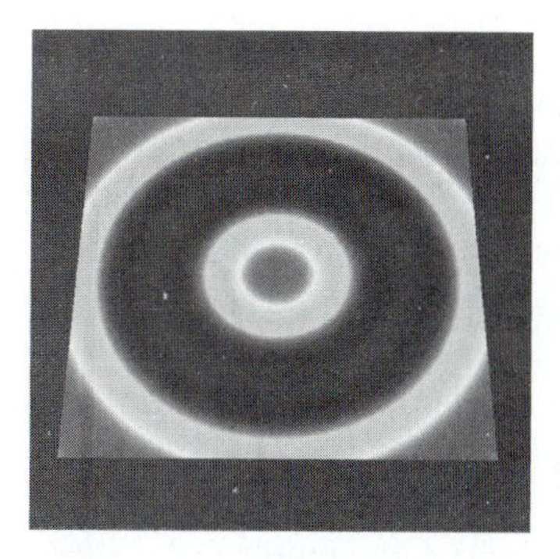 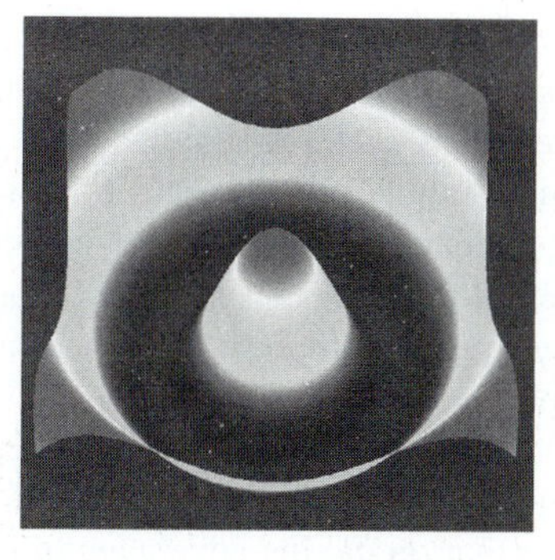 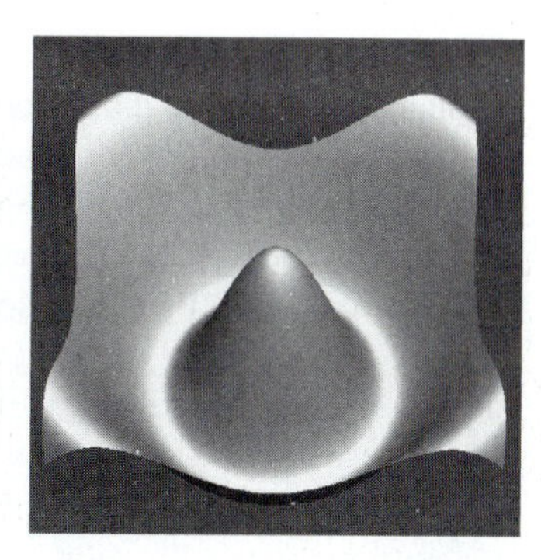

Figure 0.1 Three views of a function of two variables: artificially coloring the domain (*left*), building a surface with the artificial coloring (*center*), and building a naturalistically presented surface (*right*).

Understand and Respect the Cultural Context of Your Audience

When you create images to communicate with an audience, that audience can understand the images only in its own context. This context comes as part of the audience's culture, such as a professional culture (engineering, medicine, high-energy physics, publishing, education, management), a social culture (small-town, major urban, agricultural), a geographical culture (North American, western European, Chinese, Japanese), an ethnic culture (Native American, Chicano, Zulu), or a religious culture (Buddhist, Islamic, Roman Catholic, fundamentalist Protestant). Each of these colors may have a meaning that is different from your experience, or some symbols or images may mean something significantly different from those meanings you would expect. You must be careful to ensure that your images have the meaning you intend for their audience and not some accidental message caused by your failure to understand the context in which the images are received.

Make Your Interactions Reflect Familiar and Comfortable Relationships Between Action and Effect

If your audience is used to a particular kind of controls, simulate those controls and make the actions given by a control mimic the behavior that the control provides in the user's world. The controls you have available are probably familiar from various applications that most people have used, so you can begin by looking at these examples. Some of the controls would naturally be presented in their own control panel; some would be applied in the image itself.

Let's start by looking at some of the control panel vocabulary for interactions. If you want a user to select one among several distinct options in a program, it is natural to select from a series of a radio buttons—a list of the options with a button by each, with each button displaying whether it has been selected, and with a selection of one button canceling any other selection. If you want a user to select zero or more options from a list of options that are not mutually exclusive, then you can use an ordinary button for each, with each button capable of being selected independently of the others. If you want to set a value for a parameter from a continuous range of possible values, you can use a slider or dial to select the value (and you should display the value as it is changed to show what value is selected). Finally, if you want your user to enter some text (for example, the name of a color if you have used certain names for colors, such as the X Window color naming system, or the name of a file the program is to use), you can use a text box to allow text entry. Examples of all these controls are displayed in the chapter on interaction (Chapter 7).

If you want the controls to be applied directly in the scene, however, then there is another vocabulary for that kind of interaction. This vocabulary depends on understanding that the scene represents a certain kind of space, usually a three-dimensional space containing models of physical objects, and that behaviors can be specified in terms of that space. Here we will find object selection by clicking a mouse on a scene and identifying the object that the mouse click has identified, for example. We will also find that we can specify rotations in both latitude and longitude by clicking the mouse in the scene and holding down the button while moving the mouse vertically or horizontally, respectively. We will also find that we can zoom into a scene by specifying that a mouse motion as seen above should be interpreted as a one-dimensional zoom instead of as a two-dimensional rotation. And finally, any of these behaviors could be replaced by using the keyboard to convey the same information, taking advantage of the very large number of degrees of freedom represented by all the keys. This also has the semantic strength of identifying actions with words, and words with key characters. You may also build on familiar key patterns such as the cursor controls from text editors or motion controls from older games.

In all, recognizing that interaction is another form of language and that there are interaction vocabularies from users' backgrounds provides a form of communication that you can build on to create effective interactive programs.

Throughout the book we make a number of points about visual communication and computer graphics. We believe that as you get started in computer graphics, you need to recognize these points so you will understand them when you see them in the subsequent chapters. These include the following:

- Shape is a powerful tool that needs to be used carefully to present accurate ideas.
- Color offers many choices that are critical to effective images, and more than anything else, color is how you guide your audience to important parts of your images and convey the exact information you need to give them.
- The choice between naturalistic or artificial shapes and colors is important in communicating appropriate information to your audience.
- There are techniques of color and motion that can convey up to five dimensions of information to your audience, but you need to think carefully about how you encode different kinds of information into each dimension.
- An audience may need to see your scene from the right viewpoint and have the right context with the image in order to understand the ideas you are presenting.
- Modern graphics APIs and computers have made animated images much simpler to create, and it can be very helpful to take advantage of motion to make your images work better.
- Not only can your images move, but you can create images that let your audience interact with the information you are presenting and explore the ideas themselves.
- Motion and interaction are your ways to present the behavior of your models and must be considered an integral part of your communication.
- Your audience will always see your images in the context of their culture, so you must develop an understanding of that culture as part of designing your work.

Keep these communication issues in mind as you create your images. They may not all apply in any single piece of work; some take a good bit of work that is outside computer graphics; and many of them take some experience before you can apply them confidently and skillfully. But if you understand their importance, you will create much more effective work.

3D Geometry and the Geometry Pipeline

Computer graphics is fundamentally three-dimensional, at least as we treat it in this book, so a graphics system must deal with three-dimensional geometry. Computer graphics systems do this by creating the *3D geometry pipeline*, a collection of processes that convert 3D points, the basic building blocks of 3D geometry, into 2D points. Doing this also converts 3D graphics objects to 2D objects. This process transforms the objects from those that are most convenient for the application programmer into those that are most convenient for the display hardware. We will explore the details of the steps for the geometry pipeline in Chapter 1, which deals with viewing and projection, but here we outline the steps of the geometry pipeline to help you understand how it operates. This pipeline is diagrammed in Figure 0.2, and we will start to sketch some stages in the pipeline in this chapter. A great deal more detail will be given in the next few chapters.

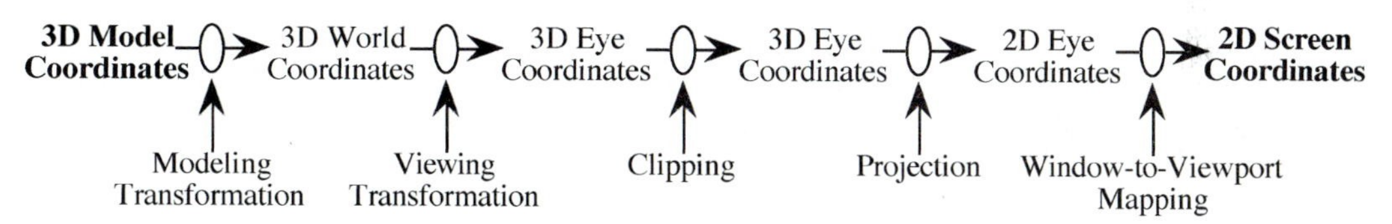

Figure 0.2 The geometry pipeline's stages and mappings.

The Scene and the View

The scene and the view are two basic concepts we will use repeatedly in describing how graphics is done. The *scene* is the collection of objects in the shared 3D space that will be displayed in our image. It contains the geometry of all the objects placed in it as well as of all the lights that illuminate the objects. The *view* is the set of information needed to create an image and is a space containing a scene, the coordinate system for the scene, an eyepoint in that coordinate system with a known direction of view, and a specified projection that is to map the viewable part of the space onto a 2D plane where it is to be viewed. The scene defines what is in the world, while the view defines what part of the world is to be seen and how the viewer is to see it. The geometry pipeline, in fact, captures the way the scene and view are defined and created, and these are the real subject of this section.

3D Model Coordinate Systems

To create an image we must define the geometry that represents each part of the image. The process of creating and defining this geometry is called *modeling,* and it is described in the chapters on principles of modeling and on modeling in OpenGL (Chapters 2 and 3, respectively). Modeling is usually done by defining each object in terms of a particular coordinate system that makes sense for that object and then using a set of *modeling transformations* to place that object in a single coordinate system that represents the common space in which all the objects are seen. We can think of the original model as a template for a graphics object, with the modeling transformations making the object the right size, with the right orientation, in the right location in the world space.

It is common to define a single template object to be used in creating number of other objects. The template object can be part of other objects or can be resized, reoriented, or relocated to use in a scene. Modeling transformations are used to change the template object into the actual objects to be used, and these transformations can be modified over time or through interaction to give your models the behavior they may need.

3D World Coordinate System

Recall that a scene contains a collection of graphics objects in a common 3D coordinate system shared by everything in the scene. This coordinate system is called the *world coordinate system*. By placing every component of the scene in this single shared world, we can treat the scene uniformly as we develop the presentation of the scene through the graphics display device to the user. Note that the world coordinate system can represent the actual coordinate dimensions of a model of the space of a real-world environment. This coordinate system and the scene it contains exist on their own, independent of any reference to a viewer, as is the case with any real-world scene. In order to create an image from the scene, a viewer is added at the next stage.

Let's look at a scene that we'll use soon to discuss viewing. For the scene we build a model by starting with 3D model coordinates and moving to 3D world coordinates. The scene shows a forest with a number of evergreen trees. To model this, we first build a tree in model coordinates as a trunk (cylinder) and top (cone). The trunk is one unit long, with its base at the origin, while the treetop is three units long and is placed at the top of the trunk. So the tree is centered at the origin and its height is four units. But a forest contains many trees, so we want to draw 100 trees placed in the rectangular region of the X-Y plane with x between -4 and 4, and y between 0 and 8. The trees are placed in the world space by translations that move them from the origin to a point determined randomly in the region. Such a forest is shown in Figure 0.3.

Figure 0.3 A forest.

3D Eye Coordinate System

Once you have created your 3D world, you want to be able to view it from any location. But the model of viewing in computer graphics typically has a specific default orientation and/or position for the eye. For example, the system might specify the default eye position to be at the origin, looking in the $-Z$ (or sometimes $+Z$) direction, with the Y-axis oriented upward. The *viewing transformation* takes the chosen eye location and all the objects that have been defined in the 3D world space and slides them around to realign the coordinates so that the eye is at the proper place, looking in the proper direction. The relative positions between the eye and the other objects are not changed; everything in the scene is simply anchored in a different spot in 3D space. When we apply the viewing transformation to the world coordinate system, we get the *3D eye coordinate system*. The viewing transformation is specified in a variety of ways, depending on the graphics API. A common approach is to specify the location of the eye, the direction the eye is facing, and the direction that is "up" to the view; this is enough information to allow the graphics system to calculate the viewing transformation.

Projections

The 3D eye coordinate system must next be converted to a 2D coordinate system before it can be mapped onto a graphics display device. The next stage of the geometry pipeline does this operation, called a *projection*. Projections map the view volume to a 2D rectangle, called the *view plane*, that is parallel to the X-Y plane in the eye coordinate space and contains the 2D eye coordinates. Before we discuss the actual projection, let's think about what the displayed image will actually look like. Imagine your eye placed at a particular point in the scene, looking in a particular direction, and imagine what you will see when you look at the scene through a rectangular window. You do not see the entire scene; you see only the space that lies in the view volume for your scene.

Two projections are most commonly used in computer graphics and are supported by standard graphics APIs. One maps all the points in the eye space to the view plane by projecting each point in your model onto the X-Y plane in a direction parallel to the Z-axis. All points on a line parallel to the direction of the eye are mapped to the same point on the viewing plane, which has the effect of keeping the x- and y-coordinates and ignoring the z-coordinate of each point. This is called a *parallel* projection, and it lets you read accurate dimensions in the x- and y-coordinates. In the most common parallel projection, called the *orthographic* projection, the lines along which projection is done are parallel to the Z-axis. A graphics API will usually provide orthographic projections and may provide other parallel projections as well. It is common for engineering drawings to present two parallel projections, with one as described above and with the second including a 90° rotation of the world space so that accurate z-coordinates can also be seen.

The second common projection acts as if the eye were a single point and each point in the scene were mapped to the view plane along a line from the eye to that point, which is the classic technique of perspective drawing. This is called a *perspective* projection. In a parallel projection, an object is drawn the same size, no matter how far away it is from the viewing plane. In a perspective projection, an object is drawn smaller as it is placed farther away from the eye. Perspective projections tend to look more realistic, while parallel projections allow you to line up and measure objects in space. And just as there are parallel and perspective projections, there are orthographic and perspective view volumes. Figure 0.4 shows us the view volumes for the parallel and orthographic projections. On the left we see the view volume of a parallel projection. This has the shape of a pyramid that is truncated at the front. On the right we see the view volume of an orthographic projection. This has the shape of a rectangular region. In both cases, the eye positions are shown as white spheres. The view plane for both projections is the front face of the view volume, while the back plane for the view volumes is the back face.

Figure 0.4 Perspective and orthographic viewing volumes from the front (*top*) and from above (*bottom*); both views show the entire forest.

The truncated pyramid shape of the view volume for the perspective projection is known as a *frustum*.

While the view volume describes the visible region in space, the actual view is the geometry as it is displayed in the 2D eye space of the view plane. Figure 0.5 shows the scene of Figure 0.4 seen with both perspective and orthographic projections and their view volumes. These views

Figure 0.5 The scene in Figure 0.4 as presented by a perspective projection (*left*) and an orthographic projection (*right*) using the view volumes of the previous figure.

should be compared carefully with the parts of the scene in the view volumes in the earlier figure so you can see exactly how each fits with the overall scene. Each part of the figure shows some unique features. In the left-hand side, part of the tree at the left is clipped by the front of the view volume. In the right-hand side, you do not see a ground plane because that plane is parallel to the view volume, and you cannot see a plane edge-on. You also see all the trees having the same height because this is an orthographic projection; you also see a small part of a tree at the back edge of the scene because the rest of the tree lies behind the viewable space.

Clipping

Just as your eye or a camera cannot see the entire 3D world around you, a graphics image does not show the entire 3D eye space. The *3D view volume* is the part of the scene that can be viewed, and this volume is determined by the projection as defined in the next section. This volume is specified by setting the left, right, bottom, top, near, and far boundaries of the view. When we know these, we can *clip* the object against the viewing volume by identifying the parts of the scene that lie inside the view volume and the parts that lie outside. We then discard everything that is outside the view volume and pass to the projection step everything inside. In a perspective projection, some of the trees (or parts of the trees) lie outside the viewable space to the left, right, top, or bottom. You may not have thought about it, but the graphics system must make sure these are not seen. An example of this from another view of the forest is shown in Figure 0.6. Besides things that are to the side of the scene, or above or below it, some things in the scene are outside the viewable space because they are too near to or too far from the eyepoint. Note that the front of the tree to the left in the figure is clipped, or made invisible in the scene, because it is too close to the viewer's eye. There are also some trees in the scene behind those shown in the figure; they are also clipped because they are too far from the eye.

This clipping on the view volume is done in the same space as viewing, the 3D eye coordinate space, and before the scene is projected to the 2D eye coordinates with the projection.

Figure 0.6 Clipping on a scene.

Besides ensuring that the view includes only the things that should be visible, clipping also makes the graphics system more efficient because it eliminates parts of the geometry from the rest of the display process.

Choosing Perspective or Orthographic Projections

One common question beginners have about computer graphics is whether to use perspective or orthographic projections for an image. Each has its strengths and its weaknesses. As a quick start, here are some guidelines on the two approaches.

Orthographic projections are best used when:

- items in the scene need to be checked to see if they line up or are the same size,
- items in the scene need to be measured, or
- lines need to be checked to see if they are parallel.

Perspective projections are best used when:

- you want your image to be more realistic,
- you want to be able move through a scene and have a view such as a person would have, or
- you do not need to measure or align parts of the image.

When you have some experience with each and when you know what your audience expects, you will find that the choice is quite natural and will have no problem knowing which is better for a specific image.

2D Eye Coordinates

Projection maps a three-dimensional real-coordinate space to a two-dimensional real-coordinate space and lets the viewer see a 2D view of the geometry of the original scene. Because a single point in 2D eye coordinates corresponds to an entire line segment in the 3D eye space, depth information is lost in any projection. It can then be difficult for a viewer to perceive depth in a scene, particularly if a parallel projection was used and there are no depth cues from the relative sizes of objects. For perspective projections, the differences between the size of the image of objects that are known to be of similar size but are at different distances from the viewer will help the viewer recognize the objects' positions in space. If we further display the scene with a hidden-surface technique, the way nearer objects cover farther objects will help the viewer recognize the depth of objects in the scene—even for orthographic projections.

2D Screen Coordinates

The final step in the geometry pipeline is to change the coordinates of objects in the 2D eye space so that the object is in a coordinate system appropriate for the 2D display device. Because the screen is a digital device, this requires that the real numbers in the 2D eye coordinate system be converted to integer numbers that represent screen coordinates. This is done with a proportional mapping followed by a truncation of the coordinate values. It is called the *window-to-viewport mapping,* and the new coordinate space is referred to as *screen coordinates,* or *display coordinates*. When this step is done, the entire scene is now represented by integer screen coordinates and can be drawn on the 2D display device.

Note that this entire pipeline process converts *geometry,* as expressed by vertices of objects, from one form to another with several different transformations. These transformations preserve a consistent vertex geometry of the scene among the different representations, but computer graphics also assumes that the *topology* of the scene stays the same. For instance, if two points are connected by a line in 3D model space, then the converted points are assumed to still be connected by a line in 2D screen space. Thus the geometric objects (points, lines, polygons, or programmer-defined objects) and the relationships of the edges and vertices that were specified in the original model space are all maintained until we get to screen space, and are actually drawn only there.

Appearance

Along with geometry, computer graphics allows you to define the *appearance* of objects, so you can make them appear naturalistic or can give them colors that can communicate a particular meaning to the user.

So far we have talked only about the coordinates of the vertices of a model. Many other properties of vertices are needed to create the image defined by your scene. You set these properties when the vertex is defined, and they are preserved as the vertex is processed through the geometry pipeline. Some of these properties involve concepts that we have not yet covered. They include:

- a depth value for the vertex, defined as the distance of the vertex from the eye point in the direction of the view reference point,
- a color for the vertex,
- a normal vector at the vertex,
- material properties for the vertex, and
- texture coordinates for the vertex.

These properties are used to develop the appearance of each of the objects in the image. They allow the graphics system to do hidden-surface displays and to calculate the color of each pixel in the image on the screen after the vertices are converted to 2D screen coordinates.

Appearance is handled by the rendering pipeline operations that are applied after the geometry is mapped to screen space. In order to do this, the geometric primitives described previously are broken down into very simple pieces that are processed by setting the pixels in the window that make up each one. Appearance information is associated with each vertex, and as the vertex information is processed, appearance information is also processed to create the colors used for each pixel. Processes such as depth buffering are also handled at this stage, creating the appropriate visible-surface view of a scene. So processes handling the appearance information follow processes handling the geometry information, and the presentation of appearance issues will follow most of the geometry chapters. Here we introduce a few appearance topics that will be expanded later.

Color

Color can be defined directly by the programmer or can be computed from a lighting model if your scene is defined in terms of lights and materials. Most graphics APIs support RGBA color: color defined in terms of the emissive primary colors—red, green, and blue—and with an alpha channel that allows you to blend items with the background when they are drawn. These systems also allow a very large number of colors, typically on the order of 16 million. So there is a large number of possible colors you can use, as described in later chapters on color and on lighting (Chapters 5 and 6, respectively).

Textures

Among the most powerful ways to add visual interest to a scene is texture mapping, which allows you to add visual content to objects in a scene from images such as photographs. With texture mapping you can achieve photographic surface effects or other kinds of images that will make your images much more interesting and realistic. This should be an important capability for you.

Depth Buffering

As your scene is developed, you want only the objects nearest the eye to be seen; anything that is behind these objects will be hidden by nearer objects. This can be managed in the rendering stage by keeping track of the distance from the eye to each pixel that has been drawn and each pixel that is being drawn. If a pixel in an object being drawn is nearer to the eye than the pixel that was previously drawn, then the new pixel's color will replace the previous one; otherwise, the previous pixel's color is retained. Depth buffering is a straightforward computation that is supported by essentially all modern graphics systems.

The Viewing Process

Let's look at the overall operations on your geometry as the graphics system works on that scene and eventually displays it to your user. Referring again to Figure 0.2 and omitting the clipping and window-to-viewport process, we see that we start by defining our basic geometry, apply the modeling transformation(s), apply the viewing transformation, and finally apply the projection to the screen. This can be expressed in terms of function composition as the sequence

```
projection(viewing(modeling(geometry)))
```

or, writing function composition as multiplication and applying the associative law,

```
projection*(viewing*(modeling(geometry)))=
                              (projection*viewing*modeling)(geometry).
```

The operations nearest the geometry are performed before operations further from the geometry, so we want to define the projection first, the viewing next, and the modeling transformations last before we define the geometry on which they are to operate. This is independent of whether we want to use a perspective or parallel projection. This sequence is a key *factor* in the way we structure a scene through the scene graph later in the book.

Different Implementation, Same Result

Up to this point, we have not provided any details on how a vertex travels through the geometry pipeline. There are several ways of implementing this travel, any of which will produce a correct display. Don't be surprised if your particular computer graphics system doesn't manage the geometry pipeline in exactly the way we show here. The basic principles and stages of the operation will be fundamentally similar.

For example, OpenGL combines the modeling and viewing transformations into a single transformation known as the *modelview transformation*. When we talk about OpenGL, this makes us take a little different approach to modeling and viewing. Also, graphics hardware systems typically perform a window–to–normalized-coordinates operation prior to clipping so that hardware can be optimized around a particular coordinate system. In this case, everything else stays the same except that the final step would be normalized-coordinate–to–viewport mapping.

In many cases, we simply will not be concerned about how the stages are carried out. We will represent the correct geometry at the modeling stages, will be sure to define the right appearance information with the geometry, will specify the eye position appropriately, and will define our window and projections correctly. The graphics system will carry out the geometry pipeline and appearance processes for us. We will leave the many details of graphics fundamentals to more advanced graphics courses.

Graphics Cards

While computer graphics was originally done with the same processor and memory as other computations, almost all interactive computer graphics systems now use graphics cards that have special-purpose processors and memory to speed the computations needed to create images. These cards, especially the high-end, high-performance cards, are also called *graphics accelerators*. These contain special-purpose hardware designed especially for the operations geometry data into images in graphics memory. They also contain special memory to hold images being computed (sometimes called color buffers) and other data needed for graphics computation (depth buffers, shadow buffers, texture memory, and more). Because they are designed for very special computations they can be very fast, and one of the roles of a graphics API is to map the functions you call through your graphics API to the capabilities of these cards.

At this time, graphics cards and graphics APIs are developing in close parallel. Cards are designed to support the kinds of computation needed for the API, and APIs are developing to take advantage of the increasing performance and flexibility of graphics cards. The continuing development of graphics APIs is clearly in the direction of providing access to new features being built into cards.

A Basic OpenGL Program

The example programs in this book that use OpenGL have some strong similarities. Each is based on the GLUT (*G*raphics *L*ibrary *U*tility *T*oolkit) toolkit that usually accompanies OpenGL systems. If your version of OpenGL does not include GLUT, you can find its source code online; check the page at http://www.opengl.org/resources/libraries/glut.html to get to the download pages. You will need to download the code, compile it, and install it in your system. Similarly, when we get to the section on event handling, we will use the MUI (micro user interface) toolkit, although this is not part of some releases of OpenGL. Many other resources for GLUT and user interface functionality are available and are linked through this Web page.

Like most worthwhile APIs, OpenGL is quite complex and offers you many different ways to express a solution to a graphical problem using code. Our examples use a modest subset of OpenGL that works well for interactive programs, because we strongly believe that computer graphics and user interaction should be learned together. If you make highly realistic graphics it may take a long time to create a single image, so you may not be able to make this work interactive.

What is the typical structure of a program that uses OpenGL to make interactive images? We will display this structure-only example in C, as we will with all our examples. We don't use C++ because OpenGL's operations do not fit well with object-oriented programming. OpenGL maintains an extensive set of state data that cannot be encapsulated in graphics classes, while object-oriented design usually calls for objects to maintain their own state. Many functions such as event callbacks cannot even deal with parameters and must work with global variables, so the usual practice in applications is to create an environment through global variables and use these variables instead of parameters to pass information in and out of functions.

In the code below, you will see that the `main()` function is mostly made up of operations that set up the OpenGL system. This is done in two ways: first, setting up GLUT to create and place the system window in which your work will be displayed, and second, setting up the event-handling system by defining the callbacks to be used when events occur. It also initializes the models and environment for your display. After this is done, `main()` calls the main event loop that will drive all of the program operations, as described in the chapter on event handling (Chapter 7).

The `display()` function is particularly important because it creates the display of the model you define. When we discuss scene graphs in Chapter 2, you will see that the task of the `display()` function is to walk through the scene graph and carry out the operations it specifies by defining geometry, setting appearance, and applying transformations.

The event-driven approach of GLUT is described in the later chapter on events, but you should understand that GLUT operates entirely from events. For each event the program is to handle, you need to define a callback function in `main()`. A **callback function** is one that is called by the system event handler when its associated event occurs. When the main event loop is started, a **reshape** event creates the window and a **display** event draws the initial image in the window using its callback function. If any other events have callbacks defined, they are invoked when their events happen. The reshape callback lets you move the window or change its size, and it is called whenever you do any window manipulation. The **idle** callback lets the program create a sequence of images by recomputing the image whenever the system is idle (when it is not creating an image or responding to another event) and then redisplaying the changed image.

The full code example that follows this outline discusses many of the details of these functions and of the callbacks. For now, note that the reshape callback sets up the window parameters for the system, including the size, shape, and location of the window, and defines the projection to be used in the view. This is called first when the main event loop is entered as well as when any window activity (such as resizing or dragging) happens. The reshape requests a redisplay when it finishes, which calls the display callback, whose task is to set up the view and define the geometry for the scene. When this is finished, the OpenGL operations are finished and the graphics system goes back to your computer to see if there has been any other graphics-related event. If there has, your program should have a callback to manage it. If there has not, then the idle event is generated and the idle callback function is called; this may change some of the geometry parameters, and then a redisplay is again called.

```
#include <GL/glut.h>      // Windows; other includes for other systems
    // other includes as needed

//  typedef and global data section
    // as needed

//  function template section
    void doMyInit(void);
    void display(void);
    void reshape(int,int);
    void idle(void);
    // others as defined

//  initialization function
    void doMyInit(void) {
        set up basic OpenGL parameters and environment
        set up projection transformation (ortho or perspective)
    }

//  reshape callback function
    void reshape(int w, int h) {
        set up projection transformation with new window
            dimensions w and h
        post redisplay
    }

//  display callback function
    void display(void) {
        set up viewing transformation as in later chapters
        define the geometry, transformations, appearance you need
        post redisplay
    }

//  idle callback function
    void idle(void) {
        update anything that changes between steps of the program
        post redisplay
    }
```

```
//  other graphics and application functions
    // as needed

//  main function - set up the system, turn it over to events
    void main(int argc, char** argv) {

//      initialize system through GLUT and your own initialization
        glutInit(&argc,argv):
        glutInitDisplayMode(GLUT_DOUBLE | GLUT_RGB);
        glutInitWindowSize(windW,windH);
        glutInitWindowPosition(topLeftX,topLeftY);
        glutCreateWindow("A Sample Program");
        doMyInit();

//      define callback functions for events; this is pretty minimal
        glutDisplayFunc(display);
        glutReshapeFunc(reshape);
        glutIdleFunc(idle);

//      go into main event loop
        glutMainLoop();
    }
```

Now that we have seen a basic OpenGL program structure, we will look at a complete working program and analyze the way it represents the geometry pipeline, while describing the details of OpenGL it uses. The program is a simple simulation of temperatures in a uniform metal bar and is described in the later chapter on graphical problem-solving in science (Chapter 9). We will analyze only the program structure, not its function. It creates the image shown in Figure 0.7. The code is listed following the figure. We segment the code so you may see the ways the individual pieces contribute to the overall graphics operations, and then we will discuss the pieces after the listing.

Figure 0.7 Heat distribution in a bar. See the figure in the color insert.

In the following code, each boxed section carries out a specific OpenGL function. It may be initialization, modeling, viewing, or a callback, but highlighting the separate parts should help you find and focus on them. The OpenGL functions are straightforward, but the overall program may seem complex. However, after the first few chapters of the book you will find that most of the code is actually pretty simple.

```
//   Example - temperature change in a thin rectangular body
//            with fixed hot and cold spots

//   declarations and initialization of variables and system
#include <GL/glut.h>      // for windows; can change for other systems
                          // this also includes gl.h and glu.h
#include <stdlib.h>
#include <stdio.h>
#include <math.h>
#define ROWS 10       //    body is ROWSxCOLS (unitless) squares
#define COLS 30

#define AMBIENT 25.0;       // ambient temperature, degrees Celsius
#define HOT 50.0            // hot temperature of heat-source cell
#define COLD 0.0            // cold temperature of cold-sink cell
#define NHOTS 4             // number of hot cells
#define NCOLDS 5            // number of cold cells

GLfloat angle = 0.0;
GLfloat temps[ROWS][COLS], back[ROWS+2][COLS+2];
GLfloat theta = 0.0, vp = 30.0;

//   set locations of fixed hot and cold spots on the bar
int hotspots[NHOTS][2] =
    { {ROWS/2,0},{ROWS/2-1,0},{ROWS/2-2,0},{0,3*COLS/4} };
int coldspots[NCOLDS][2] =
    { {ROWS-1,COLS/3}, {ROWS-1,1+COLS/3}, {ROWS-1,2+COLS/3},
      {ROWS-1,3+COLS/3}, {ROWS-1,4+COLS/3} };
int myWin;

void myinit(void) {
    int i,j;

glEnable(GL_DEPTH_TEST);
glClearColor(0.6, 0.6, 0.6, 1.0);

//   set up initial temperatures in cells
    for (i-0; i<ROWS; i++) {
        for (j=0; j < COLS; j++) {
            temps[i][j] = AMBIENT;
        }
    }
    for (i=0; i<NHOTS; i++)
        temps[hotspots[i][0]][hotspots[i][1]]=HOT;
    for (i=0; i<NCOLDS; i++)
        temps[coldspots[i][0]][coldspots[i][1]]=COLD;
}

//   create a unit cube in first octant in model coordinates
void cube(void) {
```

```
typedef GLfloat point[3];

point v[8] = {
    {0.0, 0.0, 0.0}, {0.0, 0.0, 1.0},
    {0.0, 1.0, 0.0}, {0.0, 1.0, 1.0},
    {1.0, 0.0, 0.0}, {1.0, 0.0, 1.0},
    {1.0, 1.0, 0.0}, {1.0, 1.0, 1.0} };

glBegin(GL_QUAD_STRIP);
    glVertex3fv(v[4]);
    glVertex3fv(v[5]);
    glVertex3fv(v[0]);
    glVertex3fv(v[1]);
    glVertex3fv(v[2]);
    glVertex3fv(v[3]);
    glVertex3fv(v[6]);
    glVertex3fv(v[7]);
glEnd();

    glBegin(GL_QUAD_STRIP);
    glVertex3fv(v[1]);
    glVertex3fv(v[3]);
    glVertex3fv(v[5]);
    glVertex3fv(v[7]);
    glVertex3fv(v[4]);
    glVertex3fv(v[6]);
    glVertex3fv(v[0]);
    glVertex3fv(v[2]);
glEnd();
}
```

```
void display(void) {
    #define SCALE 10.0
    int i,j;
```

```
glClear(GL_COLOR_BUFFER_BIT | GL_DEPTH_BUFFER_BIT);
//  This short section defines the viewing transformation
    glMatrixMode(GL_MODELVIEW);
    glLoadIdentity();
    //    eye point    center of view    up
    gluLookAt(vp, vp/2., vp/4., 0.0, 0.0, 0.0, 0.0, 0.0, 1.0);

    // Set up a rotation for the entire scene
    glPushMatrix();
    glRotate(angle, 0., 0., 1.);
```

```
    // Draw the bars
    for (i = 0; i < ROWS; i++) {
```

```
        for (j = 0; j < COLS; j++) {
            setColor(temps[i][j]);
//  Here is the modeling transformation for each item in the display

     glPushMatrix();
     glTranslatef((float)i - (float)ROWS/2.0,
                  (float)j - (float)COLS/2.0,0.0);
     // 0.1 cold, 4.0 hot
     glScalef(1.0, 1.0, 0.1+3.9*temps[i][j]/HOT);
     cube();
     glPopMatrix();

            }
        }

 //  Wrap up the scene by popping the rotation and swapping buffers
 glPopMatrix();
 glutSwapBuffers();

    }
}

void reshape(int w,int h) {
//  This defines the projection transformation

 glViewport(0,0,(GLsizei)w,(GLsizei)h);
 glMatrixMode(GL_PROJECTION);
 glLoadIdentity();
 gluPerspective(60.0, (float)w/(float)h, 1.0, 300.0);
 glutPostRedisplay();

}

void setColor(float t) {
//  Color is based on HOT=red (1,0,0) and COLD=blue (0,0,1)
//  with the assumption that COLD <= t <= HOT at all times
    float r, g, b;
    r = (t-COLD)/(HOT - COLD); g = 0.0; b = 1.0 - r;

 glColor3f(r, g, b);

}

void animate(void) {
//  This function is called whenever the system is idle; it calls
//  iterationStep() to change the data so the next image is changed
```

```
    iterationStep();
    glutPostRedisplay();
}

void iterationStep(void) {
int i, j, m, n;

    float filter[3][3]={{ 0.    , 0.125, 0.    },
                         { 0.125 , 0.5,   0.125 },
                         { 0.    , 0.125, 0.    } };

    // increment temperatures throughout the material
    for (i=0; i<ROWS; i++)// backup temps up to recreate it
        for (j=0; j<COLS; j++)
            back[i<1][j+1] < temps[i][j]; // leave boundaries on back

    // fill boundaries with adjacent values from original temps[][]
    for (i=1; i<ROWS+2; i++) {
        back[i][0]=back[i][1];
        back[i][COLS+1]=back[i][COLS];
        }
    for (j=0; j<COLS+2; j++) {
        back[0][j] = back[1][j];
        back[ROWS+1][j]=back[ROWS][j];
        }
    for (i=0; i<ROWS; i++)// diffusion based on back values
        for (j=0; j<COLS; j++) {
            temps[i][j]=0.0;
            for (m=-1; m<=1; m++)
                for (n=-1; n<=1; n++)
                    temps[i][j]+=back[i+1+m][j+1+n]*filter[m+1][n+1];
        }
    for (i=0; i<NHOTS; i++) {
        temps[hotspots[i][0]][hotspots[i][1]]=HOT;
        }
    for (i=0; i<NCOLDS; i++) {
        temps[coldspots[i][0]][coldspots[i][1]]=COLD;
        }
    // update the angle for the rotation
    angle += 1.0;}

int main(int argc, char** argv) {

//  Initialize the GLUT system and define the window
    glutInit(&argc,argv);
    glutInitDisplayMode(GLUT_DOUBLE | GLUT_RGB | GLUT_DEPTH);
    glutInitWindowSize(500,500);
    glutInitWindowPosition(50,50);
    myWin = glutCreateWindow("Temperature in bar");
```

```
    myinit();

//  define the event callbacks and enter main event loop
    glutDisplayFunc(display);
    glutReshapeFunc(reshape);
    glutIdleFunc(animate);
    glutMainLoop(); /* enter event loop */
```

The Structure of the `main()` Function in OpenGL

The `main()` function in an OpenGL-based application may look different from that in the programs you have seen before. This function has several key operations: It sets up the display mode, defines the window in which the display will be presented, and does whatever initialization is needed by the program. It then does something that may not be familiar to you: It defines a set of event callbacks, which are functions that are called by the system when an event occurs. Finally, it passes control to the computer's event system through the main event loop function.

When you set up the display mode, you tell the system the features that your program will use at some point. In the example here,

```
glutInitDisplayMode(GLUT_DOUBLE | GLUT_RGB | GLUT_DEPTH);
```

tells the system that you will be working in double-buffered mode, will use the RGB color model, and will be using depth testing. Some of these have to be enabled before they are actually used, as the depth testing is in the `myInit()` function with

```
glEnable(GL_DEPTH_TEST)
```

Details on depth testing and how this is managed in OpenGL are Chapter 1.

Setting up the window (or windows; OpenGL will let you have multiple windows open and active) is handled by a set of GLUT function calls that position the window, define the size of the window, and give a title to the window. As the program runs, an active window may be reshaped by the user using the standard techniques of the window system being used. This is handled by the GLUT `reshape()` function that uses the underlying window system.

Model Space

The function `cube()` in the code defines a unit cube with sides parallel to the coordinate axes, one vertex at the origin, and one vertex at (1,1,1). This cube is created by defining an array of points that are the eight vertices of such a cube, and then using the `glBegin() . . . glEnd()` construction to draw the six squares that make up the cube through two quad strips. This is discussed in the chapter on modeling with OpenGL (Chapter 3); for now, note that the cube uses its own coordinates, which may or may not have anything to do with the space where we will define the heat transfer simulation.

Modeling Transformation

Modeling transformations are found in the `display()` function or functions called from it, and they define the fundamental transformations to be applied to the basic geometry as it is placed in the world. In our example, the basic geometry is a unit cube, scaled in Z (but not in X or Y) to define the height of each cell and then translated by X and Y (but not Z) to place the cell in the right place. The order of the transformations, the way each is defined, and the operations `glPushMatrix()/glPopMatrix()` you see in the code are described in Chapter 3, which deals with modeling in OpenGL. For now you should just see that the transformations are defined in order to make a rectangular object whose height represents its temperature.

3D World Space

The 3D world space for this program is the space where the graphical objects are placed by the modeling transformations. The translations give us one hint as to this space; we see that the x-coordinates of the translated cubes will lie between –ROWS/2 and ROWS/2, while the y-coordinates of these cubes will lie between –COLS/2 and COLS/2. Because ROWS and COLS are 30 and 10, respectively, the x-coordinates will lie between –15 and 15 and the y-coordinates between –5 and 5. The low z-coordinate is 0 because that is never changed when the cubes are scaled, while the high z-coordinate is never larger then 4. Thus the entire bar lies in the region between –15 and 15 in x, –5 and 5 in y, and 0 and 4 in z. (This is not quite correct, but it is good enough for now; you are encouraged to find the small error.)

Viewing Transformation

The viewing transformation is defined at the beginning of the `display()` function. This sets up the modelview matrix, sets that matrix to the identity (a transformation that makes no changes to the world), and then specifies the view. A view is specified in OpenGL with the `gluLookAt()` call:

```
gluLookAt(ex, ey, ez, lx, ly, lz, ux, uy, uz);
```

with parameters that include the coordinates of eye position `(ex, ey, ez)`, the coordinates of the point at which the eye is looking `(lx, ly, lz)`, and the coordinates of a vector that defines the "up" direction for the view `(ux, uy, uz)`. This is discussed in Chapter 1.

3D Eye Space

There is no specific representation of the 3D eye space in the program, because this is simply an intermediate stage in the production of the image. We can see, however, that we set the center of view to the origin, which is the center of our image, and we set our eye point to look at the origin from a point somewhat above and to the right of the center, so after the viewing transformation the object seems to be tilted up and to the side. This is the representation in the final 3D eye space that will be used to project the scene to the view plane.

Projections

In this example, the projection operation is defined in the `reshape()` function. It may be done in other places, but this is a good location and clearly separates the operation of projection from the operation of viewing.

Projections are specified fairly easily in OpenGL. An orthographic projection is defined with the function:

```
glOrtho(left, right, bottom, top, near, far);
```

where left and right are the x-coordinates of the left and right sides of the orthographic view volume, bottom and top are the y-coordinates of the bottom and top of the view volume, and near and far are the z-coordinates of the front and back of the view volume. A perspective projection can be defined with the function:

```
gluPerspective(fovy, aspect, near, far);
```

Here the first parameter is the field of view in degrees, the second is the aspect ratio for the window, and the near and far parameters are as above. In this projection, your eye is assumed to be at the origin so there is no need to specify the other four clipping planes; they are determined by the field of view and the aspect ratio. The field of view defines the width of the view, and the aspect ratio defines the ratio of the width to height of the view so that, for example, an aspect ratio of 0.5 specifies a view that is twice as wide as it is high.

When the window is reshaped, you can take the width and height of the changed window from the reshape event and define your projection to have the same aspect ratio (ratio of width to height) as the window. This is done in the sample code. This introduces no distortion into the scene as it is seen through the newly shaped window. If you use a fixed aspect ratio but change the window's shape, the original scene will be distorted as it is displayed in the new window, which can be confusing to the user.

2D Eye Space

This is the real 2D space in the view plane to which the 3D world is projected, and it corresponds to the forward plane of the view volume. The actual dimensions of the 2D eye space depend on the API. OpenGL scales the eye space so it has dimension –1 to 1 in each coordinate.

2D Screen Space

When the system was initialized in the example, the window for this program was defined to be 500×500 pixels in size with a top corner at (50, 50), or 50 pixels down and 50 pixels over from the upper-left corner of the screen. Thus the screen space for the window is the set of pixels in that area of the screen. In fact, though, the window maintains its coordinate system independently of its location, so the point that had been (0, 0, 0) in 3D eye space is now (249, 249) in screen space. Screen space has discrete integer coordinates that represent individual pixels, and its coordinates start at 0.

The Science in the Program

Most of the program deals with modeling the geometry, setting up the viewing, and handling the events that control the animation of the image. This is not unusual; graphics has a good deal of overhead that just goes into making the images. But this program also contains science in the way it models the heat flow in the bar. This is managed by the `iterationStep()` function and the `filter[][]` data element. The key point in the filter is that the elements of the array are all nonnegative and sum to 1, so the filter conserves energy. This kind of diffusion model is discussed later in the chapter on science applications (Chapter 9), but we want to point out that there *is* science in this program. The code in this function could be replaced if we wanted to work with a different model of heat flow or if we wanted to describe a different kind of diffusion problem.

Appearance

The appearance of the objects in this program is defined by the function `setColor()`, called from the `display()` function. If you recall that `display()` is also the place where modeling is defined, you will see that appearance is really part of modeling—you model both the geometry of an object and its appearance. The value of the temperature in each cell is used to compute a color for the cell's object as it is displayed, using the OpenGL `glColor3f()` function and individual calculations for each of the red, green, and blue components of the color. This is about the simplest way to define the color for an object's appearance, but it is quite effective.

Another Way to See the Program

Another way to see how this program works is to consider the code function-by-function instead of by the properties of the geometry pipeline. We will do this briefly here.

The task of `myinit()` is to set up the program environment. This is a good place to compute values for arrays that define the geometry, to define specific named colors, or perform any other operation that needs to be done only once. At the end of this function you should set up the initial projection specifications.

The task of `display()` is to do everything needed to create the image. This can involve manipulating a significant amount of data, but the function cannot have any parameters. The data for graphics problems must be managed through global variables. We treat the global data as a programmer-created environment, with some functions manipulating the data and the graphical functions using that data to define and present the display. In most cases, the global data is changed only through well-documented side effects, so this use of the data is reasonably clean. (This argues strongly for an emphasis on documentation in your projects, which most people believe is not a bad thing.) Of course, some functions can create or receive control parameters, and it is up to you to decide whether these parameters should be managed globally or locally, but even in this case the declarations are likely to be global because of the wide number of functions that may use them. OpenGL also maintains its own environment, called its system state, and some of your functions will also manipulate that environment.

The task of `reshape()` is to handle user manipulation of the window in which the graphics are displayed. The function takes two parameters, which are the width and height of the window in screen space (or in pixels) as it is resized by the user's manipulation and should be used to reset the projection information for the scene. GLUT interacts with the window manager of the system and allows a window to be moved or resized very flexibly without the programmer's having to manage any system-dependent operations directly. This kind of system independence is a very good reason to use GLUT!

The task of `animate()` is to respond to the **idle** event—the event that nothing has happened. This function defines what the program is to do without any user activity and is a way we can get animation in our programs. Without going into detail that should wait for our better discussion of events, `animate()` makes any desired changes in the global environment and then requests that the program make a new display with these changes by invoking `glutPostRedisplay()`. This posts a "redisplay" event to the system to ask the display function to be performed when the system can next do it.

The execution sequence of a simple program with no other events would then look something like that shown in Figure 0.8. Note that `main()` does not call the `display()` function directly; instead, `main()` calls the event-handling function `glutMainLoop()`, which never terminates but waits for events to be posted to the system event queue and then dispatches appropriate event callbacks. Because the graphics window's state has not yet been set, the display event

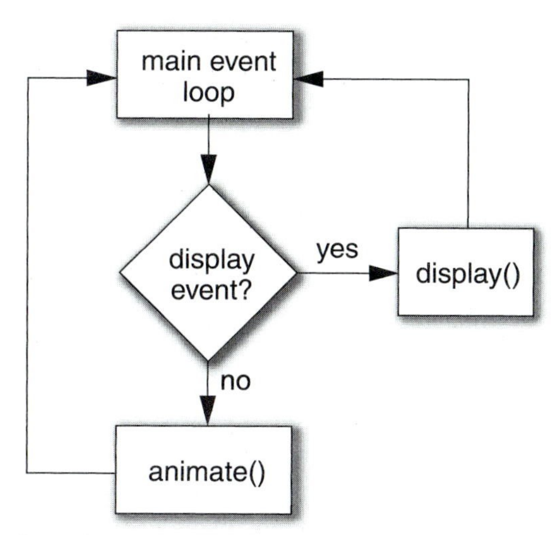

Figure 0.8 The event loop for the idle and display events.

is set by the system so the callback function `display` is called immediately when `glutMainLoop` starts. With no other event activity, the program will continue to apply the `idle()` function as time progresses, leading to an image that changes over time—that is, to an animated image.

A few words on the details of the `animate()` function might help you to see what it does. The program presents the behavior of heat in a bar, and the transfer of heat from one place to another is described by the heat equation. In this program we model heat transfer by a diffusion process. This sets the current heat of each cell to a weighted average of the heat of the cell's neighbors, with the weighting given by the filter array. At each time step, or each time when the program becomes idle, this diffusion process is applied to compute a new set of temperatures, and the angle of rotation of the display is updated. The call to `glutPostRedisplay()` at the end of this function then generates a call to the `display()` function that draws the image with the new temperatures and new angle.

In looking at the execution sequence for the functions in this simple program, it can be useful to consider a graph that shows which functions are called by which other functions. Because the program is event-driven, the event callback functions `animate()`, `display()`, and `reshape()` are not called directly by the program. We thus have the function caller/callee graph in Figure 0.9.

In this program, as in most programs using OpenGL, functions are called only by event callbacks or the `init()` initialization function, the `init()` function is called only once from `main()`, and all the event callbacks are called from the event handler. For most OpenGL programs, this is the general shape of the graph: A callback function may use several functions, but any function except a callback will be called only as part of program initialization or from an event callback. Functions may be called by both initialization and callbacks, though, or by other functions, so the caller/callee graph really is a graph and not the simple tree it looks like in the figure.

Now that we have an idea of the geometry pipeline and know what a program can look like, we can move on in later chapters to discuss how we specify the viewing and projection environment, how we define the fundamental geometry for our image, and how we create the image in the `display()` function with the environment that we define through the viewing and projection.

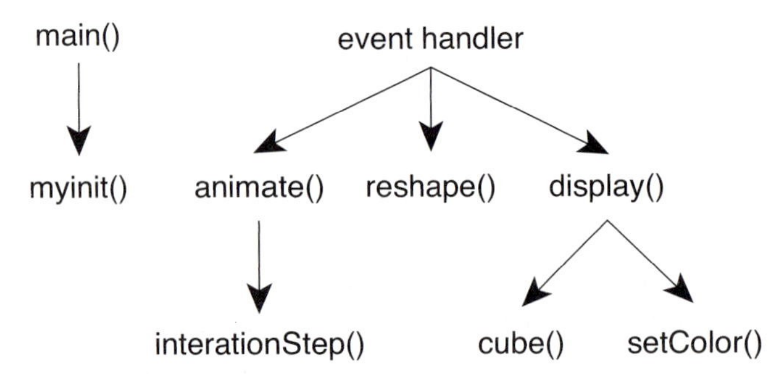

Figure 0.9 The function caller/callee graph for the example program.

OpenGL Extensions

In this chapter, and throughout this book, we take a tightly focused view of the OpenGL graphics API and focus on the basic features of computer graphics and of OpenGL. We do not work with most of the advanced features of the system, and we consider only the more straightforward uses of the parts we cover. But OpenGL is capable of very sophisticated kinds of graphics, both in its original version and in versions that are available for specific kinds of graphics. As you develop your graphics skills, you may find that the "vanilla" OpenGL that we cover here will not do everything you want.

Advanced features of OpenGL include a number of special operations to store or manipulate information on a scene. These include modeling via polygon tessellation, NURBS surfaces, and defining and applying your own special-purpose transformations; the scissor test and the more general stencil buffer and stencil test; rendering in feedback mode to get details on what is being drawn; and facilities for client/server support. OpenGL 2.0 also includes the specification of vertex and fragment shader languages to allow you to write custom shaders for your scenes. Remember, however, that this is a general text, not a detailed presentation of OpenGL, and be ready to look further (see the references) for more information. In addition to standard OpenGL, a number of extensions support more specialized kinds of operations. You can get information on extensions at the standard OpenGL Web site whose URL was given previously.

Summary

In this chapter we discussed the geometry pipeline and have indicated what each step involves and how it contributes to creating your final image. We have also shown how appearance fits into the geometry pipeline, although it is actually implemented in the rendering pipeline, and how all of this is implemented through a complete sample OpenGL program. In fact, you actually have a significant tool in this sample program, because it can be modified and adapted to serve as a basis for a great deal of other graphics programming. We do not have any programming projects in this chapter, but these will come along quickly and you will be able to use this sample program to get started on them.

OpenGL Glossary for the Chapter

In this chapter we used several OpenGL functions and definitions. This section recalls those that were used and gives a very short summary of what each does. In subsequent chapters we will have similar glossaries that will include new terms as we introduce them.

Types

`Glfloat`: a floating-point definition that is used to be system-independent

OpenGL Functions

`glBegin(xxx)`: identifies the kind of geometry that will be defined by vertex functions

`glClear(parms)`: clears data in the window as defined by the parameters

`glClearColor(r,g,b,a)`: sets the background color for the graphics window

`glColor3f(r,g,b)`: sets the color to be used for subsequent vertex calls to the RGB values given

`glEnable(parm)`: enables the capability defined by the parameter that is used

`glEnd()`: ends a geometry-defining section; paired with `glBegin(...)`

`glLoadIdentity()`: writes an identity matrix into whatever matrix has been specified by `glMatrixMode`

`glMatrixMode(parm)`: identifies the system matrix to be used for subsequent operations

`glPopMatrix()`: removes the top entry of the active matrix stack specified by `glMatrixMode`

`glPushMatrix()`: duplicates the top entry of the active matrix stack so that future operations on the stack will be applied to the copy; when the top entry is removed with `glPopMatrix`, the matrix is restored to the value it had when `glPushMatrix` was last called

`glRotate(angle,x,y,z)`: rotates geometry through the specified angle around the line whose parametric coefficients are (x, y, z)

`glScalef(dx,dy,dz)`: scales geometry by multiplying each vertex's coordinates by the values given

`glTranslatef(tx,ty,tz)`: translates geometry by adding the values given to each vertex's coordinates

`glVertex3fv(array)`: specifies a geometry vertex based on a 3D array

`glViewport(x,y,width,height)`: using integer window coordinates, specifies the portion of the graphics window in which drawing will be done

GLU functions

`gluLookAt(eyepoint,viewpoint,up)`: sets the environment for viewing by defining the eyepoint, the point the eye is looking at, and a point that is in the up direction from the viewpoint

`gluPerspective(fieldOfView,aspect,near,far)`: defines the perspective projection by giving four values that define the view volume based on the viewing environment

GLUT Functions

`glutCreateWindow(title)`: creates the graphics window and defines the window title

`glutDisplayFunc(function)`: specifies the callback function for the display event

`glutIdleFunc(function)`: specifies the callback function for the idle event

`glutInit(parms)`: initializes the GLUT system based on parameters that are part of the parameters to the `main()` function

`glutInitDisplayMode(parms)`: sets up the system display mode based on the symbolic parameters that are passed to it

`glutInitWindowPosition(x,y)`: specifies the screen coordinates of the top left corner of the window `glutInitWindowSize(x,y)`: specifies the width and height of the window in screen coordinates

`glutMainLoop()`: enters the GLUT event processing loop

`glutPostRedisplay()`: sets a redisplay event to cause the display to be generated again

`glutReshapeFunc(function)`: specifies the callback function for the reshape event

`glutSwapBuffers()`: copies the content of the back color buffer into the front color buffer so it can be displayed

Parameters:

`GL_COLOR_BUFFER_BIT`: used with `glClear`, indicates that the color buffer is to be cleared

`GL_DEPTH_BUFFER_BIT`: used with `glClear`, indicates that the depth buffer is to be cleared

`GL_DEPTH_TEST`: specifies that depth testing is to be done

`GL_MODELVIEW`: specifies that the matrix to be used is the modelview matrix

`GL_QUAD_STRIP`: specifies that vertices are to be interpreted as belonging to a sequence of quads in a specified order

`GLUT_DEPTH`: specifies that a window is to have a depth buffer (so depth testing can be done)

`GLUT_DOUBLE`: specifies that a window is to have a back buffer (so double buffering can be done)

`GLUT_RGB`: specifies that a window is to operate in RGB (or RGBA) mode

Questions

1. There are other ways to do graphics besides API-based programming, such as various modeling, painting, and other end-user tools. Distinguish between API-based graphics and graphics done with a tool such as Photoshop or a commercial paint program. The sample program in this chapter can give you an idea of how API-based graphics can look, although it is only a simple program and much more complex programs are discussed in later chapters.
2. Trace the 3D geometry in the sample program through the geometry pipeline from the point where you define a unit cube in model space, through the transformations that place that point into world space, through the viewing transformation that places the point in 3D eye space, to the projection that places the point in 2D eye space. Without doing any of the mathematics, identify and describe the changes that are made in the points' coordinates as these operations are performed.
3. We are surrounded by visual communication, often using very specialized vocabularies. Write a short paper on an example of a class of visual communication with a special vocabulary. One example might be the visual vocabularies in reporting financial data; another might be the visual vocabularies for weather reports. Include a number of examples and an analysis of how shape, color, geometric relationships, and behavior are used in this field.
4. The visual communication around us also involves scientific communication, and the vocabulary is often even more specialized for each of these. Use *Science*, *Scientific American,* or another high-end general science journal and write a science-focused paper as in the previous question.

Exercises

1. (Drawing) Visual communication is much broader than computer graphics, and skills in one part of this communication can lead to skills in others. As directed by your instructor, pick a

view in your local environment and draw this view by hand in a way that focuses on communicating the important parts of that view to others. When the drawings are done, share them with others and discuss what you were trying to communicate and to what degree the drawings achieved that. Try to identify the parts of the drawing that lead to the best communication and discuss how these parts can be created using computer graphics techniques.

2. Compile and execute the sample program in the chapter so you can become familiar with the use of your compiler for graphics programming. Exercise the `reshape()` function in the code by dragging and resizing the window. Change the shape of the window (make it narrower but not shorter, for example, or make it shorter but not narrower) and see how the window and image respond.

Experiments

1. There are many ways you can experiment with the full sample program in this chapter. A few of these experiments, along with the functions you need to modify to carry them out, are
   a. Change the size and upper left corner coordinates of the window [function `main()`].
   b. Change the locations of the hot and cold spots in the bar [function `myinit()`].
   c. Change the `filter()` function so that heat is transferred differently from the way it is in the example. This might make heat transferred differently in different directions, or might involve heat migrating to all eight adjacent cells instead of just the four cells right beside the original cell.
   d. Change the way the color of each bar is computed by changing the function that determines the color [function `setColor()`]. Be sure that each of the color values is a real number between 0 and 1.
   e. Change the rate at which the image rotates by changing the amount the angle is increased [function `animate()`].
   f. Change the way the edge of the bar is treated, so that instead of simply repeating the values at the edge, you get the values at the opposite edge of the bar, effectively allowing temperatures to move from one edge to the other as if the bar were a torus [function `iterationStep()`].
   g. Change the view of the bar from a perspective view to an orthogonal view [function `reshape()`] (you will probably need to look up the details of orthogonal projections in Chapter 1 on projection and viewing.

   Take as many of these experiments as you can, add appropriate code changes to the code of the previous exercise, and observe the changes in the images and program behavior that result. Draw as many conclusions as you can about the role of these various functions in creating the final animated image.

2. Experiment with the science in this program by changing the values in the filter array to modify the model of how heat diffuses in the bar [function `iterationStep()`]. As we noted in the discussion of the program, the filter needs to conserve energy by having all non-negative values that sum to 1, but you can change the values to have energy only flow in one direction or along one line. This could model something like a fibrous material where energy flows along the fiber but not between fibers, for example. You may need to change hot and cold spots to reflect this behavior, however.

3. Continuing with the `reshape()` function, look at the code of that function and think about how you might make it respond differently. The current version uses the window dimensions w and h in defining the perspective projection to ensure that the aspect ratio of the original image is preserved, but the window may cut off part of the image if it is too narrow. You might think about changing the projection angle to increase as the window is narrower, for example. Change the code in `reshape()` to try to change the behavior in the window.
4. Some sample programs are available for this book, and an enormous number of OpenGL programs are available on the Web. Find several of these and create the graph of function calls described in this chapter to verify (or refute) the claim we made that functions tend to operate in either program initialization or a single event callback. What does this tell you about the way you develop a graphics program with OpenGL? Where in this graph do most of the user-defined functions operate within the program?

1 Viewing and Projection

This chapter looks at two important stages of the geometry pipeline in detail. It presents the fundamental models for viewing and projection and discusses the operation of each. Viewing is considered in the context of the overall scene, and the key information needed to define a view is presented in terms of the scene. Both perspective and orthographic (or parallel) projections are also discussed, and again the key information needed for each is presented. The chapter assumes a basic understanding of 2D and 3D analytic geometry and some familiarity with simple linear mappings. If you have questions about these you should review the relevant part of Chapter 4.

After discussing the pipeline as a general feature of computer graphics, the chapter discusses how each stage is created in OpenGL. We discuss the OpenGL functions that allow you to define the viewing transformation and the orthographic and perspective projections, and we show how they are used in a program and how they can respond to window manipulation.

In addition to discussing viewing and projection, this chapter includes some topics related to basic steps in the geometry pipeline. These include clipping performed during projection (as well as the concept of clipping in general), defining the screen window where the image is presented, and specifying the viewport that will contain the actual image. Other topics include double buffering (creating the image in an invisible window and then swapping it with the visible window) and managing hidden surfaces. Finally, we show how you can create a stereo view with two images, computed from viewpoints that represent the left and right eyes, presented in adjacent viewports so they may be fused by someone with appropriate vision skills.

This chapter also includes a brief discussion of some of the ways views are important to creating effective visual communications. These are not complex, but you need to think of them as you design your overall image.

When finished with this chapter, you should be able to choose an appropriate view and projection for a scene and should be able to define the view and projection and write the necessary code to implement them in OpenGL. You should also understand the function of double buffering and hidden surfaces in 3D graphics and be able to use them in graphics programming.

Introduction

We emphasize 3D computer graphics because we believe computer graphics should be learned through 3D processes and that 2D graphics are best seen as a special case of 3D graphics. However, almost all of the viewing technologies that are readily available to us are 2D—monitors, printers, video, and film—and eventually even the active visual retina of our eyes presents a 2D environment. So in order to present the images of our scenes, we must create a 2D representation of 3D scenes. As we saw in the previous chapter, you begin by developing a set of models for your scene and place the models in the scene, giving you a set of objects in your world space. You then define the way the scene will be viewed and the way that view is presented on the screen.

We set the scene for this in the previous chapter, when we defined the geometry pipeline. We begin at the point where we have the 3D world coordinates—that is, where we have a complete scene fully defined in a 3D world. This point comes after we have done the modeling and model transformations that will be discussed in detail in the two chapters after this one. To remind ourselves of the steps in this process as shown in Figure 0.1, the geometry pipeline without the modeling stage is shown in Figure 1.1.

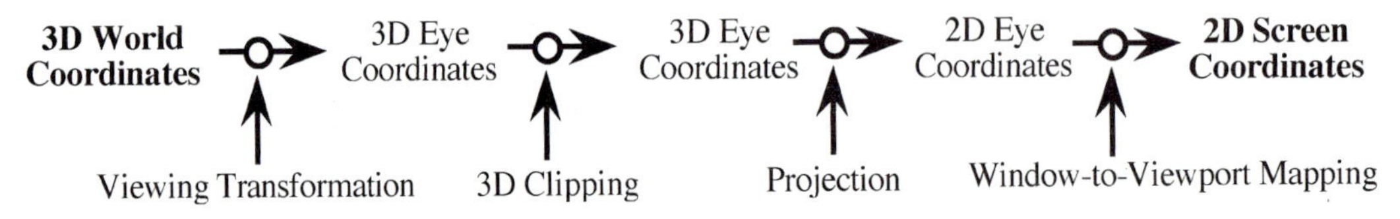

Figure 1.1 The geometry pipeline for creating an image of a scene.

Let's consider an example of an actual world space and look at what it means to present that space. One of the author's favorite places is Yosemite National Park, a wonderful example of a 3D world. There is a basic geometry in the park, made up of stone, wood, and water, and this geometry can be seen from a number of points. In Figure 1.2 we see the classic piece of Yosemite geometry, the Half Dome monolith, from below in the valley and from above at Glacier Point. This gives us an excellent example of two views of the same geometry.

In photographs we see the essential components of viewing. First, your view depends on where you are standing. If you are standing on the valley floor, you see the face of the monolith in the classic view shown on the left in Figure 1.2; if you are standing on the rim of Yosemite Valley, you see the profile of the rock on the right. So your view depends on your position, which we call your *eye point*. Second, the view also depends on the point you are looking at, which we will call the *view reference point*. Both photos look toward the Half Dome monolith, with the classic left-hand view looking directly at the dome and the right-hand view from Glacier Point looking at a point in space behind the dome. This changes not only the view of the dome, but also the view of the region around the dome. In the classic view from the valley, at the right you see the south wall of the valley; in the view from Glacier Point, at the right you see Vernal and Nevada falls on the Merced River and, farther to the right, the high Sierra in the south of the park. Finally, although this may not be obvious at first because our minds process images in context, the view

Figure 1.2 Two views of half dome from Yosemite Valley (*left*) and Glacier Point (*right*).

depends on your sense of the *up direction* in the scene: whether you are standing with your head upright or tilted. This might be easier to grasp if you think of the view as being defined by a camera instead of by your vision; it's clear that if you tilt a camera at a 45° angle you get a very different photo from one that's taken by a camera held horizontally or vertically.

The view also depends on the *breadth of field* of your view, or whether you are looking at a wide part of the scene or a narrow part. The left-hand photograph is a view of just Half Dome, while the right-hand one is a panoramic view that includes the dome. While both photos are essentially square, you can visualize the left-hand photo as part of a photo that is more vertical in layout, whereas the right-hand photo looks as if it could come from a horizontal layout; this represents an *aspect ratio* for the image. The world is the same in all of this discussion, but the things that determine the image are where your eye is, the point you are looking toward, the way your view sees as up, the breadth of your view, and the aspect ratio of your view. In computer graphics, you must specify all of these in order to define an image.

Once you have set your view, it must be converted into an image that can be presented on a 2D device. This is like recording an image with a digital camera: Each point of the view space (each pixel in the image) must be given a specific color. With the digital camera this involves only capturing the light that comes through the lens to that point in the camera's sensing device, but with computer graphics we must calculate exactly what will be seen at that particular point in 2D screen space. Defining the way the 3D scene is transformed into 2D space involves a number of steps: what parts of the scene are in front of what other parts, what parts are within view from the viewer's eye point, and how the scene is brought to the 2D viewing space. The best way to think about the last step is to compare how two very different kinds of lenses work: One is a standard lens that gathers light from a cone in front of a camera, and the other is a high-altitude photography lens that gathers light only from a very tight cylinder and processes light rays that are essentially parallel as they are transferred to the sensor.

This model of viewing is paralleled quite closely by a computer graphics system, and it follows the geometry pipeline of the previous chapter. You begin by modeling your scene with a collection of objects in their own modeling spaces, and you place each in the world space with its own modeling transformations. We saw an example of this in the temperature example of the previous chapter, and it is outlined in detail in Chapters 2 and 3. The result is your completed model in 3D world space. The fundamental task of the viewing operation is to define a view within your world space so that the viewer can see the things in your modeling space that you want to be seen. Defining the view places the eye in world space and creates a coordinate system relative to the eye. This lets you transform the 3D world space into this coordinate system, which creates the 3D eye space. Projection, in turn, defines a 2D plane within the 3D eye space where the scene is to be presented, defines a mapping that projects the model space into that plane, and displays that plane on the viewing surface. We will usually think of a that plane as a screen, but it could be a page, a video frame, or a number of other spaces.

It is sometimes useful to "cut away" part of a scene so that you can see things that would otherwise be hidden behind some objects in the scene. This chapter includes a brief discussion of clipping planes, a technique for accomplishing this action that we will describe in more detail in later chapters. This is related to the system's task of clipping parts of the scene that lie outside the view volume.

The mechanics of the modeling transformations, viewing transformation, and projection are managed by the graphics API, and the task of the graphics programmer is to provide the API with the correct information and call the API functionality in the correct order to make these operations work. We will now describe the general concepts of viewing and projection and will then tell you how to specify the various parts of this process to OpenGL. However, we don't need to focus on the details of transformations at this point. For now, we can simply treat the transformations of computer graphics as functions that operate on points in space and that preserve geometry. In Chapter 4 we will see how these are represented to the computer and how they work.

Fundamental Model of Viewing

We can create a physical model of the viewing process by looking through a rectangular frame that you hold in front of your eye. You can move around, setting your eye into whatever position and orientation you wish to see the world. This defines your viewpoint and view reference point. The shape of the frame and the orientation you give it determine the aspect ratio and the up direction for the image. Once you have set your position in the world, you can hold the frame up to your eye and this will set a perspective projection; by moving the frame nearer to or farther from the eye you change the breadth of field for the projection. And finally, if you put a piece of transparent material that is ruled in very small squares behind the cardboard and you fill in each square to match the color you see in the square, you create a copy of the image to take away with you.

Consider the situation shown in the left-hand side of Figure 1.3. Here we have a world coordinate system oriented in the usual way, and within this world we have both a (simple) model and an eyepoint. The original *X*, *Y*, and *Z* coordinate axes are shown in the usual orientations. At the eyepoint we have a small white sphere, the view reference point is shown as a small dark-gray sphere, and the view-up point is shown as a small light-gray sphere. Lines of the same color connect

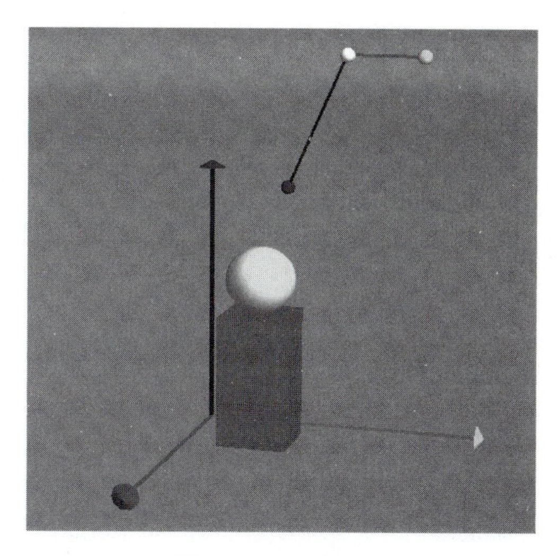

Figure 1.3 The viewing setup within the world coordinate system (*left*) and the actual view that it sets up (*right*).

the spheres to the eyepoint. From this, you should try to visualize how the model will look once it is displayed with the view. To make it easier for you to start, the right-hand side of Figure 1.3 shows the same model as displayed from the eyepoint of the left-hand side (cropped to fit the space better), without the original axes. An exercise at the end of the chapter suggests that you explore this further.

When you place your eye, you define a coordinate system within the world space relative to the eye. Once this eye coordinate system is specified, it defines an operation to change everything in the view from world coordinates into the eye coordinate system. This is a straightforward mathematical transformation, performed by creating a change-of-basis matrix from the world coordinate system to the eye coordinate system and then applying it to everything in the world space geometry. This transformation places the eye at the origin, looking along the Z-axis, and with the Y-axis pointed upward. This is the *viewing transformation* that moves the geometry from the world coordinate system to the eye coordinate system, preserving all the geometric relations in your model. Once the eye is in standard position and all your geometry is adjusted with the viewing transformation, the system can easily project the geometry to the viewing plane in the next stage of the pipeline.

In Chapter 2 we discuss modeling, and part of modeling is using transformations to place an object defined in one position, orientation, and size in model space into a different position, size, and orientation in world space. The eyepoint can be defined with this kind of modeling, and we can think of starting with the eye in standard position and applying transformations to place the eye where you want it.

Once you have organized the viewing information, you must organize the way your scene is projected to the screen. The graphics system gives you ways to define the projection, and once the projection is defined, the system will carry out the computations that map the scene to the display space. This will be discussed later in this chapter.

Definitions

You must consider a small number of things when you think of how you will view your scene. These are independent of the particular API you are using, but later in the chapter we will talk about how they are handled in OpenGL. These are the following:

- Your world must be seen, so you need to define the view of your model, including the eye position, view direction, field of view, and orientation. This defines the viewing transformation.
- Your world must usually be seen on a 2D surface such as a screen, so you must define how the 3D world is projected to a 2D space. There will be different ways to do this for different kinds of projections.
- The region of the viewing device where you will see the image must be defined. This is the *graphics window,* which should not be confused with the concept of a window on your screen, though they may both refer to the same space.
- When your view is seen, it must be seen at a particular place in the window, so you must define its location. This defines the *viewport* within the window, and the window-to-viewport mapping that takes the 2D eye space to screen space.

These four things are called setting up your viewing environment, defining your projection, and defining your window and viewport, respectively, and they are discussed in that order in the sections below.

Setting Up the Viewing Environment

A scene is built in world space with modeling primitives and transformations, as described in Chapter 2. This world space is then transformed by the viewing transformation into a 3D space with the eye in standard position. Within that world, you define three critical components for your eye setup: where your eye is located, what point your eye is looking toward, and what direction is vertical with respect to your eye. When these are set, your model geometry is transformed with the viewing transformation to create the view as it would be seen in the environment you defined.

A graphics API gives you tools to define your view and then does the computations that transform your overall scene in this way. For example, OpenGL defines its modeling in a right-handed coordinate system and transforms all the geometry in your scene (*all* the geometry, including lights and directions, as we will see in Chapter 6) to place your eyepoint at the origin. The viewing is done in a left-handed coordinate system with the eye looking in the negative direction along the *Z*-axis. This orientation is illustrated in Figure 1.4: The eyepoint is located in ordinary modeling space, but the eye's coordinate system is a separate left-handed system shown attached to the eyepoint.

The information needed to define your view includes

- the (x, y, z) coordinates of your eye position,
- the direction your eye is facing or the coordinates of a point toward which it is facing, which will become the *Z*-direction for the eye coordinate system, and
- the direction your eye perceives as "up" in the world space, which will become the *Y*-direction in the eye coordinate system.

Your graphics API will give you functions that let you set your eyepoint and viewing directions as you like.

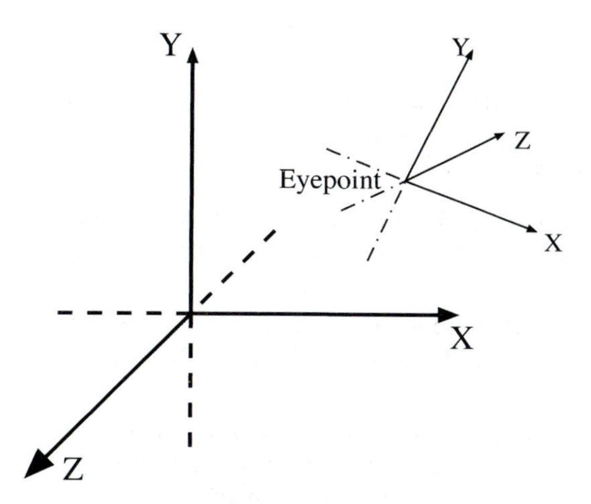

Figure 1.4 The standard openGL viewing model.

The viewing transformation takes the scene as you define it in world space and aligns the eye position with the standard model, giving you the eye space we discussed in the previous chapter. The key actions of the viewing transformation are to rotate the world to align your personal up direction with the *Y*-axis, to rotate it again so the look-at direction is in the direction of the negative *Z*-axis, to translate the world so the eyepoint lies at the origin, and finally to scale the world so the look-at point or look-at vector has the value (0, 0, –1). These operations are the inverses of the modeling transformations that you would use to move the eyepoint from the standard position to the position you define with your API function. This is very important in Chapter 2 on modeling, and is discussed in some depth later in this chapter in terms of defining the view environment for the OpenGL API.

Defining the Projection

The viewing transformation defines the 3D eye space, but that space cannot be viewed on our standard devices. The scene must be mapped to a 2D space that corresponds to your display device—a computer monitor, a video screen, or a sheet of paper. The technique for moving from the three-dimensional world to a two-dimensional world uses a projection operation that is defined based on straightforward principles.

When you (or a camera) view something in the real world, everything you see is the result of light that reaches the retina (or the CCD cell on the film) through a lens that focuses the light rays onto that viewing surface. This process is a projection of the natural (3D) world onto a two-dimensional space. A dramatic illustration of a perspective view is shown in Figure 1.5. This projection operates by light passing through the lens of the eye (or camera) and has the property that parallel lines going into the distance seem to converge at the horizon so things in the distance are seen as smaller than the same things when they are close to the viewer. The exact way things converge depends on the field of view of the projection. This kind of projection, where everything is seen by being projected onto a viewing plane through or toward a single point, is called a *perspective projection.*

On the other hand, you may want to have objects of the same size in the scene be shown as the same size in the image. For example, you may need to take careful measurements from the image, as in engineering drawings. An *orthographic projection* accomplishes this by projecting all the

Figure 1.5 A photograph of an architectural feature showing very strong perspective.

objects in the scene to the viewing plane by parallel lines. In orthographic projection, objects that are the same size are seen in the projection at the same size, no matter how far they are from the eye.

In Figure 1.6 we show two images of a house and its modeling coordinate system from the same viewpoint. The house has been drawn with partly transparent surfaces so you can see the "hidden" back parts of the model through the front parts. The left-hand image of the figure uses a perspective projection, and you can see the difference in the apparent sizes of the front and back ends of the building and the way that the sides and roof of the building appear smaller as they recede from the viewer. The right-hand image of the figure uses an orthographic projection, as

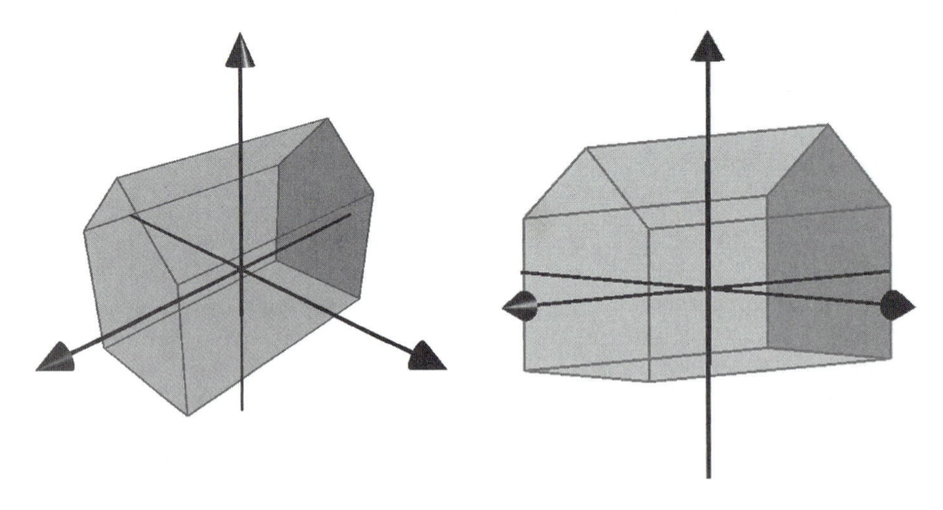

Figure 1.6 Perspective image (*left*) and orthographic image (*right*) of a simple model of a house.

shown by the equal sizes of the front and back ends of the building and the parallel lines outlining the sides and roof of the building. The difference between these two images is modest but should be easy to grasp. It could be useful to have both projections for some of your scenes and compare the results to see how each of the projections works in different situations; we explore this in an experiment described at the end of the chapter.

These projections operate on points in 3D space in different ways. For the orthographic projection, all points are projected to the *XY*-plane in 3D eye space by considering only the *X*- and *Y*- coordinates. If the point (x,y,z) is projected to the point (x',y'), we have $x'=x$ and $y'=y$. Each point in 2D eye space is the image of a line parallel to the Z-axis, so the orthographic projection is a *parallel projection.*

For the perspective projection, each point is projected onto the plane Z=1 in 3D eye space at the point where the line from the point to the origin meets that plane. Each point in the 2D eye space represents the line through that point and the origin in 3D eye space. If the point (x,y,z) is projected to the point (x',y'), we must have $x'=x/z$ and $y'=y/z$ by similar triangles. The mathematics of the perspective projection are considered further later in this chapter, but the basic setup and the similarity diagram that give us these equations is shown in Figure 1.7.

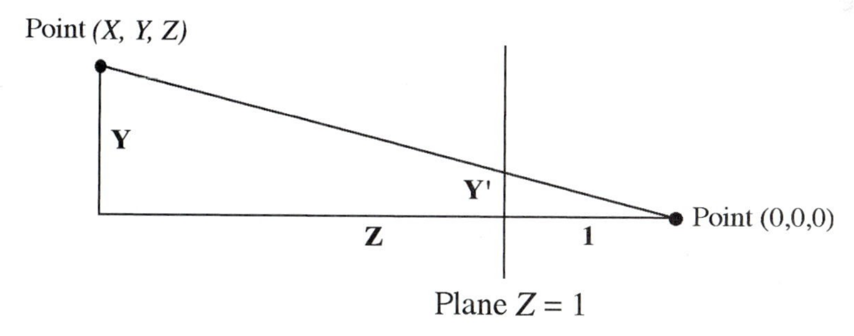

Figure 1.7 The diagram for the perspective projection calculation.

Applying a projection maps your scene to 2D eye space, as discussed in the previous chapter, but the *z*-values in your scene need not be lost. As each point is transformed, its *z*-value is retained for later computations such as depth tests or perspective-corrected textures. In some APIs, the *z*-value is converted to an integer and its sign is changed so that points farther from the eye (farther from the origin in 3D eye space) have larger positive *z*-values, consistent with a left-hand coordinate system. This lets the system use positive integers in depth operations.

View Volumes

A projection is often thought of in terms of its *view volume,* the region of space that is to be visible in the scene after the projection. With any projection, the fact that the image is viewed on a rectangular viewing device implicitly defines a set of boundaries for the left, right, top, and bottom sides of the scene; these correspond to the left, right, top, and bottom of the viewing space. The conventions of viewing do not display objects that are too close to or too far from the eyepoint, and the ideas of too close or too far give us the front and back sides of the region that can be viewed. We will use the names ZNEAR and ZFAR for the front and rear boundaries, respectively, of the view volume; the other boundaries will depend on whether we use perspective or orthographic perspectives. Note that we must always have $0 \leq \text{ZNEAR} \leq \text{ZFAR}$.

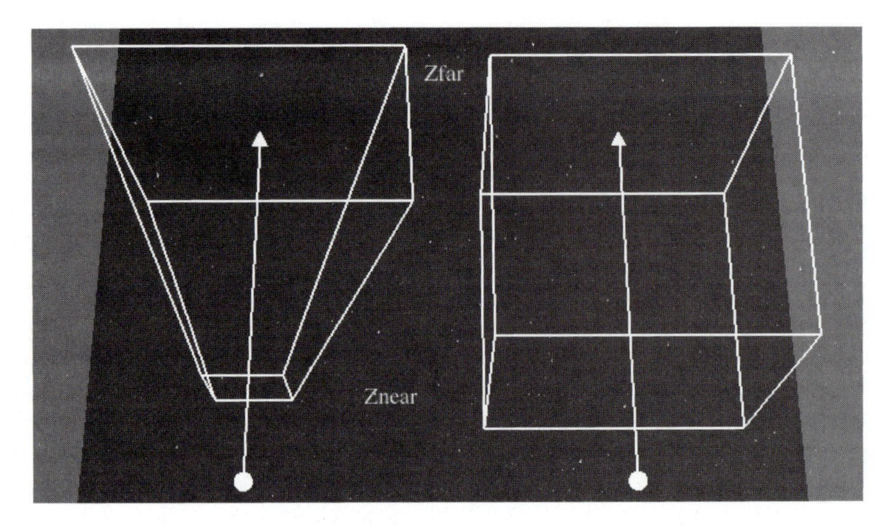

Figure 1.8 The viewing volumes for the perspective (*left*) and orthographic (*right*) projections.

This region in three-dimensional space which contains all the scene that can be viewed is called the *view volume* for the projection. The view volumes for the perspective and orthographic projections are shown in Figure 1.8, with the eyepoint shown as a white sphere; this region is the space within the rectangular volume behind the *X-Y* plane (right, for the orthographic projection) or the pyramid frustum behind the *X-Y* plane (left, for the perspective transformation). These view volumes show the regions of 3D eye space that map to the viewplane in 2D eye space, and each includes the *Z*-axis in the left-handed viewing coordinate system shown in Figure 1.4. In the standard positions shown, the eye is at the origin and is looking into the screen, so the figures show the left-handed coordinates with the *Z*-axis pointing in the opposite direction from the familiar coordinate axis. Note that both view volumes lie behind the *X-Y* plane that contains the eyepoint.

The perspective view volume is generally defined only with a specific position in your model space because it makes assumptions about the view's being symmetric around the *Z*-axis. In contrast, an orthographic view volume may be defined wherever you need it. This lets you set up an orthographic view of any part of your space, or to move your orthographic view volume around to view any part of your model. This ability to place your viewing volume for the orthographic projection might be useful but is probably less important than it seems, because you can always use simple translations to move the region you want to see into standard position.

We emphasize the view volume because only objects inside your projection's view volume will be displayed, as you saw in the previous chapter. Anything else in the scene will be clipped—that is, it will be identified as invisible for the projection process, so it will not be handled further by the graphics system. Any object that is partly within and partly outside the viewing volume will be clipped so that precisely those parts inside the volume are seen. The sides of the viewing volume are to the projections of the sides of the visible rectangular space, and the front and back of the volume correspond to the nearest and farthest spaces that are visible in the projection. These let you ensure that your image presents only the part of space that you want and prevent things that might lie behind your eye or too far away from being projected into the visible space.

The Orthographic Projection

To define an orthographic projection we must specify the left, right, top, bottom, back, and front planes for its view volume. Each of these planes is defined by an equation of the form

$$\text{coordinate} = \text{value}$$

so each plane is defined by a single real number. For example, an orthographic view volume that is two units in each coordinate can be defined by the six equations of the bounding planes:

$$x = -1; \qquad x = 1;$$
$$y = -1; \qquad y = 1;$$
$$z = 0.1; \qquad z = 2.1;$$

Changing each value simply includes more or less of the space at one side of the view volume. So to see more of the space to the left of the volume, we would decrease the value that specifies the left plane of the volume; to see less of that space, we would increase the value. For the right side, these are reversed: Decreasing the value shows less of the space, and increasing it shows more of the space.

The Perspective Projection

The perspective projection is more complicated than the orthographic projection. The perspective projection is always centered on the Z-axis, and the actual volume is defined by the field of view (horizontally, often measured in degrees) and the aspect ratio (vertically). The aspect ratio is the ratio of the height to the width of the view, so an aspect ratio of 1 means that the width equals the height; a ratio of .75 means that the ratio is 3:4, the standard U.S. television ratio. For many images, you want to make the aspect ratio of your projection equal to the aspect ratio of your window so that your view accurately represents your model. The field of view itself determines how much of the model is seen in the window, as shown in Figure 1.9. If the field of view is broader, the effect is like that of a wide-angle lens; if it is narrower, the effect is like that of a telephoto lens.

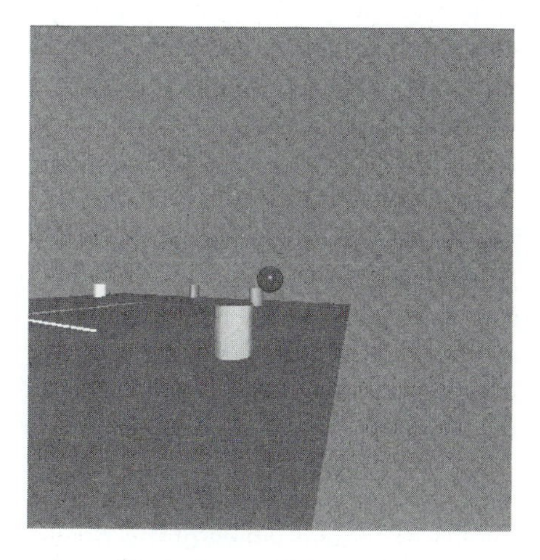
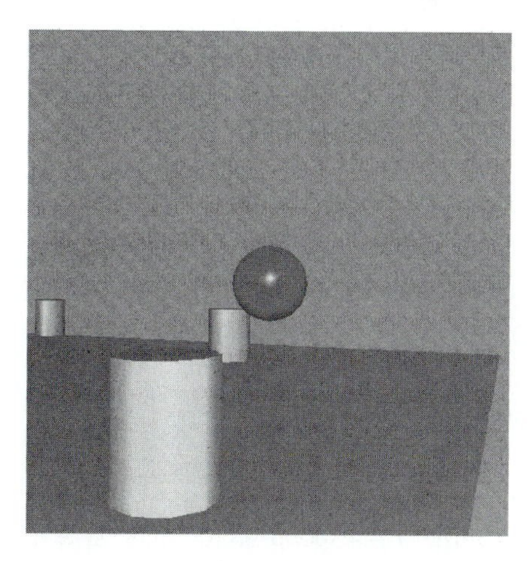

Figure 1.9 Two views of the same simple scene from the same viewpoint with a wide field of view (*left*) and narrow field of view (*right*), both looking toward the red ball.

The other parameters for the perspective projection are the front and back planes. These work like the planes in the orthographic transformation: If the front plane value is decreased, objects closer to the eye are seen instead of being clipped; if the back plane value is increased, objects farther from the eye are seen instead of being clipped.

Because the farther parts of the view volume are larger than the nearer parts, objects that are farther away are smaller in comparison to the overall space and so are reduced more when the view volume is mapped to the screen. They are thus displayed in a smaller part of the image, and this makes them smaller in screen space. If a plane containing two objects is parallel to the *XY*-plane in the 3D eye space, the perspective transformation affects them both the same way. However, if one of the objects is farther from the eye, the farther object seems to shrink in the view. This effect provides views that show objects getting smaller as they recede into the distance. The discovery of perspective was one of the most important developments in art in the Renaissance, and it is an important tool for making effective images. This is often used to show distance by its effect on a set of objects that are aligned; standard examples include a highway, a row of telephone poles, and a row of buildings.

The basic kinds of perspective drawings are one-point, two-point, and three-point perspective. This classification models the world as laid out in a regular two- or three-dimensional coordinate system and is based on a simple fact: If two objects the same size are in a plane that is not parallel to the viewing plane, then one object is farther from the viewing plane than the other and is seen as being smaller.

In the simplest kind of scene layout, two coordinate directions are parallel to the viewing plane and one coordinate is not parallel to it. Then only objects that have changes in that coordinate and that move directly away from the viewer will seem to grow smaller. This kind of view is called *one-point perspective,* and the point toward which the direction is leading is called the *vanishing point.* Of course, the back clipping plane for the view volume will not let your view go all the way to the horizon, but you will certainly see the tendency toward the vanishing point as shown in the left-hand image of Figure 1.10.

In a slightly more complex layout, one coordinate is parallel to the viewing plane and two coordinates are not parallel to it. Then objects having changes in either of these two coordinates will look as though they are smaller when they are farther from the viewer. This

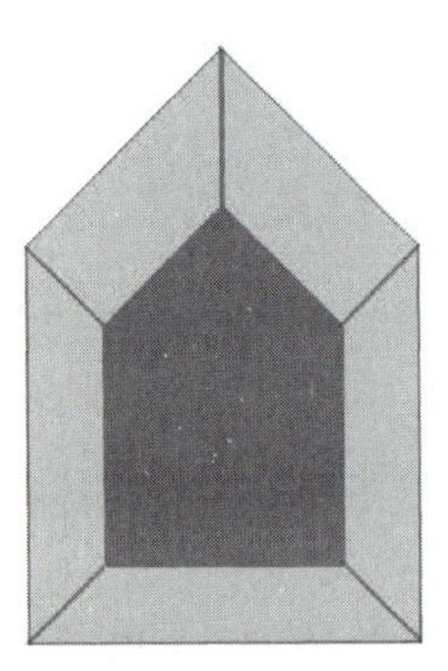
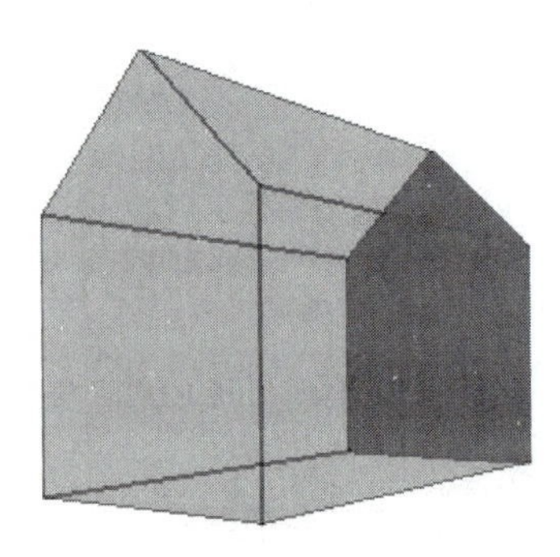
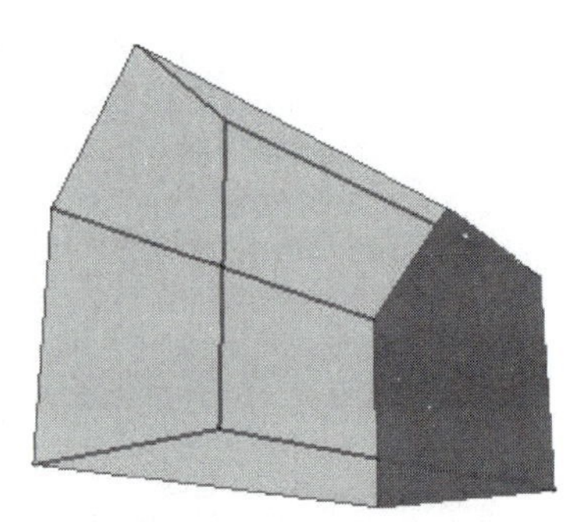

Figure 1.10 One-point, two-point, and three-point perspective views of the house in Figure 1.6.

kind of view is called *two-point perspective,* and there are two vanishing points, although they may not both show up inside the frame of the image. This is illustrated in the center image of Figure 1.10. Of course, if objects in the world have multiple parallel lines that are not parallel to the view plane, the image can have multiple vanishing points; you can see this if you look at an orchard or a cemetery with a regular grid of gravestones. And in a third named case, if none of the coordinates is parallel to the view plane, objects that are aligned with any of the world space axes will also seem to grow smaller as they recede. This gives a third vanishing point and leads to *three-point perspective,* as shown in the right-hand image of Figure 1.10.

Calculating the Perspective Projection

The perspective projection is straightforward to compute. Although you do not need to carry out this computation yourself, you will find it very useful later on to understand how it works. With the general setup for the perspective viewing volume, let's look at a 2D version of perspective shown in Figure 1.11, repeated from Figure 1.7. Here we see from similar triangles that $Y/Y' = Z$ or $Y' = Y/Z$. A similar calculation shows that $X' = X/Z$. Thus with the standard viewing conventions we have defined, the perspective projection defined on 3D eye space simply divides the original X and Y values by Z. If we write this projection as a matrix, we have:

$$\begin{bmatrix} 1/Z & 0 & 0 \\ 0 & 1/Z & 0 \\ 0 & 0 & 1 \end{bmatrix}$$

This 3×3 matrix defines a transformation from 3-space to 3-space, changing the X and Y values while leaving the Z value fixed. However, if you want your projection to go strictly to 2D space, you can omit the right-hand column.

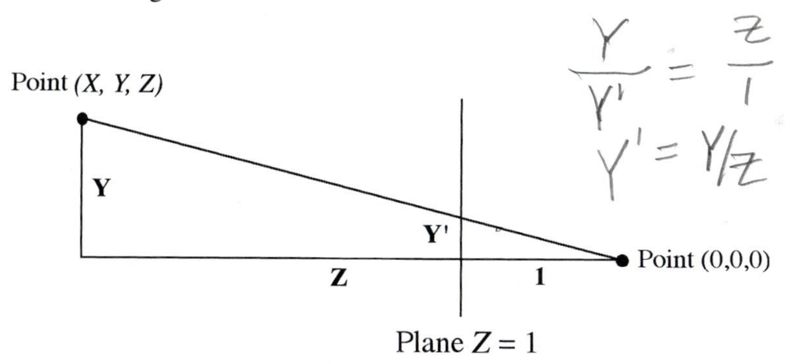

Figure 1.11 The diagram for the perspective projection calculation.

This matrix represents a transformation called the *perspective transformation*. Because the matrix entries have a variable in the denominator, this transformation is not a linear mapping. That will be important later when we must perform perspective corrections when interpolating some object properties. If we have the transformed values of X' and Y' and know the original value of Z, we can reconstruct the original values as $X = X'*Z$ and $Y = Y'*Z$. This suggests that projection computations should retain depth values in some form, an important idea we will see when we discuss hidden surfaces and texture mapping. The perspective projection applies the perspective transformation and has only X' and Y' as output. While we can clip on the perspective view volume before we apply the perspective transformation, we can also apply the perspective transformation to the whole world first, and then use a parallel projection and its simpler clipping in the transformed space second.

Clipping on the View Volume

We saw that parts of an image outside the view volume are clipped, or removed from the active scene, before the scene is displayed. Clipping for an orthographic projection is easy because the boundary planes are defined by constant values of single coordinates: $X = Xleft$, $X = Xright$, $Y = Ybottom$, $Y = Ytop$, $Z = Znear$, and $Z = Zfar$. Clipping a line segment against any of these planes checks to see whether the line is all inside, is all outside, or crosses the plane. If it is all inside, it is kept. If it is all outside, it is discarded. If it crosses the plane, the line segment is replaced with the part of the line segment that does not include the part outside the volume.

On the other hand, clipping on the view volume for the perspective projection is not as simple. This requires making clipping tests against the sloping side planes, and this is more complex. This can be avoided by being clever: apply the perspective transformation before carrying out the clipping. This transforms the sloping side planes of the perspective view volume into planes parallel to the Z-axis, just like those of the orthographic view volume. Then clipping can be carried out just as it was for the orthographic projection.

Clipping as part of projection is generally done after the perspective projection so that all the work is performed on a region defined by planes having one of the coordinate values constant. Clipping generally focuses on line segments, because most of the work we do is based on line segments or areas bounded by them. Polygons must also be clipped, of course, but polygon clipping is based on clipping the line segments in the polygon's boundary.

Clipping works with individual line segments and starts by working with the segment's endpoints. It is simple to tell if a vertex is in a rectangular view volume; simply compare the coordinates of the vertex with the values that define the bounding planes. If both endpoints of the line segment are in the volume, the entire segment must be also. If an endpoint is outside the volume, at least one coordinate of the vertex must be outside the boundary, so you can substitute the boundary value in the parametric equation of the line segment and solve for the parameter that defines the intersection point. That parameter defines a new vertex. You then replace the previous endpoint with the new vertex and get a line segment that is shorter than the original segment. You continue this process until either both endpoints of the line segment are in or no line segment is left. If any line segment is left, you can draw it. This is illustrated in a 2D example as the left-hand diagram in Figure 1.12.

If you are working with a polygon, you work on one face of the view volume at a time and clip each of the polygon edges on that face. When an edge goes from inside the volume to outside the volume, you calculate the vertex where the edge meets the face as above. You not only use this new vertex for the edge but save it, and when an edge next comes back into the volume on that side you also calculate its new entry vertex. You then take the saved vertex and the new entry vertex and create a new edge that you add to the polygon before you add the edge whose entry point you just calculated. The result of this work on all faces in a 2D example is shown in the right-hand side of Figure 1.12, where the heavy lines show what is kept from the original object in light lines.

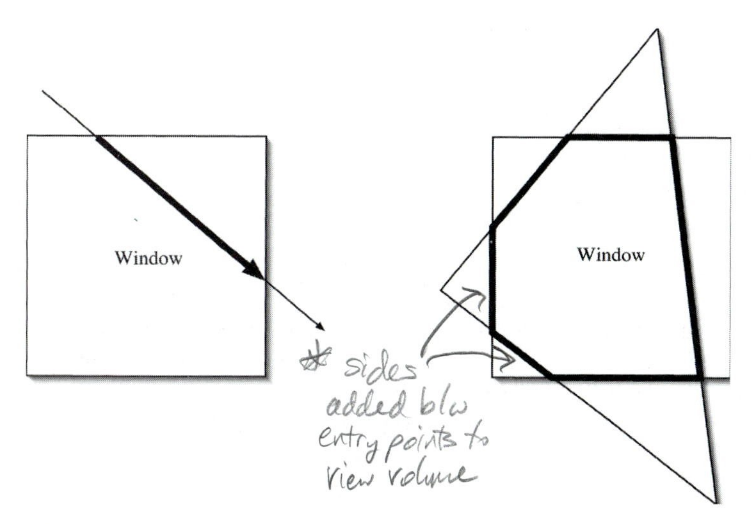

Figure 1.12 Line segment and polygon clipping.

Finally, if you are working with a polyhedron, you must work with each of the polygon faces separately and clip each face to the view volume. After clipping, the polyhedron will not be complete if, for example, a corner of the polyhedron should lie outside the view volume. Holes such as this are generally not filled, so a clipped polyhedron may no longer be a polyhedron, strictly speaking. If you want to fill in any such hole, you will need to save the line segments that are generated on each boundary of the view volume and assemble them into one or more new polygons that will be part of the boundary of the polyhedron.

This simple approach is slow because each vertex is tested against each bounding plane, but there are other approaches that make it more efficient. Perhaps the simplest is the Cohen-Sutherland approach [FO] of computing an *outcode* for each vertex and using the outcodes to determine what operations are needed to clip a line segment. Briefly, an outcode is a six-tuple of true/false values (or 1/0 values, if you prefer) where each position indicates whether the point lies on the side of a view volume edge that is to be clipped. If the point is clippable on that edge, the code for that edge is true, or 1; if the point is on the viewable side, the value given is false, or 0. As an example, if the view volume has bounds $-2 \le X \le 2$, $-2 \le Y \le 2$, and $-3 \le Z \le -1$, the point $(-3, 3, -2)$ has the outcode (1,0,0,1,0,0).

To clip a line segment, the outcodes of both endpoints of the segment are computed and logical tests are made on them. If the logical OR of the two outcodes is all zero, the entire segment is kept. If the logical AND of the two outcodes is not all zero, then the entire segment is discarded. If not, then the position of the 1s in each outcode tell you exactly what edges you must intersect the segment with, so you need not make any other comparisons. After the intersections are computed and old endpoints replaced with new, as above, a new outcode is computed for the new endpoint and the process is repeated.

With the advent of high-speed graphics hardware, the classic approach to clipping has become less important for the programmer because clipping is done at the graphics card. This is optimized for vertex processing and is doubtless faster (and simpler for the programmer) than doing your own clipping. Unless you can eliminate large chunks of geometry and keep from sending them into the pipeline, let the specialized hardware do the work for you.

Defining the Window and Viewport

The scene presented by the projection is still in 2D eye space, and the objects are all defined by real-valued coordinates. However, the display space is discrete, so the next step in creating the image is converting the geometry from 2D eye coordinates into integer-valued discrete coordinates. This requires identifying discrete screen points to replace the real-valued geometry points and introduces sampling issues that must be handled carefully, but graphics APIs do this work for you. The actual display space used by the image depends on the window and the viewport you have defined.

To a graphics system, a window is a rectangular region in your viewing space in which all of the drawing from your program will be done. The window is defined in terms of the display device's coordinate system, but it has its own internal coordinate system. A window used for drawing is different from a window used in a desktop display window system, although the drawing window may in fact occupy a desktop window. We will consistently be careful to reserve the term *window* for the region used for the graphic display. The graphics API provides the interface between your graphics windows and the device's window manager. The space in the graphics window is called *screen space* and uses the 2D screen coordinates as described in the geometry pipeline. The smallest displayed unit in this space will be called a *pixel*, a shorthand for *picture element.* This separate coordinate system is defined relative to the window, not the overall display, and does not change if the display window is moved on the screen. We will consistently think of the display space in terms of pixel coordinates because they are all that matter to our image.

Recall that the geometry pipeline has a final transformation from the 2D eye coordinate system to the 2D screen coordinate system. To understand that transformation, you need to understand the relation between points in two corresponding rectangular spaces. The rectangle for the scene in 2D eye space is one, and the rectangle in 2D screen space is another. The same processes apply to other cases of corresponding points in two rectangular spaces, such as the relation between the cursor position in screen space and the corresponding point in 2D eye space, or points in the world space and points in a texture space.

In Figure 1.13, we see the 2D window and viewport with boundaries and points named as shown. We assume that the lower left corner of each rectangle has the smallest coordinate values

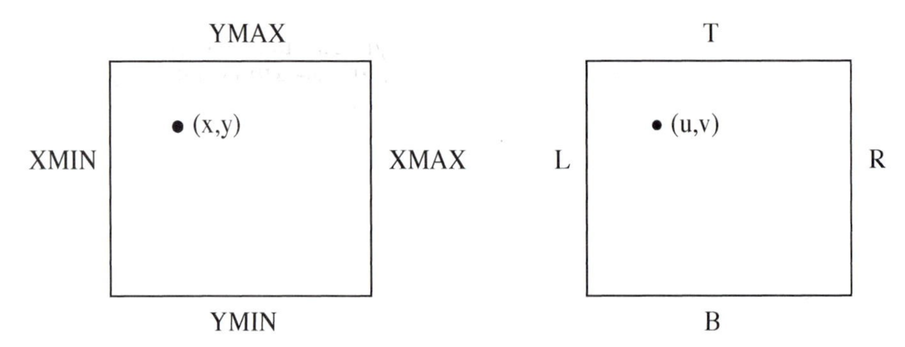

Figure 1.13 Correspondences between points in the 2D window (*left*) and viewport (*right*).

in the rectangle. The left-hand rectangle has a smallest X-value of $XMIN$ and a largest X-value of $XMAX$, and a smallest Y-value of $YMIN$ and largest Y-value of $YMAX$. The right-hand rectangle has a smallest X-value of L and a largest X-value of R, and a smallest Y-value of B and a largest Y-value of T, for example (think *left*, *right*, *top*, and *bottom* in this case).

With the names used in the figures, the width WW and height WH of the windows are, respectively,

$$WW = XMAX - XMIN \quad \text{and} \quad WH = \text{YMAX} - \text{YMIN}$$

for the window, and the width VW and height VH of the viewport are

$$VW = R - L \quad \text{and} \quad VH = T - B$$

for the viewport. Then the relations in the rectangles give us two sets of equal ratios:

$$(x - XMIN)/WW = (u - L)/VW$$

and

$$(y - YMIN)/WH = (v - B)/VH$$

These equations can be solved for the variables of either point in terms of the other, giving u and v in terms of x and y as:

$$u = L + (x - XMIN) * VW/WW$$
$$v = B + (y - YMIN) * VH/WH$$

or the dual equations can be used to solve for (x,y) in terms of (u,v). As an example of how we can use these calculations, if the (u,v) coordinates represent a point in screen space such as a mouse click location, the calculations give us the location (x,y) in 2D eye space for that event. This calculation assumes that all our ratios of screen-space coordinates are treated as real values, but we must realize that the real-valued coordinates we compute are aliased because they come from discrete screen-space coordinates, and so the actual 2D eye space coordinates are aliased.

In our discussion of the graphics display window's coordinate system, we were not specific about how it is organized. Your graphics API may use one of two conventions for window coordinates. The window may have its origin, or (0,0) value, at either the upper left or lower left corner. In the previous discussion, we assumed the usual mathematics convention that the origin was at the lower left, but graphics hardware may put the origin at the top left because that usually corresponds to the lowest address of the graphics memory. If your API puts the origin at the upper left, you can make a simple change of variables $Y' = YMAX - Y$, and using the Y' values instead of Y will put you back into the situation described in the figure.

Many graphics systems include an intermediate step in going from 2D eye space to 2D screen space. They go from 2D eye coordinates to *normalized device coordinates* (NDC), a square in real-valued 2D space with coordinates between 0. and 1. in each direction, and then to 2D screen space. Mapping 2D eye coordinates to NDC coordinates is a simple linear mapping, and mapping NDC coordinates to 2D screen coordinates is a similar mapping. Using NDC space makes it easier to handle changes in window sizes and is usually handled by the graphics hardware. Most graphics APIs do not include it as a separate step, so we will not discuss it further here.

You can choose to present your image in a distinct subrectangle of the window called a *viewport* instead of in the entire window. A viewport is a rectangular region within the graphics window to which you can restrict your image. In any window or viewport, the ratio of its width to its height is called its *aspect ratio*. A window can have many viewports, even overlapping viewports if needed, and each viewport can have its own image. Mapping an image to a viewport is done with exactly the same calculations we described previously, except that the boundaries of the drawing area are the viewport's boundaries instead of the window's. The default behavior of most graphics systems is to have the viewport equal to the entire graphics window. A viewport is usually defined in the same terms as the window it occupies, so if the window is specified in terms of physical units, the viewport probably will be also. However, a viewport may be defined relative to the window, in which case its boundary values are calculated from the window's.

If your graphics window is presented in a windowed desktop system, you may want to manipulate your graphics window just as you would any other window on the desktop. You may want to move it, change its size, and click in it to bring it to the front. Window management can be a difficult task, but the graphics API can provide this to make your graphics windows compatible with the behavior of all other windows. When you manipulate the desktop window containing the graphics window, the contents of the window are managed by the graphics API to maintain a consistent view. If you change the aspect ratio of a window or viewport, the image in the viewport may seem distorted, because the program is trying to draw to the originally defined viewport. This can be managed by allowing your program to change its projection to respond to window changes. A single program can manage several different windows, drawing to each as needed. Individual windows will be defined with different identifiers, and these are used to specify which window will get drawing commands.

Some Aspects of Managing the View

Once you define the basic features for viewing your model, a number of other things also affect how the image is created and presented. We will talk about many of these over the next few chapters, but here we discuss hidden surfaces and double buffering because you need them to make your images more effective.

Hidden Surfaces

Most things in our world are opaque, so we see only the things that are nearest to us. This can be challenging for computer-generated images, however, because a graphics system simply draws what we tell it to draw in the order we tell it to draw it. To create images that have the simple "show me only what is nearest" property, we must use appropriate tools in viewing our scene.

Most graphics systems can use the depth information in the geometry of a scene to decide what objects are in front of other objects and then to draw only the parts of the objects that are in front. This general technique is called *depth buffering*. If the depth information is directly based on the z-coordinates in the scene, this can also be called *z-buffering*. A depth buffer has one value for each pixel so it has the same dimension as the window, and the value for each pixel is the depth of the nearest point that has used that pixel so far in the color buffer. This depth value is computed from the z-values of the items in the scene, or the distance from the eyepoint to the point in the scene in modified eye coordinates. This depth value is the value after the viewing transformation; we noted earlier that this is retained for each vertex during projection.

When a polygon is processed in the geometry pipeline, depth values are kept. Then when the polygon is rendered as described in Chapter 10, interpolation is applied to the depth values of each vertex to get the depth of each pixel. When a new point is to be plotted, the depth value of the pixel to be plotted is compared to the depth value currently held for that pixel in the depth buffer. When using depth buffering, if the new pixel is closer to the viewer than the current pixel in the image buffer, the current pixel is replaced in the frame buffer by the new pixel and the depth buffer stores the new depth at that point. If the new pixel is not closer than the depth buffer value, it is discarded. This can be done in hardware by a graphics board or in software by simple data structures.

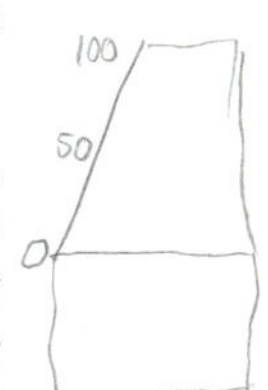

There are subtleties in this process for some graphics APIs that you should understand, however. One is that it is more efficient to compare integers than floating-point numbers so the depth values may be kept internally as unsigned integers, scaled to fit the range between the near and far planes of the viewing volume with 0 as the front plane and the largest positive integer as the back plane. This integer conversion can cause a phenomenon called *z-fighting* because of the aliasing introduced when floating-point depth values are converted to integers. This can make the depth buffer show inconsistent values for things that are at an equal distance from the eye. Integer conversion is particularly a problem if the front and back planes are far apart, because in that case the integer depth is coarser than if the planes are close. This problem is best controlled by trying to fit the near and far planes of the view as closely as possible to the actual items being displayed. This makes each integer depth unit represent a smaller real number, and so there is less likelihood of two real depths having the same integer representation. You can also try to avoid the problem by avoiding using coplanar objects in your modeling, so that (for example) a sign that is to be seen on a wall is actually placed slightly in front of the wall.

Another subtlety is that directly converting the z-values from the 3D eye space into depth values is not linear in the way values are spaced. If there is a large difference between the near distance and the far distance, then the nonlinearity in how z is interpolated causes most of the z-buffer resolution to be allocated to near objects and less to far objects. Thus, far objects might unfairly exhibit z-fighting. A kind of depth buffer called a *w-buffer* stores $1/z$ in the buffer instead of z. Because $1/z$ interpolates more linearly than z, this treats far objects more fairly.

You can use other techniques to ensure that only the genuinely visible parts of a scene are presented to the viewer. If you can compute the depth (the distance from the eye) of each object in your model, then you may be able to sort a list of the objects so that you can draw them from back to front—that is, draw the farthest first and the nearest last. This covers anything that is hidden by nearer objects, giving a scene that shows just the visible objects. This is a classic technique called the *painter's algorithm* that mimics the way a painter could create an image using opaque paints. This was widely used in more limited graphics systems, but it sometimes has real advantages over depth buffering. It is faster because it doesn't require the pixel depth comparison for every pixel that is drawn, and sometimes depth buffering has problems, as we will see when we discuss modeling transparency with blending in Chapter 6. Because the painter's algorithm requires that you know the depth of each object in 3D eye space, it can be difficult if your image includes overlapping objects, moving parts, or a moving eyepoint. More sophisticated modeling is required in those cases, such as the space partitioning discussed in Chapter 4. Getting depths in eye space is discussed with scene graphs in Chapter 2.

Double Buffering

A buffer, such as the depth buffer, is a set of memory that is used to store the result of computations. One such buffer holds the pixel values you see on your graphics screen. If you use a single buffer, this is the color buffer. As you generate your image, it is written into this buffer pixel by pixel. Because the image buffer is automatically displayed continuously to the screen, clearing the buffer and writing new parts of your image to the buffer will be visible to your audience.

Most graphics APIs let you use two image buffers to store the results of your work. These are called the *front buffer* and the *back buffer*. Because it can take time to create an image and it is distracting to watch an image being built, it is unusual to use a single image buffer unless you are creating only one image. Most of the time you want to write your graphics to the back buffer instead of to the front buffer. When your image is completed, you switch the buffers so that the back buffer (with the new image) becomes the front buffer and the viewer sees the new image. When graphics is done this way, we say that we are using *double buffering*. This is essential to animated images because you want your viewer to see only a sequence of completed images. It is also used frequently for other graphics because it is more satisfactory to present a completed image to a viewer. When an image is completed, you must remember to swap the buffers or the viewer will never see the new image!

Stereo Viewing

Stereo viewing lets us see some of these viewing processes in action. Stereo viewing should not be your first goal in creating images; it requires experience with the basics of viewing before it makes sense. Here we describe binocular viewing—viewing that requires you to converge your eyes beyond the computer screen or printed image but gives you the full 3D effect when the images are converged. Other techniques for creating stereo views are described in Chapters 10 and 15.

Stereo viewing develops two views of a model from two viewpoints that represent the positions of a viewer's eyes and then presents those views so the eyes can see them individually and the brain's visual processing can resolve them into a single image. This was once done with two photographs that are printed side by side for a viewing system such as a stereopticon or a stereo slide viewer. Two kinds of stereopticon are shown in Figure 1.14, and you may want to build a simple version of one to help people view your stereo images. If you actually have or can borrow an antique stereopticon, it can be very interesting to use modern technology to create the images for this early viewing technology! Another antique viewing technology for animated images is described in Chapter 11, on animation.

These two images can be presented in two viewports in a single window on the screen to create a stereo view as shown in Figure 1.15. To do this, you need to identify two eyepoints offset by a suitable value in a plane perpendicular to the up direction of your view. It is simplest to define your up direction to be one axis (perhaps the z-axis) and align your overall view with one of the axes perpendicular to that (perhaps the x-axis). We choose to define the model this way because we see the surface defined in terms of an equation on two variables, and it seems more natural (at least at first) to think of those two variables as x and y and of the result as the variable z. This is discussed more in Chapter 9, where we look at surface plotting in detail.

After you define your model, you can define an offset that is about the distance between the eyes of the observer and move each eyepoint from a central point by half that offset. This makes

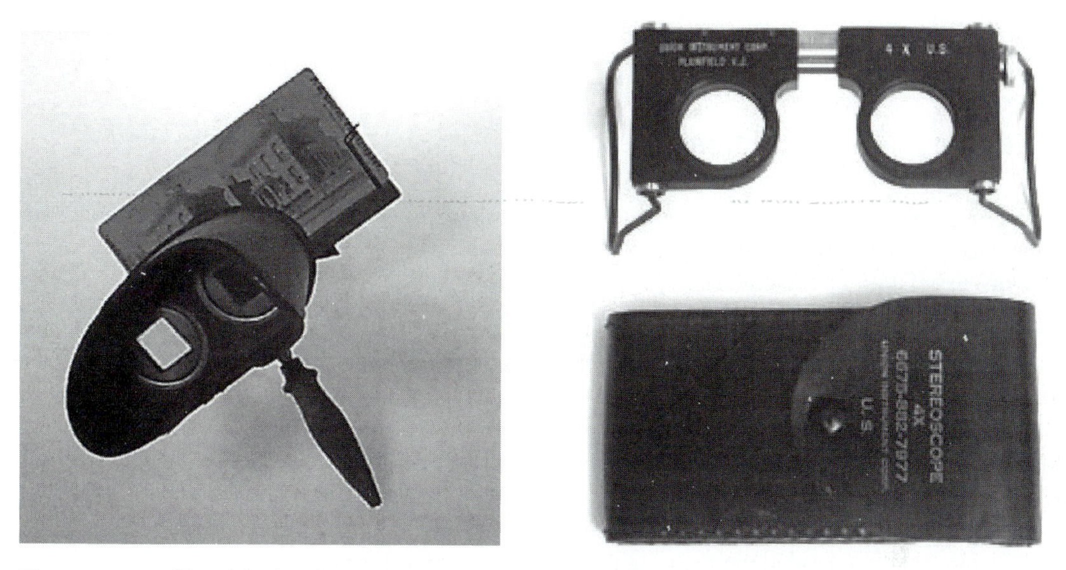

Figure 1.14 Two kinds of stereopticons: antique (*left*) and modern (*right,* used for reading pairs of aerial photographs).

it easier for each eye to focus on its individual image and let the brain's convergence create the merged stereo image. It is also quite important to keep the overall display small enough so that the distance between the centers of the images in the display is not larger than the distance between the viewer's eyes, so that he or she can focus each eye on a separate image.

A significant number of people have physical limitations that do not allow their eyes to perform the convergence needed by this kind of stereo viewing. Some have general convergence problems that do not allow the eyes to focus together to create a merged image, and some cannot seem to see beyond the screen to the point where convergence would occur. In addition, if you do not get the spacing of the stereo pair right, or if you have the viewpoints misaligned, or if you allow the two sides to refresh at different times, or . . . well, it can be difficult to get stereo viewing

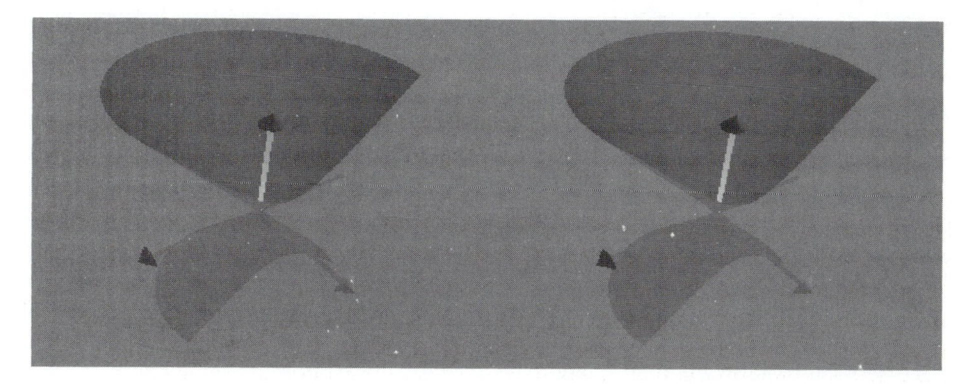

Figure 1.15 A stereo pair that can be viewed by merging individual eye images. See the figure in the color insert.

to work well for users. If some of your users can see the converged image and some cannot, that's probably as good as it's going to be.

Viewing and Visual Communication

Choosing an appropriate view for a scene is critical in creating effective visual communication. When you present information to an audience, you must focus their attention on what you want them to see. There are a number of ways you can do this, though some of these techniques won't be discussed until later chapters.

- If you want the viewer to see some detail in its overall context, you might want to start with a broad image showing the context and then provide a zoom operation into the image to see the detail. This effect might be predefined or might be something that the user can control.
- If you want the viewer to see how a particular portion of the image works as part of a moving environment, you might want to have that part fixed in the audience's view while the rest of your model moves as needed to illustrate the moving environment.
- If you want the viewer to see the entire model from all possible viewpoints, you might want to move the eye around the model, either under user control or through an animated viewpoint.
- If you want the audience to follow a particular path or object that moves through the model, you can create a moving viewpoint in the model.
- If you want the viewer to see internal structure of your model, you can create clipping planes that move through the model and allow the audience to see internal details, or you can vary the way the colors blend to make the areas in front of your structure seem partly or completely transparent so that the audience can see through them.

But no matter what kind of effect you want your audience to see, plan your image very carefully and be very conscious of how your audience will see the images so you can be sure that they see what you need them to see.

Implementation of Viewing and Projection in OpenGL

The following OpenGL code fragment captures much of the discussion in this section. It could be taken from a single function or could be assembled from several functions; in the sample structure of an OpenGL program in the previous chapter we suggested that the viewing and projection operations be separated, with the first part being at the top of the `display()` function and the latter part being at the end of the `init()` and `reshape()` functions.

```
//  Define the projection for the scene
    glMatrixMode(GL_PROJECTION);
    glLoadIdentity();
    gluPerspective(60.0,(GLsizei)w/(GLsizei)h,1.0,30.0);

//  Define the viewing environment for the scene
    glMatrixMode(GL_MODELVIEW);
    glLoadIdentity();

    // eye point  center of view  up
    gluLookAt(10.0, 10.0, 10.0, 0.0, 0.0, 0.0, 0.0, 1.0, 0.0);
```

You will notice that this fragment has two parts, and they are fairly similar. In both we choose an operation mode (projection or modelview) with the `glMatrixMode()` function and then call the function `glLoadIdentity()` before using a function to define the specific operation. The `glLoadIdentity()` function sets the operation initially to do nothing (by setting the operation's matrix to the identity), and then the detail-setting function can set the necessary values for the projection or viewing transformation without interference from past operation data.

Defining a Window and Viewport

The window was defined in the previous chapter's example by functions that initialize the window size and location and create the window. The details of window management are intentionally hidden from the programmer so that an API can work with many different platforms. In OpenGL, it is easiest to do the window setup with the GLUT toolkit, where much of the system-dependent parts of OpenGL are defined. The functions to do this are usually found in the `main()` program:

```
glutInitWindowSize(width,height);
glutInitWindowPosition(topleftX,topleftY);
thisWindow = glutCreateWindow("Your window name here");
```

The integer value `thisWindow` returned by the `glutCreateWindow` function is the window's identifier and can be used to set this window as the active window to which you will draw. This is done with the `glutSetWindow` function, as in

```
glutSetWindow(thisWindow);
```

which sets the window identified with `thisWindow` as the current window. If you need to check which window is active, you can use the `glutGetWindow()` function, which returns the value of the window's identifier. In any case, no window is active until the main event loop is entered, as described in the previous chapter.

A viewport is defined by the `glViewport` function, which specifies the lower left coordinates and the upper right screen coordinates for the portion of the window that will be used by the display. This function will normally be used in your initialization function for the program if you want a viewport smaller than the full graphics window.

```
glViewport(VPLowerLX,VPLowerLY,VPWidthX,VPHeightY);
```

You can see the use of the viewport in the stereo viewing example below to create two separate images within one window.

Reshaping the Window

The window is reshaped when it is created or whenever it is moved to another place or made larger or smaller. These operations are handled easily by OpenGL because the computer generates an event for any of these window reshapes, and there is an event callback for window reshaping. We will discuss events and event callbacks in more detail in Chapter 7, but the reshape callback is registered by the function `glutReshapeFunc(reshape)`, which identifies a function `reshape(GLint w, GLint h)` that is executed whenever the window reshape event occurs and that does whatever is needed to regenerate the image in the window.

The work done when a window is reshaped can involve defining the projection and the viewing environment and updating the definition of the viewport(s) in the window, or some of these actions can be delegated to the `display()` function. The reshape callback gets the dimensions of the window as it has been reshaped, and you can use these to control the way the image is presented in the reshaped window. For example, if you are using a perspective projection, the second parameter of the projection definition is the aspect ratio, and you can set this with the ratio of the width and height you get from the callback, as

```
gluPerspective(60.0,(GLsizei)w/(GLsizei)h,1.0,30.0);
```

This will let the projection compensate for the new window shape and retain the proportions of the original scene. On the other hand, if you really want to present the scene only in a given aspect ratio, you can simply define a viewport that has the aspect ratio you want. If you want a square presentation, for example, simply take the smaller of the two values and define a square in the middle of the window as your viewport, and then do all your drawing to that viewport.

Any viewport you may define probably needs to be defined either inside the `reshape()` callback function, so it can be redefined for resized windows, or in the display function where the changed window dimensions can be used. The viewport probably should be designed relative to the size or dimensions of the window, using the parameters of the reshape function. For example, if the window is defined to have integer dimensions `(width,height)` as in the definition above, and if the viewport is to comprise the right-hand half of the window as in the stereo pair example, then the viewport's coordinates are

```
(width/2, 0, width/2, height)
```

and the aspect ratio of the window is `width/(2*height)`. If the window is resized, you may want to adjust the width of the viewport. This might be no larger than the larger of half the new window width, to preserve the concept of occupying only half of the window. Alternately, it might be the new window height times the original aspect ratio, to preserve the basic look of your images.

Defining a Viewing Environment

To define the viewing projection, you must ensure that you are working with the GL_MODELVIEW matrix, set that matrix to be the identity, and then define the viewing environment by specifying two points and one vector. The points are the eyepoint and the center of view (the point you are looking at), and the vector is the up vector—a vector that will be projected to define the vertical direction in your image. The only restrictions are that the eyepoint and center of view must be different, and the up vector must not be parallel to the vector from the eyepoint to the center of view. As we saw earlier, some sample code to do this is:

```
glMatrixMode(GL_MODELVIEW);
glLoadIdentity();
//    eye point    center of view    up
gluLookAt(10.0, 10.0, 10.0, 0.0, 0.0, 0.0, 0.0, 1.0, 0.0);
```

The `gluLookAt()` function may be invoked from the `reshape()` function, or it may be put in the `display()` function. Variables may be used as needed for the viewing parameters. In general, we will lean toward including the `gluLookAt` operation at the start of the `display` operation. This will make it easier to modify the view as the program runs and will let you use interactive techniques to change the view.

The `gluLookAt(...)` function defines a transformation that moves the eyepoint from the default position and orientation described earlier. These are the same as if we called the `gluLookAt()` function with the parameters

```
gluLookAt(0., 0., 0., 0., 0., -1., 0., 1., 0.).
```

If we place the eyepoint by transforming this default position into the one we want, we define a set of transformations for the eyepoint. The transformations supported by graphics APIs will be discussed in Chapter 2, but those used for defining the eyepoint are:

1. a rotation about the *Z*-axis that aligns the *Y*-axis with the projection of the up vector on the view plane,
2. a scaling to place the center of view at the correct distance along the negative *Z*-axis,
3. a translation that moves the center of view to the origin,
4. two rotations, about the *X*- and *Y*-axes, that position the eyepoint correctly relative to the center of view, and
5. a translation that puts the center of view at the right position.

As we will see when we discuss transformations in the next chapter, order is critical in this sequence and the next sequence of questions.

To orient the overall scene to create the view you have defined, the viewing transformation adjusts the scene to have the standard eye position and orientation. The viewing transformation makes this happen by being the inverse of the transformation that placed the eye. Because functions have the property that the inverse of a product is the product of the inverses in reverse order, $(f \cdot g)^{-1} = g^{-1} \cdot f^{-1}$ for any functions *f* and *g*. We build the viewing transformation by inverting each of the five transformations above and applying them in the reverse order. Because this must be done on all the geometry in the scene, it must be applied last, so it must be specified before any of the geometry is defined. Thus the `gluLookAt(...)` function is one of the first things to appear in the `display( )` function, and its operation is the same as applying the following transformations:

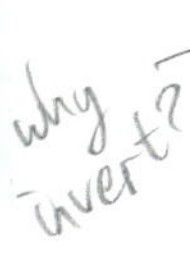

1. Translate the center of view to the origin.
2. Rotate about the *X*- and *Y*-axes to put the eyepoint on the positive *Z*-axis.
3. Translate to put the eyepoint at the origin.
4. Scale to put the center of view at the point (0., 0., –1.).
5. Rotate around the *Z*-axis to restore the up vector to the *Y*-axis.

We will need to know about this in Chapter 2 when we need to control the eyepoint as part of our modeling when we place the eye relative to an object within our scene.

Defining a Perspective Projection

A perspective projection is defined by first specifying that you want to work on the GL_PROJECTION matrix and setting that matrix to the identity. You then specify the properties that will define the perspective transformation. In order, these are:

1. the field of view (an angle, in degrees, that defines the width of your viewing area),
2. the aspect ratio,
3. the zNear value (the distance from the viewer to the front clipping plane), and
4. the zFar value (the distance from the viewer to the back clipping plane).

This is not very complicated, and once you've set it up a couple of times you'll find it very natural. For example, we might see

```
glMatrixMode(GL_PROJECTION);
glLoadIdentity();
gluPerspective(60.0,1.0,1.0,30.0);
```

This defines a perspective view with a 60° field of view, equal width and height in 3D eye space, a front clipping plane 1 unit from the eye, and a back clipping plane 30 units from the eye.

It is interesting to vary the field of view to see the effect on the image. If you decrease the field of view angle you will get more of a telephoto lens effect, and if you increase that angle you will get more of a wide-angle lens effect.

You can also define your perspective projection by using the glFrustum() function that defines the projection in terms of the viewing volume containing the visible items. This is written as

```
glFrustum(left, right, bottom, top, near, far);
```

The gluPerspective() function is usually more natural, so we will not discuss the glFrustum() function further but leave it to the student who wants to explore it.

Defining an Orthographic Projection

An orthographic projection is defined much like a perspective projection except that the parameters of the projection are different. To define the view volume for an orthographic projection, we define the boundaries of the box as shown in Figure 1.3, and the OpenGL system does the rest.

```
glOrtho(xLow, xHigh, yLow, yHigh, zNear, zFar);
```

The viewing space is the same left-handed space as noted earlier, so the zNear and zFar values are the distance of the front and back clipping planes, respectively, from the *X–Y* plane. Note that because of the way OpenGL defines the viewing environment, these distances are measured in the direction away from the eye. Thus positive values of zNear and zFar refer to distances in front of the eye and have the same effect as we considered when we were looking at the perspective projection.

Managing Hidden Surface Viewing

In the previous chapter we introduced a program that uses OpenGL and saw that we can use GLUT to define properties of the display with the glutInitDisplayMode() function, called from main(). This function allows the use of hidden surfaces if you specify GLUT_DEPTH as one of its parameters:

```
glutInitDisplayMode(GLUT_DOUBLE | GLUT_RGB | GLUT_DEPTH);
```

You must also enable the depth test. Enabling is a standard feature of OpenGL; many capabilities of the system are available only after they are enabled through the glEnable function:

```
glEnable(GL_DEPTH_TEST);
```

From that point the depth buffer is in use and you need not be concerned about hidden surfaces; they will either be overwritten if something nearer is displayed after them, or they will not be drawn if something nearer has been displayed before them.

While depth testing is automatic if you have enabled it, it uses implementation ideas you should understand in order to use it effectively. OpenGL uses integer values for the depth test, not real values, and this introduces some granularity into the depth buffer. As each pixel is scanned into the depth buffer, its z-value is converted to an unsigned integer that represents the proportion of the maximum unsigned integer value for your system. The proportion is

```
(z-zfront)/(zback-zfront)
```

with *zfront* being the depth of the front clipping plane and *zback* being the depth of the back clipping plane, as specified in the projection definition. OpenGL depth testing has a granularity that makes it vulnerable to Z-fighting. The default test is that a point passes the depth test and is recorded in the scene if its z-value is greater than zero and less than the z-value stored in the depth buffer, but this can be changed by using the glDepthFunc(value) function, where value is a symbolic constant. We will use the depth test in its default form only, but you can see OpenGL references for more details.

If you want to turn off the depth test, there is a glDisable function as well as the glEnable function. Note the use of the enable and disable functions in enabling and disabling the clipping plane in the example code for stereo viewing.

Setting Double Buffering

Double buffering is a standard facility. The glutInitDisplayMode() function takes a parameter GLUT_DOUBLE to set up double buffering. This indicates that you will use both the back buffer and front buffer for your drawing. The content of the front buffer is displayed, and all drawing takes place to the back buffer. Your display() function calls glutSwapBuffers() when you finish creating the image; this causes the back buffer to be exchanged with the front buffer, and your new image will be displayed. An added advantage of double buffering is that a few techniques examine the back buffer's contents without swapping the buffers, so the work done in the back buffer may not always be seen.

Implementing a Stereo View

This section describes the implementation of binocular viewing as described earlier. We will generate two views of a single model as if they were seen from the viewer's separate eyes, presented in two viewports in a single window on the screen. These two images are manipulated by transforming the model as a whole, while the viewer resolves the two viewports into a single image by focusing each eye on a separate image.

This process is fairly simple. First, create a window that is twice as wide as it is high and whose overall width is twice the distance between your eyes. Display your model twice, with two different viewports that occupy the left and right halves of the window. Each display is identical except that the eyepoints in the left and right halves represent the position of the left and right eyes, respectively. This can be done by creating a window with space for both viewports with the window initialization function

```
#define W 600
#define H 300
width = W; height = H;
glutInitWindowSize(width, height);
```

The initial values set the width to twice the height. We set up the view with the overall view at a distance ep from the origin in the x-direction, looking at the origin with the z-axis pointing up, and set the eye positions to a given offset distance from the overall viewpoint in the y-direction. We then define the left- and right-hand viewports in the `display()` function:

```
left-hand viewport
glViewport(0, 0, width/2, height);
     ...
//   eye point center of view up
     gluLookAt(ep, -offset, 0.0, 0.0, 0.0, 0.0, 0.0, 0.0, 1.0);
     ... code for the actual image goes here
     ...
//   right-hand viewport
     glViewport(width/2, 0, width/2, height);
     ...
//   eye point center of view up
     gluLookAt(ep, offset, 0.0, 0.0, 0.0, 0.0, 0.0, 0.0, 1.0);
     ... the same code as above for the actual image goes here
     ...
```

This example responds well to a `reshape(width, height)` operation because it uses the window dimensions to set the viewport sizes, but it is susceptible to distortion problems if the user does not maintain the 2:1 aspect ratio as the window is reshaped. It is left to you to work out how to create square viewports within the window if the window aspect ratio is changed.

Summary

In this chapter we discussed topics in viewing and projection that are basic to computer graphics and that must be addressed in graphics programming. The viewing transformation is determined by the eyepoint, view reference point, and up direction; the perspective projection is determined by the width and height of the view (often expressed as the angle of the view and the aspect ratio) and by the front and back clipping plane; the orthographic projection is determined by the width and height of the viewspace and by the front and back clipping plane.

The viewing and projection operations can be expressed in terms of OpenGL functions. These were presented along with a number of other OpenGL functions to provide window and viewport management, double buffering, depth testing, and more general clipping operations.

With these concepts and operations, you can write a graphics program that has all its modeling done in world space, and you can implement such techniques as stereo viewing. In the next few chapters we will introduce several general modeling techniques that will extend these abilities so that you can write very general and capable graphics programs.

OpenGL Glossary for the Chapter

In this chapter we introduced some new OpenGL functions, as well as some new GLU and GLUT functions and system parameters. Here we outline these and give a short indication of their meaning. You should go to the OpenGL manuals if you need more details.

OpenGL Functions

`glDepthFunc(parm)`: uses a symbolic parameter to specify the function that will be used to determine if a vertex replaces the current vertex in the drawing buffer; The usual function for depth testing is GL_LESS, as discussed in the chapter

`glDisable(parm)`: as with the `glEnable()` function you saw in the previous chapter, uses a symbolic parameter to specify an OpenGL capability that is to be disabled

`glFrustum(left, right, bottom, top, near, far)`: specifies the viewing frustum for a perspective projection by specifying the left, right, bottom, and top vertical clipping planes and the distances from the eyepoint to the near and far clipping planes (which must both be positive)

`glGetFloatv(parm, *params)`: uses a symbolic name to specify a parameter whose value is to be returned and specifies a variable (by reference) which is to receive that value. The value may be a scalar or an array, depending on the symbolic name

`glLoadMatrixf(array)`: copies the array parameter (which must contain 16 floats) into the currently active matrix—either the projection matrix or the modelview matrix, depending on the most recently set value with `glMatrixMode()`

`glOrtho(left, right, bottom, top, zNear, zFar)`: defines the view volume for an orthographic projection by defining its six clipping planes

`glViewport(lowX,lowY,width,height)`: defines the viewport within the graphics window by identifying its lower left corner, its width, and its height; all these are taken as integer screen coordinates

GLUT Functions

`glutGetWindow()`: returns the number of the currently active window

`glutSetWindow(winName)`: sets the number (often called the name) of the current window

Parameters

`GL_DEPTH_TEST`: the symbolic name used by the `glEnable()` function to enable depth testing

`GL_MODELVIEW_MATRIX`: the matrix that holds the current value of the modeling and viewing transformation

`GL_PROJECTION`: the symbolic name used by the `glMatrixMode()` function to specify that the active matrix is to be the projection matrix

`GL_PROJECTION_MATRIX`: the matrix that holds the current value of the projection transformation

Questions

These questions cover your recognition of issues in viewing and projection in your personal environment. They will help you see the effects of defining views and applying projections and the other topics in this chapter.

1. Find a comfortable environment and examine the ways in which your view of that environment depends on your eyepoint and your viewing direction. Note how objects seem to move in front of and behind other objects as you move your eyepoint, and notice how objects move into the view from one side and out of the view on the other side as you rotate your viewing direction. It may help if you look through a paper or cardboard rectangle.
2. Because of the way our eyes work, we cannot see an orthographic view of a scene. However, if we keep our eyes oriented in a fixed direction and move around in a scene with your eyes in a fixed direction, the view directly ahead of us will approximate a small piece of an orthographic view. For your familiar environment as in the previous question, try this and see if you can sketch what you see at each point and put the sketches together into a single image.
3. Consider a painter's algorithm approach to viewing your environment; write down the objects you see in the order of farthest to nearest to your eye. Now move to another position in the environment and imagine drawing the things you see in the same order in which you wrote them down from the other viewpoint. Is anything out of order so that the farther thing would be drawn on top of the nearer thing? Where must you move in order to see this kind of change in the scene? What conclusions can you draw about the calculations you would need to do for the painter's algorithm?
4. Imagine defining a plane through the middle of your environment so that everything on one side of the plane is not drawn. Make this plane go through some of the objects you would see, so that one part of the object would be visible and another part invisible. What would the view of the environment look like? What would happen to the view if you switched the visibility of the two sides of the plane?
5. Discuss some issues in choosing an appropriate viewpoint for presenting a scene so that the viewer can get the best information from it. Consider issues such as whether key information in the scene is visible, whether you show the right relationships in the scene, or whether some key issues may be difficult to distinguish from the viewpoint. Consider also issues that could help you decide whether your image should be static or should provide different views by moving the eyepoint in the scene.

Exercises

In these exercises you carry out some calculations that are involved in creating a view of a scene and in defining the projection of the scene to the screen.

1. Take a standard perspective viewing definition with, say, a 45° field of view, an aspect ratio of 1.0, a distance to the front plane of the view volume of 1.0, and a distance to the back plane of the view volume of 20.0. For a point P = $(x,y,1.)$ in the front plane, derive the parametric equation for the line segment within the frustum that all projects to the point *P*. Hint: The line segment goes through both the origin and *P*, and these two points define a line that contains the segment. Then use the front and back planes of the view volumes to identify the endpoints of the line segment for the final parametric equation.
2. Create an *X-Y-Z* grid as shown here on a piece of paper using the convention that *X* is to the right, *Y* is up, and *Z* is into the page.

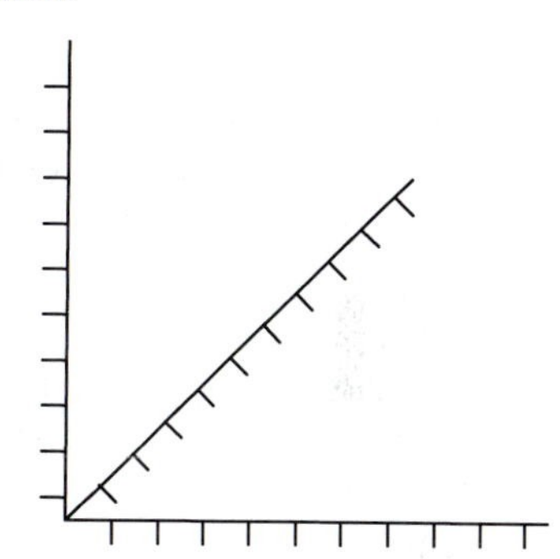

   a. In your familiar environment from question 1, define your units for the grid and place a number of things from that environment into the grid with measured coordinates, to become familiar with coordinate systems to define positions. For this example, put everything into the space with non-negative coordinates (the first octant in 3D Cartesian coordinates) to make it easier to deal with the coordinates.
   b. Define a position and direction for your eye in that same space and visualize what will be seen with that viewing definition, and then go to your space and see if your visualization was accurate. If not, then work out what was causing the inaccuracy.
3. In the numerically modeled environment above, place your eyepoint in the (X,Z)-center of the space (the middle of the space left to right and front to back) and have your eye face the origin at floor height. Calculate the coordinates of each point in the space relative to the eye coordinate system and try to identify a common process for each of these calculations.
4. The model of Figure 1.3 is defined by the following simplified code fragment (with a number of OpenGL details omitted) that you might find in the `display()` function:

```
glPushMatrix();
    glTranslatef(1., 1., 1.);
    glScalef(1., .5, .5);
    cube();
glPopMatrix();
glPushMatrix();
    glTranslatef(-.5, 1., 1.);
    glScalef(.5, .5, .5);
    Sphere(1.); // parameter is radius
glPopMatrix();
```

   This is getting a bit ahead of ourselves, but see if you can figure out what this modeling code does. Define several views of this model as shown in the figure and try to visualize how the model will look for each view before you actually implement the view in a working program. If you want to work with the actual code for the figure that is included with the resources for the book, you can modify it to try out your ideas.

5. Create a program that will display a simple model in a viewport that is one-half the dimension of the graphics window. Animate the model by drawing it in the viewport while the idle callback continually changes the viewport's position in the window. Be careful that as you move the viewport, you keep the viewport entirely within the window.

Experiments

1. In the first chapter you saw the complete code for a simple program to display the concept of heat transfer in a bar, and in the exercises you saw some discussion of the behavior of the program when the window was manipulated. Working with the projection in the `reshape()` function in that program, create other displays for the program: Create an orthographic projection, and create a perspective projection that will always fit the image within the window.
2. In the chapter you saw the `glEnable(...)` function for depth testing, and you saw the effect of depth testing in creating images where the objects that are nearer to the eye obscure objects that are farther from the eye. In this experiment, disable depth testing with the function `glDisable(GL_DEPTH_TEST)` and draw the same scene that you drew with depth testing enabled. View the scene from several points of view and draw conclusions about why you will get very different images from the same scene with different viewpoints.

In the next two experiments, we will work with a very simple line drawing version of the model of the house in Figure 1.5, although you are encouraged to replace this model with a more interesting model of your own. The code for a function to create the house centered around the origin that you can call from your own `display()` function is given below to help you get started. The drawing mode `GL_LINE_STRIP` is described in Chapter 3; it draws a connected sequence of line segments that start at the first vertex and continues from there to each vertex in turn until it reaches the `glEnd()` function.

```
void drawHouse(void) {
  point3 myHouse[10]= { { -1.0, -1.0,  2.0 }, { -1.0,  1.0,  2.0 },
                        {  0.0,  2.0,  2.0 }, {  1.0,  1.0,  2.0 },
                        {  1.0, -1.0,  2.0 }, { -1.0, -1.0, -2.0 },
                        { -1.0,  1.0, -2.0 }, {  0.0,  2.0, -2.0 },
                        {  1.0,  1.0, -2.0 }, {  1.0, -1.0, -2.0 } };

int i;
glBegin(GL_LINE_STRIP);
  for (i=0; i<5; i++)
    glVertex3fv(myHouse[i]);
  glVertex3fv(myHouse[0]);
glEnd();
glBegin(GL_LINE_STRIP);
  for (i=0; i<5; i++)
    glVertex3fv(myHouse[i+5]);
  glVertex3fv(myHouse[5]);
glEnd();
```

```
for (i=0; i<5; i++) {
  glBegin(GL_LINE_STRIP);
    glVertex3fv(myHouse[i]);
    glVertex3fv(myHouse[i+5]);
  glEnd();
}
```

3. Create a program to draw the house with this function or to draw your own scene, and note what happens to the view as you move your eyepoint around the scene, always looking at the origin (0, 0, 0). Define both perspective and orthographic projections for the scene and compare the images that are created with the different projections.
4. As in the project above, draw the house with the eyepoint fixed but change the view reference point so that you look in different directions. Note the effect as you move the view reference point around the scene.
5. With the same program as above and a fixed eyepoint, experiment with the other parameters of the perspective view: the front and back view planes, the aspect ratio of the view, and the field of view of the projection. For each, note the effect so you can control these when you create more sophisticated images later.

In the next two experiments, you will consider the matrices for the projection and viewing transformations described in this chapter. For more on these matrices, see the discussion in Chapter 4 of transformations and matrices.

In OpenGL, the general `glGet*v(...)` inquiry functions return the values of many different system parameters. These can retrieve the values of some of the transformations that are discussed in this chapter. Specifically, we can get the values of the projection transformation and viewing transformation for any projection or any view that we define. In the following two problems we explore this possibility. The transformations you will get back will be represented by 4×4 matrices, so you should write a small function to display a 4×4 matrix so that you can see its components clearly. The actual transformation values will be in the 3×3 submatrix in the first three rows and first three columns of the full matrix.

6. To get the value of the projection transformation, we use the function

   ```
   glGetFloatv(GL_PROJECTION_MATRIX, v)
   ```

   where *v* is an array of 16 floats that could be defined as

   ```
   GLfloat v[4][4];
   ```

   To see the matrix for any projection, whether perspective or orthographic, simply insert the function call above into your code any time after you have defined your projection and print out the matrix that is returned. If the projection is orthographic, you should be able to identify the parameters of the projection from components of the matrix; if the projection is perspective, this will be harder but you should start with the simple discussion of the perspective matrix in this chapter. The experiment, then, is to take the matrix returned by this process from your projection definition, change some of its values, and reset the projection transformation with this new matrix with

   ```
   glMatrixMode(GL_PROJECTION);
   glLoadMatrixf(v);
   ```

This will redefine the projection transformation to the transformation whose matrix is v. You may then observe the difference between your original projection and the new projection.

7. To get the value of the viewing transformation, you can get the value of the OpenGL modelview matrix, which is a product of the viewing and modeling transformations. So if you have defined a view but have not defined any modeling transformations (that is, you have not yet applied any scaling, rotation, or translation operations), you can use the function

```
glGetFloatv(GL_MODELVIEW_MATRIX, v)
```

where v is the same as defined above. This matrix is complicated, but if you set only a few simple parameters from the default view (change only the view point, change only the up vector, etc.), you should be able to identify the components of the viewing transformation matrix that come from each part of the view definition. As in the previous experiment, take the viewing transformation matrix returned by this process from your viewing definition, change some of its values, reset the modelview matrix with this new matrix by the process above but using the GL_MODELVIEW_MATRIX instead of GL_PROJECTION_MATRIX, and then observe the difference between your original view and the new view.

Principles of Modeling

Modeling is the first step in the graphics pipeline. It is how you define the geometry for a scene and how you implement that geometry with the tools of your graphics system. This chapter is critical in understanding the standard polygon-based approach to modeling and in developing your ability to create graphical images. It takes you from modeling simple objects to fairly complex hierarchical modeling. Many graphics APIs' modeling is based on polygons. However, there are other kinds of modeling in computer graphics, and some involve more sophisticated kinds of constructions than we include in this chapter. One of the other common approaches, ray tracing, is discussed in Chapter 14.

This chapter has four distinct parts because there are four distinct parts of modeling that you will use as you create images. We begin with simple geometric modeling directly in world space: modeling where you define the coordinates of each vertex directly in the world coordinate system. This is straightforward, but modeling complex objects can be very time consuming, so we also discuss importing models from various kinds of modeling tools.

The second section describes the next step in modeling: creating objects in standard position in their own individual model spaces and using modeling transformations to place them in world space with any size, any orientation, and any position. This step lets you create a set of simple models and use them very generally. It uses a standard set of modeling transformations you can apply to create more general model components in your scene. These transformations are also critical to using motion in your scenes because it is typical to move parts of your scene, such as objects, lights, or the eyepoint, with transformations that use parameters that change with time. This can let you extend your modeling to define animations that can represent time-varying concepts.

These first two sections cover concepts in modeling but give no specific information on implementing modeling using a graphics API. In Chapter 3 you will see how to implement all these concepts with OpenGL and will see several examples of how this is done.

The third section considers the role of modeling in creating effective visual communications. It gives examples of different types of modeling you might use, with most of the emphasis on communicating scientific ideas. We focus on shape and dimension, with several examples of how different shapes can carry different ideas. We also discuss using labels and legends as modeling objects that carry text and other information for an image.

The final section of the chapter gives you an important tool for organizing complex images: the scene graph. The scene graph provides a unified approach to defining all the objects and transformations in a scene and specifying how they are related and presented. We then show how you work from the scene graph to write the code to implement your model. This concept makes modeling much more straightforward for anything beyond a very simple scene. The scene graph is particularly valuable for hierarchical modeling, where one designs an object by assembling other objects. Hierarchical objects can let you simulate actual physical assemblies and develop models of structures such as physical machines. Scene graphs let you build a structure in which individual components can move relative to each other in ways that would be difficult to define from first principles.

For this chapter, you need an understanding of simple three-dimensional geometry, knowledge of how to represent points in three-dimensional space, enough programming experience to be comfortable writing code that calls API functions to do required tasks, ability to design a program in terms of simple data structures such as stacks, and an ability to organize things in 3D space. When you finish this chapter you should be able to organize the geometry for a scene based on simple model components and combine them with modeling transformations. You should also be able to create complex hierarchical scenes with a scene graph and to express such a scene graph in terms of graphics primitives.

A number of code fragments are included in this chapter to help you see how the general concepts we discuss can be realized in code. These fragments use C syntax and look a lot like OpenGL, but they are not; in Chapter 3 we cover the OpenGL modeling functions, and almost everything we discuss in this chapter is repeated in its OpenGL implementation there.

Simple Geometric Modeling

Computer graphics is based on geometry and on how the geometry can be represented so that it can be manipulated and displayed by a computer. In this book the geometry is simple and uses familiar concepts of three-dimensional space. When you work with a graphics API, as we do in this book, you will need to work with the kinds of object representations the API understands, so you must design your image in ways that fit the API's tools. Most graphics APIs are polygon-based, and this means that you will use only a few simple graphics primitives, such as points, line segments, and polygons, to build your scenes.

The application programmer starts by defining an object based on specific points or vertices with respect to a coordinate system, including a local origin and x-, y-, and z-directions. This is called the object's *modeling space*. This object definition naturally happens if the object is created with a modeling or computer-aided design system or is defined by a mathematical function. Examples of these operations are described for some specific cases in Chapter 9. Modeling an object in its local coordinate system involves defining it in terms of *model coordinates*. Model coordinates are defined by specifying each point by defining constant coordinates or by computing them from some algorithm. This could use code that looks something like

```
vertex(x1, y1, z1);
vertex(x2, y2, z2);
...
vertex(xN, yN, zN);
```

Because each object can be designed in its own coordinate system, each part of a scene may be defined in a different modeling space. To integrate all the objects into a single overall 3D world space, the objects must be placed in the world space through the use of *modeling transformations*. Modeling transformations, like all the transformations we describe in this book, are functions that move objects while preserving basic geometric relationships. The transformations usually available to us in a graphics system are *rotations, translations,* and *scaling*. These are the fundamental transformations of computer graphics. Rotations rotate all the points they act on by a fixed angle around a fixed line, translations add fixed values to each of the coordinates of each point they act on, and scaling operations multiply each coordinate of each point they act on point by fixed values. All transformations may be represented as matrices, so sometimes in a graphics API you will see a discussion of matrices; this almost always means that a transformation is involved.

In practice, graphics programmers build up model transformations through a sequence of simple, standard transformations. Because each transformation works on the geometry it sees, it follows the associative law for functions; in a piece of code represented by metacode such as

```
transformOne(...);
transformTwo(...);
transformThree(...);
geometry(...);
```

the effect is that `transformThree` is applied to the original geometry, `transformTwo` to the results of that transformation, and `transformOne` to the results of the second transformation. Letting `t1`, `t2`, and `t3` be these three transformations, respectively, we see by the associative law for function composition that

```
t1(t2(t3(geometry))) = (t1*t2*t3)(geometry)
```

This shows us that in a product of transformations applied by multiplying on the left, the transformation on the right is applied first. This will be very important in the overall understanding of the overall order in which we operate on scenes.

The modeling transformations for objects in a scene can change over time to create motion. For example, in a rigid-body animation, an object can be moved through the scene just by changing a translation in its model transformation between frames.

Definitions

We need some common terminology as we talk about modeling. We think of modeling as the process of defining the objects that are part of the scene you want to create to make an image. There are many ways to model a scene for an image, and a number of commercial programs let you model scenes with very high-level tools. However, for much graphics programming, and certainly as you are beginning to learn about this field, you will want to do your modeling by defining your geometry in terms of simple primitive objects so that you can be fully in control of the modeling process.

The space we will use for our modeling is simple Euclidean 3-space with standard *X*-, *Y*-, and *Z*-coordinates. Figure 2.1 illustrates a point, a line segment, a triangle, a polygon, and a polyhedron—the basic elements of the computer graphics world that we use for most of our graphics in this book. In this space a *point* is simply a single location in 3-space, sometimes called a *vertex,* whose coordinates are a triple of real numbers (*vx, vy, vz*). A point is drawn on the screen by lighting a single pixel at the screen location that best represents the location of that point in space. To draw the point, you will specify that you want to draw points and specify the point's coordinates, usually in 3-space. The graphics API will calculate the coordinates of the point on the screen that best represents that point and light that pixel. A point is usually presented on the screen as a square, not a dot, as indicated in the figure.

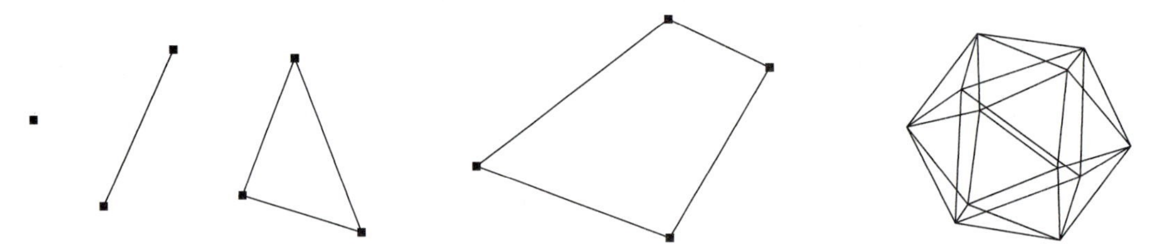

Figure 2.1 A point, a line segment, a triangle, a polygon, and a polyhedron.

A *line segment* is determined by its two specified endpoints, so to draw the line segment you indicate that you want to draw lines and define the two points or vertices that are the endpoints. Again, these points are specified in 3-space, the graphics API calculates their representations on the screen and then draws the line segment between them by calculating the pixels that best represent the points on the segment and lighting these pixels.

A *polygon* is a region of space that lies in a plane and is bounded by line segments. It is determined by a sequence of points (called the *vertices* of the polygon) that specify the line segments which form its boundary. We generally assume that a polygon lies in a plane, but if vertices are points in 3D space this may not be true; because of this, and because a triangle is the simplest (and most useful) polygon, most polygon drawing actually consists of drawing triangles. To draw the polygon you indicate that you want to draw polygons and specify the sequence of vertex points The graphics system calculates the pixels that represent points inside the polygon and lights these pixels.

A *polyhedron* is a region of 3-space bounded by polygons, called the *faces* of the polyhedron. A polyhedron is defined by specifying a sequence of faces, each of which is a polygon. Because figures in 3-space determined by more than three vertices cannot be guaranteed to lie in a plane, polyhedra are often defined to have triangular faces; a triangle always lies in a plane because three points in 3-space determine a plane. As we will see when we discuss lighting and shading in Chapter 6, the direction in which we go around the vertices of each face of a polygon is very important.

Before you can create an image, you must define the objects in that image through some kind of *modeling process*. Perhaps the most difficult, or at least the most time-consuming, part of beginning graphics programming is creating the models for your images. One difficulty is in designing the objects themselves, which may require that you sketch parts of your image by hand so you can determine the correct vertex coordinates. You may be able to determine the coordinates by some other technique, such as an analytical calculation. Another difficulty is actually entering the data for the points in an appropriate data structure and writing the code that will interpret this data as points, line segments, and polygons for the model. But until you get the points and their relationships right, you cannot get the image right.

Graphics APIs also let you define larger objects that are made up of several simple objects. These can involve disconnected sets of objects such as points, line strips, quads, or triangles, or they can involve connected sets of points, such as line segments, quad strips, triangle strips, or triangle fans. Some of these techniques use a concept called *geometry compression,* which lets you define a geometric object while sending fewer vertices to the graphics system than might be normally needed. The following discussions and examples show you how to build a repertoire of techniques you can use for modeling.

Before going forward, however, we need to mention another way to specify vertices for your models. It can be helpful to think of your three-dimensional space as being embedded in four-dimensional space. Because 4-space is difficult to think about, let's first consider the simpler case of a two-dimensional space embedded in 3-space. Specifically, there is a clear correspondence between each point (x, y) in 2-space and the line $\{(xw, yw, w) \mid \text{all } w \neq 0\}$ in 3-space. This line intersects the plane $Z = 1$ in exactly the point $(x, y, 1)$, an element of the two-dimensional *affine plane* in 3-space, as shown in Figure 2.2. If we identify the point (x, y) with the *homogeneous point* $(x, y, 1)$ in 3-space, we can carry out all computer graphics transformations on 2-space with 3×3 matrices. A similar correspondence between points (x, y, z) and $(x, y, z, 1)$ embeds 3-space in the affine 4-space of all points in 4-space with the fourth coordinate 1, and this correspondence lets us carry out all computer graphics transformations on 3-space with 4×4 matrices.

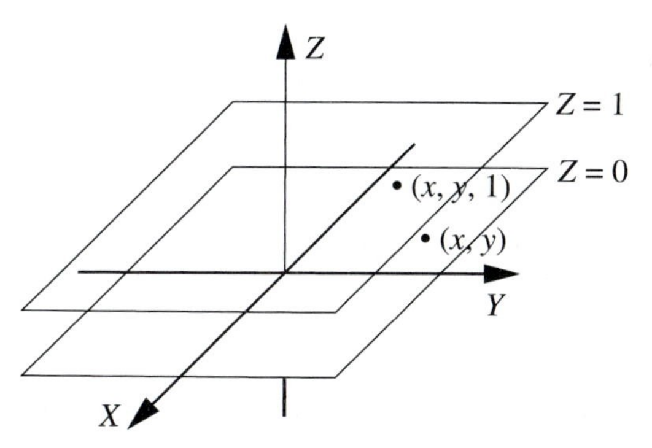

Figure 2.2 The 2D affine plane in 3-space.

If we think of four-dimensional space as having X, Y, Z, and W components, this identifies the three-dimensional space with the affine subspace $W = 1$ of four-dimensional space, so the point (x, y, z) is identified with the four-dimensional point $(x, y, z, 1)$. Conversely, the four-dimensional point (x, y, z, w) is identified with the three-dimensional point $(x/w, y/w, z/w)$ whenever $w \neq 0$. The four-dimensional representation of vertices with a nonzero w component is called *homogeneous coordinates,* and calculating the three-dimensional equivalent for a homogeneous representation by dividing by w is called *homogenizing* the point. This representation is useful for general transformations on three-dimensional space, as we will see in Chapter 4. When we think of transformations as matrices, they will usually be 4×4 matrices because they operate on points in homogeneous coordinates.

Not all points in four-dimensional space can be identified with points in 3-space, however. The point $(x, y, z, 0)$ is not identified with a point in 3-space because it cannot be homogenized, but it can be identified with the direction defined by the vector $<x, y, z>$. This can be thought of as a "point at infinity" in a certain direction. This has an application in the discussion of lighting when we discuss directional instead of positional lights, but we will not deal with homogeneous coordinates often in our discussion of graphics.

Some Examples

In this section we describe the simple objects that are directly supported by most graphics APIs. We begin with very simple objects and proceed to more complex ones, but you will find that you will need both simple and complex objects in your work. With each simple object we will describe how you specify that object, and in later examples we will create a set of points and then show a function that can draw the object we have defined.

Point and Points

To draw a single point, we define the coordinates of the point and pass them to the graphics API function that draws points. Such a function can typically handle one point or a number of points, so if we want to draw only one point, we provide only one vertex; if we want to draw more points, we provide more vertices. Points are extremely fast to draw, and it is not unreasonable to draw tens of thousands of points if a problem needs that kind of modeling. On a modestly fast machine without much graphics acceleration, a 50,000-point model can be redrawn in a fraction of a second.

Line Segments

To draw a line segment, we pass the endpoint vertices to the graphics API function that draws lines. This function will also probably let you specify a number of line segments and will draw them all. For each segment you give the endpoints of the segment, so you need to specify twice as many vertices as the number of line segments you need.

The way a graphics API handles line segments hides an important concept, however. A line is a continuous object with real-valued coordinates, but it is displayed in screen space with integer screen coordinates. This is the difference between model space and eye space on the one hand and screen space on the other. While we focus on geometric thinking in 3D space and overlook the details of conversions from eye space to screen space, you should realize that algorithms for such conversions lie at the foundation of computer graphics and that your ability to think in higher-level terms is built on these foundations.

Sequence of Line Segments

Connected line segments—segments joined "head to tail" to form a longer connected group—are shown in Figure 2.3. These are often called *line strips* and *line loops,* and your graphics API will probably provide a function for drawing them. Your vertex list will define the line segments by using the first two vertices for the first line segment, and then by using each new vertex to define each additional segment from its predecessor. The difference between a line strip and a line loop is that the former does not connect the last vertex defined to the first vertex, leaving the figure

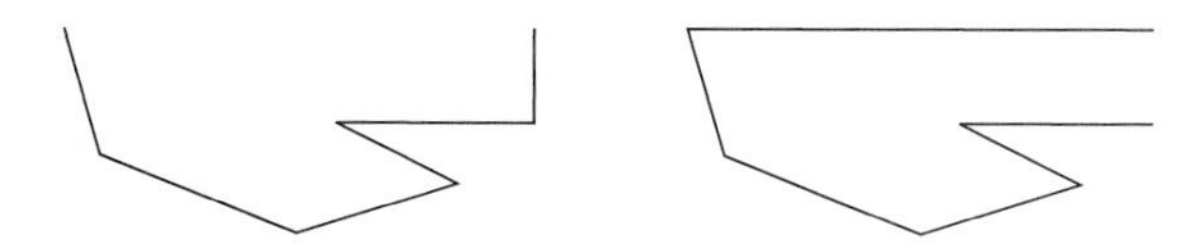

Figure 2.3 A line strip and a line loop.

open; the latter includes this extra segment and creates a closed figure. The number of line segments drawn by a line strip will be one fewer than the number of vertices in the vertex list, while a line loop will draw the same number of segments as vertices. This is a geometry compression technique because instead of needing to define two points per line segment, for each segment after the first, only one vertex needs to be defined. To define a line strip with N segments you specify only $N + 1$ vertices instead of $2N$ vertices.

Triangle

To draw one or more unconnected triangles, your graphics API will have a simple triangle-drawing function. With this function, each set of three vertices defines an individual triangle, so the number of triangles defined by a vertex list is one-third the number of vertices in the list. The humble triangle may be the most simple of the polygons, but it is the most important. No matter how you use a triangle, and no matter what points form its vertices, it is always convex and it always lies in a plane. Moreover, any polygon, convex or not, can be represented as a collection of triangles. Because of this, most polygon-based modeling really comes down to triangle-based modeling, and almost every kind of graphics tool knows how to manage objects defined by triangles. So treat this humblest of polygons well and learn how to think about polygons and polyhedra in terms of the triangles that make them up.

Sequence of Triangles

Triangles are the foundation of most useful polygon-based graphics, and it is common to define large objects in terms of triangles that make up their boundary or surface. Graphics APIs often provide two different geometry compression techniques for sequences of triangles: *triangle strips* and *triangle fans*. These techniques can be very helpful in defining a large graphic object in terms of triangles. The behavior of each is shown in Figure 2.4. This figure shows simple geometric primitives as if they were drawn in 2D space. In fact they are not, but to make them look three-dimensional we would need to use some kind of shading, which we have not covered yet. So we ask you to think of these as three-dimensional, even though they look flat.

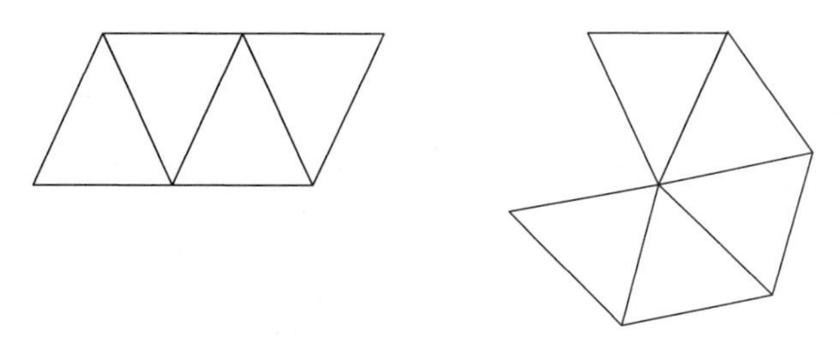

Figure 2.4 Triangle strip and triangle fan.

Most graphics APIs support both techniques by interpreting the vertex list in different ways. To create a triangle strip, the first three vertices in the vertex list create the first triangle, and each subsequent vertex creates a new triangle with the two vertices immediately before it. To create a triangle fan, the first three vertices create the first triangle and each vertex after that creates a new triangle with the point immediately before it and the first point in the list. In each case, the number of triangles defined by the vertex list is two less than the number of vertices in the list, so these are very efficient ways to specify triangles. These two techniques behave quite differently with respect to polygon order; for triangle fans, the orientation of all the triangles is the same (clockwise or counterclockwise), while for triangle strips, the orientation of alternate triangles is reversed. This may require some careful coding when lighting models are used.

Quadrilateral

A convex quadrilateral, often called a *quad* to distinguish it from a general quadrilateral because the general quadrilateral need not be convex, is any convex four-sided figure. Examples of convex and nonconvex quadrilaterals are shown in Figure 2.5. Your graphics API function that draws quads will probably let you draw a number of them. Each quad requires four vertices in the vertex list—the first four vertices define the first quad, the next four the second quad, and so on, so your vertex list will have four times as many points as there are quads. The sequence of vertices is that of the points as you go around the perimeter of the quad. In an example later in this chapter, we will use six quads to define a cube we will use in later examples.

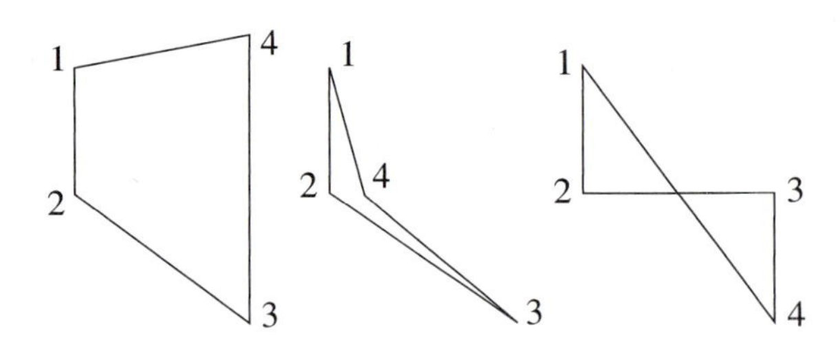

Figure 2.5 Convex quad (*left*) and nonconvex (*center, right*) quadrilaterals.

The sequence you use to specify the vertices in a quadrilateral can be important. In the convex quad in Figure 2.5, the sequence of vertices goes around the quad in counterclockwise order. This is the standard ordering because it supports the correct computations for lighting, as you will see in Chapter 6. More generally, if the polygon is a face of a polyhedron, the ordering of the vertices should be counterclockwise as seen from outside the polyhedron.

Sequence of Quads

Many large objects can be defined by a number of connected quads, so most graphics APIs have functions that allow you to define a particular sequence of quads called a *quad strip*. The vertices in the vertex list are taken as vertices of a sequence of quads that have common sides. The first four vertices define the first quad; the last two of these, together with the next two, define the next quad; and so on. The order in which the vertices are presented is shown in Figure 2.6. Note the order carefully; instead of the expected sequence around the quads, the points in each pair have the same order. Thus the sequence 3–4 is the opposite order than would be expected, and this same sequence goes on in each additional pair of extra points. This difference is critical when you are implementing quad strip

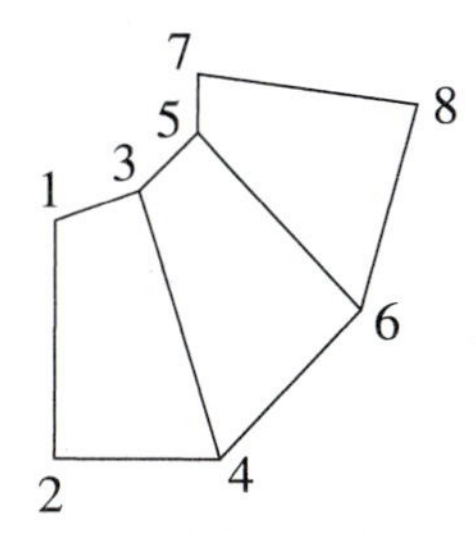

Figure 2.6 Sequence of points in a quad strip.

constructions. It is helpful to think of this in terms of triangles, because a quad strip treats its vertices as if it were really a triangle strip—vertices 1/2/3 followed by 2/3/4 followed by 3/4/5, and so on.

As an example of the use of quad strips and triangle fans, let's create a model of a unit sphere. The sphere is a familiar object and it is common to have a built-in sphere function, but it can be helpful to see how to create familiar things with basic tools. There may also be times when you need to do things with a sphere that are difficult with the prebuilt objects, so it is useful to have this example in your "bag of tricks."

In Chapter 4 we will describe the use of spherical coordinates in modeling. We will use spherical coordinates to model the sphere at first, and then we can later convert to Cartesian coordinates as we describe in that chapter to present the model to the graphics system for actual drawing. Let's think of creating a model of the sphere with *N* divisions around the equator and *N*/2 divisions along the prime meridian. In each case, then, the angular division will be *theta* = 360/*N* degrees. Let's also think of the sphere as having a unit radius, so it will be easier to work with later when we have transformations. Assuming we can define a vertex in spherical coordinates with a function scvertex(. . .), the basic code structure would be:

```
//  create the two polar caps with triangle fans
doTriangleFan()   // north pole
    set scvertex at (1, 0, 90)
    for i = 0 to N
        set scvertex at (1, 360/i, 90-180/N)

endTriangleFan()
doTriangleFan()        // south pole
    set scvertex at (1, 0, -90)
    for i = 0 to N
        set scvertex at (1, 360/i, -90+180/N)

endTriangleFan()
//  create the body of the sphere with quad strips
for j = -90+180/N to 90 - 180/2N
    // one quad strip per band around the sphere
    // at a given latitude
    doQuadStrip()
        for i = 0 to 360
            set scvertex at (1, i, j)
            set scvertex at (1, i, j+180/N)
```

```
            set scvertex at (1, i+360/N, j)
            set scvertex at (1, i+360/N, j+180/N)
    endQuadStrip()
```

Because we're working with a sphere, the quad strips we have defined are planar, so we do not need to divide each quad into two triangles to get planar surfaces as we might do for other objects. Note the order in which we set the points in the triangle fans and in the quad strips, as we described when we introduced these concepts.

A coarse-grained wireframe sphere is shown in Figure 2.7, along with triangle fans at a polar cap shown in the middle and a quad strip around the sphere shown at the right. Look carefully at the way the quad strips go around the sphere.

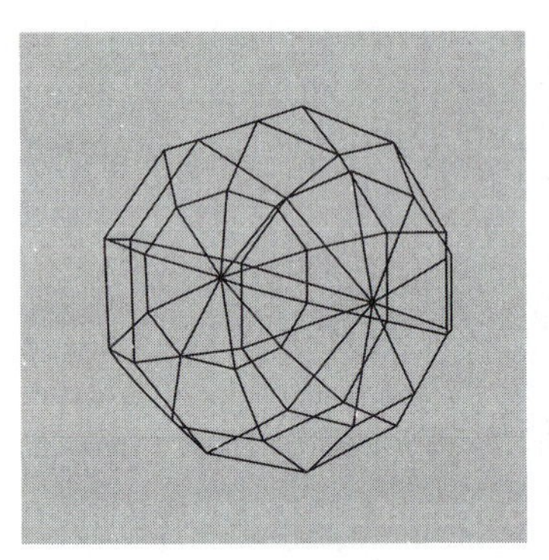
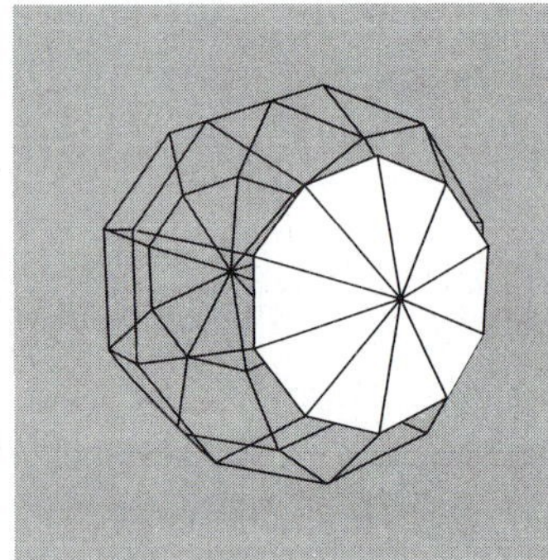
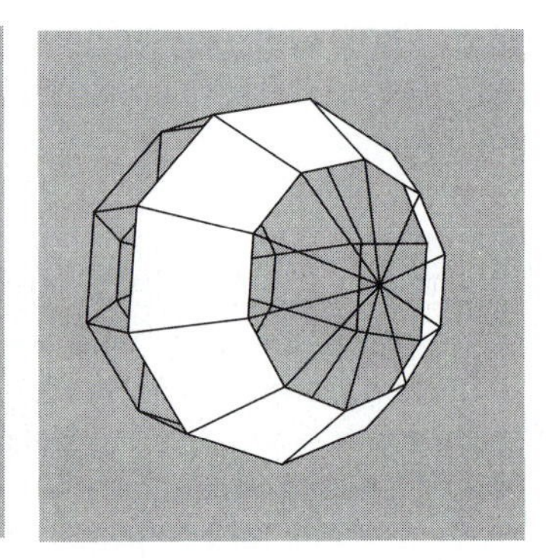

Figure 2.7 A wireframe sphere (*left*) with triangle fans (*middle*) and quad strips (*right*) making up parts of the sphere.

General Polygon

Some images need to include more general kinds of polygons. While these can be created by constructing them manually as collections of triangles and/or quads, it might be easier to define them simply as polygons. Many APIs can handle only *convex* polygons—polygons for which any two points in the polygon also contain the entire line segment between them. This is because many APIs implement polygons through triangle fans, and this does not work unless the polygon is convex.

A graphics API will allow you to define a single polygon by specifying its vertices, and the vertices in the vertex list are taken as the vertices of the polygon in sequence order. An interesting property of convex polygons is that if you take any two adjacent vertices and write the remaining vertices in order as they occur around the polygon, you have exactly the same vertex sequence you would have if you were defining a triangle fan. In fact, this can be taken as a definition of a convex polygon. This gives you a way to implement a convex polygon as a triangle fan, just as you can for quad strips and triangle strips. (You may be able to do this for some vertices in nonconvex polygons, as would be the case if you started with special cases in the middle polygon in Figure 2.5 or Figure 2.8, but you cannot do it for *any* adjacent pair of vertices.) We saw convex and nonconvex quadrilaterals in Figure 2.5, and Figure 2.8 shows the difference for general polygons. The center object in Figure 2.8 is not convex because the segment between vertices 2 and 4 is not contained in the figure, and the right-hand object is similarly not convex.

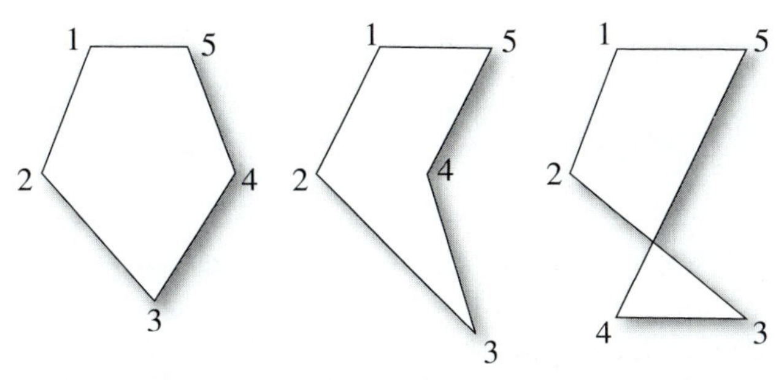

Figure 2.8 Convex (*left*) and nonconvex (*center, right*) polygons.

Because a polygon is a plane figure, it has two sides called the *front* side and *back* side. These are defined by the normal vector for the polygon's plane, and we will discuss normals shortly. We want the normal to always point toward the outside of a polyhedron, or to always point up on a surface defined as a function of two variables. The side of the polygon that is on the outside of a polyhedron is called the front side. If there is no polyhedron, the front side (of a convex polygon) is the side from which the vertices are seen in a counterclockwise order. This distinction is important in several graphical computations. Another way to identify a front side of a convex polygon is to take any interior point and the line from the interior point to the first vertex. Then the angle from that line to the line from the point to any other vertex will always increase as the vertex index increases.

Polyhedron

In Figure 2.1 we noted that a polyhedron is a basic object for modeling, especially when we focus on 3D computer graphics. We specify a polyhedron by specifying all the polygons that make up its boundary. In general, most graphics APIs leave the specification of polyhedrons up to the user, and they can be fairly difficult to define as you are learning the subject. With experience, however, you will develop a set of polyhedra that you're familiar with and can use with comfort.

While a graphics API may not have a general set of polyhedra available for you to use, most have a set of basic polyhedra that can be very useful. These depend on the API, and Chapter 3 includes a description of the polyhedra in OpenGL and its standard toolkits.

Aliasing and Antialiasing

When you create a point, line, or polygon in your image, the system defines the pixels in 2D screen space that represent the geometry. This process is described in detail in Chapter 4. Pixels are defined by integer coordinates in 2D screen space, while the geometry in model space is defined in real numbers. Representing a continuous line in model space with a set of discrete pixels in screen space is an example of *aliasing*. Generally, aliasing means representing a quantity by a value that is sampled from the quantity, an idea that comes up in many places both within computer graphics and outside it.

The standard way of selecting pixels is all-or-none: A pixel is computed to be either in the geometry, so it is colored as the geometry specifies, or not in the geometry, so it is left as whatever color it already was. Because of the relatively coarse nature of screen space, this all-or-nothing approach can leave jagged edges along the space between geometry and background. This appearance is an example of aliasing and is shown in the left-hand image of Figure 2.9.

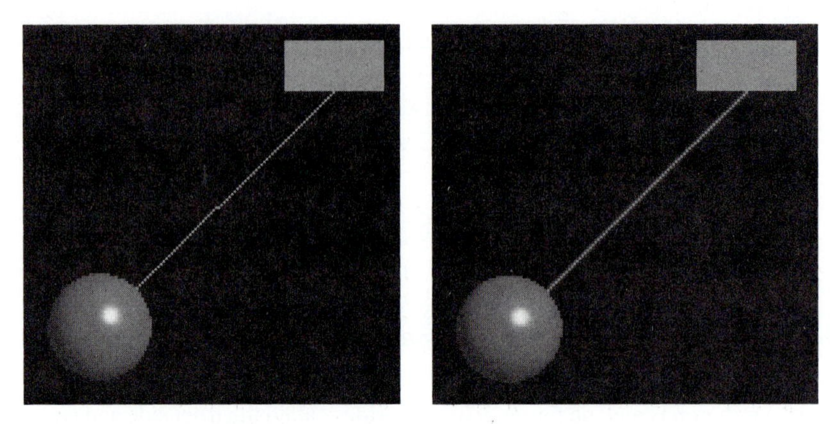

Figure 2.9 Aliased lines (*left*) and antialiased lines (*right*).

There are a number of techniques to reduce the effects of aliasing, and collectively the techniques are called *antialiasing*. They all work by recognizing that the boundary of a true geometry can go through individual pixels in a way that only partially covers a pixel. Each technique finds a way to account for this varying coverage and then lights the pixel according to the amount of coverage of the pixel with the geometry. Because the background may vary, this variable lighting can be managed by controlling the blending value for the pixel's color, using the color (R, G, B, A) where (R, G, B) is the geometry color and A is the proportion of the pixel covered by the object's geometry. An image that uses antialiasing is shown in the right-hand image of Figure 2.9. Antialiasing may be available with your graphics API. For more detail on color and blending, see Chapter 5.

One way to calculate the color for a pixel that is often used for very high-quality images is to *supersample* the pixel. This assumes a much higher image resolution than is really present and calculates how many of these "subpixels" lie in each pixel. The proportion of subpixels that are covered is taken as the proportion of the new color that is mixed with the original pixel color. A simpler technique takes advantage of the linear geometry of polygon-based modeling and calculates exactly how the 2D eye space line intersects each pixel and then how much of the pixel is covered. This is a fairly common API computation, though the details will vary among APIs and even among different implementations of an API. You may want to look at your API's manuals for more details.

In Figure 2.9, antialiasing was used to smooth the shape of a line segment, but it can also be used to smooth the drawing of points on the edge of a polygon. The same techniques are used for handling the drawing of the new geometry on top of previously drawn geometry.

Normals

As you define the geometry of an object, you may need to define not only the vertex coordinates but also a direction that is perpendicular to the object at that vertex. This is a key to creating shaded images, for example. You specify this perpendicular direction by defining a *normal* for the object. Normals are often fairly easy to obtain. You can calculate normals for plane polygons fairly easily using a cross product technique on adjacent edges, as we will describe in Chapter 4.

For many of the objects that are available with a graphics API, normals are built into the object definition. If an object is defined by mathematical formulas, you can often get normals by using calculus techniques.

The sphere described earlier as a sequence of quads gives us a good example of getting normals by calculation. For a sphere, the normal to the sphere at a given point has the same direction as the radius vector at that point. For a unit sphere with center at the origin, the radius vector to a point has the same components as the coordinates of the point. Thus if you know the coordinates of the point, you know the normal at that point. This is illustrated in Figure 2.10.

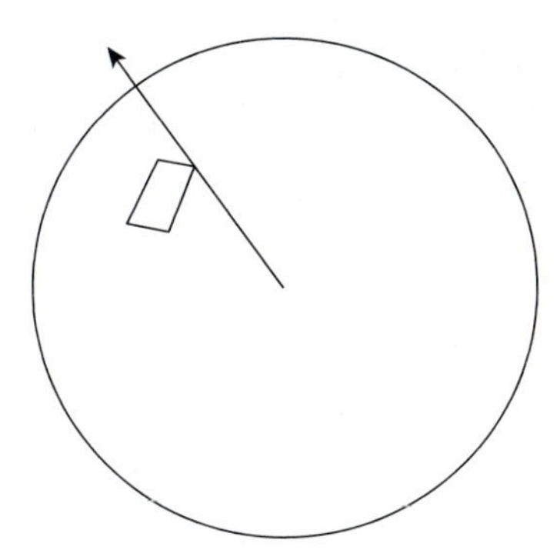

Figure 2.10 A normal at a vertex of a surface quad on a sphere.

To add the normal information to the modeling definition, then, you can simply use functions that set the normal for a geometric primitive, as you would expect to have from your graphics API, and you get code that looks like the following excerpt from the sphere example, where we use a spherical representation for a normal as well as a vertex:

```
for (float j=-90.+180./M; j<=90.-180./M; j+=latstep)      // latitude
    doQuadStrip()
    //  one quad strip per band around the sphere at any latitude
        for (float i=0.; i<=360.; i+=longstep)     // longitude
            set scnormal to (1., i, j)
            set scvertex at (1., i, j)
            set scvertex at (1., i, j+180./M)
            set scvertex at (1., i+360/N, j)
            set scvertex at (1., i+360/N, j+180./M)
    endQuadStrip()
```

Because we are working with a unit sphere, this normal has unit length. However, a normal defined in this way may not be of unit length, so we would want to normalize it (make it have length 1) before we use it. We don't include this calculation here because a graphics API might provide automatic normalization of normal vectors for you. You could be even more accurate with your normal if you were to use the center of each quad for the normal instead of a vertex; the principle is the same, but you find the center of the quad by averaging each coordinate of the quad's vertices.

Clipping

Clipping defines a plane in the model space and draws an image that shows everything in the model that lies on one side of the plane or on the plane, but none on the model on the other side of the plane. Clipping defines parts of the scene that you do *not* want to display. As we have seen, projection operations automatically include clipping because they must leave out objects in the space to the left, right, above, below, in front, and behind the viewing volume. Each of the planes bounding the viewing volume for the projection is a clipping plane for the image. A plane is defined by a linear equation

$$Ax + By + Cz + \mathrm{D} = 0$$

so it can be represented by the four-tuple of real numbers (A, B, C, D) as described later in Chapter 4. Your graphics API will probably let you define other clipping planes in an image and might let you define the plane by giving the four coefficients of the plane equation. One reason to use clipping might be to see what is inside an object instead of just seeing the object's surface; you can define clipping planes that go through the object and display only the part of the object on one side of the plane.

Clipping is handled by the graphics API, but you should know something about how it is done. Because we generally think of graphics objects as built of polygons, clipping operates by testing vertices against the clipping plane. With the plane equation above, you can tell what side of a plane contains a point (x, y, z) by testing the algebraic sign of the expression $Ax + By + Cz + D$. If this is negative for both endpoints of a line segment, the entire line segment lies on the "wrong" side of the clipping plane and is discarded. If the expression is positive for both endpoints, the line segment lies on the "right" side and is kept. If the expression is positive for one endpoint and negative for the other, then you find the point for which the equation $Ax + By + Cz + D = 0$ is satisfied and keep the line segment from that point to the point whose value in the expression is positive. If the line segment is defined by a linear parametric equation, this is a linear equation in one variable and is easy to solve. This line segment clipping is then extended to polygons as described in Chapter 1.

Clipping introduces a different kind of geometry into a model—a geometry that defines what is visible and what is not. Any transformations that are applied to a model before a clipping plane is defined are also applied to the clipping plane; any transformations applied after a clipping plane is defined are not.

Data Structures for Modeling

You will often have a number of vertices that make up an object you are modeling, and it is natural to ask how you might hold the vertices and their attributes so you can work on them. The most natural way to do that is through lists, where each list would hold the information for the model on a vertex-by-vertex basis. You can use any data structure you want to implement these lists, as long as the data structure allows easy (usually sequential) access to the list items. Your choice of lists is not important to the graphics, so we will restrict ourselves to arrays in this text. But you can be as free as you like in your own work.

As an example, when you define a polyhedron, there are many ways you can organize the information that describes it. One of the simplest is the *triangle list*—an array of triangles, where each triangle is an array of three vertices. A sample declaration would be

```
float triangles[N][3][3];
```

where each entry is three triples—that is, three triangles. Drawing the object is a simple matter of reading one array entry from the list and drawing the triangle using the three vertices. A good example of this kind of list is the STL graphics file format discussed in Chapter 15.

A more effective, though a bit more complex, approach is to create three lists. The first is a *vertex list,* and it is simply an array of vertices that contains all the vertices in the object. If the object is a polygon or contains polygons, the second list is an *edge list* and contains one entry for each edge of the polygon. Each entry of the edge list is an ordered pair of numbers that are indices of points in the vertex list. To draw a line from point *i* to point *j,* you use `vertex[i]` and `vertex[j]`. If the object is a polyhedron, the third list is a *face list,* containing information on each face in the polyhedron. Each face is defined by a list of the indices of the edges that make up the face, in the order needed by the orientation of the face. You can then draw the face by using the indices as an indirect reference to the edges, and these then have indirect references to the actual vertices. To draw the object, you loop across the face list to draw each face; for each face you loop across the edge list to determine each edge, and for each edge you get the two vertices that determine the actual geometry.

As an example, let's consider the classic case of a cube that is centered at the origin and has sides of length two. We define the vertex array, edge array, and face for the cube, and we outline how we could organize the actual drawing of the cube. We will return to this example later in this chapter and from time to time as we discuss other examples throughout the book.

We begin with the data and data types for the cube. The vertices are points, which are arrays of three points, while the edges are pairs of indices of points in the point list and the faces are quadruples of indices of faces in the face list. The normals are vectors, one per face, but these are also given as arrays of three points. In C, these might be given as follows:

```
typedef float point3[3];
typedef int edge[2];
typedef int face[4];      // each face of a cube has four edges

point3 vertices[8] = {{-1.0, -1.0, -1.0},
                      {-1.0, -1.0,  1.0},
                      {-1.0,  1.0, -1.0},
                      {-1.0,  1.0,  1.0},
                      { 1.0, -1.0, -1.0},
                      { 1.0, -1.0,  1.0},
                      { 1.0,  1.0, -1.0},
                      { 1.0,  1.0,  1.0} };

point3 normals[6] =   {{ 0.0, 0.0, 1.0},     // one normal for each face
                       {-1.0, 0.0, 0.0},
                       { 0.0, 0.0,-1.0},
                       { 1.0, 0.0, 0.0},
                       { 0.0,-1.0, 0.0},
                       { 0.0, 1.0, 0.0} };

edge edges[24]     =  {{ 0, 1 }, { 1, 3 }, { 3, 2 }, { 2, 0 },
                       { 0, 4 }, { 1, 5 }, { 3, 7 }, { 2, 6 },
                       { 4, 5 }, { 5, 7 }, { 7, 6 }, { 6, 4 },
                       { 1, 0 }, { 3, 1 }, { 2, 3 }, { 0, 2 },
                       { 4, 0 }, { 5, 1 }, { 7, 3 }, { 6, 2 },
                       { 5, 4 }, { 7, 5 }, { 6, 7 }, { 4, 6 }};
```

```
face cube[6] = {{  0, 1,  2,  3 }, {  5,  9, 18, 13 },
                { 14, 6, 10, 19 }, {  7, 11, 16, 15 },
                {  4, 8, 17, 12 }, { 22, 21, 20, 23 }};
```

In the edge list, each edge is actually listed twice—once for each direction in which the edge can be drawn. We need this distinction to let us orient our faces properly: using edges in a counter-clockwise direction as seen from outside that face of the cube. To draw the cube we work our way through the face list and determine the actual points that make up the cube and send them to the generic `vertex(...)` and `normal(...)` functions. In this pseudocode, we assume that there is no automatic closure of the edges of a polygon, so we must list the vertex at both the beginning and the end of the face when we define the face; if this is not needed by your API, then you may omit the first `vertex()`call.

```
void cube(void) {
    for faces 1 to 6
        start face
            normal(normals[i]);
            vertex(vertices[edges[cube[face][0]][0]);
            for each edge in the face
                vertex(vertices[edges[cube[face][edge]][1]);
        end face
}
```

We added a simple structure for a list of normals with one normal per face. This supports flat shading, or shading where each face has a single color. In many applications, though, you might want to use smooth shading, where colors blend smoothly across each face of your polygon. For this, each vertex would need an individual normal. In this case, you specify the normal each time you specify a vertex, and a normal list that follows the vertex list would let you do that easily. For the code above, for example, we would not have a per-face normal, but instead each `vertex` operation could be replaced by the pair of operations:

```
normal(normals[edges[cube[face][0]][0]);
vertex(vertices[edges[cube[face][0]][0]);
```

You will see some techniques for computing normals at polygon vertices in Chapter 4.

Modeling Surfaces

A very useful kind of modeling is the modeling of surfaces. A surface is a set of points in 3-space that is the image of a function or process that operates on a region in 2-space. We think of a *function surface* when a function is used, and often in the sciences we will use these to look at the behavior of continuous functions.

We can draw surfaces by creating a grid of points $P_{ij} = (x_i, y_j)$ in 2-space and calculating a point $(u, v, w)_{ij}$ in 3-space for each. Then for each set of four points P_{ij}, $P_{i(j+1)}$, $P_{(i+1)j}$, $P_{(i+1)(j+1)}$, you choose two triangles that make up the quadrilateral they define, identify the points in 3-space that correspond to these mesh points, and draw the two triangles in the 3-space they define. This process is much harder to discuss than to implement and is presented in more detail in Chapter 9, where we look at graphics examples in the sciences.

As a particular case of this, let's look at a surface defined by a function of two variables. If the function is reasonably well behaved, computer graphics can make this very straightforward. The general idea of a graph of a function of two variables presented as a surface is straightforward. For each point (x, y) in the domain we calculate a value $f(x, y)$, and the set of triples $(x, y, f(x, y))$ is the graph of the function. As we saw above, however, we do not need to draw every point in the graph; we can choose regularly spaced values in the domain, calculate the function for each value, and join the vertices defined by these points to make a piece of the surface. If we take the points four at a time over the grid in the domain, we can make the associated piece of the surface with two triangles. Any triangle is planar and you can display it with your choice of either solid color or color determined by a lighting and shading model, depending on the results you want. The process is described by Figure 2.11 for a very coarse grid. In this figure you can see that the basis for the surface is the set of rectangles in the domain, with each rectangle defining two triangles in the actual surface.

Figure 2.11 Mapping a set of domain rectangles to surface triangles.

Additional Sources of Graphic Objects

Interesting and complex graphic objects can be difficult to create, because it can take a lot of work to measure or calculate the detailed coordinates of each of their vertices. More automatic techniques have been developed, including 3D scanning and laser rangefinding, but they are out of the reach of most college classrooms. What can we do to get interesting objects? There are four approaches.

The first way to get models is to buy them: Go to the commercial providers of 3D models. There is a serious market for some kinds of models, such as models of human anatomy, from medical and legal sources. This can be expensive, but it avoids having to develop the expertise to do professional modeling and then putting in the time to create the actual models. If you are interested, an excellent commercial source (as of this book's publication) with a few free samples is `http://www.digimation.com/ModelBankCollection/`.

A second way to get models is to find them in places where people share them with others. If you have friends in the graphics world, you can ask them about any models they know of.

As an example, the Protein Data Bank (`http://www.wwpdb.org/`) has a wide range of structure models available at no charge. If you want models of all kinds of different things, try the site `http://avalon.viewpoint.com;` it has many public domain models that have been contributed to the community by generous people. You will need to write or find a file reader that reads in data in one of the modeling formats into your programs' data structures. Models you get in this way may use many different formats for their data, so you may also need to write or find functions to translate these formats into one you can use.

A third way to get models is to digitize physical objects yourself with appropriate kinds of digitizing devices. A number of these are available, but their accuracy is often related to their cost. If you need to digitize specific physical objects, you can compare the cost and accuracy of different kinds of equipment. This will probably come with software tools that capture the points and store the geometry in a standard format, which may or may not be compatible with your graphics API or data structures. As above, you may need format translators.

A fourth way to get models is to create them yourself from your own imagination. A number of free or commercial graphics products let you do your own high-quality interactive 3D modeling. Again we find issues of file formats, but a good modeling system should be able to save the models in several formats, one of which you should be able to use fairly easily with your graphics API. It is also possible to create interesting models analytically, using mathematical approaches to generate the vertices. You have final control over the form and quality of these models, so this approach can give you extremely good results.

If you get models from modeling tools, digitizers, or other sources, you will find that they use a number of different data formats. Sometimes it seems as though every graphics tool uses its own unique data format. Some file or modeling tools will open models with many formats and allow you to save them in a different format, acting as format converters. But you are likely to end up needing to understand some model file formats and to write your own functions to read these formats and produce the kind of internal data that you need for your models. It may take some work to write filters that will translate formats; things that are "free" but use a unique format might cost more than things you buy if you can save the work of the conversion, but that's up to you to decide. An excellent resource on file formats is the *Encyclopedia of Graphics File Formats* [MUR], and we refer you to that book for details on particular formats.

Modeling Behavior

Geometry is the basis for traditional computer graphics that typically focuses on creating one image at a time. But we need to present the behavior of models in order to communicate many ideas to our audience. By *behavior* we mean how the objects we are modeling move or change over time, or how they react in response to internal forces or to stimuli that come from external inputs. For example, we can look at a model of the solar system. A single picture does not tell us much about planetary behavior, so it is not enough to create a geometric model of the sun, planets, and moons, even if we use texture mapping to make each planet and moon look very realistic. The solar system is much more about motion than about position.

We can model planetary motion two ways. One is to use equations for each planet's and moon's position over time, with a known initial position of each part at the start, and use an animation that increments the clock and generates positions for each time and then draws a sequence of images that show the motion. This will be quite accurate but will depend on how good the equations of motion are. Equations that capture the planets' elliptical orbits and include the interaction of planets and moons can be quite complex.

On the other hand, we can start with an initial set of positions and velocities and can apply the laws of physics to tell us the acceleration on each object caused by the gravitational effect of each other object. This is the way the solar system works, after all, and if we update the planets' and moons' positions based on their new velocity after acceleration is applied, we should get a model that has not only the behavior of the equations above but also effects such as the wobble of Neptune that suggested the existence of Pluto in the 1930s. The price you pay is that the model is described by a very complex set of differential equations that take a good deal of knowledge of numerical analysis to program, and the model is prone to numerical errors even with the best kind of numerical methods. This is likely beyond the experience of most students (and a large number of instructors) in a beginning graphics course.

But whatever kind of modeling you do, you are likely to find yourself dealing with questions such as this: How does the model behave over time or in response to different inputs, and how can you capture that behavior in your program so that your graphics accurately reflects the model's behavior? The answers probably are outside the field of computer graphics because they lie in the field from which the model comes, but computer graphics needs to give you the tools to program behaviors you have identified.

A Word to the Wise

Modeling can be the most time-consuming part of graphics, but you aren't going to create a useful or interesting image unless the modeling is done carefully and well. If you are concerned about the programming part of modeling, it might be best to create a simple version of your model and do the programming (and other things we haven't talked about yet) for that simple version. Once you are satisfied that the programming works and that you have gotten the other parts right, you can replace the simple model—the one with just a few polygons in it—with the one that represents what you really want to present.

TRANSFORMATIONS AND MODELING

This section requires some mathematical background. You need to understand the general concept of functions and of function composition, as well as an understanding of 3D geometry and what it means for objects to be moved around in 3-space. You should also have a general understanding of the stack data structure.

Transformations are a key point in creating significant images in any graphics system. It is extremely difficult to model everything in a scene in its actual place in the world space, and it is even more difficult if you want to move objects in your scene with animation and user control. Modeling transformations let you define each object you will use in any space that makes sense for that object, and you can then place it and move it around in the world space however you wish. Modeling transformations also allow you to place your lights or eyepoint in the scene and move them around as needed.

There are several kinds of transformations in computer graphics: projection transformations, viewing transformations, and modeling transformations. Your graphics API should support all of these. Projection transformations specify how your scene in 3-space is mapped to the 2D screen space and are defined when you define your perspective or orthogonal projections. Viewing transformations let you view your scene from any point in space and are set up when you define your viewing environment. We have discussed these in previous chapters. Modeling transformations are used to place objects in your scene and are set up as you define the size, orientation, and position of each of those objects. Together, these transformations make up the graphics pipeline that we discussed in Chapter 0.

There are three fundamental modeling transformations: rotations, translations, and scaling. These maintain the basic geometry of any object to which they may be applied and are fundamental tools you use to build more complex and sophisticated models than you can create with only simple modeling techniques. Later in this chapter we will see how you can use scene graphs to define and maintain the relationships among parts of these complex models.

The power of modeling transformation, though, does not come from using simple transformations on their own but from combining them to achieve complete control over your modeled objects. Simple transformations are combined into a composite modeling transformation that is applied to your geometry when the geometry is specified. These composite transformations can be saved and later restored to let you build up transformations that place groups of objects consistently. One of the powerful features of a graphics API is its ability to support this transformation composition without detailed work by the programmer, as you will see in the discussion of OpenGL modeling operations in Chapter 3. In this section we will see several examples of modeling with composite transformations.

Finally, simple modeling and transformations work together to let you generate more complex graphical objects, but these objects can take time to display. Graphics APIs let you store precompiled objects that can execute much more quickly than objects that are simply defined, and these compiled objects are usually simple to create and use.

Definitions

In this section we outline the general concept of geometric transformations and describe the fundamental transformations used in computer graphics. We then describe how the fundamental transformations can be used to build general graphical object models for your scenes.

Transformations

A *transformation* is a function that acts on *n*-dimensional space. The linear transformations we use in computer graphics preserve many geometric relationships, so we view them as taking geometry and producing new geometry. The geometry can be anything a computer graphics systems works with—a projection, a view, a light, a direction, or an object to be displayed. We have already talked about projections and views, so in this section we will talk about transformations as modeling tools. These are the three transformation types we mentioned earlier: rotation, translation, and scaling. Below we look at each of these transformations individually and then together to see how we can use transformations to create the scenes we will display.

Our first example of transformations will be the creation and movement of a rugby ball. Because the ellipsoid is longer on one axis, it is easy to see its rotations around one of its short axes, and of course it is easy to see its translations. This ball is easy to create from a sphere using scaling. We first discuss scaling and show how it is used to create the ball, then rotation and show how the ball can be rotated around one of its short axes, and then translation and show how the ball can be moved to any location we wish. We finally see how the transformations work together to create a rotating, moving ball such as we might see when the ball is kicked. The ball is shown with very simple lighting and shading as described in Chapter 6.

Scaling changes the objects it acts on by multiplying each coordinate of each vertex by a fixed value. Each time a scalar transformation is applied, it changes each dimension of everything it acts on. A scaling transformation requires three values, each of which multiplies one of the three coordinates. A graphics API scaling function takes three real values as its parameters. If we have a point with coordinates (x, y, z) and specify the three scaling values as Sx, Sy, and Sz, then applying the scaling transformation changes the point's coordinates to $(x*Sx, y*Sy, z*Sz)$. If we take a simple sphere centered at the origin, scale it by 2.0 in one direction (in our case, the z-coordinate or vertical direction), and translate it upward by 2.0 so its bottom is even with the ground plane, using functions such as

```
translate(0.0, 0.0, 2.0);
scale(1.0, 2.0, 1.0);
sphere(1.0);
```

we get the rugby ball shown in Figure 2.12 next to the original sphere. It is important to note that this scaling operates on everything in the space, so if we happen to also have a unit sphere at a position away from the origin, scaling will move the sphere farther away from the origin and will also multiply each of its coordinates by the scaling amount. This shows that it is most useful to apply scaling to an object defined at the origin so only the dimensions of the object will be changed. The standard approach to modeling defines objects at the origin and applies scaling closest to the actual geometry because that's the best way to create objects of known dimensions.

Figure 2.12 A sphere shown unscaled (*left*) and scaled by 2.0 in the *y*-direction and translated by 1.0 upward to make a rugby ball (*right*).

Rotation takes the objects it acts on and changes each vertex by rotating it around a line in that space. A rotation transformation will always have a fixed line through the origin. To define a rotation transformation, you need to specify the amount of the rotation (in degrees or radians, as needed) and the line about which the rotation is done. A graphics API function to apply a rotation transformation, then, will take the angle and the line as its parameters; remember that a line through the origin can be specified by three real numbers that are the coordinates of the direction vector for that line. An example function for the rotation of the rugby ball in our example would be

```
rotate(angle, 0.0, 1.0, 0.0);
```

because the vector (0.0, 1.0, 0.0) specifies the *y*-axis. It is most useful to apply rotations to objects centered at the origin in order to change only the orientation with the transformation. The standard approach to modeling applies rotation immediately next to scaling to give correctly sized objects the needed orientation for the scene.

Translation takes the objects it acts on and changes each vertex's coordinates by adding a fixed value to each coordinate. This moves all the parts of the object by the same amount. A translation transformation needs the three values that are to be added to the coordinates of each point. A graphics API function to apply a translation, then, will take these three values as its parameters and might look like

```
translate(tx, ty, tz);
```

A translation treats all the parts of an object uniformly, and in the standard approach to modeling, a translation is applied after any scaling or rotation in order to take an object with the right size and right orientation and place it correctly in space.

Finally, we put these transformations together to create a sequence of images of the rugby ball as it moves through space, rotating as it goes, as shown in Figure 2.13. This sequence is created by defining the rugby ball as a sphere with scaling, and using a translation to put it on the ground. Then rotation and translation transformation values are computed at several times in the flight of the ball, rotating the ball by slowly increasing amounts *angle* and translating it by values *Tx*, *Ty*, and *Tz* using standard gravitational calculations. Each separate image is created with transformations that can be described generically by

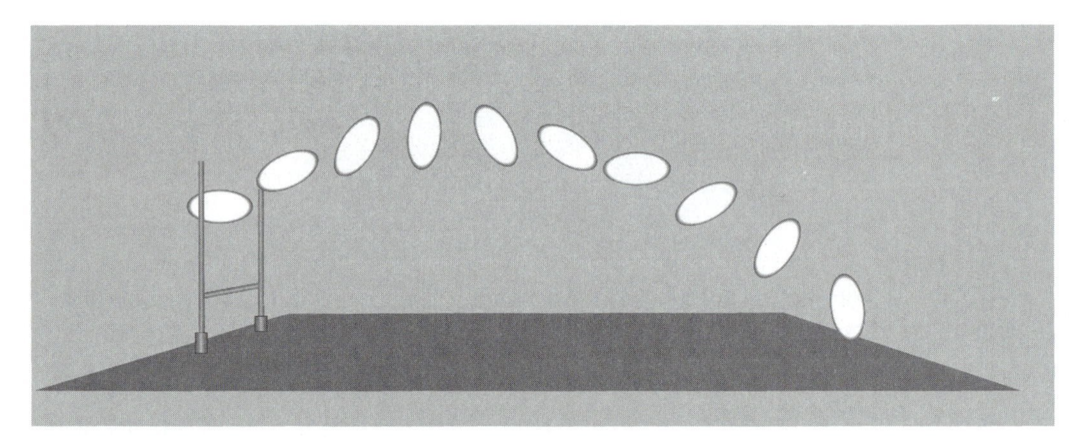

Figure 2.13 A sequence of images of the rugby ball as transformations move it through space.

```
translate(Tx, Ty, Tz)
rotate(angle, x-axis)
drawBall()
```

where the function `drawBall()` is defined as follows, based on a generic `drawSphere()` function that draws a sphere with radius 1 centered at the origin:

```
scale(1., 2., 1.)
drawSphere()
```

Notice that the ball rotates in a slow counterclockwise direction as it travels from left to right, while the position of the ball describes a parabola as it moves, modeling the effect of gravity on the ball's flight. This kind of composite transformation construction is described in the next section, and the order of these transformations is critical to achieve the correct results.

The transformations of computer graphics all have simple inverses, or transformations that undo the result of the original transformation. These are easy to write down: The inverse of a rotation by an angle Θ around a given line is a rotation by $-\Theta$ around the same line; the inverse of a scaling by values (Sx, Sy, Sz) is a scaling by values $(1/Sx, 1/Sy, 1/Sz)$; and the inverse of a translation by (Tx, Ty, Tz) is a translation by $(-Tx, -Ty, -Tz)$. Combined with the fact that if S and T are two transformations, the inverse of the composition ST is the composition of the inverses of S and T in reverse order: $(ST)^{-1} = T^{-1}S^{-1}$, this gives you complete control over the inverses of all graphics transformations.

Because transformations are mathematical operations that map 3D space to 3D space, mathematics has standard ways to represent and manipulate them as arrays of real numbers. You do not need to master the array form to think about how you use transformations to create images, but it is needed to some do more advanced kinds of graphics operations. This representation is discussed in Chapter 4. Processes such as creating composite transformations are linked there to the standard operations on the matrices that represent transformations.

Composite Transformations

In order to model your objects, you may need to apply more than one simple transformation as you model your scene. This uses what is called a *composite transformation*. For example, if you want to create a rectangular box with height A, width B, and depth C, with center at (C_1, C_2, C_3) and oriented at an angle α relative to the Z-axis, you could start with a cube one unit on a side and with center at the origin. You can then create the box you want by applying the following sequence of operations:

- First, scale the cube to the right size to create the rectangular box with dimensions A, B, and C.
- Second, rotate the cube by the angle α around the line with direction (0, 0, 1) to produce the right orientation.
- Third, translate the cube to the position C_1, C_2, C_3.

This is what we call the standard approach to modeling because it works predictably to produce a well-understood result. In terms of code for the box, this looks like

```
translate(...);
rotate(...);
scale(...);
cube();
```

This standard sequence is critical because of the way transformations work. For example, if we rotated first and then scaled with different scale factors in each dimension, we would introduce distortions in the box because the edges would not be aligned with the coordinate axes, so the different scale factors would change the x-y proportions. If we translated first and then rotated, the rotation would move the box to an entirely different place. Because the order is very important, certain sequences of operations give predictable, workable results, and the order above is the one that works best: Apply scaling first, rotation second, and translation last.

The order in which we apply transformations is important in ways that go well beyond the translation and rotation example above. In general, transformations are an example of *noncommutative* operations, operations for which $f*g \neq g*f$ (that is, $f(g(x)) \neq g(f(x))$). Unless you have some experience with noncommutative operations from courses such as linear algebra, this may be a new concept for you. But let's look at the operations we described above: If we take the vertex (1, 1, 0) and apply a rotation by 90° around the Z-axis, we get the point (−1, 1, 0). If we then apply a translation by (2, 0, 0) we get the point (1, 1, 0) again. However, if we start with the vertex (1, 1, 0) and first apply the translation, we get (3, 1, 0), and if we then apply the rotation, we get the point (−1, 3, 0), which is certainly not the same as (1, 1, 0). That is, using some pseudocode for rotations, translations, and vertex definition, the two code sequences

```
     rotate(90, 0, 0, 1)                translate(2, 0, 0)
(1)  translate(2, 0, 0)            (2)  rotate(90, 0, 0, 1)
     setVertex(1, 1, 0)                 setVertex(1, 1, 0)
```

produce different results, so the rotate and translate operations are not commutative. In an exercise at the end of the chapter you are asked to try this for yourself with different vertices and different transformations to see the results.

This noncommutative behavior is not limited to different kinds of transformations. Different order of rotations around different lines can result in different images as well. If you consider rotations in different order, one around the Y-axis and one around the Z-axis

```
     rotate(60, 0, 0, 1)                rotate(90, 0, 1, 0)
(1)  rotate(90, 0, 1, 0)           (2)  rotate(60, 0, 0, 1)
     scale(3, 1, .5)                    scale(3, 1, .5)
     cube()                             cube()
```

then the results are again quite different, as is shown in Figure 2.14.

Figure 2.14 The results from two different orderings of the same rotations.

Transformations are implemented for computational purposes as matrices. Recall that we can represent points as four-tuples of real numbers by using homogeneous coordinates; transformations are implemented as 4×4 matrices that map the space of four-tuples into itself. (For reasons we discuss in Chapter 4 on mathematics for modeling, it is not enough to use 3×3 matrices for our modeling transformations.) Although we don't use this representation often in this book, it is used by graphics APIs and helps explain how transformations work; for example, transformations are not commutative because matrix multiplication is not commutative. (Try it out for yourself!) While you do not need to master matrix operations for transformations for most API-based graphics programming there may be times when you'll need to manipulate transformations in ways that go beyond your API, so be aware of this.

To save current modeling transformations and restore the transformation to a saved value, you might use a *transformation stack.* A stack is a data structure that stores a sequence of things with the property that when we take something from the structure, it is the most recent thing that was stored in the structure. Adding something to the stack is called *pushing* it onto the stack; taking it out of the stack is called *popping* the stack. The object most recently pushed onto the stack is said to be at the *top* of the stack. A transformation stack, then, holds a sequence of transformations, and we adopt the convention that the transformation at the top of the stack is the current active transformation. When we apply a rotation, translation, or scaling, then, we multiply the current active transformation (at the top of the stack) by the new transformation. We can save the current transformation by making a copy of the top of the stack and pushing it onto the stack, saving the current transformation right below the top. We can restore the previous transformation by popping the stack, taking the current transformation off the top. We will discuss how the stack is used in more detail later in this chapter. Later (in Chapter 4) we will see that a transformation is represented for computation as a 4×4 real-valued matrix and that this is equivalent to an array of sixteen real numbers, so we can think of transformation stacks as stacks of such arrays.

When you apply transformations to your models, you need to think about how to represent the transformations and models for computational purposes. Mathematical notation can be applied in many ways, so your mathematical experience may help you think about this problem. There are three ways to think about how transformations are applied to your models. In the first approach, you simply define the sequence of transformations as *last-specified, first-applied.* A second way of thinking about it is to apply transformations so that the transformation specified nearest to the geometry is applied first. A third way to think about this is in terms of building composite functions by multiplying the individual functions, and we compose each new function by multiplying it on the right of the previous functions. With any of these conventions, the standard operation sequence

```
translate(...);
rotate(...);
scale(...);
geometry();
```

would be achieved by the algebraic sequence of operations

```
translate * rotate * scale * geometry
```

or, thinking of multiplication as function composition, as

```
translate(rotate(scale(geometry())))
```

At first glance, this sequence looks to be exactly the opposite of the standard operation sequence above. But we see that the scaling operation is the function physically closest to the geometry (the function `geometry()`) as the code is written. This is also the right place for the scaling transformation because of the last-specified, first-applied nature of transformations. In Figure 2.15 we see the sequence of operations to create a long, thin, rectangular bar that is oriented at a 45° angle upward and lies above the definition plane. We proceed from the plain cube (at the left), to the scaled cube next, then to the scaled and rotated cube, and finally to the translated object that uses all the transformations (at the right).

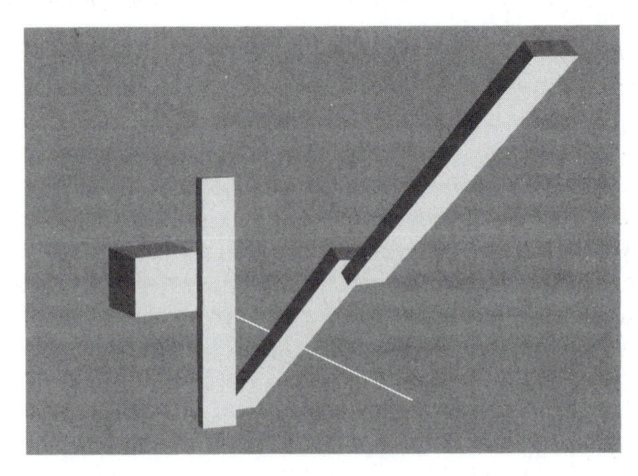

Figure 2.15 The sequence of figures as a cube is transformed.

If P is the projection transformation, V is the viewing transformation, and `T0, T1, ... Tlast` are the transformations specified in the program to model the scene, in the order in which they appear in the code (`T1` is first, `Tlast` is last), then the operation sequence is

`P→V→T0→T1→T2→ ... →Tn→Tn+1→ ... →Tlast→ ... →geometry`

In the example code from the previous chapter, we saw the projection transformation defined in the `reshape()` function, and the viewing transformation is defined at the beginning of the modeling process in the `init()` function or at the beginning of the `display()` function. These two transformations are specified before any of the modeling transformations. But the sequence is applied as we saw above: `Tlast` is actually applied first, and V and finally P are applied last. The code has the definition of P first, the definition of V second, the definitions of `T0, T1, ... Tlast` in order, and the definition of the geometry last. Go back to the actual code example in the first chapter and trace out this sequence there. You need to understand this sequence very well, because it's critical to building, complex hierarchical models.

Using Transformation Stacks

In defining a scene, we may want to define some standard pieces and assemble them in specific ways and then use the combined pieces to create additional parts or objects for your scene. This process can be repeated to create more and more complex objects, and the overall process is usually captured in functions that express the modeling. To create such complex models, we need to create individual parts through functions that are independent of how the parts will be used later and then be able to assemble them into a whole. Eventually, we can see that the entire image will be a single whole that is composed of its various parts.

As we saw above, there is always some kind of transformation in place. even just the projection and viewing transformations, when you define the geometry of an object in your scene. When you begin to put the simple parts of a composite object in place you will use some transformations to place each part, but you may need to undo some of those transformations when you define the next part. In effect, you need to save the state of the transformations when you begin a new part, and then return to that transformation state, discarding any transformations you added past that mark, to begin the next part. Note that you always add and discard transformations at the end of the list we described above, so this operation acts like a stack. We may define a stack of transformations and use it to manage this process as follows:

- As transformations are defined, they are right-multiplied into the transformation.
- To save the state of the transformation, we copy the current version of the transformation and push the copy onto the stack, and apply all subsequent transformations to the top of the stack. To return to the original transformation we pop the stack, giving us the original transformation so we can work with it again.

Because all transformations are applied to the one at the top of the stack, when we pop the stack we return to the original context.

In the rugby ball example, we defined the playing field and goal posts and placed them in our model only once, but we need to place the ball in the model many times. For each individual ball in the scene we have saved the current modeling transformation by pushing a copy of that transformation onto the transformation stack; applied modeling transformations to translate, rotate, and scale the sphere; drawn the sphere; and popped the transformation stack. Thus each instance of the ball is placed separately into the scene with its own transformations, and these transformations have no effect outside the task of drawing that single ball.

Designing a scene that has a large number of pieces of geometry and the transformations that define them can take some slow and painstaking work. In the next section we introduce the concept of the scene graph as a design tool to help you create complex and dynamic models both efficiently and effectively.

Compiling Geometry

Creating a model and transforming it into world space can take a good deal of work. You may need to compute vertex coordinates in model space and you will need to apply modeling transformations to these coordinates to get the final vertex coordinates. These are finally sent to the viewing and projection processes to determine the vertices in eye space and finally screen space. If the model is complex and is used frequently, and if it must be re-calculated each time it is drawn, it can make a scene quite slow to display. Applying a transformation involves a matrix multiplication that could use as many as sixteen floating-point operations for each transformation and each vertex.

As a way to save time in displaying the image, many graphics APIs allow you to "compile" the geometry in a model in a way that allows it to be displayed much more quickly. This compiled geometry is basically the *display list,* sent to the rendering pipeline as described in Chapter 10. When the compiled model is displayed, no re-calculation of vertices and no computation of transformations are needed; only the saved result of these computations is sent to the graphics system. Geometry that is to be compiled should be carefully chosen so that it is not changed between displays; if changes are needed, you will need to recompile the object. Once you have seen what parts you can compile, you can compile them and use the compiled versions to make the display faster. We will discuss how OpenGL compiles geometry in display lists in Chapter 3. If you use another graphics API, look for details in its documentation.

An Example

To help us see how you can make useful graphical objects from simple modeling, let's consider a 3D arrow that we could use to point out things in a 3D scene. Our goal is to make an arrow such as the one in Figure 2.16, with the arrow oriented downward and aligned with the *Y*-axis. A generic arrow like this could be reused easily whenever you need an arrow by scaling it to create the desired size, rotating it to orient it as desired, and then translating it to have its point wherever it is needed.

Figure 2.16 The 3D arrow in standard position.

In order to make this arrow, we start with two simpler shapes that are themselves useful. (These are sufficiently useful that they are provided as built-in functions in the GLU and GLUT toolkits described in Chapter 3.) These simpler shapes are designed to be in standard positions and have standard sizes. These templates are not necessarily designed to be convenient for this application but are designed with an eye toward being simple to understand and to use.

The first of our simple shapes is a cylinder. This will be a template object that can be made into a general cylinder of any size and any orientation by simple transformations. Our template will have the centerline of the cylinder parallel to the *X*-axis, one end centered at the origin and the other end on the positive *X*-axis, and a radius of 1 and a length of 1. The cylinder will have the cross-section of a regular polygon with *NSIDES* sides. This is a reasonable approximation of an actual cylinder and is easy to scale. The template is shown in the left-hand side of Figure 2.17. The second simple shape is a cone whose centerline is the *Y*-axis and whose point is at the origin, with a base of radius 1 and a height of 1, and having a filled-in base. As with the cylinder, this template is easy to scale and orient as needed. We again use a regular polygon of *NSIDES* sides for the base of the cone. The template shape is shown in the right-hand side of Figure 2.17.

Figure 2.17 The templates of the parts of the arrow: the cone (*left*) and the cylinder (*right*).

A sketch of the code for the cylinder template function `cylinder()` is:

```
angle = 0.;
anglestep = TwoPI/(float)NSIDES;
for (i = 0; i < NSIDES; i++) {
    nextangle = angle + anglestep;
    beginQuad();
        vertex(0., cos(angle), sin(angle));
        vertex(1., cos(angle), sin(angle));
        vertex(1., cos(nextangle), sin(nextangle));
        vertex(0., cos(nextangle), sin(nextangle));
    endQuad();
    angle = nextangle;
}
```

A sketch of the code for the cone template `cone()` is:

```
angle = 0.;
anglestep = TwoPI/(float)NSIDES;
beginTriangleFan();
    vertex(0., 0., 0.);
    for (i = 0; i < NSIDES; i++) {
        angle += anglestep;
        vertex(cos(angle), 1., sin(angle));
}

endTriangleFan();
angle = 0.;
beginPolygon();
```

```
    for (i = 0; i < NSIDES; i++) {
        angle += anglestep;
        vertex(cos(angle), 1., sin(angle));
    }
endPolygon();
```

Notice that we have not set the color of either the cylinder or the cone, even though the figure shows them white and red, respectively. We also have not defined any shading such as you see in the figure. These are appearance issues that we will discuss in Chapter 6, and the figure shows these appearances only to help you see the shapes and the relations better.

Now that we have created both template shapes, we can build a template 3D arrow function `arrow3D()`. We use a cylinder twice as long and with half the radius of the original cylinder template, oriented along the *Y*-axis, and translated so it lies one unit above the origin. We combine this with the cone in its original form to form the shape of the arrow. The result is an arrow three units long, so we will scale it uniformly by 0.33 so that it will have overall length 1 in order to make it easier to use in any application.

```
//  scale arrow as a whole
    pushTransformStack();
    scale(.33, .33, .33);      //  1/3 original size
//  scale and orient cylinder part of arrow
    pushTransformStack();
    translate(0., 1., 0.);         //  placed as specified
    rotate(90., 0., 0., 1.);       //  90 degrees around z-axis
    scale(2., 0.5, 0.5);           //  cylinder of right dimensions
    cylinder();
    popTransformStack();
//  now use the cone as defined without any transforms
    cone();
    popTransformStack();
```

A Word to the Wise

As we saw above, you must be careful of transformation order. It can be difficult to look at an image that is obviously incorrect and see what errors, such as misordered transformations, could have caused the problems. You need to develop skill in what we call "visual debugging"—looking at an image and seeing that it is not correct, and then figuring out what errors might have created these problems in the image. However, you cannot tell that an image is wrong unless you know what the correct image should be, so you must know what you should be seeing. As an obvious example, if you are doing scientific images, you must know the science well enough to know when an image makes sense.

MODELING FOR VISUAL COMMUNICATION

Shape is probably the fundamental part of any image. All our images are built from modeling, and modeling is based on creating geometric objects that have shape. Behavior is also important because static images do not give us as good an idea about their subject as dynamic or interactive images. Visual communication begins with the shapes we create in our images and with the behavior we give them. Here we focus on shape, and we go into behavior in depth in discussions of events in Chapter 7 and animation in Chapter 11.

All sorts of shapes and all sorts of arrangements of basic shapes are available to you as you create images. You may use simple shapes, emphasizing a basic simplicity in the ideas you are communicating. There is a visual clarity to an image built of simple (or at least apparently simple) shapes; the image will seem uncluttered and it will be easy for your viewer to see what you are presenting. If you need to use a more complex shape to communicate your ideas, you may be able to find a pre-built shape you can use, or you can design the shape using basic transformations and the geometry supported by the API to create the shape yourself.

Shapes are not used arbitrarily, of course. Sometimes your images will describe physical objects, and you will want to create shapes that represent those objects either by being an accurate version of the objects or by representing the objects in a recognizable but simplified way. These shapes may be smooth, if you know that your theoretical or data values change smoothly across the display, or they may be coarse and irregular if you have only discrete data and do not know that it is correct to display it smoothly. Sometimes your images will deal with concepts that are not physical objects, and you will want to create abstract shapes that give your viewer something to represent the concepts. These shapes carry ideas through their position and through properties such as size, shape, color, and motion.

Be careful about the cultural context of shapes you might use as symbols. If you need to use a simple shape to show the position of a data point, for example, you could use a circle, a square, a cross, a pentagram, or a hexagram. The last three shapes have cultural associations that may or may not be appropriate for your use, and you need to think about that before using them. In general, be sensitive to the cultural context of shapes and recognize that a choice that seems innocent to you may have a strong impact on someone else.

Recognizing the Meaning of Shapes

A viewer can get information from an image only if the image is presented in ways the viewer has already learned to understand. This is almost self-evident, but someone developing an image can easily assume that the viewer shares the developer's visual vocabulary and can understand the meaning the developer intended. In fact, each of us has a rich visual vocabulary; for example, we understand many shapes of signs and we are used to reading simple line graphs. But if we think about the mathematics and science courses we have taken, we see that they emphasize being able to read and create many different graphs and diagrams; this emphasis is meant to give the student the visual vocabulary needed for the field. The meaning of shapes is, in fact, part of the cultural context a viewer brings to an image.

To think concretely about the way shapes represent information, we will use Coulomb's law of electrostatic potential. This law states that the potential at any point in the plane is the sum of the potentials at the point from each of the point charges, and the potential from each point charge is the point charge divided by the square of the distance between the point and the charge. As a formula expressing the potential at a point (x, y) we have:

$$P(x, y) = \sum \frac{Q_i}{\sqrt{(x - x_i)^2 + (y - y_i)^2}}$$

where each charge Q_i is positioned at point (x_i, y_i). This example is discussed in more detail in Chapter 9, but in this chapter we will look at some representations of this problem as examples of visual presentation.

If we look at the Coulomb's law function on a rectangular surface with three fixed point charges, one positive and two negative, we can compute the potential at each point in the surface. This is a function of two variables over a domain in the real 2D plane, and we can present its graph as a surface in three-dimensional space. In Figure 2.18, we show the function by presenting its 3D surface graph in a fairly traditional way, with an emphasis on the shape of the surface. If the emphasis is on the surface itself, this might be a good way to present the graph, because lighting shows the shape well. This can be presented as a smooth shape because the theory tells us that the potential is continuous across the space except at points where a term in the denominator is zero. The only lie we tell with this surface is that the surface is bounded because there are discontinuities at the points where the fixed charges lie. In fact, the graph goes to infinity at these points. This view shows two minima and one maximum for the surface, corresponding to two negatively charged points and one positively charged point. The viewpoint that is used for the figure lets us see these three points and shows us a good representation of the shape. The viewpoint is critical to getting the best understanding of the surface because another view might hide the smaller of the minima or the details of the region between the minima.

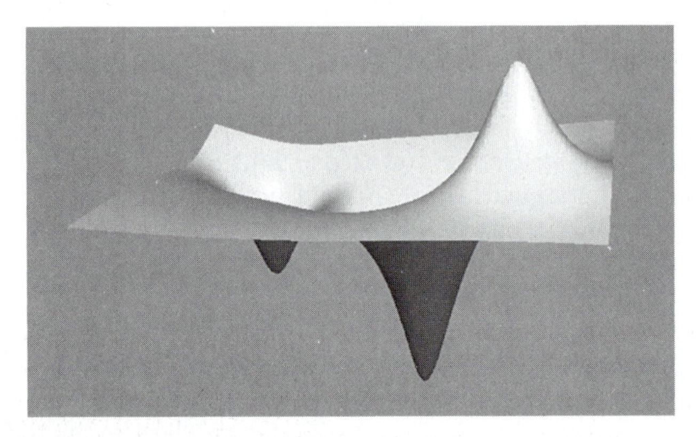

Figure 2.18 Traditional surface graph presented with three lights to show its shape. See the figure in the color insert.

There is a potential problem with this kind of representation, depending on the experience of the viewer. The viewer must be familiar with surface representations of functions are because there is no actual surface in this problem; instead, for each point (x, y) in 2D space, the value of the electrostatic force at that point is represented by the height. The peaks of the graph represent points where the force is large and positive; the valleys represent points where the force is large and negative (and so are simply downward-facing peaks). But both peaks and valleys are, as we have seen, inaccurate because these include discontinuities, and the viewer should understand that. Finally, because the viewer must see abstract values from the surface, this is not necessarily a good representation for novice users or for use when no other discussion of the situation is presented. This is discussed further in Chapter 9.

How might we have presented this concept differently? Because we are discussing something that works in a plane, we might have used a two-dimensional image that showed its values by using colors to stand for the potential, or we might have used the three-dimensional view but instead of using naturalistic color we could have used a color ramp as we did with the temperature change example. This question of how to represent a concept graphically is one of the most important parts of designing an image, and we consider it several times throughout the book.

Dimensions

We think of computer graphics as being 2D or 3D, because we think of creating images in either a plane or in 3-space. But we actually can use more than three dimensions for images, and understanding this can help us select from options that can make our images more effective.

Three dimensions we can use are obvious: the three coordinates of ordinary space. Because we can create motion over time, we have some control over a fourth dimension: time. We will see how we can use color to represent a numeric value, so we can think of color as yet another dimension, our fifth. A color used this way is often called a *pseudocolor,* or false color. Let's consider how we might use these dimensions to represent a particular problem: representing the temperature of an object. We use some color in our representation; a more complete discussion of color will be found in Chapter 5, but it is easy to include here.

We will look at several versions of this problem, so let's start with the simple one-dimensional concept: temperature along a wire. In this example, there is one dimension (length) in the physical object, and one more dimension in the temperature at each point. There is no "temperature" dimension, but we can represent temperature by either number or color. If we use number, we can make a graph whose horizontal axis is length and whose vertical axis is temperature; this is a familiar graph in mathematics and science textbooks. If we use color, we have a line that shows different colors at different points on the line, a very different representation but one that might look a bit like an actual heated wire. These two representations are shown in Figure 2.19 for a wire that is initially at a uniform temperature and is cooled at both ends.

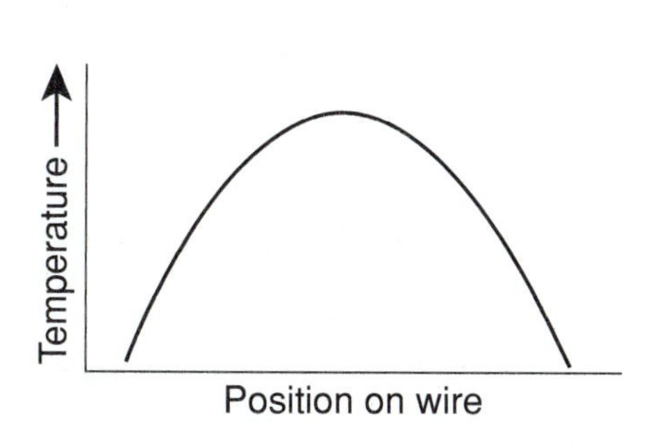

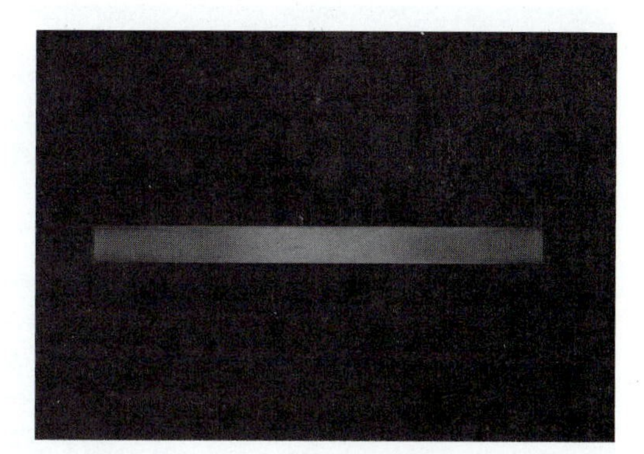

Figure 2.19 Two representations of temperature on a wire: curve (*left*) and color (*right*).

These two representations have one thing in common: The viewer must understand that we are using an abstraction for temperature, though the abstractions are fundamentally different. In the left-hand image the abstraction is that the temperature is a second coordinate value, while in the right-hand image the abstraction is that the temperature is a color. The first is more quantitative and the viewer can get more exact values from the image, while the second is more expressive and gives a better sense of hot and cold. You must decide which you want to express.

If we want to consider how the temperature on the wire changes over time, we add a third dimension of time to the question. Again, we can ask how we would represent that third dimension, and again we have two different answers: as a third numerical dimension, or by animating the original image in time. Because the original image has two choices, we actually have four possible answers for this problem:

1. Use a numerical curve for the temperature at any point in time, extended with numerical values for the third dimension to produce a three-dimensional surface; in this surface, slices parallel to the original curve are the temperatures at any time, while slices perpendicular to the original curve are temperatures at a particular point over time.
2. Use a numerical curve for the temperature at any point in time, extended by animation so the curve changes over time.
3. Use a colored line for the temperature at any point in time, extended with numerical values for the third dimension to produce a colored plane; in this plane, slices parallel to the original curve are the temperatures at any time, while slices perpendicular to the original curve are temperatures at a particular point over time.
4. Use a colored line for the temperature at any point in time, extended by animation so that the colors change over time.

Figure 2.20 shows the two representations that add a third dimension of time. Here the third dimension is shown by adding a horizontal axis toward the right of the scene. Unfortunately a printed book does not let us show animations, so the options that include time by animating the two-dimensional representation are not shown.

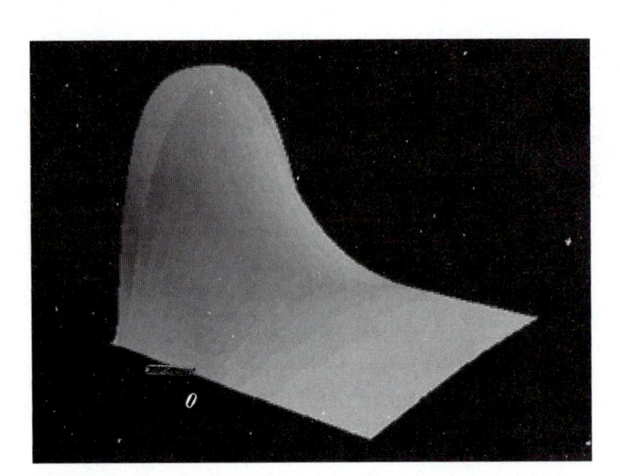

Figure 2.20 Change in temperature over time from solutions 1 and 3. See the figure in the color insert.

If we go one step further, we can consider temperature in a 3D space such as a room. Here our choices of the fourth dimension are very limited, because time simply does not work differently for different points in the space. Thus we would probably use color as the representation of temperature, our fourth dimension, and we would have to use some kind of higher-dimensional approach to viewing the scene (e.g., 2D slices showing color, or equitemperature surfaces). To see how the temperatures would change over time, we would almost certainly animate the display.

Higher Dimensions

This kind of modeling (including the use of color) works well when you are working with processes or functions that operate in 2D space. Here the 2D points can serve as the domain, and the process or function value can provide a third dimension that can be associated with a height or a color at the point. However, you may find yourself working beyond that level with processes or single-valued functions in 3D space, with processes or functions that produce 2D information in 2D space, or in other areas such as time-varying processes in 3D space where you exceed the ability to illustrate information in 3D space. In these cases you must find other ways to describe your information. All we can do is offer some examples. These examples include color as part of the modeling, so you should refer to Chapter 5 for the color details.

Perhaps the simplest higher-dimensional problem is to consider a process or function that operates in 3D space and has a simple real value. This could be a process that produces a value at each point in space, such as temperature or pressure. There are two simple ways to look at such a situation. The first asks, "For what points in space does this function have a given value?" This leads to what are called *isosurfaces* in the space, and there are complex algorithms for finding isosurfaces for volume data or for functions of three variables. The left-hand part of Figure 2.21 shows a simple approach to the isosurface problem, with the space divided into a number of small cubic cells and the function evaluated at each vertex on each cell. If the cell has some vertices where the value of the function is larger than the target value and some vertices where the function is smaller, the continuous function has the target value somewhere in that cell and a sphere is drawn in the cell. The second way to look at the problem asks for the values of the function in some 2D subset of the 3D space, typically a plane. For this, we can pass a *cutting plane* through the 3D space, measure the values of the function in that plane, and plot those values as colors on the plane displayed in space. The right-hand part of Figure 2.21 shows an example of a cutting

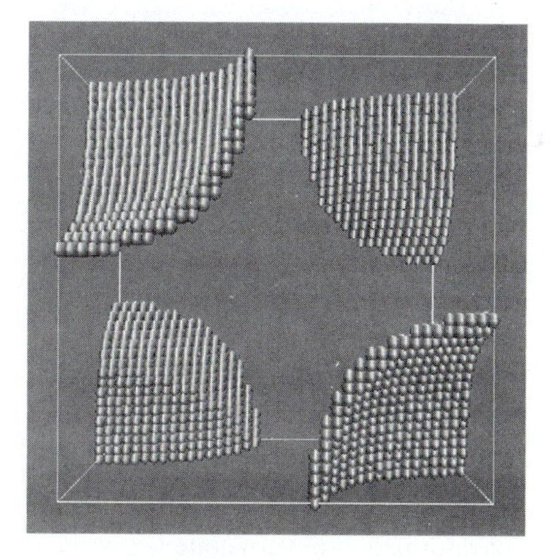

Figure 2.21 A fairly simple isosurface of a function of three variables (*left*); values of a function in 3D space viewed along a 2D plane in the space (*right*).

plane display for a function $f(x, y, z) = x*y*z$ that is hyperbolic in all three of the x, y, and z components in space. The pseudocolor coding is the uniform luminance ramp described above.

A different problem considers functions with a two-dimensional domain and a two-dimensional range and tries to find ways to display this four-dimensional information to your audience. Two examples of this problem are vector-valued functions on a rectangular real space, or complex-valued functions of a single complex variable. Figure 2.22 presents two such examples: a system of two first-order differential equations of two variables (left) and a complex-valued function of a complex variable (right). The domain is the standard rectangular region of two-dimensional space, and we have taken the approach of encoding the range in two parts based on considering each value as a vector with a length and a direction. We represent the magnitude of the vector or complex number as a color, and the direction of the vector or complex number as a fixed-length vector in the appropriate direction. The fact that fundamentally different concepts can have very similar presentations comes from the fundamental similarity of their vector-valued results and emphasizes the importance of having experience with presentations in order to see what you can do yourself.

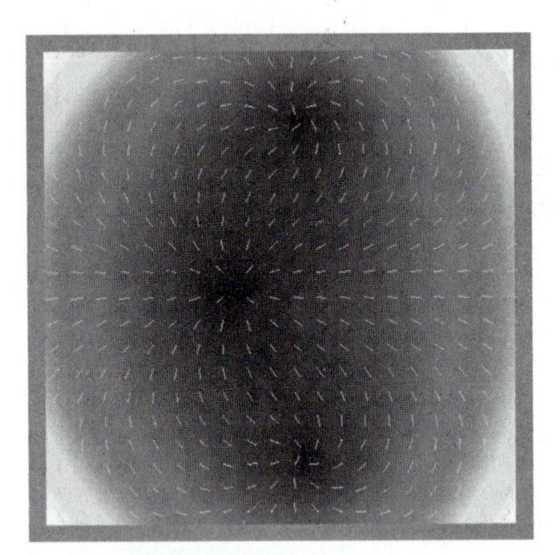

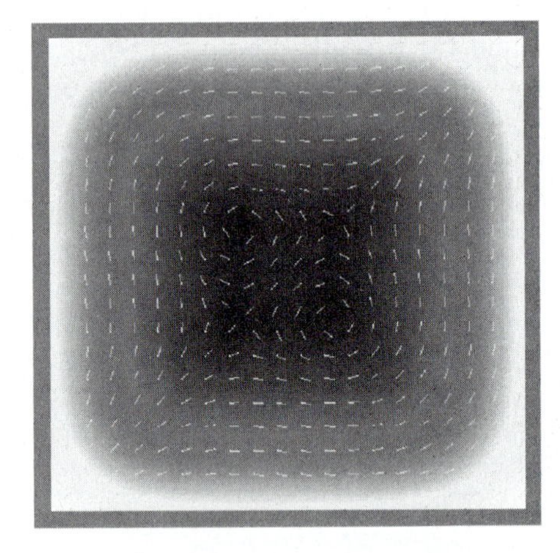

Figure 2.22 Two visualizations: a function of a complex variable (*left*); a differential equation (*right*).

The displays in Figure 2.22 that combine color and shape are fundamentally 2D images, with the domain of the functions given by the display window and the range of the functions represented by the color of the domain and the direction of the vector. There have been similar visualizations where the range had dimension higher than two, and the technique for these is often to replace the vector with an object having more information. Such an object is called a *glyph*, a relatively complex plotting symbol that can be varied in different ways to show values on several variables simultaneously. An example is shown in Figure 2.23, modeled from Donna Cox's work in [ELL], built from triangles that show temperature (from a color ramp as discussed in Chapter 5), pressure (as length), and direction (direction of the object) in an injection mold at different times (heights). These objects are placed at the locations where these measures are taken. Glyphs are abstract constructions and need to be designed carefully, because they combine shape and color information in very complex ways. However, they can be effective in carrying a great deal of information, particularly when the entire process being visualized is dynamic and is presented as an animation with the glyphs changing with time.

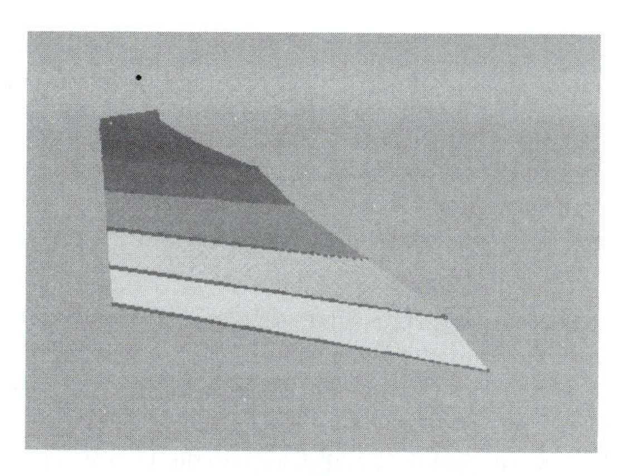

Figure 2.23 A glyph that could be used in an application.

Of course, there are other techniques for working with higher-dimensional problems. One of these extends the concept of projection. We understand the projection from three-dimensional eye space to two-dimensional viewing space in standard 3D graphics, but you can think about projections from spaces of four or more dimensions into three-dimensional space where they can be manipulated in familiar ways. An example of this is the image in Figure 2.24, a image of a hypercube or tessaract (four-dimensional cube) whose vertices have coordinates (x, y, z, w) where each of these components is either 1 or -1. In this particular example, each vertex in 4-space is projected into 3-space by projecting a constant proportion of the fourth coordinate into each of the other coordinates, which is essentially an orthogonal projection of 4-space into 3-space:

```
newVertex[0] = oldVertex[0]-0.3*oldVertex[3];
newVertex[1] = oldVertex[1]-0.3*oldVertex[3];
newVertex[2] = oldVertex[2]-0.3*oldVertex[3];
```

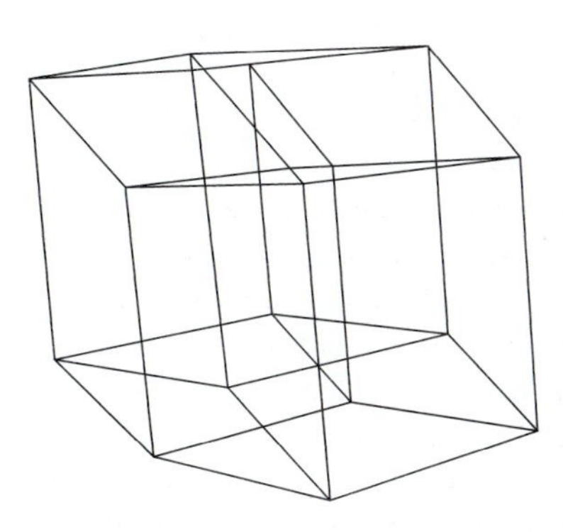

Figure 2.24 A hypercube projected into 3-space.

Other kinds of projections are possible, of course. Figure 2.24 comes from an example where the four-dimensional cube rotates in four-dimensional space and is then projected into 3-space. The code for this example is included with the book's resources so that you can examine it.

So we see that there are many meanings for a dimension, and we have many different ways to represent and show various dimensions. If you have a model that includes more than a simple three dimensions, look carefully at your options in designing a scene.

Legends and Labels

Legends and labels are text or simple graphics that are placed in an image in order to communicate information about the image and its model to the viewer. They are part of the model you create, even though they describe the primary image rather than being part of it. We give an example that is discussed at more length in Chapter 9. This example models the spread of a contagious disease through a diffusion process and includes a legend and label to help the viewer understand the image.

Legends are small graphics that include text and some kind of image that help the viewer interpret the meaning of your scene. They help your audience understand the information in your images, and you should always provide legends when they will help your audience understand your displays. If you use pseudocolor, show color scales to help a viewer interpret the color information. This lets people understand the relationships shown by your color and understand the context of your problem, which is an important part of the distinction between pretty pictures and genuine information. Creating images without scales or legends is one of the ways people create misleading visualizations.

An image alone makes up only part of the idea of using images to present information. A *label* is text information presented on the screen to put the image into context. Figure 2.25 shows an image with a label in the main viewport (a note that this image is about the spread

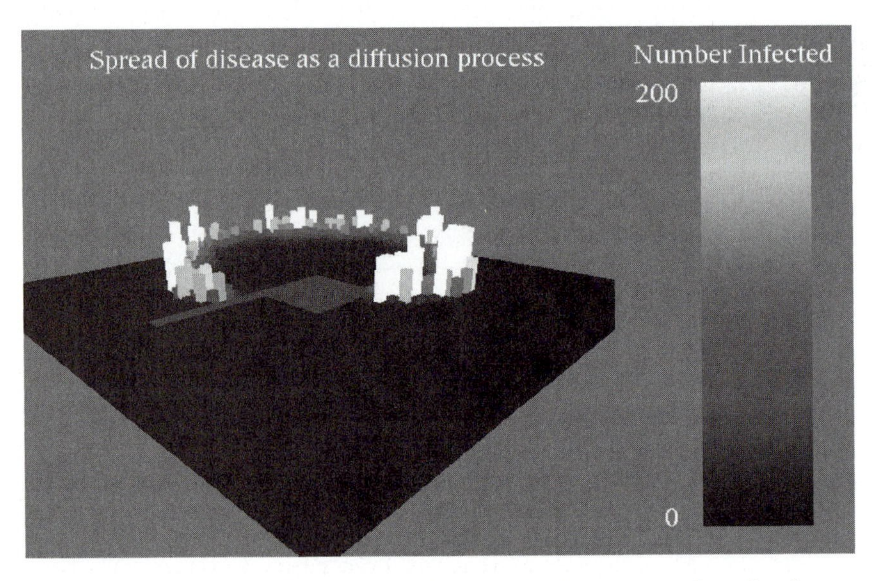

Figure 2.25 An example of a figure with a label and a legend to allow the figure to be interpreted.

of disease) and a legend in a separate viewport to the right of the main display (a note that says what the color means and how to interpret the color as a number). The label puts the image in a general context, and the legend shows that the different colors tell the numbers of persons infected in a region. This helps the viewer understand the results of this simulation as the bars in the main figure rise and fall, showing how the disease spreads from a single initial infection point.

Another very useful form of label could be text placed on a billboard in the scene. Billboards are simple 2D rectangles in space that are always oriented toward the viewer and that carry some texture-mapped information. Billboards are described in Chapter 8 on texture mapping and can give you the effect of floating text in a scene. If this is combined with a line or arrow from the billboard to the particular object being described, it can be an effective way to highlight something as animation or interaction moves the scene around.

Accuracy

When you create a model to represent with an image, you must think about the accuracy of the representation. This is part of modeling, but it is particularly important in thinking about how your audience will understand your image. You want to present images that show your information in a way that helps your audience understand it clearly and accurately. You must respect your data and not try to go beyond what it can give you. Your goal is not particularly to present pretty pictures; it is to present your data or theory as accurately as possible while helping the viewer to convert data to information. Of course, making attractive *and* accurate images is useful, especially when you are creating images for public presentation.

The key to accuracy is to work hard to understand what the data or theory you are working with really tells you, and what it doesn't. You can then create your presentation to emphasize those things that the data or theory needs to show. For data presentation, the issues are fairly straightforward. If you have data that is organized on a regular mesh, then it is straightforward to use polygons based on the mesh to present that data. If your data is not organized regularly, then you may have to create a polygonal representation of the data for most graphics APIs. If you do not know *a priori* that there is a smooth variation to the population from which you get your data, then you need to present the data as discrete values and not use smooth interpolations or smooth shading to make your data look smoother. If your data values are spatially distributed and there is no reason to assume anything about the values of the data between your samples, then the best approach might be to display the data in the sampled space as simple shapes at the sample locations using different sizes and/or colors to show the values at those positions.

On the other hand, when you display theoretical concepts, you may be able to calculate the exact theoretical values of your displayed information at some points (or some times), but the behavior between these points or these times is based on operations that cannot readily be solved exactly. This is common, for example, when the theory leads to systems of differential equations that cannot be solved in closed form (that is, whose solutions are not exact expressions). Here you must pay careful attention to the numerical solutions for these operations to be sure that they give you enough accuracy to be meaningful and, in particular, that they do not diverge from accurate results as your solution points or times move further from the known values. It can be very useful to have a good knowledge of numerical techniques such as you would get from a study of numerical analysis in order to develop accurate presentations of the theory.

SCENE GRAPHS AND MODELING GRAPHS

In this chapter we have defined modeling as the process of defining and organizing the geometry and behavior in a scene. While modern graphics APIs can provide you with a great deal of assistance in rendering your images, modeling is usually less well supported and programmers may have difficulty with modeling when they begin to work in computer graphics. Organizing a scene with transformations, particularly when that scene involves hierarchies of components and when some of those components are moving, involves relatively complex concepts that need to be organized very systematically in order to create a successful scene. This is even more difficult when the eyepoint is one of the moving parts, especially when it is defined relative to other moving objects. Hierarchical modeling has long been done by using trees or treelike structures to organize the components of the model, and we will find this approach to be very useful.

Recent graphics systems, such as Java3D and VRML 2, have formalized the *scene graph* as a powerful tool for both modeling scenes and organizing scene drawing. By understanding and adapting the structure of the scene graph, we can organize a formal tree approach to both the design and the implementation of hierarchical models. This can give us tools to manage not only modeling the geometry of such models but also the behavior of these models and their components' animation and interactive control. This section introduces the scene graph concept and structure and adapts scene graphs to a slightly simplified *modeling graph* that you can use to design scenes. We also show how the modeling graph gives us the three key transformations that go into creating a scene: the projection transformation, viewing transformation, and modeling transformation(s). This structure is very general and lets us manage all the fundamental principles in defining a scene and translating it into code for a graphics API. Our terminology is based on the scene graph of Java3D and should help anyone using that system understand the way its scene graph works.

A Brief Summary of Scene Graphs

The fully developed scene graph of the Java3D API has many parts and can be complex to understand, but we can abstract it to get an excellent model to help us think about scenes that we can use in developing the code to implement our modeling. A brief outline of the Java3D scene graph in Figure 2.25 will help us discuss the general approach to graph-structured modeling as it can be applied to beginning computer graphics. Remember that we will simplify some parts of this graph before applying it to our modeling.

A *virtual universe* holds one or more (usually one) *locales*, which are positions in the universe to put scene graphs. Each scene graph has two branches: a *content branch*, which contains shapes, lights, and other content; and a *view branch*, which contains viewing information. The division is flexible, but we will use this standard approach to build a framework for our modeling work.

The *content branch* of the scene graph is a collection of nodes, including group nodes, transform groups, and shape nodes, as seen in the left-hand branch of Figure 2.26. A *group node* is a grouping structure that can have any number of children; besides simply organizing its children, a group node can include a switch that selects which children to present in a scene. A *transform group* is a collection of modeling transformations that affect all the geometry that lies below it. The transformations will be applied to any of the transform group's children with the convention that transforms "closer" to the geometry (defined in shape nodes that are leaves in the graph) are applied first. Transform groups traditionally have the same representation in the scene graph as general group nodes, though their function is quite different. A *shape node*

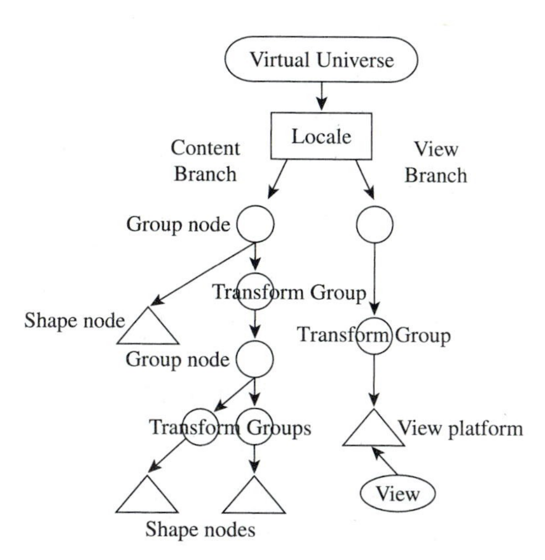

Figure 2.26 The structure of the scene graph as defined in java3D.

includes both geometry and appearance data for an individual graphic unit. The geometry data includes standard 3D coordinates, normals, and texture coordinates, including points, lines, triangles, and quadrilaterals, as well as triangle strips, triangle fans, and quadrilateral strips. The appearance data includes color, shading, or texture information. Lights and eyepoints are included in the content branch as a particular kind of geometry, having position, direction, and other appropriate parameters. Scene graphs also include shared groups, or groups that are included in more than one branch of the graph. Shared groups are groups of shapes that are included indirectly in the graph, and any change to a shared group affects all references to that group. This allows scene graphs to include the kind of template-based modeling that is common in graphics applications. The notation for scene graphs is that circles denote group nodes, ovals denote transforms or transform groups, and triangles represent shape nodes.

The *view branch* of the scene graph includes the specification of the display device, and thus the projection appropriate for that device, as shown in the right-hand branch of Figure 2.26. It also specifies the user's position and orientation in the scene and includes abstractions of different viewing devices that can be used. It supports viewing the same scene on any kind of display device, including sophisticated virtual-reality devices, and part of the device support is the use of appropriate projection transformations for the device. This is a much more general approach than we need for our relatively simple modeling. We consider the eyepoint as part of the geometry of the scene, so we set the view by including the eyepoint in the content branch, and the transformation information that placed the eyepoint is used to create the view transformations in the view branch. This is an important point, and its effect in our work is to make the view branch simply represent the projection operation.

Besides using the scene graph for modeling, Java3D also uses it to organize the processing as the scene is rendered. Because the scene graph is processed from the bottom up, the content branch is processed first, followed by the viewing transformation and then the projection transformation. However, Java3D does not guarantee the sequence for processing the node's branches, so it can optimize processing by selecting a processing order for efficiency, or it can distribute the computations over a networked or multiprocessor system. Thus the Java3D programmer must be careful to make no assumptions about the state of the system when any shape node is processed. In this book we will use the scene graph only to help us develop our modeling code, so we will not ask the system to process the scene graph. Developing a simple scene graph parser is left as a project for anyone who wants to carry this out.

Clipping in the Scene Graph

Clipping is something of an odd operation in graphics, because it defines visibility, not geometry. It is possible that different graphics APIs will treat clipping differently, but you can probably think of clipping as being set anywhere in the scene graph and being applied to everything below the point of definition. This assumes that you "unset" clipping (whatever that means in your API) when you have traversed the graph and come back to the point where you set it originally.

There is no specific notation in the standard scene graph for setting and unsetting clipping. You can define your own notation or simply note informally "here we set a clipping plane" on the graph. Of course, if you are going to formally define a scene graph data structure and operate on it through code, you will need to make this more formal so that your graph parser can take the correct action. This is the subject of project 1 in this chapter.

Examples of Modeling with a Scene Graph

We will develop the scene graphs for two example scenes to show how this process can work. To begin, we present already completed scenes so we can analyze how they were created, and we will take these analyses and show how the scene graph can give us other ways to present the scenes.

Let's start by considering a simple example that emphasizes transformations. Let's make a simple model of a rabbit's head as shown in Figure 2.27. This scene includes a large ellipsoidal head, two small spherical eyes, and two middle-sized ellipsoidal ears. We will use the ellipsoid (actually a scaled sphere, as we saw earlier) as our basic part and will use modeling transformations to put this object in various places with various orientations and colors as needed.

Figure 2.27 The rabbit's head.

The modeling graph for the rabbit's head is shown in Figure 2.28. This includes all the transformations needed to assemble the parts (eyes, ears, main part) into a unit. The basic geometry for all these parts is the sphere. Note that the transformations for the left and right ears include rotations; these can easily be designed to use a parameter for the angle of the rotation to make the rabbit's ears wiggle back and forth.

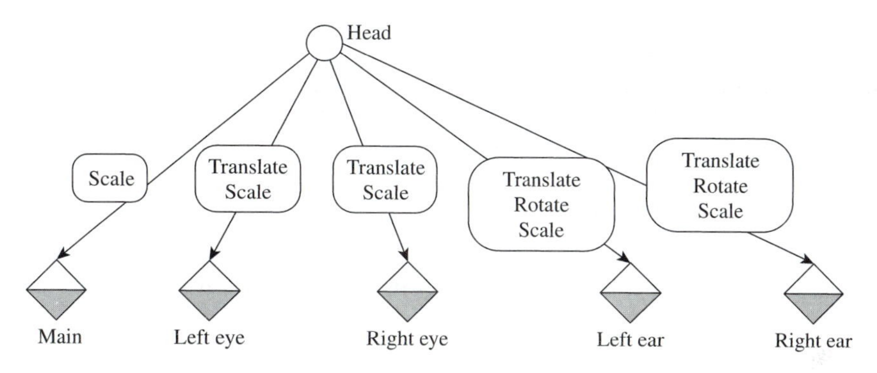

Figure 2.28 The modeling graph for the rabbit's head.

The transformations in this graph, particularly the transformations for the ears, can be built with parameters that allow animation. This is discussed below when we consider using the modeling graph to write code for the scene.

Next, consider the scene as shown in Figure 2.29, where a helicopter is flying above a landscape and the scene is viewed from a fixed eyepoint. This scene contains two principal objects: a helicopter and a ground surface. The helicopter is made up of a body and two rotors, and

Figure 2.29 A scene that we will describe with a scene graph. See the figure in the color insert.

the ground surface is modeled as a set of polygons (from a 3D map of Crater Lake, Oregon). There is some hierarchy to the scene because the helicopter is made up of smaller components, and the scene graph can help us identify this hierarchy so that we can work with it in rendering the scene. In addition, the scene contains a light and an eyepoint, both at fixed locations. The first task in modeling the scene is complete: To identify all the parts of the scene, organize the parts into a hierarchical set of objects and put this set of objects into a viewing context. We next identify the relationship among the parts of the landscape so we can create the tree representing the scene. In this case, the relationship is between the ground and the parts of the helicopter. Finally, we must put this information into a graph form.

The initial analysis of the scene in Figure 2.29, organized along the lines of view and content branches, gives us an initial draft of a graph structure shown in Figure 2.30. The *content branch* of this graph captures the organization of the components for the modeling process. This describes how content is assembled to form the image, and the hierarchical structure of this branch helps us organize our modeling components. The *view branch* of this graph corresponds to projection and viewing. It specifies the eye position and orientation to develop the viewing transformation and the projection to be used.

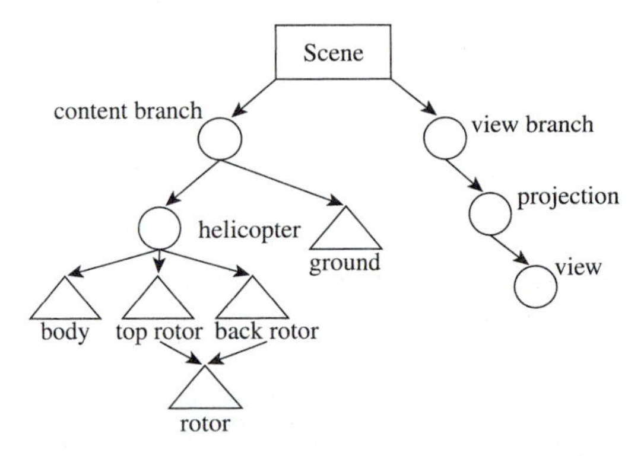

Figure 2.30 A scene graph that organizes the modeling of our simple scene.

This initial structure is compatible with the simple OpenGL viewing and modeling approaches we have seen so far, where the view is implemented with the API function that sets the viewpoint, and the modeling is built from simple primitives and transformations. This approach takes us only so far, however, because it does not integrate the eye into the scene graph. It can be difficult to compute the parameters of the viewing function if the eyepoint is embedded in the scene and moves with the other content, and in another example we will present that part of rendering the scene.

We may have started to define the scene graph, but we are not nearly finished. Figure 2.30 is incomplete because it merely includes the parts of the scene and describes which parts are associated with which other parts. To expand this to a more complete scene graph, we must add several things:

- the transformations that describe the relationship among items in a group node, to be applied separately on each branch as indicated
- the attribute information for each shape node, indicating such information as color, texture, and shading, indicated by the shaded portion of those nodes in Figure 2.31

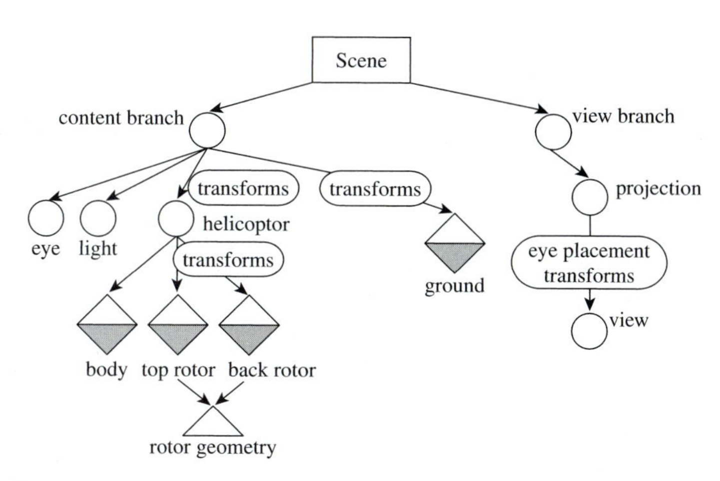

Figure 2.31 The more complete graph including transformations and appearance.

- the light and eye position, either absolute (as used in Figure 2.30 and shown in Figure 2.31) or relative to other components of the model (as described later in the chapter)
- the specification of the projection and view in the view branch

These are all included in the expanded version of the scene graph with transformations, appearance, eyepoint, and light shown in Figure 2.31. We have also added a second triangle to the shape nodes to indicate appearance information.

The content branch of this graph handles the modeling and is very much like the content branch of the scene graph. It includes the geometry nodes of the graph in Figure 2.30 as well as appearance information. Explicit transformation nodes place the geometry into correct sizes, positions, and orientations, and group nodes assemble content into logical groupings. It also contains lights and the eyepoint, shown here in fixed positions. In some models a light or the eyepoint might be attached to a group instead of being positioned independently, and this can lead to some interesting situations that we describe in an example later. In this example, it identifies the geometry of the shape nodes such as the rotors or individual trees as shared. This might be implemented, for example, by defining the geometry of the shared shape node in a function and calling this function from each of the rotor or tree nodes that use it.

The view branch of this graph is similar to the view branch of the scene graph but is treated much more simply, with only projection and view components. The projection includes the definition of the projection (orthographic or perspective) for the scene and the definition of the window and viewport. The view component includes the information needed for the viewing transformation, and because the eyepoint is placed in the content branch, this is simply a copy of the set of transformations that position the eyepoint in the scene as represented in the content branch.

The attribute part of the shape node has color, lighting, shading, texture mapping, and other properties we will see in Chapters 5, 6, and 9. Each vertex in the shape node will have not only vertex coordinates, but also normal components, texture coordinates, and other information. For now, we are concerned only with the geometry of the shape node; the later chapters just noted cover attribute properties such as appearance, because the appearance content is perhaps the most important part of graphics for high-quality images.

When you have a known set of transformations that place the eyepoint in a scene, we saw earlier that you can define the viewing transformation as the inverse of the transformation that placed the eye and simply use the default view for the scene. This lets us compute the viewing transformation and to place that at the top of the content branch. We can restructure the scene graph of Figure 2.31 as shown in Figure 2.32 so that it may take any eye position. That position can be fixed or changing, or it can be relative to the whole scene or to any part of the scene. This will be a key point as we discuss how to manage the eyepoint when it is a dynamic part of a scene.

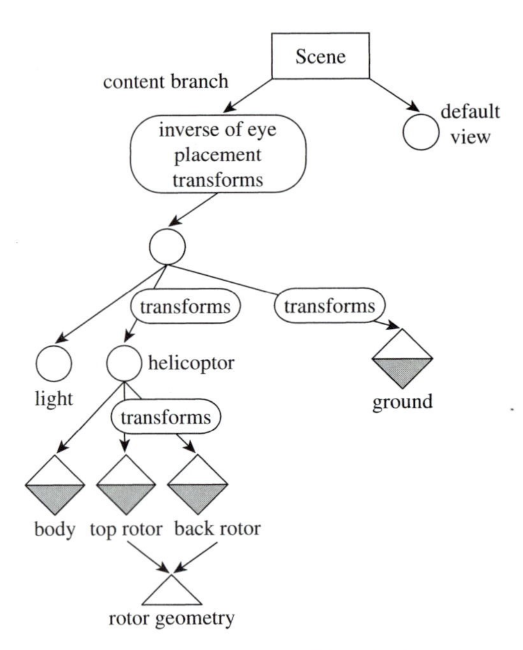

Figure 2.32 The scene graph after integrating the viewing transformation into the content branch.

The Viewing Transformation

In a scene graph with no view specified, the default view puts the eye at the origin looking in the negative z-direction with the y-axis upward. If we use a set of transformations to position the eye, then the viewing transformation is built by inverting those transformations to restore the eye to the default position. This inverse takes the sequence of transformations that positioned the eye and inverts the primitive transformations in reverse order, so if $T_1T_2T_3 \ldots T_K$ is the original transformation sequence, the inverse is $T_K^{-1} \ldots T_3^{-1}T_2^{-1}T_1^{-1}$ where T^{-1} is the inverse of T.

As we noted above, each of the primitive scaling, rotation, and translation transformations is easily inverted. For the scaling transformation `scale(Sx, Sy, Sz)`, the three scale factors multiply the values of the three coordinates when it is applied. To invert this transformation, we must divide the values of the coordinates by the same scale factors, so the inverse is

```
scale(1/Sx, 1/Sy, 1/Sz).
```

Of course, this tells us quickly that the scaling function can be inverted only if none of the scaling factors is zero.

For the rotation transformation `rotate(angle, line)` that rotates space by the value `angle` around the fixed line `line`, the inverse is obtained by simply rotating the space by the same angle around the same line in the reverse direction. So the inverse of the rotation transformation is

```
rotate(-angle, line).
```

For the translation transformation `translate(Tx, Ty, Tz)` that adds the three translation values to the three coordinates of any point, we simply subtract those same three translation values to invert the transformation. So the inverse of the translation transformation is

```
translate(-Tx, -Ty, -Tz).
```

Putting this together with the information on the order of operations for the inverse of a composite transformation above, we can see that, for example, the inverse of the set of operations (written in our pseudocode as earlier)

```
translate(Tx, Ty, Tz)
rotate(angle, line)
scale(Sx, Sy, Sz)
```

is the set of operations

```
scale(1/Sx, 1/Sy, 1/Sz)
rotate(-angle, line)
translate(-Tx, -Ty, -Tz)
```

Now let's apply this to the viewing transformation. Deriving the eye transformations from the tree is straightforward. Because we suggest that the eye be considered one of the content components of the scene, we can place the eye at any position relative to other components of the scene. When we do so, we can follow the path from the root of the content branch to the eye to get the sequence of transformations of the eyepoint. That sequence of transformations is the eye transformation, and we create the viewing transformation by inverting the sequence.

In Figure 2.33 we show how the view of Figure 2.29 is changed when we define the eyepoint to be immediately behind the helicopter and looking directly at it, and in Figure 2.34 we show how the scene graph of Figure 2.31 is changed to implement the changed eyepoint. The eye transform consists of the transforms that place the helicopter in the scene, followed by the transforms that place the eye relative to the helicopter. The eye transformations that place the eye relative to the helicopter must be made in the space where the helicopter is defined. Then the viewing transformation is the inverse of the eye positioning transformation, which in this case is

Figure 2.33 The same scene as in Figure 2.29 but with the eyepoint following directly behind the helicopter. See the figure in the color insert.

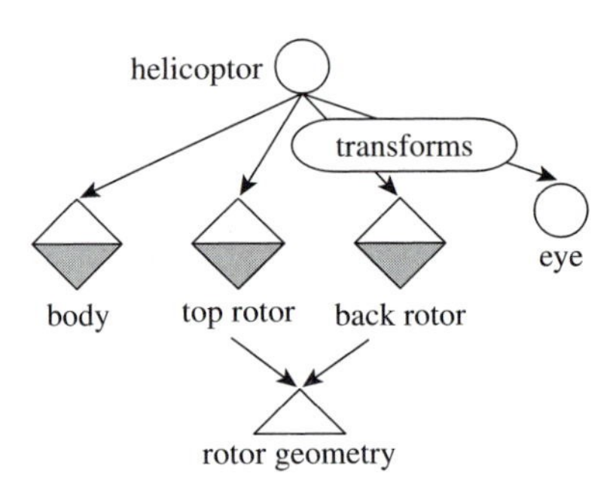

Figure 2.34 The change in the scene graph of Figure 2.30 to implement the view in Figure 2.33.

the inverse of the transformations that placed the eye relative to the helicopter, followed by the inverse of the transformations that placed the helicopter in the scene.

With this scene graph, we can identify the set of transformations $T_aT_bT_cT_d \ldots T_iT_jT_k$ that are applied to put the helicopter in the scene and the transformations $T_uT_v \ldots T_z$ that place the eye point relative to the helicopter. The implementation of the structure of Figure 2.31, then, is to begin the display code with the standard view, followed by $T_z^{-1} \ldots T_v^{-1}T_u^{-1}$ and then $T_k^{-1}T_j^{-1}T_i^{-1} \ldots T_d^{-1}T_c^{-1}T_b^{-1}T_a^{-1}$, before we begin to write the code for the standard scene that is given in Figure 2.33.

This change in the eye position means that the set of transformations that lead to the eyepoint must be changed, but the mechanism of writing the inverse of these transformations before beginning to write the definition of the scene graph still applies; only the actual transformations to be inverted will change. This is how the scene graph will help you organize the viewing process that was described earlier. You might, for example, have a menu switch that selects whether the eye is to be at a fixed point or at a point following the helicopter; then the code for inverting the eye position would be a switch statement that implemented the appropriate transformations depending on the menu choice.

Because the viewing transformation is performed before the modeling transformations, we see from Figure 2.32 that the inverse transformations for the eye must be applied before the content branch is analyzed and its operations are placed in the code. This means that the display operation must begin with the inverse of the eye placement transformations, which has the effect of moving the eye to the top of the content branch and placing the inverse of the eye path at the front of each set of transformations for each shape node.

The scene graph for an image is not unique, because there are many ways to organize a scene and many ways to organize how you carry out the operations the scene graph specifies. Once you have written a first scene graph for a scene, you may want to consider whether there is another way to organize the scene graph to make the program more efficient or to present a clearer description of the scene. Remember that the scene graph is a design tool, and there are always many ways to create a design for any problem.

We need to extract information on the three key kinds of transformations from a scene graph to create the code to implement our modeling. The projection transformation is straightforward and is built from the projection information in the view branch, and this is easily managed from tools in the graphics API. Because this is so straightforward, we really do not need to include it in our graph. The viewing transformation is readily created from the transformation information in the view when you analyze the eye placement transformations as we saw earlier. It is straightforward to extract this and, more important, to create this transformation from the inverse of the eyepoint placement transformations. Finally, the modeling transformations for the various components are built by working with the various transformations in the content branch as the components are drawn.

It is very important to understand that the scene graph can describe a dynamic geometry. The transformations in the scene graph may be defined with parameters instead of constant values, and event callbacks can affect the graph by controlling these parameters through user interaction or through computed values. This lets us capture behavior as well as geometry in a scene graph. Using transformations is discussed in the rewrite guidelines in the next section. This lets a single graph describe an animated scene or even alternate views of the scene and can let you design the effect of user inputs in the scene. The graph can be seen as having some parts with external controllers, and the controllers are the event callback functions.

Because all the information we need for the primitive geometry, the transformations, and the behavior is held in this simple graph, we will call it the *modeling graph* for our scene. This modeling graph, basically a scene graph without a view branch but with the viewing information organized at the top as the inverse of the eyepoint placement transformations, will be the basis for coding our scenes as we describe in the remainder of the chapter.

The Scene Graph and Depth Testing

In almost all of the images we create, we use the hidden-surface abilities provided by our graphics API. As we described in Chapter 1, this uses a depth buffer or *Z*-buffer, and the depth comparisons for hidden-surface resolution are done as each pixel in the scene is drawn. However, there may be times when you want to avoid depth testing and take control of the sequence of drawing your scene components. One example is described in Chapter 5, where you need a back-to-front drawing sequence to simulate transparency with blending operations. To do this you need to know the depth of each piece of your scene, or the distance of each piece from the eyepoint. This is easy enough to do if the scene is totally static, but when you allow pieces to move or the eye to move, it becomes much less simple.

The solution to this problem lies in doing a little extra work as you render your scene. After you have updated your transformations and any choices you make to draw the scene but before you actually draw anything, apply the same operations but use a tool called a *projection* that you find in most graphics APIs. This calculates the coordinates of any point in model space when the viewing and projection transformations map it into 3D eye space. The depth of a point is the Z-coordinate of the projected value. You can process the entire scene using the projection operation instead of the rendering operation, get the depth values for each piece of the scene, and use the depth values to determine the order in which you will draw the parts. The scene graph will help you make sure you have the right transformations when you project each of the parts, ensuring that you have the right depth values.

Using the Modeling Graph for Coding

Because the modeling graph is intended as a learning tool and not a production tool, we will resist the temptation to formalize its definition beyond the terms we used when we introduced the concept:

- shape node containing two components
    - geometry content
    - attribute content
- transformation node
- group node
- projection node
- light node
- eye node

At this point we don't want to parse the modeling graph automatically to create the scene, although you certainly could do that. Instead we will use the graph to organize the structure and the relationships in the model to help you write your code to implement your simple or hierarchical modeling.

Once you organize all the components of the model in the modeling graph, you need to write the code to implement the model. This is quite straightforward because we can make a simple set of re-write guidelines that allow you to write the graph into code. In this set of rules, we assume that transformations are applied in the reverse of the order they are declared, as they are in OpenGL. This should be consistent with your experience with tree handling in your programming courses, because you have probably discussed an expression tree which is parsed in leaf-first order (post-order). It is also consistent with the Java3D and OpenGL convention that transformations that are "closer" to the geometry (nested more deeply in the scene graph) are to be applied first.

The informal rewrite guidelines are as follows, including the rewrites for the view branch as well as the content branch:

- Nodes in the view branch involve only the window, viewport, projection, and viewing transformations. The window, viewport, and projection are handled by simple functions in the API and should be at the top of the display function or in the reshape function.
- The viewing transformation is built from the transformations of the eyepoint in the content branch by inverting those transformations to place the eye at the top of the content branch. This sequence should be next in the display function.
- The content branch of the modeling graph is usually maintained within the display function, but parts of it may be handled by other functions called from within the display, depending on the design of the scene. A function that defines the geometry of an object may be used by one or more shape nodes. The basic modeling may be affected by parameters set by event callbacks, including selections of the eyepoint, lights, or objects to be displayed in the view.
- Group nodes assemble several elements into a single object. Each separate object is a different branch from the group node. Before writing the code for a branch that includes a transformation group, you need to save the state of the modeling transformation before you go down a branch from which you will need to return as the graph is traversed. Because of the simple nature of each transformation primitive, it is straightforward to undo each as needed to create the viewing transformation. This can be handled through a transformation stack that allows you to save the current transformation by pushing it onto the stack, and then restore that transformation by popping the stack.
- Transformation nodes include translations, rotations, and scaling used in normal ways, including any transformations that are part of animation or user control. In writing code from the modeling graph, write the transformations in the same sequence as they appear in the tree, because the bottom-up nature of the transformation design corresponds to the last-defined, first-used order of transformations.
- Shape nodes involve both geometry and attributes, and appearance attributes must be set before the geometry is defined because appearance is applied when geometry is drawn.

  An attribute node can contain appearance specifications such as texture, color, blending, or material specifications that will control how the geometry is rendered and thus how it will appear in the scene.

  A geometry node contains vertex information, normal information, and geometry structure information such as strip or fan organization.
- Most nodes in the content branch can be affected by any interaction or other event-driven activity. This can be done by defining the content with parameters that are modified by the event callbacks. These parameters can control location (by parametrizing rotations or translations), orientation (by parametrizing rotations), size (by parametrizing scaling), appearance (by parameterizing appearance details), or even content (by parametrizing switches in the group nodes).

We have some examples of writing graphics code from a modeling graph in the sections that follow, so look for these principles as they are applied there.

Two Examples of Coding from Scene Graphs

For the simple rabbit's head example of Figure 2.27, we repeat in Figure 2.35 the modeling graph that was shown in Figure 2.28. This includes all the transformations needed to assemble the parts (eyes, ears, main part) into a unit. The basic geometry for all these parts is the sphere. Note that the transformations for the left and right ears include rotations; these can easily be designed to use a parameter for the angle of the rotation to make the rabbit's ears wiggle back and forth.

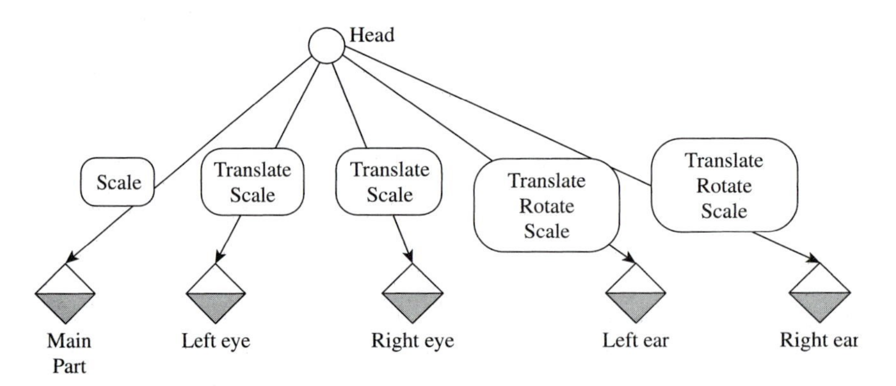

Figure 2.35 The modeling graph for the rabbit's head.

To write the code from the modeling graph for the rabbit's head, we apply the following sequence of actions on the modeling transformation stack:

1. Push the modeling transformation stack.
2. Apply the transformations to create the head, and define the head:
   scale
   draw sphere.
3. Pop the modeling transformation stack.
4. Push the modeling transformation stack.
5. Apply the transformations that position the left eye relative to the head, and define the eye:
   translate
   scale
   draw sphere.
6. Pop the modeling transformation stack.
7. Push the modeling transformation stack.
8. Apply the transformations that position the right eye relative to the head, and define the eye:
   translate
   scale
   draw sphere.
9. Pop the modeling transformation stack.

10. Push the modeling transformation stack.
11. Apply the transformations that position the left ear relative to the head, and define the ear:
    translate
    rotate
    scale
    draw sphere.
12. Pop the modeling transformation stack.
13. Push the modeling transformation stack.
14. Apply the transformations that position the right ear relative to the head, and define the ear:
    translate
    rotate
    scale
    draw sphere.
15. Pop the modeling transformation stack.

Trace this sequence of operations carefully and watch how the head is drawn. If you were to put the rabbit's head on a body, you could treat this whole set of operations as a single function `rabbitHead()` that is called between push and pop operations on the transformation stack, and put the code to place the head and move it around before the function call. This is the fundamental principle of hierarchical modeling—to create objects that are built of other objects, finally reducing the model to simple geometry at the lowest level. For the modeling graph, that lowest level is the leaves of the tree, in the shape nodes.

The transformation stack we used informally here is a very important consideration for the scene graph. It may be provided by your graphics API or it may be something you create yourself; even if it is provided by the API, there may be limits on the depth of the transformation stack that make it inadequate for some projects, and you may need to create your own. We will discuss transformation studies in the OpenGL API in Chapter 3.

In the helicopter example from Figure 2.33, we would traverse the tree with the rewrite rules above to write code as shown in skeleton form in below. Most of the details have been omitted, such as the inversion of the eye placement transformation, the parameters for the modeling transformations, and the details of the appearance of individual objects, but we have used indentation to show the pushing and popping of the modeling transformation stack so that we can easily see the operations between these pairs.

Animation is simple to add to this example. The rotors can be animated by adding an extra rotation in their definition plane immediately after they are scaled and before the transformations place them on the helicopter body, and by updating angle of the extra rotation each time the idle event callback executes. These are shown in the code. The helicopter's behavior itself can be animated by updating the parameters of transformations that are used to position it, again with the updates coming from the idle callback. The helicopter's behavior may be controlled by the user if the positioning transformation parameters are updated by callbacks of user interaction events. The code for the helicopter behavior are not included here; you should work out how to do this. So there are ample opportunities to have this graph represent a dynamic environment and to include the dynamics in creating the model from the beginning. The modeling for Figures 2.33 and 2.34 is shown in the following code fragment.

```
display()
    set the viewport and projection as needed
    initialize modelview matrix to identity
    define viewing transformation
        invert the transformations that set the eye location
    set eye through gluLookAt with default values
    define light position // note absolute location
    push the transformation stack      // ground
        translate
        rotate
        scale
        define ground appearance (texture)
        draw ground
    pop the transformation stack
    push the transformation stack      // helicopter
        translate
        rotate
        scale
        push the transformation stack  // top rotor
            translate
            rotate   // placement
            rotate   // movement
            scale
            define top rotor appearance
            draw top rotor
        pop the transformation stack
        push the transformation stack  // back rotor
            translate
            rotate   // placement
            rotate   // movement
            scale
            define back rotor appearance
            draw back rotor
        pop the transformation stack
        // assume no transformation for the body
        define body appearance
        draw body
pop the transformation stack
swap buffers
```

Other variations in this scene could by developed by changing the position of the light from a fixed position to a position relative to the ground (by placing the light as a part of the branch group containing the ground) or relative to the helicopter (by placing the light as a part of the branch group containing the helicopter). Similarly, the eyepoint could be placed relative to another part of the scene, or either or both could be placed with transformations controlled by user interaction, with the event callbacks setting the transformation parameters.

We remind you that you should include appearance content with each shape node. Many appearance parameters involve a saved state in graphics APIs, so parameters set for one shape will be retained unless they are reset for the new shape. You can design your scene so that shared appearances will be used consecutively to increase the efficiency of rendering the scene, but this is a specialized organization that is inconsistent with APIs such as Java3D. Thus it is very important to reset the appearance with each shape to avoid accidentally retaining an appearance that you do not want for objects presented in later parts of your scene.

Using Standard Objects to Create More Complex Scenes

The way we built the rabbit head is, in fact, part of a much larger example—using a collection of standard objects to define a larger object. In a program that defined a scene that needed rabbits, we could create the rabbit head with a function rabbitHead() that has the code we used and apply whatever transformations would be needed to place a rabbit head properly on each rabbit body. The rabbits themselves could be part of a larger scene, and you could proceed in this way to create as complex a scene as you wish.

Summary

In this chapter you saw all the concepts you need for polygon-based modeling as used in many graphics APIs. You know how to define an object in model space (that is, in a 3D space that is set up just for the object) in terms of graphics primitives such as points, line segments, triangles, quads, and polygons; how to apply the modeling transformations of scaling, translation, and rotation to place objects into a common world space so that the viewing and projection operations can be applied to them; and how to organize a hierarchy of objects in a scene with the scene graph so that the code for the scene can be written easily. You also know how to change transformations so that you can add motion to a scene. You are now ready to look at how the OpenGL graphics API implements these concepts so you can begin doing solid graphics programming, and we will take you there in the next chapter.

Questions

1. We know that we can model any polyhedron with triangles, but why can you model a sphere with triangle fans for the polar caps and with quad strips for the rest of the object? Can you think of an object that could not use any quads in its model?
2. Put yourself in a familiar environment, but imagine the environment simplified so that it is made up of only boxes, cylinders, and other very basic shapes. Imagine further that your environment has only one door and that everything in the room has to come in that door. Write the sequence of transformations to put everything in its place in your environment. Now imagine that each of these basic shapes starts out as a standard shape: a unit cube, a cylinder with diameter 1 and height 1, and the like; write the sequence of transformations to make each object from these basic objects. Finally, if the door admits only basic objects, put together these two processes to write the full set of transformations to create the objects and place them in the space.
3. We said that transformations are generally not commutative, but that leaves room for some transformations A and B to commute, or to have $A*B = B*A$. For example, if both transformations are of the same primitive type (rotation, scaling, or translation), then they commute, or if either A or B is the identity, they commute. Can you either find

examples of other transformations that commute or justify a statement that any "mixed pair" of transformations cannot commute?

4. Consider the environment around you and identify several processes that would require more than three dimensions to display. An example might be wind direction and magnitude at different locations and times (a 2D environment with 2D data over an extra 1D of time) on your university campus or in your region. For each process you identify, write a description of a way to model this for some kind of display; if you find that you cannot display the entire process, describe how you would choose the part of the process you would display.
5. In the discussion of higher-dimension viewing, we showed a representation of a complex-valued function f of a complex variable z and showed the value of the function with the polar representation (r, θ) of the complex variable $f(z)$, with the direction θ as a vector and magnitude r as a color. Discuss the effectiveness of that representation and whether these visualizations show you the nature of the functions.
6. Take the environment described in question 2 and write a scene graph that describes the whole scene, using the basic shapes and transformations you identified in the previous question. Also place your eye in the scene graph starting with a standard view of you standing in the doorway and facing directly into the room. Now imagine that on a table in the space there is a figure of a ballerina spinning around and around, and identify the way the transformations in the scene graph would handle this moving object.

Exercises

1. Calculate the vertex coordinates of the simpler regular polyhedra: the cube, the tetrahedron, and the octagon. For the octagon and tetrahedron, try using spherical coordinates and converting them to rectangular coordinates; see Chapter 4 for modeling for more details.
2. Verify that for any x, y, z, and w, the point $(x/w, y/w, z/w, 1)$ is the intersection of the line segment between (x, y, z, w) and $(0, 0, 0, 0)$, and the hyperplane

   $$\{ (a, b, c, 1) \mid \text{arbitrary } a, b, c \}.$$

   Show that this means that an entire line in 4D space can be represented by a single point in homogeneous coordinates in 3D space.
3. Show how you can define a cube as six quads. Show how you can refine that definition to write a cube as two quad strips. Can you write a cube as one quad strip?
4. Show how you can write any polygon, convex or not, as a set of triangles. Show further how you can write any *convex* polygon as a triangle fan. Does it matter which vertex you pick as the first vertex in the triangle fan? Can you think of a way to find out whether OpenGL actually creates polygons as triangle fans? (Hint: Look at how OpenGL handles a nonconvex polygon if you try to draw it as a polygon.)
5. An approach to antialiasing polygon edges considers how much of each pixel is covered by the polygon and sets the color of the pixel based on that value. Define a polygon in 2D space that is reasonably large and that has a side that is not parallel to one of the axes. Find a unit square in the 2D space that intersects that side and calculate the proportion of the

polygon that lies within the unit square. If the square represents a pixel, suggest what proportion of the pixel's color should come from the polygon and what proportion should come from the background.

6. The code for the normals to a quad on a sphere as shown in Figure 2.10 is not accurate because it uses the normal at a vertex instead of the normal in the middle of the quad. How should you calculate the normal so that it is the face normal and not a vertex normal?
7. Design a simple object that has no symmetries, so you can distinguish any two positions it may take. Apply simple rotation, translation, and scaling to the object and describe the change you see in the object's shape. Then define two transformations T_1 and T_2 and apply them to the object in order $T_1 * T_2$ and in order $T_2 * T_1$ and observe whether the results are the same. Do this if T_1 and T_2 are different transformations, and if T_1 and T_2 are rotations around different lines. If T_1 is a scaling transformation, does it matter if it scales coordinates by different amounts?
8. Consider a scene created by placing a few objects of different shapes, representing buildings, on a simple grid that could represent a street map. Sketch how the modeling for this would look, including a label that defines this as a building locator map and a legend that would show each shape as indicating a particular building.
9. Scene graphs are simular to trees, though different branches may share common shape objects. As trees, they can be traversed in any way that is convenient. Show how you might choose the way you would traverse a scene graph in order to draw back-to-front if you knew the depth of each object in the tree.
10. Add a mouth and a tongue to the rabbit's head and modify the scene graph for the rabbit's head to have the rabbit stick out its tongue and wiggle it around.
11. Define a scene graph for a carousel, or merry-go-round. This object has a circular disk as its floor, a cone as its roof, a collection of posts that connect the floor to the roof, and a collection of animals in a circle just inside the outside diameter of the floor, each parallel to the tangent to the floor at the point on the edge nearest the animal. The animals will go up and down in a periodic way as the carousel goes around. You may assume that each animal is a primitive and not try to model it, but you should carefully define all the transformations that build the carousel and place the animals.

Experiments

1. Get some models from the `avalon.viewpoint.com` site and use a text editor to examine the model file. See how the geometry in the file is presented so that you can read the model file and read the data into your programs as a sequence of triangles or other graphics primitives so it can be used.
2. Write the code for the scene graph of the familiar space from question 3, including the code that manages the inverse transformations for the eyepoint. Now identify a simple path for the eye, created by parametrizing some of the transformations that place the eye, and create an animation of the scene as it would be seen from the moving eyepoint.

As we saw in the problems for Chapter 1, the general function

```
glGetFloatv(GL_MODELVIEW_MATRIX, v)
```

can be used to retrieve the sixteen real-number values of the modelview matrix and store them in an array v defined by

```
GLfloat v[4][4];
```

If we leave the viewing transformation in its default state and apply modeling transformations one at a time, we can get the values of the various modeling matrices using this technique. In each of the problems below, be sure that your modeling transformation is the only thing on the modelview stack by setting the modelview matrix to the identity before calling the modeling transform function you are looking at. It will help greatly if you write a function that will display a 4×4 array nicely so that you can see the elements easily. The matrices you produce in this section should be compared with the matrices for scaling, rotation, and translation that are described in Chapter 4

As we did with viewing and projection transformations in Chapter 1, you can manipulate modeling transformations explicitly. If you get the modelview matrix for the simple transformations, you can change appropriate values in the matrix and reset the modelview matrix to this modified matrix. You can then redraw the figure with the modified matrix and compare the effects of the original and modified matrix to see the graphic effects, not just the numerical effects. Use the default values for viewing so they do not interfere with the modeling transformations in OpenGL's modelview matrix.

3. Start with a simple scaling, set for example with the function `glScalef(α, β, γ)`, and then get the values of the modelview matrix. You should be able to see the scaling values as the diagonal values in this matrix. Try using different values of the scale factors and first get and then print out the matrix in good format.
4. Do as above for a rotation, set for example with the function `glRotatef(α, x, y, z)` where x, y, and z are set to be able to isolate the rotation by the angle alpha around individual axes. For the x-axis, for example, set $x = 1$ and $y = z = 0$. Print out the matrix in good format and identify the components of the matrix that come from the angle through trigonometric functions. Hint: Use some simple angles such as 30°, 45°, or 60°.
5. Do as above for a translation, set with the function `glTranslatef(α, β, γ)` for example, and then get the values for the modelview matrix. Identify the translation values as a column of values in the matrix. Experiment with different translation values and see how the matrix changes.
6. Now that you have seen the individual modeling matrices, combine them to see how making composite transformations compares with the resulting matrix. In particular, take two of the simple transformations you have examined above and compose them, and see if the matrix of the composite is the product of the two original matrices. Hint: You may have to think about the order of multiplication of the matrices.
7. We claimed that composing transformations was not commutative and justified our statement by noting that matrix multiplication is not commutative. However, you can verify this much more directly by composing two transformations and getting the resulting matrix, and then composing the transformations in reverse order and getting the new resulting matrix. The two matrices should not be equal under most circumstances; check this and see. If you happened to get the matrices equal, check whether your simple transformations might not have been too simple, and, if so, make them a bit more complex and try again.

Projects

1. (A scene graph parser) Define a scene graph data structure as a graph (or tree) with nodes that have appropriate modeling or transformation statements. Write a tree walker that generates the appropriate sequence of statements to present a scene to a graphics API. For now, these can be pseudocode statements as we have used them in this chapter. Can you see how to make some of the transformations parametric so that you can generate motion in the scene? Can you see how to generate the statements that invert the eyepoint placement transformations if the eyepoint is not in standard position?

3 Implementing Modeling in OpenGL

This chapter discusses the way you implement the general modeling discussion of the previous chapter using the OpenGL graphics API and is intended to parallel that chapter closely. This includes functions for specifying geometry, specifying vertices for that geometry in model space, specifying normals for these vertices, and specifying and managing transformations that move these objects from model space into world space. It also includes functions that implement polygons, including the geometry compression described in the previous chapter. Finally, it discusses some prebuilt geometric models in OpenGL and GLUT to help you create your scenes more easily. When you have finished this chapter, you should be able to write graphics programs with OpenGL that implement the modeling you saw in the previous chapter, though the appearance information to make your scenes more interesting will not be covered until the chapters on lighting, shading, and texture mapping.

To see how the content of this chapter fits into an overall graphics program with the OpenGL API, recall that we discussed the OpenGL viewing model in Chapter 1 and outlined an example OpenGL-based program in Chapter 0. You may want to review these discussions. In general, we expect the functions presented in this chapter to be used in the display event callback, although this is not necessary.

The OpenGL Model for Specifying Geometry

To define a model for your program, you use a single function to specify its geometry to OpenGL. This function specifies that geometry is being defined by means of a vertex list, and its parameter defines how the geometry is to be interpreted:

```
glBegin(mode);
//   vertex list: point data to create a primitive object in
//   the drawing mode you have indicated
```

```
//  appearance information such as colors, normals, and texture
//  coordinates may also be specified here
glEnd();
```

This pattern of `glBegin(mode) - vertex list - glEnd()` uses different values of mode to establish the way the vertex list is used in creating the image. The drawing modes and the interpretation of the vertex list are described in the discussions that follow. Because you may use a number of different objects in an image, you may use this pattern several times for different kinds of drawing. We will see examples of this pattern throughout the book.

In OpenGL, vertex data is defined by a set of functions that go under the general name of `glVertex*(...)`. These functions enter the numeric value of the vertex coordinates into the OpenGL pipeline to convert them into image information. We say that `glVertex*(...)`is a *set* of functions because there are many functions that differ only in the format of their vertex data. You may specify your vertex data in any standard numeric type, and these functions let the system respond to your needs.

- If you specify your vertex data as three separate real numbers, or floats (we'll use the variable names x, y, and z, although they could also be constants), you can use `glVertex3f(x,y,z)`. Here the number 3 says that the vertex is three-dimensional and the character f indicates that the arguments are floating-point. Other data formats may also be specified for vertices, and other dimensions besides three are possible.
- If you define your coordinate data in an array, you can declare your data in a form such as `glFloat x[3]` and then use `glVertex3fv(x)` to specify the vertex. Adding the letter v to the function name specifies that the data is in array form.

Other versions of these functions let you specify the coordinates of your point in two dimensions (`glVertex2*`); in three dimensions specified as integers (`glVertex3i`), doubles (`glVertex3d`), or shorts (`glVertex3s`); or as four-dimensional points (`glVertex4*`). The four-dimensional version uses homogeneous coordinates, described in the previous chapter. You will see some of these in code examples later in this chapter.

In OpenGL you can call your own functions between a `glBegin(mode)` and `glEnd()` pair to determine vertices for your vertex list. This lets you do whatever computation you need to calculate vertex coordinates within the `glBegin/glEnd` pair instead of outside it. For example, you may include various kind of loops to calculate a sequence of vertices, or you may include logic to decide which vertices to generate. Any vertices defined by a `glVertex*(...)` function will be added to the vertex list for this drawing mode.

A great deal of other information can go between a `glBegin(mode)` and `glEnd()` pair. We will see the importance of including vertex normals in Chapter 6, and of including texture coordinates in the chapter on texture mapping. So this simple construct can do much more than just specify vertices. The available OpenGL operations here include `glVertex`, `glColor`, `glNormal`, `glTexCoord`, `glEvalCoord`, `glEvalPoint`, `glMaterial`, `glCallList`, and `glCallLists`, although this is not a complete list.

Point and Points Mode

The mode for drawing points with the `glBegin` function is named `GL_POINTS`, and any vertex data between `glBegin(GL_POINTS)` and `glEnd()` is used as the coordinates of a point to be drawn. If you want to draw only one point, give only one vertex between `glBegin` and `glEnd`; if you want more points, give more vertices. Points are usually one pixel in size, but if you want to make each point more visible, the function `glPointSize(float size)` lets you set the size of each point in pixels, where `size` is any non-negative real value and the default size is 1.0.

Following is a code fragment that generates a sequence of points in a spiral. This code uses ordinary programming to define geometry, showing we need not hand calculate points when we can compute them. We specify the vertices of a point by computing the coordinates and calling the `glVertex*()` function within a standard `for` loop inside the `glBegin/glEnd` pair. The functions calculate points on a spiral in the z-direction with x- and y-coordinates determined by simple trigonometric functions. The result of the code is shown as the left-hand image of Figure 3.1. The full source code is available online and includes the ability to rotate the spiral under keyboard control. You are encouraged to try some similar curves on your own based on other mathematics functions you may know. These are some specific parametric curves as discussed in Chapter 4.

```
#define PI 3.14159
#define N 100.0
void pointSet(void) {
    int i;
    float step, zstep;

    step = 2.0*PI/N;
    zstep = 2.0/N;
    glPointSize(2.0);
    glBegin(GL_POINTS);
        for (i=0; i<(int)(3*N); i++)
        glVertex3f(2.0*sin(step*i),2.0*cos(step*i),-1.+zstep*i);
    glEnd();
}
```

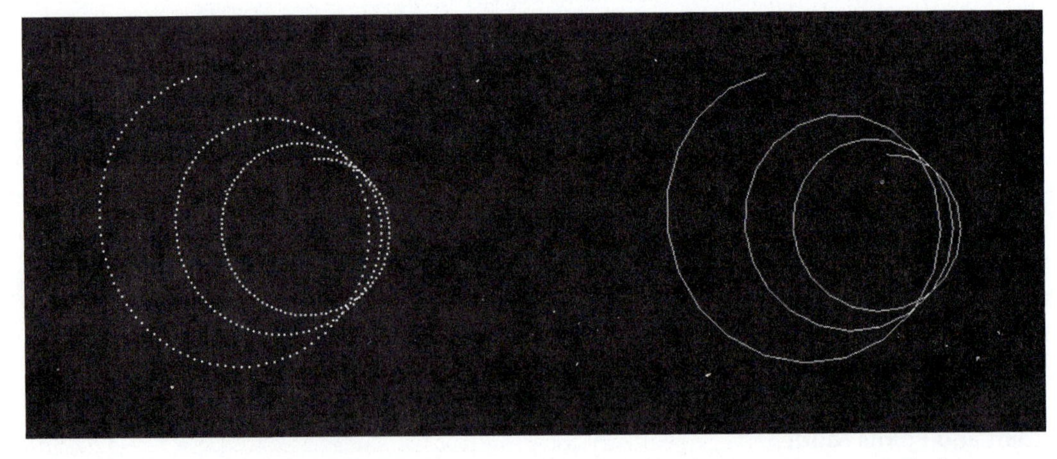

Figure 3.1 The spirals in 3-space made by the code fragments above—spiral of points (*left*) and of line segments (*right*).

Line Segments

To draw line segments, use the GL_LINES mode for glBegin/glEnd. For each segment to be drawn, define the vertices for the two endpoints of the segment. So between glBegin(GL_LINES) and glEnd, each pair of vertices in the vertex list defines a separate line segment. Ordinarily each line segment is drawn with width one pixel, but this can be changed by calling glLineWidth(width), where width is any non-negative value. The effect of different line widths may be different if you specify antialiased lines. The following code fragment specifies four simple parallel line segments:

```
glBegin(GL_LINES);
     glVertex3f(0., 0., 0.); glVertex3f(5., 5., 5.); // first segment
     glVertex3f(1., 0., 0.); glVertex3f(6., 5., 5.); // second
     glVertex3f(0., 1., 0.); glVertex3f(5., 6., 5.); // third
     glVertex3f(0., 0., 1.); glVertex3f(5., 5., 6.); // fourth
glEnd();
```

Line Strips

Connected lines are called *line strips* in OpenGL, and they are specified by using the mode GL_LINE_STRIP. The vertex list defines the line segments as in the earlier discussion of connected lines, so if you define N vertices you have N-1 line segments. With either line segments or connected lines, we can set the line width to emphasize (or deemphasize) a line. Heavier line widths give more emphasis than lighter line widths. The line width is again set with glLineWidth(float width). The default value of width is 1.0, but any non-negative width can be used.

As an example of a line strip, we can create a parametric curve by taking the point spiral code above and changing the drawing mode from GL_POINTS to GL_LINE_STRIP. These two curves are shown in Figure 3.1. The number of steps in the point spiral is 100, but the number of steps in the line segment spiral is reduced to 20. This reduction lets you see the individual line segments better than you could with a smaller granularity, but you can look at the source code of the previous example and experiment with the number of steps or the parametric equations of the curve.

Line Loops

A *line loop* is just like a line strip except that an additional line segment is drawn from the last vertex in the list to the first, creating a closed loop. There is little more to be said about line loops; they are specified by the mode GL_LINE_LOOP.

Triangle

To draw unconnected triangles, you use glBegin/glEnd with the mode GL_TRIANGLES. This is treated exactly as discussed in the previous chapter and produces a collection of triangles, one for each three vertices specified.

Sequence of Triangles

OpenGL has both of the standard geometry compression techniques for sequences of triangles: triangle strips and triangle fans. Each has its own mode for glBegin/glEnd: GL_TRIANGLE_STRIP and GL_TRIANGLE_FAN, respectively. These behave exactly as described earlier.

Because there are two different modes for drawing sequences of triangles, we will look at two examples. The first is a triangle fan, used to define an object whose vertices radiate from a central point. An example of this is the top or bottom of a sphere, where a triangle fan can create a cone at the north or south pole. The second is a triangle strip, often used to define surfaces, because most surfaces have a curvature that keeps rectangles of surface points from being planar. In this case, triangle strips are much better than quad strips as a basis for creating curved surfaces.

Our triangle fan example defines a cone that has its vertex at point (0.0, 1.0, 0.0) and a circular base of radius 0.5 in the X–Z plane. The cone is oriented toward the y-direction and is centered on the y-axis. This surface is shown in Figure 3.2 with simple lighting and flat shading as described in Chapter 6, although the code shown here does not reflect this. When the cone is used, it can easily be defined to have whatever size, orientation, and location you need by applying modeling transformations.

Figure 3.2 The cone produced by the triangle fan.

```
#define numStrips 20
glBegin(GL_TRIANGLE_FAN);
    glVertex3f(0., 1.0, 0.);      // the point of the cone
    for (i=0; i < numStrips; i++) {
        angle = 2. * (float)i * PI / (float)numStrips;
        glVertex3f(0.5*cos(angle), 0.0, 0.5*sin(angle));
        // code to calculate normals would go here
    }
glEnd();
```

The triangle strip example shown in Figure 3.3 is a function surface defined on a grid for the parametric function with parameter t:

$$y = \frac{x^2 + 2z^2}{e^{(x^2+2z^2+t)}}$$

This function's domain is in the X–Z plane and its value is the Y-value of each vertex. The grid points in the X–Z plane are given by simple functions `XX(i)` and `ZZ(j)` that step across the

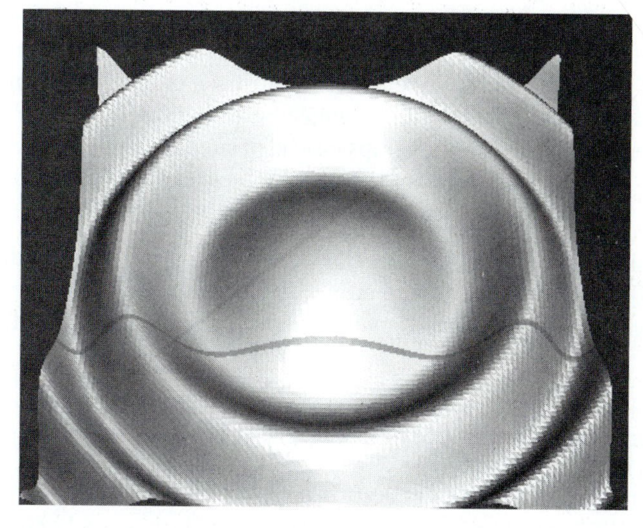

Figure 3.3 The full surface created by triangle strips, with a single strip highlighted in cyan.

grid, and the values of the function are held in an array, with `vertices[i][j]` giving the value of the function at the grid point `(XX(i), ZZ(j))` as defined in the following code fragment, taken from the full code that is included with the book's online resources. Typical values for `XSIZE` and `YSIZE` are between 100 and 250.

```
for (i=0; i<SIZE; i++)
     for (j=0; j<ZSIZE; j++) {
     x = XX(i);
     z = ZZ(j);
     vertices[i][j] = (x*x+2.0*z*z)/exp(x*x+2.0*z*z+t);
}
```

The surface rendering can be organized as a nested loop, where each iteration of the loop draws a triangle strip that is one section of the surface which is one unit in the *X* direction and extends across the domain in the *Z* direction. The code for the surface follows, and the surface is shown in Figure 3.3. Again, the code that calculates the normals is omitted; this example is discussed further and the normals are developed in the later chapter on shading. This kind of surface is explored in more detail in Chapter 9.

```
for (i=0; i<XSIZE-1; i++)
     for (j=0; j<ZSIZE-1; j++) {
          glBegin(GL_TRIANGLE_STRIP);
               glVertex3f(XX(i),vertices[i] [j],ZZ(j));
               glVertex3f(XX(i+1),vertices[i+1] [j],ZZ(j));
               glVertex3f(XX(i),vertices[i][j+1],ZZ(j+1));
               glVertex3f(XX(i+1),vertices[i+1][j+1],ZZ(j+1));
          glEnd();
     }
```

This example shows a white surface lit by three lights of different colors, a technique we describe in Chapter 6. This surface example is also briefly revisited in the quads discussion that follows. Note that the sequence of points is slightly different here from what it is in the following quad example because of the way quads are specified. In this example instead of one quad we have two triangles—and if you rework the example to use quad strips instead of simple quads to display the mathematical surface, it is simple to make the change noted here and do the surface with extended triangle strips.

Quads

To create a set of one or more distinct quads, you use `glBegin/glEnd` with the GL_QUADS mode. As described earlier, this takes four vertices for each quad. An example of an object based on quads would be the function surface above. For quads, the code for the surface looks like this:

```
for (i=0; i<XSIZE-1; i++)
    for (j=0; jZSIZE-1; j++) {
        // quad sequence: points (i,j),(i+1,j),(i+1,j+1),(i,j+1)
        glBegin(GL_QUADS);
            glVertex3f(XX(i),vertices[i][j],ZZ(j));
            glVertex3f(XX(i+1),vertices[i+1][j],ZZ(j));
            glVertex3f(XX(i+1),vertices[i+1][j+1],ZZ(j+1));
            glVertex3f(XX(i),vertices[i][j+1],ZZ(j+1));
        glEnd();
    }
```

Quad Strips

To create a quad strip, the mode for `glBegin/glEnd` is GL_QUAD_STRIP. This operates as we described earlier, and the order of the vertices is different from that in the GL_QUADS mode because a quad strip can be implemented as a triangle strip. Be careful of this when you define your geometry or you may get a very unusual display!

In the application of making a hollow beam, we can use quad strips to create long, narrow tubes with square cross-section as shown in Figure 3.4. The quad strip defined here creates the tube oriented along the *Z*-axis with the cross-section centered on that axis. The dimensions given make a unit tube—a tube that is one unit in each dimension, making it actually a cube with two opposite ends open. These dimensions make it easy to scale for any use.

```
#define RAD 0.5
#define LEN 1.0
glBegin(GL_QUAD_STRIP);
    glVertex3f( RAD, RAD, LEN ); // start of first side
    glVertex3f( RAD, RAD, 0.0 );
    glVertex3f(-RAD, RAD, LEN );
    glVertex3f(-RAD, RAD, 0.0 );
    glVertex3f(-RAD,-RAD, LEN ); // start of second side
    glVertex3f(-RAD,-RAD, 0.0 );
    glVertex3f( RAD,-RAD, LEN ); // start of third side
    glVertex3f( RAD,-RAD, 0.0 );
    glVertex3f( RAD, RAD, LEN ); // start of fourth side
    glVertex3f( RAD, RAD, 0.0 );
glEnd();
```

Figure 3.4 A beam made with quad strips.

General Polygon

The GL_POLYGON mode for glBegin/glEnd lets you display a single convex polygon. The vertices in the vertex list are taken as the vertices of the polygon in sequence order (we remind you that this order is counterclockwise from the front, and we also remind you that the polygon must be convex). It isn't possible to display more than one polygon with this operation because the function assumes that all the points it receives go in the same polygon.

What if your points come from a nonconvex polygon? (Examples of convex and nonconvex polygons are given in Figure 3.5; we also saw this figure in the previous chapter.) As we saw before, a convex polygon can be represented by a triangle fan so OpenGL tries to draw the polygon using a triangle fan. This will cause very strange-looking figures if the original polygon is not convex! If you must work with nonconvex polygons, you need to reorganize your geometry so that these polygons are presented as a set of convex polygons.

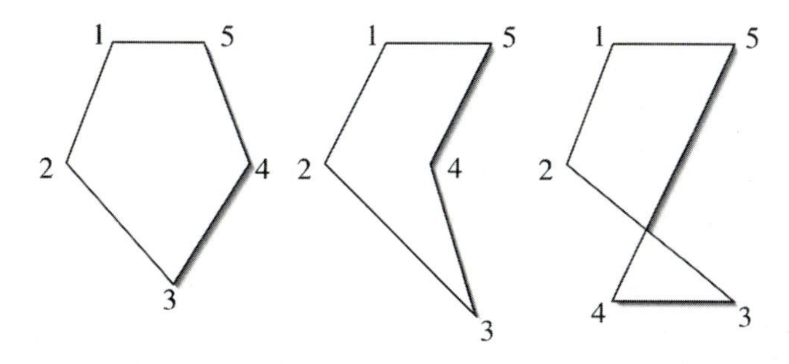

Figure 3.5 A convex polygon (*left*) and nonconvex polygons (*center and right*).

The simplest kind of multi-sided convex polygon is the regular N-gon, an N-sided figure with all edges of equal length and all interior angles equal. This is simply created (in this case, for $N = 7$) using trigonometric functions to determine the vertices.

```
#define PI 3.14159
#define N 7
glBegin(GL_POLYGON);
	for (i=0; i<=N; i++)
		glVertex3f(2.0*sin((float)(i*360)/(float)N),
			2.0*cos((float)(i*360)/(float)N),0.0);
glEnd();
```

This polygon lives in the X–Y plane because all the Z-values are zero. This polygon also has a default color (white) because we have not specified a color. This is an example of a "canonical" object—an object defined not primarily for its own sake but as a template that can be used to build other objects with transformations. An interesting application of regular polygons is to create regular polyhedra—closed solids whose faces are all regular N-gons. These polyhedra can be created by writing a function for a simple N-gon and then using transformations to place these properly in 3-space to be the boundaries of the polyhedron.

Vertex Arrays

The approach we used above to define geometry has some inefficiencies because it needs a large number of function calls and each vertex is processed individually by the graphics hardware. Individual vertex processing comes not only from the `glVertex*()` functions but also from other functions such as `glNormal*()` and `glTexCoord*()` that associate additional information with each vertex, such as the normal vector and texture coordinates. OpenGL lets us use arrays, called *vertex arrays*, that can hold vertex, normal, texture, or other information. These let you reduce the number of function calls because it takes only one function to process an entire array. Modern graphics accelerators have a special architecture to process arrays that makes this especially valuable. You must set up the use of vertex arrays with appropriate `glEnable()` functions, and you use them differently from the way you use individual vertex functions. Because the main reason for using vertex arrays is to increase the efficiency of your program, this capability is discussed in Chapter 12.

Antialiasing

As we saw in the previous chapter, geometry drawn with antialiasing is smoother and less "jaggy" than geometry drawn in the usual all-or-nothing pixel mode. OpenGL provides some capabilities for antialiasing by letting you enable point smoothing, line smoothing, and/or polygon smoothing. These are straightforward to specify, but they operate with color blending and there may be some problems with the order in which you draw your geometry. OpenGL calculates the coverage factor for antialiasing based on the proportion of a pixel that is covered by the geometry, as described in the previous chapter, and blending the edge according to that proportion. Color blending and drawing order are covered in Chapter 5.

To use built-in OpenGL antialiasing, choose the various kinds of point, line, or polygon smoothing you want with the `glEnable(...)` function. Each implementation of OpenGL will define a default behavior for smoothing, so you may want to override that default by defining your choice with the glHint(...) function. The appropriate enable/hint pairs are:

```
glEnable(GL_LINE_SMOOTH);
glHint(GL_LINE_SMOOTH_HINT,GL_NICEST);
glEnable(GL_POINT_SMOOTH);
glHint(GL_POINT_SMOOTH_HINT,GL_NICEST);
glEnable(GL_POLYGON_SMOOTH);
glHint(GL_POLYGON_SMOOTH_HINT,GL_NICEST);
```

A more sophisticated kind of polygon smoothing involves antialiasing the entire image, done by drawing the scene into the accumulation buffer with slight offsets so that boundary pixels will be chosen differently for each version. This is a time-consuming process and is a more advanced use of OpenGL than we assume in this book. We discuss the accumulation buffer in a Chapter 11 when we discuss motion blur.

The Cube We Will Use in Many Examples

Because a cube can be made up of six quads, it is tempting to try to make a cube from a single quad strip. It is impossible to make a single quad strip go around the cube, however; the largest quad strip you can create from a cube's faces has only four quads. You can create two quad strips of three faces each for the cube (think of how a baseball is stitched together), but here we use a set of six quads specified by the eight vertices of the cube. Below we repeat the declarations of the vertices, normals, edges, and faces of the cube from the previous chapter.

```
typedef float point3[3];
typedef int  edge[2];
typedef int  face[4];     // each face of a cube has four edges

point3 vertices[8]   = {{-1.0, -1.0, -1.0},
                        {-1.0, -1.0,  1.0},
                        {-1.0,  1.0, -1.0},
                        {-1.0,  1.0,  1.0},
                        { 1.0, -1.0, -1.0},
                        { 1.0, -1.0,  1.0},
                        { 1.0,  1.0, -1.0},
                        { 1.0,  1.0,  1.0} };

point3 normals[6]    = {{ 0.0, 0.0, 1.0},
                        {-1.0, 0.0, 0.0},
                        { 0.0, 0.0,-1.0},
                        { 1.0, 0.0, 0.0},
                        { 0.0,-1.0, 0.0},
                        { 0.0, 1.0, 0.0} };

edge edges[24]       =  {{ 0, 1 }, { 1, 3 }, { 3, 2 }, { 2, 0 },
                         { 0, 4 }, { 1, 5 }, { 3, 7 }, { 2, 6 },
                         { 4, 5 }, { 5, 7 }, { 7, 6 }, { 6, 4 },
                         { 1, 0 }, { 3, 1 }, { 2, 3 }, { 0, 2 },
                         { 4, 0 }, { 5, 1 }, { 7, 3 }, { 6, 2 },
                         { 5, 4 }, { 7, 5 }, { 6, 7 }, { 4, 6 }};
```

```
face cube[6]          = {{  0, 1,  2,  3 }, {  5,  9, 18, 13 },
                         { 14, 6, 10, 19 }, {  7, 11, 16, 15 },
                         {  4, 8, 17, 12 }, { 22, 21, 20, 23 }};
```

Drawing the cube proceeds by working through the face list and determining the actual vertices for the cube. We expand the function we gave earlier for the OpenGL code. Each face is defined individually in a loop within the `glBegin/glEnd` pair, and with each face we include that face's normal. Because the GL_QUADS drawing mode takes each set of four vertices as the vertices of a quad, it isn't necessary to close the quad by including the first point twice.

```
void cube(void) {
     int face, edge;
     glBegin(GL_QUADS);
          for (face = 0; face<6; face++) {
               glNormal3fv(normals[face];
               for (edge = 0; edge<4; edge++)
                    glVertex3fv(vertices[edges[cube[face][edge]][0]]);
          }
     glEnd();
}
```

This cube is shown in Figure 3.6, showing the six steps of adding individual faces colored in the sequence Red-Green-Blue-Cyan-Magenta-Yellow so you can see each added in turn. This is a fairly elegant way to define a cube and takes very little coding. However, there are other ways to define a cube. Because the cube is a regular polyhedron with six square faces, we can define the cube by defining a standard square and then using transformations to create the faces from this square. Carrying this out is left as an exercise for the student.

Figure 3.6 The cube as a sequence of quads.

Defining Clipping Planes

In addition to the clipping OpenGL performs in projection, OpenGL allows lets you define at least six clipping planes of your own, named `GL_CLIP_PLANE0` through `GL_CLIP_PLANE5`, to carry out the clipping discussed in the previous chapter. The clipping planes are defined by the function `glClipPlane(plane, equation)`, where `plane` is one of the predefined clipping planes and `equation` is a vector of four `GLfloat` values. Once you have defined a clipping plane, it is enabled or disabled by the enable function `glEnable(GL_CLIP_PLANEn)` or the equivalent disable function. Clipping is done on any modeling primitive when a clip plane is enabled; it is not performed when the clip plane is disabled. The clip planes are enabled or disabled as needed to take effect in the scene. Some example code for defining a clipping plane (by specifying the coefficients of its equations; this must be in array form) and turning it on and off follows; the geometry that is to be displayed with clipping would go between the enable and disable functions.

```
GLfloat myClipPlane[] = { 1.0, 1.0, 0.0, -1.0 };
glClipPlane(GL_CLIP_PLANE0, myClipPlane);
glEnable(GL_CLIP_PLANE0);
...
glDisable(GL_CLIP_PLANE0);
```

Additional Objects with the OpenGL Toolkits

Modeling with polygons alone would make you write many standard graphics elements that are so common that any reasonable graphics system should include them. OpenGL includes the OpenGL Utility Library, GLU, with many useful functions, and most releases of OpenGL also include the OpenGL Utility Toolkit, GLUT. We saw that GLUT includes system-specific functions, such as window management functions, in a standard way so you can move code between systems. Both GLU and GLUT include a number of built-in graphical elements that you can use. The objects these toolkits provide are defined with several parameters, such as the resolution in each dimension of the object. Many details are specific to each kind of object and are described in more detail when we describe each object.

GLU Quadric Objects

The GLU toolkit provides several quadric objects, or objects defined by quadric equations (polynomial equations in three variables with degree no higher than two in any term). These include spheres (`gluSphere`), cylinders (`gluCylinder`), and disks (`gluDisk`). Each GLU primitive is declared as a GLU quadric and is allocated with the function

```
GLUquadric* gluNewQuadric(void)
```

Each quadric object is a surface of revolution around the *Z*-axis and is modeled in terms of subdivisions around the *Z*-axis, called *slices,* and subdivisions along the *Z*-axis, called *stacks*. Slices and stacks let you determine the *granularity,* or degree of smoothness, of the models. Figure 3.7 shows an example of a typical prebuilt quadric object, a GLUT wireframe sphere, modeled with a small number of slices and stacks so that you can see the basis of this definition. A full example that uses GLU and GLUT objects is given at the end of this section.

The GLU quadrics are very useful because you can use transformations to create many common objects from them. The GLU quadrics also usefully support many OpenGL

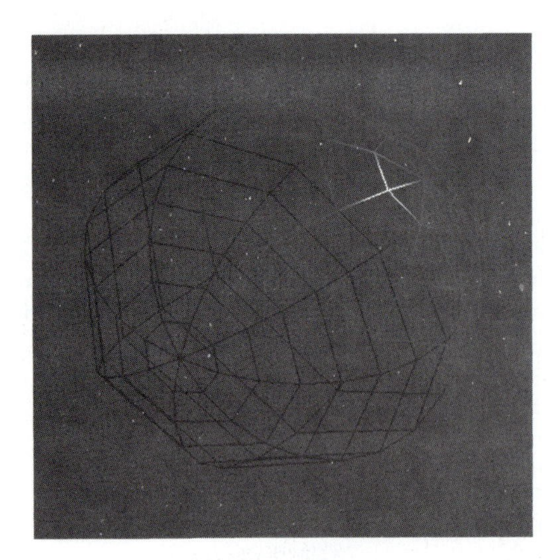

Figure 3.7 A GLUT wireframe sphere with 8 slices and 12 stacks.

rendering capabilities for making interesting images. You can set the drawing style with `gluQuadricDrawStyle()`, so the object can be filled, wireframe, silhouette, or drawn as points. You can get normal vectors to the surface for lighting models and smooth shading with the `gluQuadricNormals()` function, which lets you choose whether you want no normals, normals for flat shading, or normals for smooth shading. Finally, with the `gluQuadricTexture()` function you can specify whether you want to apply texture maps to the GLU quadrics to create objects with visual interest. See Chapters 6 and 8 for details. Below we describe each of the GLU primitives by listing its function prototype; more details may be found in the GLU section of your OpenGL manual.

GLU Cylinder

```
void gluCylinder(GLUquadric* quad, GLdouble base, GLdouble top, GLdouble
height, GLint slices, GLint stacks)
```

quad identifies the quadrics object you previously created with `gluNewQuadric`

base is the radius of the cylinder at $z = 0$, the base of the cylinder

top is the radius of the cylinder at $z =$ height

height is the height of the cylinder.

GLU Disk

The GLU disk is different from the other GLU primitives because it is only two-dimensional, lying entirely within the *X–Y* plane. Thus instead of being defined in terms of stacks, the second parameter is loops, the number of concentric rings that define the disk.

```
void gluDisk(GLUquadric* quad, GLdouble inner, GLdouble outer, GLint
slices, GLint loops)
```

quad identifies the quadrics object you previously created with `gluNewQuadric`

inner is the inner radius of the disk (may be 0)

outer is the outer radius of the disk

GLU Sphere

`void gluSphere(GLUquadric* quad, GLdouble radius, GLint slices, GLint stacks)`

quad identifies the quadrics object you previously created with `gluNewQuadric`

radius is the radius of the sphere

The GLUT Objects

Models provided by GLUT are geometric solids. They do not have as wide a usage in general situations because they have fixed shapes and cannot be readily adapted for general modeling situations. There is no general way to create a texture map for these objects except for the teapot.

The GLUT models include

- cone (`glutSolidCone/glutWireCone`),
- cube (`glutSolidCube/glutWireCube`),
- dodecahedron (`glutSolidDodecahedron/glutWireDodecahedron`), a 12-sided regular polyhedron,
- icosahedron (`glutSolidIcosahedron/glutWireIcosahedron`), a 20-sided regular polyhedron,
- octahedron (`glutSolidOctahedron/glutWireOctahedron`), an 8-sided regular polyhedron,
- sphere (`glutSolidSphere/glutWireSphere`),
- teapot (`glutSolidTeapot/glutWire/glutWireTeapon`), the Utah teapot, an icon of computer graphics, sometimes called the "teapotahedron,"
- tetrahedron (`glutSolidTetrahedron/glutWireTetrahedron`), a 4-sided regular polyhedron, and
- torus (`glutSolidTorus/glutWireTorus`).

Each of these has a standard position and orientation, typically being centered at the origin and lying within a standard volume. If it has an axis of symmetry, it is aligned with the z-axis. As with the GLU primitives, the GLUT cone, sphere, and torus allow you to specify the granularity of the modeling, but the others do not because they have a fixed geometry. You should not take the term "solid" for the GLUT objects too seriously; they are not actually solid but are simply bounded by polygons. "Solid" merely means that the shapes are filled in, in contrast with the wireframe objects that give you only a wireframe view. If you clip the "solid" objects you will find that they are hollow.

If you have GLUT with your OpenGL, check your GLUT manuals for the details on these solids and on many other important capabilities that GLUT adds to your OpenGL system. If you do not already have it, you can download the GLUT code from the OpenGL Web site (http://www.opengl.org/resources/libraries/glut) for many different systems and install it in your OpenGL area so you may use it with your system.

Selections from the overall collection of GLU and GLUT objects are shown in Figure 3.8 to show the range of items you can create with these tools. From top left and moving clockwise,

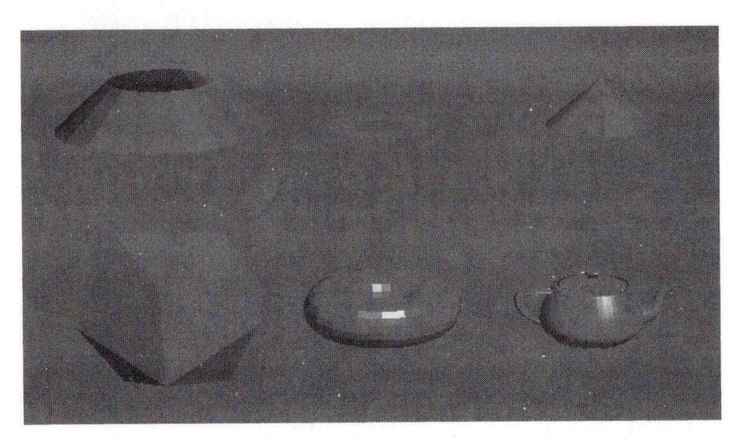

Figure 3.8 Several GLU and GLUT objects as described in the text.

we see a gluCylinder, a gluDisk, a glutSolidCone, a glutSolidIcosahedron, a glutSolidTorus, and a glutSolidTeapot. You should think about how you might use various transformations to create other figures from these basic parts.

An Example

This example is the `display()` function for a simple application that displays the objects shown in Figure 3.8. The objects that use slices and stacks for granularity set them as literal constants, but it is easy to change these in the example code. The code leaves in the color and shading specifications that are used for the figure even though we will not see them until Chapter 6.

```
// Global variables
...
    GLUquadric *Q;

void myinit(void) {
    ...
}

void display(void)
{
    int i;
    ...

glClear(GL_COLOR_BUFFER_BIT | GL_DEPTH_BUFFER_BIT);
for (i = 0; i<6; i++) {
    glPushMatrix();
    glTranslatef(positions[i][0],positions[i][1],positions[i][2]);

    switch(i) {
    case 0: {Q=gluNewQuadric();
    gluCylinder(Q, 2., 1., 1., 20, 1); break; }
```

```
case 1: {Q=gluNewQuadric();
         gluDisk(Q, 0.5, 1., 20, 10); break; };
case 2: {
         glutSolidCone(1., 1., 20, 10); break; };
case 3: {
         glPushMatrix();
         glScalef(2., 2., 2.);
         glutSolidIcosahedron();
         glPopMatrix();
         break; };
case 4: {glutSolidTorus(0.5,1.,20,20); break; };
case 5: {
         glPushMatrix();
         glRotatef(90.,1.,0.,0.);
         glutSolidTeapot(1.);
         glPopMatrix();
         break; };
}
glPopMatrix();
}
glutSwapBuffers();
}
```

Transformations in OpenGL

OpenGL uses only two active transformations in creating images: projection transformations and modelview transformations. The projection transformation is created by the projection you define, and the modelview transformation is built up from the viewing transformation you define and all the modeling transformations you apply in your programming. We have already discussed projections and viewing, so here we will focus on the transformations used in modeling.

There are three fundamental kinds of modeling transformations: rotations, translations, and scaling. In OpenGL, these are applied with the function sets `glRotate`, `glTranslate`, and `glScale`, respectively. As we have found with other OpenGL function sets, there are different versions of each of these, varying only in the kind of parameters they take.

The most common `glRotate` function is

```
glRotatef(angle, x, y, z)
```

where angle is the angle of rotation, in degrees, and x, y, and z specify the coordinates of a vector, all as floats (f). The rotation function `glRotated`, operates in exactly the same way, but the arguments must all be doubles (d). The vector in the parameters defines the fixed line for the rotation. This rotation follows the right-hand rule, so the rotation will be counter-clockwise as viewed from the direction of the vector (x, y, z). The simplest rotations are those around the three coordinate axes, so that `glRotatef(angle, 1., 0., 0.)` will rotate the model space around the X-axis. This function can be applied to either the projection or modelview transformation, depending on the value of `glMatrixMode`, allowing you to define a rotated projection if you are in projection mode or to rotate objects in model space if you are in modelview mode. You can use `glPushMatrix` and `glPopMatrix` to save and restore the unrotated coordinate system.

The most common `glTranslate` function is

```
glTranslatef(Tx, Ty, Tz)
```

where *Tx*, *Ty*, and *Tz* are the coordinates of a translation vector as floats `(f)`. Again, the translation function `glTranslated` operates the same, but has doubles `(d)` as arguments. As with `glRotate`, this function can be applied to either the projection or modelview transformation depending on the value of `glMatrixMode`, so you may define a translated projection if you are in projection mode or translate objects in model space if you are in modelview mode. You can again use `glPushMatrix` and `glPopMatrix` to save and restore the untranslated coordinate system.

The most common `glScale` function is

```
glScalef(Sx, Sy, Sz)
```

where *Sx*, *Sy*, and *Sz* are the coordinates of a scaling vector as floats `(f)`. Again, the translation function `glScaled` operates the same, but its arguments are doubles `(d)`. This function can be applied to either the projection or modelview transformation, depending on the value of `glMatrixMode`, so you can define a scaled projection if you are in projection mode or scaled objects in model space if you are in modelview mode. You can again use `glPushMatrix` and `glPopMatrix` to save and restore the unscaled coordinate system. Because scaling changes geometry in non-uniform ways, a scaling transformation may change the normals of an object. If scale factors other than 1.0 are applied in modelview mode and lighting is enabled, automatic normalization of normals should probably also be enabled. See Chapter 6 for details.

OpenGL has several tools for working with transformations. A transformation for 3D computer graphics is represented by a 4×4 array stored as an array of 16 real numbers. You may save the current modelview matrix with the function

```
glGetFloatv(GL_MODELVIEW_MATRIX, trans)
```

with an array `GLfloat trans[16]`. You do not restore the modelview matrix directly, but if your transformation mode is set to modelview by `glMatrixMode(GL_MODELVIEW)` you can multiply the current modelview matrix by `myMatrix`, saved as a 16-element array, with the function `glMultMatrix(myMatrix)`. To set the modelview matrix to a saved value, you can clear the matrix and multiply by the saved matrix as follows:

```
glMatrixMode(GL_MODELVIEW);
glLoadIdentity();
glMultMatrix(myMatrix);
```

You can similarly manipulate the OpenGL projection matrix. This kind of operation requires that you be comfortable with expressing and manipulating transformations as matrices, but OpenGL provides enough transformation tools that the need to handle transformations this way is rare.

As we saw earlier, you may use many transformations to define an object in a graphics scene. When we consider the overall order of transformations for the entire model, we must consider not only the modeling transformations but also the projection and viewing transformations.

If our code uses transformations T_0, T_1, . . . T_{last}, in that order, then the overall sequence of transformations in the order in which they are specified at the point when we define the object is:

$$P \rightarrow V \rightarrow T_0 \rightarrow T_0 \rightarrow \ldots \rightarrow T_n \rightarrow T_{n+1} \rightarrow \ldots \rightarrow T_{last}$$

with P being the projection transformation, V the viewing transformation, and T_0, T_1, . . . T_{last} the transformations specified in the program to model the scene, in order (T_0 is first, T_{last} is last and is closest to the geometry). The effect is to apply the composition sequence

$$P(V(T_0\ (T_0\ (\ldots (T_{last}) \ldots))))(\text{vertex})$$

to the vertices that specify the geometry. The projection transformation is probably defined in the `reshape()` function, and the viewing transformation is probably defined in the `init()` function, in the `reshape()` function, or at the beginning of the `display()` function. In any case, viewing is defined at the beginning of the modeling process. You need to understand this sequence very well, because it's critical to understand how you build complex, hierarchical models.

Legends and Labels

In this short section we describe how OpenGL handles text. We also show how to handle a legend in a separate viewport, which is probably the simplest way to deal with a legend. This code was used in creating the image in Figure 2.25, although a couple of functions used in that example are not included here.

The text in either a legend or label is created with a handy function that encapsulates the tools for presenting text. The function `doRasterString (...)` displays bitmapped characters defined with the GLUT `glutBitmapCharacter()` function at a position you set with the `glRasterPos()` function. In this example we chose a 24-point Times Roman bitmapped font, but other sizes and styles of fonts are available to each version of GLUT. Check your system for other options.

```
void doRasterString(float x, float y, float z, char *s) {
    char c;

    glRasterPos3f(x,y,z);
    for (; (c = *s) != '\0'; s++)
        glutBitmapCharacter(GLUT_BITMAP_TIMES_ROMAN_24, c);
}
```

The rest of the code used to produce a legend for the example is straightforward and is given below. The color of the text is set and lighting is disabled in order to control the presentation of the legend. These are discussed in Chapter 6. Note that the `sprintf` function in C needs a character array as its target instead of a character pointer. This code includes a function to build color ramps using smooth shading that will be covered in the color chapter. It could be part of the `display()` callback function where it would be redrawn.

```
//  draw the legend in its own viewport
    glViewport((int)(5.*(float)winwide/7.),0,
                    (int)(2.*(float)winwide/7.),winheight);
glClear(GL_COLOR_BUFFER_BIT, GL_DEPTH_BUFFER_BIT);
...
```

```
//  set viewing parameters for the viewport
    glPushMatrix();
    glEnable(GL_SMOOTH);
    glColor3f(1.,1.,1.);
    doRasterString(0.1, 4.8, 0., "Number Infected");
    sprintf(s,"%5.0f",MAXINFECT/MULTIPLIER);
    doRasterString(0.,4.4,0.,s);

//  color is with the heat ramp, with cutoffs at 0.3 and 0.89
    glBegin(GL_QUADS);

        glColor3f(0.,0.,0.);
        glVertex3f(0.7, 0.1, 0.);
        glVertex3f(1.7, 0.1, 0.);
        colorRamp(0.3, &r, &g, &b);
        glColor3f(r,g,b);
        glVertex3f(1.7, 1.36, 0.);
        glVertex3f(0.7, 1.36, 0.);
        glVertex3f(0.7, 1.36, 0.);
        glVertex3f(1.7, 1.36, 0.);
        colorRamp(0.89, &r, &g, &b);
        glColor3f(r,g,b);
        glVertex3f(1.7, 4.105, 0.);
        glVertex3f(0.7, 4.105, 0.);
        glVertex3f(0.7, 4.105, 0.);
        glVertex3f(1.7, 4.105, 0.);
        glColor3f(1.,1.,1.);
        glVertex3f(1.7, 4.6, 0.);
        glVertex3f(0.7, 4.6, 0.);

    glEnd();
    sprintf(s,"%5.0f",0.0);
    doRasterString(.1,.1,0.,s);
    glPopMatrix();
    glDisable(GL_SMOOTH);

//  now return to the main window to display the actual model
```

Labels are implemented in much the same way, but they are simpler because you need not include a graphic. You simply create text that is to go into the image wherever your design dictates, and write that text to the screen with similar raster positioning and text output.

Code Examples for Transformations

Simple Transformations

Figure 3.9 shows the effect of the three simple transformations on a given square that is initially placed several units out on the *X*-axis. This square is rotated at left, scaled in the center (and notice that scaling also affects the distance from the origin as well as the size of the square), and translated at right. These are all shown in separate viewports in the same window in the full example code.

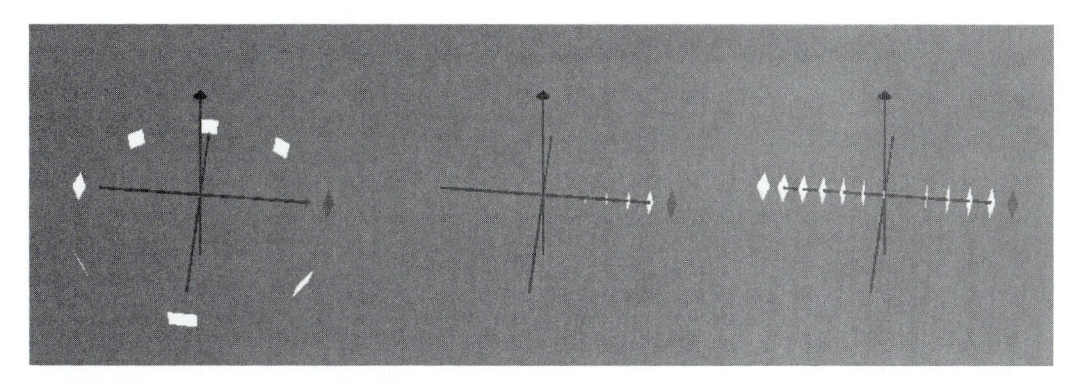

Figure 3.9 The square with the three simple transformation operations—rotations (*left*), scaling (*center*), and translations (*right*).

All the code examples use the following definition of the simple square.

```
void square(void)
{
    typedef GLfloat point [3];
    point v[8] = {{12.0, -1.0, -1.0},
                  {12.0, -1.0,  1.0},
                  {12.0,  1.0,  1.0},
                  {12.0,  1.0, -1.0} };

    glBegin(GL_QUADS);
      glVertex3fv(v[0]);
      glVertex3fv(v[1]);
      glVertex3fv(v[2]);
      glVertex3fv(v[3]);
    glEnd();
}
```

To display the simple rotations example, you can use the following display function. This function, or any of the other `display()` functions below, can be placed in the general function template at the beginning of the book.

```
void display(void)
{  int i;
   float theta = 0.0;

   glClear(GL_COLOR_BUFFER_BIT | GL_DEPTH_BUFFER_BIT);
   axes(10.0);
   for (i=0; i<8; i++) {
      glColor3f(1.0, 1.0, 1.0);
      glPushMatrix();
      glRotatef(theta, 0.0, 0.0, 1.0);
      if (i==0) glColor3f(1.0, 0.0, 0.0);
      square();
```

```
      theta += 45.0;
      glPopMatrix();
  }
  glutSwapBuffers();
}
```

To display the simple translations example, you can use the following display function:

```
void display(void)
{  int i;

   glClear(GL_COLOR_BUFFER_BIT | GL_DEPTH_BUFFER_BIT);
   axes(10.0);
   for (i=0; i<=12; i++) {
     glColor3f(1.0, 1.0, 1.0);
     glPushMatrix();
     glTranslatef(-2.0*(float)i, 0.0, 0.0);
     if (i==0) glColor3f(1.0, 0.0, 0.0);
     square();
     glPopMatrix();
  }
  glutSwapBuffers();
}
```

To display the simple scaling example, you can use the following display function:

```
void display(void)
{  int i;
   float s;

   glClear(GL_COLOR_BUFFER_BIT | GL_DEPTH_BUFFER_BIT);
   axes(10.0);
   for (i=0; i<6; i++) {
       glColor3f(1.0, 1.0, 1.0);
       glPushMatrix();
       s = (6.0-(float)i)/6.0;
       glScalef(s, s, s);
       if (i==0) glColor3f(1.0, 0.0, 0.0);
       square();
       glPopMatrix();
   }
   glutSwapBuffers();
}
```

Transformation Stacks

The OpenGL functions that manage the transformation stack are `glPushMatrix()` and `glPopMatrix()`. Technically, they apply to the stack of whatever transformation is the current matrix mode, set by the `glMatrixMode` function with parameter GL_PROJECTION or GL_MODELVIEW. We rarely want to use the stack of projections (and the projection stack

Figure 3.10 The rabbit head.

holds only two transformations), so we almost always work with the modelview stack. The rabbit head example of the previous chapter, as shown in Figure 3.10 as a reminder, used the display function below. This code makes the stack operations more visible by using indentations; this is intended for emphasis and is recommended practice. We have defined only very simple display properties (just a simple color) for each of the parts, but we could have defined a more complex set of properties and made the parts more visually interesting. We could also have used a more complex object than a simple `gluSphere` to make the parts more geometrically interesting. The sky's the limit. . . .

```
void display(void)
{
//   Indentation level shows the level of the transformation stack
//   The basis for this example is the unit gluSphere; everything
//   else is done by explicit transformations

     glClear(GL_COLOR_BUFFER_BIT | GL_DEPTH_BUFFER_BIT);
     glPushMatrix();

          //  model the head
          glColor3f(0.4, 0.4, 0.4);     //     dark gray head
          glScalef(3.0, 1.0, 1.0);
          myQuad = gluNewQuadric();
          gluSphere(myQuad, 1.0, 10, 10);

     glPopMatrix();
     glPushMatrix();

          //  model the left eye
          glColor3f(0.0, 0.0, 0.0);     //     black eyes
          glTranslatef(1.0, -0.7, 0.7);
          glScalef(0.2, 0.2, 0.2);
          myQuad = gluNewQuadric();
          gluSphere(myQuad, 1.0, 10, 10);
```

```
    glPopMatrix();
    glPushMatrix();

        //  model the right eye
        glTranslatef(1.0, 0.7, 0.7);
        glScalef(0.2, 0.2, 0.2);
        myQuad = gluNewQuadric();
        gluSphere(myQuad, 1.0, 10, 10);

    glPopMatrix();
    glPushMatrix();

        //  model the left ear
        glColor3f(1.0, 0.6, 0.6);    //    pink ears
        glTranslatef(-1.0, -1.0, 1.0);
        glRotatef(-45.0, 1.0, 0.0, 0.0);
        glScalef(0.5, 2.0, 0.5);
        myQuad = gluNewQuadric();
        gluSphere(myQuad, 1.0, 10, 10);

    glPopMatrix();
    glPushMatrix();

        //  model the right ear
        glColor3f(1.0, 0.6, 0.6);    //    pink ears
        glTranslatef(-1.0, 1.0, 1.0);
        glRotatef(45.0, 1.0, 0.0, 0.0);
        glScalef(0.5, 2.0, 0.5);
        myQuad = gluNewQuadric();
        gluSphere(myQuad, 1.0, 10, 10);

    glPopMatrix();
    glutSwapBuffers();
}
```

In OpenGL, the modelview matrix stack must be at least 32 deep, but this might not be enough to handle complex models. OpenGL stores a transformation as a 4×4 matrix of `GLfloat` values that is stored in a single array of 16 elements. If you exceed that depth, or if you want to treat transformations differently, you can create your own structure to hold these arrays and use it as you wish to manage transformations. To deal with the modelview transformation itself, you can use functions that let you save and set the modelview transformation yourself. You can capture the current value of the transformation with the function

```
glGetFloatv(GL_MODELVIEW_MATRIX, myTran);
```

(here we have declared `GLfloat myTran[16]`), and if you are in modelview mode you can use the functions

```
    glLoadIdentity();
    glMultMatrixf(myTran);
```

to set the current modelview matrix to the value of the matrix `myTran`.

Inverting the Eyepoint Transformation

In the previous chapter we talked about the relationship between the transformations that set up a view and showed that we could get the same effect by using the standard view and applying the inverse transformations for viewing to the model space. This is straightforward to implement in OpenGL. We wrote a small program in which the eye follows a moving object in a scene rather than being at a fixed position. In this example, the eye follows a red sphere at a distance of 4 units as the sphere flies in a circle above some geometry. The geometry is a cyan plane on which are placed several cylinders at the same distance from a central point, along with some coordinate axes. The Y-axis is up, and the cyan plane is the X-Z plane. A snapshot from this very simple model is shown in Figure 3.11. The display function code for this is also provided.

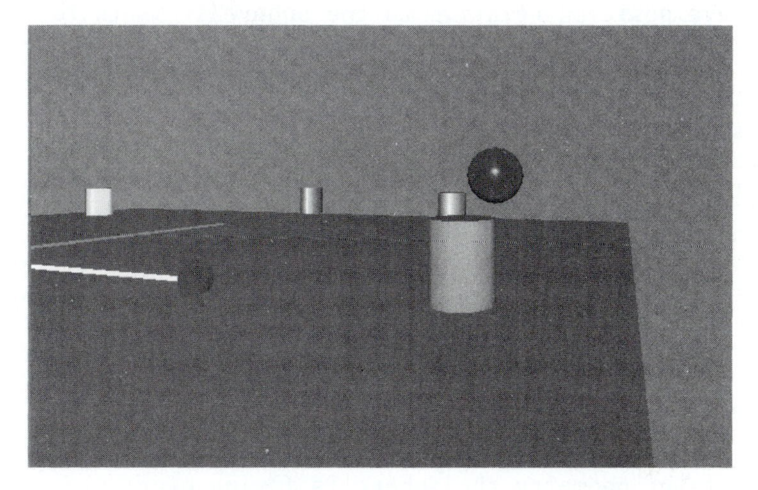

Figure 3.11 The eye following a sphere flying over some cylinders on a plane.

In this model, the sphere is placed by:

rotate by *theta* around Y
translate by 5 in X and .75 in Y

and then the eye is placed relative to the sphere by

translate by 4 in Z

When the sphere is on the X-axis, for example, the eye is at –4 units in the Z-direction. So the display function begins with the default view and is followed by the inverses of these transformations in reverse order, namely

translate by –4 in Z
translate by –5 in X and –.75 in Y
rotate by *-theta* around Y

These are the inverses of the cylinder placement and eye placement and are applied to the whole world space to get the effect of the viewing transformation. Because of our approach to viewing by inverting the eye placement, you will see no explicit viewing specification in the code, but you will see the correct viewing behavior in the running program.

```
void display(void)
{
	...
	glClear(GL_COLOR_BUFFER_BIT | GL_DEPTH_BUFFER_BIT);

	glMatrixMode(GL_MODELVIEW);
	glLoadIdentity();

//	Define eye position relative to the sphere it is to follow
//	gluLookAt(0.,0.,0., 0.,0.,-1., 0.,1.,0.); this is the default
//	and is not needed
//	invert transformations that place the eye
	glTranslatef(0.,0.,-4.);
	glTranslatef(-5.,-0.75,0.);
	glRotatef(-theta,0.,1.,0.);

//	draw the sphere we're following around...
	glPushMatrix();   // save the current modeling transformation
	glRotatef(theta, 0., 1., 0.);
	glTranslatef(5., 0.75, 0.);
	glColor3f(1., 0., 0.);
	myQuad = gluNewQuadric();
	gluSphere(myQuad, .25, 20, 20);
	glPopMatrix();

//	draw whatever geometry the sphere is flying over...
	...
	glutSwapBuffers();
}
```

Creating Display Lists

In the previous chapter we discussed the idea of compiling geometry to make display operations more efficient. In OpenGL, graphics objects can be compiled into a *display list,* which will contain the final geometry of the object as it is ready for display. A display list captures a branch of your modeling graph that can contain as much or as little of the display as you want, and some guidelines on how much you can include are given below.

Display lists are relatively easy to create in OpenGL. First, choose an unsigned integer (usually a small integer constant, such as 1, 2, . . .) to serve as the name of your list. Before you define the geometry for your list, call the function `glNewList(i)`. Code whatever geometry you want into the list, including geometry, transformations, and appearance, and at the end call the function `glEndList()`. Everything between the new list and the end list functions will be executed whenever you call `glCallList(i)` with a valid list name as parameter, and only the actual set of instructions to the drawing portion of the OpenGL system will be saved. When the display list is executed, those instructions are simply sent to the drawing system; any operations needed to generate these instructions aren't included because their work has already been captured in the display list.

Display lists are designed to be defined only once but used often, so you do not want to create a list in a function that is called often, such as `display()`. It's common to create them in the `init()` function (as shown below) or in a function called from `init()`. Some sample code is given below, with most of the content omitted and only the display list operations remaining.

```
GLint displayListIndex 1;

void Build_lists(void) {
   glNewList(displayListIndex, GL_COMPILE);
     glBegin(GL_TRIANGLE_STRIP);
        glNormal3fv(...); glVertex3fv(...);
        ...
     glEnd();
   glEndList();
}
static void Init(void) {
   ...
   Build_lists();
   ...
}
void Display(void) {
   ...
   glCallList(displayListIndex);
   ...
}
```

The display list is created in GL_COMPILE mode and is not executed (the object is not displayed) until the list is called. You can have the list displayed as it is created if you create the list in `GL_COMPILE_AND_EXECUTE` mode.

OpenGL display lists are named by nonzero unsigned integer values (technically, `GLuint` values), and OpenGL has several tools to manage name values. We'll assume here that you won't need many display lists and that you can manage a small number of list names yourself, but if you begin to use a number of display lists in a project, look into the `glGenLists`, `glIsList`, and `glDeleteLists` functions to help you manage the lists.

Distance to the Eyepoint

As we saw in Chapter 1 and will see in Chapter 5 when we talk about ordering objects from the eye position, it can be very useful to know the distance from the eyepoint to the objects in your scene. This is particularly useful if you are using depth ordering to draw your scene, as we discuss in Chapter 12. OpenGL has some handy functions that can give you this distance. In particular, the function and parameter

```
glGetFloatv(GL_CURRENT_RASTER_DISTANCE)
```

return the distance from the eye to the current raster position. See Chapter 12 for more details on this.

Summary

In this chapter we described how OpenGL lets you define geometry and transformations for the modeling presented in the previous chapter. We saw how OpenGL implements the point, line segment, triangle, quad, and polygon primitives as well as the line strip, triangle strip, triangle fan, and quad strip geometry compression techniques. We also saw a number of geometric objects available through the GLU and GLUT utilities and how they are used in creating scenes. This chapter focused only on geometry, but we will see in Chapters 6 and 8 that the GLU and GLUT primitives are also easy to use with OpenGL appearance tools.

We have also seen how OpenGL gives you scaling, translation, and rotation transformations and how OpenGL manages the modelview transformation stack, letting you implement scene graphs easily. Finally, OpenGL lets you compile geometry into display lists that are more efficient than immediate mode.

At this point you should have a good understanding of all the steps in the graphics pipeline for polygon-based graphics, so you should be able to write complete graphics programs. The only additional modeling in this book will be surface interpolation for splines. The focus of most of the coming chapters will be the appearance of graphics objects.

OpenGL Glossary for the Chapter

This chapter deals almost exclusively with OpenGL functions for modeling, so this chapter's glossary is pretty extensive. Because some of these functions have extensive parameter lists, we will generally omit the parameters and leave them to be looked up. We generally list only those functions that are new in this chapter and that are actually used here, not just mentioned here, and we remind the reader that we have had OpenGL functions in previous chapters that will not be duplicated here.

OpenGL Functions

`glCallList(int)`: specifies by the parameter the index of the compiled display list to be executed

`glClipPlane(int, vector)`: defines a clipping plane whose number is the first parameter and whose plane equation is given by the 4-vector that is the second parameter

`glEndList()`: ends the creation of a display list

`glGetFloatv(parm, array)`: gets the values of the system matrix indicated by the first parameter and store the values in the array that is the second parameter

`glHint(parm, parm)`: specifies to the system that the process indicated by the first parameter is to be carried out according to the value of the second parameter

`glLineWidth(float)`: specifies the width of a line, in pixels, with the parameter value

`glMultMatrix(array)`: multiplies the current matrix (projection or modelview) by the array

`glNewList(int, parm)`: begins saving commands to the display list whose index is the first parameter, either saving only or saving and executing, depending on the second parameter

`glNormal*(...)`: one of a family of functions that specify the normal at a vertex for OpenGL geometry; the normal can be two- or three-dimensional, it can be float or integer valued, and it can be given as scalars or vectors

`glPointSize(float)`: specifies the size of a point, in pixels, with the parameter value

`glRasterPos3f(x,y,z)`: specifies the x, y, and z values that the system is to associate with the current raster position. This is one of a quite extensive family of functions that can set the current raster position values

`glVertex*(...)`: one of a family of functions that specify the coordinates of a vertex for OpenGL geometry; the vertex can be two- or three-dimensional, the coordinates can be float or integer valued, and the coordinates can be given as scalars or vectors

GLU Functions

`gluCylinder(...)`: with the first parameter an existing GLU quadrics object and the rest of the parameters specifying details associated with a cylinder, defines the geometry for a cylinder and draws it

`gluDisk(...)`: with the first parameter an existing GLU quadrics object and the rest of the parameters specifying details associated with a disk, defines the geometry for a disk and draws it

`gluNewQuadric()`: creates and returns a pointer to a new GLU quadrics object

`gluQuadricDrawStyle()`: with a symbolic parameter, specifies the style in which GLU quadrics objects will be drawn

`gluQuadricNormals()`: specifies whether and what kind of normals will be generated as a GLU quadric object is defined

`gluQuadricTexture()`: specifies whether texture coordinates will be generated as a GLU quadric object is defined

`gluSphere()`: with the first parameter an existing GLU quadrics object and the rest of the parameters specifying details associated with a sphere, defines the geometry for a sphere and draws it

GLUT Functions

For most of the GLUT objects included here, both a solid and a wireframe version are available. We will list the solid version (that includes the word "Solid"), but you can get the wireframe version by substituting the word "Wire" for the word "Solid."

`glutBitmapCharacter(font, char)`: renders a bitmapped character in the named bitmapped font

`glutSolidCone(...)`: with the parameters specifying details associated with a cone, defines the geometry for a cone and draws it

`glutSolidDodecahedron()`: defines the geometry of a dodecahedron and draws it

`glutSolidIcosahedron()`: defines the geometry of an icosahedron and draws it

`glutSolidOctahedron()`: defines the geometry of an octahedron and draws it

`glutSolidSphere(...)`: with the parameters specifying details associated with a sphere, defines the geometry for a sphere and draws it

`glutSolidTeapot(size)`: defines the geometry of a teapot of specified size and draws it. The normals and texture coordinates for the teapot are also generated

glutSolidTetrahedron(): defines the geometry of a tetrahedron and draws it

glutSolidTorus(...): with the parameters specifying details associated with a torus, defines the geometry for a torus and draws it

Symbolic Parameters

GL_CLIP_PLANEi: the parameter to the glEnable() function that specifies a specific clipping plane to be used

GL_COMPILE: the second parameter to the glNewList() function which specifies that the list is to be created but not yet executed

GL_COMPILE_AND_EXECUTE: the second parameter to the glNewList() function which specifies that the list is to be created and the commands are to be executed as they are entered in the list

GL_DONT_CARE: as the second parameter to the glHint() function, specifies that system may use the default technique

GL_FASTEST: as the second parameter to the glHint() function, specifies that the fastest technique is to be used (generally meaning that antialiasing will not be done)

GL_LINE_LOOP: as a parameter to the glBegin() function, specifies that the following vertex definitions are to be taken as vertices of a line loop

GL_LINES: as a parameter to the glBegin() function, specifies that the following vertex definitions are to be taken as vertices of individual lines

GL_LINE_SMOOTH: as a parameter to the glEnable() function, specifies that line smoothing is to be applied

GL_LINE_SMOOTH_HINT: as the first parameter to the glHint() function, specifies that the following hint is to be applied to line smoothing

GL_LINE_STRIP: as a parameter to the glBegin() function, specifies that the following vertex definitions are to be taken as vertices of a line strip

GL_NICEST: as the second parameter to the glHint() function, specifies that the technique giving the highest-quality result is to be used (generally meaning that antialiasing will be done)

GL_POINT_SMOOTH: as a parameter to the glEnable() function, specifies that point smoothing is to be applied

GL_POINT_SMOOTH_HINT: as the first parameter to the glHint() function, specifies that the following hint is to be applied to point smoothing

GL_POINTS: as a parameter to the glBegin() function, specifies that the following vertex definitions are to be taken as vertices of individual points

GL_POLYGON: as a parameter to the glBegin() function, specifies that the following vertex definitions are to be taken as vertices of a single (convex) polygon

GL_POLYGON_SMOOTH: as a parameter to the glEnable() function, specifies that polygon smoothing is to be applied

GL_POLYGON_SMOOTH_HINT: as the first parameter to the glHint() function, specifies that the following hint is to be applied to polygon smoothing

GL_QUADS: as a parameter to the glBegin() function, specifies that the following vertex definitions are to be taken as vertices of separate quads

`GL_QUAD_STRIP`: as a parameter to the `glBegin()` function, specifies that the following vertex definitions are to be taken as vertices of a quad strip

`GL_TRIANGLE_FAN`: as a parameter to the `glBegin()` function, specifies that the following vertex definitions are to be taken as vertices of a triangle fan

`GL_TRIANGLES`: as a parameter to the `glBegin()` function, specifies that the following vertex definitions are to be taken as vertices of individual triangles

`GL_TRIANGLE_STRIP`: as a parameter to the `glBegin()` function, specifies that the following vertex definitions are to be taken as vertices of a triangle strip

Questions

1. The OpenGL primitives include quads as well as triangles, but is it really necessary to have a quad primitive? Is there anything you can do with quads that you couldn't do with triangles?
2. The GLU objects are handy, but they can be created pretty easily from the OpenGL triangle and quad primitives. Describe how to do this for as many of the objects as you can, including at least the gluSphere, gluCylinder, gluDisk, glutSolidCone, and glutCube.
3. The GLU objects and some GLUT objects use parameters, called *slices* and *stacks* or *loops,* to define the granularity of the objects. For objects defined with these parameters, can you think of another way you could define the granularity? What are the advantages of using small values for these parameters? What are the advantages of using large values for these parameters? Are there any GLU or GLUT objects that don't use slices and stacks? Why is this so?
4. Are the values for the parameters on the scaling and translation transformations in OpenGL in model space, world space, or 3D eye space? Give reasons for your answer.
5. The angle of the OpenGL rotation transformation is given in degrees around a fixed line. What is the space in which the fixed line for the rotation is defined? In many application areas, angles are expressed in radians instead of degrees; how do you convert radians to degrees?
6. In the heat diffusion example in Chapter 0, print the source code and highlight each OpenGL function that it uses. For each, explain what it does and why it's at this point in the code.
7. Consider the model in the `display()` function in the heat diffusion example. Compare the number of operations needed to create and display this model, including all the transformations, with the number of `glVertex(...)` function calls that would be used in a display list. Draw conclusions about the relative efficiency of display lists and simple modeling.
8. In actual fact, we could not use a display list for the whole model in the `display()` function of the heat diffusion example because the model in that example changes with each `idle()` callback. Why does it not make sense to try to use display lists for the heat diffusion problem?
9. In the carousel exercise in the previous chapter, place the eyepoint on one of the objects in the carousel and change the scene graph from the previous exercise to include this eye placement. Then write the scene graph that inverts the eyepoint to place it in standard position.
10. We said that the modelview matrix stack must be at least 32 layers deep, and we saw that we need to push that stack whenever we go down the modeling graph for a scene and meet a transformation group. Relate these two facts by describing how you can tell if you exceed the depth of the modelview matrix stack in terms of properties of the modeling graph.

Exercises

1. The 3D arrow that we used as an example in the previous chapter used general modeling concepts, not specific functions. Use the GLU and GLUT modeling tools to implement the 3D arrow as a working function that you could use in an arbitrary scene.

2. Earlier we said that we could write the cube as two quad strips instead of as six separate quads. Using the declarations of vertices and edges we had in that discussion, rewrite the cube as two quad strips. Compare the number of vertices that have to be set with the `glVertex*(...)` function in these two implementations of the cube, and give the ratio of these numbers. Can you use this number as a measure of geometry compression? Why?

   Modeling is all about creating graphical objects, so the following sequence of exercises involves making some general graphical objects you can use.

3. Define a "unit cartoon dumbbell" as a thin cylinder on the x-axis with endpoints at 1.0 and -1.0, and with two spherical ends of modest size, each centered at one end of the cylinder. We call this a cartoon dumbbell because early children's cartoons always seemed to use this shape when they involved weightlifters.

4. Let's make a more realistic set of weights with solid disk weights of various sizes. Define a set of standard disks with standard weights (5kg, 10kg, 20kg, say) with the weight of the disk as a parameter to determine the thickness and/or radius of the weight, assuming that the weight is proportional to the volume. Define a function that creates a barbell carrying a given weight that is a combination of the standard weights, placing the disks appropriately on the bar. (Note that we are not asking you to create realistic disks with a hole in the middle—yet.)

5. Let's create an object that is a cylinder with a cylindrical hole, with both having the same center line. Define the object to have unit length with inside and outside cylinders of defined radii and with disks at the ends to close the pipe. Show how you could use this object to create a more realistic kind of weight for the previous exercise.

6. All the cylinder-based objects we've defined so far have a standard orientation, but we need to have cylinders with any starting point and any ending point so we need to be able to give the cylinder any orientation. Consider a cylinder with one end at the origin and the other end at a point $P = (x, y, z)$ that is one unit from the origin. Write a function that rotates a unit cylinder with one end at the origin so that the other end is at P. (Hint: You need to use two rotations, and you should think about arctangent functions.)

7. With the orientation problem for a cylinder solved by the previous exercise, write a function to create a *tube strip* that connects points $p_0, p_1, p_2, \ldots p_n$ with tubes of radius r and with spheres of the same radius at the points in order to join the tubes with a smooth transition from one tube to another. Use this to create a flexible bar between the two weights in the cartoon dumbbell in exercise 13, and show this structure supported in the middle with a bending bar in between.

8. Create a curve in the X–Y plane by defining a number of vertices and connecting them with a line strip. Then create a general surface of revolution by rotating this curve around the Y-axis. Make the surface model some object you know, such as a wine glass or a baseball bat, that has rotational symmetry. Can you use transformations to generalize this to rotate a curve around any line? How?

9. An exercise in the previous chapter asked us to design a building locator map that included a label and legend. Now implement that map, including writing the code that creates the label and legend.
10. (Class project) Each student in the class will sketch a simple model he or she would like to see and will give these to the instructor. Some of these will be chosen by the instructor as either class projects or as in-class examples. Some examples of such models, from one of the author's classes, are shown here.

Experiments

1. Design a nonconvex polygon in 2D space (e.g., the *X-Y* plane) and experiment with trying to draw it with a triangle fan. Can you find a triangle fan from a single vertex that will draw the polygon accurately? Can you find a triangle fan that will *not* draw the polygon accurately? Can you show that if you can draw the polygon accurately as a triangle fan from any single point in the polygon, then the polygon must be convex?

Projects

1. Implement the carousel discussed in question 9, using some kind of standard object as the carousel horses—use a model from an outside source or make a very simple "horse" object. Create two views of the carousel, one from outside and one from the eyepoint on the horse.
2. (The small house) Design and create a simple house with exterior and interior walls, doors, windows, ceilings in the rooms, and a simple gable roof. Use different colors for various walls so that they can be distinguished in any view. Set several different viewpoints around and within the house and show how the house looks from each.
3. (A scene graph parser) Implement the scene graph parser that was designed in a project in the previous chapter. Each transformation and geometry node is to contain the OpenGL function names and arguments needed to carry out the transformations and implement the geometry. The parser should be able to write the `display()` function for your scene.

Mathematics for Modeling

The primary mathematics background needed for API-based computer graphics programming is 3D analytic geometry. Most students pick up this background in courses such as introductory physics or multivariate calculus. Another source is a linear algebra course if it is oriented toward geometry, but not many of them are. Because we cannot assume a common mathematics background, this chapter outlines the general concepts used in computer graphics and in this book. Some of these are needed regularly in computer graphics programming and some are included for completeness and because we need them for particular applications. With these geometric tools in hand, for example, we will be able to do such things as compute the normals to a triangle as we set up a scene with lighting.

We begin with an overview of rectangular 3D Cartesian space and the way points, lines, line segments, and parametrics are represented for computation. These topics are extended to a discussion of vectors and vector computation, including dot and cross products and their geometric meanings. Using a vector view of 3D space, we introduce linear transformations and show how the basic modeling transformations of scaling, translation, and rotation are represented in matrix form and how transformation composition can be done as matrix operations. We then discuss planes and computations based on planes, including polygons and convexity. Other coordinate systems such as polar and cylindrical coordinates are introduced because they can be more natural for some modeling than rectangular coordinates. The chapter closes with some considerations in collision detection.

In order to be able to work through this chapter successfully, you need to be able to multiply two matrices, take the transpose of a matrix, and be familiar and comfortable thinking about points, lines, polygons, and polyhedra in 3D space.

Coordinate Systems

The real number line is modeled as a Euclidean straight line with two uniquely identified points. One point is identified with the number 0.0 (we will write all real numbers with decimals, to meet the expectations of programming languages), called the *origin,* and the other is identified with the number 1.0, called the *unit point*. The direction of the line from 0.0 to 1.0 is called the positive direction; the opposite direction of the line is called the negative direction. These directions identify the parts of the lines associated with positive and negative numbers, respectively.

If we have two straight lines that are perpendicular to each other and meet in a point, we can define that point to be the origin for both lines and choose two points the same distance from the origin on each line as the unit points. This defines a unit of distance measurement for both lines. This gives us the classic 2D coordinate system, often called the *Cartesian coordinate system*. The vectors from the intersection point to the right-hand point (respectively the point above the intersection) are called the unit X- and Y-direction vectors and are named $\boldsymbol{i}$ and $\boldsymbol{j}$ respectively, so we have the vector notation of $\boldsymbol{i} = <1, 0>$ and $\boldsymbol{j} = <0, 1>$. Points in this system are represented by an ordered pair of real numbers, (x, y). These points may also be represented by a vector $<X, Y>$ from the origin to the point, and this vector may be expressed in terms of the unit direction vectors as $X\boldsymbol{i} + Y\boldsymbol{j}$.

In 2D Cartesian coordinates, any two lines that are not parallel will meet in a point. The lines make four angles when they meet, and the acute angle is called the angle between the lines. If two line segments begin at the same point, they make a single angle that is called the angle between the line segments. These angles let us use the usual trigonometric functions, and we assume that you have some familiarity with trigonometry. We will need these trigonometric functions for discussions on polar and spherical coordinates, and in the description later in this chapter of the dot product and cross product.

The 3D world in which we will do most of our work is based on 3D Cartesian coordinates that extend the ideas of 2D coordinates. This is based on three lines that meet at a point, the origin for all three lines, that have their unit points the same distance from that point and that are mutually perpendicular. Each point in this space is represented by an ordered triple of real numbers (x, y, z). The three lines give three unit direction vectors, each from the origin to the unit point of its respective line; these are named $\boldsymbol{i}, \boldsymbol{j}$, and $\boldsymbol{k}$ for the X-, Y-, and Z-axis, respectively, and are named $\boldsymbol{i} = <1, 0, 0>, \boldsymbol{j} = <0, 1, 0>$, and $\boldsymbol{k} = <0, 0, 1>$. These are called the canonical basis for the space, and the point (x, y, z) can be represented as $x\boldsymbol{i} + y\boldsymbol{j} + z\boldsymbol{k}$. This is all illustrated in Figure 4.1.

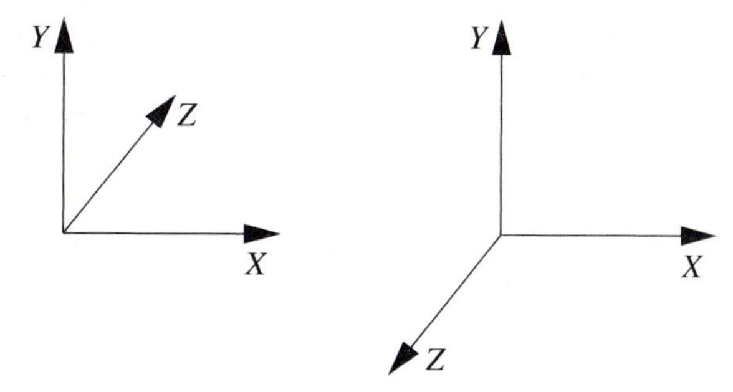

Figure 4.1 Left-hand coordinate system (*left*) and right-hand coordinate system (*right*).

Recall from the discussion of the viewing space in Chapter 1 that 3D coordinate systems can be either right-handed or left-handed: The third axis can be the cross product of the first two axes, or it can be the negative of that cross product, respectively. (We will talk about cross products a little later in this chapter.) The "handed-ness" comes from a simple technique: If you hold your hand in space with your fingers along the first axis and curl your fingers toward the second axis, your thumb will point in a direction perpendicular to the first two axes. If you do this with the right hand, the thumb points in the direction of the third axis in a right-handed system. If you do it with the left hand, the thumb points in the direction of the third axis in a left-handed system. Try this with standard *X*-*Y* coordinates (*X* is right, *Y* is up) and see how it matches the figure.

Most computer graphics systems use right-handed coordinates, and this is probably the most natural coordinate system for most uses. For example, this is the coordinate system that naturally fits electromagnetic theory, because the relationship between a moving current in a wire and the magnetic field it generates is a right-hand coordinate relationship. The modeling in Open GL is based on a right-hand coordinate system.

On the other hand, there are places where a left-handed coordinate system is natural. The RenderMan shader language assumes a left-handed coordinate system, for example. If you consider a space with a standard *X*-*Y* plane as the front of the space and define *Z* as the distance back from that plane, then the values of *Z* naturally increase as you move back into the space. This is a left-hand relationship.

Quadrants and Octants

In 2D space, you may be familiar with the division of Cartesian space into four *quadrants,* each having points with the same algebraic signs in each component. The first quadrant contains points for which x and y are both positive; the second quadrant, points for which x is negative but y is positive; the third quadrant, points for which both x and y are negative; and the fourth quadrant, points for which x is positive but y is negative.

The same idea applies in 3D space, but there are eight such regions and they are called *octants*. The names for each octant are less standardized than are those for the four quadrants in 2D space, but the region in which all of x, y, and z are positive is called the first octant, and we will sometimes think about views in which the eyepoint is in this octant.

Points, Lines, and Line Segments

In a one-dimensional space, any real number is identified with the unique point on the line that is

- at the distance from the origin which is that number times the distance from the origin to the unit point, and
- in the direction of the number's sign.

We know that a line is determined by two points; let's see how that works. Let the first point be $P_0 = (X_0, Y_0, Z_0)$ and the second point be $P_1 = (X_1, Y_1, Z_1)$. Call P_0 the origin and P_1 the unit point of the line. Points on the line are determined by starting at the origin P_0 offset by a fraction of the difference vector $P_1 - P_0$. This difference vector is sometimes called the *direction vector* for the line, especially if it has been normalized, or made to have length 1. Then any point $P = (X, Y, Z)$ on the line segment can be expressed in vector terms by

$$P = P_0 + t(P_1 - P_0) = (1 - t)P_0 + tP_1$$

for a single value of a real variable t that lies between 0 and 1. This computation is actually done for each coordinate, with a separate equation for each of X, Y, and Z as follows:

$$X = X_0 + t(X_1 - X_0) = (1 - t)X_0 + tX_1$$
$$Y = Y_0 + t(Y_1 - Y_0) = (1 - t)Y_0 + tY_1$$
$$Z = Z_0 + t(Z_1 - Z_0) = (1 - t)Z_0 + tZ_1$$

So any line segment can be determined by a single parameter, and the line segment represented by any linear parametric equations

$$x = a + bt$$
$$y = c + dt$$
$$z = e + ft$$

is called a *parametric line segment*. Points along the segment are determined by values of the parameter, as illustrated in Figure 4.2. This figure shows the coordinates of the points along a line segment determined by values of t from 0 to 1 in increments of 0.25.

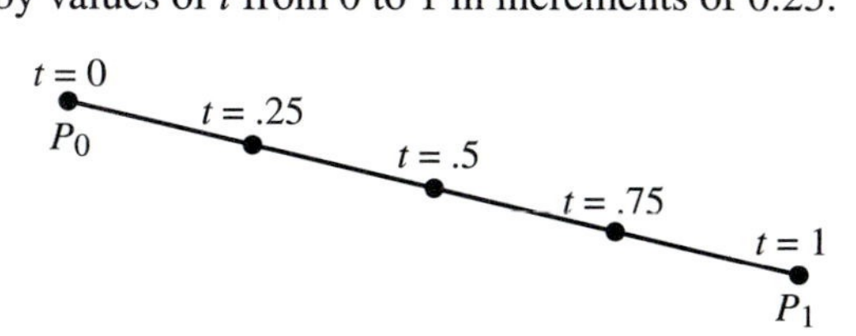

Figure 4.2 A parametric line segment with points determined by some values of the parameter.

This representation for a line segment lets you compute intersections of lines. The reverse concept is also useful; if you have a known point on the line, you can calculate the value of the parameter t that gives that point. For example, if a line intersects a plane or another geometric object at a point Q, a vector calculation of the form $Q = P_0 + t(P_1 - P_0)$ lets you calculate the value of t that gives the intersection point on the line. This calculation might involve only a single equation or all three equations, depending on the situation. This is often the basis for geometric computations such as that of the intersection of a line and a plane.

As an example of this kind of calculation, we'll take two points and calculate the parametric equations for the line segment for which they are endpoints. Let $P_0 = (3.0, 4.0, 5.0)$ and $P_1 = (5.0, -1.5, 4.0)$. Then $P_1 - P_0 = (2.0, -5.5, -1.0)$, so a set of equations for the line is

$$x = 3.0 + 2.0t$$
$$y = 4.0 - 5.5t$$
$$z = 5.0 - t$$

We will see below that a plane can be represented as the set of points (x, y, z) with

$$Ax + By + Cz + D = 0.$$

If we consider a plane $6.0x - 2.0y + 1.5z - 4.0 = 0.0$, the point where the line intersects the plane is given by

$$6.0(3.0 + 2.0t) - 2.0(4.0 - 5.5t) + 1.5(5.0 - t) - 4.0 = 0.0$$

Combining terms yields $21.5t - 13.5 = 0$, or $t = 13.5/21.5 = 27/43$, from which the intersection point for the line and the plane is $(183/43, -41/86, 188/43)$. Of course, you will rarely do this kind of calculation manually but will code such computations as you need them in your program.

Line Segments, Rays, and Parametric Curves and Surfaces

In the same way we talked about any line having unique origin identified with 0.0 and unit point identified with 1.0, any *line segment* (the points on the line between these two given points), can be identified as the points corresponding to values between 0 and 1. If the two points are P_0 and P_1, we can identify any point between them as $P = (1 - t)P_0 + tP_1$ for a unique value of t between 0 and 1. This is a parametric form for the line segment between the points. If we change the limits on the value of t, we can get other variations on the idea of a line. For example, if we take the equation for all values of t we get a complete line. If we take the equation for all non-negative values of t we get a line that has an initial point P_0 but no ending point; such a line is called a *ray*.

The parametric line segment is a special case of determining a continuous set of points by functions from the interval [0, 1] to 3-space. If we consider any continuous functions $x(t)$, $y(t)$, and $z(t)$ defined on [0, 1], the set of points $\{(x(t), y(t), z(t)\}$ they generate is called a *parametric curve* in 3-space. There are some very useful applications of such curves. For example, you can display the locations of a moving point in space, you can compute the positions along a curve from which you will view a scene in a flythrough, or you can describe the behavior of a function of two variables on a domain that lies on a curve in 2-space.

A parametric surface is a two-dimensional version of a parametric curve. Starting with a square two-dimensional domain $\{(u, v) \mid u, v \text{ in } [0,1]\}$, take any three continuous functions of two variables $x(u, v)$, $y(u, v)$, and $z(u, v)$. The set of such points $\{(x(u, v), y(u, v), z(u, v))\}$ forms a continuous surface, and again, there are many examples where this model describes important principles and ideas. This is explored in Chapter 9.

Distance from a Point to a Line

As an application of parametric lines, let's compute the distance from a point in 3-space to a line. If the point is $P_0 = (u, v, w)$ and the line is given by parametric equations

$$x = a + bt$$
$$y = c + dt$$
$$z = e + ft$$

then for any point $P = (x, y, z)$ on the line, the square of the distance from P to P_0 is given by

$$(a + bt - u)^2 + (c + dt - v)^2 + (e + ft - w)^2$$

which is a quadratic equation in t. This quadratic is minimized by taking its derivative and looking for the point where the derivative is 0. This happens when

$$2b(a + bt - u) + 2d(c + dt - v) + 2f(e + ft - w) = 0$$

and this is a simple linear equation in t. Its unique solution for t lets you compute the point P on the line that is nearest point P_0 by substituting in the parametric equations above.

Vectors

Vectors in three-dimensional space are triples of real numbers written as $<a, b, c>$. These may be identified with points, or they may be viewed as representing the motion needed to go from one point to another in space. The latter viewpoint will be one we use often.

The *length* of a vector is defined as the square root of the sum of the squares of the vector's components, written $\|\langle a,b,c \rangle\| = \sqrt{a^2 + b^2 + c^2}$. A *unit vector* is a vector whose length is 1, and unit vectors are very important in a number of modeling and rendering computations because a unit vector can be treated as a pure direction. If $V = <a, b, c>$ is any vector and L is its length, we can make it a unit vector by dividing each of its components by its length: $<a/L, b/L, c/L>$. Doing this is called *normalizing* the vector.

The angle between two vectors is defined as the angle between the line segments through the origin with the vectors as direction vectors. If the vectors are normalized, then the angle between them has cosine equal to their dot product, as discussed in the next section.

Dot and Cross Products of Vectors

There are two computations on vectors that we will need to understand, and sometimes to perform, in developing the geometry for our images. The first is the *dot product* or *scalar product* of two vectors. The dot product computation is quite simple: It is simply the sum of the componentwise products of the vectors. If the two vectors A and B are

$$A = <X_1, Y_1, Z_1>$$
$$B = <X_2, Y_2, Z_2>$$

then their dot product is computed as

$$A \cdot B = X_1 * X_2 + Y_1 * Y_2 + Z_1 * Z_2$$

A simple consequence of this definition is that the length of any vector A is the square root of the dot product $A \cdot A$ of the vector with itself.

There is an important alternate meaning of the dot product. A straightforward calculation shows that $U \cdot V = \|U\| * \|V\| * \cos(\Theta)$, where $\|V\|$ denotes the length of a vector and Θ is the angle between the vectors. This is the projection of one vector on the other and links the algebraic calculation of the dot product with geometric properties of vectors, and it is very important. For example, if two vectors are parallel, the dot product is simply the product of their lengths with the sign saying whether they are oriented in the same or opposite directions. However, if the vectors are orthogonal—the angle between them is 90°—then the dot product is zero. If the angle between them is acute, then the dot product will be positive, no matter what the orientation of the vectors, because the cosine of any acute angle is positive; if the angle between them is obtuse, then the dot product will be negative. Another useful application of the dot product is that you can compute the angle between two vectors if you know the vectors' lengths and their dot product.

It is not uncommon to do vertex computations as you set up polygons, so you should know that you can calculate the angle at any vertex by $\cos^{-1}((U \cdot V)/(\|U\| * \|V\|))$ where U and V are the two edge vectors at the vertex. This value may be useful in doing per-vertex normal computations and it may be retained as vertex data in your polygon data structures.

The relationship between the dot product and the cosine of the included angle also lets us look at the component of any vector that lies in the direction of another vector, or the *projection* of one vector on another. As we see in Figure 4.3, for any two vectors we can construct a right triangle where one side is one of the vectors and another is the projection of the first on the second. Because the side of the triangle in the direction of V has length $\|U\|*\cos(\Theta)$, and because the dot product uses the cosine of the included angle, the length of the projection of U onto V is $U \cdot V/\|V\|$. This is especially useful when V is a unit vector, because then the dot product alone gives the length of the projection. This is one of the reasons for normalizing the vectors we use.

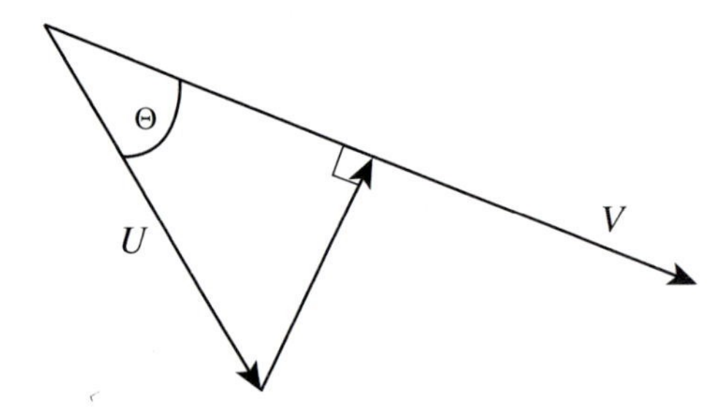

Figure 4.3 The projection of *U* onto *V*.

The second computation is the *cross product,* or *vector product,* of two vectors. Cross products use determinants of square matrices; these are defined simply for square 2 × 2 matrices and are defined recursively for larger matrices. For the determinant of a square 2 × 2 matrix, we have

$$\det\begin{vmatrix} a & b \\ c & d \end{vmatrix} = ad - bc$$

And for the determinant of a square 3 × 3 matrix we have

$$\det\begin{vmatrix} a & b & c \\ d & e & f \\ g & h & k \end{vmatrix} = a*\det\begin{vmatrix} e & f \\ h & k \end{vmatrix} - b*\det\begin{vmatrix} d & f \\ g & k \end{vmatrix} + c*\det\begin{vmatrix} d & e \\ g & h \end{vmatrix}$$

Note the alternating plus and minus signs in the expansion of the larger determinant. We will not need determinants of arrays larger than 3 × 3, but the pattern may not be too difficult to see.

The cross product of two vectors is a third vector that is perpendicular to each of the original vectors and whose length is the product of the two vector lengths times the sine of the angle between them. So if two vectors are parallel, the cross product is zero; if they are orthogonal, the cross product has length equal to the product of the two lengths; if they are both unit vectors, the cross product is the sine of the included angle. The cross product can be expressed as the determinant of a matrix whose first row is the three standard unit vectors, whose second row is the first vector of the product, and whose third row is the second vector of the product. Denoting the unit direction vectors in the X, Y, and Z directions as $\boldsymbol{i}, \boldsymbol{j}$, and $\boldsymbol{k}$, as above, we can express the cross product of two vectors in terms of a determinant:

$$\langle a,b,c\rangle \times \langle u,v,w\rangle = \det\begin{vmatrix} i & j & k \\ a & b & c \\ u & v & w \end{vmatrix} = i\det\begin{vmatrix} b & c \\ v & w \end{vmatrix} - j\det\begin{vmatrix} a & c \\ u & w \end{vmatrix} + k\det\begin{vmatrix} a & b \\ u & v \end{vmatrix}$$

$$= \langle bw - cv,\ cu - aw,\ av - bu\rangle$$

As you may remember from determinants, if two adjacent rows or columns of a matrix are switched, the determinant's sign is changed. This shows that $U \times V = -V \times U$.

As an example of cross products, consider the two points we saw earlier treated as vectors: u = <3.0, 4.0, 5.0> and v = <5.0, −1,5, 4.0>. The length of u is the square root of the dot product $u \cdot u$, or 7.071, and the length of v is the square root of $v \cdot v$, or 6.576. So we see that

$$u \cdot v = 15.0 - 6.0 + 20.0 = 29.0.$$

and the cosine of the angle between u and v is 29.0/(7.071*6.576) or 0.624. The cross product of the two vectors is

$$u \times v = \begin{vmatrix} i & j & k \\ 3 & 4 & 5 \\ 5 & -1.5 & 4 \end{vmatrix} = i\begin{vmatrix} 4 & 5 \\ -1.5 & 4 \end{vmatrix} - j\begin{vmatrix} 3 & 5 \\ 5 & 4 \end{vmatrix} + k\begin{vmatrix} 3 & 4 \\ 5 & -1.5 \end{vmatrix}$$

Calculating the 2×2 determinants gives us $u \times v = 23.5\boldsymbol{i} + 13.0\boldsymbol{j} - 24.5\boldsymbol{k}$ as the cross product. Check to see that this product is orthogonal to both u and v by computing the dot products, which should be 0.

The cross product has a "handedness" property and is said to be a right-handed operation. That is, if you align the fingers of your right hand with the direction of the first vector and curl your fingers toward the second vector, your right thumb will point in the direction of the cross product. Thus the order of the vectors is important; as we saw above, if you reverse the order, you reverse the sign of the product, so the cross product operation is not commutative. As a simple example, with $\boldsymbol{i}, \boldsymbol{j}$, and $\boldsymbol{k}$ as above, we see that $\boldsymbol{i} \times \boldsymbol{j} = \boldsymbol{k}$ but that $\boldsymbol{j} \times \boldsymbol{i} = -\boldsymbol{k}$. If you consider the arrangement of Figure 4.4, and if you think of the three direction vectors as being wrapped around as if they were visible from the first octant of 3-space, the product of any two is the third direction vector if the letters are in counter-clockwise order around the circle in Figure 4.4, and the negative of the third if the order is clockwise.

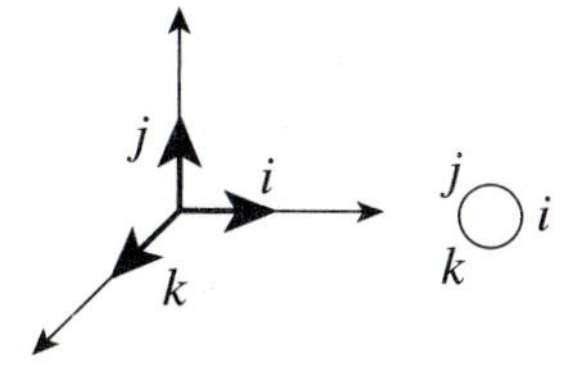

Figure 4.4 The direction vectors and a device to help you remember their order.

The cross product can be very useful when you need to compute a vector perpendicular to two given vectors. The most common application of this is computing a normal vector to a polygon by calculating the cross product of two edge vectors. For a triangle as in Figure 4.5 with vertices A, B, and

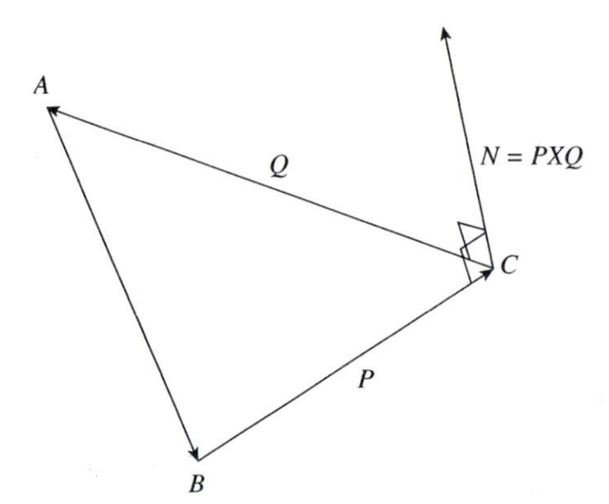

Figure 4.5 The normal to a triangle as the cross product of two edges.

C in counterclockwise order from the "front" side of the triangle, the normal vector can be computed by creating the two difference vectors $P = C-B$ and $Q = A-C$. The cross product is $P \times Q$ and is a vector N normal to the plane of the triangle. This normal vector and any point on the triangle let us generate the equation of the plane that contains the triangle. When we need to use this normal for lighting we will need to normalize it, or make it a unit-length vector as we described above, but that is easily done by calculating the vector's length and dividing each component by that length.

Reflection Vectors

There are times in computer graphics when it is important to calculate a *reflection vector*—that is, a vector that is a reflection of another vector in some surface. One example is in specular light calculations needed for the lighting model of Chapter 6. The brightness of specular light at a point (a shiny-reflection from a surface similar to a mirror reflection) depends on the angle between the vector to the eye from that point and the reflection of the vector from that point to the light. Another example is in any model where an object hits a surface and is reflected from it, so the object's velocity vector after the bounce is the reflection of its incoming velocity vector. To calculate reflections we need to know the normal to the surface at the point where the vector to be reflected hits the surface, and the calculation is fairly straightforward. Figure 4.6 shows the situation we are working with.

In this figure we assume that N is a unit vector perpendicular to the surface and P is a vector coming into the surface. We want to compute the vector Q reflected out from the sur-

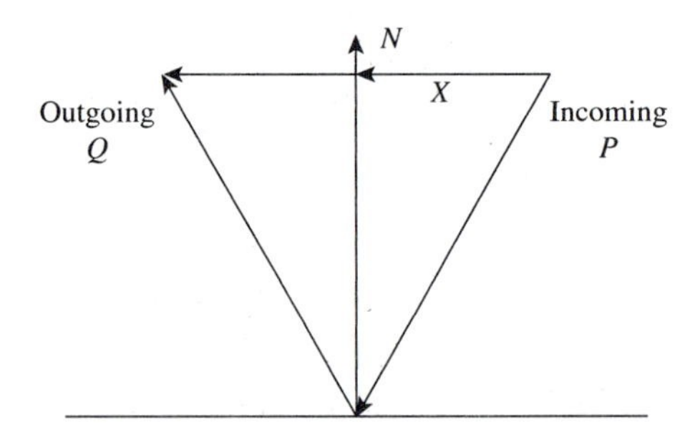

Figure 4.6 Incoming vector P, outgoing vector Q, and normal vector N.

face. Let N^* be the vector that Q makes when it is projected on N. Because of symmetry in the figure, N^* is the negative of the vector that P makes when it is projected on N, so $N^* = -(N \cdot P)N$, which gives us $X = P + N^* = P - (N \cdot P)N$. But from the figure we see that $Q + P = 2X$, from which $Q = 2(P - (N \cdot P)N) - P$, so $Q = P - 2(N \cdot P)N$. This is simple and is easy to code.

Transformations

In the two previous chapters we discussed transformations rather abstractly: as functions that operate on 3D space to produce given effects. In the spirit of this chapter, however, we describe how these functions are represented as matrices for computation and, in particular, the representation of each of the basic scaling, rotation, and transformation matrices.

To begin, we recall that we earlier introduced the notion of homogeneous coordinates for points in 3D space: We identify the 3D point (x, y, z) with the homogeneous point $(x, y, z, 1)$. We will see when we discuss the translation transformation why we need to use 4D space instead of 3D space when we compute transformations. The transformations T are all linear functions on 4D space and so may be represented as 4×4 matrices:

$$T = \begin{pmatrix} t_{00} & t_{01} & t_{02} & t_{03} \\ t_{10} & t_{11} & t_{12} & t_{13} \\ t_{20} & t_{21} & t_{22} & t_{23} \\ t_{30} & t_{31} & t_{32} & t_{33} \end{pmatrix}$$

Applying two transformations in order, or *composing* the transformations, is accomplished by multiplying the transformations' matrices. So if we have transformations S and T, represented by real-valued arrays `S[i] [j]` and `T[i] [j]`, respectively, then the composition of the transformations is given by $C = S*T$; in terms of code for multiplying the matrices, this is

```
for (int i = 0; i < 4; i++)
    for (int j = 0; j < 4; j++) {
        C[i][j] = 0.;
        for (int k = 0; k < 4; k++)
            C[i][j] += S[i][k]*T[k][j];

}
```

This is a straightforward matrix multiplication. Geometrically, this treats the matrices as sets of vectors, with the left-hand matrix composed of row vectors and the right-hand matrix composed of column vectors. The product of the matrices is made up of the dot products of each row matrix from the left by each column matrix on the right.

The effect of a transformation on a vector is given by multiplying the transformation, as a matrix, on the left of the point, stored as a column vector. This uses similar code to the matrix multiplication, but is simpler. To apply the transformation whose matrix is `T[i][j]` to the vector V_1 to get the vector V_2, we have

```
for (int i = 0; i < 4; i++)
    V2[i] = 0.;
    for (int k = 0; k < 4; k++)
        V2[i] += T[i][k]*V1[k];
    }
```

With this background, let's see how the basic transformations look as matrices. For scaling, the transformation defined by the OpenGL function `glScalef(sx, sy, sz)` is expressed as

```
sx   0    0    0
0    sy   0    0
0    0    sz   0
0    0    0    1
```

For translation, the OpenGL function `glTranslatef(tx, ty, tz)` actually needs the full 4 × 4 matrix. We need to go to 4D space for this transformation because a translation cannot be a linear transformation in 3D space: any translation takes the origin to the point (*tx*, *ty*, *tz*) while any linear transformation must take the origin to (0, 0, 0). In order to make translation work, we have to use homogeneous coordinates and look at a shear transformation in 4D space that takes (0, 0, 0, 1) to (*tx*, *ty*, *tz*, 1). This is given by

```
1    0    0    tx
0    1    0    ty
0    0    1    tz
0    0    0    1
```

Rotation is more complex. To see the general case, let's start with a rotation around the origin in 2D space. If we rotate by the angle theta around the origin, the point $U = (1, 0)$ moves to the point $(\cos \Theta, \sin \Theta)$ and the point $V = (0, 1)$ moves to the point $(-\sin \Theta, \cos \Theta)$ as shown in Figure 4.7. Because any point (x, y) in 2D space can be written as a linear combination $xU + yV$, the behavior of the rotation is completely determined by what it does to U and V. It is easy to check that the matrix

$$R = \begin{bmatrix} \cos\Theta & -\sin\Theta \\ \sin\Theta & cos\Theta \end{bmatrix}$$

gives the appropriate results when multiplied on the right by U and V, and thus R is the matrix form for the rotation by Θ around the origin.

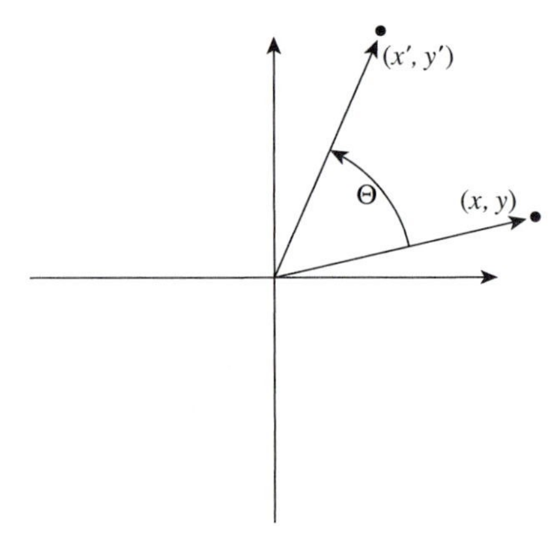

Figure 4.7 A rotation by the angle Θ around the origin in 2D space.

OpenGL gives you a rotation around any specified line through the origin with the function `glRotatef(angle,x,y,z)` where *angle* is the amount or rotation (in degrees) and <*x*, *y*, *z*> is the direction vector of the line around which the rotation is to be done. We can write a simple matrix for the rotations around the coordinate axes. For the rotation around the *Z*-axis, `glRotatef(angle,0.,0.,1.)`, the *Z*-coordinate is fixed so that the operation is basically a 2D rotation in the *X*-*Y* plane. With the 2D rotation we saw above, it is easy to see that the matrix for the rotation is:

```
cos(angle) -sin(angle)     0       0
sin(angle)  cos(angle)     0       0
0               0          1       0
0               0          0       1
```

For the rotation around the *X*-axis, `glRotatef(angle,1.,0.,0.)`, the *X*-coordinate is fixed and the rotation is basically in the 2D space of the *Y*-*Z* plane. This is much the same as the *Z*-axis rotation above, and the matrix representing the rotation is:

```
1        0           0          0
0    cos(angle) -sin(angle)     0
0    sin(angle)  cos(angle)     0
0        0           0          1
```

For rotation around the *Y*-axis, there is a difference because the cross product of the *X*- and *Z*-axes is in the opposite direction to the *Y*-axis. This means that the angle relative to the *Y*-axis is the negative of the angle relative to the cross product, and the change in the sign of the angle changes only the sign of the sine function. So the matrix that represents the function `glRotatef (angle,0.,1.,0.)` is:

```
 cos(angle)     0     sin(angle)     0
     0          1     0              0
-sin(angle)     0     cos(angle)     0
     0          0     0              1
```

The formula for a rotation around an arbitrary line through the origin is more complex and is given in the OpenGL manual, so we will not present it here.

Planes and Half-Spaces

We saw above that a line could be defined in terms of a single parameter, so it is a one-dimensional space. A plane is determined by two parameters and is a two-dimensional space. Any two nonparallel lines that meet in a single point *P* determine a plane: the set of points that are translations of *P* by linear combinations of the direction vectors of the lines. Thus any plane is two-dimensional, with each of the lines contributing a dimension. In practice, we usually don't define a plane by two lines. Instead, we take three points that do not lie in a straight line, and we get the two lines by letting two pairs of points determine two lines. Because each pair of points lies in the plane, so do the lines they generate, and so we have the two lines described above.

To get an equation for a plane, consider the vector $N = \langle A, B, C\rangle$ that is the cross product of the vectors determined by the two lines. The vector N is perpendicular to each of the two vectors and so to any line in the plane. In fact, this can define the plane: all lines through the fixed point perpendicular to $<A, B, C>$. If we take a fixed point in the plane with coordinates (U, V, W) and a variable point in the plane (x, y, z), we get a line in the plane with direction vector $<x-U, y-V, z-W>$. We can use the dot product to express the perpendicular relation as

$$<A, B, C> \cdot <x - U, y - V, z - W> = 0$$

When we expand the dot product we have

$$A(u - X) + B(y - V) + C(z - W) = Ax + By + Cz + (-AU - BV - CW) = 0$$

This gives an equation for the plane:

$$Ax + By + Cz + D = 0$$

for a value of D that depends on the fixed point in the plane. So the coefficients of the variables in the plane equation exactly match the components of the vector normal to the plane, a fact that can be useful from time to time. Notice that there are only two independent variables in this equation, because if two are fixed, the value of the third is also fixed. This reinforces the idea that the plane has dimension two.

We know that a plane divides 3D space into two half-spaces, but we need to know how to tell which points in the plane are in which half-space. To see how to do this, let's look first at 2D space. Any line divides the plane into two parts. If we know the equation of the line

$$ax + by + c = 0,$$

we can tell whether a point (x, y) lies on, above, or below the line by evaluating the function $f(x, y) = ax + by + c$ and seeing whether the result is zero, positive, or negative, respectively. Similarly, the equation for a plane does more than just identify the plane; it allows us to determine on which side of the plane any point lies. If we create a function from the plane equation

$$f(x,y,z) = Ax + By + Cz + D,$$

then the plane contains all points (x, y, z) where $f(x, y, z) = 0$. All points with $f(x, y, z) > 0$ lie on one side of the plane, called the *positive half-space* for the plane, while all points with $f(x, y, z) < 0$ lie on the other, called the *negative half-space* for the plane. OpenGL uses the coordinates A, B, C, D to identify a plane and uses the half-space concept and the sign of the function above to decide what can be displayed when the plane is used for clipping.

Let's consider an example that illustrates both these ideas. If we take three points $A = (1.0, 2.0, 3.0)$, $B = (2.0, 1.0, -1.0)$, and $C = (-1.0, 2.0, 1.0)$, we can easily see that they do not lie on a straight line in 3D space. These three points define a plane; let's calculate its equation. The difference vectors are $A-B = <-1.0, 1.0, 4.0>$ and $B-C = <3.0, -1.0, -2.0>$, so these two vectors acting on any one of the points define two lines in the plane. We compute the cross product $(B-C) \times (A-B)$ of these two vectors through the 2×2 determinants outlined above, and we get

$$<-2.0, -10.0, 2.0>$$

So the equation of the plane is $-2X - 10Y + 2Z + D = 0$. When we put in the coordinates of B we calculate the constant D as -12.0, giving the final equation $-2X - 10Y + 2Z - 12 = 0$. Any point for which the plane equation $f(x, y, z) = -2x - 10y + 2z - 12$ yields a positive value lies in the side of the plane's positive half-space, and any point that yields a negative value lies in the plane's negative half-space.

Distance from a Point to a Plane

Just as we earlier could compute the distance from a point to a line, we also want to be able to compute the distance from a point to a plane. This will be useful when we discuss collision detection and may also have other applications.

Given a plane $Ax + By + Cz + D = 0$ with normal vector $N = <A, B, C>$, unit normal (direction) vector $n = <a, b, c>$, and an arbitrary point $P = (u, v, w)$. Select any point $Q = (d, e, f)$ in the plane and consider the relationships shown in Figure 4.8. The distance from the point to the plane is the length of the projection of the vector $P-Q$ on the unit normal vector n, or $|(P-Q) \cdot n|$. This gives us an easy way to compute this distance, especially because we can choose the point Q any way we wish.

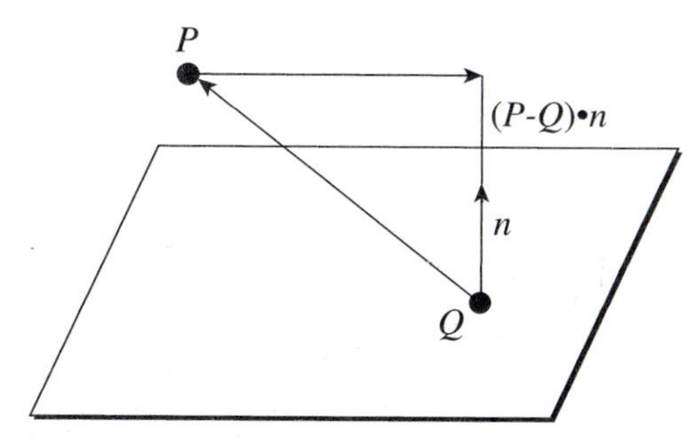

Figure 4.8 The computation of the distance from a point to a plane.

Polygons and Convexity

Most simple graphics systems, including OpenGL, are based on modeling and rendering using polygons and polyhedra. A *polygon* is a plane region bounded by a sequence of line segments with the property that the endpoint of one segment is the same as the starting point of the next segment, and the endpoint of the last line segment is the starting point of the first segment. A *polyhedron* is a region of 3-space that is bounded by a set of polygons. Because polyhedra are composed of polygons, we will focus on modeling with polygons.

The reason to base modeling on polygons is that many fundamental problems for computer graphics have simple solutions for polygons. These algorithms operate by interpolating values across the polygon; you will see this in later chapters on shading (Chapter 6), texture mapping (Chapter 8), and rendering (Chapter 10). In order for a property to be interpolated correctly across a polygon, the polygon must be convex. Informally, a polygon is *convex* if it has no indentations; formally, a polygon is convex if for any two points in the polygon (either the interior or the boundary) the line segment between them lies entirely within the polygon.

Because a polygon bounds a region of the plane, we can talk about the *interior* or *exterior* of the polygon. In a convex polygon, it is enough to determine which side of each is "inside" the figure. General polygons can be nonconvex, and we would like to define the concept of "inside" for them. We start with convex figures and note that if a point is inside the figure, any ray from an interior point (line extending in only one direction from the point) must exit the figure in precisely one point.

(Polygon vertices are special cases and are handled by the convention that only one edge at the vertex actually contains the vertex.) But if a point is outside the figure, whenever a ray hits the polygon it must both enter and exit, and so the ray crosses the boundary of the figure in either 0 or 2 points. In general polygons we see that if a point is inside the polygon, any ray from the point must cross the boundary of the polygon an odd number of times, and for a point outside the polygon, any ray from the point must cross the boundary of the polygon an even number of times. This is illustrated in Figure 4.9. In the figure, points A and E are outside the polygons and points B, C, and D are inside. Note carefully the case of point E; according to our definition of inside and outside, this point is outside the polygon because of the even number of intersections, even though it is surrounded by polygon edges. Thus our definition of inside and outside might not be intuitive in some cases.

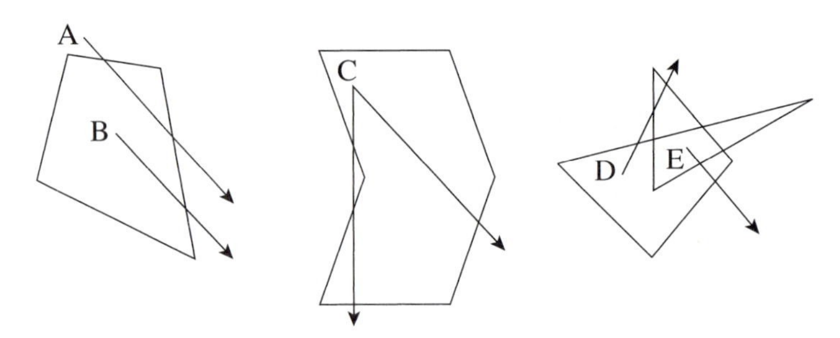

Figure 4.9 Interior and exterior points of a convex polygon (*left*) and two nonconvex polygons (*center and right*).

Another way to think about convexity is in terms of linear combinations of points. We can define a *convex sum* of points $P_0, P_1, \ldots P_n$ as a sum $\sum c_i P_i$ where each of the coefficients c_i is non-negative and the sum of the coefficients is exactly 1. If we recall that the parametric definition of a line segment is $(1-t)P_0 + tP_1$, we note that this is a convex sum. If a polygon is convex, all line segments between vertices in the polygon must lie in the polygon and so all convex sums of vertices of the polygon also lie in the polygon. The converse is also true; if all convex sums of vertices lie in the polygon, then the polygon is convex. This is one way to generate a convex polygon: Take any set of points and include all of their convex sums. This polygon is called the *convex hull* of the vertices and is the smallest convex polygon that includes all of them. There are other, more geometrically oriented, ways to generate convex hulls, and you may find it interesting to find or create algorithms for them.

Because the entire interior of the polygon can be expressed as a convex sum of the vertices, interpolation processes such as depth and color smoothing can be expressed by the same convex sum of these properties for the vertices. Thus convexity is a very important property for geometric objects in computer graphics systems.

As we said above, most graphics systems, and certainly OpenGL, require that all polygons be convex in order to be rendered correctly. If you need to use a polygon that is not convex, you may always subdivide it into triangles or other convex polygons and work with them instead of with the original polygon. As an alternative, OpenGL provides a facility to tesselate a polygon—divide it into convex polygons—automatically, but this is a complex operation that we do not cover in this book.

Polyhedra

Polyhedra are volumes in 3D space that are bounded by polygons. To work with a polyhedron, you define the polygons that form its boundaries. In terms of the scene graph, a polyhedron is a group node whose elements are polygons. Most graphics APIs do not provide a rich set of predefined polyhedra that you can use in modeling; in OpenGL, for example, you have only the Platonic solids and a few simple polyhedral approximations of other objects (sphere, torus, etc.).

A convex polyhedron is one for which any two points in the object are connected by a line segment that is completely contained in the object. Because polyhedra are almost always defined in terms of polygons, we will not focus on them but will rather focus on polygons. So when we talk about collision detection, the most detailed level of testing will be to identify polygons that intersect.

Polar, Cylindrical, and Spherical Coordinates

Up to this point we have emphasized Cartesian, or rectangular, coordinates for describing 2D and 3D geometry, but there are times when other kinds of coordinate systems are very useful. The coordinate systems we discuss here are based on angles, not distances, in at least one of their terms. Because graphics APIs generally do not handle non-Cartesian coordinate systems directly, when you want to use these coordinates you will need to translate points between these forms and rectangular coordinates.

In 2D space, we can identify any point (X, Y) with the line segment from the origin to that point. This identification allows us to write the point in terms of the angle Q the line segment makes with the positive X-axis and the distance R of the point from the origin as:

$$X = R*\cos(\Theta)$$
$$Y = R*\sin(\Theta)$$

or, inversely,

$$R = \mathrm{sqrt}(X^2 + Y^2)$$
$$\Theta = \arctan(Y/X)$$

where Θ is the value between 0 and 2π that is in the proper quadrant to match the signs of X and Y. The representation (R, Θ) is known as the *polar coordinates* for the point. This is illustrated in the left-hand image in Figure 4.10.

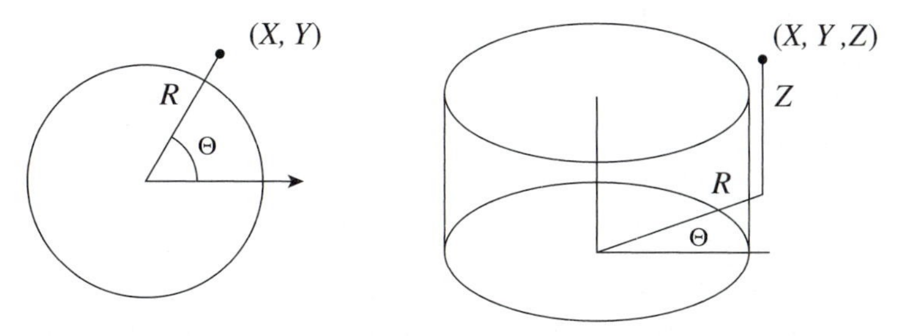

Figure 4.10 Polar coordinates (*left*) and cylindrical coordinates (*right*).

There are two alternatives to Cartesian coordinates for 3D space. *Cylindrical coordinates* add a third linear dimension to 2D polar coordinates, giving the angle between the *X-Z* plane and the plane through the *Z*-axis and the point, along with the usual *Z*-coordinate value of the point. Points in cylindrical coordinates are represented as (R, Θ, Z) with R and Θ as above and with the *Z*-value as in rectangular coordinates. The right-hand image of Figure 4.10 shows the structure of cylindrical coordinates for 3D space.

Cylindrical coordinates are an extension of the 2D polar coordinate model to 3D space. They are not particularly common in graphics modeling, but they can be very helpful when appropriate. For example, if you have a planar object that has to remain upright in a vertical direction but must rotate to face the viewer in a scene as the viewer moves around the scene, then it would be appropriate to model the object's rotation using cylindrical coordinates. An example of such an object is a *billboard* and is discussed in Chapter 8. Spherical coordinates can be very useful when you want to control motion to achieve smooth changes in angles or distances around a point.

Spherical coordinates represent 3D points in terms much as latitude and longitude represent points on the surface of the Earth. The *latitude* of a point is the angle from the equator to the point and ranges from 90° south to 90° north, or −90° to 90°. The *longitude* of a point is the angle from the "prime meridian" to the point, where the prime meridian is determined by the half-plane that runs from the center of the Earth through the Greenwich Observatory just east of London, England. This runs from 0° to 360°. The latitude and longitude values uniquely determine any point on the surface of the Earth. In addition, any point in space can be represented relative to the Earth by determining the point on the Earth's surface met by a line from the point to the center of the Earth, and then identifying the point by the latitude and longitude of the point on the Earth's surface and the distance to the point from the center of the Earth. Spherical coordinates are based on the same principle: Start with a unit sphere centered at the origin, with the sphere having a polar axis and a prime meridian. For a point P in space, determine the latitude F (angle north or south from the equatorial plane) and longitude Q (angle from the prime meridian through the diameter of the sphere perpendicular to the equatorial plane) of the point where the half-line from the origin to P meets the sphere, and determine the distance R from the origin to P. The spherical coordinates of the point P are then $(\mathrm{R}, \Theta, \Phi)$.

It is straightforward to convert spherical coordinates to 3D Cartesian coordinates. The relationship between spherical and rectangular coordinates is shown in Figure 4.11 with the

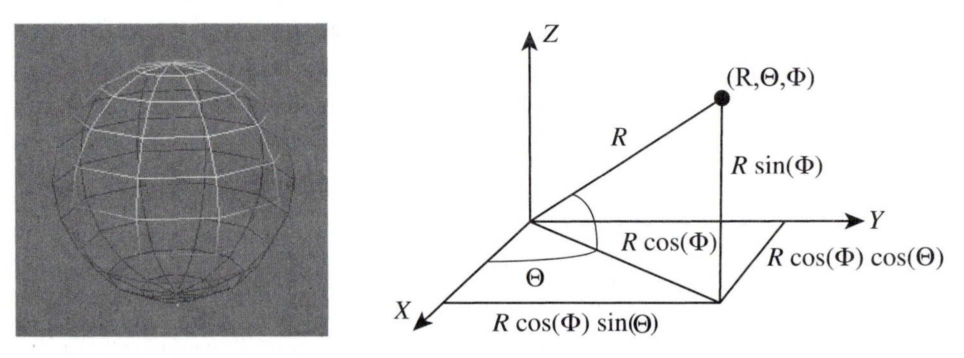

Figure 4.11 Spherical coordinates (*left*) the conversion from spherical to rectangular coordinates (*right*).

Z-coordinate as the vertical axis, so we have the following conversion equations from polar to rectangular coordinates:

$$x = R\cos(\Phi)\cos(\Theta)$$
$$y = R\cos(\Phi)\sin(\Theta)$$
$$z = R\sin(\Phi)$$

Converting from rectangular to spherical coordinates is also straightforward. Again referring to Figure 4.11, we see that R is the diagonal of a rectangle and that the angles can be described in terms of the trigonometric functions based on the sides. So we have the equations

$$R = \mathrm{sqrt}(x^2 + y^2 + z^2)$$
$$\Phi = \mathrm{Arcsin}(z/R)$$
$$\Theta = \arctan(y/x)$$

Note that the inverse trigonometric function is the principal value for the longitude (Φ), and the angle for the latitude (Θ) is chosen between 0° and 360° so that the sine and cosine of Θ match the algebraic sign (+ or −) of the X and Y coordinates. Figure 4.11 depicts a sphere showing latitude and longitude lines and containing an inscribed rectangular coordinate system, as well as the figure needed to make the conversion between spherical and rectangular coordinates.

Collision Detection

There are times when we need to know whether two objects meet in order to apply the logic of a model, particularly when the logic involves moving and interacting with objects in physical space. Collision detection involves a little extra modeling and several stages of logic, and we outline several techniques here without too much detail because there isn't any one right way to do it.

The first thing you must ask yourself is exactly what kind of collision you want to detect, and what objects in your model could collide. You will see shortly that a lot of logic is involved in this process, and the two best ways to speed up the process are to avoid making tests when you can and to make the simplest possible tests when you must test at all.

When you test for collisions, you need to know the actual coordinates of various points in 3D world space. You can track the world space or eye space coordinates of a point in model space as you apply the modeling transformation to an object, but this requires computation and works against the high-level graphics approach we have been taking. But your API may have the capability to give you the world coordinates of a point with a simple inquiry function. In OpenGL, for example, the function `glGetFloatv(GL_MODELVIEW_MATRIX)` allows you to get the current value of the modelview matrix at any point; this returns a column-major array of 16 real values that represents the matrix to be applied to your model vertex coordinates at that point. If you treat this as a 4×4 matrix and multiply it by the original model coordinates of any vertex, you get the coordinates of the transformed vertex in 3D eye space. This will give you a consistent space in which to make your tests.

To simplify collision detection, think of *possible* collisions instead of actual collisions. Quick rejection of possible collisions will make a big difference in speeding up handling actual collisions. One standard approach is to use a substitute object instead of the real object, such as a sphere or a box that surrounds the object closely. These are called *bounding objects*, such as bounding spheres or bounding boxes, and they are chosen to make collision testing easier. A bounding sphere is a sphere that is centered on the object and contains the object; it is specified by a center and a radius. A bounding box is the space bounded by six planes, two parallel to each axis, and containing the object. It is easy to see if two spheres collide, because this happens precisely when the distance between their centers is less than the sum of the radii of the spheres. It is also easy to see if two bounding boxes intersect because in this case, you can test the relative values of the larger and smaller boundaries of each box in each direction. Of course, you must be careful that the bounding objects are defined in 3D eye space, or your modeling transformations may distort the bounding object and make the tests more difficult. To do this you will need to see how the original object definition in its modeling space is changed as you go to eye space.

As you test for collisions, you start by testing for collisions between the bounding objects of your original objects. When you find a possible collision, you move to more detailed tests based on the actual objects. We assume that your objects are defined by a polygonal boundary, and in fact we will assume that the boundary is composed of triangles. Thus the next set of tests is for collisions between triangles. Unless you know which triangles in one object are closest to which triangles in another object, you may need to test all possible pairs of triangles, one in each object, so we start with a quick rejection of triangles.

Just as we can tell when two bounding objects are too far apart to collide, we can tell when a triangle in one object is too far from the bounding object for the other object to collide. If that bounding object is a sphere, you can see whether the coordinates of the triangle's vertices (in world space) are farther from that sphere than the longest side of the triangle. If you have more detailed information on the triangle, such as its circumcenter, you can test for the circumcenter to be farther from the sphere than the radius of the circumcircle. The *circumcenter* of a triangle is the common intersection of the three perpendicular bisectors of the sides of the circle; the *circumcircle* is the circle with center at the circumcenter that goes through the vertices of the triangle. See Figure 4.12.

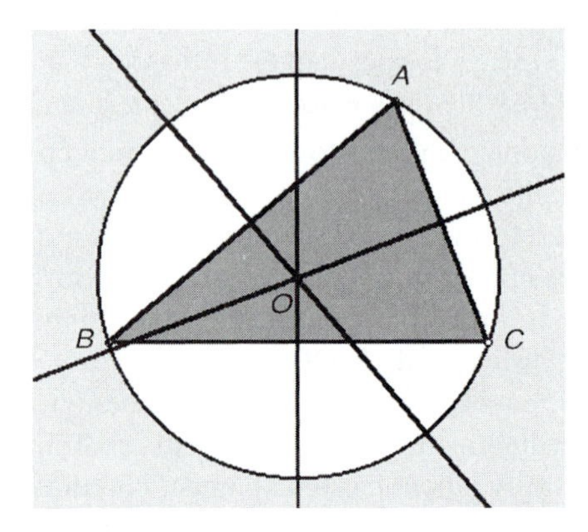

Figure 4.12 The circumcenter and circumcircle of a triangle.

If we cannot rule out triangle collisions, we must consider the possible intersection of a triangle in one object with a triangle in the other object. The simplest test is whether one triangle meets the plane defined by the other triangle. Let the plane of the second triangle be given by $f(x, y, z) = Ax + By + Cz + D = 0$. If this function has the same sign for all the vertices of the first triangle, then they cannot intersect the plane. If a triangle intersects the plane of the other triangle, we work with each line segment bounding one triangle and with the plane containing the other triangle, and we compute the point where the line meets the plane of the triangle. If the line segment is given by the parametric equation $Q_0 + t(Q_1 - Q_0)$ and the plane of the triangle is given as above, we can readily calculate the value of the parameter t that gives the intersection of the line and the plane. If this value of t is not between 0 and 1, then the segment does not intersect the plane, and we are finished. If the segment does intersect the plane, we need to see if the intersection is within the triangle. This is shown in Figure 4.13.

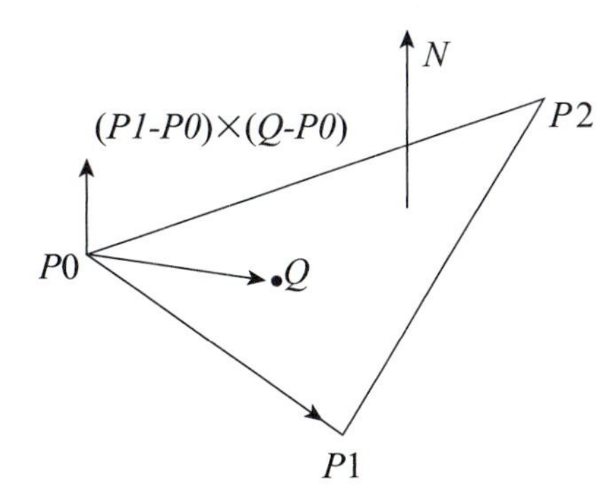

Figure 4.13 A point inside a triangle.

Once we know that the line is close enough to have a potential intersection, we move on to test whether the point where the line meets the plane lies inside the triangle, as shown in Figure 4.13. Assuming that the triangle has a counterclockwise orientation, any point inside the triangle is to the left (that is, counterclockwise) from the oriented edge for each edge of the triangle. This can be characterized by the cross product of the edge vector and the vector from the vertex to the point; if this cross product has the same orientation as the normal vector to the triangle for each vertex, then the point is inside the triangle. If the point at the intersection of the line segment and the plane of the triangle plane is Q, this means that we must have all of the relations

$$N \cdot ((P1-P0) \times (Q-P0)) > 0$$
$$N \cdot ((P2-P1) \times (Q-P1)) > 0$$
$$N \cdot ((P0-P2) \times (Q-P2)) > 0$$

to express the interior relation between the point and each edge of the triangle.

Higher Dimensions?

While our perceptions and experience are limited to three dimensions, there is no such limit to the kind of information we may want to display with our graphics system. Of course, we cannot deal with these higher dimensions directly, so we will have other techniques to display higher-dimensional information. There are some techniques for developing three-dimensional information by projecting or combining higher-dimensional data, and some techniques for adding extra non-spatial information to 3D information in order to represent higher dimensions. We will discuss some ideas for higher-dimensional representations in Chapter 9 in terms of visual communications and science applications.

Summary

This chapter presented some parts of 3D analytic geometry that can be very useful when doing computer graphics. Whether you are laying out the geometry of objects, defining other properties such as normal vectors, or defining the motion of objects in your scene or the relationship between them, it is very helpful to have experience with the mathematical or geometric behaviors that let you represent them so that your program can manipulate them effectively. With the tools from this chapter, you will be able to do this comfortably and fluently.

Questions

1. If you have any two Cartesian coordinate systems defined in 2D space, show how you can convert either one into the other by applying a scaling, rotation, and translation to either one, where the operations are defined relative to the target coordinate system.
2. Can you do the same as asked in the previous question when you have two coordinate systems in 3D space? Why or why not? (Hint: Consider right-handed and left-handed coordinate systems.) Can you do this if you use a new kind of transformation, called a reflection, that reverses the sign of one particular coordinate while retaining the value of any other coordinate? What might the 3×3 matrix for a reflection look like?
3. Pick any two distinct points in 3D space and do the hand calculations to write the parametric equations for a line segment that joins the points. How do you modify these equations in case you want a ray that starts at one point and goes through the other? How do you modify them in case you want the equations for a complete line through the two points?

Exercises

1. For several pairs of vectors, compute their dot and cross products as in the chapter. Do this particularly for some pairs of vectors that are parallel and some that are orthogonal. Also define some vectors for which you know the angle between them, and verify the trigonometric relationships in the dot and cross products.
2. Write the matrices for two rotations around different axes or for a rotation and a translation. Model the composition of these transformations by multiplying the matrices. Show that the composition is not commutative by showing that these two matrix products are different.
3. Write the complete set of functions for converting among Cartesian, cylindrical, and polar coordinate systems. Make these general so you can use them as utilities if you want to model an object using any of these coordinates.
4. In Chapter 2 you saw a spherical-coordinate modeling approach to the sphere using quad strips and triangle fans. Implement the sphere with this approach, writing a function `scvertex()` that converts the spherical coordinates to Cartesian coordinates and then calling `glVertex()`.
5. Model a problem using polar or cylindrical coordinates and create a display for the problem by building triangles, quads, or polygons in these coordinates and converting to standard OpenGL geometry using the coordinate system conversions in the previous exercise.

Experiments

1. In case you have an object with dimension higher than three, there are many ways you might be able to project it into 3D space so it could be viewed. For example, if you look at the 4D "cube"—the object in 4D space with 16 vertices, and with each component of each vertex being either 0 or 1—and project it to 3D space, you can get an image such as the following:

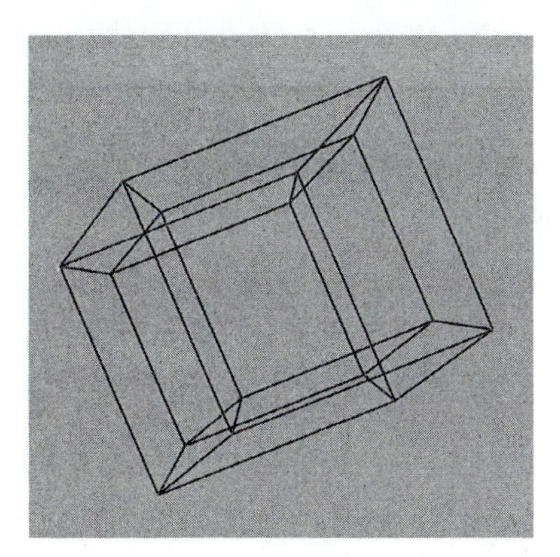

   Work out several ways that you could project a 4D object into 3D space by working with the coordinates of each vertex; for each way you come up with, implement a view of the 4D cube with that projection.

2. Write a function that implements the "point inside a triangle" test and apply this function to test whether a particular line of your choice intersects a particular triangle of your choice, all in 3D space. Extend this function to test whether two triangles intersect.

5

Color and Blending

This chapter describes how you specify and use color in computer graphics. We introduce the RGB model for specifying color, the most common model for digital color work, along with the concept of luminance of colors so you can work with persons who have color vision deficiencies. We discuss two other color models, HLS and HSV, which are sometimes useful for color specification, and we give the conversion functions from these models to RGB. We give the RGBA extension to the RGB model that permits color blending and show how that can be used to simulate transparency, and we introduce the use of color anaglyphs as a color-based 3D viewing technique. We then show how color is implemented for OpenGL graphics programming. When you finish this chapter, you will be able to include color in your graphics programming to make it more interesting and informative.

Introduction

Color is a fundamental concept in computer graphics. We need to be able to define for our graphics colors that represent good approximations of real-world colors, and we need to be able to manipulate colors as we develop our applications. We can get color in our image in two ways: by directly setting the color for our objects, or by defining material properties of objects and having the color generated by a lighting model. This chapter covers only direct colors of objects, and color from lighting models is saved for Chapter 6.

The human eye and perception of light are much more complex than the models we see in standard computer graphics. The retina of the eye contains two types of cells that respond to light. One type of cell, the *rods,* is sensitive to brightness but not to color. Rods are densest in areas outside the center of the retina and are the main source of vision in low light. They do not contribute to sharp vision because they are not wired individually to neurons. The other type of cell, the *cones,* are of three kinds, each kind sensitive to a different wavelength of light. Each kind gives us the sense of one of the colors red, green, or blue, and this is the source of the tristimulus concept for color. These cells are clustered around the center of the retina, called the *fovea*. Each of these cells has its own neuron in the visual system, and so they are able to distinguish fine detail. The technology of computer graphics uses pure red, green, and blue colors on the display surface to stimulate the three kinds of cones in the eye and to simulate the appearance of objects in the real world.

It would be simplistic, however, to assume that the RGB display can actually represent the colors around us. Objects reflect a whole spectrum of colors, not just the pure wavelengths of the RGB phosphors, and we respond to the spectra in complex ways. You may think of our color models in terms of sampling, as we saw that a display on an integer-coordinate screen is a sample of the real-valued geometry we define. Thus the colors we produce are quite susceptible to aliasing issues, just as the geometry is. We need to realize that the color models we use in this book are simply ways to approximate the colors around us.

One result of color aliasing comes from a peculiar behavior of the neurons in the human visual system. While we talk about single neurons above, what we really perceive comes from the whole network of neurons. Among the behaviors of the network is an inhibition effect in which a strong stimulus in one area inhibits the effect of a stimulus in nearby areas. This is called *lateral inhibition,* and it is the cause of many of the visual illusions (see Figure 5.19) and Mach banding (see Figure 5.9) you will see in this chapter. There isn't a lot you can do about this, but you should be aware of it as you design your images.

There are many ways to specify colors, but all depend principally on the tristimulus nature of the three kinds of cones in the retina of the eye. This fundamental fact of three kinds of stimulus is maintained by all the color models in computer graphics. The usual color model for computer graphics is the RGB (Red, Green, Blue) color model that matches in software the physical design of computer monitors, which are made with a pattern of three kinds of phosphor that emit red, green, and blue light when they are excited by an electron beam. There are a number of other models of color, and we discuss a few of these in this chapter. However, we refer you to textbooks and other sources, especially [Foley *et al.*], for additional discussions on color models and for more complete information on converting color representations from one model to another.

Because the computer monitor uses three kinds of phosphor and each phosphor emits light levels based on the energy of the electron beam that is directed at it, a common approach is to specify a color by the level of each of the three primaries. These levels are a proportion of the maximum light energy that is available for that primary, so an RGB color is specified by a triple (r, g, b) where each of the three components represents the amount of that particular component in the color and where the ordering is the red-green-blue that is implicit in the name RGB. In this book we specify each component by the proportion of the maximum intensity we want for the color. This proportion for each primary is represented by a real number between 0.0 and 1.0, inclusive, that represents the proportion of the available color of that primary hue that is desired for the pixel. The higher the value for a component, the brighter the light in that color is. Black is represented by (0.0, 0.0, 0.0) and white by (1.0, 1.0, 1.0), and the RGB primaries are represented by red (1.0, 0.0, 0.0), green (0.0, 1.0, 0.0), and blue (0.0, 0.0, 1.0), respectively—that is, colors that are fully bright in a single primary component and dark in the other primaries. Other colors are a mix of the three primaries as needed.

Some graphics APIs, particularly older ones, may use an integer-based color representation. In these, each color component is represented by an integer that depends on the color depth for the system. For example, if you have eight bits of color for each component, which was a common property, the integer values would be in the range 0 to 255. However, a real number approach is used more commonly in current graphics APIs because it is more device-independent and the trend in graphics cards is to use 16- to 32-bit floating-point values for R, G, and B. This distinction may come up in the details of color operations in your API, but you can usually ignore it. The color-generation process itself is surprisingly complex because the monitor or other viewing device must generate perceptually linear values. These representation and hardware issues are hidden from the API programmer, however, and are translated from the API representations of the colors, allowing API-based programs to work very much the same across a wide range of platforms.

In addition to the three color components of light, modern graphics systems add a fourth component called the *alpha channel* that represents the opacity of material. As with color, this is represented by a real number between 0.0 (no opacity—completely transparent) and 1.0 (completely opaque—no transparency). This lets you create objects that show their background when drawn, and it can be very valuable when you want to see more than just the things at the front of a scene. This is called *alpha blending*. Alpha blending works by compositing the new object with whatever is already present in the Z-buffer, and models transparency for an object only when compared with things that are already drawn. If you want to create an image with many levels of transparency, you need to pay careful attention to the sequence in which you draw your objects, drawing them in order from farthest to nearest to get the correct attenuation of the colors of background objects. This is discussed in more detail later in this chapter.

Principles

Specifying Colors for Geometry

The basic principle for using simple color is straightforward: Once you have specified a color, all the geometry defined after that point will be drawn in the specified color until the color is changed. This means that if you want different parts of your scene to be presented in different colors, you will need to re-specify the color for each distinct part. This is not difficult, but it requires attention.

In terms of the scene graph, color is part of the appearance node that accompanies each geometry node and is our first appearance issue. When you write your code from the scene graph, you need to write the code that manages the appearance before you write the code for the geometry so that you will have the correct appearance information in the system before the geometry is drawn.

Color can be represented in the appearance node any way you wish. In the following sections we discuss three different kinds of color models, and in principle you can represent color with any of these. Because most graphics APIs support RGB color, if you use any other color model you may have to convert your color specifications to RGB before you can write the appearance code. Later in this chapter we include code to do two such conversions.

The RGB Cube

The RGB color model is a geometric presentation of the color space. That space is represented by a cube consisting of all points (r, g, b) with each of r, g, and b being a real number between 0 and 1. Because of the easy analogy between color triples and points in 3D space, every point in the unit cube is identified with a color whose red, green, and blue values are the *r*, *g*, and *b* coordinates of the point. This identification is very natural, and most people in computer graphics think of the color space and the color cube interchangeably.

The RGB cube is shown in diagram form in Figure 5.1 and again from two points of view in color form in Figure 5.1 in the color insert, from the white vertex and from the black vertex, so that you can see the full range of colors on the surface of the cube. As you can see from the figure, the three vertices closest to the white vertex are the cyan, magenta, and yellow vertices, while the three vertices closest to the black vertex are the red, green, and blue vertices. This shows a key feature of the RGB color model, with the colors getting lighter as the amounts of the primary colors increase. Of course, all points interior to the cube also correspond to colors. For example, the center diagonal of the RGB cube from (0, 0, 0) to (1, 1, 1) corresponds to the colors with equal amounts of each primary; these are the gray colors which provide the neutral backgrounds that are very useful in presenting colorful images.

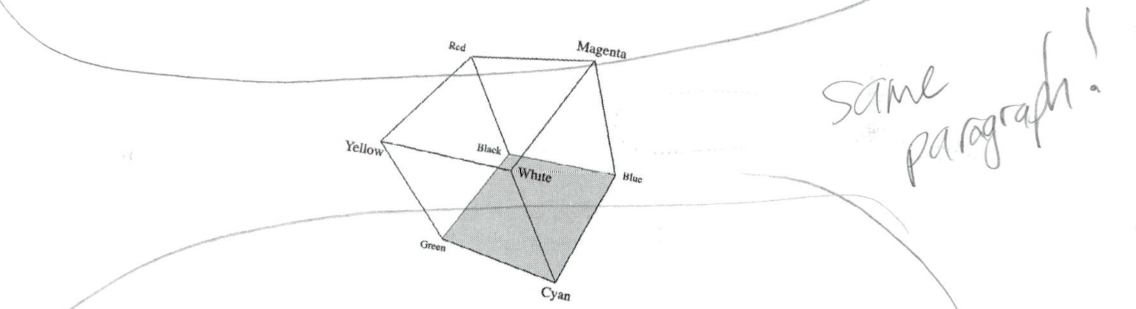

Figure 5.1 Diagram of the RGB cube. See the color figure in the color insert.

This figure suggests the nature of the RGB cube, but the entire RGB cube is more informative. It is shown from two points of view in Figure 5.1, from the white vertex and from the black vertex, so that you can see the full range of colors on the surface of the cube. As you can see from the figure, the three vertices closest to the white vertex are the cyan, magenta, and yellow vertices, while the three vertices closest to the black vertex are the red, green, and blue vertices. This shows a key feature of the RGB color model, with the colors getting lighter as the amounts of the primary colors increase. Of course, all points interior to the cube also correspond to colors. For example, the center diagonal of the RGB cube from (0, 0, 0) to (1, 1, 1) corresponds to the colors with equal amounts of each primary; these are the gray colors which provide the neutral backgrounds that are very useful in presenting colorful images.

As an example of specifying colors using the RGB system, let's look along the line in the RGB cube from yellow, with color (1, 1, 0), to blue, with color (0, 0, 1). These would have color (*a*, *a*, 1–*a*) for any value of *a* between 0 and 1. In Figure 5.2 we see six of these colors with values of *a* of 0, .2, .4, .6, .8, and 1, from left to right. Notice that the colors change as the yellow (that is, red and green) gets brighter and the blue gets dimmer (see the color section to see the figure in color). The colors are presented against a 0.5 gray background with no space between them, and you should pay particular attention to the edges between the colors because they show the visual effect of two adjacent, nearly equal colors that we discuss later in this chapter as Mach bands.

Figure 5.2 A sequence of six colors between yellow and blue. See the figure in the color insert.

Luminance and Color Deficiency

Luminance of a color is the color's brightness or intensity, without regard for its actual color. This concept is particularly meaningful for emissive colors on the screen, because in this case luminance actually is the amount of light emitted from the screen. For RGB images, luminance is quite easy to compute. Of the three primaries, green is the brightest, and so it contributes most to the luminance of a color. Red is the next brightest, and blue is the least bright. The actual luminance will vary from system to system and even from display device to display device because of differences in the way color numbers are translated into voltages and because of the way the phosphors respond. For standard TV-based displays, we are relatively accurate if we use the luminance formula

```
luminance = 0.30*red + 0.59*green + 0.11*blue
```

so the overall brightness ratios are approximately 6:3:1 for green:red:blue. If you want more precise factors, the red, green, and blue coefficients are .299, .587., and .114, respectively. For the HDTV standard, the factors are a little different, and green dominates even more; they are .2125, .7154, and .0721, respectively.

To see the effects of constant luminance, we can pass a plane $0.30R + 0.59G + 0.11B + t$ through the RGB color space and examine the plane it exposes in the color cube as the parameter t varies. An example of this is shown in Figure 5.3 but you will need to see the figure in the color insert. You will see that this plane in the grayscale figure isn't exactly uniform, though; the conversion to grayscale seems to show green as even brighter than the formula would indicate. We do not give this as an experiment at the end of this chapter, though there are others that deal with luminance; you might see what results you get if you do this on your system.

As you work with color, you must keep in mind that a significant part of your audience may have difficulties distinguishing certain colors or color combinations. Between 8 and 10 percent of Caucasian males have a color vision deficiency; this number is about 4 percent for non-Caucasian males and only about 0.5 percent for females. These persons confuse colors, whatever kind of display is used, but most can distinguish colors whose luminance is different even if they have difficulty distinguishing differences in chroma. If your audience includes significant numbers of Caucasian males, make sure that elements of your image that your audience needs to distinguish are presented with colors having different luminance, not just different chroma.

Luminance is also important because part of the interpretation of an image deals with the brightness of its parts, and you need to understand how to use colors with the right luminance to ensure that brightness is handled correctly. For example, in the discussion of color ramps later in

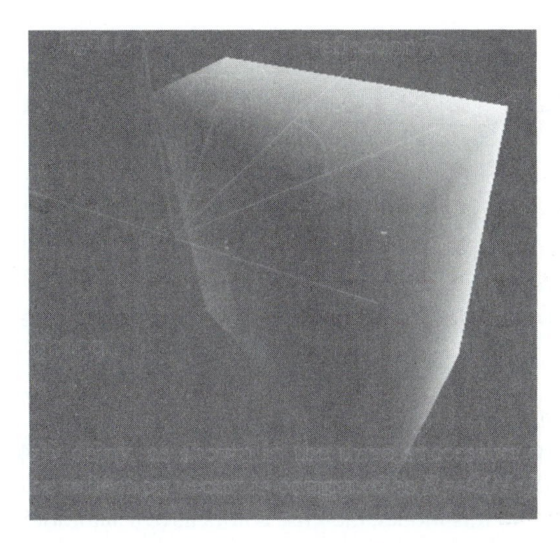

Figure 5.3 A plane of constant luminance in the RGB cube in grayscale. See the color figure in the color insert.

this chapter we will use luminance information to get color scales that are approximately uniform in having the brightness of the color show the numerical value the color represents.

Other Color Models

There are times when the RGB color model is not the easiest or most natural to use. When we want to capture a particular color, few of us think of the color in terms of the proportions of red, green, and blue needed to create it. Other color models give us different ways to think about color that may make it more intuitive to specify a color. The RGB model also does not fit the reality of color production. We need to have a wider range of ways to model color.

A more intuitive approach to color is given by two other color models: the HSV (Hue-Saturation-Value) and HLS (Hue-Lightness-Saturation) models. These models represent color as a *hue* (intuitively, a descriptive variation on a standard color such as red, magenta, blue, cyan, green, or yellow) that is modified by setting its *value* or *lightness* (a property of the color's darkness or lightness) and its *saturation* (a property of the color's purity). This lets us find numerical ways to say "The color should be a dark, vivid reddish-orange" by using a hue that is to the red side of yellow, has a relatively low value or lightness, and has a high saturation.

Let's look first at the HSV model. Just as there is the cube model for RGB color space, there is a geometric model for HSV color space: a cone with a flat top, as shown in the diagram form in Figure 5.4 and, in more detail, in the color figure of the same number in the color insert. The distance around the circle in degrees represents the hue, starting with red at 0, moving to green at 120 and blue at 240. The distance from the vertical axis to the outside edge represents the saturation, or the amount of the primary colors in the particular color. This varies from 0 at the center (no saturation, only gray) to 1 at the edge (fully saturated bright colors). The vertical axis represents the value, from 0 at the bottom (black) to 1 at the top (white). So an HSV color is given by a triple representing a point in or on the cone, and the "dark, vivid reddish-orange" color would be something like (40.0, 1.0, 0.7). Code to display this geometry interactively is discussed at the end of this chapter.

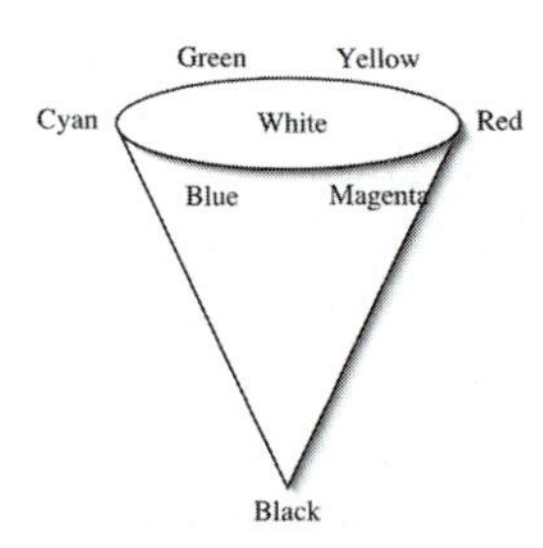

Figure 5.4 Diagram of the HSV color model. See the color figure in the color insert.

The shape of the HSV model space can be confusing. The top surface represents all the lighter colors based on the primaries, because colors getting lighter look the same as colors becoming less saturated. The model tapers to a point at the bottom because there is no noticeable color variation near black. In this model, the gray colors have a saturation of 0 and are on the vertical center line of the cone. Their hue is meaningless, but it still must be included.

In the HLS color model, shown in diagram form in Figure 5.5 and in color form in the color insert, the geometry is much the same as for the HSV model, but the top surface is stretched into a second cone. Hue and saturation have the same meaning as HSV, but lightness replaces value and the brightest colors have a lightness of 0.5. The rationale for the dual cone is that as colors get lighter, they lose their distinctions of hue and saturation, much as colors behave as they get darker. The HLS model comes closer to the language of *tints* and *tones* used when describing paints, with the strongest colors at lightness 0.5 and becoming lighter (tints) as the lightness increases, and becoming darker (tones) as the lightness decreases. Just as in the HSV case above, the grays form the center line of the cone with saturation 0, and their hue is meaningless.

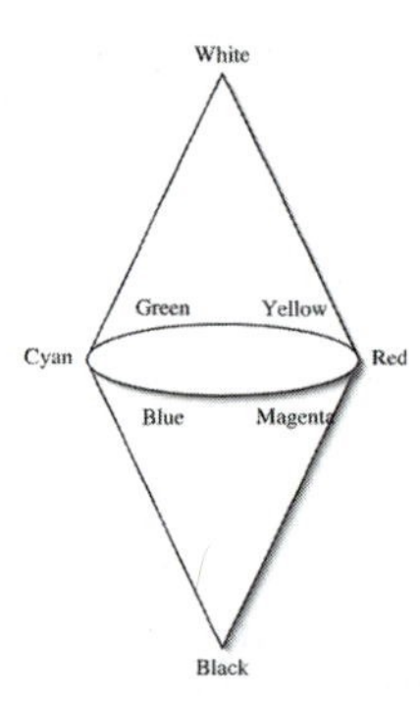

Figure 5.5 Diagram of the HLS double cone color model. See the color figure in the color insert.

The top and bottom views of the HLS double cone look just like those of the HSV single cone, but the side views of the HLS double cone are quite different. Figure 5.5 shows the HLS double cone from the three primary-color sides: red, green, and blue, respectively. Notice that because of the approximate 120° coverage of each image, the edges of adjacent images match up. The views from the top or bottom are exactly those of the HSV cone. The images in the figure do not show the geometric shape as well as you may like; the code examples later in this chapter will show you how this can be presented interactively.

There are relatively simple functions that convert a color defined in one space into the same color as defined in another space. The functions to convert HSV to RGB and to convert HLS to RGB are included in the code discussions later in this chapter about producing these figures. The full set of conversion functions is found in [FO].

The color models above are based on colors seen on a computer monitor or other device where light is emitted to the eye. These are called *emissive* colors, and they work by adding light at different wavelengths as different phosphors in screen cells emit light. Most color presented by programming comes from a screen, so this is the main way we think about color in computer graphics. This is not the only way that color is presented to us, however. When you read these pages in print, the colors you see are generated by light that is reflected from the paper through the inks on the page. These can be called *transmissive* colors, and they operate by subtracting colors from the light being reflected from the page. This is a totally different process and needs separate treatment. Figure 5.6 illustrates this principle, shown best in the color insert. The way the RGB add to produce CMY and eventually white shows why emissive colors are sometimes called *additive* colors, while the way CMY produce RGB and eventually black shows why transmissive colors are sometimes called *subtractive* colors.

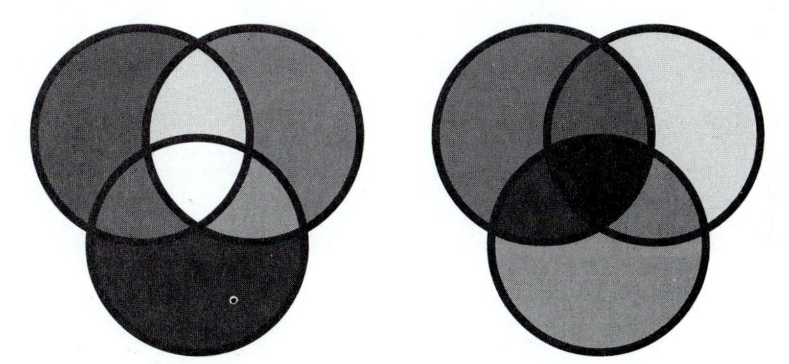

Figure 5.6 Emissive colors (*left*) and transmissive colors (*right*). See the figure in the color insert.

Transmissive color processes use inks or films that transmit only certain colors while filtering out all others. The primary values for transmissive color are cyan (which transmits both blue and green), magenta (which transmits both blue and red), and yellow (which transmits both red and green). In principle, if you use all three inks (cyan, magenta, and yellow) you should have no light transmitted and so you should see only black. In practice, actual materials are not perfect and allow a little off-color light to pass, so using all three makes a dark and muddy gray (called "process black" by printers); you need to add extra black to parts that are intended to be really black. This cyan-magenta-yellow-black model is called *CMYK color* and is the basis for printing and other transmissive processes. It is used to create color separations that combine to form full-

Figure 5.7 Color separations for printing. See the figure in the color insert.

color images as shown in Figure 5.7 in the color insert (shown as black and white in the text because of color limitations), which shows a full-color image (top) and the sets of black, cyan, yellow, and magenta separations (middle and bottom, clockwise from top left) that are used to create plates to print the color image. We will not consider the CMYK model further here because its use is in printing and similar technologies, not in graphics programming. We will meet this approach to color again in Chapter 15 when we discuss graphics hardcopy, however.

Color Depth

The color models we have seen are device-independent; they assume that colors are represented by real numbers, so an infinite number of colors are potentially available to be displayed. This is, of course, not correct for real devices. Instead, graphics devices use color capabilities based on the amount of memory allocated to holding color information.

The basic model for computer graphics is based on screen displays and is called *direct color.* For each pixel on the screen we store its color information directly in the image buffer. The number of bits of storage we use for each pixel is called the *color depth* for the device. It is probably most common to use eight bits of color for each of the R, G, and B primaries, so we talk about 24-bit color. This is not universal, however; some systems use fewer or more bits per pixel to store colors, and not all systems use an equal number of bits for each color. Graphics systems now often use 36-bit or 48-bit color, and some are as high as 128-bit color. However, some image formats do not allow greater depth; the GIF format, for example, specifies 8-bit indexed color in its standard [MUR].

As we noted earlier, *color aliasing* comes from representing real-world colors with only three primaries. But this is made worse by the limitation on the number of distinct values that each primary can assume, as is the case if your system has a limited color depth. The exact color from your color computations may not be displayed on the screen but is aliased by being rounded to a value that can be represented with the color depth of your system. This is especially true if you have a limited number of colors in the system. This can lead to serious effects called *Mach bands,* shown in Figure 5.8. Mach bands occur when you have regions of solid color that differ only slightly, or when you have piecewise linear intensity that changes across a polygon boundary, and are common when you have a limited number of colors. The human eye is exceptionally able to see edges, possibly as an artifact of evolution, and will identify even a small change in color as an edge. These perceived edges can disrupt the perception of a smooth image. Look carefully for Mach banding in your work, and when you see it, use antialiasing techniques from geometric antialiasing, applied to color, to

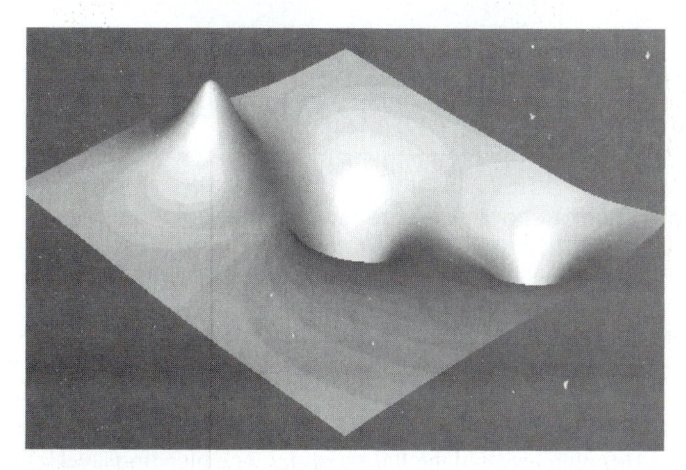

Figure 5.8 An image showing mach banding.

make it less visible. Figure 5.8 shows a small image created with a reduced color depth that contains some Mach bands, most visible in the tan areas toward the front of the image.

Color Gamut

Color is limited not only by the number of colors that can be displayed but also by limitations in the technology of display devices. No matter what display technology you use—phosphors on a video-based screen, ink on paper, or LCD cells on a flat panel—the technology can present only a limited range of colors. This is true of all color technologies, such as print, video, or color film. The range of a device is called its *color gamut,* and we must realize that the gamut of our devices limits our ability to represent certain kinds of images. A significant discussion of the color gamut of different devices is beyond the scope of the first course in computer graphics, but it is important to realize that there are serious limitations on the colors you can produce on any device. Figure 5.9, best seen in the color insert, shows the most commonly used color reference space, the 1931 CIE space, along with three specific color points for R, G, and B values and the triangular space that is the color gamut for a monitor with these values. (Note that this is only an approximation of the actual color space because it is, itself, printed on a device with a limited color gamut.)

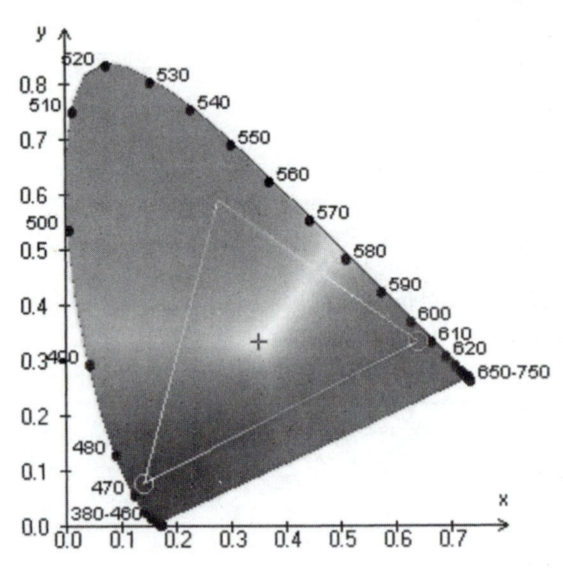

Figure 5.9 The CIE color space. See the figure in the color insert.

Color Blending with the Alpha Channel

In most graphics APIs, color can be represented as more than just a RGB triple; it can also include a blending level (sometimes thought of as a transparency level) so that anything with this color will have a color blending property. Color is represented by a quadruple (r,g,b,a), and the color model that includes blending is called the *RGBA model*. The blending level a for a color is called the *alpha value,* and its value is a number between 0.0 and 1.0, usually representing opacity instead of transparency. That is, if you use standard kinds of blending functions and if the alpha value is 1.0, the color is completely opaque, but in the same situation if the alpha value is 0.0, the color is completely transparent. The alpha channel was invented to permit image compositing [POR] in which an image could be laid over another image and have part of the underlying image show through. So while we may say (or sometimes even think) "transparent" we really mean *blended.* Blending compares the color of a pixel being drawn with the current color of that pixel in the color buffer and sets a color for the pixel by blending the object color and the current color according to whatever blending function you choose. A common blending function is to take the simple average of the two colors. This blending capability builds up an image by merging the colors of parts in the order in which they are rendered, and we will see in an example later in this chapter that the results can be quite different if objects are received in a different order.

This difference between blended and transparent colors can be very significant. If we think of transparent colors, we are modeling the logical equivalent of colored glass. This kind of material embodies transmissive, not emissive, colors, because only certain wavelengths are passed through while the rest are absorbed. But this is not the model for the alpha value; blended colors operate by averaging emissive RGB colors, which is the opposite of the transmissive model of transparency. The difference can be important in creating the effects you need in an image. There is an additional issue to blending because averaging colors in RGB space may not result in the intermediate colors you would expect; the RGB color model is one of the worst color models for perceptual blending, but we have no real choice in most graphics APIs.

Modeling Transparency with Blending

Blending has some challenges if we want to model transparency. To begin, we note that if something is intended to seem transparent, you must be able to see things that are behind it. This suggests a simple first step: If you are trying to model transparency with blending, it is important to allow the drawing of things that are behind other objects. To do that, you might want to try drawing all opaque objects (objects with alpha component equal to 1.10) before drawing the things you want to seem transparent, turn off the depth test while drawing items with blended colors, and turn the depth test back on again after drawing them.

But it may not be enough to do this, and in fact trying to get the effect of transparency in this way may lead to more confusing images than leaving the depth test intact. Assume that you have three objects to draw, as described in Figure 5.10. Assume that the objects are numbered 1, 2, and 3, that they have colors C_1, C_2, and C_3, that you draw them in the sequence 1, 2, and 3, that they line up from the eye but have a totally white background, and that each color has alpha = 0.5. Assume further that we are not using the depth buffer and that the blend function is standard. What color will be drawn to the screen where these objects lie?

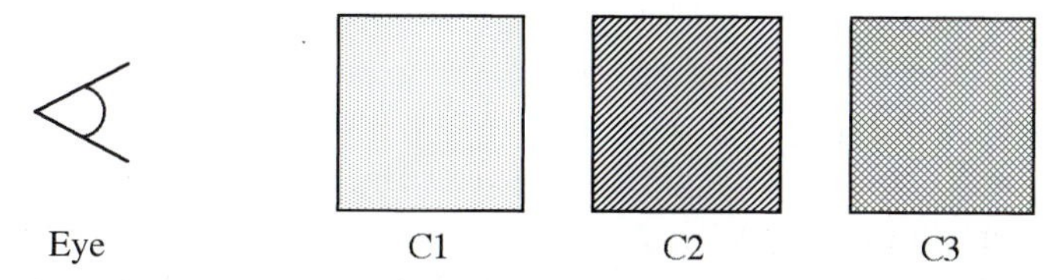

Figure 5.10 The sequence for drawing the objects.

When we draw the first object, the frame buffer will have color C_1; no other coloring is involved. When we draw the second object on top of the first, the frame buffer will have color $0.5*C_1 + 0.5*C_2$, because the foreground (C_2) has alpha 0.5 and the background (C_1) is included with weight $0.5 = 1 - 0.5$. Finally, when the third object with color C_3 is drawn on top of the others, the color will be

$$0.5*C_3 + 0.5*(0.5*C_1 + 0.5*C_2), \text{ or } 0.5*C_3 + 0.25*C_2 + 0.25*C_1.$$

That is, the color of the most recent object drawn is emphasized much more than the color of the other objects. This shows up clearly in the right-hand part of Figure 5.19, where the red square is drawn after the other two squares. On the other hand, if you had drawn object 3 before object 2, and object 2 before object 1, the color would have been

$$0.5*C_1 + 0.25*C_2 + 0.25*C_3,$$

so the order in which you draw the objects, not the order in which they are in space, determines the color.

This emphasizes a difference between blending and transparency. If we were genuinely modeling transparency, it would not make any difference which object were placed first and which last; each would subtract light in a way that is independent of its order. So this represents another challenge if you want to create an illusion of transparency with more than one nonsolid object.

The problem with this approach, and with the results shown in Figure 5.19, is that the most recently drawn object is not necessarily the object that is nearest the eye. This model of transparency using blending works generally only if the order of drawing is back-to-front in the scene. If we consider the effect of actual partial transparency, we see that the colors of objects farther away from the eye really are of less importance in the final scene than nearer colors. So if we draw the objects in back-to-front order, our blending will model transparency much better. We will address this with a detailed OpenGL example later in this chapter.

Indexed Color

On some systems, the image buffer is not large enough to handle three bytes per pixel. This was common on systems before the late 1990s, and such systems are still supported by graphics APIs. In these systems, we have what is called *indexed color,* where the frame buffer stores a single integer value per pixel, and that value is an index into an array of RGB color values called the *color table*. Typically the integer is simply an unsigned byte and there are 256 colors available to the system, and the programmer must define the color table for the application.

Indexed color creates some difficulties with scenes containing large numbers of colors, such as shaded objects. These often require that the scene be generated as RGB values, and the colors in the RGB scene are analyzed to find the set of 256 that are most important or are closest to the colors in the full scene. Algorithms for this are found in many traditional graphics texts. The color table is then built from that analysis.

Besides the extra computational difficulties caused by having to use color table entries, systems with indexed color are very vulnerable to color aliasing problems. Mach banding is one such color aliasing problem, as are color approximations when pseudocolor is used in scientific applications.

Color and Visual Communication

Color is one of your most important tools in creating effective communications with computer graphics. It enriches the image and attracts the eye, and it gives you many tools with which to present information to your audience. It can even let you present an additional dimension in your images. However, if it is misused, color can work against effective images, so you must use it carefully. Your goal is to use color in a way that makes sense to the viewer, even if it is completely artificial. In this section we describe many approaches to using appropriate color so you can think about the meaning of color and how you can use it to create strong and effective communication.

When you use color you must consider carefully the information it is to convey. Color is critical to convey the relation between a synthetic image and the real thing the image is to portray, of course, but it can be used in many more ways. One of the most important is to convey the value of some property associated with the image itself. As an example, the image can be of some kind of space (such as interstellar space) and the color can be the value of something that occupies that space or happens in that space (such as jets of gas emitted from astronomical bodies where the value is the speed or temperature of that gas). Or the image can be a surface such as an airfoil (an airplane wing) and the color can be the air pressure at each point on that airfoil. Color can even be used for displays in a way that carries no meaning in itself but is used to support the presentation, as in the Chromadepth display above. But never use color without understanding how its use will further the message you intend in your image. In the next few sections we will talk about several ways you can use color.

Emphasis Colors

An image you create will include whatever information you want to present to the viewer, including all the structure and details for your model. As you design your image, however, you may want to draw the viewer's attention to specific points in order to highlight the critical features of the display.

There are many ways to draw attention to a specific feature in a graphics image, but one effective technique is to use a strong, contrasting color for that feature. Such a color will probably be bright and clear, and will be chosen to stand out from the other colors in the scene. If you want this kind of emphasis you need to do two things: design the scene with muted colors so that a bright color can stand out from it, and choose emphasis colors that contrast strongly with the overall colors and can be quickly seen.

As an example of this, Figure 5.11 shows a freeform surface defined by a number of control points, and one of the control points is highlighted. Here the background, surface top and bottom, and standard control points are in low-saturation colors, but the highlighted control point is in red (shown darker in the grayscale image but correctly in the color insert) and can easily be identified.

Background Colors

Images include more than just the objects being emphasized. They also include a background color against which your scene is drawn. Background colors should recede in the viewer's perception so that the scene stands out against them. In general, a good background color is a dark or neutral color, but black is often a poor choice because anything dark will fade into it. White can be a good background color because it is neutral, but just like black, if objects are too light they may not show up well against white.

Constant-color backgrounds may not be the best approach to presenting images. Professional photographers and videographers don't use a constant-color background; they use a background with a central highlight that focuses attention on the subject. Try to use a brighter

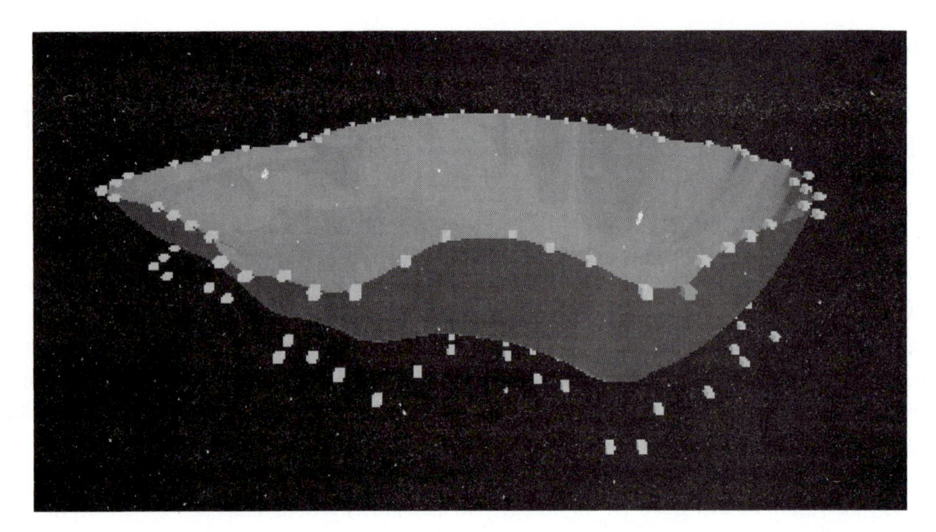

Figure 5.11 An image with one item highlighted for emphasis. See the figure in the color insert. Courtesy of Ben Eadington.

spot at the center of your background, or possibly a brighter slash of light through the background (usually lower left to upper right) to pull the eye to the part of the image where you put your critical content. This kind of background is not directly provided by graphics APIs, but you can create your own background by putting a texture map on a plane behind your model. Ideas such as these from photo and video professionals can help you focus your viewer's attention on the critical part of your images, as demonstrated in Figure 5.12.

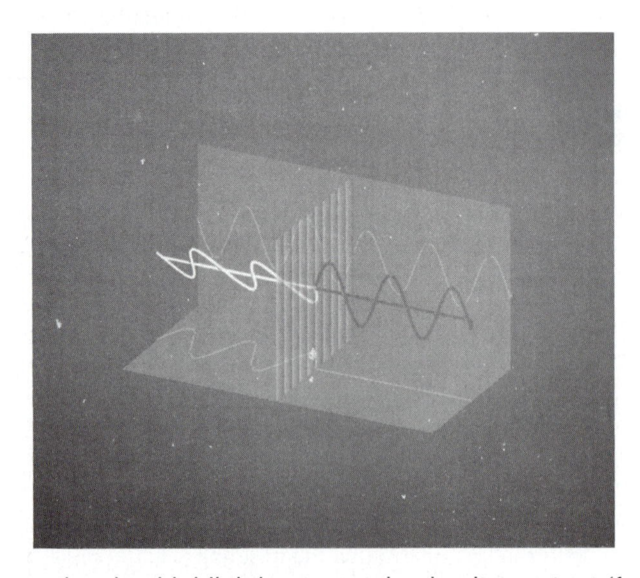

Figure 5.12 Image showing highlighting to emphasize its content (for example, with a polarization figure courtesy of Virginia Muncy) by creating some kind of spotlighted background.

Naturalistic Color

If you are working with images of actual objects, you may want to make them look realistic to the user. When you do, you can use your API's modeling, lighting, and shading tools to create appropriately colored images. You can also apply texture mapping to give realism to your display. Modeling was discussed in Chapters 2 and 3, and lighting and shading will be discussed in Chapter 6 and texture mapping in Chapter 8, so we will not discuss them further here. There are limitations on the realism you can get from graphics APIs, however, because most of them use only simple approximations to realistic coloring. This is an interesting topic of study after you complete the first graphics course.

Pseudocolor and Color Ramps

If you think of color as a separate property of objects, you can use it to convey extra information in your images. One of the important uses of color is to represent a property of the objects being displayed. This property could be temperature, velocity, distance, or almost anything you could think of that can be represented by a number. This numerical value can be translated to a color, and then displaying the object in this color carries the information that the property has the value represented by the color. Color that represents another value is called a *pseudocolor*.

Pseudocolor separates the shape of an object from the colors of the object. In Figure 5.13, a normal view of a house is shown at left, and at right the house is shown with the heat it emits. Note how the heat-emitting photo highlights the windows of the house, which are more poorly insulated than the walls between them. This example was created with thermal imaging, not computer graphics, but the principle of showing a property along with the shape is the key to pseudocolor imaging—and this photo shows a good example of pseudocolor corresponding to the physical property of temperature.

This representation of values by colors is managed by creating *color ramps,* which are one-dimensional sequences of colors such that any value between 0.0 and 1.0 corresponds to a particular color. Color ramps link color to number, so they must be chosen carefully to help the user

Figure 5.13 A house shown in a normal photograph (*left*) and with thermal imaging (*right*); from [MCC]. Courtesy of FLIR systems.

understand the numeric values shown by the colors. These ramps may use colors that are customary in the field whose content is being displayed, so there are aspects of cultural context for the ramps. They may be developed to show changes smoothly or to have strong boundaries, depending on the meaning they are to convey. There is an art to creating the relation between colors and values for a particular application, and you are encouraged to design your applications so you can change color ramps easily so you can experiment with different ramps and the meanings they convey.

Building Color Ramps

Building color ramps is straightforward and is independent of your graphics API. The following sample code shows how two color ramps were created so you can build ramps for your projects. Each assumes that the numerical values have been scaled to this range and returns an array of three numbers that represents the RGB color that corresponds to that value according to the particular representation it uses. This code assumes only that your API uses the RGB color model. The first ramp provides color in a rainbow sequence, red-orange-yellow-green-blue-violet. A second color ramp uses colors that vary uniformly in luminance as the numeric values range from 0.0 to 1.0. The uniform-luminance ramp runs from black through red through yellow to white. Other uniform-luminance color sequences are also possible and are discussed in the exercises for this chapter. You should notice that these functions operate by setting a global real variable `myColor[3]` that is used by other functions. Examples of these ramps' use are given later in the chapter.

```
//  rainbow color ramp
void calcRainbow(float yval)
{  if (yval < 0.2)                          // purple to blue ramp
      {myColor[0]=0.5*(1.0-yval/0.2);myColor[1]=0.0;
       myColor[2]=0.5+(0.5*yval/0.2);return;}
   if ((yval >= 0.2) && (yval < 0.40))  // blue to cyan ramp
      {myColor[0]=0.0;myColor[1]=(yval-0.2)*5.0;myColor[2]=1.0;return;}
   if ((yval >= 0.40) && (yval < 0.6))  // cyan to green ramp
      {myColor[0]=0.0;myColor[1]=1.0;myColor[2]=(0.6-yval)*5.0;return;}
   if ((yval >= 0.6) && (yval < 0.8)          // green to yellow ramp
      {myColor[0]=(yval-0.6)*5.0;myColor[1]=1.0;myColor[2]=0.0;return;}
   if (yval >= 0.8)                         // yellow to red ramp^
      {myColor[0]=1.0;myColor[1]=(1.0-yval)*5.0;myColor[2]=0.0;}
   return;
}

// uniform-luminance color ramp
void calcLuminance(float yval)
{  if (yval < 0.30)
      {myColor[0]=yval/0.3;myColor[1]=0.0;myColor[2]=0.0;return;}
   if ((yval>=0.30) && (yval < 0.89))
      {myColor[0]=1.0;myColor[1]=(yval-0.3)/0.59;myColor[2]=0.0;return;}
   if (yval>=0.89)
      {myColor[0]=1.0;myColor[1]=1.0;myColor[2]=(yval-0.89)/0.11;}
   return;
}
```

Figure 0.7 and Figure 9.2 Heat distribution in a bar.

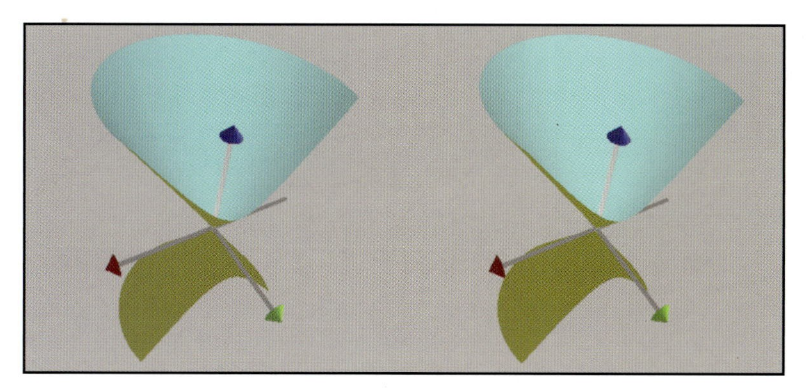

Figure 1.15 A stereo pair that can be viewed by merging individual eye images.

Figure 2.18 Traditional surface graph presented with three lights to show its shape.

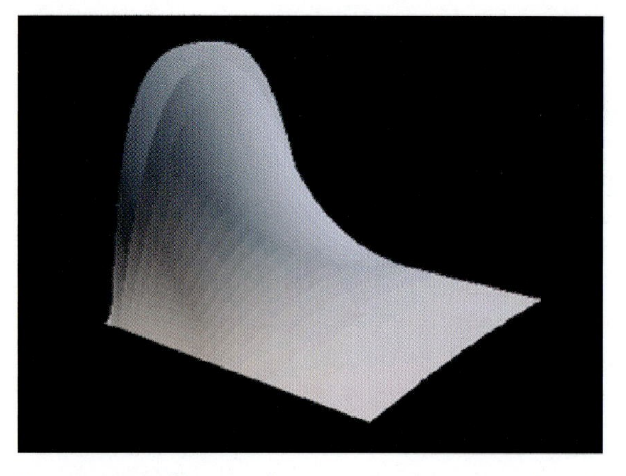

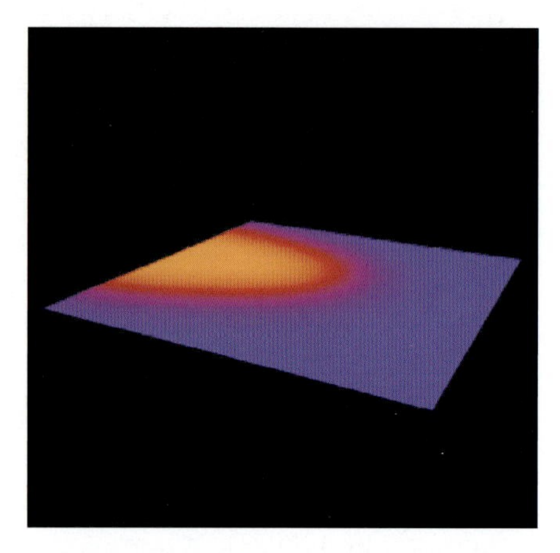

Figure 2.20 Change in temperature over time from solutions 1 and 3.

Figure 2.29 A scene that we will describe with a scene graph.

Figure 2.33 The same scene as in Figure 2.29 but with the eyepoint following directly behind the helicopter.

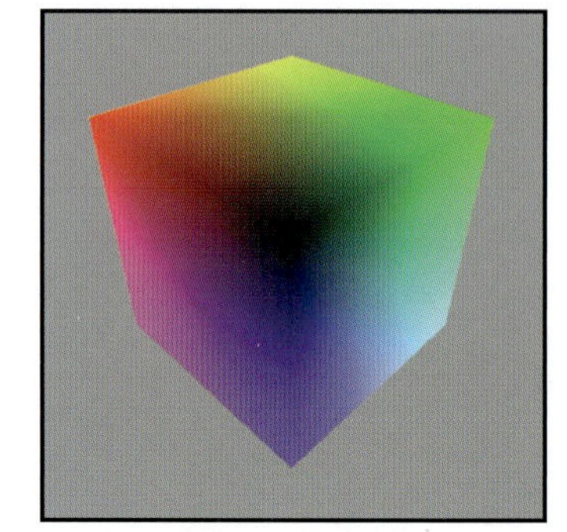

Figure 5.1 Two views of the RGB cube—from the white (*left*) and black (*right*) corners.

Figure 5.2 A sequence of six colors between yellow and blue.

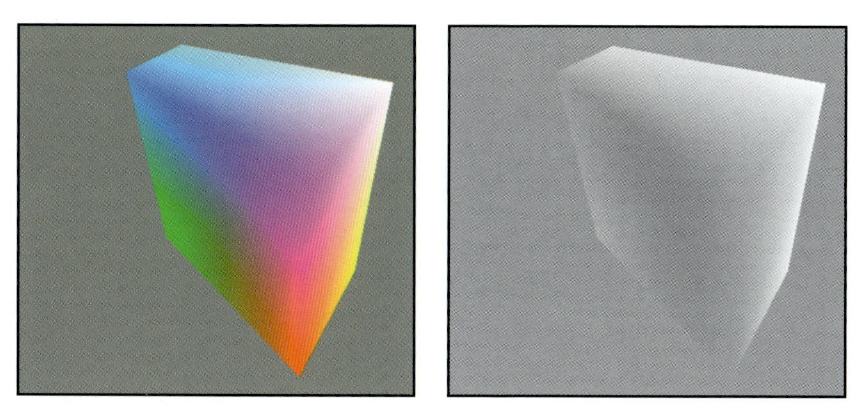

Figure 5.3 A plane of constant luminance in the RGB cube in both color (*left*) and grayscale (*right*).

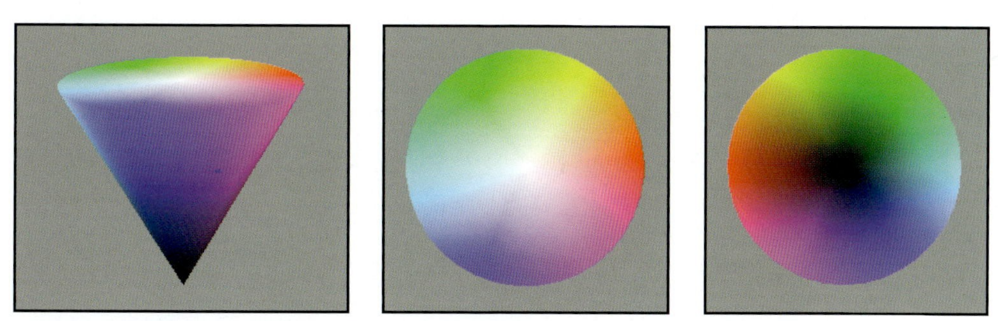

Figure 5.4 Diagram of the HSV color model.

Figure 5.5 Approximately 120 degree views of the HLS double cone from the directions of red (*left*) green (*middle*), and blue (*right*).

Figure 5.6 Emissive colors (*left*) and transmissive colors (*right*).

Figure 5.7 Color separations for printing.

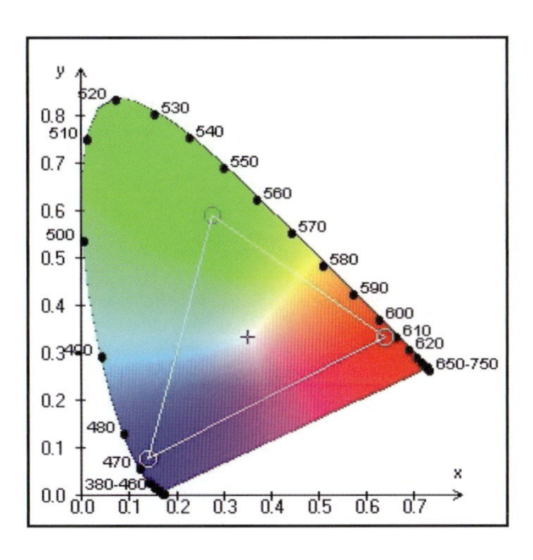

Figure 5.9 The CIE color space.

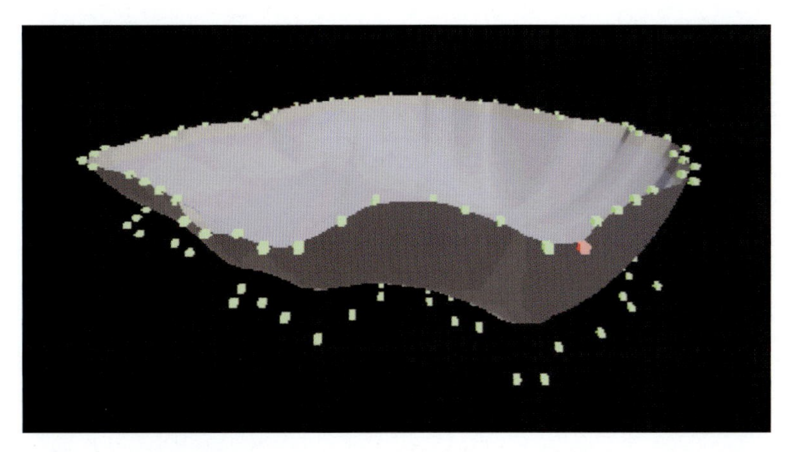

Figure 5.11 and Figure 7.7 An image with one item highlighted for emphasis. Courtesy of Ben Eadington.

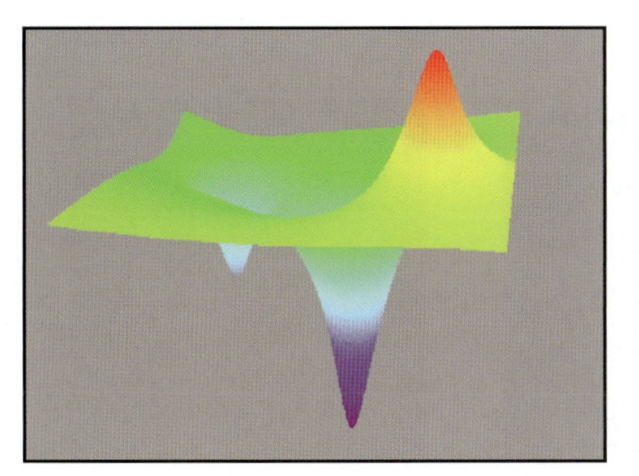

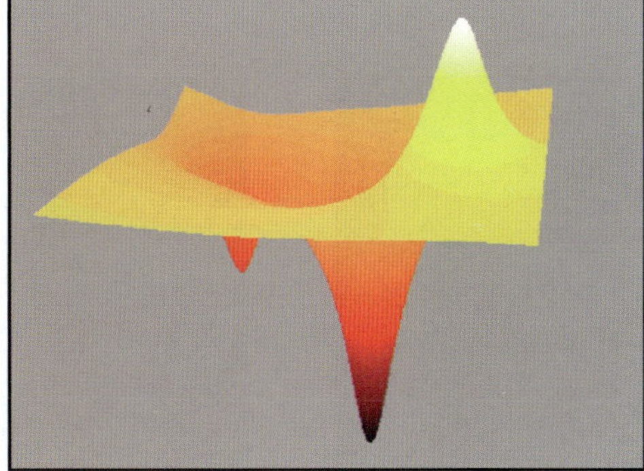

Figure 5.14 Electrostatic potential surface model presented with "rainbow" color ramp to emphasize the extreme values (*left*) and with a uniform-luminance distribution of colors (*right*).

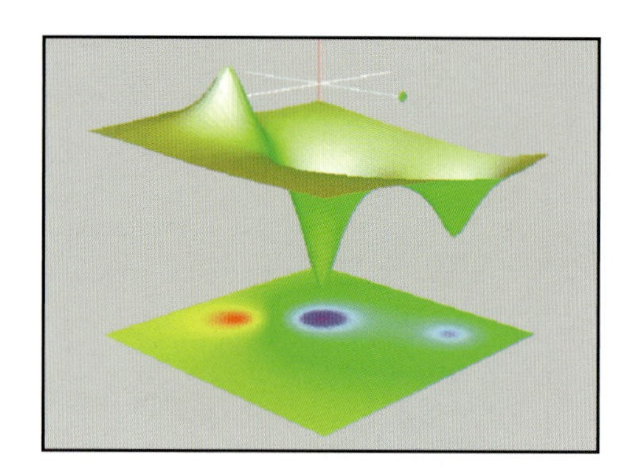

Figure 5.15 and Figure 9.5 A pseudocolor plane with the lighted surface.

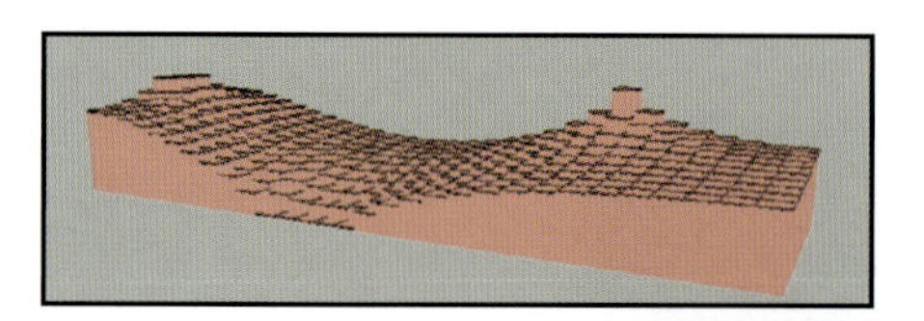

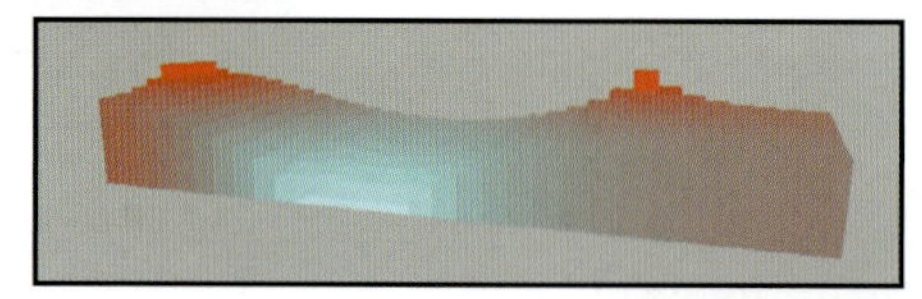

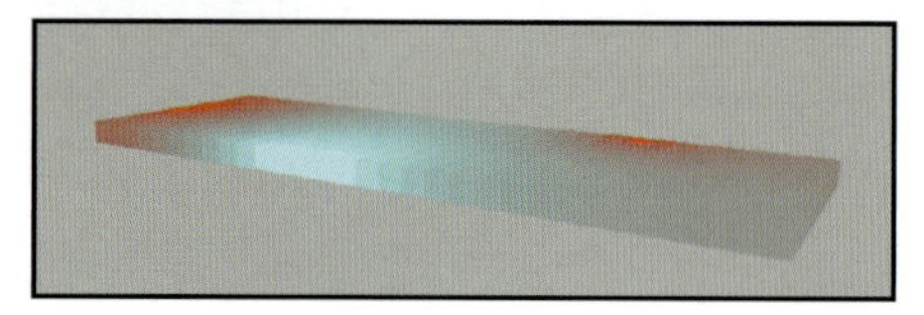

Figure 5.16 Three encodings of the same information: temperature in a bar, encoded only through geometry (*top left*), only through color (*bottom right*), and through both (*center*).

Figure 5.19 The partially transparent coordinates planes (*left*); the same coordinate planes fully transparent but with same alpha (*center*); the same coordinate planes with adjusted alpha (*right*).

Figure 5.20 The partially transparent planes broken into quadrants and drawn back-to-front.

Figure 6.5 A scene with different lighting on the sun and the earth.

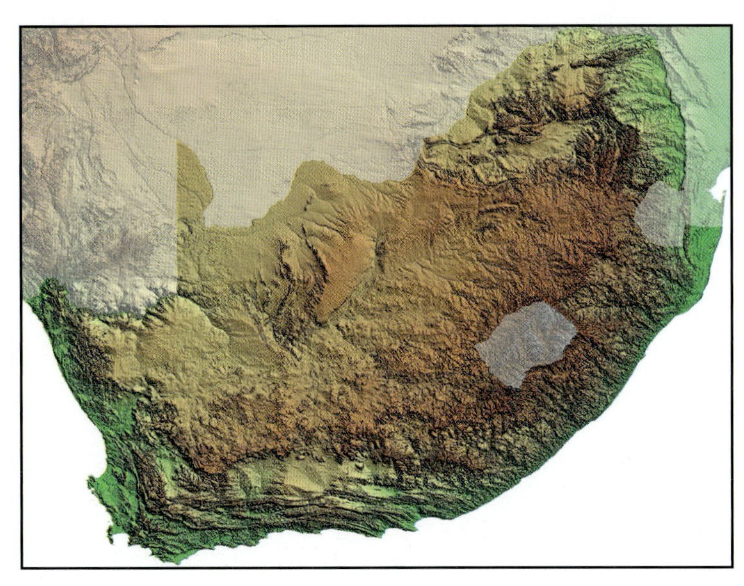

Figure 6.6 A lighted, false-color map of South Africa. Courtesy of ComputaMaps, South Africa.

Figure 6.12 A scene rendered with the radiosity model, from [LI]. Courtesy of Dani Lischinslci.

Figure 6.13 A scene rendered with the photon mapping model. Courtesy of Henrik Wann Jensen.

Figure 6.14 The white cube viewed with three colored lights.

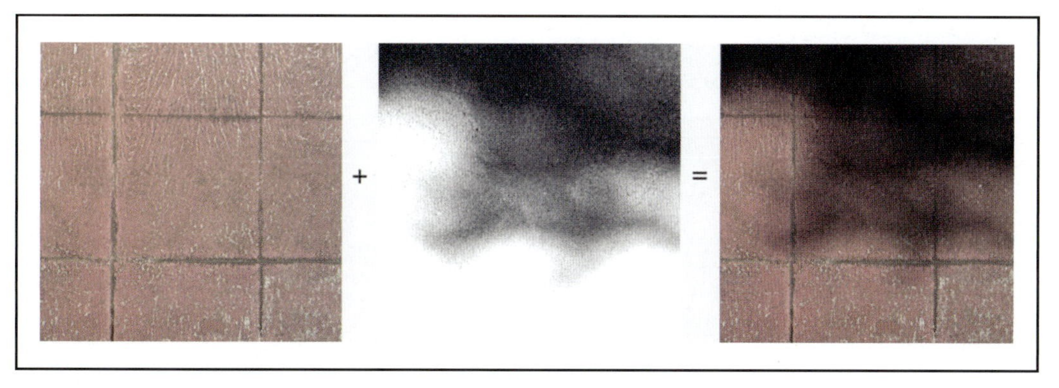

Figure 8.10 Multitexturing in use.

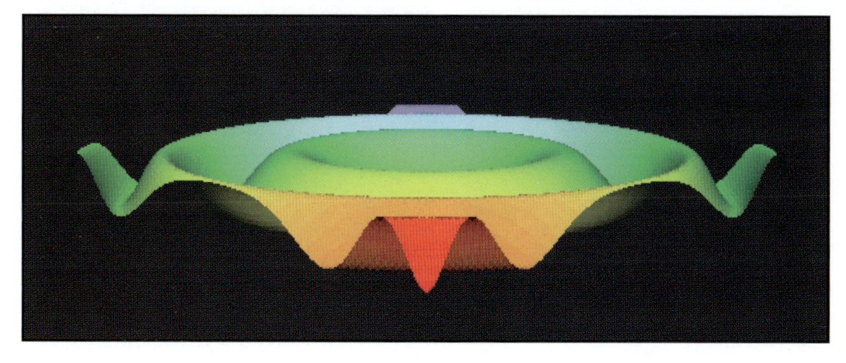

Figure 8.13 A ChromaDepth-colored image of a mathematical surface.

Exercise 8.4

Exercise 8.5 Courtesy of Vali Lalioti.

Figure 9.15 Photograph of cave site with photogrammetric reference card and laser scan point. Courtesy of Alan Chalmers.

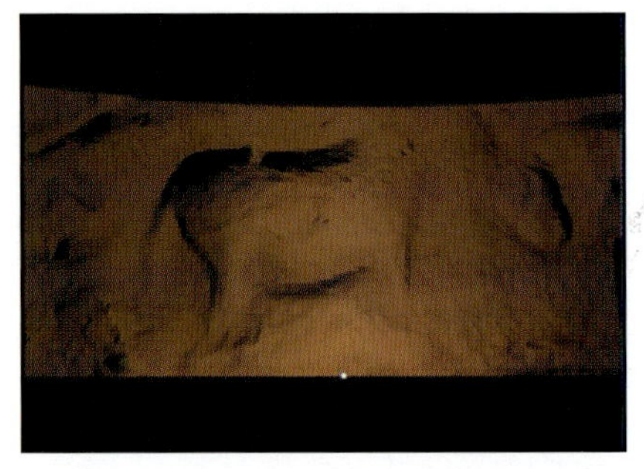

Figure 9.17 The cave wall shown with a simulated animal-oil lamp. Courtesy of Alan Chalmers.

Figure 9.18 A "fractal forgery" landscape with shading and transparent water. Courtesy of Ben Eadington.

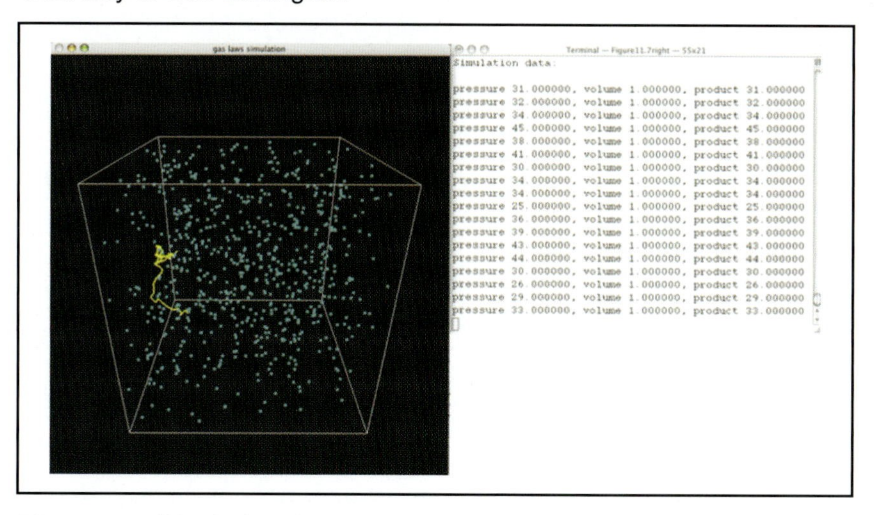

Figure 9.19 Displaying the gas as particles in the fixed space, including simulation printout.

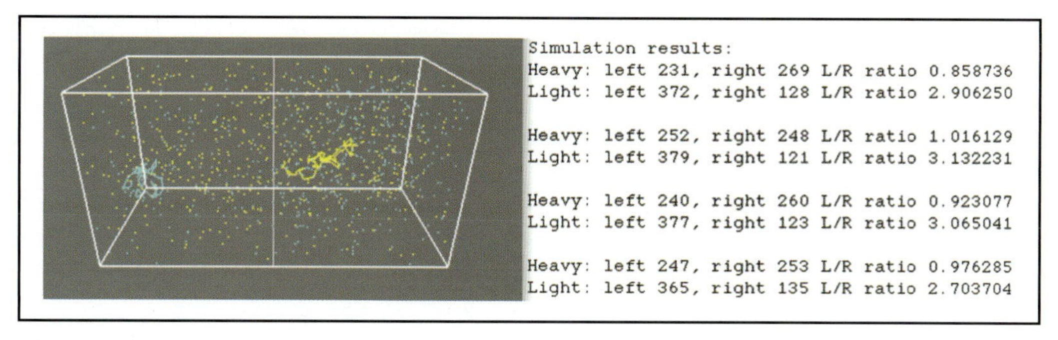

Figure 9.20 Display of the diffusion simulation, directly across the membrane (including data output from the simulation).

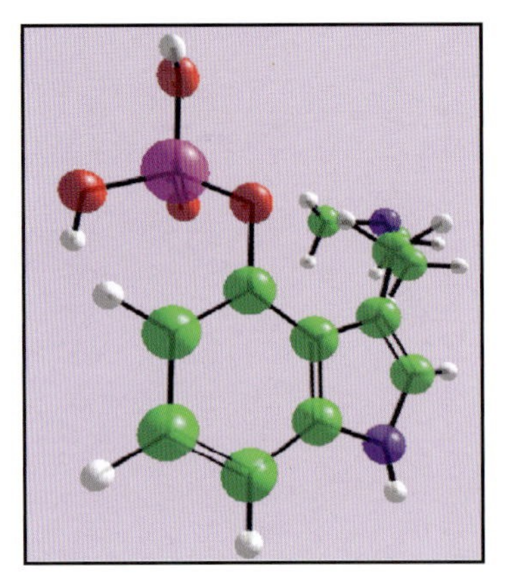

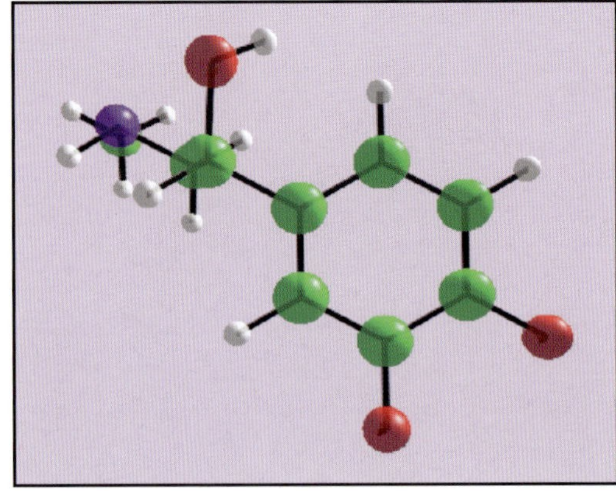

Figure 9.21 Displays from psilocybin.mol (*left*) and adrenaline.pdb (*right*).

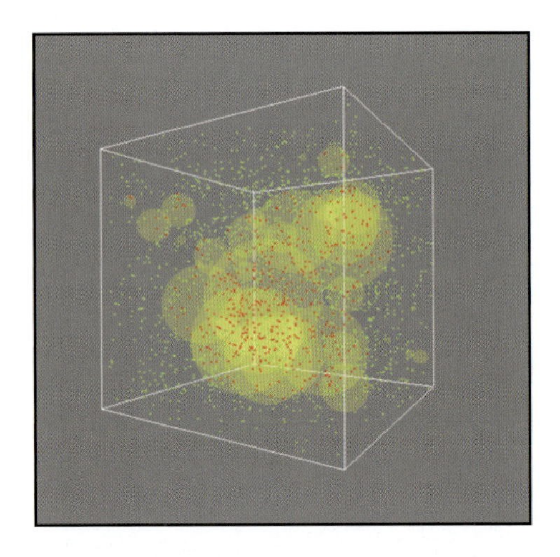

Figure 9.23 A Monte Carlo estimate of a complex volume.

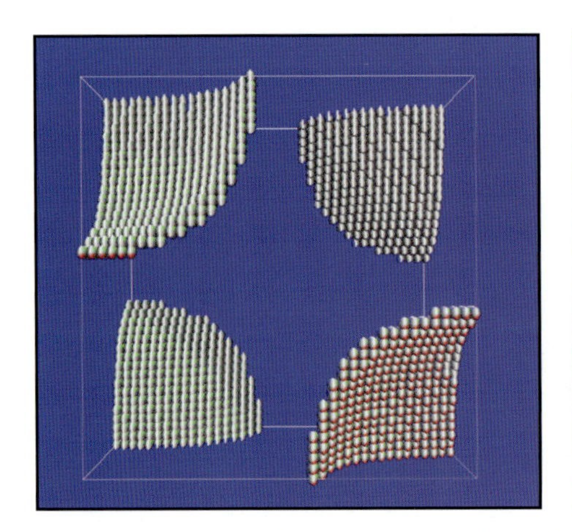

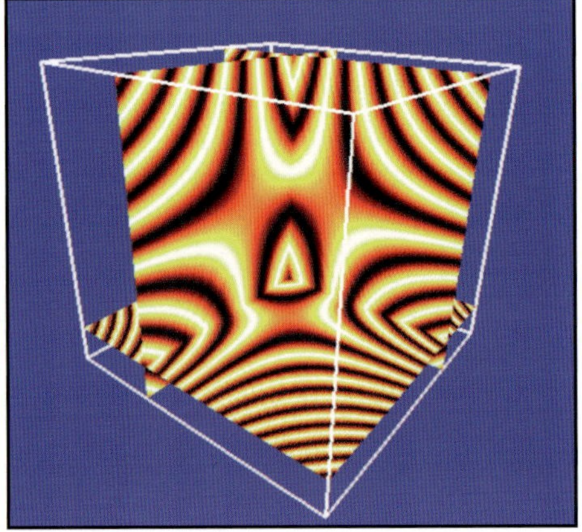

Figure 9.24 An implicit surface approximation that uses spheres to locate a surface (*left*) and cross-sections of a function's values (*right*).

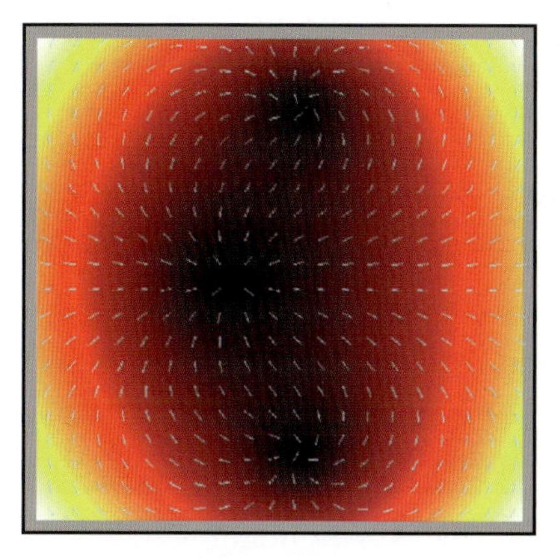

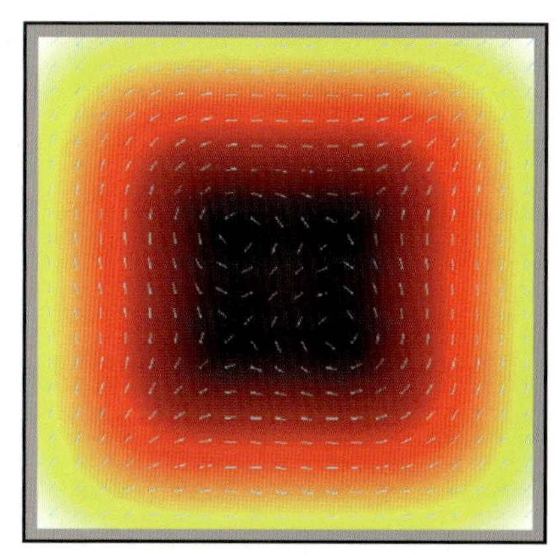

Figure 9.25 Two visualizations with a constant theme: a complex-valued function of a complex variable (*left*) and the direction vectors for a differential equation (*right*).

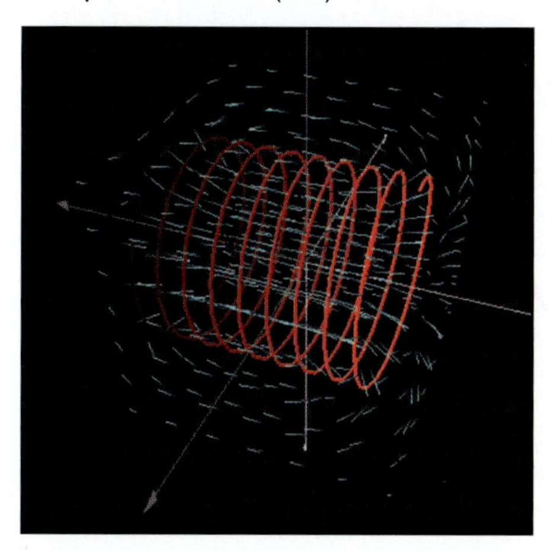

Figure 9.26 A magnetic field around a coil with a moving current. Courtesy of Jordan Maynard.

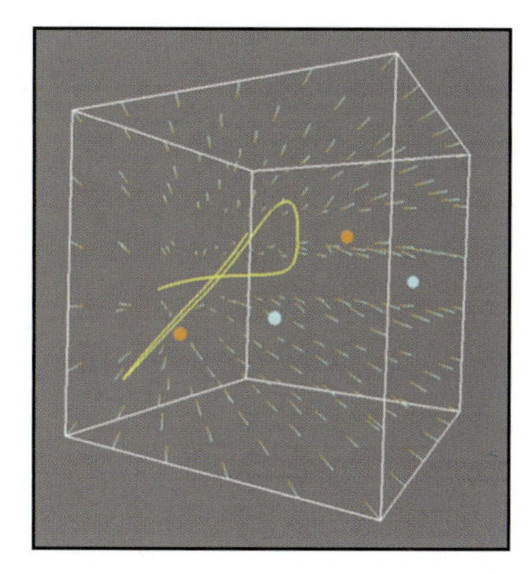

Figure 9.27 The 3D Coulomb's law simulation with a 3D vector field.

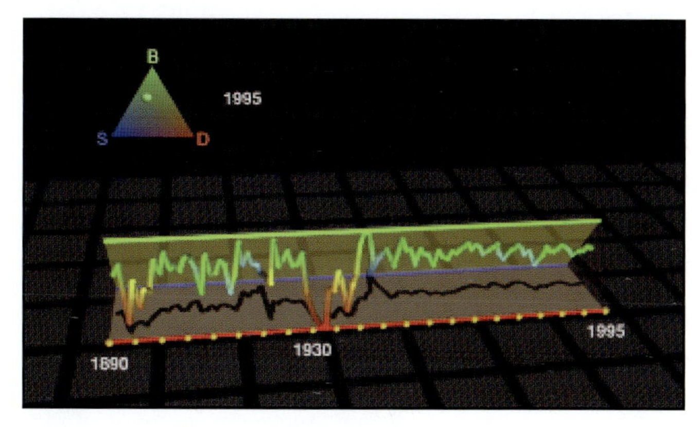

Figure 9.28 The economic data presentation. Courtesy of the San Diego Supercomputer Center.

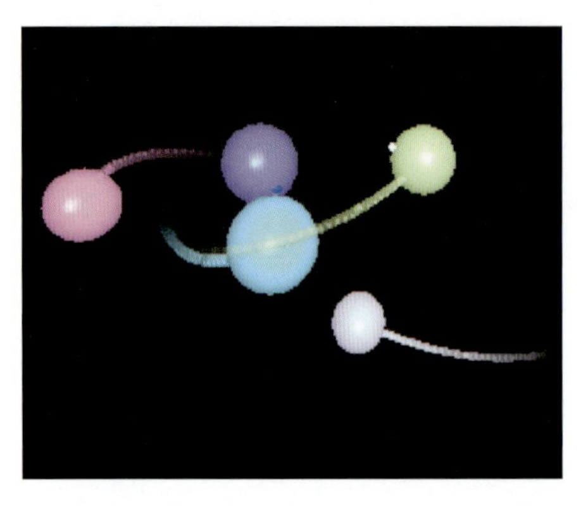

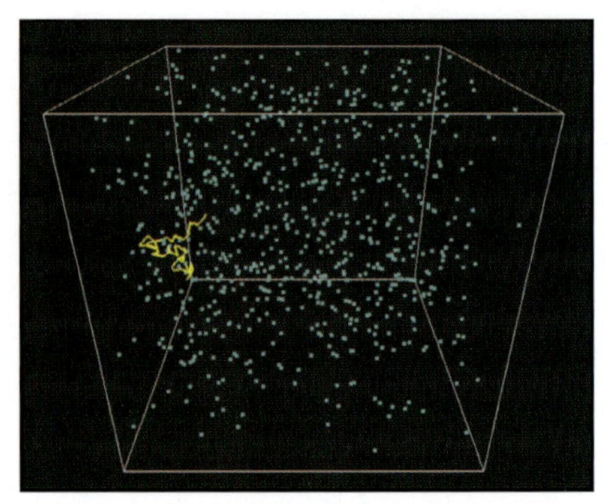

Figure 11.7 Two kinds of traces of moving objects. Figure on the left is courtesy of Ben Eadington.

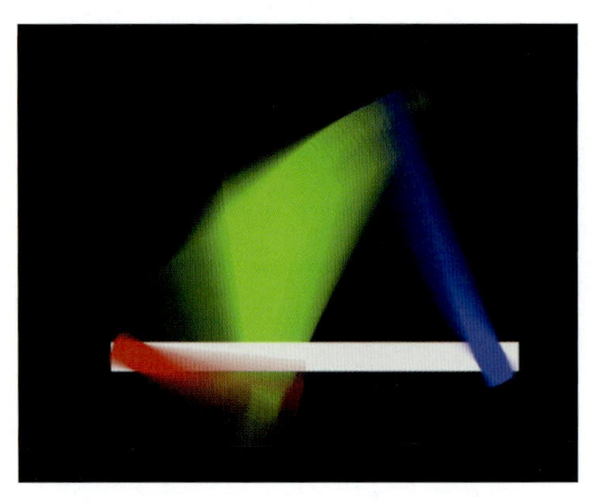

Figure 11.8 A moving mechanism shown with one part fixed and the rest blurred from motion. Courtesy of Mike Bailey.

Figure 12.2 A foggy cube (including a texture map on one surface).

Figure 12.7 The cube drawn with both vertex and normal arrays.

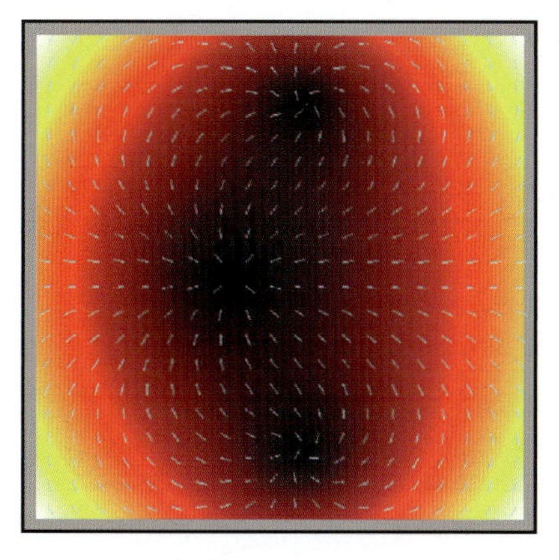

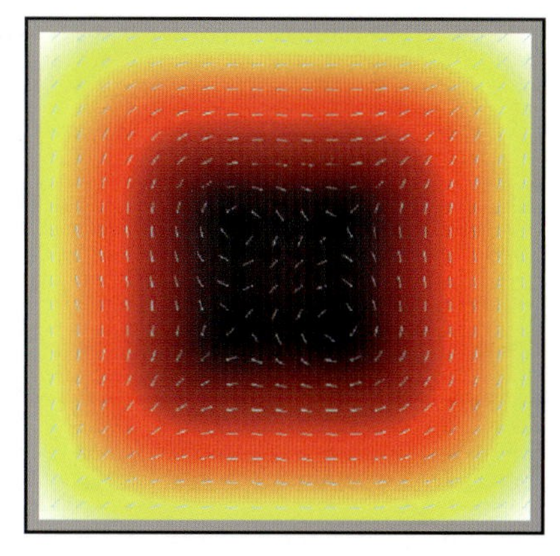

Figure 9.25 Two visualizations with a constant theme: a complex-valued function of a complex variable (*left*) and the direction vectors for a differential equation (*right*).

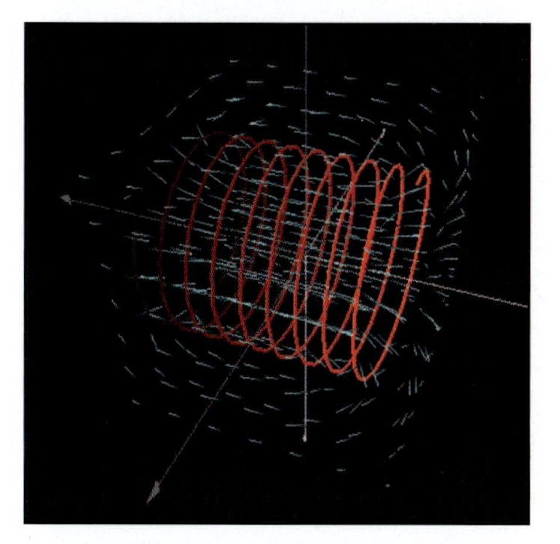

Figure 9.26 A magnetic field around a coil with a moving current. Courtesy of Jordan Maynard.

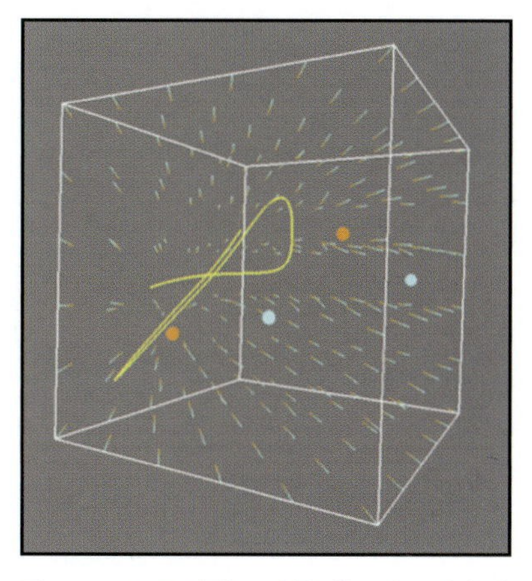

Figure 9.27 The 3D Coulomb's law simulation with a 3D vector field.

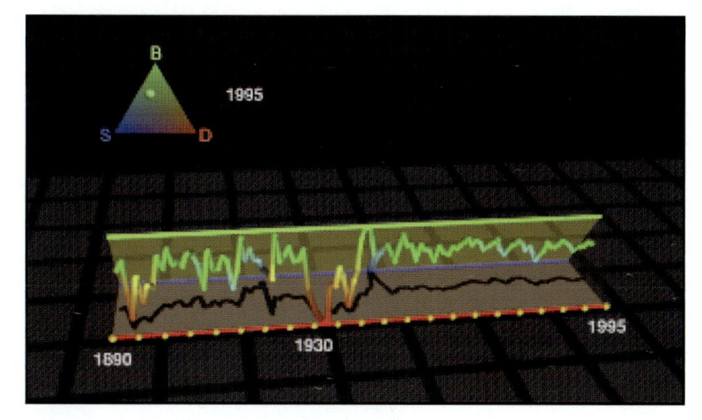

Figure 9.28 The economic data presentation. Courtesy of the San Diego Supercomputer Center.

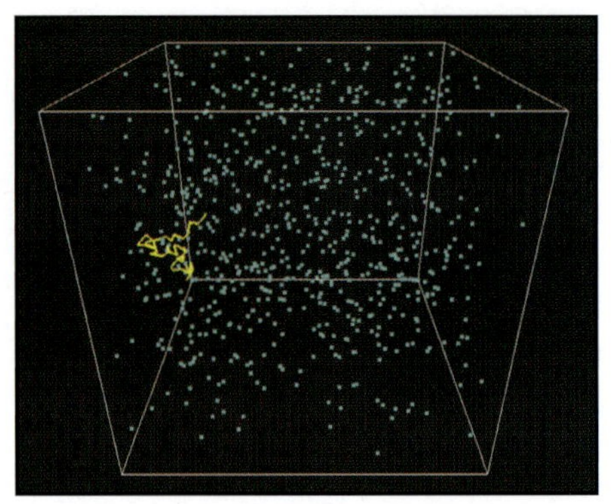

Figure 11.7 Two kinds of traces of moving objects. Figure on the left is courtesy of Ben Eadington.

Figure 11.8 A moving mechanism shown with one part fixed and the rest blurred from motion. Courtesy of Mike Bailey.

Figure 12.2 A foggy cube (including a texture map on one surface).

Figure 12.7 The cube drawn with both vertex and normal arrays.

Figure 14.4 A ray-traced image created with POVRay.

Figure 14.5 A volume visualization of a model of the Orion nebula. Courtesy of Courtesy of David R. Nadeau.

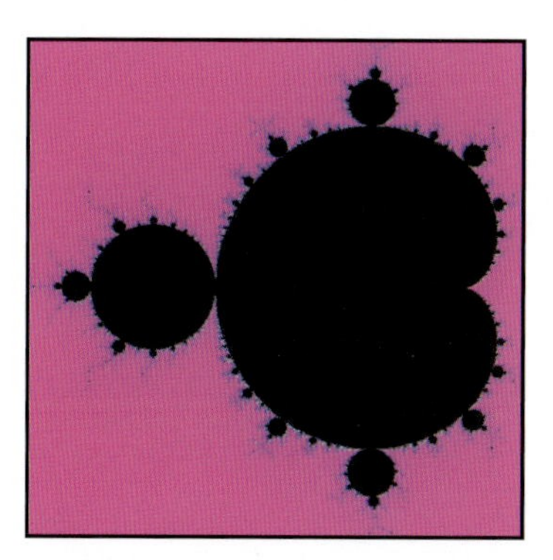

Figure 14.12 The full mandelbrot set (*left*) and a detail (*right*).

Figure 14.13 A Julia set for a particular fixed value c.

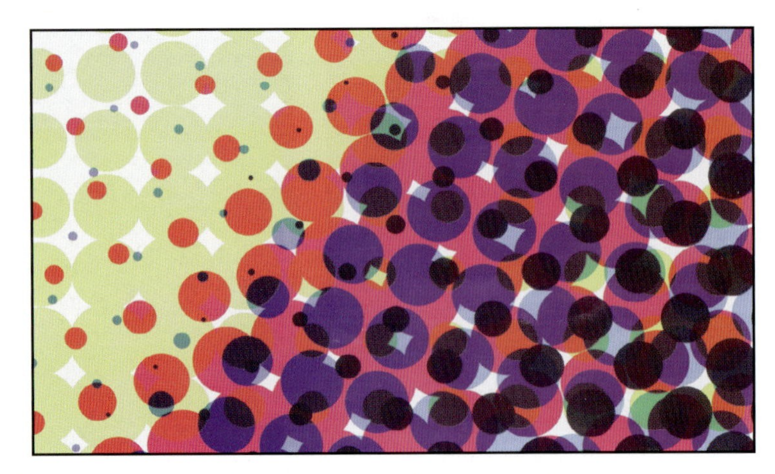

Figure 15.1 C, M, Y, and K screens in a color image, greatly enlarged.

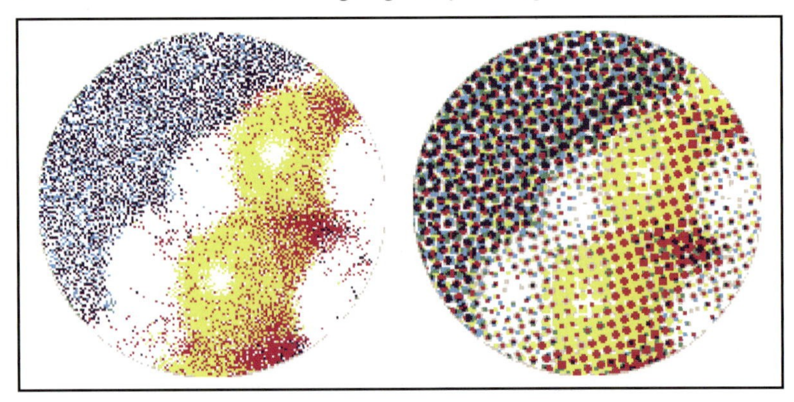

Figure 15.2 A comparison of a stochastic screen (*left*) with a fixed-angle screen (*right*). Courtesy of Weiser Litho, Inc.

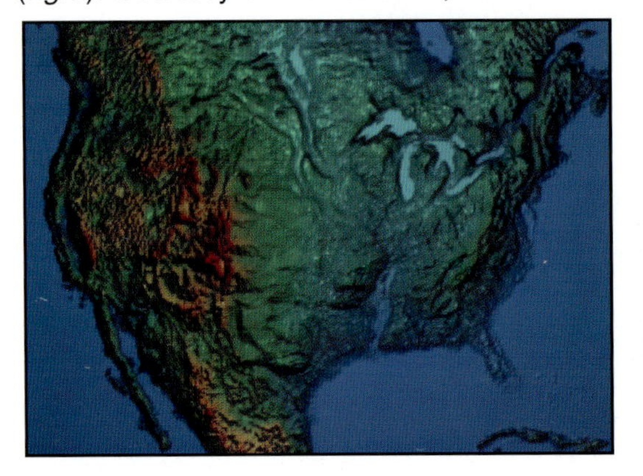

Figure 15.4 A ChromaDepth display. Courtesy of Mike Bailey.

Figure 15.6 An example of a color anaglyph; when it is viewed with red/blue or red/green glasses, a 3D color image is seen. Clouresty of Rolf Henkel.

The color ramp in the thermal imaging of Figure 5.13 is different from either of these. In the original color image, the interval from 0 to 13.9 (degrees Celsius) runs from black (lowest value) through dark blue to magenta, then to red and on to yellow, and finally to white. This could be implemented by segmenting the range from 0 to about 6 as a ramp from black to blue, then adding red and reducing blue from 6 to 9, then adding yellow to about 12, and then adding blue on up to 13.9. Here blue is used for the low values because blue is a customary color for cold or cool things, and red is added as blue is decreased because redder colors are associated with warmer things. Finally the red is moved to yellow by adding green, and yellow is moved to white by adding blue, because as metals are heated their colors move from red to yellow and finally to white (as in "white-hot"). Thus the thermal imaging ramp uses a familiar representation of temperatures in Western cultures.

Using Color Ramps

A color ramp is a one-dimensional space whose values are colors, not numbers. It creates a relationship between numbers between 0 and 1 and colors by the way the ramp is coded. The color is used to make the number visible, so when you show an object with a particular value, you display it in the color given by the color ramp. You can use this color as an absolute color in a display without lighting or as a material color if you use lighting; once the color is set by the numeric value, you can treat the colored model any way you want.

When we discussed shapes, we gave an example that showed how either shapes or colors can encode information. That example used a simple blue-to-red color change without explicit color ramps. A combination of colors and shapes can be used in the Coulomb's law presentation described earlier. The electrostatic potential on a rectangle was shown as a pure surface, but if we use color ramps to show potential values we get the images shown in Figure 5.14 (see the figure in the color insert). The left-hand image shows the surface with the rainbow color ramp and the right-hand image shows a uniform-luminance ramp. Look at the figure carefully to see if you can get the numeric value of the potential at a given point in each image. In an actual application, you would not simply display the colored surface but would also include a legend that identified colors with numeric values, as described earlier.

Figure 5.14 Electrostatic potential surface model presented with "rainbow" color ramp to emphasize the extreme values (*left*) and with a uniform-luminance distribution of colors (*right*). See the figure in the color insert.

However, perhaps these examples might not be the only way to approach the problem. If we think of the surface and the color ramp as different representations of the same space, it might be useful to think of them as separate displays that are linked in space. Figure 5.15 shows one way that might be done, with a lighted surface and a 2D pseudocolor plane displayed together. Here the rainbow color ramp is used, but others are possible.

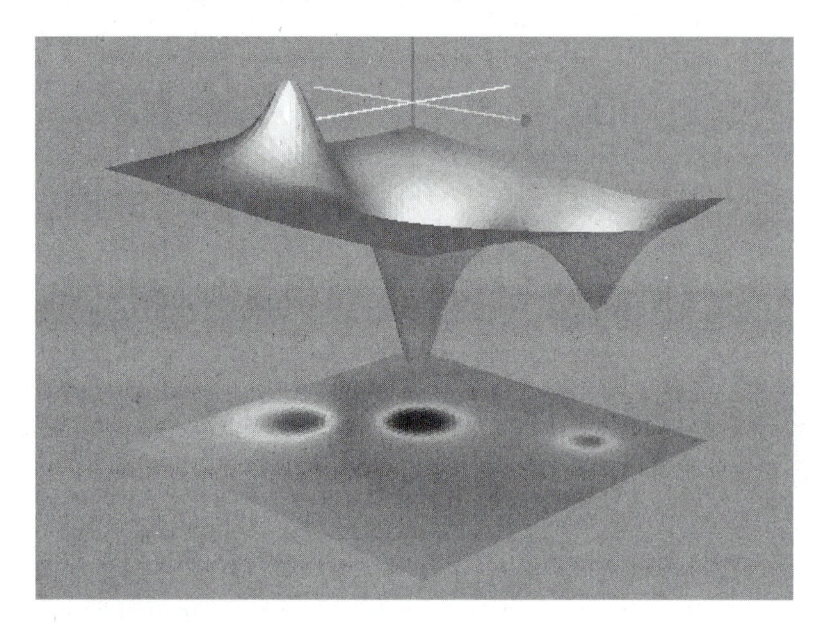

Figure 5.15 A pseudocolor plane with the lighted surface. See the figure in the color insert.

Comparing Shape and Color Codings

We talked about combining shapes and colors to communicate your model. Figure 5.16 shows three different ways to represent temperatures for the heat diffusion program introduced in the first chapter of the book. In the figure we see this temperature information presented three ways: using both geometric and color encoding (center), using only geometric coding (top and left), and using only color encoding (bottom and right). These use higher bars and redder values for higher temperatures, while lower bars and more cyan values represent lower temperatures. Each encoding communicates the same basic information, but they emphasize different things. Height alone suggests that the bar itself actually changes shape, so it might confuse someone who is not used to the problem. The color-only encoding seems easier for a novice to understand because we are used to this color coding for heat. The combined image reinforces the color-only image with the more numerically related height. Thus the way we encode information may depend on the experience of our users and on the conventions they are accustomed to in understanding information.

Cultural Context of the Audience

When members of your audience try to understand an image you have created, they will be working from within the frame of reference of their individual culture. This is a complex issue, with many different facets: professional cultures, social cultures, geographic cultures, and many others.

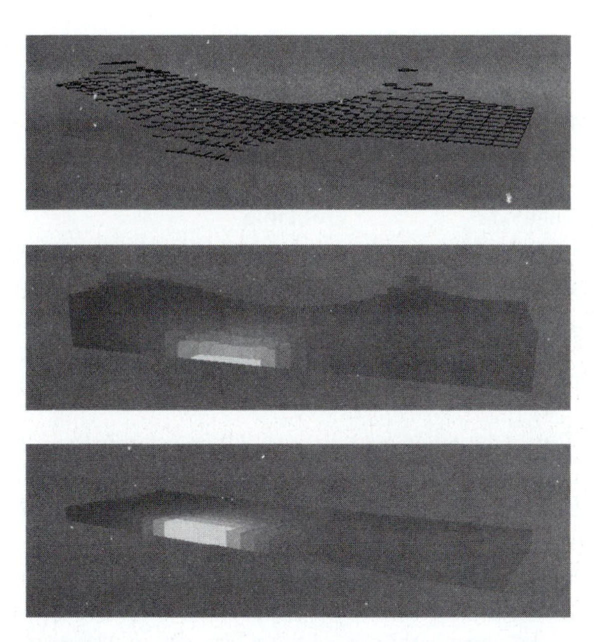

Figure 5.16 Three encodings of the same information: temperature in a bar, encoded only through geometry (*top left*), only through color (*bottom right*), and through both (*center*). See the figure in the color insert.

If someone has to *learn* how to understand your image (for example, if you use features that mean something different to you than they would to the audience) then your image will be less effective. You must learn how to express your ideas in the audience's context.

To communicate with your audience using images, you must understand their visual vocabularies. You must understand the symbols used in the culture, the color schemes and their meanings in the culture, and the way graphic design is used in the culture. For example, we are familiar with the traditional spare and open Japanese design, but Japan's present culture may be more accurately represented by the crowded, banner-laden Japanese Web sites, similar to Japanese newspapers and magazines. If you are reaching a Japanese audience, you will have to choose which of these two approaches to use in laying out your image.

Most of your work will probably be oriented more toward a professional group than a cultural group, however. You will need to understand the use of images to represent concepts in physics, chemistry, biology, or engineering more than their use in an ethnic or religious culture. To do this, you will need to know how physicists, chemists, biologists, or engineers are accustomed to using and interpreting images. There are references on the meaning of color in various contexts that could be useful to you, especially [THO] and [BR95]. Figure 5.17 gives one look at this, and the reference contains other ideas about color meanings in context.

How can you learn about the visual frame of reference of a particular culture? Research the culture you're reaching by reading the magazines, newspapers, or professional publications of that group. You can develop a bank of images that are commonly found in this culture by taking images from these sources, and you can test the role of these images with people deeply familiar with the

Color	Process Control Engineers	Financial Managers	Health Care Professionals
Blue	Cold Water	Corporate Reliable	Death
Turquoise (Cyan)	Steam	Cool Subdued	Oxygen deficient
Green	Nominal Safe	Profitable	Infected
Yellow	Caution	Important	Jaundiced
Red	Danger	Unprofitable	Healthy
Purple	Hot Radioactive	Wealthy	Cause for concern

Figure 5.17 Associations of color by profession.

culture, such as persons from an ethnic or religious culture or professionals from a scientific culture. Similarly, you can develop standard layouts, color schemes, and symbol sets for the culture that have been reviewed and shaped by experts. When you are finished, you will have a collection of images, layouts, symbols, and color sets—that is, a design vocabulary—for your target audience and can be comfortable that you have the basis for effective communication with that group.

Also remember that color is not seen by itself; it is always seen in the context of other colors in the scene, and the context-sensitive nature of color can lead to some surprises. A description of color in context is found in [BR95]. As a very simple but dramatic example of this impact of context on perception, the image in Figure 5.18 consists of a sequence of black squares, separated by gray lines with a bright white spot at each junction. Why do you see only the spot you're looking at as white, when the white spots away from the one you're looking at appear gray or black?

Figure 5.18 A figure which shows artifacts that aren't there.

Some Examples

Example: An Object with Partially Transparent Faces

If you were to draw a piece of the standard coordinate planes made with transparent plastic, you would be able to see through each coordinate plane to the other planes. We have modeled a set of three squares in the primary RGB colors, each lying in a coordinate plane and centered at the origin, and each defined as having a rather low alpha value of 0.5 so that the other squares are supposed to show through. In this section we try to model transparency in this geometry to consider the effects of different drawing options on this view.

The left-hand side of Figure 5.19 shows the image we get with these colors when we use the depth test. What you can "see through" depends on the order in which you draw the objects. With the depth test enabled, a transparent object close to your eye prevents an object farther away from being blended with a nearer object that was drawn before. The first coordinate plane you draw is completely opaque to the other planes, even though we specified it as being partly transparent. You can see through a second coordinate plane, to the first plane, but it is fully opaque to the third plane. We drew the blue plane first, and it is transparent only to the background (and is darker than it would be because the black background shows through). The green plane was drawn second, and that allows only the blue plane or background to show through. The red plane was drawn third, and it shows the background and both other planes. In the working example, you can use keypresses to rotate the planes in space. As you do, the squares have the same transparency properties in any position because they are always drawn in the same order.

Figure 5.19 The partially transparent coordinates planes (*left*); the same coordinate planes fully transparent but with same alpha (*center*); the same coordinate planes with adjusted alpha (*right*). See the figure in the color insert.

For the image in the center of Figure 5.19 we disabled the depth test, and this presents a different situation. The result is more like transparent planes, but the transparency is very confusing because the last plane drawn, the red plane, always seems to be on top because its color is the brightest. This figure shows that the OpenGL blending is not transparency; it is quite difficult to get information about the relationship of the planes from this image. This figure is created by exactly the same code as the one above with blending disabled instead of enabled.

In the final image we change the alpha values of the three squares to account for the difference between the weights. We use 1.0 for the first color (blue), 0.5 for the second color (green), but only 0.33 for red, and we see that the right-hand image in Figure 5.19 has the following color weights in its various regions:

- 0.33 for each of the colors in the region they all share
- 0.5 for each of blue and green in the region they share
- 0.33 each for red and green in the region they share
- 0.33 for red and 0.67 for blue in the region they share
- the original alpha values for the regions where there is only one color

The original alpha values give us a solid blue, a fairly strong green, and a weak red. The modified colors give us a closer approximation to the appearance of actual transparency, with a particular attention to the clear gray in the area they all cover, but some areas still don't work. To get even this close, however, we must analyze the rendering carefully and we still cannot quite get a perfect appearance.

Consider this example again with the concept of depth-sorting the things we will draw. In this case, the three planes intersect one another and each plane must be subdivided into four pieces each so that there is no overlap. Once there is no overlap of the parts, we can sort them so that the pieces farther from the eye will be drawn first. This lets us draw in back-to-front order, so as we described earlier in the chapter, blending provides a better model of how transparency operates. Figure 5.20 shows how this would work. The technique of adjusting your model is not always as easy as this because it can be difficult to subdivide parts of a figure, but this figure shows its effectiveness.

Figure 5.20 The partially transparent planes broken into quadrants and drawn back-to-front. See the figure in the color insert.

There is another issue with depth-first drawing, however. If you create a scene that lets the user rotate all or part of the scene, the model will not always have the same parts closest to the eye. In this case, you need to use a feature of your graphics API to identify the distance of each part from the eyepoint. There are three ways you might do this.

- The function and parameter `glGet(GL_CURRENT_RASTER_DISTANCE)` returns the distance from the eyepoint to the current raster position, so it can be used.
- You can use the `gluProject()` function with the original model coordinates of points in each part and get the *z*-value of the point in the window from that function as the distance to the part.
- You may use the space-partitioning techniques from Chapter 4 to order the parts.

In each case you can get the distance of each from each part to the eye and sort the parts before you draw them. This process can be seen as changing the order in which you traverse the scene graph.

As you look at this figure, note that although each of the three planes has the same alpha value of 0.5, the difference in luminance between the green and blue colors is apparent because the plane with the green in front looks different from the plane with the blue (or the red, for that matter) in front. This goes back to the difference in luminance between colors that we discussed earlier.

Color in OpenGL

OpenGL uses the RGB and RGBA color models with real-valued components. These colors follow the RGB discussion above very closely, so there is little need for any special comments on color itself in OpenGL. Instead, we will discuss blending in OpenGL and then give some examples of code that uses color for its effects.

Specifying Colors

In OpenGL, colors are specified with the `glColor*(...)` functions. These follow the usual OpenGL pattern of including information on the parameters they will take, including a dimension, the type of data, and whether the data is scalar or vector. Specifically we will see functions such as

```
glColor3f(r, g, b)-three real scalar color parameters, or
glColor4fv(V)     -four real color parameters in a vector V.
```

These allow us to specify either RGB or RGBA color with either scalar or vector data, as we wish. You will see several examples of this kind of color specification throughout the book.

Enabling Blending

To use RGBA colors, you must specify that you want blending enabled and you must identify the way the pixel color will blend the color in the color buffer with the color of the new object. This is done with two simple function calls:

```
glEnable(GL_BLEND);
glBlendFunc(GL_SRC_ALPHA, GL_ONE_MINUS_SRC_ALPHA);
```

The first is a case of general enabling for OpenGL; the system has many capabilities and you select those you want by enabling them. This lets your program be more efficient by carrying out only the operations you choose in the rendering pipeline. The second allows you to specify how the color of the object you are drawing is blended with the color that has already been set for each pixel. The blend functions above are the most commonly used to simulate transparency. If you use these functions and your object has an alpha value of 0.7, then the color of a pixel after your object has been drawn is 70 percent the color of the new object and 30 percent the color of whatever had been drawn up to that point.

The OpenGL blending function has many options. The format for the blending function specification is

```
glBlendFunc(src, dest)
```

and there are many symbolic options for the source (`src`) and destination (`dest`) blending values; the OpenGL manual covers them all.

Code Examples

A Model with Parts Having a Full Spectrum of Colors

This example is the code that draws the edges of the RGB cube. It uses translation and scaling to create a number of small cubes that make up the edges. In this code, we create a cube function whose parameters are its location, and it sets its color by its location.

```
#define NUMSTEPS 20
#define SIZE 20.0
typedef GLfloat color[4];

void cube(float r, float g, float b) {
     color cubeclr;
     ...
     cubeclr[0]=r; cubeclr[1]=g; cubeclr[2]=b; cubeclr[3]=1.0;
     glColor4fv(cubecolor);
     glBegin(GL_QUADS);
          ...
     glEnd();
}

void ribboncube() {
     ...
     for (i=0; i<=NUMSTEPS; i++) {        // one of the red parts
          glPushMatrix();
          glScalef(scale,scale,scale);
          glTranslatef(-SIZE+(float)i*2.0*scale*SIZE,SIZE,SIZE);
          cube((float)i/(float)NUMSTEPS,1.0,1.0);
          glPopMatrix();
     }
}
```

We use the transformation stack technique of pushing the current modeling transformation onto the transformation stack, applying translation and scaling, drawing the cube, and then popping the transformation stack to restore the previous modeling transformation.

The HSV Cone

There are two functions of interest for the program that displays this color model. The first is the conversion from HSV colors to RGB colors; this is taken from [FO] and is based on a geometric relationship between the cone and the cube that is clearer if you look at the cube along a diagonal between two opposite vertices. The second function does the actual drawing of the cone with colors generally defined in HSV and converted to RGB for display, and with color smoothing handling most of the problem of shading the cone. For each vertex, the color of the vertex is specified before the vertex coordinates, allowing smooth shading to give the effect in Figure 5.4 in the color insert. For more on smooth shading, see Chapter 6.

```
void
convertHSV2RGB(float h,float s,float v,float *r,float *g,float *b)
{
// conversion from Foley et.al., fig. 13.34, p. 593
float f, p, q, t;
int k;

if (s == 0.0) {   // achromatic case
    *r = *g = *b = v;
}
else {   // chromatic case
        if (h == 360.0) h=0.0;
        h = h/60.0;
        k = (int)h;
        f = h - (float)k;
        p = v * (1.0 - s);
        q = v * (1.0 - (s * f));
        t = v * (1.0 - (s * (1.0 - f)));
        switch (k) {
            case 0: *r = v; *g = t; *b = p; break;
            case 1: *r = q; *g = v; *b = p; break;
            case 2: *r = p; *g = v; *b = t; break;
            case 3: *r = p; *g = q; *b = v; break;
            case 4: *r = t; *g = p; *b = v; break;
            case 5: *r = v; *g = p; *b = q; break;
        }
    }
}

void HSV(void)
{
#define NSTEPS 36
#define steps (float)NSTEPS
#define TWOPI (2.*M_PI)

    int i;
    float r, g, b;

    glBegin(GL_TRIANGLE_FAN);    // cone of the HSV space
        glColor3f(0.0, 0.0, 0.0);
        glVertex3f(0.0, 0.0, -2.0);
        for (i=0; i<=NSTEPS; i++) {
            convert(360.0*(float)i/steps, 1.0, 1.0, &r, &g, &b);
            glColor3f(r, g, b);
            glVertex3f(2.0*cos(TWOPI*(float)i/steps),
                2.0*sin(TWOPI*(float)i/steps),2.0);
        }
    glEnd();
    glBegin(GL_TRIANGLE_FAN);    // top plane of the HSV space
        glColor3f(1.0, 1.0, 1.0);
        glVertex3f(0.0, 0.0, 2.0);
```

```
        for (i=0; i<=NSTEPS; i++) {
            convert(360.0*(float)i/steps, 1.0, 1.0, &r, &g, &b);
            glColor3f(r, g, b);
            glVertex3f(2.0*cos(TWOPI*(float)i/steps),
                2.0*sin(TWOPI*(float)i/steps),2.0);
        }
    glEnd();
}
```

The HLS Double Cone

The conversion itself takes two functions, while the function to display the double cone is so close to that for the HSV model that we do not include it here. The source of the conversion functions is again Foley et al. This code was used to produce the images in Figure 5.5 in the color insert.

```
void
convertHLS2RGB(float h,float l,float s,float *r,float *g,float *b)
{
// conversion from Foley et.al., Figure 13.37, page 596
        float m1, m2;

        if (l <= 0.5) m2 = l*(1.0+s);
        else      m2 = l + s - l*s;
        m1 = 2.0*l - m2;
        if (s == 0.0) {   // achromatic cast
            *r = *g = *b = l;
        }
        else {   // chromatic case
            *r = value(m1, m2, h+120.0);
            *g = value(m1, m2, h);
            *b = value(m1, m2, h-120.0);
        }
    }

    float value(float n1, float n2, float hue) {
    // helper function for the HLS-≥RGB conversion
        if (hue > 360.0) hue -= 360.0;
        if (hue < 0.0) hue += 360.0;
        if (hue < 60.0) return(n1 + (n2 - n1)*hue/60.0);
        if (hue < 180.0) return(n2);
        if (hue < 240.0) return(n1 + (n2 - n1)*(240.0 - hue)/60.0);
        return(n1);
    }
```

An Object with Partially Transparent Faces

The code that draws the three images in Figure 5.19 has a few points that are worth noting. These three squares are colored by:

```
GLfloat         color0[]={1.0, 0.0, 0.0, 0.5}, // R
                color1[]={0.0, 1.0, 0.0, 0.5}, // G
                color2[]={0.0, 0.0, 1.0, 0.5}; // B
```

These are the full red, green, and blue colors with a 0.5 alpha value, so when each square is drawn it uses 50 percent of the background color and 50 percent of the square color. You will see that blending in the left-hand image of the figure for this example.

The geometry for each of the planes is defined as an array of points, each of which is, in turn, an array of real numbers:

```
typedef GLfloat point3[3];
point3 plane0[4]= {{-1.0, 0.0, -1.0}, // X-Z plane
                   {-1.0, 0.0, 1.0},
                   { 1.0, 0.0, 1.0},
                   { 1.0, 0.0, -1.0} };
```

As we saw in the example above, the color of each part is specified as the part is drawn. This would not be needed if many of the parts had the same color; once a color is specified, it is used for anything that is drawn until the color is changed.

```
glColor4fv(color0);     // red
glBegin(GL_QUADS);     // X-Z plane
    glVertex3fv(plane0[0]);
    glVertex3fv(plane0[1]);
    glVertex3fv(plane0[2]);
    glVertex3fv(plane0[3]);
glEnd();
```

To extend this to the example of Figure 5.20 with back-to-front drawing, you first break each of the three squares into four pieces so that there is no intersection between any of these parts. You then arrange the order of drawing these twelve parts so that the parts farther from the eye are drawn first. For a static view this is simple, but to do this for a dynamic image with the parts or the eyepoint moving, you need to do depth calculations on the fly. This may not be simple to do. In OpenGL, this uses the function

```
GLint gluProject(objX,objY,objZ,model,proj,view,winX,winY,winZ)
```

where `objX, objY`, and `objZ` are the `GLdouble` coordinates of the point in model space, `model` and `proj` are `const GLdouble *` variables for the current modelview and projection matrices (obtained from `glGetDoublev` calls), `view` is a `const Glint *` variable for the current viewport (obtained from a `glGetIntegerv` call), and `winX, winY`, and `winZ` are `GLdouble *` variables that return the coordinates of the point after projection into 3D eye space.

With this information, you can determine the depth of each component of your scene and build sequence information based on the depth. You can use this sequence information to draw the components in back-to-front order if you have structured your data with techniques such as arrays of structs that include quads and depths.

Indexed Color

In addition to the RGB and RGBA color we have discussed in this chapter, OpenGL can operate in indexed color mode. However, we don't discuss this further here because it introduces few new graphics ideas and it is difficult to create high-quality images with indexed color. If you have a system that supports only indexed color, please refer to the OpenGL reference material for this information.

Color Ramps in OpenGL

Because color ramps make color represent a numeric value, you use a color ramp by calculating the value and setting the color of a vertex or object to the color determined by the value. Using the notion of a ramp developed earlier in this chapter, a code segment like that which follows calculates the RGB components of the global variable `myColor[]` from a function `calcRamp(float)` as discussed earlier, and then sets either a material color or an absolute color to the values of `myColor` that is set by the ramp function. The following code calculates absolute colors for a grid of triangles, where the value used to determine the color is the average height of the triangle's three vertices.

```
for (i=0; i<XSIZE-1; i++)
    for (j=0; j<YSIZE-1; j++){
        // first triangle in the quad
        glBegin(GL_POLYGON);
            zavg = (height[i][j]+height[i+1][j]+height[i+1][j+1])/3.0;
            calcRamp((zavg-ZMIN)/ZRANGE);
            glColor3f(myColor[0],myColor[1],myColor[2]);
            // now give coordinates of triangle
        glEnd();

        // second triangle in the quad
        glBegin(GL_POLYGON);
            zavg = (height[i][j]+height[i][j+1]+height[i+1][j+1])/3.0;
            calcRamp((zavg-ZMIN)/ZRANGE);
            glColor3f(myColor[0],myColor[1],myColor[2]);
            // now give coordinates of triangle
        glEnd();
    }
```

Summary

In this chapter we presented a general discussion of color that includes the RGB, RGBA, HLS, and HSV color models. We included information on color luminance and techniques for simulating transparency with the blending function of the alpha channel, and we introduced a way to generate 3D images using color. Finally, we showed how color is specified and implemented in OpenGL. You should now be able to use color easily in your images, creating much more interesting and meaningful results than you can get with geometry alone.

OpenGL Glossary for the Chapter

OpenGL, like any graphics API, has its functions to specify color. In this chapter we saw a few of these, and they are listed here for reference. The number of these in this chapter is quite small because much of the emphasis in computer graphics is on color derived from lighting models rather than color that is directly specified. As always, we do not include any functions or constants that have been seen previously.

OpenGL Functions

`glColor*()`: a family of functions that define the color the system will use to draw anything until the color is changed; the color can be specified by three or four values, and the values can be scalars or arrays

`glBlendFunc(const, const)`: specifies what scale factors are to be applied to the source (first literal constant) and destination (second literal constant) to determine the blended color for a pixel

Literal Constants

`GL_BLEND`: used with `glEnable()` and `glDisable()` to specify that color blending is enabled or disabled

`GL_ONE_MINUS_SRC_ALPHA`: the scale factor for the `glBlendFunc()` function which specifies that the multiplier for the color is $1-\alpha_{source}$

`GL_SRC_ALPHA`: the scale factor for the `glBlendFunc()` function which specifies that the multiplier for the color is α_{source}

Questions

1. Look at a digital photograph or scanned image of a real scene and compare it with a grayscale version of itself (for example, print the image on a monochrome printer, change your computer monitor to show only grayscale, or connect it to gray with a tool such as Photoshop). What parts stand out more in the color image? In the monochrome image?
2. Look at a standard color print with good magnification (a large magnifying glass, a loupe, etc.) and examine the individual dots of each CMYK color. Is there a pattern defined for the individual dots of each color? How do varying amounts of each color make the actual color you see in the image?
3. On your computer system find ways to displays colors of different depth. (The usual options are 256 colors, 4,096 colors, and 16.7 million colors.) Display an image on the screen, change among these color depth options, and observe the differences; draw some conclusions. Do this for both natural and synthetic images. Pay particular attention to whether you see Mach bands at some of these color depths.
4. Several different color ramps were discussed in this chapter. Discuss some scientific issues that could make one or another color ramp preferable for a particular problem. Include such things as whether changes in the ramp's colors show changes in the value being shown, whether the ramp has discontinuities while the data is smooth, whether the ramp can readily be shown in a legend, and whether the ramp highlights particular values that are important for the viewer to understand.
5. In the previous question we asked you to discuss scientific issues in color ramps; in this question we ask you to discuss cultural issues in color ramps. Consider some places you see color ramps used, such as elevation maps in atlases, temperature maps in weather forecasts, or weather threat maps in news broadcasts. Discuss these color ramps in terms of the cultural issues in the things they display and see if you can identify other ramps that could represent the same information but have other cultural meanings.
6. We discussed using a surface with lights and lighting to show how a function varies in a region, and we also discussed using a surface whose color is determined by a color ramp to show the same information. Compare the information in the pseudocolor surface, where you can see the color at each point, with the information in the lighted surface, where lighting shows the variations in the surface. Is it worthwhile considering a presentation

that includes a surface with both lighting and pseudocolor? Can you think of a way to implement that idea?

7. How easy is it to determine a value from a color in a pseudocolor image? If an image uses a color ramp and includes a legend that shows the relation between colors and values, can you match the color of a point in the image with a numeric value? Could you do anything to the color ramp or the legend to make it easier to match the color and value?

Exercises

1. Identify several different colors with the same luminance and create a set of squares next to each other on the screen that are displayed with these colors. View this display on a monochrome environment and see whether the colors of the squares are differentiable. Discuss the results.
2. Create a model of the RGB color cube in OpenGL, with the faces modeled as quads and colored by blending the colors at the vertices. View this RGB cube from several points to see how the various faces look. Modify the full RGB cube by scaling the vertices so that the largest color value at each of the vertices is C, where C lies between 0 and 1, for a value of C you determine however you like. Find other ways to look at subspaces of the full RGB cube.
3. Many computers or computer applications have a "color picker" capability that allows you to choose a color by RGB, HSV, or HLS specifications. Choose one or two specific colors; use the color picker to find the RGB, HSV, and HLS color coordinates for each; and then hand-execute the color-conversion functions in this chapter to verify that each of the HSV and HLS colors converts to the correct RGB.
4. You can use the color picker as in the previous exercise to find the RGB values for a given color and compare the given color (for example, the color of a physical object) with the color given by the color picker. Make an initial estimate of the color, and then change the RGB components little by little to get as good a match as you can.
5. Go back to the beginning of the book and the temperature distribution example shown in Figure 0.7. That image involved a color ramp for temperature. Create another color ramp for that problem to replace the simple red-to-cyan ramp and examine whether your color ramp is as good as, better than, or not as good as the original. Try to make one that is better, of course!
6. Create two planes that are very close and that cross at a very shallow angle, and color them in quite different colors. See if you get z-fighting at the intersection of these two planes. Now take exactly the same planes, offset by a very small amount, and see what kind of z-fighting you observe. How does the color help you see what the geometry is doing?
7. (Class project) There is a technique called the Delphi method for estimating an answer to a numeric question. In this technique, a number of people each give independent answers, and the answers are averaged to create an overall estimate. Do this with RGB values for the colors of objects: Have everyone in the class estimate the RGB colors of an object and average the individual estimates, then see how close the combined estimate is to the RGB color as you would determine it by exercise 4.

8. (Painter's algorithm) Take any of your images that use only a modest number of polygons, and instead of using depth buffering to accomplish hidden surfaces, use the Painter's Algorithm: Draw the polygons in order from the farthest to the nearest. Do this by creating an array or list of all the polygons you will use and get their distances from the eye with the OpenGL `gluProject(...)` function as described in this chapter, then sort the array or list by depth and draw the polygons in distance order.
9. We talked about color ramps whose values have luminance that varies uniformly with the data being represented, and we gave an example of a ramp that ranged from black to red to yellow to white. Create other examples of uniform-luminance color ramps and compare the feeling of those color ramps with the feeling of the very warm black-red-yellow-white ramp.

Experiments

1. (Blending) Draw two or three planar objects on top of each other, with different alpha values in the color of the different objects. Verify the discussion about what alpha values are needed to simulate equal colors from the objects in the final image, and try changing the order of the different objects to see how the alpha values must change to restore the equal color simulation.
2. In the chapter we suggested that there is a different formula for the luminance in HTDV than for regular monitors. Do the same work as in exercise 1 with this different luminance formula and compare the results with the results of that exercise. Which formula works better for your system?
3. Take any image you have created and make a monochrome image from it by reading the color buffer into a RGB array and replacing each pixel with a grayscale image with the same luminance by computing the luminance and writing that into each of the R, G, and B components. Then copy the new image into the color buffer and display it. What is the effect of this process? Is it the same as or different from viewing your original image on a monochrome monitor or converting the image in Photoshop?
4. Create an image that uses the black-red-yellow-white color ramp discussed above to implement its pseudocolor, and then change that color ramp to other ramps; try those discussed in the chapter as well as others from exercise 9. Compare the feelings of the resulting images; you may find that changing the color ramp changes the overall sense of the image.
5. For the heat diffusion program illustrated in Figure 0.7, and using the code included in the introductory chapter, change the temperature-to-color function `setColor()` to use different color ramps, and examine how well the different ramps show the temperature changes across the bar.
6. Simulate color deficiencies in your viewer by modifying the colors you present in an image, and consider the effect on whether the image can be understood. For example, simulate red-green color blindness, one of the most common deficiencies, by changing all colors to have both red and green values equal to the average of the original red and green values. (You can do this in a color ramp by changing the ramp computation; you can do this in a lighted surface by changing the colors of the lights and materials.)

Projects

1. (The small house) For the small house project you have seen before, modify the colors of the walls to include an alpha value and arrange the modeling so that you can see the structure of the house from the outside by using blending.
2. (A scene graph parser) Modify the scene graph parser you began in Chapter 2 to let you specify the color of an object in the appearance node of a geometry node for the object, and write the code for that appearance before the geometry code is written. For efficiency, check whether the color has changed before writing a code statement to change the color, because color is generally retained by the system until it is specifically changed.

6

Lighting and Shading

This chapter introduces the next level beyond color for creating more attractive and realistic computer graphics images. It focuses on two related areas that give improved images: lighting based on a simple model of the interaction of lights and surfaces, and shading based on a simple model of how color changes across an object's surface. The lighting model is based on three components of light that model indirect, direct, and reflective lighting, and introduces both the idea of a light and of an object's material properties. The shading model is based on the idea of averaging the color of the vertices of a polygon to get the color of the interior of the polygon. With these techniques, you can make images that look much more realistic than the images you could make with simple color.

In order to get the most from this chapter, you need to have an understanding of color at the level of the previous chapter, a careful observation of the way light and colors work in the world around you, and an understanding of the concept of polygons and of simple averaging across a polygon.

Lighting

There are two ways to think of how we see things. The first is that things have an intrinsic color and we simply see that color. The model for this in computer graphics is that you define a color in RGB space and instruct the graphics system to draw things with that color. This approach is simplistic, but it's very easy to create images this way because we simply set a color when we define and draw our geometry. In fact, when objects don't have an intrinsic color but we use color to represent some value or other property, as we discussed in the previous chapter, this is an appropriate approach.

However, it's clear that you don't simply see the color things in the real world; what you see depends on the lighting conditions in which you see the things, so you must take light into account in presenting a scene. So the second way to think about how we see things is to recognize that we see light that reaches us after a physical interaction between light and objects in the world. Lights emit energy that reaches the objects, and the energy then comes to us by reflections that involve both the color of the light and the physical properties of the objects. In computer graphics, lighting that considers only lights in the scene is called a *local illumination model.* The usual local illumination model is Phong illumination; it breaks illumination down into three components and is the lighting model supported by most simple graphics APIs. This is handled by an API by the graphics programmer's defining the lights and the materials of objects in the scene, and the color seen on the screen is derived from these. In this chapter we discuss how this approach to light models how we see the world, and how computer graphics distills the model into simple definitions and computations to produce images that have a relationship to the lights and materials in the scene.

A first step in developing graphics with the local illumination model depends on modeling the nature of light. In the simplified but workable model of light used by basic APIs, light has three fundamental components: the ambient, diffuse, and specular components. We can think of each of these as follows:

Ambient: light that is present in the scene because of the overall illumination in the space; this is independent of any particular light and models the general distribution of reflected light in the scene

Diffuse: light that comes directly from a light source to an object, where it interacts with the object and is then sent directly to the viewer; an object reflects a subset of the wavelengths it receives that depends on its material, with the effect of creating the color of the object

Specular: light that comes directly from a light source to an object, where it is reflected directly to the viewer without interacting with the material; because the light does not interact with the material, specular light is generally the color of the light source, not that of the object that reflects the light

These three components are computed based on properties of lights, properties of object materials, and the geometric relationship between the lights and the objects. All three components contribute to the overall light, and the graphics system models this by calculating them for the RGB components separately. The sum of these three light components is the light that is actually seen from an object.

You model a light for computer graphics by defining its position, its color, and other properties. The properties a light can have can vary between different graphics APIs, but they always include position and color, along with others that might or might not be present with different systems. A light might be a spotlight, with a direction and a breadth of beam. The light might be modeled as being so distant that it is a directional light, with all light beams parallel, instead of a positional light. The energy from the light may fall off with distance in different ways. So there may be several ways you can experiment with the properties of lights to get your scene to look like you want.

Just as the lights are modeled to create an image, the material of objects in a scene is modeled to reflect how they contribute to the light. Each object will have properties that show how it responds to each of the three components of light. The ambient property will define the color of the object in ambient light, the diffuse property the color in diffuse light, and the specular property the color in specular light. Our simple models of realistic lighting assume that objects behave the same in ambient and diffuse light, and that objects simply take on the light color in specular light. However, because of the kind of calculations that are done to display a lighted image, each of the light and material properties is treated separately.

So to use lighting in a scene, you must define one or more lights in terms of the three kinds of color they provide, and you must define material properties for each of your objects. This is different from the way you use simple color and will take more thought as you model your scenes, but the changes are not difficult. Graphics APIs have their own ways to specify lights and materials, and we will discuss these for OpenGL when we talk about implementing lighting for your work.

Ambient, Diffuse, and Specular Light

Ambient light is light that seems to come from no apparent source but is simply present in a scene. This is the light you would find in parts of a scene that are not directly illuminated by the lights in the scene. There are contributions to ambient light from reflections among the objects in the scene, creating an overall ambient light value. The amount of ambient light on an object due to single light is simply $A = L_A * C_A$ for a constant C_A that depends on the material of the object and the ambient light L_A present in the scene. The light L_A and constant C_A are RGB triples, not simple constants, and the calculation yields another RGB value. If you have multiple lights, the total ambient light is $A = (L_0 + \sum L_A)*C_A$, where L_0 is the overall ambient light value and the sum is over all the lights. All of the ambient light values are just general approximations and can be tuned for appearance. For example, if you want to emphasize direct lights, you probably want to set your ambient light coefficients to a fairly low level (so you get the effect of lights at night or in a dim room). On the other hand, to see everything in the scene with a relatively uniform light, you can use fairly high ambient light coefficients. If you want to emphasize shapes, use relatively low ambient light coefficients so that the shading we discuss later in this chapter can bring out variations in the surface.

Diffuse light comes directly from light sources and is reflected by the surface of the object at a particular wavelength that depends on the object's material. The general model for diffuse light, used by OpenGL and other APIs, is based on the idea of brightness, or light energy per unit area. A light emits a certain amount of energy per unit area in the direction it is shining, and when this falls on a surface, the intensity of light seen on the surface is proportional to the surface area illuminated by the unit area of the light. As Figure 6.1 shows, one unit of area as seen

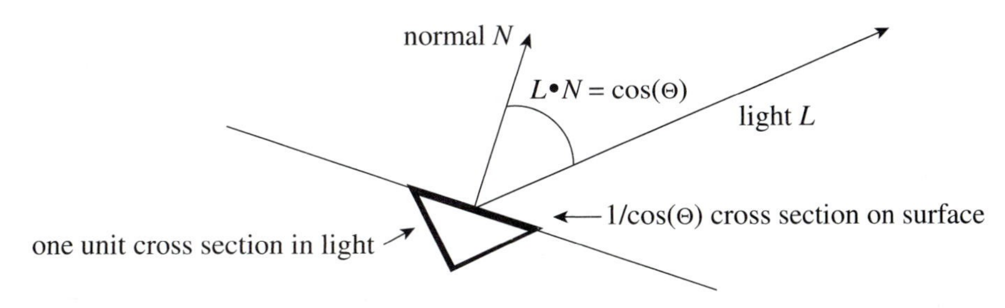

Figure 6.1 Diffuse lighting.

by the light, or one unit of area perpendicular to the light direction, illuminates an area of $1/\cos(\Theta)$ in the surface. So if we have L_D light energy per unit of area in the light direction, we have $L_D\cos(\Theta)$ units of light energy per unit of area on the surface. As the angle of incidence of the light on the surface decreases, the amount of light at the surface becomes reduced, going to zero when the light is parallel to the surface. Because it is impossible to talk about "negative light," if the cosine is negative we replace it with zero, which eliminates diffuse light on surfaces facing away from the light.

Now that we know the amount of diffuse light energy per unit of surface, how does that appear to the eye? Diffuse light is reflected from a surface according to Lambert's law:

> The amount of light reflected in a given direction is proportional to the cosine of the angle from the surface in that direction.

If the amount of diffuse light per unit surface is D and the unit vector from the surface to your eye is E, then the energy reflected to your eye from one unit of surface is proportional to $D*\cos(\Theta) = D*(E \cdot N)$. But this surface area is not seen by your eye to be a unit of area; its area is $\cos(\Theta) = E \cdot N$ and decreases as the angle to your eye increases. So the intensity of light you perceive at the surface is the ratio of the energy your eye receives and the area your eye sees, and this intensity is simply D—which is the same, no matter where your eye is. This means that the location of the eyepoint does not matter in the diffuse light computation, which fits our observation that things don't change color as we move around.

From these discussions, the diffuse lighting calculation that computes the intensity of diffuse light is

$$D = L_D*C_D*\cos(\Theta) = L_D*C_D*(L \cdot N)$$

for the value of the diffuse light L_D from each light source and the ambient property of the material C_D. The presence of the $L \cdot N$ dot product term shows why we must have surface normals in order to calculate diffuse light. If you have several lights, the total diffuse light is given by $D = \sum L_D*C_D*(L \cdot N)$ where the sum is over all the lights (including a different light vector L for each light). Using the dot product instead of the cosine assumes that our normal vector N and light vector L are of unit length, as we assumed previously.

Direct light interacts with the objects it illuminates in a way that produces the color we see in the objects. The object does not reflect all the light that hits it; rather, it absorbs certain wavelengths (or colors) and reflects the others. The color we see in an object, then, comes from the light that is reflected instead of being absorbed, and this behavior is what we specify when we define the diffuse property of materials.

Specular light is a surface phenomenon that produces bright highlights on shiny surfaces. Specular light depends on the smoothness and electromagnetic properties of the surface, so smooth metallic objects (for example) reflect light well. The energy in specular light is not reflected according to Lambert's law but is reflected with no interaction with the material so that the angle of incidence is equal to the angle of reflection, as illustrated in Figure 6.2. This light has a small amount of "spread" as it leaves the object, depending on the smoothness of the object's surface, so the standard model for specular light allows you to define a property called the *shininess* of an object to model that spread. Shininess is modeled by a parameter called the *shininess coefficient,* which gives smaller, brighter highlights as it increases and makes the

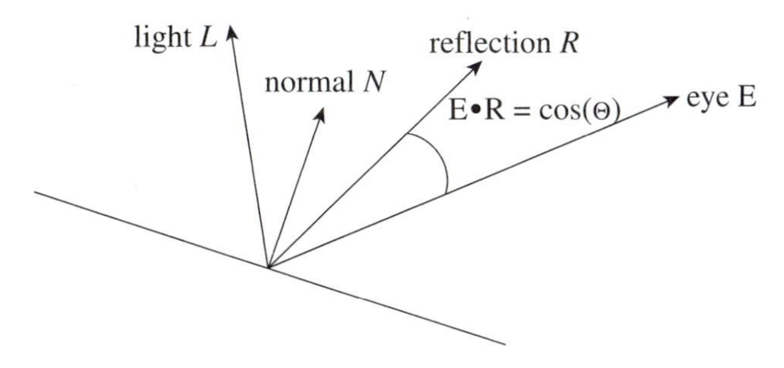

Figure 6.2 Specular lighting.

material seem increasingly shiny, as shown in the three successive images in Figure 6.3. In Figure 4.6, we saw that the reflection vector is computed as $R = 2(N \cdot L)N - L$ with the notation of Figure 6.2.

The specular light seen on an object is computed by the equations

$$S = L_s{}^*C_s{}^*\cos^M(\Theta) = L_s{}^*C_s{}^*(E \cdot R)^M$$

for a light's specularity value L_S, the object's specular coefficient C_S and shininess coefficient M. Again, the eye vector E and reflection vector R must have unit length. Specular light depends on the angle between the eye and the light reflection, because it is reflected directly from the surface in a mirrorlike way and falls off as a power of the cosine of this angle. Because it describes the extent to which the surface acts shiny, larger values give shinier materials. *Shininess* is a relative term, because even rather shiny materials may have small surface irregularities that keep the reflection from being perfectly mirrorlike. As the shininess coefficient increases, the highlight gets smaller and more focused—that is, the sphere looks shinier and more polished. Thus the shininess coefficient is part of the definition of a material. This produces a fairly good model of shininess, because for relatively large values of M (for example, M near or above 30) the function $\cos^M(\Theta)$ has a value very near one if the angle Θ is small and drops off quickly as the angle increases, with the speed of the dropoff increasing as the power is increased.

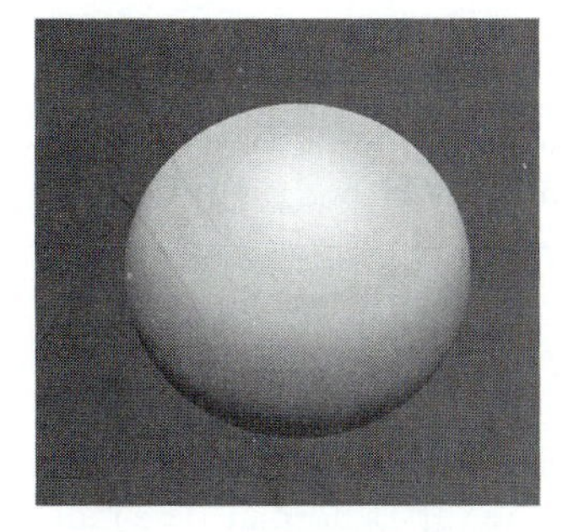

Figure 6.3 Specular highlights with specular coefficients 20, 50, and 80 (*left*, *center*, and *right*), respectively.

The specular light computation is done separately for each light and each object. This calculation depends fundamentally on both the direction from the object to the light and the direction of the object to the eye, so you should expect to see specular light move as objects, lights, or your eyepoint moves.

Specular light interacts with objects quite differently from the way diffuse light does. We generally assume that no light is absorbed by specular reflection so that the color of the specular highlight is the same as the color of the light, and you model this by defining a material to have white specular color. You can specify a material that colors specular highlights if you want, but in order to appear at all realistic, that color should be the same as the object's diffuse color.

Because both diffuse and specular lighting use normals to the surface in their computation, we need to review how we get surface normals. One way to do this is analytically. For a sphere, the normal at any given point is in the direction from the center of the sphere to the point, so we just need to know the center and the point to calculate the normal. If we have a surface that is the graph of a smooth function of two variables, you can calculate the function's directional derivatives at a point and take the cross product of these derivatives, because the derivatives define the tangent plant to the surface and the normal is perpendicular to that plane. But if we cannot use analytical computations, we must calculate the normal from the coordinates of the polygon. This calculation was described in the discussion of mathematical fundamentals in Chapter 4 by taking the cross product of two adjacent edges of the polygon in the direction the edges are oriented.

Now that we know how to compute these three light values, let's consider the constants in the light calculations. The ambient constant is the product of the ambient light component and the ambient material component, calculated separately for the red, green, and blue light components. Similarly, the diffuse and specular constants are the products of their respective light and material components. So a white light and any color of material will produce the color of the material, and a red or yellow light and a red material will produce a red color. But a red light and a blue material will produce black because there is no blue light to go with the blue material and there is no red material to go with the red light. The final light at any point is the sum of the ambient, diffuse, and specular values, each computed for all three RGB components. If any component has a final value larger than one, it is clamped to have value 1.

If you have multiple lights, they are treated additively—the ambient light in the scene is the sum of any overall ambient light for the entire scene plus the ambient lights from the individual lights, the diffuse light in the scene is the sum of the diffuse lights from the individual lights, and the specular light in the scene is the sum of the diffuse lights from the individual lights. As above, if any component of these sums exceed one, the value is clamped to unity.

Later in this chapter we discuss shading models, but for now all our lighting computations calculate the light at a single point on a model. We can calculate the light at one point on each polygon or we can do it at each vertex of the polygon. If we choose to do this at only one point on each polygon, we can get only one color for the entire polygon, which gives us *flat* shading. If we do this for each vertex we can get *smooth* shading, which can give a much more realistic kind of image. If a vertex is part of several polygons and we want to calculate a normal for the vertex that we can use for each of these polygons, we can do an analytical calculation or we can calculate the normal based on each polygon and average them to get the vertex normal. The individual colors for the vertices are then used to calculate colors for all the points in the polygon.

But none of our light computation handles shadows because shadows depend on light that reaches the surface, which is very different from the way light is reflected from the surface.

Shadows are difficult and are handled in most graphics APIs with very specialized programming. We discuss a simple approach to shadows based on texture mapping in Chapter 8.

Surface Normals

We have seen that you need to have surface normals in order to compute diffuse and specular light. This is done by including normal vectors in the geometry specifications in the shape node. Processes for computing normals can involve analysis of an object, so you can compute exact normals for analytically defined objects. If you can't do an analytic calculation, you can use cross products of the edges of the polygon. However, it is not enough merely to specify a normal; you need to have unit normals, or normals that are one unit long (usually called *normalized vectors*). It takes some computation to scale the normals yourself, and it is not enough to do this when you define your geometry because scaling or other transformations can change the length of the normals. Your graphics API may help by giving you a way to say that all normals are to be normalized before they are used.

We saw that the cross product of two vectors is another vector that is perpendicular to both of them. If we have a polygon, we can calculate a vector parallel to an edge by taking the difference of the endpoints of the edge. If we do this for two adjacent edges, we get two vectors that lie in the polygon's plane, so their cross product is a vector perpendicular to both edges. This vector is perpendicular to the plane of the polygon, so we have a normal to the polygon.

As we saw in Chapter 2, each polygon has two sides called the *front* side and *back* side. We want the normal to always point out of a polyhedron; the side toward which the normal points is called the *front* side, and this distinction is important in lighting computations as well as other graphical computations. We will also see that materials can have separate definitions for the front and back sides of polygons.

Materials

Lighting involves both the specification of the lights in a scene and the light-related properties of the objects in the scene. To use lighting in a scene, you must specify both of these: the properties of your lights, and the material properties of your objects. In this section we discuss material specifications. Implementing lighting for a scene involves putting lights and materials together as we show in an example at the end of this chapter.

Each object in your scene contributes to the reflected light that determines its color when it is displayed. When we discussed the three components of light, we found four properties of materials: C_A, the reflectivity of the material in ambient light; C_D, the reflectivity of material in diffuse light; C_S, the reflectivity of the material in specular light; and M, the shininess coefficient for specular light. The three reflectivity terms involve color, so they are specified by giving their RGB components, while the shininess coefficient is the scalar exponent of the dot product $R \cdot E$ in specular light. These properties are the material specifications of an object and must be defined for each object in your scene so the system can carry out the lighting calculations. Your graphics API will probably let you define these as part of your modeling work; they should be considered part of the appearance information in a shape node. The API may have some other material behavior, such as separate specifications of the front and back sides of a material; this is the case for OpenGL, but it may vary between APIs.

All of our discussions of lighting have assumed that an object is only reflective, but an object can also be *emissive*—that is, it can send out light of its own. An emissive light adds to the light of the object but does not add extra light to the scene, letting you define a bright spot to present something like an actual light in the scene. This is managed by defining a material to have an emissive light property, and the final lighting calculations for this object add the components of the light emission to the other lighting components when the object's color is computed.

When we introduced scene graphs in Chapter 2, we talked about the appearance part of a shape node. There we noted that color and shading were among the appearance factors that we could include, but materials are also appearance properties. While we should define materials separately for each shape node—as we should also define color or shading separately for each—it's usually much more convenient to use the facilities of your graphics API to define them for groups of shapes. However, this depends on how your API retains data between geometry definitions. But it reminds us that we can vary our shading across a scene in the same way we can change the color or materials we are drawing.

Light Properties

Because all the lighting comes from lights you provide, lights are critical components of your modeling work. In Chapter 2, we saw how to include lights in a scene graph. Along with the location of each light, which is directly supported by the scene graph, you want to define other aspects of the light, and these are discussed in this section.

Your graphics API allows you to define a number of properties for a light. Typically, these can include its position or its direction, its color, how it is attenuated (diminished) over distance, and whether it is an omnidirectional light or a spotlight. We will cover these properties generally here but will not go into depth for them all, but the properties of position and color are critical. The other properties are primarily useful if you are trying to achieve a particular kind of effect in your scene. Details on lights in OpenGL are covered in the OpenGL section of this chapter, and the position and color properties are illustrated in the example at the end of this chapter.

Light Color

Light color is usually seen as having a single value, which like all colors can be expressed in terms of the RGB color model. Because the lighting model separates ambient, diffuse, and specular components, however, some graphics APIs allow you to specify the ambient, diffuse, and specular colors of a light separately. You will want to look at your API carefully to see what model it uses for colors and for the lighting model components.

Positional Lights

When you want to use a light that is located within the scene, you want to give your light an actual position in the scene. To define a light position, simply use standard modeling coordinates and define the position at the correct place in your model, as discussed in the OpenGL section.

Spotlights

A positional light will shine in all directions, but if you want a light that shines only in a specific direction, define the light to be a spotlight. A spotlight has not only a position but also other properties such as a direction, a cutoff angle, and a dropoff exponent, as shown in Figure 6.4. The direction is a 3D vector that is parallel to the light direction, the cutoff angle is a value between 0.0 and 90.0 that represents half the spread of the spotlight and determines whether the light is focused

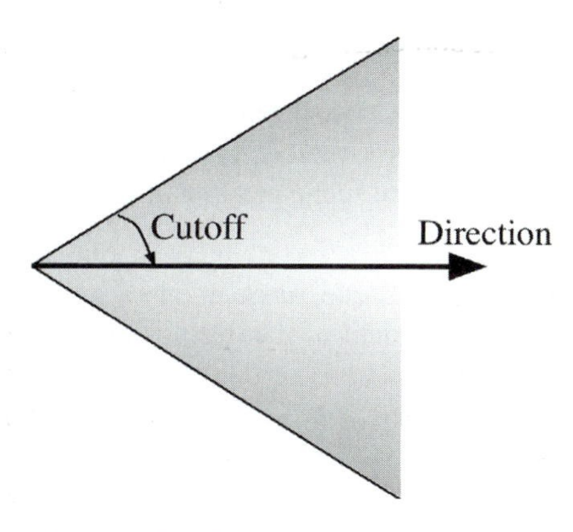

Figure 6.4 Spotlight direction and cutoff.

tightly or spread broadly (a smaller cutoff represents a more focused light), and the dropoff exponent controls how the intensity drops off between the centerline of the spotlight and the intensity at the edge.

In more detail, if a spotlight has position P, dropoff d, direction D, and cutoff Θ, the light energy at a point Q in a direction V from the spotlight is zero if the absolute value of the dot product $(Q-P) \cdot D$ is larger than $\cos\Theta$, or is multiplied by $((Q-P) \cdot D)^d$ if the absolute value of the dot product is less than $\cos(\Theta)$.

Attenuation

Physics tells us that the energy from a light source on a unit surface diminishes as the square of the distance from the light to the surface. This diminishing is called attenuation, and computer graphics models that behavior in a number of ways. An accurate model would give a light that diminishes as the square of the distance d from the light, multiplying the light energy by k/d^2, and the graphics system would diminish the intensity of the light accordingly. However, the human perceptual system is more nearly logarithmic than linear in the way we see light, so this light does not seem as realistic, and we probably need to use an attenuation that drops off more slowly. Your graphics API will probably give you some options in modeling attenuation.

Directional Lights

For lights that are at a specific position in the scene, the lighting model takes the light direction in the lighting model as the direction from the light position to that point. However, if we were looking for an effect like that of sunlight, we would want light that comes from the same direction at all points in the scene. In effect, we would want to have a light at a point at infinity. If the fourth coordinate of the position is zero, which would be invalid for actual coordinates, the light is treated as a *directional* light and the first three values are the direction of the light. All lighting calculations are then done with this light direction. If your graphics API supports directional lights, there will be a way to specify that the light is directional instead of positional and that simply defines the direction from which the light will be received.

Positioning and Moving Lights

Lights can be critical components of a scene, because they can show objects' shapes and contours. Lights are affected by all the transformations that are active when the light position is defined. A summary of the concepts from the scene graph will remind us of the issues with lights in models:

- If the light is at a fixed place in the scene, its geometry is at the top level of the scene graph. This creates a light that is independent of the eye position or of any other modeling in the scene.
- If the light is at a fixed place relative to the eyepoint, the light's geometry is modified by the viewing transformation, but not by any subsequent modeling transformations. To get this placement you can specify the light in the view branch of the scene graph if you adopt the convention that the viewing is set by the inverse of the eyepoint-setting transformation.
- If the light is at a fixed place relative to an object in the scene, you define the light's geometry in a branch of the group node that defines the object. Anything that affects the object will be done above that group node and will affect the light's geometry in the same way as the rest of the object.
- If the light is to move around in the scene on its own, the light is a separate content node of the scene graph, and the geometry of the light is defined when that node is set.

The concept for this modeling is that the geometry of a positional light is simply another part of the modeling process and is managed in the same way as any other object. The other appearance properties of each light are set at any legal point, probably as part of the light's definition.

Using Lights for Effect

If we think about a simple scene, it may be most natural to think of creating a single set of lights that will be used to show everything in that scene. But there may be reasons to use different lights for different parts of a scene. Doing so will let you highlight one thing in the scene differently from other things to make it stand out by showing its shape, it brightness, or anything else you want to bring out. In order to use this kind of lighting, you will need to define lights in your scene that you can turn on and off as you display different parts of the scene. Most of the scene might be drawn with a standard set of lights to create an overall idea, but to draw the object you are highlighting you turn on its key light, draw the object, and turn off the light. You can get other effects this way, such as featuring several items one at a time by creating an animation that highlights each in turn.

A simple example of this highlighting is shown in Figure 6.5. This is part of an animation of the Earth moving around the sun that illustrates the equinoxes, and the Earth is lighted with a light that is placed at the center of the sun. The sun is lighted with a light at the eyepoint, however, so it will look like the large luminous sphere that we think of it as. This lighting shows how the Earth is lighted realistically, including emphasizing when the sun focuses on the northern or southern hemisphere (the figure shows summer in the southern hemisphere), but the sun is shown iconically with no attempt to be realistic. The code for this example is included in the resources with the book.

Figure 6.5 A scene with different lighting on the sun and the earth. See the figure in the color insert.

Lights in Scene Graphs

Lights are graphics objects that are part of the scene, and they are placed in scene graphs just as any other graphics objects are. Each can be represented by a shape node that gives its geometric position and, if appropriate, its direction, and also includes appearance data that includes the light color, light type, and any other light parameters. However, enabling and disabling lights is not an appearance property of the light's shape node because each object may decide for each light whether or not the light should affect it. If you carefully choose the lights that affect each object, you can use lights to highlight objects for the viewer. Thus we could see the list of enabled lights as part of the appearance part of the shape nodes that represent the visible graphics objects in a scene.

Shading

Shading is the process of computing the color for the components of a scene based on the effect of light on the surface of each object. The shading process is based on the physics of light, and the most detailed kinds of shading computation can involve deep subtleties of the behavior of light, including the way light scatters from various kinds of materials with various surface details. A great deal of research has been done in these areas, and any genuinely realistic rendering must take a number of surface details into account.

Most graphics APIs do not have the capability to do these detailed kinds of computation. The usual beginning API such as OpenGL supports only the simple local illumination model we saw previously and only two shading models for polygons: flat shading and smooth shading. Flat shading gives a constant color for each polygon, and smooth shading gives color variations by averaging colors at the vertices. You may use either, but smooth shading is often more pleasing and can be more realistic. Unless there is a sound reason to use flat shading because you must represent data or a discontinuous concept more accurately, you may want to use smooth shading for your images. We will briefly discuss some more sophisticated kinds of shading, even though a beginning API cannot usually support them.

Shading Considerations for Visual Communication

If you are developing an image that represents actual objects and uses naturalistic colors, you will want to make that image as realistic as you can. Drawing actual objects is often enhanced by making the objects seem realistic—though sometimes you may want to highlight a particular feature by using special lighting or a nonrealistic color. If the things you display in your scene do not represent actual objects, however, and particularly if you use synthetic colors to represent some property, then you need to think carefully about whether you should use lighting and shading for your image.

If you are working with synthetic colors, lighting a scene will make shapes stand out, but colors in the shaded image may not represent the data values accurately. This can be minimized by using the same color for ambient and diffuse lighting (especially if that color is white), and using a material color from a color ramp that maintains relatively constant luminance and simply changes chroma, so the shading provided by the lighting model will change brightness but not color as we discussed such ranges in the previous chapter. This is shown by the shaded relief map of South Africa in Figure 6.6, where the colors represent the height (altitude) of the land but the image is shaded as though there were a light low in the eastern sky, north of the country—as in fact the sun would be shining on the country in the morning. But if the model for your synthetic-color image doesn't have physical meaning for its geometric shapes, there is no reason to use lighting and shading when you present it.

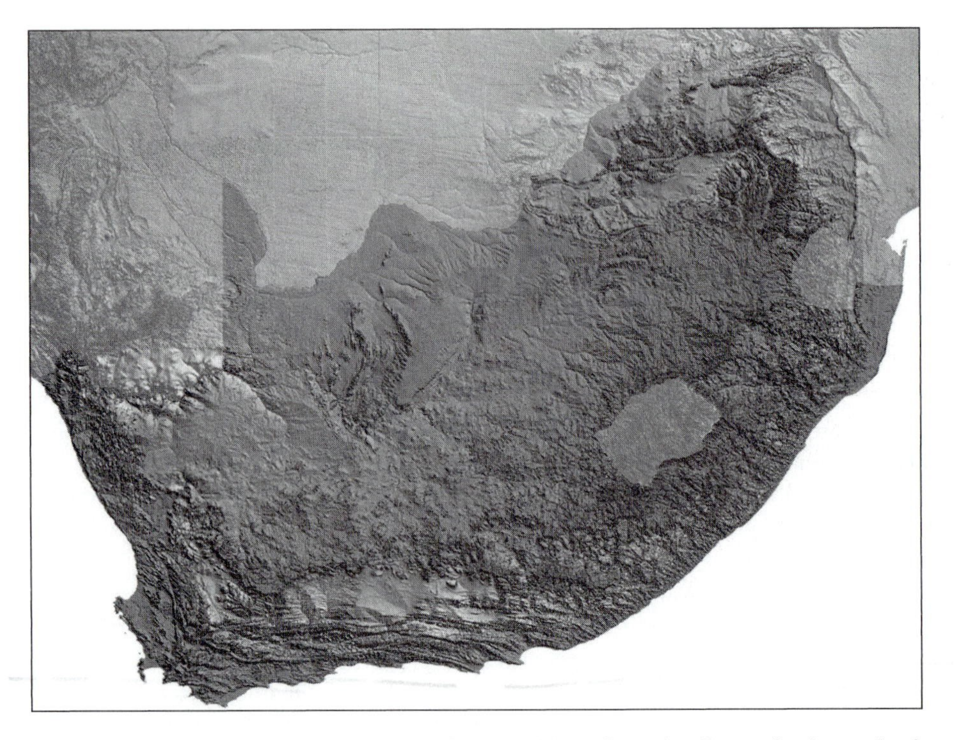

Figure 6.6 A lighted, false-color map of South Africa. See the figure in the color insert. Image courtesy of ComputaMaps, South Africa.

Definitions

Flat shading of a polygon presents each polygon with a single color. This assumes that all the points on the polygon have exactly the same kind of lighting treatment. The term *flat* can be taken to mean that the color is flat (does not vary) across the polygon, or that the polygon is colored as though it were flat (planar) and thus does not change color as it is lighted. This is the effect you will get if you simply set a color for the polygon and do not use a lighting model (the color is flat), or if you use lighting and materials models and then display the polygon with a single normal vector (the polygon is flat). This single normal allows you only a single lighting computation for the entire polygon.

Smooth shading of a polygon displays the pixels in the polygon with smoothly changing colors across the surface of the polygon. This requires that you have a separate color for each vertex of your polygon, because the smooth color change is computed when the graphics system linearly interpolates the vertex colors across the interior of the triangle. The interpolation is done in screen space after the vertices' position has been set by the projection, so the linear calculations can easily be done in graphics cards. This per-vertex color can be provided by setting a different color for each vertex, but it is often produced by per-vertex lighting computations. In order to compute the color of each vertex separately, you must define a separate normal vector for each vertex of the polygon so that the lighting model will produce different colors at each vertex.

Every graphics API supports flat shading in a consistent way. Different graphics APIs may treat smooth shading somewhat differently, however, so you need to understand how your particular API handles this. The simplest smooth shading is done by calculating color at the vertices of each polygon and then interpolating the colors smoothly across the polygon. This is the Gouraud shading model discussed in the next section. If the polygon is a triangle, you may recall that every point in the triangle is a convex combination of the vertices, so you may simply use that same convex combination of the vertex colors. As computer graphics becomes more sophisticated, however, we will see more complex kinds of polygon shading in graphics APIs so that the determination of colors for the pixels in a polygon will become increasingly flexible.

Examples of Flat and Smooth Shading

We have seen many examples of polygons earlier in the book, but we have not been careful to distinguish between whether they were presented with flat or smooth shading. Figure 6.7 illustrates

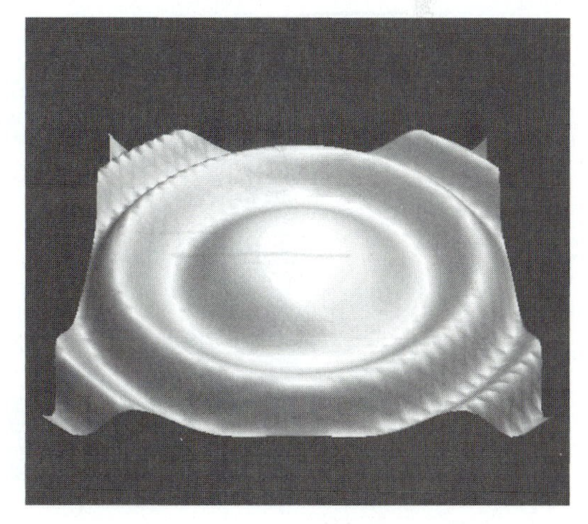

Figure 6.7 A surface with flat shading (*left*) and the same surface with smooth shading (*right*).

the difference by showing two images of the same relatively coarsely defined function surface with flat shading (left) and with smooth shading (right). The smooth-shaded image is much cleaner, but there are still some areas where the triangles change direction very quickly and the color interpolation between adjacent triangles can differ visibly in the smoothly shaded image. Smooth shading is very nice—often nicer than flat shading—but it isn't perfect.

In the computation for this smooth shading, each vertex has its own normal, computed using the analytic techniques described in the next section, so the lighting model computes a different color for each vertex. The interpolation then calculates colors for each pixel in the polygon that vary smoothly across the polygon interior, providing a smooth color graduation across the polygon. This interpolation is called *Gouraud shading*. It is quick to compute, but because it depends on colors only at the polygon vertices, it can miss lighting effects within polygons. Visually, it is susceptible to showing the color of a vertex more strongly along an edge of a polygon than a genuinely smooth shading would suggest, as you can see in the right-hand image in Figure 6.7. Other kinds of interpolation do not show some of these problems, though they are not often provided by a graphics API. One of these, Phong shading, is discussed later in this chapter.

An interesting experiment to help you understand the properties of shaded surfaces is to consider the relationship between smooth shading and the resolution of the display grid. In principle, you should be able to use a fairly fine grid with flat shading or a much coarser grid with smooth shading to achieve similar results. You should define a particular grid size and flat shading, and try to find the smaller grid that would give an image similar to the original grid with smooth shading. Figure 6.8 is an example of this experiment. The surface still shows a small amount of the faceting of flat shading but avoids much of the problem with quickly varying surface directions of a coarse-grained smooth shading and is superior in many ways to the smooth-shaded polygon of Figure 6.7. Increasing the grid size may make your program either faster or slower than the original smooth shading, depending on the efficiency of the polygon interpolation in the graphics pipeline. This is an example of a very useful experimental approach to computer graphics: if you have several

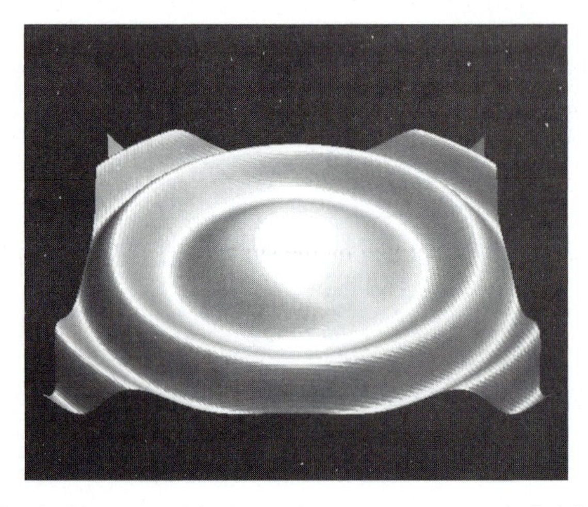

Figure 6.8 A flat-shaded image with three times as many subdivisions in each direction as in the previous figure.

different ways to approximate an effect, try all of them that make sense and see which works best, both for effect and for speed, in a particular application!

This decrease in the granularity of the mesh can be continued until you come to the level of one polygon for each pixel in the image. At that level you effectively don't have shading across the polygon but have a separate normal per polygon, giving you Phong shading.

Calculating Per-Vertex Normals

The only real difference between the programming for the two parts of Figure 6.7 is that the image with flat-shaded polygons uses only one normal per polygon, while the image with smooth-shaded polygons uses a separate normal per vertex. Because this is a mathematical surface, the normal is calculated by analytic processes to determine the exact value of the normal at the vertex. It can take a bit more work to compute the normal at each vertex instead of only once per polygon, but that is the price you pay for smooth shading. Here we discuss techniques for calculating normals either as a weighted average of the normals of each of the polygons that includes the vertex, or as an analytic computation.

Averaging Polygon Normals

If you have a vertex shared by several polygons in a model, you can calculate a single normal N at the vertex that takes all the polygons into account by computing the weighted average of the normals for all the polygons that meet at the vertex as

$$N = \left(\sum a_i N_i\right) \Big/ \left(\sum a_i\right),$$

with the sum taken over all indices i of polygons P_i that include this vertex, where each polygon P_i has a normal N_i and has weight a_i at the vertex. (Note that this is a sum of vectors, so we are really doing x, y, and z calculations for each normal.) Each weight can be calculated in any way you want to represent the importance of the polygon in determining the normal to the vertex. If all the weights are equal, you are simply averaging all the vertex normals. A common approach is to take the weight as the angle of the polygon at the vertex. This angle a_i is the inverse cosine of the dot product of the two normalized edges of the polygon P_i that meet at the vertex because that dot product is the cosine of the angle between the edges. These angles can be retained with the vertex information for the polygon and used in cases such as this.

Analytic Computation of Normals

In the example of Figure 6.7, an analytic approach to computing the normal N at each vertex is possible because the surface was defined by the simple closed-form equation

$$f(x,y) = 0.3 * \cos(x * x + y * y + t).$$

We can calculate the analytic directional derivatives at each vertex: In the x direction and y direction respectively they are

$$fx(x,y) = \partial f / \partial x = -0.6 * x * \sin(x * x + y * y + t) \text{ and}$$
$$fy(x,y) = \partial f / \partial y = -0.6 * y * \sin(x * x + y * y + t).$$

These are used to calculate tangent vectors in these directions, and their cross product was computed to get the vertex normal. If you have a function f with partial derivatives fx and fy, as we have above, the tangent vectors to the surface in the x and y directions are $<1, 0, fx>$ and $<0, 1, fy>$, respectively. Taking the cross product through determinants as we discussed in Chapter 4, we see that a normal vector to the surface at a point is $<-fx, -fy, 1>$. Normalizing this, either through direct computation or by enabling `GL_NORMALIZE`, completes the calculation of the surface normal. This is shown in the code sample at the end of this chapter.

You can also get exact normals from other kinds of models; we saw earlier that the normals to a sphere are simply the radius vectors for the sphere, so a purely geometric model may also have exact normals. In general, when models permit you to carry out analytic or geometric calculations for normals, these will be more exact and will give you better results than an interpolation technique.

Other Shading Models

You cannot and must not assume that the smooth shading model of a simple API such as OpenGL represents smooth surfaces accurately. It assumes that the surface of the polygon varies uniformly, it includes only per-vertex information in calculating colors across the polygon, and it relies on a linear behavior of the RGB color space that isn't accurate. Like many of the features of any computer graphics system, it approximates reality, but there are better ways to achieve smooth surfaces. For example, a shading model called *Phong shading* takes a normal for each vertex and interpolates the normals themselves to compute the color at each pixel in the polygon, instead of simply interpolating the vertex colors. Interpolating normals is much more complicated than interpolating colors, because the uniformly spaced pixels in screen space do not come from uniformly spaced points in 3D eye space or 3D model space; the perspective projection involves a division by the Z-coordinate of the point in eye space. This makes normal interpolation more complex—and much slower—than color interpolation and takes it out of the range of simple graphics APIs. However, the Phong shading model behaves like a genuinely smooth surface across the polygon and will pick up specular highlights within the polygon and will behave smoothly along the edges of the polygon. The details of Gouraud and Phong shading are discussed in other graphics textbooks. We encourage you to read them as an excellent example of the use of interpolation for many computer graphics processes.

Figure 6.9 illustrates the visual difference between flat, smooth, and Phong shading. Notice that the flat-shaded sphere shows each facet clearly, the smooth-shaded sphere shows some facet

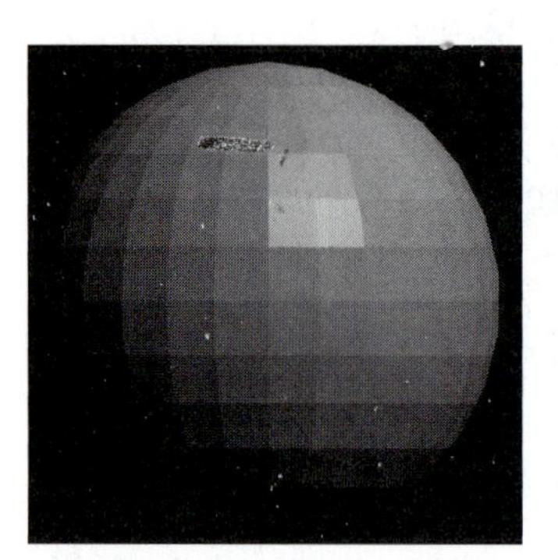 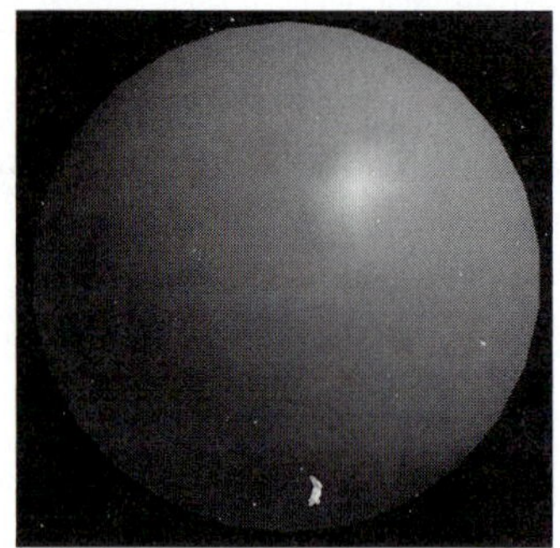 

Figure 6.9 A sphere presented with flat shading (*left*), smooth shading (*center*), and phong shading (*right*).

edges and the specular reflection is not quite smoothly distributed over the surface, while the facet edges and the specular reflection in the Phong shaded sphere are much smoother.

The Phong shading model is based on smoothly changing normals across the polygon, but another shading model is based on controlling the normals across the polygon. Like the texture map that we describe later and which creates effects that change across a surface, we can create a mapping that alters the normals inside the polygon so the shading model can create the effect of a bumpy surface. This is called a *bump map,* and like Phong shading the normal for each individual pixel is individually defined. The normal for a pixel is computed by combining the normal from Phong shading and a normal computed from the bump map by the gradient of the color. The color of each individual pixel is then computed with this normal by the standard lighting model. Figure 6.10 shows an example of the effect of a bump map. Note that the bump map itself is simply a 2D image wherein the height of each point is defined by the gray level; this is called a *height field.* Normals are computed from the changes in colors in the field.

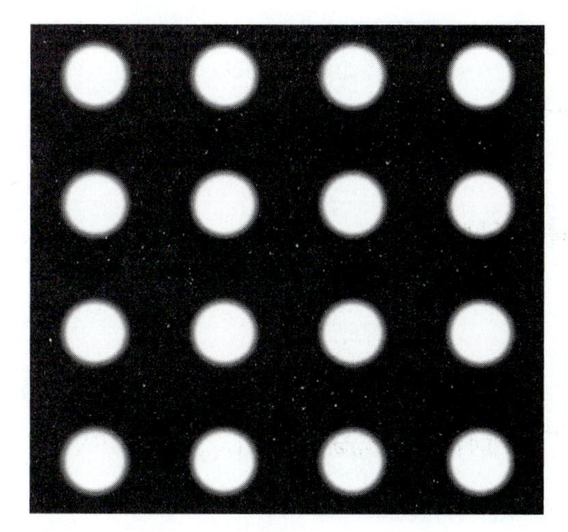

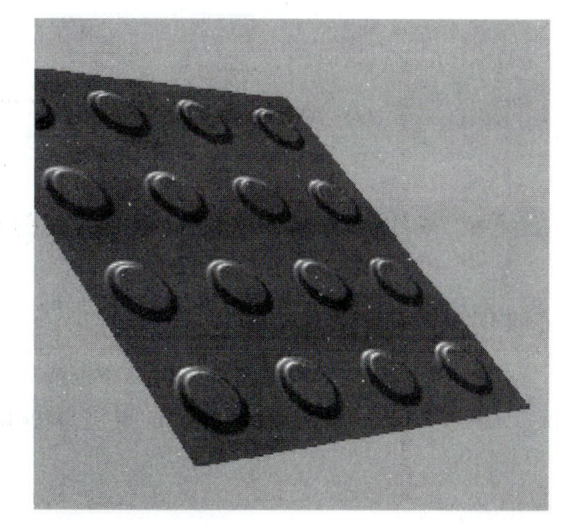

Figure 6.10 A bump map defined as a height field (*left*) and the bump map applied to a surface with specular lighting (*right*).

This representation of heights through a grayscale image can be seen as if it were given by an application of a grayscale color ramp to a surface. In cartography, this representation of a region is called a *digital elevation map,* and the combination of aerial photographs and digital elevation maps can let you create a detailed 3D view of the region. An example of this is given in Chapter 9.

Anisotropic Shading

The shading models described so far are all based on the simple lighting model of the previous chapter, which assumes that light is reflected uniformly from the surface normal (the lighting is *isotropic*). However, there are some materials where the lighting parameters differ depending on the angles of the light and eye around the normal. Such materials include brushed metals or the nonlabel surface of a CD, and the shading for these materials is called *anisotropic* because the reflections are different in different directions. Here the role in lighting calculations of the usual angles, the angle from the normal of the diffuse reflection, and the angle from the reflected light in the specular reflection, are replaced by a more complex function called the *bidirectional reflection distribution function* (or *BRDF*), here named ρ, that typically depends on both the latitude Θ and longitude Φ angle of the eye and of the light from the point being lighted: $\rho(\Theta_e,\Phi_e,\Theta_l,\Phi_l)$. The BRDF may also take into account behaviors that differ for different wavelengths (or different colors) of light. The lighting calculations for such materials take much more complex computation than the standard isotropic model and are beyond the scope of simple graphics APIs, but you will find this kind of shading in some professional graphics tools. Figure 6.11 shows the sphere of Figure 6.9 with an anisotropic shading. Such a shading can be simulated by modifying the surface normal to represent the appropriate BRDF and, if you go do the one-polygon-per-pixel level, this simulation becomes the real shading.

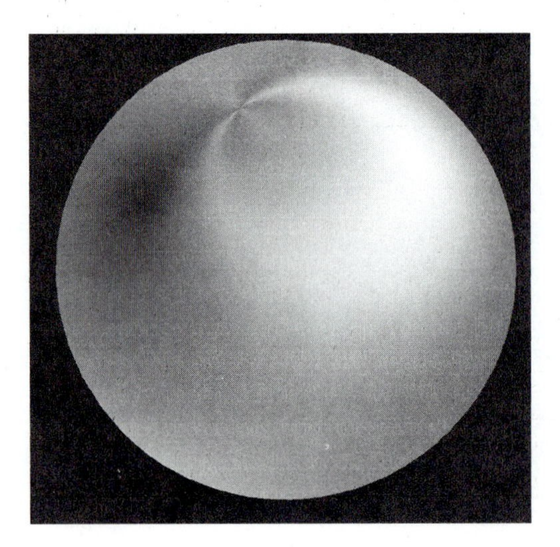

Figure 6.11 A sphere presented with an anisotropic shading.

Vertex and Pixel Shaders

An important recent advance in shading is the development of shading languages that let the programmer define shading at a much more detailed level than we have discussed so far. These languages give you a programmatic way to access the capabilities of programmable graphics cards and allow custom work on both vertices and individual pixels. This lets you develop anisotropic shaders, motion blur, bump mapping, clever textures, and many other sophisticated effects. There is ongoing research in developing shader languages that can be part of a graphics API to make them accessible to the programmer, and in Chapter 10 we see how they can fit into the structure of the rendering pipeline. The latest version of OpenGL (OpenGL 2.0) includes a shading language, but covering it in any detail is beyond the scope of this text.

The OpenGL shading language, GLSL, is a high-level procedural language, somewhat similar to C but with some specialized data and operations that reflect the nature of programmable graphics. It replaces some of the functions of graphics cards that we don't discuss until Chapter 10, but the principles are simple: Vertices are sent to the card and are processed to convert them to pixel locations, and polygon scanlines (called *fragments*) are processed to set the colors of individual pixels. GLSL includes both vertex shaders (used to manipulate coordinates, normals, texture coordinates, or colors) and fragment shaders (used to provide more realistic effects as well as various nonphotorealistic effects). Both let you use the card's texture memory for other operations and let you significantly increase the amount of work you can do in the graphics card. These will be very important tools for advanced graphics work, and you are encouraged to try to use them after you've gotten a start in this book.

Global Illumination

We have been describing the local illumination model for computer graphics, but there is another approach to lighting that can make more realistic images. In the world around us, light does not only come from direct lights and have a single ambient value; it is reflected from every object and every surface in the scene, and this indirect light varies widely throughout a scene. Lighting that accounts for this uses a *global illumination model,* so called because light is computed globally for the entire scene independent of the viewpoint rather than being computed for each polygon separately in a way that depends on the viewpoint, as we did earlier in this chapter. Global illumination processes do not involve shading models. Any unique kinds of shading come out in the way the light energy arriving at a surface is passed on to other surfaces.

One of the advantages of global illumination is that once you have computed the lighting at each point in the scene, you can display the scene very quickly. This is a good example of an asymmetric graphics process: You put in a large amount of processing one time to create the lighting for your model, and once you have done so, you need not do much processing to display the model many times from many viewpoints. Global illumination has a number of interesting and useful applications but is not yet supported by basic graphics APIs—though it may be in the future. We will describe two widely used models for global illumination.

Radiosity

The classical global illumination model is *radiosity,* which is basically built on the transfer of radiant energy within a closed space. This assumes that every surface can radiate energy and calculates the emission in a sequence of steps that converges to an eventual stable light. In the first step, light sources radiate their light energy and any other source radiates zero. The light energy arriving at each surface is calculated and stored with the surface, and it is available to be radiated in future steps. In subsequent steps, each surface radiates energy according to the energy it has received and properties of the material. These steps are repeated until the difference between energies at each point from one step to the next is small. When the scene is displayed, each point is given a color consistent with the energy emitted at that point. Figure 6.12 is an example of an image computed with radiosity.

In practice, the scene must be modeled as a set of many small regions, each of which is a perfect diffuse reflector (that is, reflects light as described in Figure 6.1). Every object in the scene is subdivided into a number of these regions so that the light is roughly equal across each region. One of the challenges of defining a radiosity model is subdividing the scene in this way. Each region gathers energy from all the other regions and emits energy to all the other regions, and the main computational work in radiosity is calculating this energy transfer. This is done by

Figure 6.12 A scene rendered with the radiosity model, from [LI]. See the figure in the color insert. Courtesy of Dani Lischinslci.

creating a hemisphere (or an approximation, such as a half-cube) for each region and calculating the projection of each other region on this hemisphere. Because you are working with diffuse reflection, the amount of energy received from a given region is proportional to the area of the projection of the region and the amount of energy emitted from that region. After the energy is stable, the energy is translated into lighting and the scene is rendered.

Photon Mapping

Another global illumination model is called *photon mapping*. This uses a technique similar to ray tracing (see Chapter 14) to model the overall light energy in a scene. The basic process of photon mapping involves generating a large number of randomly directed rays from each emissive light source in a scene. Each ray represents the path of a photon of a particular color (depending on the properties of the source) from the light source. When the ray meets an object, the object records the fact that a photon of that color has arrived, and the number of photons meeting an object is a measure of the illumination of that object. But because the main premise of global illumination is that every object not only receives illumination but also emits illumination, each photon that meets an object may also be emitted from the object, based on probability calculations that represent the material making up the object. If a photon is emitted, it is given a random direction and a color determined by the initial light and by the material. This process continues recursively for each photon until it ends because of probability computations or when a given number of steps has occurred. The actual number of photons that are emitted and traced can be surprisingly small.

After the full set of photons is emitted and all the objects in the scene have accumulated information on the photon intersections, the scene is processed to determine an illumination value for each object. Like most global illumination techniques, the illumination needs to be done only once unless objects move in the scene. Once the illumination is known, the scene can be rendered by ray casting (if there is no reflective or refractive material in the scene), ray tracing (if there is reflective or refractive material), or by other techniques to present it to the viewer. Because the illumination computation may not need to be redone each time the image is rendered, it is possible to get good frame rates for displays such as walkthroughs in such scenes. See Jensen [JEN] for a complete discussion of photon mapping; Figure 6.13 was rendered with this process.

Figure 6.13 A scene rendered with the photon mapping model. See the figure in the color insert. Courtesy of Henrik Wann Jensen.

Local Illumination and OpenGL

In contrast to global illumination, where the energy reflected from every surface is taken into account, local illumination assumes that light energy comes only from light sources that you define. This is the approach taken by OpenGL, where the light at any point is only that accounted for by the ambient, diffuse, and specular light components described earlier in this chapter. In this section we describe how this is carried out in OpenGL.

The OpenGL graphics API supports most of the local illumination lighting capabilities we have discussed. Here we outline the OpenGL support for lighting and materials. Some of the OpenGL functions such as `glLightf(light, pname, set_of_values)` use separate real (or integer) parameters, while others such as `glLightfv(light, pname, vector_values)` use the vector parameter form. If you have a choice, you may use whichever form fits your particular design and code best.

As is often the case in OpenGL, you must use particular names for some of these values. Lights must be named GL_LIGHT0 through GL_LIGHT7 for standard OpenGL (some implementations may allow more lights, but eight lights are required by the standard). The parameters define properties that are part of the appearance of a light. The parameter name pname must be one of the available light parameters

```
GL_AMBIENT,
GL_DIFFUSE,
GL_SPECULAR,
GL_POSITION,
GL_SPOT_DIRECTION,
GL_SPOT_EXPONENT,
GL_SPOT_CUTOFF,
GL_CONSTANT_ATTENUATION,
GL_LINEAR_ATTENUATION, or
GL_QUADRATIC_ATTENUATION
```

In this section we discuss the properties of OpenGL lights that use these parameters.

Specifying and Defining Lights

When you design your scene and your lighting, you may define your light model with the function `glLightModel(...)` to set some fundamental properties of your lighting. Perhaps the most important use of this function is defining is whether your scene will use one-sided or two-sided lighting, defined with the function

```
glLightModel[f|i](GL_LIGHT_MODEL_TWO_SIDE, value).
```

where `[f|i]` means that you use either the letter `f` or the letter `i` to indicate whether the parameter value is real or integer. If the (real or integer) value of the numeric parameter is 0, one-sided lighting is used and only the front side of your material is lighted; if the value is nonzero, both front and back sides of your material are lighted.

Another use of the function is choosing whether specular calculations are done by assuming the view direction is parallel to the Z-axis or the view direction is toward the eyepoint. This is determined by the function

```
glLightModel[f|i](GL_LIGHT_MODEL_LOCAL_VIEWER, value).
```

A value of 0 means that the view direction is parallel to the Z-axis, and a nonzero value means that the view direction is toward the eyepoint; this was the case that we discussed when we talked about specular lighting earlier in the chapter. The default value is 0.

Finally, you can use the function to set a global ambient light. In addition to the ambient light that is contributed to your scene from each light's ambient components, you can define an overall ambient light for the scene that is independent of any particular light. This is done with the function

```
glLightModelf(GL_LIGHT_MODEL_AMBIENT, r, g, b, a)
```

or the equivalent vector-parameter version, and the value of this light is added into the overall ambient lighting computation.

OpenGL lets you define up to eight lights for any scene. These have the symbolic names `GL_LIGHT0 ... GL_LIGHT7`, and you create them by defining their properties with the `glLight*(...)` functions before they are available for use. You define the position and color of your lights (including their ambient, specular, and diffuse contributions) as illustrated by the following position definition and definition for the light LIGHT0:

```
glLightfv(GL_LIGHT0, GL_POSITION, light_pos0); // light 0
glLightfv(GL_LIGHT0, GL_AMBIENT, amb_color0);
glLightfv(GL_LIGHT0, GL_DIFFUSE, diff_col0);
glLightfv(GL_LIGHT0, GL_SPECULAR, spec_col0);
```

Here we use a light position and specific light colors for the specular, diffuse, and ambient colors that we would define in separate statements such as

```
GLfloat light_pos0 = { ..., ..., ... };
GLfloat diff_col0 = { ..., ..., ... };
```

In principle, both of these vectors are four-dimensional, with the fourth value in the position vector being a homogeneous coordinate value and with the fourth value of the color vector being the alpha value for the light. For a positional light, the homogeneous coordinate should be 1.0; for a directional light it should be 0.0. We have used alpha values for colors, of course, but the default value for alpha in a color is 1.0 and we suggest you use that value for the alpha component of light colors, which you can do simply by using RGB-only light definitions.

As we noted earlier in this chapter, you must define normals for your objects' surfaces in order for lighting to work successfully. Because the lighting calculations involve cosines that are calculated with dot products, you must make sure that your normal vectors all have unit length. You can ensure this by enabling automatic normalization with the function `glEnable(GL_NORMALIZE)` before any geometry is specified in your display function. This should probably be done in your initialization function.

Before any light is available to your scene, lighting must be enabled and each of the individual lights to be used must also be enabled. This is an easy process in OpenGL. First, you must specify that you will use lighting by invoking the enable function

```
glEnable(GL_LIGHTING);  // so lighting models are used
```

Then you must identify the lights you will be using by invoking an enable function for each light, as illustrated by the following setup of three lights:

```
glEnable(GL_LIGHT0);        //use LIGHT0
glEnable(GL_LIGHT1);        //and LIGHT1
glEnable(GL_LIGHT2);        //and LIGHT2
```

Lights may also be disabled with the `glDisable(...)` function, so you may choose when to have a particular light active and when to have it inactive. Lights can be enabled or disabled to create emphasis or to highlight a part of a scene. This could be done by using a separate light just for the emphasized object, or you could use it in an animation or when designing a display so that a light may be chosen, say, by a user interaction.

The other properties of lights we discussed earlier are also straightforward to set in OpenGL. If you want a particular light to be a spotlight, you need to set the direction, cutoff, and dropoff properties as we described them, as well as the standard position property. These additional properties are set with the `glLightf*(...)` functions as follows:

```
glLightf(light, GL_SPOT_DIRECTION, -1.0, -1.0, -1.0);
glLightf(light, GL_SPOT_CUTOFF, 30.0);
glLightf(light, GL_SPOT_EXPONENT, 2.0);
```

If you do not specify the spotlight cutoff and exponent, these are 180° (which means that the light really isn't a spotlight at all) and the exponent is 0. If you do set the spotlight cutoff, its parameter is the cutoff angle in degrees, and the value is trimmed to between 0° and 90°.

Attenuation is not modeled realistically by OpenGL but is set up in a way that can make it useful. There are three attributes to attenuation: constant, linear, and quadratic. The value of each is set separately as noted above with the symbolic constants `GL_CONSTANT_ATTENUATION`, `GL_LINEAR_ATTENUATION`, and `GL_QUADRATIC_ATTENUATION`. If these three attenuation coefficients are A_C, A_L, and A_Q, respectively, and the distance of the light from the surface is D, then the light value is multiplied by the attenuation factor

$$A = 1/(A_C + A_L{*}D + A_Q{*}D^2)$$

where D is the distance between the light position and the vertex where the light is calculated. The default values for A_C, A_L, and A_Q (think of constant, linear, and quadratic attenuation terms) are 1.0, 0.0, and 0.0, respectively. The actual values of the attenuation constants can be set by the functions

```
glLightf(GL_*_ATTENUATION, value)
```

where the wildcard * is replaced by `CONSTANT, LINEAR, or QUADRATIC,` as above.

A directional light is specified by setting the fourth component in its position to be zero. The direction of the light is set by the first three components, and these are transformed by the modelview matrix. A directional light cannot have any attenuation properties, but otherwise it works just like any other light: Its direction is used in any diffuse and specular light computations but no distance is ever calculated. An example of the way a directional light is defined would be

```
glLightf(light, GL_POSITION, 10.0, 10.0, 10.0, 0.);
```

Selectively Choosing Lights

In order to use lights selectively you must define two or more lights, and you can enable or disable them as you wish to activate whatever set of lights you desire. In the equinox example shown in Figure 6.5, two lights were used, and in the `display()` function we see the following code excerpt that displays the sun with `GL_LIGHT1` and the Earth and equatorial plane with `GL_LIGHT0`.

```
//   the sun
     glEnable(GL_LIGHT1);
     glDisable(GL_LIGHT0);
...
```

```
//  the earth
    glDisable(GL_LIGHT1);
    glEnable(GL_LIGHT0);
...
//  the earth's equatorial plane
...
```

Defining Materials

For OpenGL to model the way a light interacts with an object, the object must be defined in terms of the way it handles ambient, diffuse, and specular light. This means that you must define the color of the object in ambient light and the color in diffuse light. You do not define the color of the object in specular light, because specular light is the color of the light instead of the color of the object, but you must define the way the material handles the specular light, which really means how shiny the object is and what color the shininess will be.

OpenGL takes advantage of the two-sided nature of polygons and lets you specify that for your material you are lighting the front side of each polygon, the back side of each polygon (refer to the earlier discussion of front and back sides), or both the front and back sides. You do this by specifying materials with the parameters `GL_FRONT`, `GL_BACK`, or `GL_FRONT_AND_BACK`. If you use two-sided lighting, you must specify both the front side and back side properties of the material. You can make these properties the same by defining the material with the parameter `GL_FRONT_AND_BACK` instead of defining `GL_FRONT` and `GL_BACK` separately. This can let you use separate colors for the front side and back side of an object, for example, and make it clear which side is being seen if the object is not closed.

To let us define an object's material properties we have the `glMaterial*(...)` function family. These have the general form

```
glMaterial[i|f][v](face, pname, value)
```

and can take either integer or real parameter values (`[i|f]`) in either individual or vector (`[v]`) form. The parameter `face` is a symbolic name that must be one of `GL_FRONT`, `GL_BACK`, or `GL_FRONT_AND_BACK`. The value of pname is a symbolic constant whose values can include `GL_AMBIENT`, `GL_DIFFUSE`, `GL_SPECULAR`, `GL_EMISSION`, `GL_SHININESS`, or `GL_AMBIENT_AND_DIFFUSE`. Finally, the value parameter is either a single number, a set of numbers, or a vector that sets the value for the symbolic parameter depending on the parameter name. Following is a short example of setting these values.

```
GLfloat shininess[]={ 50.0 };
GLfloat white[] = { 1.0, 1.0, 1.0, 1.0};
glMaterialfv(GL_FRONT, GL_AMBIENT, white);
glMaterialfv(GL_FRONT, GL_DIFFUSE, white);
glMaterialfv(GL_FRONT, GL_SPECULAR, white);
glMaterialfv(GL_FRONT, GL_SHININESS, shininess);
```

This gives the material a very neutral property that can pick up the light's colors.

Most of the parameters and values are familiar from the earlier discussion of the different aspects of the lighting model, but the `GL_AMBIENT_AND_DIFFUSE` parameter is worth noting because it is very common for a material to have the same properties in both ambient and diffuse light. In both cases, the light energy is absorbed by the material and is then re-radiated with the color of the material itself. This parameter lets you define both properties to be the same, which supports this assumption.

Using GLU Quadric Objects

As we discussed when we first saw the GLU quadric objects, OpenGL can generate automatic normal vectors for these objects. This is done with the function

```
gluQuadricNormals(GLUquadric* quad, GLenum normal)
```

which lets you set `normal` to either `GLU_FLAT` or `GLU_SMOOTH`, depending on the shading model you want to use for the object.

An Example: Lights of all Three Primary Colors Applied to a White Surface

Some lighting situations are easy to see. When you put a white light on a colored surface, you see the color of the surface, because the white light contains all the light components and the surface has the color it reflects among them. Similarly, if you shine a colored light on a white surface, you see the color of the light because only that color is available. When you use a colored light on a colored surface, however, it gets more complex because a surface can reflect only colors that come to it. So if you shine a (pure) red light on a (pure) green surface you get no reflection at all, and the surface seems black. You don't see this in the real world because you don't see lights of pure colors, but it can readily happen in a synthetic scene.

Let's look at an example of the effect of shining colored lights on a white surface. A white surface will reflect all the light that it gets, so if it gets only a red light, it should reflect only red. So if we take a simple shape (a cube) in a space with three colored lights (red, green, and blue), we should see it reflect these different colors. In the following example, the lights shine from three different directions on a white cube. There is a significant difference between the cube used in this example and the cube used in the simple lighting example in a previous module. This cube includes not only the vertices of its faces but also the normals to each face. If you add code that lets you rotate the cube to expose each face to one or more of the three lights, you will be able to see all the lights on various faces and to experiment with their reflection properties. This may let you see the effect of having two or three lights on one of the faces, as well as seeing the effect of a single light. You may also want to move the lights around and recompile the code to achieve other lighting effects.

Code for the Example

Defining the light colors and positions in the initialization function:

```
GLfloat light_pos0[]={ 0.0, 10.0, 2.0, 1.0 }; //up y-axis
GLfloat light_col0[]={ 1.0,  0.0, 0.0, 1.0 }; //light is red
GLfloat amb_color0[]={ 0.3,  0.0, 0.0, 1.0 };

GLfloat light_pos1[]={ 5.0, -5.0, 2.0, 1.0 }; //lower right
GLfloat light_col1[]={ 0.0,  1.0, 0.0, 1.0 }; //light is green
GLfloat amb_color1[]={ 0.0,  0.3, 0.0, 1.0 };

GLfloat light_pos2[]={-5.0,  5.0, 2.0, 1.0 }; //lower left
GLfloat light_col2[]={ 0.0,  0.0, 1.0, 1.0 }; //light is blue
GLfloat amb_color2[]={ 0.0,  0.0, 0.3, 1.0 };
```

Defining the light properties and the lighting model in the initialization function:

```
glLightfv(GL_LIGHT0, GL_POSITION, light_pos0); // light 0
glLightfv(GL_LIGHT0, GL_AMBIENT, amb_color0);
glLightfv(GL_LIGHT0, GL_SPECULAR, light_col0);
glLightfv(GL_LIGHT0, GL_DIFFUSE, light_col0);

glLightfv(GL_LIGHT1, GL_POSITION, light_pos1); // light 1
glLightfv(GL_LIGHT1, GL_AMBIENT, amb_color1);
glLightfv(GL_LIGHT1, GL_SPECULAR, light_col1);
glLightfv(GL_LIGHT1, GL_DIFFUSE, light_col1);

glLightfv(GL_LIGHT2, GL_POSITION, light_pos2); // light 2
glLightfv(GL_LIGHT2, GL_AMBIENT, amb_color2);
glLightfv(GL_LIGHT2, GL_SPECULAR, light_col2);
glLightfv(GL_LIGHT2, GL_DIFFUSE, light_col2);

glLightModeliv(GL_LIGHT_MODEL_TWO_SIDE, &i);    // two-sided
```

Enabling the lights in the initialization function:

```
glEnable(GL_LIGHTING);    // so lighting models are used
glEnable(GL_LIGHT0);      // we'll use LIGHT0
glEnable(GL_LIGHT1);      // ... and LIGHT1
glEnable(GL_LIGHT2);      // ... and LIGHT2
```

Defining the material color in the function that draws the surface: We must define the ambient and diffuse parts of the object's material specification, as shown below; note that the shininess value must be an array of length one (that is, a pointer to a number). Higher values of shininess will create more focused and smaller specular highlights on the object. This example doesn't specify the properties of the material's back side because the object is closed and all the back side of the material is invisible.

```
GLfloat shininess[] =      { 50.0 };
GLfloat white[] =          { 1.0, 1.0, 1.0, 1.0 };
GLfloat mat_specular[] =   { 0.8, 0.8, 0.8, 1.0 };
glMaterialfv(GL_FRONT, GL_AMBIENT, white);
glMaterialfv(GL_FRONT, GL_DIFFUSE, white);
glMaterialfv(GL_FRONT, GL_SHININESS, shininess);
glMaterialfv(GL_FRONT, GL_SPECULAR, mat_specular);
```

Figure 6.14 shows the cube when it is rotated so that one corner points toward the viewer. Clearly the red light is above, the green light is below and to the right, and the blue light is below and to the left of the viewer's eyepoint. You are encouraged to experiment with the code to look at these effects.

Shading Example

To use OpenGL shading you must select the shading model to be used and set a color at each verex, either explicitly with the `glColor*(...)` function or by setting a normal per vertex with the `glNormal*(...)` function and using lighting. The default shading model for OpenGL is smooth, but you won't get the visual effect of smooth shading unless you specify the appropriate normals for your model. OpenGL lets you select the shading model with the `glShadeModel` function, and the only values of its parameter are the symbolic constants `GL_SMOOTH` and

Figure 6.14 The white cube viewed with three colored lights. See the figure in the color insert.

GL_FLAT. You can use the `glShadeModel` function to switch back and forth between smooth and flat shading any time you wish.

If we were to use flat shading, for each triangle with vertex points `P[0]`, `P[1]`, and `P[2]`, we would compute its normal and use the calculated normal. In this case we would see code something like this:

```
glBegin(GL_POLYGON);
// calculate the normal Norm to the triangle
    calcTriangleNorm(p[0],P[1],P[2],Norm);
    glNormal3fv(Norm);
    glVertex3fv(P[0]);
    glVertex3fv(P[1]);
    glVertex3fv(P[2]);
glEnd();
```

to compute a single normal for each triangle. This assumes that we have defined a function `calcTriangleNorm(...)` that uses a process such as the cross product that we discussed in Chapter 4.

However, we want to use smooth shading for our example. In the following sample code, we look at the surface defined by $f(x,y) = 0.3(x^2 + y^2 + t)$ for a single parameter t. We set up smooth shading by defining an analytic normal vector at each vertex. To begin, we use the following function call in the `init()` function to ensure that we automatically give all our normals unit length in order to avoid having to do this computation ourselves:

```
glEnable(GL_NORMALIZE);//make unit normals after transforms
```

We use the analytic nature of the surface to generate the normals for each vertex. We compute the partial derivatives $\partial f/\partial x$ and $\partial f/\partial y$ for the function in order to get tangent vectors at each vertex:

```
#define f(x,y)    0.3*cos(x*x+y*y+t)      // original function
#define fx(x,y) -0.6*x*sin(x*x+y*y+t)   // partial derivative in x
#define fy(x,y) -0.6*y*sin(x*x+y*y+t)   // partial derivative in y
```

In the display function, we first compute the values of x and y with the functions that compute the grid points in our domain, here called `XX(i)` and `YY(j)`, to calculate the tangent vectors <1, 0, *fx*> and <0, 1, *fy*>. Then we do an inline cross product operation for each triangle in the surface as shown in the following code. We are careful to compute the triangle surface normal as (*X*–partial)*x*(*Y*–partial), in that order, so that the right-hand rule for cross products gives the normal the correct direction. We could have used the analytic form for the cross product and avoided the cross product calculation, but this approach is more general and can be used if we do not have analytic forms available.

```
glBegin(GL_POLYGON);
    x = XX(i);
    y = YY(j);
    vec1[0] = 1.0;
    vec1[1] = 0.0;
    vec1[2] = fx(x,y); // partial in X-Z plane
    vec2[0] = 0.0;
    vec2[1] = 1.0;
    vec2[2] = fy(x,y); // partial in Y-Z plane
    Normal[0] = vec1[1] * vec2[2] - vec1[2] * vec2[1];
    Normal[1] = vec1[2] * vec2[0] - vec1[0] * vec2[2];
    Normal[2] = vec1[0] * vec2[1] - vec1[1] * vec2[0];
    glNormal3fv(Normal);
    glVertex3f(XX(i),YY(j),vertices[i][j]);
    ... // do similar code two more times for the other vertices
    ... // of the triangle
glEnd();
```

This would probably be handled more efficiently by setting up the `vec1` and `vec2` vectors and then calling a utility function to calculate the cross product. This example produces the smooth-shaded surface shown in Figure 6.7.

A Word to the Wise

The OpenGL lighting model lacks some very important capabilities that could let you achieve effects you would want if you tried to get genuine realism in your scenes. One of the most important things lacking in this lighting model is shadows; while OpenGL has techniques that can let you create shadows, they are tricky and require some special effort. Another important missing part is the kind of "hot" colors that seem to radiate more of a particular color than they could possibly get in the light they receive, and there is no way to fix this because of the limited gamut of the phosphors in any computer screen, as described in many textbooks. Finally, OpenGL does not allow the kind of directional (anisotropic) reflection that you would need to model materials such as brushed aluminum, which can be created on the computer with special programming. So do not take the OpenGL lighting model as the correct way to do color; take it as a way that works pretty well and realize that it would you take much more effort to do better.

Summary

This chapter showed you how to create images using the Phong lighting model for vertex color and the Gouraud shading model with simple linear color averaging for creating smoothly changing color across polygons. This gives you a significant advantage in dealing with the appearance part of an image and lets you make much more interesting and informative images for your audience. From here, the only simple extension to appearance is texture mapping, as presented in Chapter 8.

OpenGL Glossary for the Chapter

OpenGL has a number of functions to specify lighting and shading, and they are listed here for reference. The number of new OpenGL functions in this chapter is relatively modest, but the number of parameters they use is fairly large. As always, we do not include any functions or constants that have been seen previously.

OpenGL Functions

`glLight*(light, pname, value[s])`: family of functions that set the value of the named parameter for the specified light; the function names reflect whether the value is integer or float

`glLightModel*(pname, value[s])`: family of functions that set the parameters for the lighting model you will use; the function names reflect whether the values are integer, float, or a vector, and the number of values needed depends on the parameter you are setting

`glMaterial*(face, pname, value)`: family of functions that specify material properties for your lighting model; the function names reflect whether the values are integer, float, or a vector, and the number of values needed depends on the parameter you are setting

`glShadeModel(pname)`: selects either the flat or smooth shading model, depending on the parameter chosen

`gluQuadricNormals(quad, pname)`: selects either the flat or smooth shading model for GLU objects, depending on the parameter chosen

Literal Constants

`GL_AMBIENT`: parameter to define the ambient component of a light or the ambient reflectance of a material

`GL_CONSTANT_ATTENUATION`: parameter which specifies that a light is to have a constant attenuation

`GL_DIFFUSE`: parameter to define the diffuse component of a light or the diffuse reflectance of a material

`GL_FLAT`: parameter to choose flat shading in the `glShadeModel()` function

`GL_LIGHT*`: parameter to identify the particular light being enabled, disabled, or defined

`GL_LIGHT_MODEL_LOCAL_VIEWER`: parameter to define whether the specular lighting is to be calculated relative to the viewer's eye position or relative to the z-axis

`GL_LIGHT_MODEL_TWO_SIDE`: parameter to the `glLightModel()` function to choose either the one-sided or two-sided lighting model

`GL_LINEAR_ATTENUATION`: parameter which specifies that a light is to have a linear attenuation

`GL_POSITION`: parameter that specifies the location of a light in four-dimensional homogeneous coordinates

`GL_QUADRATIC_ATTENUATION`: parameter which specifies that a light is to have a quadratic attenuation

GL_SMOOTH: parameter to choose smooth shading in the glShadeModel() function

GL_SPECULAR: parameter to define the specular component of a light or the specular reflectance of a material

GL_SPOT_DIRECTION: parameter which specifies that the values are to define the direction of a spotlight

GL_SPOT_EXPONENT: parameter which specifies that the value is to define the intensity distribution of light from a spotlight

GL_SPOT_CUTOFF: parameter which specifies that the value is to define the maximum spread angle of a spotlight

GLU_FLAT: parameter to choose flat shading for GLU objects

GLU_SMOOTH: parameter to choose smooth shading for GLU objects

Questions

This set of questions covers your recognition of issues in lighting and shading as you see them in your environment. These will help you see the different kinds of light used in the OpenGL simple local illumination model and will also help you understand some of the limitations of this model.

1. In your environment, identify examples of objects that show only ambient light, that show diffuse light, and that show specular light. Note the relationship of these objects to direct light sources and draw conclusions about the relationships that give only ambient light, that give both ambient and diffuse light, and that give specular light. Observe the specular light and see whether it has the color of the object or the color of the light source.
2. In your environment, identify objects that show high, moderate, and low specularity. What seems to be the property of the materials of these objects that makes them show specular light?
3. In your environment, find examples of positional lights and directional lights and discuss how your observations affect your choice of these two kinds of lights in a scene.
4. In your environment, select some objects that seem to be made of different materials and identify the ambient, diffuse, and specular properties of each. Try to define each of these materials in terms of the OpenGL material functions.
5. In your environment, find examples where the ambient lighting seems to be different in different places. What contributing factors make this so? What does this say about the accuracy of local illumination models as compared with global illumination models?

Exercises

This set of exercises asks you to calculate some of things that are important in modeling or lighting, and then often to draw conclusions from your calculations. The calculations should be straightforward based on information from the chapter.

1. Given a triangle whose vertices are $V_0 = (0, 0, 0)$, $V_1 = (5, 0, 5)$, and $V_2 = (0, 5, 5)$, in that sequence, calculate the appropriate edge vectors and then calculate the unit normal to this triangle based on a cross product of the edge vectors. It might help to draw the

triangle in some 3D technique to look at the space, and this will also help with exercises 4 and 5 below.

2. If you have a surface given by a function of two variables, $f(x,y) = e^{xy} \sin(ax)\cos(by)$, calculate the partial derivatives in x and y. For the point $P = (1, 2, 3)$, calculate the two directional tangents and, using the cross product, calculate the unit normal to the surface at P.
3. For some special objects, the surface normal is particularly easy to compute. Show how you can easily calculate the normals for a plane, a sphere, or a cylinder.
4. Going back to exercise 1, switch the values of vertices V_0 and V_2 and do the calculations of that exercise again. What do you observe about the relation between the new unit normal you have just computed and the unit normal you computed originally?
5. We saw in exercise 1 that the orientation of a polygon defines the direction of a surface normal, and the direction of the surface normal affects the sign of the dot product in the diffuse and specular equations. For the normals of exercise 1, assume that you have a light at the point (5, 5, 5) and calculate the diffuse and specular light components for each of the two normals. Which orientation makes sense, and what does that tell you about the way you define the sequences of vertices for your geometry?
6. In the equation for diffuse light, assume a light has unit energy and calculate the energy reflected at different angles from the normal using the diffuse lighting equation. Use the standard angles of $\pm 30°$, $\pm 45°$, and $\pm 60°$. Similarly, calculate the area of a unit square of surface when it is projected onto a plane at different angles to the surface. Then calculate the ratio of the energy to the projected surface area; this should be a constant. Using your calculations and the discussion of diffuse lighting in the chapter, describe why this is so.
7. Based on the specular light equation, write the equation that would let you find the angle Θ at which the energy of the specular light would be 50 percent of the original light energy. How does this equation vary with the specularity coefficient (the shininess value) N?
8. In exploring the effect of dropoff for spotlights, define a spotlight with a cutoff of 45° and constant attenuation and calculate the light energy over 5° increments from 0° to 45° with dropoff exponents 1, 2, and 4. What does this tell you about the central and edge energies of spotlights?
9. In exploring the effect of attenuation for lights, consider the OpenGL equation for attenuation: $A = 1/(A_C + A_L * D + A_Q * D^2)$. Define a set of points at distances 1, 2, 3, 4, and 5 units from a light, and calculate the light energy at each of these points using values of 1 for each of the lighting coefficients. Calculate the attenuation coefficient A in three cases:
   (a) only constant attenuation, $A_L = A_Q = 0$,
   (b) only linear attenuation, $A_C = A_Q = 0$, and
   (c) only quadratic attenuation, $A_C = A_L = 0$.
   What conclusions do you draw about the effect of linear and quadratic attenuation as you observe positional lights in the world around you?
10. For the merry-go-round scene graph defined in the questions in Chapter 2, show how you would place a light in the scene graph if the light were
   (a) at the center of the merry-go-round,
   (b) on a post at the outside of the base of the merry-go-round, or
   (c) on top of the head of a horse on the merry-go-round.

11. True or False: For a model with lighting, flat shading for a polygon is exactly the same as smooth shading if the smooth-shaded model uses the face normal at each vertex. Why is your answer correct?
12. Define a triangle with specific colors at each vertex and animate the effect of smooth shading by changing the color of one vertex over time. Observe the way that colors change across the entire surface of the triangle. Do this with a selection of colors and see if the behavior is the same for all colors or shows up more strongly for some particular choices.
13. If a triangle is very small—that is, if the number of pixels in the rendered triangle is small—does it really matter whether you use flat or smooth shading for the triangle? Why or why not?

Experiments

1. We have talked about enabling a number of properties or attributes in the discussion of creating lighted, shaded images. In order to really understand what each does, take a program that uses lighting and shading well and systematically disable (rather than enable) each of the properties or attributes to see what happens. For example, disable `GL_NORMALIZE` to see what happens when you do not have unit normals. Take notes on the results so you can recognize the problems caused when you do not properly enable a property.
2. We discussed the principle that if you use very small polygons, both flat and smooth shading would quite closely approximate Phong shading. Create a surface built on a mesh in the 2D domain and experiment with the granularity of the mesh and the quality of the surface shading. Can you approximate a one-polygon-per-pixel mesh and either verify or dispute the principle?
3. Consider the gluCylinder you met in Chapter 3; our goal is to create a shaded cylinder whose color varies smoothly from one end to the other. In order to do this, represent the cylinder by a set of quads whose vertices are on the two end circles of the cylinder. Define the colors for the two ends of the shaded cylinder and set smooth shading for your image. For each quad, use the appropriate color for the vertices on each end and see whether your cylinder has the same kind of shading properties you'd expect for a smooth-shaded quad. Try various numbers of quads in order to get the best possible look with the smallest possible number of quads.

Define a hemisphere from scratch using spherical coordinates or any other modeling techniques from Chapter 2 or Chapter 3. Design the hemisphere so you can easily control the resolution of the figure in all dimensions, just as the GLU and GLUT models let you define slices and stacks. This hemisphere will be the basis of experiments 4 to 8.

4. From the question above in which you were asked to try to define material properties that matched some real-world materials, use these material definitions in the image of the hemisphere and see how closely the image approximates the actual appearance of the object. If the approximation is not very good, see if you can identify why this is so and modify the material definitions to make it better.
5. Because we are working with a hemisphere, it is simple to get analytic normals for each vertex. However, a normal for a face is not the same as the normal for a vertex; show how you can get a normal for each face of the hemisphere.

6. Using routine code for displaying polygonal models and using a relatively coarse definition of the hemisphere, compare the effect of flat shading (using the face normal) with the effect of smooth shading (using vertex normals). Compare the effect of using coarsely modeled smooth shading with using flat shading with much higher resolution.
7. For the display of flat shading, choose a vertex normal for each face instead of the face normal, always choosing the same vertex relative to the face, and compare the view you get each way. Why is the vertex normal view less accurate than the face normal view? Is the difference important?
8. Because the display code allows us to rotate the hemisphere and see the inside as well as the outside, we can consider different light models:

```
GL_LIGHT_MODEL_TWO_SIDE
GL_LIGHT_MODEL_LOCAL_VIEWER
```

   and different face parameters for materials:

```
GL_FRONT
GL_BACK
GL_FRONT_AND_BACK
```

   Try out all or most of these options, and for each, note the effect of the option on the image you see.

Projects

1. (The simple house) Returning to the simple house we created as a project for Chapter 3, add a few lights within and outside the house, replace the colored walls with a reasonable material description for walls, and show how the previous views of the house now look with lighting and shading.
2. (A scene graph parser) Add light information in the scene graph parser of Chapter 3 so that each light can be placed with appropriate transformations. Also store the properties of each light with the light node so that appropriate lighting information can be generated by the parser.
3. (A scene graph parser) Add appearance information into the scene graph parser of Chapter 3. The code the parser will generate should now include appropriate material definition functions as well as the previous geometry functions. Also include shading information so that each piece of geometry may independently be smooth or flat shaded. See if you can keep track of current material definitions as you parse the graph so that you can avoid generating new materials definitions if they would be redundant with the ones in place at the time the new definitions are read.

7

Events and Interactive Programming

Graphics programming goes much further than creating images or animations. More and more we see the value of creating applications that let the user interact with a graphical presentation, that allow the user to control the way an image is created, or that interact with a graphical model of a process to control the process itself. These interactive images can be used in entertainment, in education, in engineering, or in the sciences. These *interactive* computer graphics applications offering the ability to interact with an image are critically important to the success of this field.

The set of capabilities for interaction in an application is called a *user interface,* and there is a science of creating and evaluating interfaces for interactive applications. However, the emphasis in this chapter is on techniques for graphical interaction, not on user interfaces. Many user interfaces use graphical presentations that give information to the user, take graphical interactions, and interpret the results for program control, but we view these interactive presentations as part of our graphics. Many interface toolkits work with OpenGL, and each has its advantages; if you want to develop genuine interactive applications, you will want to pick a toolkit carefully and learn it, though you must realize that some of the toolkits are complex and take some effort to learn.

In this book wc focus on simplicity and choose a widely available and easy-to-use interface toolkit to support the programming for this chapter. Toward the end of this chapter we introduce the MUI (micro user interface) system for OpenGL, which lets you add a primitive interface to your OpenGL programs, and we believe very strongly that you should understand the communication about images that can be supported by a user interface. However, a solid discussion of user interfaces is much too deep for us to undertake here. We subscribe to the view that computer interaction should be designed by persons who are specially trained in human factors, interface design, and evaluation, and not by computer scientists. But computer scientists will implement the design, and this chapter describes how you can implement graphical interactions.

Programming interactive computer graphics generally takes advantage of the event-handling capabilities of modern systems, so we must understand something about what events are and how to use them in order to write interactive graphics programs. Events are fairly abstract and there are several kinds of events, so we will go into some detail as we develop this idea. But modern graphics APIs handle events pretty cleanly, and you will find that once you are used to event concepts it is not difficult to write event-driven graphics programs. Some basic graphics APIs do not include event handling on their own, so you may need to use an extension to the API for this.

When you have finished working through this chapter, you should understand the range of interactive capabilities offered by a standard graphics API and should be able to implement an interactive graphics program using appropriate event-driven tools.

Definitions

An *event* is a transition in the control state of a computer system. Events can come from many sources and can cause any of a number of actions to take place as the system responds to the transition. We will treat an event as an abstract concept that we use to design interactive applications, that provides a concrete piece of data to the computer system. An *event record* is a formal record of some system activity, often an activity from an input device such as a keyboard or mouse. This record is a data structure that identifies the event and holds data corresponding to the event. This data structure is not accessible by the programmer, but its values are returned to the system and the application by appropriate system functions. For example, a keyboard event record contains the identity of the key that was pressed and the location of the cursor when it was pressed, for example; a mouse event record contains the mouse key that was pressed, if any, and the cursor's location on the screen when the event took place.

Event records are stored in the *event queue,* which stores event records and is managed by the operating system. The event queue keeps track of the sequence in which events happen and serves as a resource to processes that deal with events. When an event occurs, its event record is entered into the event queue and we say that the event is *posted* to the queue. As each event gets to the front of the queue and a process requests an event record, the operating system passes the record to the process that should handle it. This is illustrated in Figure 7.1. In general, events that involve a screen location get passed to whatever program owns that location, so if the event happens outside a program's window, that program does not get the event.

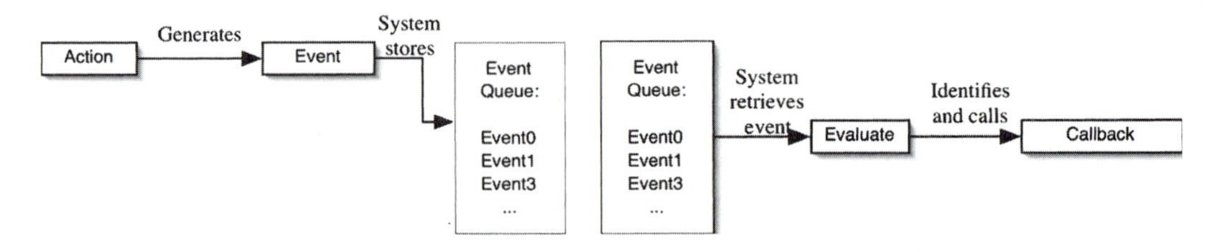

Figure 7.1 An event causes an entry in the event queue (*left*), and the system retrieves and processes an event (*right*).

Programs that use events for control, as most interactive programs do, manage that control through functions called *event handlers*. While these can gain access to the event queue in a number of ways, most APIs use functions known as *callbacks* to handle events. Associating a callback function with an event is called *registering* the callback for the event. When the system passes an event record to the program, the program determines what kind of event it is. If any callback function has been registered for the event, control is passed to that function. This kind of interactive program contains initialization and action functions, callback functions, and a *main event loop*. The main event loop invokes an event handler whose function is to get an event, determine the callback needed to handle the event, and pass control to that function. When that function finishes its operation, control is returned to the event handler.

The action of the main event loop is straightforward: The program passes control of the flow of execution to the event handler so that this control is effectively in the hands of the user. From this point on, the user will cause events to which the program will respond through the callbacks that you have created. We will see many examples of this approach in this chapter.

A callback is a function that is executed when a particular event is recognized by the program. This recognition happens when the event handler takes an event off the event queue and the program has *expressed an interest* in the event. The key to being able to use a certain event in a program, then, is to express an interest in the event by registering for the event and indicating what function is to be executed when the event happens.

Some Examples of Events

Events are often categorized based on the kind of action that causes the event. One possible way of classifying events for traditional computer devices gives you the flavor of this concept. This is:

Keypress Events, such as *keyDown, keyUp, keyStillDown, . . .* Keypress events store the fact that a key has been pressed and the value of the key. Note that there may be two different kinds of keypress events—those that use the regular keyboard and those that use the so-called "special keys" such as the function keys or the cursor control keys. There may also be different event handlers for these different kinds of keypresses. You should be careful when you use special keys, because different computers may have different special keys, and those that are the same may be laid out in different ways.

Menu Events, such as selection of an item from a pop-up or pull-down menu or submenu. These are based on your menu definition and the values you assign to menu devices.

Mouse Events, such as *leftButtonDown, leftButtonUp, leftButtonStillDown, . . .* Note that different "species" of mice have different numbers of buttons, so for some kinds of mice some of these events are expressed in different ways, such as double-clicking or shift-clicking.

Software Events These are posted by programs themselves in order to cause a specific kind of processing to occur next. An example is the redisplay event.

System Events, such as an idle event and a timer event. These are generated by the system based on the state of the event queue or the system clock, respectively.

Window Events, such as moving or resizing a window. These are based on the usual set of window manipulations.

These events are very detailed, and many of them are not used in some APIs or API extensions commonly found with graphics. However, all could be used by going deeply enough into the system on which programs are being developed.

The Vocabulary of Interaction

Interaction can take many forms, but in computer graphics interaction is generally visual and you should think of it in terms of visual communication. We discuss that aspect of interaction later in this chapter. Here we want to focus on the relation of interaction to events caused by computing devices, both hardware and software.

When users work with your application, they want to focus on the content of their work, not on the way you designed or programmed the application. The best applications are those that feel invisible to their users. Users usually want to communicate with the program and their data in ways that feel natural and comfortable to them and that let them easily do what they need to do. The interface designer's task is to create an interface that feels very natural and that doesn't interfere with the user's work. Interface design is the subject of a different course from computer graphics, but it is useful to understand something about the vocabulary of interaction.

We have talked about interaction based on the devices commonly found with current computers: keyboards or mice. These two devices have distinctly different kinds of behaviors in users' minds. As interaction devices, keyboards give discrete input that can cause different operations depending on the keys that are pressed. They let the user make abstract selections, including selecting actions as well as objects. The keyboard input for navigation in simple text games is an example of action selection. The mouse buttons can also be selection devices, although they are primarily used to select and control graphical objects on the screen. The fact that there is no standard number of buttons on a mouse (the Macintosh mouse typically has one, the Windows mouse typically has two, and the Unix mouse has three) can challenge programmers writing portable programs that use mouse interactions. The keyboard and mouse buttons both are discrete devices, providing only a limited number of well-defined actions.

The mouse itself has a different kind of meaning. It provides a more continual input, and can be used to control continual motion on the screen. This can be the motion of a selected object as it is moved into a desired position, or it can be another input that controls a property for the display (e.g., a translation or a rotation) or for the model (e.g., temperature at some point). The mouse event also has information on the mouse key or keys the user presses. When you plan the interaction for your application, you should decide whether the user should see the interaction as a discrete selection or as a continuous control, and then you should implement the interaction with the keyboard or mouse, as determined by the user's expected vocabulary for the activity and the task. There are several kinds of mice, as shown in Figure 7.2; mice with even more buttons are sometimes used.

There are a number of other devices that are not ordinarily found on most computers, but that may well be more common in the future. Let's consider as an example the 6DF joystick,

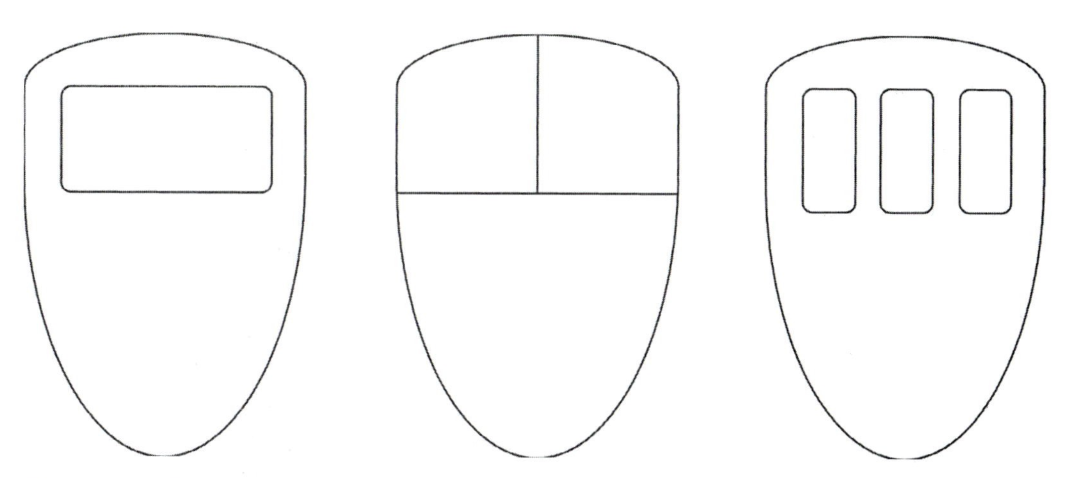

Figure 7.2 Different kinds of computer mice with one, two, and three buttons, respectively.

which can replace the mouse. Mouse motion has only four degrees of freedom represented by changes in X and Y, both positive and negative. This can let us control things in a display such as the direction we are looking, either up or down, left or right, but it cannot at the same time let us move forward or backward. For that we need two more degrees of freedom, and these cannot come from the mouse. However, there are devices that will allow you to move left and right, up and down, and forward and back; these 6DF (six degrees of freedom) devices such as the 6DF SpaceBall shown in Figure 7.3 are sometimes used for controlling virtual environments and could readily be adapted to a graphics API and to graphics applications.

Figure 7.3 A 6DF device, the SpaceBall 5000™. Courtesy of 3D Connexion.

Object Selection

Earlier we saw that a graphics API can support user inputs into your applications through menus, keystrokes, and mouse functions. These inputs can be used to manipulate images by selecting objects for actions. If you want to identify a particular object in a scene to act on, you cannot identify it simply by clicking on it; the click must be interpreted by the program to make the selection. In this section we show you how you can select an object in a scene. This lets the user interact with a scene in a much more direct way than is possible with events such as menu selections or key presses, which are more abstract and less closely related to what the user is seeing. With object selection we can get the kind of direct manipulation we are familiar with from graphical user interfaces, where the user selects a graphical object and then applies operations to it. Conceptually, selection lets your user identify an object with the cursor and choose it by clicking a mouse button when the cursor is on the object. The program must be able to identify what object was selected so it can apply to that object whatever action the user chooses.

To understand how selection works, let's start with the mouse click. When you get a mouse event, the event callback gets four pieces of information: the button that was clicked, the state of that button, and the integer coordinates of the point in the window where the event happened. To identify the object that was indicated by the click, we convert the window coordinates to 2D eye coordinates and then reverse the projection and go back to 3D eye space. However, a single point in 2D eye space becomes a line in 3D eye space, as shown in Figure 7.4. Our problem then becomes how to identify the objects that meet this line segment and tell which of these objects was chosen by the user.

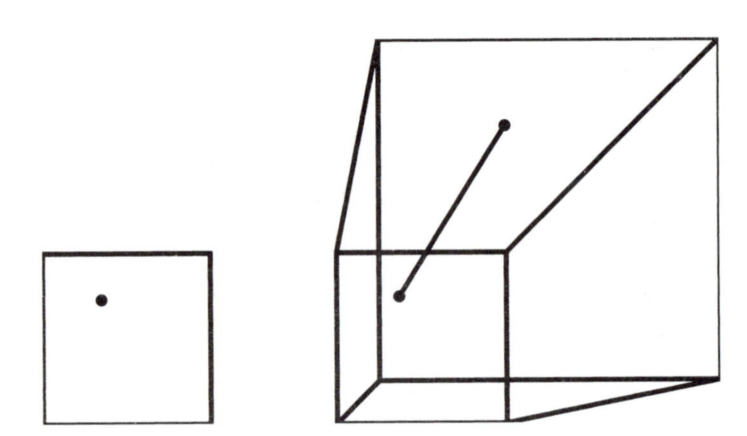

Figure 7.4 A point in 2D eye space and the line segment in the view volume that corresponds to it.

We can make this computation directly from the geometry using collision detection logic. For each object in the scene, we calculate whether the line and object intersect. When we have done all these calculations, we can say which objects lie under the chosen point and where each intersection happens in 3D eye space. We may then choose the object that is the closest to the eye, which is the one the user would see at the place the mouse click was made, or we may choose any other intersection that our logic demands. This is very computation-intensive, however, and requires us to go back to eye space, and that makes it difficult to implement.

Another way to identify the objects that lie on the line is to invert this logic. Instead of focusing on the objects that lie under the selected point, we see that any object that meets the line will use the chosen pixel when it was rendered. So if we keep track of that pixel and save information on any object that uses it, we can identify all the objects that lie under the pick point. Because the rendering process keeps track of depth values, we can also get information on the depth of the object in the view volume. Note that many different kinds of information might be saved about the point, so there are some interesting opportunities to think about what you might be able to do here.

We cannot say which of these techniques might be used by any particular graphics application, nor can we say which might be used by a particular graphics API. But OpenGL uses the second technique, and later in this chapter we will see how that is done.

Interaction and Visual Communication

In this chapter we talk about designing and implementing interactive graphics applications to help the user understand the concepts they display. This interaction is a communication between the user and the program and lets the user affect the image through that communication, so it requires good visual communication. This interaction may give the user ways to understand the information present in an image by manipulating it. An interactive application needs to consider how the user and the application communicate about interactions so that the user can make the most productive use of this capability.

One common interactive application is viewing a scene or an object from a number of different viewpoints. This lets the user move around the scene and zoom in or out of it. Another way to think of moving around a scene is to rotate the scene in world space while you hold your eye fixed. In either case, you are determining a rotation around a fixed point, either for your eyepoint or for the scene, with your eye moving toward or away from the point. This rotation, in effect, changes the latitude and longitude of the eyepoint, and it is straightforward to see this as moving the mouse vertically (changing latitude) or horizontally (changing longitude). A natural control for this might be using the mouse so that when the mouse button is held down, vertical motion of the mouse is translated into changes in latitude and horizontal motion is translated into changes in longitude. This mouse use is common in applications, and it may be familiar to you. The other control is zooming into or out of the scene, which is a one-dimensional motion. You might want to model this with a horizontal mouse motion with a different mouse button pressed, although it might be confusing to have different meanings for the same action with different buttons. Another approach is to use a keyboard action, such as pressing the *f* and *b* keys, to move the user forward and back in the scene. This is simple to implement and works well for a single-language application, though it might not work as well if your users had languages other than English. However, if you allow other key pairs to work in addition to *f* and *b*, this might still work.

Another kind of application involves working with an individual part of an image by selecting and manipulating the part. Here the communication problems are showing that the part may be selected, creating the selection, showing that the part has been selected, and giving the user natural ways to manipulate the part. One way to show that something may be selected is by changing the cursor shape when it is the selectable object. This can be implemented by using a passive mouse motion and setting a new cursor shape if your graphics API allows it, and it is most practical when the selectable object is always in the same position in the view. If the cursor shape cannot be changed, then the object's display might be different for selectable things than for nonselectable things, or perhaps a label or legend can say what is selectable. The actual selection will probably be done with a mouse click, and the manipulations will be chosen to fit the need of the application. We have described the use of a highlight color to show that something was selected, and we have talked about ways to provide 1D and 2D manipulations. Menus can be used for more complex kinds of manipulation, and we encourage you to think about having menu shortcuts to aid the expert user.

Events and the Scene Graph

As we design the interaction for an application, it can be very useful to use the scene graph to design our event handling. You should incorporate events and interaction into your scene graph and use it to manage the actions of your interaction. The scene graph has four kinds of nodes: group nodes, transformation nodes, geometry nodes, and appearance nodes. Interactions can be used to affect many of these:

- We can change transformations to move objects in a scene or to change the view.
- We can change appearance to indicate what has been selected, to add or remove objects, or to give a different look to a scene.
- We can change geometry to select an appropriate geometry for an object or to replace an object with another object or collection of objects.

So there are many ways we can attach events and interactions to things in the scene graph.

An important way an event can affect a scene graph is in selecting a particular geometric object or group of objects to have special treatment, whether in motion (transformations) or appearance or presentation. This kind of action requires triggering particular objects for action and so will need to have triggers in various scene graph nodes, with the trigger activated by the selection. This goes beyond the original modeling context of the scene graph but can be added informally by putting a boolean choice item before the node or in the data for the node.

A Word to the Wise

This section discusses the mechanics of interaction through event handling, but it does not cover the critical questions of creating natural user control for an interactive application. Many deep and subtle issues are involved in designing a user interface, and we did not begin to cover them. The extensive literature in user interfaces will help you get a start in this area, but a professional application needs a professional interface, one designed, tested, and evolved by persons who focus in this area.

The following examples do their best to present user controls that are not too clumsy, but they are designed to focus on the event and callback rather than on a useful way for a user to work. When you write your own interactive projects, think carefully about how a user might perceive the task, not just about the approach that is easiest for you to program.

Events in OpenGL

The OpenGL API generally uses the Graphics Library Utility Toolkit GLUT (or a similar extension) for event and window handling. GLUT defines a number of events and gives the programmer a way to associate a callback function with each. In OpenGL with the GLUT extension, this main event loop is quite explicit as a call to the function `glutMainLoop()` as the last action in the main program.

Callback Registering

Below we list some events for OpenGL and give the function that registers the callback for each. In later sections we give some code examples that register and use these events for some programming effects.

Event	Callback Registration Function

idle	`glutIdleFunc(functionname)`
	requires a callback function with template
	`void functionname(void)`
	as a parameter. This function is the event handler that determines what is to be done at each idle cycle. Normally this function will end with a call to `glutPostRedisplay()` as described below. This function is used to define what action the program is to take when there has been no other event to be handled and is often the function that drives real-time animations.

display	`glutDisplayFunc(functionname)`
	requires a callback function with template
	`void functionname(void)`
	as a parameter. This function is the event handler that generates a new display whenever the display event is received. Note that the display function is invoked by the event handler whenever a display event is reached; this event is posted by the `glutPostRedisplay()` function and whenever a window is opened, moved, or reshaped.

reshape	`glutReshapeFunc(functionname)`
	requires a callback function with template
	`void functionname(int, int)`
	as a parameter. This function manages any changes needed in the view setup to accommodate the reshaped window, which may include a fresh definition of the projection. The parameters of the `reshape` function are the width and height of the window after it has been changed.

keyboard	`glutKeyboardFunc(functionname)`
	requires a callback function with template
	`void functionname(unsigned char, int, int)`
	as a parameter. This parameter function is the event handler that receives the character and the location of the cursor `(int x, int y)` when a key is pressed. As is the case for all callbacks that involve a screen location, the location on the screen will be converted to coordinates relative to the

window. Again, this function will often end with a call to `glutPostRedisplay()` to redisplay the scene with the changes caused by the particular keyboard event.

special

`glutSpecialFunc(functionname)`
requires a callback function with template

```
void functionname(int key, int x, int y)
```

as a parameter. This event is generated when one of the "special keys" is pressed; these keys are the function keys, directional keys, and a few others. The first parameter is the key that was pressed; the second and third are the integer window coordinates of the cursor when the keypress occurred as described above. The usual approach is to use a special symbolic name for the key, and these are described in the keyboard callback example later in the chapter. The only difference between the special and keyboard callbacks is that the events come from different kinds of keys.

menu

`int glutCreateMenu(functionname)`
requires a callback function with template

```
void functionname(int)
```

as a parameter. The integer value passed to the function is the integer assigned to the selected menu choice when the menu is opened and a choice is made; in a later example we describe how menu entries are associated with these values.

The `glutCreateMenu()` function returns a value that identifies the menu for later operations that can change the menu choices. These operations are discussed later in this chapter when we describe how menus can be manipulated. The `glutCreateMenu()` function creates a menu that is brought up by a mouse button down event, specified by

```
glutAttachMenu(event),
```

which attaches the current menu to an identified event, and the function

```
glutAddMenuEntry(string, int)
```

identifies each of the choices in the menu and defines the value to be returned by each one. That is, when the user selects the menu item labeled with the string, the value is passed as the parameter to the menu callback function. The menu choices are identified before the menu itself is attached, as illustrated in the following lines:

```
glutAddMenuEntry("text", VALUE);
...
glutAttachMenu(GLUT_RIGHT_BUTTON)
```

The `glutAttachMenu()` function signifies the end of creating the menu.

Along with menus one can have submenus—items in a menu that cause a cascaded submenu to be displayed when it is selected. Submenus are created two ways; here we describe adding a submenu by using the function

```
glutAddSubMenu(string, int)
```

where the string is the text displayed in the original menu and the integer is the identifier of the menu to cascade from that menu item. When the string item is chosen in the original menu, the submenu will be displayed. With this GLUT function, you can add a submenu only as the last item in a menu, so adding a submenu closes the creation of the main menu. However, later in this chapter we describe how you can add more submenus within a menu.

mouse

```
glutMouseFunc(functionname)
```

requires a callback function [with template]

```
void functionname(int button, int state,
    int mouseX, int mouseY)
```

as a parameter, where button indicates which button was pressed (an integer typically made up of one bit per button, so that a three-button mouse can indicate any value from one to seven), the `state` of the mouse (symbolic values such as `GLUT_DOWN` to indicate what is happening with the mouse)—and both raising and releasing buttons causes events—and integer values `xPos` and `yPos` for the window-relative location of the cursor in the window when the event occurred.

The mouse event does not use this function if it includes a key that has been defined to trigger a menu.

mouse active motion

```
glutMotionFunc(functionname)
```

requires a callback function with template

```
void functionname(int, int)
```

as a parameter. The two integer parameters are the window-relative coordinates of the cursor in the window when the event occurred. This event occurs when the mouse is moved with one or more buttons pressed.

mouse passive motion

```
glutPassiveMotionFunc(functionname)
```

requires a callback function with template

```
void functionname(int, int)
```

as a parameter. The two integer parameters are the window-relative coordinates of the cursor in the window when the event occurred. This event occurs when the mouse is moved with no buttons pressed.

timer	`glutTimerFunc(msec, functionname, value)` requires an integer parameter, here called `msec`, that is to be the number of milliseconds that pass before the callback is triggered; a callback function with a template such as `void functionname(int)` that takes an integer parameter; and an integer parameter, here called `value`, that is to be passed to the function when it is called.

In any of these cases, the function NULL is an acceptable option for a callback function name. This lets you create a template for your code that registers all the events your system can support, and you can simply use the NULL function for any event you want to ignore.

Besides the device events we know, there are software events such as the display event, created by a call to `glutPostRedisplay()`, and the idle and timer events. There are also device events for devices that are probably not found around most undergraduate laboratories: the SpaceBall, shown in Figure 7.3, and the graphics tablet, a device familiar to the computer-aided design world and still valuable in many applications. If you want to know more about handling these devices, check the GLUT manual.

Some Details

For most of the OpenGL callbacks, the meaning of the parameters of the event callback is pretty clear. Most are either standard characters or integers such as window dimensions or cursor locations. However, the callback for the `special` event must handle the special characters by symbolic names. Many of the names are straightforward, but some are not. The full table of special keys is:

Function keys F1 through F12:	`GLUT_KEY_F1` through `GLUT_KEY_F12`
Directional keys:	`GLUT_KEY_LEFT`, `GLUT_KEY_UP`, `GLUT_KEY_RIGHT`, `GLUT_KEY_DOWN`
Other special keys:	`GLUT_KEY_PAGE_UP` (Page up) `GLUT_KEY_PAGE_DOWN` (Page down) `GLUT_KEY_HOME` (Home) `GLUT_KEY_END` (End) `GLUT_KEY_INSERT` (Insert)

To use the special keys, use these symbolic names to process the key value that is returned to the `special` callback function.

The timer event is different from any other event because it is a "one-time" event—when you register the timer event callback, the event will happen when the system clock gets to the defined elapsed time and will not happen again unless you re-register the callback. You can also register several different callbacks for the timer event that are to happen at different times. So if you want to drive a sequence of events that are separated by a fixed time, you will need to register the timer event again after each time it occurs. This is discussed in more detail when we give the timer code example in the following page.

Creating and Manipulating Menus

Menus are key parts of interactive programming, and GLUT works with your computer's window system to give you a device-independent way to provide menus for your program. These menus follow the conventions of your windowing system; for Windows and Unix the menus are pop-up menus, while for Macintosh they may be pop-up menus or may be attached to the menu bar at the top of the screen. All this is handled without difficult system-level programming. As we talk about creating menus, you should refer to the code fragment that is associated with the menu shown in Figure 7.5.

To create a menu you invoke the `glutCreateMenu(...)` function and pass to it the name of the menu event callback function that menu is to use. This callback will get the value of the menu item that is associated with each item name in the `glutAddMenuEntry(name, value)` function. The function that creates the menu returns an integer that is the name of the menu. Once you have created the menu and set it to be the active menu with the `glutSetMenu(int)` function, you can add entries with the `glutAddMenuEntry(...)` functions. These take a string and an integer as parameters, and the menu shows the string and returns the integer when the string is selected from the menu. Finally, when you have added all the menu items, you attach the menu to a mouse button so that button will invoke the menu. And that's it—you have now created a menu, and you can now write the callback function that will read the value returned from a menu choice and take the action you want.

But menus are complex resources that need more capabilities than this to respond to the dynamic needs of an application. In OpenGL, menus can be activated and deactivated, can be created and destroyed, and menu items can be added, deleted, or modified. The basic tools for this kind of manipulation are included in the GLUT toolkit and are described in this section.

You saw that when you define a menu, the `glutCreateMenu()` function returns an integer value. This value is the *menu number*. As you are creating a menu it is the *active menu*, but if you have more than one menu you will have to activate a particular menu by its number in order to work on it. To see what the active menu number is at any point, you can use the function

```
int glutGetMenu(void)
```

which simply returns the menu number. If you need to change the active menu so you can operate on a different one, you use the new menu's number as the argument to the function

```
void glutSetMenu(int menu)
```

to make the menu whose number you passed the active menu, so the operations we describe here will be done to it. Note that both main menus and submenus have menu numbers, so it is important to keep track of them.

Menus can be dynamic and can be changed as the program runs. You can change the string and the returned value of any menu entry with the function

```
void glutChangeToMenuEntry(int entry, char *name, int value)
```

where the name is the new string to be displayed and the new value is the value that the event handler is to return to the system when this item is chosen. The menu that will be changed is the active menu, which can be set as described previously.

While you may create only one submenu to a main menu with the `glutAddSubMenu()` function we described above, you may add submenus later by using the

```
void glutChangeToSubMenu(int entry, char *name, int menu)
```

function. Here the entry is the number in the current menu (the first item is numbered 1) that is to be changed into a submenu trigger, the name is the string that is to be displayed at that location, and menu is the number to be given to the new submenu. This will let you add submenus to any menu you like at any point you like.

Menus can also be destroyed. The GLUT function

```
void glutDestroyMenu(int menu)
```

destroys the menu whose identifier is passed as the parameter to the function.

The following code fragment adds items to menus and produces the menu shown in Figure 7.5. That menu also includes a submenu, and the additional code for the submenu is also included.

```
mymenu = glutCreateMenu(submenu);
mainmenu = glutCreateMenu(menu);

glutSetMenu(mainmenu);
glutAddMenuEntry("FullScreen Mode",1);
glutAddMenuEntry("Windowed Mode",2);
glutAddMenuEntry("---------------------------------",0);
glutAddMenuEntry("Toggle Lighting",3);
glutAddMenuEntry("Toggle Smoothing",4);
glutAddMenuEntry("Toggle Wireframe",5);
glutAddMenuEntry("Toggle Axes",6);
glutAddMenuEntry("Toggle Texture",7);
glutAddMenuEntry("Toggle Environment Mapping",8);
glutAddMenuEntry("---------------------------------",0);
glutAttachMenu(GLUT_RIGHT_BUTTON);
glutAddSubMenu("Function",mymenu);
glutSetMenu(mymenu);
glutAddMenuEntry("z = [empty set]/0",0);
glutAddMenuEntry("z = 0/1",1);
glutAddMenuEntry("z = x*y/2",2);
glutAddMenuEntry("z = sin[x-y]/3",3);
glutAddMenuEntry("z = sin[y*cos[x*y] div sin[x*y]]/4",4);
glutAddMenuEntry("z = cos{sqrt{x*x + y*y}}/5",5);
glutAddMenuEntry("z = {-cos{sqrt{x*x + y*y}}}/6",6);
glutAddMenuEntry("z = x*x-y*y/7",7);
glutAddMenuEntry("z = 1 div -{x*x+y*y}/8",8);
glutAddMenuEntry("z = sin{sqrt{x*x + y*y}} div x*y/9",9);
```

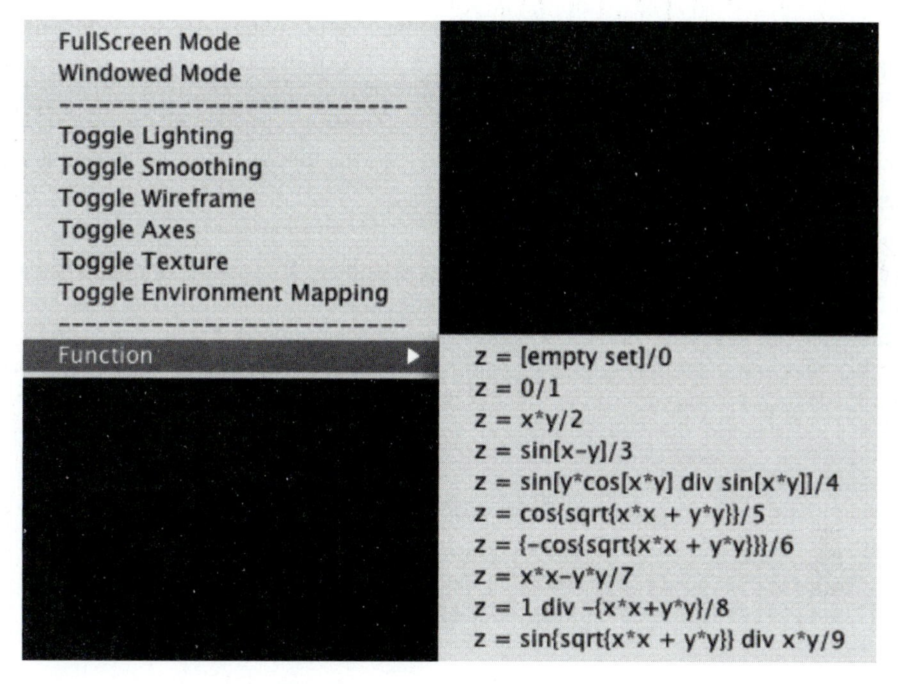

Figure 7.5 A menu with a submenu.

These details can seem overwhelming until you have a reason to want to change menus as your program runs. When you have a specific need to make changes in your menus, you will probably find that the GLUT toolkit has enough tools to let you do the job.

Code Examples

This section presents four simple examples, and the full code for all examples is included with the CD for the book. This first is a simple animation that uses the idle event to move a cube around a circle, in and out of the circle's radius, and up and down. The user has no control over this motion. When you compile and run this piece of code, see if you can imagine the volume in 3-space inside which the cube moves. This example also includes the same operation driven by the timer event rather than by the idle event, and it is interesting to see the difference in the code needed for this change.

The second example uses keyboard callbacks to move a cube up/down, left/right, and front/back by using a simple keypad on the keyboard. This uses keys within the standard keyboard instead of using special keys such as a numeric keypad or the cursor control keys. We do not use the numeric keypad because some keyboards do not have them, and we do not use the cursor control keys because we need six directions, not just four.

The third example uses a mouse callback to pop up a menu and make a menu selection, in order to set the color of a cube. This is a somewhat trivial action, but the code introduces details about menus and complements the menu discussion above.

Finally, the fourth example uses a mouse callback with object selection to identify one of two cubes that are displayed in order to change the color of that cube. Again, this is not a difficult action, but it calls upon the entire selection buffer process that we discuss later in this chapter. For now, we suggest that you focus on the event and callback concepts and postpone a full understanding of this example until you have read the discussion on selection later in this chapter.

Idle Event Callback

In this example, we assume we have a function named `cube()` that draws a simple cube with side length 2.0 centered at the origin, `(0,0,0)`. We move the cube around by changing its position with time, so we let the idle callback set the position of the cube and post a `redisplay` event. The display function then draws the cube using the positions determined by the `idle` callback. Much of the code for a complete program has been left out, but this illustrates the relation among the callback registration, the display function, and the idle callback.

```
#define deltaTime 0.05
GLfloat cubex = 0.0,cubey = 0.0, cubez = 0.0, time = 0.0;

void display(void) {
    glPushMatrix();
    glTranslatef(cubex, cubey, cubez);
    cube();
    glPopMatrix();
}

void animate(void) {
//  Position for the cube is set by modeling time-based behavior.
//  Try multiplying the time by different constants to see how
//  that behavior changes.

    time += deltaTime; if (time > 2.0*M_PI) time -= 2*0*M_PI;
    cubex = sin(time);
    cubey = cos(time);
    cubez = cos(time);
    glutPostRedisplay();
}

void main(int argc, char** argv) {
//  Standard GLUT initialization precedes the functions below
    ...
    glutDisplayFunc(display);
    glutReshapeFund(reshape);
    glutIdleFunc(animate);

    myinit();
    glutMainLoop();
}
```

Timer Callback

The timer callback can be used to drive program actions according to a schedule you can set up as you want. The callback can be registered from any point in the program, and the delay for the timer will start at the time it is registered. This can be used very flexibly; for example, you can use the parameter the callback registration sets for the callback function to control what the function does. In our example, we use the timer callback instead of the idle callback to manage the animation of the moving cube. The following code has the same code in the timer callback carrying out exactly the same action as the idle callback above; this lets you control the pace of the animation. Setting a delay value protects the animation from getting too fast if it is run on faster systems. Note that the callback function registers the next instance of the timer event. This could be placed at the top of the timer callback function so that the modeling time in that function is taken out of the delay, giving even better control over the timing between frames.

```
#define frameDelay 33
#define dTime 0.05

void timer(int i) {
    aTime += dTime; if (aTime > 2.0*PI) aTime -= 2.0*PI;
    cubex = sin(2.0*aTime);
    cubey = cos(3.0*aTime);
    cubez = cos(aTime);
    glutTimerFunc(frameDelay, timer, 1);
    glutPostRedisplay();
}

int main(int argc, char** argv) {
    ...
    glutTimerFunc(frameDelay, timer, 1);
    ...
}
```

Keyboard Callback

Again we start with the familiar `cube()` function, but this time we want to let the user move the cube up/down, left/right, or backward/forward by using simple keypresses. We will define two virtual keypads on the keyboard:

```
Q W            I O
 A S          J K
  Z X        N M
```

with the top row controlling up/down, the middle row controlling left/right, and the bottom row controlling backward/forward. So, for example, if the user presses either `Q` or `I`, the cube will move up; pressing `W` or `O` will move it down. Both upper- and lowercase letters are accepted. The other rows will work similarly. You can, of course, choose to define a different keypad or different control pattern for your own programs.

Again, much of the code has been omitted, but the display function works just as it did in the previous example: The event handler sets global positioning variables, and the display function performs a translation as chosen by the user. Note that in this example, these translations operate in the direction of faces of the cube, not in the directions relative to the window.

```
GLfloat cubex = 0.0;
GLfloat cubey = 0.0;
GLfloat cubez = 0.0;
GLfloat time  = 0.0;
```

```
void display( void ) {
     glPushMatrix();
     glTranslatef(cubex, cubey, cubez);
     cube();
     glPopMatrix();
}
void keyboard(unsigned char key, int x, int y) {
     ch = ' ';
     switch(key)
     {
          case 'q' : case 'Q' :
          case 'i' : case 'I' :
               ch = key; cubey -= 0.1; break;
          case 'w' : case 'W' :
          case 'o' : case 'O' :
               ch = key; cubey += 0.1; break;
          case 'a' : case 'A' :
          case 'j' : case 'J' :
               ch = key; cubex -= 0.1; break;
          case 's' : case 'S' :
          case 'k' : case 'K' :
               ch = key; cubex += 0.1; break;
          case 'z' : case 'Z' :
          case 'n' : case 'N' :
               ch = key; cubez -= 0.1; break;
          case 'x' : case 'X' :
          case 'm' : case 'M' :
               ch = key; cubez += 0.1; break;
     }
     glutPostRedisplay();
}
void main(int argc, char** argv) {
/*   Standard GLUT initialization */
     glutDisplayFunc(display);
     glutKeyboardFunc(keyboard);

     myinit();
     glutMainLoop();
}
```

A similar function, `glutSpecialFunc(...)`, can be used to read input from the special keys on the keyboard that we described when we discussed the special key event.

Menu Callback

When we discussed menus earlier, we had some code snippets but did not have an example that pulled all the ideas together. Again for this example we start with the familiar `cube()` function, but this time we have no motion of the cube. Instead we define a menu that allows us to choose the color of the cube, and after we make our choice the new color is applied. This example uses only one static menu so the return value of `glutCreateMenu(...)` is ignored in the `main()` function.

```
#define RED 1
#define GREEN 2
#define BLUE 3
#define WHITE 4
#define YELLOW 5

void cube(void) {
     ...
     GLfloat color[4];

//   set the color based on the menu choice
     switch(colorName) {
          case RED:
               color[0] = 1.0; color[1] = 0.0;
               color[2] = 0.0; color[3] = 1.0; break;
          case GREEN:
               ...; break;
          case BLUE:
               ...; break;
          case WHITE:
               ...; break;
          case YELLOW:
               ...; break;
     }

//   draw the cube
     ...
}

void display(void) {
  cube();
}

void options_menu(int input) {
     colorName = input;
     glutPostRedisplay();
}

void main(int argc, char** argv) {
     ...
     glutCreateMenu(options_menu);          // create options menu
     glutAddMenuEntry("Red", RED);          // 1 add menu entries
     glutAddMenuEntry("Green", GREEN);      // 2
     glutAddMenuEntry("Blue", BLUE);        // 3
     glutAddMenuEntry("White", WHITE);      // 4
     glutAddMenuEntry("Yellow", YELLOW);    // 5
     glutAttachMenu(GLUT_RIGHT_BUTTON, "Colors");

     myinit();
     glutMainLoop();
}
```

Mouse Callbacks for Mouse Motion

This example shows the callbacks for the mouse click and mouse motion events. These events can be used for anything that uses the position of a moving mouse with button pressed as control. This code might be found in a graphics program that lets the user hold down a mouse button and move the cursor around in the window, for example, and the program responds by moving or rotating the scene around the window. This is done by getting the position where the mouse button is first pressed with the mouse button callback, `mouse(...)`, and getting the updated position of the mouse with the mouse motion callback, `motion(...)`. The motion callback then keeps track of the distance between the current mouse position and the original click position and uses that distance to set the rotation in the scene by calculating global variables for the display operation. Be careful when calculating that distance to get the correct sign so that the mouse motion corresponds to the motion you want in the scene. The program that is the source for this code fragment uses the integer coordinates `spinX` and `spinY` to control spin, but the coordinates developed like this could be used for many purposes. The application code itself is not shown here.

```
float spinX, spinY;
int curX, curY, myX, myY;

void mouse(int button, int state, int mouseX, int mouseY) {
      curX = mouseX;
      curY = mouseY;
}

void motion(int xPos, int yPos) {
      spinX = (GLfloat)(curX - xPos);
      spinY = (GLfloat)(curX - yPos);
      myX = curX;
      myY = curY;
      glutPostRedisplay();
}

int main(int argc, char** argv) {
      ...
      glutMouseFunc(mouse);
      glutMotionFunc(motion);

      myinit();
      glutMainLoop();
}
```

Mouse Callback for Object Picking

This example is more complex than any of the previous examples because the use of a mouse event in object selection involves several complex steps. We begin here with a simple set of code, creating two cubes with the familiar `cube()` function, and we will select one with the mouse. When we select one of the cubes, the cubes will exchange colors.

In this code example, we start with a full `Mouse(...)` callback function, the `render(...)` function, which registers the two cubes in the object name list, and the `DoSelect(...)` function that manages drawing the scene in GL_SELECT mode and identifying the object(s) selected by the position of the mouse when the event happened. We do not include the code that registers the mouse callback function, because this was included in the preceding example.

After this example we discuss the concept of picking and extending this example. A more general version of the DoSelect() function is presented then.

```
void Mouse(int button, int state, int mouseX, int mouseY) {
    if (state = = GLUT_DOWN) { /* find which object was selected */
        hit = DoSelect((GLint) mouseX, (GLint) mouseY);
    }
    glutPostRedisplay();
}
...
void render(GLenum mode) {
//  Always draw the two cubes, even if we are in GL_SELECT mode,
//  because an object is selectable iff it is identified in the
//  name list and is drawn in GL_SELECT mode
    if (mode = = GL_SELECT)
        glLoadName(0);
    glPushMatrix();
    glTranslatef(1.0, 1.0, -2.0);
    cube(cubeColor2);
    glPopMatrix();
    if (mode = = GL_SELECT)
        glLoadName(1);
    glPushMatrix();
        glTranslatef(-1.0, -2.0, 1.0);
    cube(cubeColor1);
    glPopMatrix();
    glFlush();
    glutSwapBuffers();
}
...
GLuint DoSelect(GLint x, GLint y) {
    GLint hits, temp;

    glSelectBuffer(MAXHITS, selectBuf);
    glRenderMode(GL_SELECT);
    glInitNames();
    glPushName(0);

//  set up the viewing model
    glPushMatrix();
    glMatrixMode(GL_PROJECTION);
    glLoadIdentity();
//  set up the matrix that identifies the picked object(s), based
//  on the x and y values of the selection and the information
//  on the viewport
    gluPickMatrix(x, windH - y, 4, 4, vp);
    glClearColor(0.0, 0.0, 1.0, 0.0);
    glClear(GL_COLOR_BUFFER_BIT);
    gluPerspective(60.0,1.0,1.0,30.0);
    glMatrixMode(GL_MODELVIEW);
    glLoadIdentity();
```

```
//   eye point center of view up
     gluLookAt(7.0, 10.0, 10.0, 0.0, 0.0, 0.0, 0.0, 1.0, 0.0);

     render(GL_SELECT); // draw the scene for selection

     glPopMatrix();

//   find the number of hits recorded and reset mode of render
     hits = glRenderMode(GL_RENDER);
//   reset viewing model into GL_MODELVIEW mode
     glMatrixMode(GL_PROJECTION);
     glLoadIdentity();
     gluPerspective(60.0,1.0,1.0,30.0);
     glMatrixMode(GL_MODELVIEW);
     glLoadIdentity();
     gluLookAt(10.0, 10.0, 10.0, 0.0, 0.0, 0.0, 0.0, 1.0, 0.0);
//   return the label of the object selected, if any
     if (hits <= 0) {
          return -1;
     }
//   make any changes in the system to be caused by the selection
     ...
     return selectBuf[3];
}
```

Details on Picking

OpenGL has several ways of identifying objects that could be selected by mouse events, and we discuss two of them in this chapter. The first involves drawing in a mode that does not change the color buffer and keeping track of objects that use the selected pixel or small region around the pixel; we will call this the standard selection approach. In the second, you draw the scene with selectable objects drawn in synthetic colors that are unique to each object and look at the color of the selected pixel in the color buffer to identify the nearest object at the picked point. We will discuss the standard selection approach first.

The standard selection approach uses "invisible" drawing—drawing that does not actually write anything in the color buffer but that makes a record of all the objects that would be drawn at the selected point. This approach introduces the concepts of the *render mode* and *selection mode* for drawing. In the standard way of making an image, you draw the scene in GL_RENDER mode, which is the default drawing mode. In the mouse event callback that is executed after the mouse event, you change the rendering to GL_SELECT mode and redraw the scene with each *item of interest* given a unique name. When the scene is then drawn in GL_SELECT mode, nothing is actually changed in the color buffer, but the pixels that would be rendered are identified. When any named object is found that would include the pixel selected by the mouse, that object's name is added to the *selection buffer* data structure, actually a stack of unsigned integers, that is maintained for that name. The selection buffer holds information on all the items in a hierarchy of named items that were hit. When this rendering of the scene is finished, a list of hit records is produced, with one entry for each name of an object whose rendering included the mouse click point, and the number of such records is returned when the system is returned to GL_RENDER mode. The structure of these hit records is described in the next section. If there were any hits, you can process this list to identify the items that were hit, including the distance from the eye where the hit occurred, and you can proceed to do whatever work you need with this information.

The concept of "item of interest" is more complex than is immediately apparent. It can include a single object, a set of objects, or even a hierarchy of objects. You will see some examples of naming objects of interest in the following code fragments. Think creatively about your problem and you may be surprised at just how powerful this kind of selection can be.

Definitions

The first concept we must understand for object selection is the *name stack*. This is the structure that holds the active object names at each point in the selection rendering. In the following example we load, push, or pop names for the name stack so that the stack holds all the names of selectable objects at any point in the rendering. We will see that we can create a hierarchy of selectable objects with the stack so that we have a powerful tool for identifying objects or groups of objects to operate on. As you render the model in selection mode, each time the rendering uses the selected point, all the names on the name stack are stored in the selection buffer along with other information on the selection.

The next concept is the structure of the selection buffer, where information on selected objects is stored. This is an array of unsigned integers (`GLuint selectBuf[SIZE]`) that will hold the list of *hit records* for a mouse click. A hit record is a variable-length array of integers that contains several items as illustrated in Figure 7.6. Each item stores information from one time when

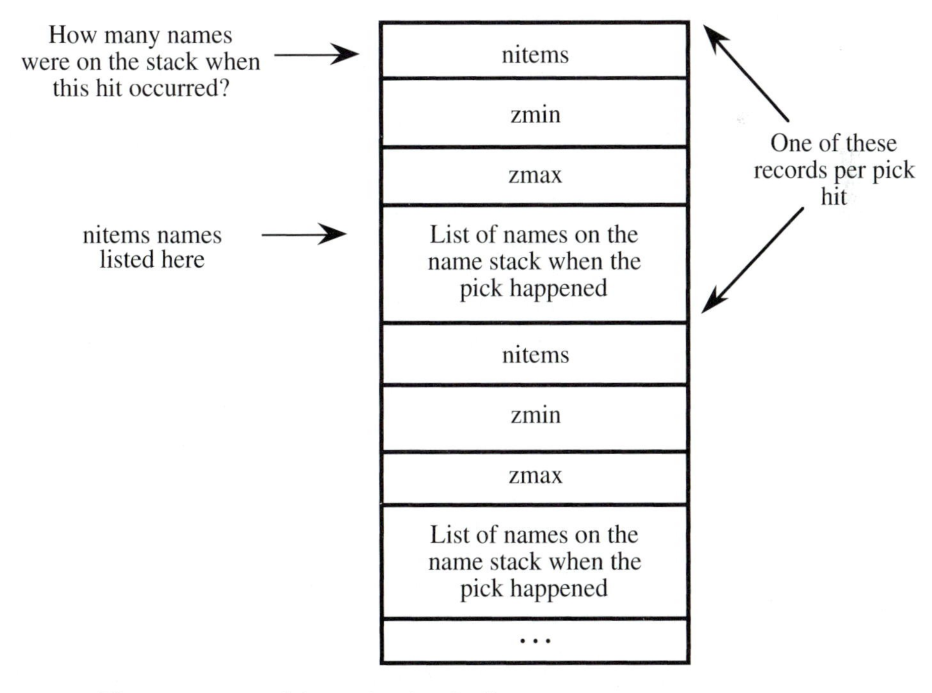

Figure 7.6 The structure of the selection buffer.

the selected point is used in a selection-mode rendering. The information stored in a hit record includes the number of items on the name stack, the nearest (`zmin`) and farthest (`zmax`) distances to objects that were rendered, and the list of all the names on the name stack for the selection. The distances are integers because they are taken from the OpenGL depth buffer, where, you may recall, distances are stored as integers in order to make comparisons more effective. These distances are determined relative to the viewing projection environment, in which the nearest points have the smallest non-negative values because this environment has the eye at the origin and distances increase as points move away from the eye.

In typical processing of the selection buffer, you would look at each hit record to find the record with the smallest value of `zmin` because that was the hit that was nearest the eye. You will then work with the names in that hit record to carry out the work needed by that hit. This work is fairly typical of handling any list of variable-length records. If the hit record starts at index N, the value at that index is the number K of names on the name stack and the first name on the stack is found at index $I = N + 3$. So you will read K names, starting at this first name index I, and for each name you will do whatever needs to be done to the scene based on that name. For example, you might set some sort of flag for each object with that name so that subsequent events (animations, mouse motions, keystrokes, etc.) will be applied to that object, or you might change a modeling transformation parameter so the selected object would be seen to move. The scene graph can help you identify how to implement the action you need. This kind of coding is not difficult, but it does require some care because of the variable size of each hit record.

Selection using the selection buffer has one key point that you must understand: You don't do anything generate the selection buffer except draw the scene in selection mode. That's it. The system does the rest of the work for you, putting all the names on the active name stack into the selection buffer whenever the drawing process operates on the selected pixel or picking region. You simply set the rendering mode to selection, generate the scene, get the number of hits from the returned value of the `glRenderMode(...)` function when you call it to restore rendering mode, and process the selection buffer to handle that many hits.

OpenGL has two ways to pick an object using the selection buffer, and both involve generating the scene either partly or fully in selection mode, as discussed in the next section. You can use the selection buffer to identify the objects that met the pixel identified by the mouse, or you can set up an additional projection with the pick matrix and clip everything that is not within the viewing volume of that projection. The first of these methods is perhaps simpler because it does not involve any changes in the basic rendering, but the second is faster because it uses clipping to avoid rendering anything except those items very near the pixel. We will begin by discussing the simpler case, and describe the use of the pick matrix later.

Making Picking Work

In the outline of selection buffer operation above, it sounds as though the drawing we create in selection mode will be the same as the one we would create in rendering mode, but this does not have to be true. There are some ways we can make select-mode drawing work more quickly or more efficiently than render-mode drawing. These include:

- If there are any objects that the user isn't allowed to select, don't draw these at all in select mode. Because they aren't drawn, they're invisible to picking.

- If you want to let the user pick a complex object, you don't need to do the work of rendering the object fully in select mode; you need only design an approximation of the object and draw that.
- You can even create invisible controls by letting the user pick things that are drawn only in select mode but not in render mode.

You can think of a separate selection scene graph that gives you an alternate model for drawing in selection mode. We could call this the *selection model.* Think creatively and you'll find that you can do interesting things with selection. In fact, you must use some of these techniques for some objects. If you want the user to be able to select a wireframe object, you probably want to replace the wireframe object with a solid version in the select-mode drawing, because a user will visualize the spaces in the wireframe as part of the object but OpenGL will not. Another important use is in selecting text, because you cannot pick raster characters in OpenGL; if you draw any raster characters in select mode, OpenGL will always think that the characters were picked no matter where you clicked. If you want to be able to pick a word that is drawn as raster characters, create a rectangle that occupies the space where the raster characters would be, and draw that rectangle in select mode instead of the text.

So how do we determine what objects will be selectable, or will be an object of interest to the selection? It's not automatic that anything you draw in selection mode will be selectable; you must decide what objects or groups of objects can be selected. An object of interest to the selection is any object that has been given a *name* for the selection. The concept of selection names is a new one to us, but there is a mechanism in OpenGL for handling names. A name is simply an integer that is used to identify a point in the modeling process; these integers are often given symbolic names through `#define` statements. Names are managed on the *name stack.* You can load a name on the name stack, replacing whatever name was on the top of the stack, with the `glLoadName(int)` function. You can push a new name onto the top of the stack using the `glPushName(int)` function. Each name on the name stack is active, so after a name is pushed, both the original name and the new name are active. Finally, when you want to make a name inactive, you can pop it off the name stack with the `glPopName()` function. When a selection occurs, all the names on the name stack are stored in the hit record, so by nesting names you can create a hierarchy of objects that can be selected.

As an example, suppose we were dealing with automobiles and we wanted someone to select parts for an automobile. We could permit the user to select parts at a number of levels—for example, to be able to select an entire automobile, or the body of the automobile, or simply one of the tires. In the following sample code fragment, we create a hierarchy of selections for an automobile ("Jaguar") and for various parts of the auto ("body," "tire," etc.). In this case, the names `JAGUAR, BODY, FRONT_LEFT_TIRE,`and `FRONT_RIGHT_TIRE` are symbolic names for integers that are defined elsewhere in the code, as suggested above, and we assume that the name stack is empty when we start this code.

```
glPushName(DUMMY); // put a dummy name on the list
glLoadName(JAGUAR);
glPushName(BODY);
    glCallList(JagBodyList);
glPopName();
```

```
glPushName(FRONT_LEFT_TIRE);
    glPushMatrix();
    glTranslatef(...);
    glCallList(TireList);
    glPopMatrix();
glPopName();
glPushName(FRONT_RIGHT_TIRE);
    glPushMatrix();
    glTranslatef(...);
    glCallList(TireList);
    glPopMatrix();
glPopName();
```

When a selection occurs, then, the selection buffer will include everything whose display involved the pixel that was chosen, including the automobile as well as the lower-level part. For example, if you selected the right front tire of the automobile, `nitems` would be 3 and your hit record would include three names: the names `FRONT_LEFT_TIRE`, `BODY`, and `JAGUAR`. Your program then would know that a hierarchy was selected that had these three parts and you can choose (or allow the user to choose) which selection or what other logic it needed to use.

The use of the name stack in organizing the objects to be selected is quite similar in some ways to the use of the transformation stack in modeling. Object names can be added to the information in the scene graph so that whenever a name is passed in going down a branch of the scene graph, the name is pushed onto the name stack, and whenever a name is passed coming back up a branch, the name stack is popped. This lets you create and manipulate the name stack as part of the modeling and makes the process more systematic.

There are a few things to watch out for in the name stack. The first is that the name stack is empty when it is initialized, so you cannot simply load a name into the stack; this will generate an error. Instead, you must push some name onto the stack so that you can load a name to replace it. In the example, we began by picking the name dummy into the stack before we loaded the first real name. The second is that you cannot load a new name inside a region of code delimited by a `glBegin(mode)-glEnd()` pair, so if you use any geometry compression in your object, all of the compression must be within a single named object. The third thing to watch for with the name stack is that loading a name replaces only the top name on the name stack. If you have finished a hierarchy and need to remove the entire hierarchy from the name stack, you will need to pop the name stack until there is only a single name left; you can then load the new name to replace that single name. But these things are straightforward to remember as you use the name stack.

The Pick Matrix

Picking using the pick matrix is almost the same operation, logically, as picking using the selected pixel, but we present it separately because it uses a different process and lets us define the concept of "near" and to discuss a way to identify the objects near the selection point.

In the picking process, you define a very small window in the immediate neighborhood of the point where the mouse was clicked, and then you can identify everything that is drawn in that neighborhood. The result is returned in the standard selection buffer and is processed in the same way we discussed previously. Because this creates a new window, the system clips everything outside the window, making this selection drawing very efficient. This is done by creating a transformation with the function `gluPickMatrix(...)` that is applied after the projection transformation (that is, defined before the projection; recall the relation between the sequence in which transformations are identified and the sequence in which they are applied). The full function call is

```
gluPickMatrix(GLdouble x, GLdouble y, GLdouble width,
              GLdouble height, GLint viewport[4])
```

where x and y are the coordinates of the point picked by the mouse, which is the center of the picking region; the width and height are the size of the picking region in pixels, sometimes called the *pick tolerance*; and the viewport is the vector of four integers returned by the function call

```
glGetIntegerv(GL_VIEWPORT, GLint *viewport).
```

The function of the pick matrix is to identify a small region centered at the point where the mouse was clicked and to select anything that is drawn in that region. The picking process returns a standard selection buffer that can then be processed to identify the objects that were picked, as described previously.

A code fragment to implement this picking follows. This corresponds to the point in the code for `doSelect(...)` above labeled "set up the standard viewing model" and "standard perspective viewing":

```
#define PICK_TOL ...        // picking tolerance
int viewport[4];            // place to retrieve the viewport numbers
    ...
dx = glutGet(GLUT_WINDOW_WIDTH);
dy = glutGet(GLUT_WINDOW_HEIGHT);
    ...
glMatrixMode(GL_PROJECTION);
glLoadIdentity();
if(RenderMode == GL_SELECT) {
    glGetIntegerv(GL_VIEWPORT, viewport);
    gluPickMatrix((double)Xmouse, (double)(dy - Ymouse),
    PICK_TOL, PICK_TOL, viewport);
}
... call glOrtho(), glFrustum(), or gluPerspective() here
```

This process uses names and the name stack in exactly the way described previously.

Using the Back Color Buffer to Do Picking

Another approach to picking avoids the selection buffer entirely by using some of the facilities of double-buffered drawing. In this approach, when you want to permit a selection, you draw your scene in render mode but you draw it into the back buffer in a unique way. You draw only the selectable objects, and you identify these objects by giving each a unique color. You can use a proxy, or replacement object, for an object to use an alternate representation as we discussed previously. When the mouse event happens and the mouse callback gets the pixel location of the pick, you look in the back buffer to see what color is at that pixel location. That color can be used to identify the object drawn at that position, giving you your picked object. If you draw with depth test enabled, you will get the object that the user sees at that point. After you have gotten the information you need from the back buffer, you simply don't swap it with the front buffer but let the next (and normal) drawing operation replace the artificial-color image in the back buffer.

The mechanics of this are pretty straightforward. After the back buffer has been filled with the artificial image, select the back buffer to be read with the `glReadBuffer(GL_BACK)` function (although the back buffer is the default buffer for reading in double-buffered mode). Then use the `glReadPixels(...)` function to read a 1×1 array of color pixels (that is, the value of the color at a single point) at the position of the selection, and the logic you used when you defined the color of each object will let you identify the object that was selected. This is a straightforward technique, but it may require some thought to make a good set of color identifications if you have a large number of objects.

A Selection Example

The selection process is well illustrated by an interactive shape-selection program by a student, Ben Eadington. This code sets up and renders a Bézier spline surface with a set of selectable control points. When an individual control point is selected, that point is highlighted and can be moved with a keyboard event callback function, and the surface responds to the adjusted set of points. A sample image from this work is given in Figure 7.7, with one control point selected (toward the front, shown as a red cube instead of the default green color. See color insert for clarity).

Selected code fragments from this project are given below, and the complete code is included in the supporting materials for the book. All the data declarations and evaluator work are omitted, as are some standard parts of the functions that are presented, and just the important functions are given with the key points described here. You will be directed to several specific points in the code to illustrate how selection works, described with interspersed text as the functions or code are presented.

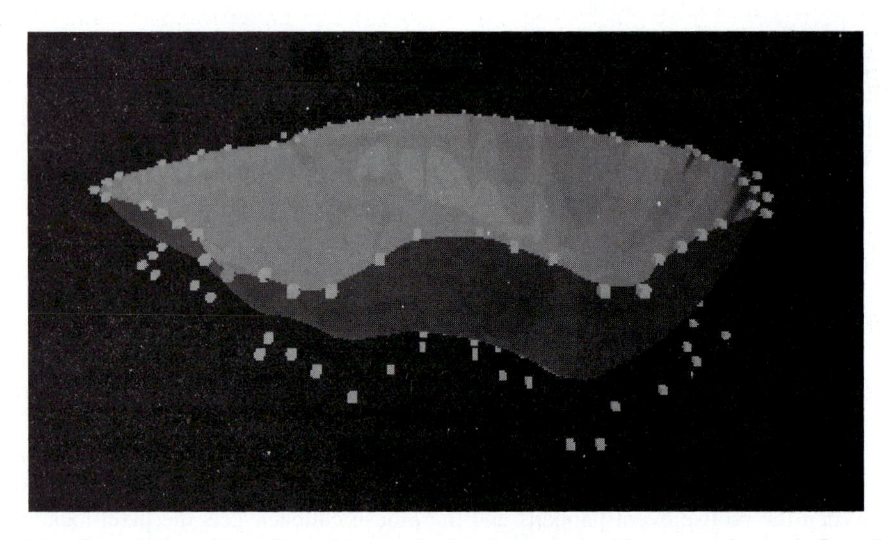

Figure 7.7 A surface with selectable control points and with one selected. See the figure in the color insert. Courtesy of Ben Eadington.

The first few lines of the program include the declaration of the global selection buffer that will hold up to 200 values. This is quite large for this particular problem, because there are no hierarchical models and no more than a very few control points could ever line up. The actual size needed would probably be no more than four `GLuints` per control point selected, and probably no more than 10 maximum points would ever line up in this problem, so the selection buffer could probably be defined to hold only 40 or 50 values. Each problem will need a similar analysis.

```
// globals initialization section
#define MAXHITS 200 // number of GLuints in hit records
// data structures for selection process
GLuint selectBuf[MAXHITS];
```

The next point is the mouse callback. This simply catches a mouse-button-down event and calls the `DoSelect` function, presented below, to handle the mouse selection. When the hit is handled (including the possibility that there was no hit at the cursor position), the control is passed back to the regular processes with a redisplay. The variable `hit` is a global that is used to identify the index of the selected control point through an array mapping function.

```
//  mouse callback for selection
void Mouse(int button, int state, int mouseX, int mouseY) {
    if (state == GLUT_DOWN) { // find which object was selected
    hit = DoSelect((GLint) mouseX, (GLint) mouseY);
    }
    glutPostRedisplay(); /* redraw display */
}
```

The control points may be drawn in either GL_RENDER or GL_SELECT mode, so the `drawpoints()` function must handle both cases. The only difference is that names must be loaded for each control point, and if any of the points had been hit previously, it must be identified so it can be drawn in red instead of in green. Note that the names are loaded sequentially as the control points are drawn; the logic `(hit == i*16+j%16)` is the array mapping function that accounts for the way names are assigned to the 16×16 array of control points. But nothing in this function says what is or is not hit in another mouse click; this is handled in the `DoSelect()` function below.

```
void drawpoints(GLenum mode) {
    int i, j;
    int name=0;
    glMaterialfv(GL_FRONT_AND_BACK, GL_AMBIENT_AND_DIFFUSE, green);
    // iterate through control point array
    for(i=0; i<GRIDSIZE; i++)
    for(j=0; j<GRIDSIZE; j++) {
        if (mode == GL_SELECT) {
            glLoadName(name); // assign a name to each point
            name++;              // increment name number
        }
        glPushMatrix();
        ... place point in right place with right scaling
```

```
            if(hit==i*16+j%16) { // selected point, need to draw it red
                glMaterialfv(GL_FRONT_AND_BACK, GL_AMBIENT_AND_DIFFUSE,
                red);
                glutSolidCube(0.25);
                glMaterialfv(GL_FRONT_AND_BACK, GL_AMBIENT_AND_DIFFUSE,
                green);
            }
            else glutSolidCube(0.25);
            glPopMatrix();
        }
}
```

The only real issue in drawing the model is to decide what you do and do not need to draw in each of the two rendering modes. The surface is drawn only if the program is in GL_RENDER mode because nothing in the surface is selectable. The only thing that needs to be drawn in GL_SELECT mode is the control points.

```
    void render(GLenum mode) {
    ... do appropriate transformations
    if (mode == GL_RENDER) { // don't render surface if mode is GL_SELECT
        surface(ctrlpts);
        ... some other operations that don't matter here
    }
    draw points(mode); // always render the control points
    ... pop the transform stack as needed and exit gracefully
    }
```

This final function is the real meat of the problem. The display environment is set up (projection and viewing transformations), the `glRenderMode` function sets the rendering mode to GL_SELECT and the image is drawn in that mode, the number of hits is returned from the call to the `glRenderMode` function when it returns to GL_RENDER mode, the display environment is rebuilt for the next drawing, and the selection buffer is scanned to find the name of the object with the smallest `zmin` value as the selected item. That number is then returned so that the `drawpoints` function can determine which control point to display in red and so other functions can determine which control point to adjust.

```
GLuint DoSelect(GLint x, GLint y) {
    int i;
    GLint hits, temphit;
    GLuint zval;
    glSelectBuffer(MAXHITS, selectBuf);
    glRenderMode(GL_SELECT);
    glInitNames();
    glPushName(0);

    // set up the viewing model
    ... standard perspective viewing and viewing transformation setup

    render(GL_SELECT); // draw the scene for selection
```

```
    // find the number of hits recorded and reset mode of render
    hits = glRenderMode(GL_RENDER);
    // reset viewing model
    ... standard perspective viewing and viewing transformation setup
    // return the label of the object selected, if any
    if (hits <= 0) return -1;
    else {
        zval = selectBuf[1];
        temphit = selectBuf[3];
        for (i = 1; i < hits; i++) { // for each hit
            if (selectBuf[4*i+1] < zval) {
                zval = selectBuf[4*i+1];
                temphit = selectBuf[4*i+3];
            }
        }
    }
    return temphit;
}
```

A Summary of Picking

To summarize the things we've seen about the standard picking process in the discussions and code examples above, we see that it involves three parts.

- Define an array of unsigned integers to act as the selection buffer.
- Design a mouse event callback that calls a function that does the following:
  sets GL_SELECT mode and draws selected parts of the image, having loaded names so these parts can be identified when the selection is made
  when this drawing is completed, returns a selection buffer that can be processed, and returns to GL_RENDER mode
- Manage the name stack as you draw objects in GL_SELECT mode so you have exactly the things on the stack you need to identify the objects the user is to be able to pick.

This is straightforward to understand and can be easily implemented with a bit of care and planning.

The MUI (Micro User Interface) Facility

Graphics APIs usually include some basic interaction capabilities, but they rarely offer a broad set of tools for building full user interfaces. These tools would include interactive graphics objects such as buttons, sliders, dials, and the like. Without a toolkit you would have to write your own functions to provide these tools for interactive program control. This can be hard work and can take quite a bit of time.

Because the APIs don't include interface toolkits, many people have built their own interface toolkits for graphics APIs, and some of these have become widely available. These provide functions that let you add interface capabilities to your programs simply by including appropriate headers and linking with appropriate libraries. In this section we introduce a very simple interface facility that is commonly available with OpenGL so that you can get some experience with programming using these interface tools. As we said at the start of this chapter, we do not believe that this will make you an effective interface designer, but it may help you understand what is involved with implementing an interface for a program using a standard toolkit.

To understand this section and be able to take advantage of an interaction toolkit for a graphics API, you should have an understanding of event-driven programming and some experience using the simple events and callbacks from the GLUT toolkit in OpenGL. You should also review the interface capabilities of a number of standard applications to see how they use buttons, sliders, text boxes, and other controls.

Introduction

We are used to seeing many kinds of interface tools in applications, but we cannot readily code many of these in OpenGL, even with the GLUT toolkit. Some of these are provided by the MUI facility (pronounced "mooey") that is a widely available extension of GLUT for OpenGL. With MUI you can create and use sliders, buttons, text boxes, and other tools that may be more natural than standard GLUT capabilities for many applications. Of course, you may choose to write your own tools as well, but you might prefer to spend your time on the problem at hand instead of writing an interface, so the MUI tools may give you what you want.

MUI has some of the look and feel of the X-Motif interface, so do not expect applications you write with it to look as if they are from either the Windows or Macintosh world. Instead, focus on the functionality you need for your application and find a way to get this functionality from the MUI tools. The visible representations of these tools are called *widgets,* just as they are in the X Window system, so you will see this term throughout this discussion.

This section is built on Steve Baker's "A Brief MUI User Guide" [BAK], and it shares similar properties: it is based on a small number of examples and some modest experimental work. It is intended as a guide, not as a manual, though we hope that it will contribute to the literature on this useful tool.

Using the MUI Functionality

Before you can use any of MUI's capabilities, you must initialize the MUI system with the function `muiInit()`, probably called from the `main()` function as described in the example code later in the chapter.

MUI widgets are managed in UI lists. You create a UI list with the `muiNewUIList(int)` function, giving it an integer name with the parameter, and add widgets to it as you wish with the function `muiAddToUIList(listid, object)`, where `listid` is the name you gave the list when you created it. You may create multiple lists and can choose which list will be active, allowing you to make your interface context-sensitive. However, UI lists are essentially static, not dynamic, because you cannot remove items from a list or delete a list once it has been created.

Any MUI capability can be made visible or invisible, active or inactive, or enabled or disabled. This adds some flexibility to your program by letting you customize the interface based on a particular context in the program. The functions for this are:

```
void muiSetVisible(muiObject *obj, int state);
void muiSetActive(muiObject *obj, int state);
void muiSetEnable(muiObject *obj, int state);
int muiGetVisible(muiObject *obj);
int muiGetActive(muiObject *obj);
int muiGetEnable(muiObject *obj);
```

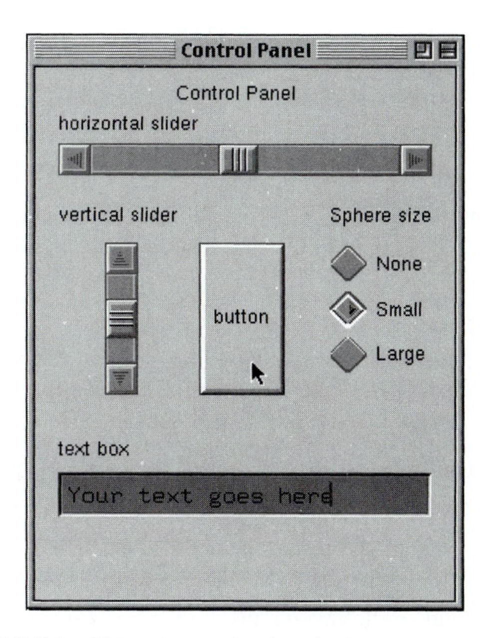

Figure 7.8 The set of MUI facilities on a single window.

Figure 7.8 shows most of the MUI capabilities: labels, horizontal and vertical sliders, regular and radio buttons (one radio button is selected and the button is highlighted by the cursor as shown), and a text box. Some text has been entered into the text box. This gives you an idea of what the standard MUI widgets look like. Because the MUI source is available, you can customize the widgets if you want, though doing so is beyond the scope of this discussion. Layout is facilitated by the ability to get the size of a MUI object with the function

```
void muiGetObjectSize(muiObject *obj, int *xmin, int *ymin,
                      int *xmax, int *ymax);
```

MUI object callbacks are optional (you would probably not want to register a callback for a fixed text string, for example, but you would with an active item such as a button). To register a callback, you must name the object when it is created and you must link that object to its callback function with

```
void muiSetCallback(muiObject *obj, callbackFn)
```

where a callback function has the structure

```
void callbackFn(muiObject *obj, enum muiReturnValue)
```

Note that this callback function need not be unique to the object; in the example below we define a single callback function that is registered for three different sliders and another to handle three different radio buttons, because the action we need from each is the same; when we need to know which object handled the event, this information is available to us as the first parameter of the callback.

If you want to work with the callback return value, the declaration of the muiReturnValue is:

```
enum muiReturnValue {
    MUI_NO_ACTION,
    MUI_SLIDER_MOVE,
    MUI_SLIDER_RETURN,
    MUI_SLIDER_SCROLLDOWN,
    MUI_SLIDER_SCROLLUP,
    MUI_SLIDER_THUMB,
    MUI_BUTTON_PRESS,
    MUI_TEXTBOX_RETURN,
    MUI_TEXTLIST_RETURN,
    MUI_TEXTLIST_RETURN_CONFIRM
};
```

so you can look at these values explicitly. For the example below, the button press is assumed because it is the only return value associated with a button, and the slider is queried for its value instead of handling the actual MUI action.

The MUI Interface Objects

The capabilities of MUI include pulldown menus, buttons, radio buttons, text labels, text boxes, and vertical and horizontal sliders. We will outline how each of these works and will include some general code to show how each is invoked.

The main thing you must realize in working with MUI is that MUI takes over the event handling from GLUT, so you cannot mix MUI and GLUT event-handling capabilities in the same window. This means that you will have to create separate windows for your MUI controls and for your display, which can feel somewhat clumsy. This is a tradeoff you must make when you design your application: are you willing to create a different kind of interface than you might expect in a traditional application in order to use the extra MUI functionality? Only you can say. But before you can make that choice, you need to know what each of the MUI facilities can do.

Menu Bars

A MUI menu bar is essentially a GLUT menu that is bound to a MUI object and then that object is added to a UIlist. Assuming you have defined an array of GLUT menus named `myMenus[ . . . ]`, you can use the function to create a new pulldown menu and then use the function to add new menus to the pulldown menu list:

```
muiObject *muiNewPulldown();
muiAddPulldownEntry(muiObject *obj,char *title,int glut_menu,
                    int is_help);
```

An example of the latter function would be

```
myMenubar = muiNewPulldown();
muiAddPulldownEntry(myMenubar, "File", myMenu, 0);
```

to add the GLUT menu myMenu to the menu bar with the value 0. The `is_help` value would be 1 for the last menu in the menu bar, because traditionally the help menu is the rightmost menu in a menu bar.

According to Baker, there is apparently a problem with the pulldown menus when the GLUT window is moved or resized. The reader is cautioned to be careful in handling windows when the MUI facility is being used.

Buttons

A button is presented as a rectangular region that sets a value or carries out a particular operation when the mouse is clicked in the region. Whenever the cursor is in the region, the button is highlighted to show that it is selectable. A button is created with the function

```
muiNewButton(int xmin, int xmax, int ymin, int ymax)
```

which has a `muiObject` * return value. The parameters define the rectangle for the button and are defined in window (pixel) coordinates, with `(0,0)` at the lower left corner of the window. In general, any layout in the MUI window will be based on such coordinates.

Radio Buttons

Radio buttons are similar to standard buttons, but they come in only two fixed sizes (either a *standard* size or a *mini* size). The buttons can be designed so that more than one can be pressed (to allow a user to select any subset of a set of options) or they can be linked so that when one is pressed, all the others are unpressed (to allow a user to select only one of a set of options). Like regular buttons, they are highlighted when the cursor is scrolled over them.

You create radio buttons with the functions

```
muiObject *muiNewRadioButton(int xmin, int ymin)
muiObject *muiNewTinyRadioButton(int xmin, int ymin)
```

where `xmin` and `ymin` are the window coordinates of the lower left corner of the button. The buttons can be linked with the function

```
void muiLinkButtons(button1, button2)
```

where `button1` and `button2` are the names of two button objects; to link more buttons, call the function with overlapping pairs of button names as shown in the following example. In order to clear all the buttons in a group, call the following function with any of the buttons as a parameter:

```
void muiClearRadio(muiObject *button)
```

Text Boxes

A text box is a facility that permits a user to enter text to the program. The text can then be used in any way the application wishes. The text box has some limitations; for example, you cannot enter a string longer than the text box's length. However, it also lets your user enter text and use the backspace or delete functions to correct errors. A text box is created with the function

```
muiObject *muiNewTextbox(xmin, xmax, ymin)
```

whose parameters are window coordinates, and there are functions to set the string:

```
muiSetTBString(obj, string)
```

to clear the string:

```
muiClearTBString(obj)
```

and to get the value of the string:

```
char *muiGetTBString(muiObject *obj).
```

Horizontal Sliders

Sliders are widgets that return a single value when they are used. The value is between zero and one, and you must manipulate that value into whatever range your application needs. A horizontal slider is created by the function

```
muiNewHSlider(int xmin,int ymin,int xmax,int scenter,int shalf)
```

where `xmin` and `ymin` are the screen coordinates of the lower left corner of the slider, `xmax` is the screen coordinate of the right-hand side of the slider, `scenter` is the screen coordinate of the center of the slider's middle bar, and `shalf` is the half-size of the middle bar itself. In the callback for the slider, the function `muiGetHSVal(muiObject *obj)` is used to return the value (as a float) from the slider to be used in the application. In order to reverse the process—to make the slider represent a particular value—use the function

```
muiSetHSValue(muiObject *obj, float value)
```

Vertical Sliders

Vertical sliders have the same functionality as horizontal sliders, but they are aligned vertically in the control window instead of horizontally. They are managed by functions that are almost identical to those of horizontal sliders:

```
muiNewVSlider(int xmin,int ymin,int ymax,int scenter,int shalf)
muiGetVSValue(muiObject *obj, float value)
muiSetVSValue(muiObject *obj, float value)
```

Text Labels

A text label is a piece of text on the MUI control window. This lets the program communicate with the user by presenting text in the interface, and a label can present either a fixed or variable string. To set a fixed string, use

```
muiNewLabel(int xmin, int ymin, string)
```

with `xmin` and `ymin` setting the lower left corner of the space where the string will be displayed. To define a variable string, you give the string a `muiObject` name via the variation

```
muiObject *muiNewLabel(int xmin, int ymin, string)
```

to attach a name to the label, and use the `muiChangeLabel(muiObject *, string)` function to change the value of the string in the label.

A text label can identify the window that contains the controls or can put a name on a button, put names beside radio buttons, or put names on sliders. In other words, labels can tell the user what your controls mean, and you can change the messages in the interface whenever these meanings change.

An Example

Let's consider a simple application and see how we can create the controls for it using the MUI facility. The application is color choice, commonly handled with three sliders (for R/G/B) or four sliders (for R/G/B/A), depending on the need of the user. This kind of application typically displays the color that is chosen in a region large enough to reduce the interference of nearby colors in perceiving the chosen color. The application we have in mind is a variant on this that shows not only the color but also the three fixed-component planes in the RGB cube and draws a sphere of the selected color (with lighting) in the cube.

The design of this application is built on an example in the science examples chapter (Chapter 9) that shows three cross-sections of a real function of three variables. We set the position of the cross-sections with controls based on MUI sliders. We also add radio buttons to let the user define the size of the sphere at the intersection of the cross-section slices.

Selected code for this application includes declarations of `muiObjects`, callback functions for sliders and buttons, and the code in the main program that defines the MUI objects for the program, links them to their callback functions, and adds them to the single MUI list we identify. The main issue is that MUI callbacks, like the GLUT callbacks we discussed earlier, have few parameters and do most of their work by modifying global variables that are used in the other modeling and rendering operations. The entire application is included in the resources for the book.

```
//  selected declarations of muiObjects and window identifiers
muiObject *Rslider, *Gslider, *Bslider;
muiObject *Rlabel, *Glabel, *Blabel;
muiObject *noSphereB, *smallSphereB, *largeSphereB;
int muiWin, glWin;

//  callbacks for buttons and sliders
void readButton(muiObject *obj, enum muiReturnValue rv) {
    if (obj = = noSphereB)
        sphereControl = 0;
    if (obj = = smallSphereB)
        sphereControl = 1;
    if (obj = = largeSphereB)
        sphereControl = 2;
    glutSetWindow(glWin);
    glutPostRedisplay();
}

void readSliders(muiObject *obj, enum muiReturnValue rv) {
    char rs[32], gs[32], bs[32];
    glutPostRedisplay();

    rr = muiGetHSVal(Rslider);
    gg = muiGetHSVal(Gslider);
    bb = muiGetHSVal(Bslider);

    sprintf(rs,"%6.2f",rr);
    muiChangeLabel(Rlabel, rs);
```

```
    sprintf(gs,"%6.2f",gg);
    muiChangeLabel(Glabel, gs);
    sprintf(bs,"%6.2f",bb);
    muiChangeLabel(Blabel, bs);

    DX = -4.0 + rr*8.0;
    DY = -4.0 + gg*8.0;
    DZ = -4.0 + bb*8.0;

    glutSetWindow(glWin);
    glutPostRedisplay();
}

void main(int argc, char** argv){
    char rs[32], gs[32], bs[32];
//  Create MUI control window and its callbacks
    glutInitDisplayMode(GLUT_DOUBLE | GLUT_RGBA);
    glutInitWindowSize(270,350);
    glutInitWindowPosition(600,70);
    muiWin = glutCreateWindow("Control Panel");
    glutSetWindow(muiWin);
    muiInit();
    muiNewUIList(1);
    muiSetActiveUIList(1);

//  Define color control sliders
    muiNewLabel(90, 330, "Color controls");

    muiNewLabel(5, 310, "Red");
    sprintf(rs,"s%6.2f",rr);
    Rlabel = muiNewLabel(35, 310, rs);
    Rslider = muiNewHSlider(5, 280, 265, 130, 10);
    muiSetCallback(Rslider, readSliders);

    muiNewLabel(5, 255, "Green");
    sprintf(gs,"%6.2f",gg);
    Glabel = muiNewLabel(35, 255, gs);
    Gslider = muiNewHSlider(5, 225, 265, 130, 10);
    muiSetCallback(Gslider, readSliders);

    muiNewLabel(5, 205, "Blue");
    sprintf(bs,"%6.2f",bb);
    Blabel = muiNewLabel(35, 205, bs);
    Bslider = muiNewHSlider(5, 175, 265, 130, 10);
    muiSetCallback(Bslider, readSliders);

//  define radio buttons
    muiNewLabel(100, 150, "Sphere size");
    noSphereB = muiNewRadioButton(10, 110);
    smallSphereB = muiNewRadioButton(100, 110);
    largeSphereB = muiNewRadioButton(190, 110);
    muiLinkButtons(noSphereB, smallSphereB);
    muiLinkButtons(smallSphereB, largeSphereB);
    muiLoadButton(noSphereB,     "None");
```

```
    muiLoadButton(smallSphereB,  "Small");
    muiLoadButton(largeSphereB,  "Large");
    muiSetCallback(noSphereB,    readButton);
    muiSetCallback(smallSphereB,readButton);
    muiSetCallback(largeSphereB,readButton);
    muiClearRadio(noSphereB);
//  add sliders and radio buttons to UI list 1
    muiAddToUIList(1, Rslider);
    muiAddToUIList(1, Gslider);
    muiAddToUIList(1, Bslider);
    muiAddToUIList(1, noSphereB);
    muiAddToUIList(1, smallSphereB);
    muiAddToUIList(1, largeSphereB);
//  Create display window and its callbacks
    ...
}
```

The presentation and interface for this application are shown in Figure 7.9. As the sliders set the R, G, and B values for the color, the numerical values are shown above the sliders and the

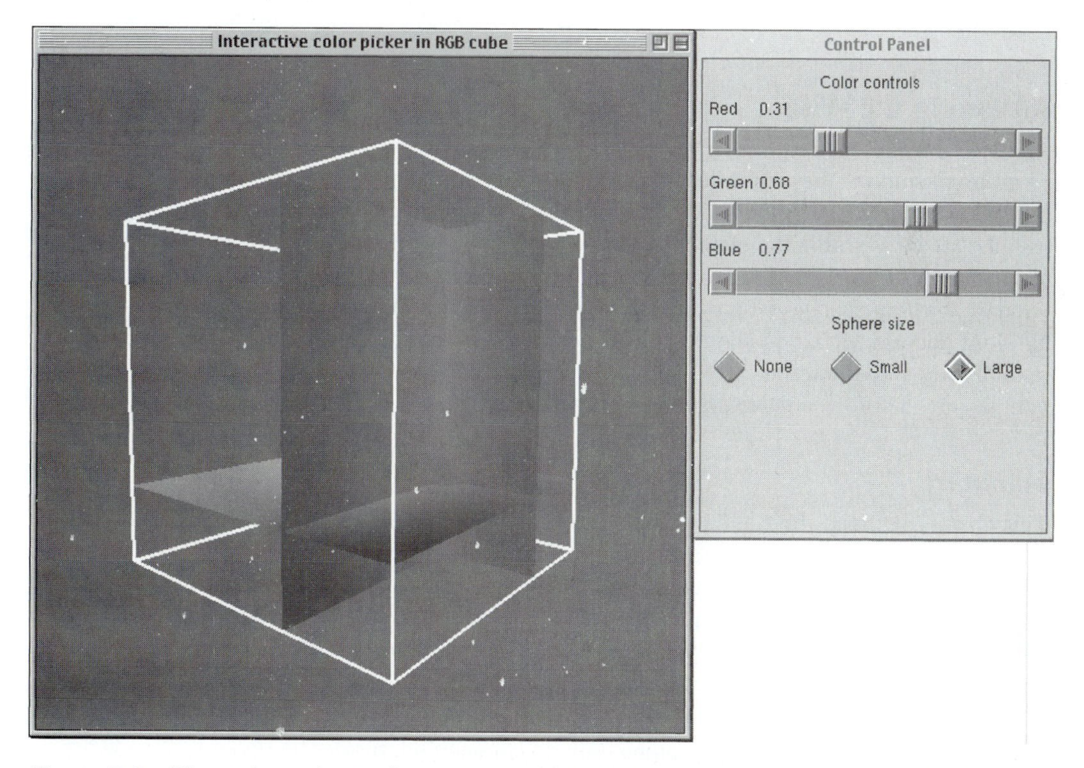

Figure 7.9 The color selector in context, with both the display and control windows shown.

three planes of constant R, G, and B are shown in the RGB cube. At the intersection of the three planes we draw a sphere of the selected color in the size chosen by the radio buttons. The RGB cube itself can be rotated by the keyboard controls described earlier so that the user can compare the selected color with nearby colors in those planes, but you have the usual issues of active windows: You must make the display window active to rotate the cube, but you must make the control window active to use the controls.

Installing MUI for Windows Systems

MUI often comes with the GLUT release, so if you have GLUT on your system you probably also have MUI. But if you do not have GLUT, when you download and uncompress the GLUT release you will have several header files (in the `include/mui` directory) and a couple of libraries: `libmui.a` for Unix and `mui.lib` for Windows. Install these in the usual places; for Windows with Visual Studio, for example, install `mui.lib` in the

```
<drive>:\Program Files\Microsoft Visual Studio\VC98\Lib\
```

directory. Place the header files also in the usual place; for Windows with Visual Studio this is

```
<drive>:\Program Files\Microsoft Visual Studio\VC98\include\
```

Then simply add `mui.lib` to your project files and you should be able to use MUI successfully.

A Word to the Wise

The MUI control window has behaviors that are outside the programmer's control, so you must be aware of some of these in order to avoid some surprises. The primary behavior to watch for is that many of the MUI elements include a stream of events (and their associated redisplays) whenever the cursor is within the element's region of the window. If your application was not careful to insulate itself against changes caused by redisplays, you may suddenly find the application window showing changes when you are not aware of requesting them or of creating any events at all. So if you use MUI, you should be particularly conscious of the structure of your application on redisplay and ensure that (for example) you clear any global variable that causes changes in your display before you leave the display function.

Summary

This chapter outlined the standard kinds of events used by a graphics system and the kinds of callbacks they use and gave several examples of programming with these events. It also discussed a user interface toolkit, both for its own value and as an example of the kind of interaction toolkits that might be found with a graphics API. With these tools, you should be able to extend your graphics programming with a broad set of interaction tools that can be used whenever your users need to be able to interact with your images.

If you find MUI to be too limiting for your work, you might try the GLUI interface toolkit. It is available in C++ source form, along with documentation, from

```
http://glui.sourceforge.net/
```

As described at that site, GLUI is a GLUT-based C++ user interface library that provides controls such as buttons, checkboxes, radio buttons, and spinners to OpenGL applications. It is window-system independent, relying on GLUT to handle all system-dependent issues, such as window and mouse management. It does not require you to separate the interface from the display window and so may be more powerful to use.

OpenGL Glossary for the Chapter

This chapter introduced the event-handling capacities of OpenGL through the GLUT toolkit. This means that we introduced a number of GLUT functions and constants that are listed here. It is possible that there are details of GLUT operations that we didn't discuss, so you are encouraged to look carefully at the GLUT documentation to be sure we didn't miss anything you need.

This chapter also talked about the MUI interface toolkit, but we don't cover that here; the material here is probably as good as any other reference and so you should simply refer to the chapter for any details.

OpenGL Functions

`glRenderMode(GL_SELECT)`: choose the mode in which you will render the scene; the `GL_RENDER` mode actually renders the scene to the color buffer, while the `GL_SELECT` mode does not render the scene but adds information to the selection buffer

`glSelectBuffer(value, buffer)`: establishes a buffer array of the given value to hold the information from `GL_SELECT` mode rendering

GLUT Functions

`glutAddMenuEntry(string, value)`: adds a menu entry to the bottom of the current menu; display the string and return the value if this menu item is selected

`glutAddSubMenu(string, value)`: adds a submenu trigger to the bottom of the current menu; display the string and use the menu whose identifier is the value as the submenu

`glutAttachMenu(event)`: associates the current menu to the event specified by the choice of mouse button events

`glutAttachMenuName(event, string)`: on the Macintosh (which has the convention of pulldown menus from a menu bar rather than from popup windows), associates the menu to the entry on the menu bar that displays the string and identify the selection of this window with the named event; the named event is to be one of the mouse button events

`void glutChangeToMenuEntry(index, string, value)`: changes the item indicated by index in the current menu into a menu item that displays the string and returns the value if chosen

`void glutChangeToSubMenu(index, string, menu)`: changes the item indicated by index in the current menu into a submenu trigger for the indicated menu that displays the given string

`int glutCreateMenu(functionname)`: sets the callback for the event that is generated if an entry is chosen from the menu

`void glutDestroyMenu(value)`: destroys the menu whose index value is passed to the function `glutDisplayFunc(functionname)`: sets the callback to the named function for a display event

`int glutGetMenu(void)`: returns the index number of the active menu

`glutIdleFunc(functionname)`: set the callback to the named function for the `idle` event

`glutKeyboardFunc(functionname)`: sets the callback to the named function for a `keypress` event

`glutMotionFunc(functionname)`: sets the callback to the named function for the mouse motion event (mouse motion in the graphics window while a button is pressed) to the named function

`glutMouseFunc(functionname)`: sets the callback to the named function for a `mouse` event

`glutPassiveMotionFunc(functionname)`: sets the callback to the named function for the mouse passive motion event (mouse motion in the graphics window while no button is pressed) to the named function

`glutReshapeFunc(functionname)`: sets the callback to the named function for a `reshape` event

`glutSetMenu(value)`: sets the menu whose index number is the value to be the active menu

`glutSpecialFunc(functionname)`: sets the callback function to the named function for the event of a `special` key event

`glutTimerFunc(msec, functionname, value)`: sets the callback to the named function for the `timer` event, set the event to be called in at least the indicated number of milliseconds, and define a value to be passed to the callback

OpenGL Parameters

`GL_RENDER`: used by `glRenderMode()` to set the system to draw to the color buffer

`GL_SELECT`: used by `glRenderMode()` to set the system to identify all the primitives that are drawn using the pixel selected to the selection buffer

GLUT Parameters

`GLUT_KEY_F*`: the symbolic names for the function keys F1 through F12

`GLUT_KEY_LEFT`: the symbolic name for the left cursor control key

`GLUT_KEY_UP`: the symbolic name for the up cursor control key

`GLUT_KEY_RIGHT`: the symbolic name for the right cursor control key

`GLUT_KEY_DOWN`: the symbolic name for the down cursor control key

`GLUT_KEY_END`: the symbolic name for the END special key

`GLUT_KEY_HOME`: the symbolic name for the HOME special key

`GLUT_KEY_INSERT`: the symbolic name for the INSERT special key

`GLUT_KEY_PAGE_UP`: the symbolic name for the PAGE UP special key

`GLUT_KEY_PAGE_DOWN`: the symbolic name for the PAGE DOWN special key

`GLUT_LEFT_BUTTON`: the symbolic name for the left button on a three-button mouse

`GLUT_MIDDLE_BUTTON`: the symbolic name for the middle button on a three-button mouse

`GLUT_RIGHT_BUTTON`: the symbolic name for the right button on a three-button mouse

Questions

1. In the chapter we alluded to 4DF and 6DF controls (DF = degree of freedom). However, we also have 2DF controls; discuss how the slider in MUI is a 2DF control. Describe further how you could create a 6DF control from three sliders (or other 2DF controls). Why is this or is this not a good way to create a 6DF control? Could you use mouse motion for 4DF and some keyboard control for the other 2DF? Again, is this a good way to create such a 6DF control?
2. When you use a mouse motion control for a rotation, it is important that the direction of the mouse be the direction of motion of the image. You can achieve image motion in two ways—by moving the eyepoint around a fixed image, or by moving the image with a fixed eyepoint. If we take increasing *x*- or *y*-coordinate values from the mouse to mean that the object moves to the right or up, how can you achieve that goal with each of these motions?
3. Imagine, or lay out, some collection of objects in a space; an example might be the carousel model you created in Chapter 2. Suppose you want only part of these objects to be selectable (for example, the posts in the carousel, but not the carousel animals). Describe how you could define your selection process to make this happen.
4. Sometimes a graphical object is made up of things that are difficult to select, such as points or line segments. How would you lay out a "selection scene" that provides alternative objects that represent the difficult original objects so you could select them more easily? What kind of alternative object might you use for a point? For a line segment?
5. Discuss the differences between picking and selection in terms of efficiency and of ease of identifying objects of various sizes. What advantages or disadvantages does each approach have?
6. Both selection and pick processes require you to analyze the selection buffer to identify which objects are closest or farthest or have another relationship to the eyepoint. Why does the back buffer approach find the object nearest the eye without any further work? Is there any way that the back buffer could find any other object?
7. Designing interaction is a very complex subject and an entire discipline in computing, HCI (human-computer interaction), is devoted to it. However, we can think about interaction in terms of the relation between controls presented in an application and controls for the area of the application in terms that are familiar to a user from the problem outside computing. For each of the following interaction techniques, identify a work area where you might find the technique in a context outside the computer.
   - a slider to control the value of a program parameter
   - a dial to control the value of a program parameter
   - a button to choose an option
   - a set of radio buttons to choose only one of a set of options
   - a mouse click to identify an item in an image
   - a mouse drag to move an image or a selected item in an image
   - a menu to make a selection from a list of options

Exercises

1. In many applications it is useful to be able to navigate around a scene by moving your eyepoint in a 2D space within your scene and directing your view in an appropriate direction in the scene. Devise a way to do this by using a diamond of keys on the keyboard controlling

motion left, right, forward, and back, and by using mouse motion to rotate the direction of view around the current eyepoint. By a diamond of keys we are referring to a set of keys such as S-E-D-X (for the left hand) or J-I-K-M (for the right hand).

2. Using examples from the science chapter (Chapter 9) or from your own work, identify a problem that uses animation to communicate an action and build an idle or timer callback that handles the necessary parameter changes to provide that animation for the image.
3. Using examples from the science chapter (Chapter 9) or from your own work, identify a problem that uses selection from a set of options and build a menu interface that allows the user to make the necessary selection(s) for the problem.
4. Using examples from the science chapter (Chapter 9) or from your own work, identify a problem that uses selection from a set of options and build a keyboard interface that allows the user to make the necessary selection(s) for the problem. Be careful that the keyboard options are understandable to the user.
5. Using examples from the science chapter (Chapter 9) or from your own work, identify a problem that uses selection from a set of options and build a MUI button interface that allows the user to make the necessary selection(s) for the problem.
6. Using examples from the science chapter (Chapter 9) or from your own work, identify a problem that involves selecting a particular graphical object to be manipulated and build a mouse selection operation that allows the user to select the graphical object for the problem.
7. Using examples from the science chapter or from your own work, identify a problem that needs a parameter or other value from the user and build a MUI interface that allows the user to enter the value from either a text input window or a slider.
8. Examine the nature of hit records by modifying any program including selection to include code that dumps the selection buffer byte-by-byte into a file when a selection is made, and examining that file by a simple file dump utility such as `Unix's od.` Identify all the components of the selection buffer within this byte array and see how these components are arranged.
9. Do the previous exercise when several objects are grouped in one name; do it again when objects are arranged in a hierarchy. These should give more complex lists of the names on the name stack when the selection is made; break these down to understand how grouping and hierarchy work.

Experiments

1. Compare the animations you create with the idle and timer callbacks by creating a very simple model (such as the cube in the included source codes) with each approach and comparing the frame rates and the rate consistency between the two examples. Then replace the simple model with a complex model and do the same. If you have access to machines with different speeds, take these codes to the other machines and look at the effect of machine speed on any difference you observed between these approaches.
2. (Class project) While full evaluation and user testing of a program interface is well beyond the scope of this book, you can get an idea of how useful program controls are by getting a few of your friends to use your program and tell you about it. These friends can, in fact, be classmates. So choose a problem involving exploring a principle or set of data that is oriented to user interaction, and each person in the class should design and implement the interactions

for the problem. Make everyone's program available to the class, and each class member should run each program and write a short evaluation of the interaction. Gather the evaluations and find the program that works best, and discuss why this program's interactions work.

3. Recall from Chapter 1 that you calculated the parametric equation of a line segment in the viewing frustum that represents the points in 3D eye space that project to a single screen point. Define a number of simple sphere and polygon primitives that lie in the visible part of a space and choose a point on the front viewing plane. Calculate the intersection of the resulting line with each of the primitives and explore the way you could tell which is nearest the eye.

4. Examine the structure of the selection buffer by creating a few scenes with different kinds of object structure, doing a selection in each, and printing and hand-parsing the buffer (which you can readily do at the point when you return the number of hits to the program). Some of the kinds of scene structure you would want include selecting a single object with no overlap or heirarchy, a selection when two individual objects overlap and the selection is made in the overlap, and a selection when a heirarchy is defined and selected. Hand-parsing will help you see how you need to code the handling of the selection buffer in these cases.

5. Experiment with the use of the back buffer for picking by setting your select-mode rendering to draw different objects in different colors and identify what object is nearest the eye at any given screen point.

6. As an experiment in different kinds of interaction, create a balance beam with an unknown weight at one end and have the user add weight to the other end in order to balance the beam. Use different kinds of interaction to add the weight and consider which kind of interaction is most effective based on either the time it takes to accomplish the task or the ease the user reports in accomplishing the task. Some possible interaction techniques are
   a. use a dial or slider to adjust the weight to achieve the balance
   b. use picking to select standard weights to achieve the balance (think of a set of weights in a physics experiment)
   c. use the keyboard to increase or decrease the weight by unit amounts to achieve the balance

7. (The scene graph) In order to be systematic about including event handling in the scene graph, you might want to include an "event node" that documents the event control over an aspect of the scene graph, such as transformations, appearance, or even geometry. Create such a new kind of node and modify the scene graph for an interactive graphics program by adding these nodes. It may be difficult to generate the code for the event handling from the scene graph, but see if you can do that.

Projects

1. (The small house) Build an interactive walkthrough of your small house by implementing the navigation scheme in exercise 1 and showing the views of the house from successive eyepoints as they are selected.

2. (A scene graph parser) Add a name node to the scene graph, to be used in the same places as the transformation node. Add pushing and popping the name stack to the set of operations that are handled by the parser.

Texture Mapping

Of all the techniques we will see in this book, texture mapping offers the best results for creating realistic and exciting images. In this chapter we look at texture mapping with 1D, 2D, and 3D textures and will see several examples of the effects you can create with 1D and 2D texture maps. We will also describe how you can make your own textures from both natural and synthetic images. Finally, we will look at how the OpenGL graphics API works with texture maps and give some working examples of code fragments for using texture maps in graphics programming. To benefit from this chapter, you need to understand the geometry of polygons in 3-space and how values in one space can map linearly to values in another space.

Introduction

We have seen how lighting and shading create the colors that fill a polygon in an image. Texture mapping is another way to define the colors in a polygon. It gives you a way to "paint" an image onto a polygon to achieve a more interesting image or to add information to the image without computing additional geometry. This is a significant addition to your tools for computer graphics and is a very useful technique for you to master. Texturing is a rich topic we will not cover in all the depth that is possible, but we will describe a useful set of capabilities as we present the topic in a way that is compatible with current graphics APIs. This will let you use texture mapping effectively in your work.

The primary reason to use texture mapping is to provide additional visual content in your images as the geometry is computed and displayed. In our APIs the geometry is primarily based on polygons, and as the pixels of the polygon are computed using texture mapping, the color of each pixel is calculated by including information from an array of values called a *texture map*. Texture maps are arrays of colors that represent information (for example, an image) that you want to display on an object in your scene. These maps can be 1D, 2D, or 3D arrays, though we will focus on 1D and 2D arrays here. *Texture mapping* is the process of identifying points on objects you define with points in a texture map to achieve images that can include strong visual interest while using simpler geometry.

This chapter focuses on how texture mapping works. Most of the time we think of the texture as an image, so that when you render your objects they will be drawn with the color values in the texture map. This lets you use many sources, such as digital or scanned photos, digital art, or synthetic images, as visually interesting things to be displayed on your objects. There are also ways to use texture maps to determine the luminance, intensity, or alpha values of your objects, adding significantly to the breadth of effects you can achieve.

Image sources are not, however, the only way we can do texture mapping. We can also compute the texture data for each pixel of an object procedurally. We will illustrate some simple procedural methods as we create texture maps for some of our examples. This will let us have a look at procedural texturing and give you an idea of the value of this approach, and you can look at these techniques further in more detail.

You must keep in mind that you are dealing with two different spaces in texture mapping. The first is your familiar 2D screen space, the space in which your objects will be displayed. The second is the *texture space,* a space that holds information to be mapped to your objects. This information is in discrete pieces that correspond to points in the texture array, often called *texels.* In order to use texture maps effectively, you must carefully consider how these two spaces will be linked when your image is created, and you must include this relationship as part of your design for the final image.

In order to coordinate the two spaces used in texture mapping and to develop the texture information to apply to each fragment, the graphics system must be given values for many individual parameters. You can think of this parameter setting as a *binding* operation, and the bindings will be set by several API functions. Among the things you will need to set are

- the name (usually a small integer) given to the texture in internal texture memory
- the dimensions of the texture map
- the format of the information the texture map contains
- what the texture map represents (a texture map may represent more than simply color)
- the way the texture and object colors are to be combined when a polygon is rendered with the texture, as described in Chapter 10
- how the texture is to be treated if the texture coordinates go outside the basic texture space
- how the texture aliasing is to be handled when the texture is applied to each fragment
- whether the texture has a border

You should look for all these bindings, and quite likely others, when you consider how your graphics API handles texture mapping.

There are many ways to create texture maps you can use. For 1D textures you may define a linear color function through various associations of color along a line segment. This is similar to the way you create a pseudocolor map as described in Chapter 5. For 2D textures you may use scanned images, digital photos, digital paintings, or screen captures to create original images, and you may use image tools such as Photoshop to manipulate the images to achieve precisely the effects you want. Your graphics API may have tools that let you capture the contents of your frame buffer in an array where it can be read to a file or used as a texture map. This 2D texture world is the richest texture environment we will meet in this book, and it is the most common texture context for most graphics work. For 3D textures you may again define your texture by associating colors with points in space, but this is more difficult because there are few tools for scanning or painting 3D objects. However, you may compute the values of a 3D texture from a 3D model, and various kinds of medical scanning will produce 3D data, so 3D textures have many appropriate applications.

Most graphics APIs are quite flexible in accepting texture maps in many different formats. You can use one to four components for the texture map colors, and you can select RGB, RGBA, or any single one of these four components of color for the texture map. Many of these look as if they have very specialized uses for unique effects, but an excellent general approach is to use straightforward 24-bit RGB color (8 bits per color per pixel) taken from an image file that does not have any compression or special file formats, such as the format Photoshop calls "raw RGB."

Finally, texture mapping is much richer than simply applying colors to an object. Depending on the capabilities of your graphics API, you may be able to apply texture to a number of different kinds of properties, such as transparency or luminance. In the most sophisticated kinds of graphics, texturing is applied to properties such as the alpha value of color to achieve effects such as clouds, or the directions of normals to achieve special lighting effects such as bump mapping and anisotropic reflection.

Definitions

In defining texture maps here, we describe them as one-, two-, or three-dimensional arrays of colors. These are the correct definitions technically, but we usually think of them more intuitively as one-, two-, or three-dimensional spaces that contain colors. When you use texture maps, the vertices in the texture map may not correspond exactly to the pixels you are filling in for the polygon, so the system must find a way to choose colors from the texture arrays. This is why it is more intuitive to think of a texture map as a space rather than as an array—we will need colors "between" the texture vertices. The graphics API interpolates the colors from the texture space and computes the value for the pixel based on the colors in the interpolated space. The interpolation techniques range from choosing the nearest point in the texture array to averaging the values of the colors for the pixel. However, this is usually not a problem when you first start using textures, so we note this for future reference and will discuss how to do it for the OpenGL API later in this chapter.

1D Texture Maps

A 1D texture map is a one-dimensional array of values that can be applied along any direction of an object, essentially as though it were extended to a 2D texture map by being replicated into a 2D array. It thus allows you to apply textures that emphasize the direction you choose, and in an example later in the chapter, a 1D texture lets us apply a texture that varies only according to the distance of an object from the plane containing the eyepoint.

2D Texture Maps

A 2D texture map is a two-dimensional array of values that can be applied to any 2D surface in a scene. This is probably the most natural and easy-to-understand kind of texture mapping, because it models the concept of "pasting" an image onto a surface. Another view of this texturing could be that the image is on an elastic sheet and it is tacked onto the surface by pinning certain points of the sheet onto the vertices of the surface. By associating points on a polygon with points in the texture space, which are actually coordinates in the texture array, we let the system associate any point on the polygon with a point in the texture space so that the polygon point can be colored appropriately. When the polygon is drawn, the value from the texture space is used as directed in the texture map definition.

3D Texture Maps

A 3D texture map is a three-dimensional array of values that can be associated with an object in 3D space. A useful visual examination of 3D textures is found in [WO00]. The 3D texture capability could be very useful in scientific work in a volume-rendering situation. Here the texture could defined by an array of colors from data (e.g., a CAT scan) or theory (e.g., a theoretical distribution of electrical charges) and the user can examine 3-space by taking slices or sections, colored by the texture, to understand higher-dimensional information in the space.

Associating a Vertex with a Texture Point

As you define your geometry, you associate a point in texture space with each vertex. This is similar to the way you associate a normal with each vertex when you set up lighting with smooth shading. This now lets us associate even more information with each vertex: the geometry of the vertex by its coordinates, the color of the vertex or the normal for the vertex that allows the color to be computed, and the coordinates of the texture point that's associated with the vertex. The vertex coordinates are used in the rendering pipeline to determine the pixel coordinates for the vertex, and the color, normal, and texture information are used to determine the appearance of the pixels within the object in the fragment processing step of the rendering pipeline.

Depending on how your graphics API works, you may either associate each vertex with actual texel coordinates of the texture point or a point with real coordinates, usually each in [0, 1], that represents a point by its proportional location in the texture map. The latter real number approach is preferable because it lets you work independently of the actual texture map size. It may seem difficult to associate geometry and texture for polygon-based objects, but if you are careful it can be straightforward. See Figure 8.1 for an illustration of this. Remember that your texture needs to be consistent with the object's geometry, and make sure you work out details such as matching the edges of adjacent faces and the like.

Figure 8.1 Associating an object with a texture. Here we see an object (*left*) and texture (*right*), and the problem is how to associate object and texture coordinates in order to get a good result.

The first question is what to do with the edges of your object. If you look at brick buildings, you will see that some corners (usually outside corners) have bricks that have sides showing on both faces, so you would want to use texture coordinates that are in the middle of bricks. Fortunately the texture shown will let you break up each brick so that the break comes between two seams, and this simulates such edges well. On the other hand, there are some corners (usually inside corners) where the mortar shows along the seam. Again, if you choose your edges carefully you can make this happen with these textures. And finally, you will probably want to make horizontal edges line up with whole bricks and make individual bricks line up along vertical corners, so you will want to choose texture coordinates carefully to make this happen. In our example, there are exactly 20 vertical and horizontal bricks in the texture, so using spacing of .05 texture units gives you whole bricks horizontally. This kind of calculation is needed in laying out any texture on any geometry.

The Relation Between the Color of the Object and the Color of the Texture Map

In a texture-mapping application, we have a graphical object and a texture. The object may be assumed to have color properties, and the texture also has color properties. Defining the color or colors of the texture-mapped object involves considering the colors of both the object and the texture map.

Perhaps the most common way to use texture mapping is to replace the color on the original object with the color of the texture map. This is certainly one of the options that a graphics API will give you. But many APIs have other options as well. If the texture map has an alpha channel, you can blend the texture map onto the object, using the kind of color blending we discuss in Chapter 5. You may also be able to apply other operations to the combination of object and texture color to achieve other effects. So don't assume that the only way to use texture maps is to replace the color of the object with the color of the texture; the options are much more interesting than that.

Other Meanings for Texture Maps

Texture maps can describe other things besides an image that is to be mapped onto an object. A texture map can be used to change the appearance of a polygon by modifying the alpha value, luminance, or intensity of the pixels in the polygon based on the values in the texture map. The details of what texture maps can do and how they do it are likely to vary for each API. This gives you a number of ways you can alter the appearance of a polygon by changing the way it is presented. This can be especially effective if it is used as part of multitexturing, where you build up an image by layering blending, luminance, and one or more textures onto an object.

Texture Mapping in the Scene Graph

A texture is basically an appearance property for a geometry object, so it should be part of the appearance part of a geometry node. However, the geometry node itself must include the texture coordinates that correspond to each vertex, so texture must also be involved in the geometry node.

The most straightforward way to achieve this is to consider all the details of the texture map, such as those used by OpenGL, when you create the appearance part of the node. This is typically expressed before the geometry of the node is defined, as would be done with the material and shading definitions for the appearance node. Then the geometry node would be expressed, but this must include texture coordinates for each vertex, just as using a lighting model needs the geometry node to include the normal vector for each vertex of the geometry. As the scene graph is traversed, either automatically or manually, the code that expresses the appearance would then be placed before the code that expresses the geometry. This is relatively straightforward and should pose few problems.

Creating Texture Maps

Any texture you use must be created before it is loaded into the texture array. You can create the texture by reading an image into an array and loading that as your texture, or by creating your texture through a computational process. In this section we consider these two options and outline how you can create a texture map through each. Later in the chapter we will have examples of both processes.

Creating a Texture Map from an Image

Using images as texture maps is very popular, especially when you want to give a naturalistic feel to a graphical object. Naturalistic textures of sand, concrete, brick, grass, trees, and ivy, to name only a few, are often based on scanned or digital photographs of these materials. Other kinds of textures, such as flames or smoke, can be created with a digital paint system and saved in a file to be used in your work. All the image-based textures are handled in the same way: The image is created and saved in a file in an appropriate format, and the file is read by the graphics program into a texture array to be used by the API's texture process. Of course, all these are 2D textures because they start with 2D images. 3D texture maps can be created from 3D scanning processes, such as medical scans, but these are much less common.

The main problem with using image files for textures is that there are an enormous number of graphics file formats. Entire books are devoted to cataloging these formats [MUR], and some formats include compression techniques that require significant computation when you re-create the image from the file. Using compressed images directly requires you to use a tool called an *RIP*—a *raster image processor*—to create the pixel array from your file, and this can be a complex tool to write yourself. However, many implementations of graphics APIs are starting to include tools to read images in various formats. Unless you have such functions available, we suggest that you avoid file formats such as JPEG, GIF, PICT, or even BMP and use only formats that store a simple sequence of RGB values. If you want to use an image that you have in a compressed file format, probably the simplest approach is to open the image in a highly capable image manipulation tool such as Photoshop, which can read images in most formats, and then re-save it in a simplified form such as interlaced raw RGB.

A sample image that we will use as a texture map is a picture of a group of African penguins created from one of the author's photographs. This is shown in Figure 8.2. Graphics APIs are likely to have restrictions on the dimensions of texture maps (for example, the OpenGL standard requires all dimensions, not including borders, to be a power of 2) so even if the format is so low-level that the image format does not store the image's dimensions, they can be recalled easily. In this text we use a raw RGB format for images to make it easy to read them into a program, though you may have utility programs to read images in other formats into a raster file. We suggest that when you use such a raw image file format, you include the dimension as part of the file name, such as `ivy.128x64.rgb`, so that the size will not need to be recorded. The process of using an image file as a source for a texture map is described in a code example later in this chapter.

Generating a Synthetic Texture Map

Because a texture map is simply an array of color, luminance, intensity, or alpha values, you can generate the values of the array by doing computation instead of reading a file. Generating a

Figure 8.2 An image that will be used as a texture map in several examples in this chapter.

texture computationally is a very powerful technique that can be either simple or complex. Here we'll describe a few techniques that you might find helpful as starting points in creating your own computed textures.

One of the simplest textures is the checkerboard tablecloth such as is shown in Figure 8.3 applied to two rectangles. For example, if we want to build a 64 × 64 texture array, we can define the color of an element *tex*[*i*][*j*] as red if (*i*/4 + *j*/4)%2 has value zero and white if the value is one:

Figure 8.3 A simple checkered tablecloth pattern as a texture map.

```
for (i = 0; i < 64; i++)
     for (j=0; j<64; j++) {
          if ((i/4+j/4)%2) tex[i][j] = red;
          else tex[i][j] = white;
     }
```

where red and white are symbolic names for color vectors. This will put a 4×4 red square at the top left of the texture and will alternate white and red 4×4 squares from there, thus creating a traditional checkerboard pattern. This kind of texture map is often used for debugging a texture-mapped image because it shows problems easily.

Noise Functions as Texture Maps

A particularly useful kind of computed texture involves using a *noise function*. A noise function is a single-valued function of one, two, or three variables that has no statistical correlation to any rotation (that is, does not seem to vary systematically in any direction) or translation (does not seem to vary systematically across the domain) and that has a relatively limited amount of change in the value across a limited change in the domain. There are a number of ways to create such functions, and we will not begin to explore them all, but we will take one relatively simple approach to defining a noise function and use it to generate a couple of texture maps.

Instead of starting with a noise function itself, let's look at a simple texture map that has some of the properties of a noise function: no correlation for rotation or translation. If we generate a random number between 0 and 1 at each point of the texture map, then the nature of random numbers will give us the lack of correlation we need. But there is also no correlation between nearby elements of the texture map, so the purely random texture map is not satisfactory for many uses.

To give us a smoother, but still uncorrelated, random texture, we can apply the kind of filter function that we will see in the examples of diffusion processes in Chapter 9. Recall that this filter replaces the value of each pixel with a weighted sum of the values of the pixels near that pixel, creating a weighted average of these values. If we start with a random texture and apply the filter process several times, we get a smoother texture that will still have the lack of correlation we need. This filtering can be done as often as you like, and the more often it is applied, the smoother the resulting texture. This is straightforward, and the results of 2D versions of the processes are shown in Figure 8.4. The texture can be created in grayscales, as shown, or colored textures can

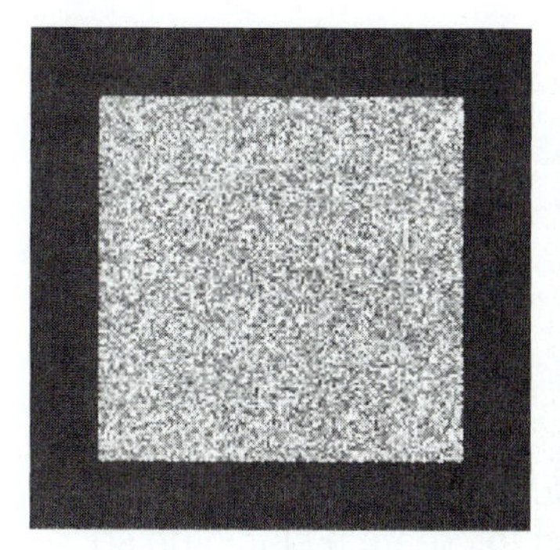

Figure 8.4 A random 2D texture (*left*) and the texture smoothed by filtering twice (*center*) and five times (*right*).

be made by creating similar textures for each of the RGB components in the color. A similar process could be used to create 3D textures by using 3D filters, a direct extension of the concept of 2D filters.

The random textures defined above are examples of noise functions that might be called *white noise,* with random values between 0 and 1. However, many other kinds of noise are possible, and one important one for texture maps is called *1/f noise*. This is a noise function that is built from a linear combination of white noise functions f_N at various frequencies M, with the amplitude of f_M adjusted to be $1/M$. If we take these functions at frequencies 2^N for positive values of N, then the amplitude of the sum of the functions is $\Sigma(1/N)$, with the sum taken over all powers of two. This sum is 1 in the limit, so the combined function also takes values from 0 to 1, just as the individual functions did. A texture map made from this technique has both large-scale properties (low frequencies) and small-scale details (high frequencies) and can be used to model some natural phenomena very well.

To see how this works, let's work our way through a simple 1D example shown in Figure 8.5. A noise function will be thought of as a piecewise linear function with values in [0,1], defined on the interval [0,1]. The *frequency* of a noise function on an interval can be defined to be the number of separate linear segments the function has over the interval. So if a function is defined by values at 0.0, 0.5, and 1.0, its frequency is 2, while if the function is defined by values at 0,0. 0.25, 0.5, 0.75, and 1.0, its frequency is 4. It should be clear how to get functions with frequencies 8, 16, or any other power of 2: For frequency 2^N, the function f_N could be piecewise linear with random values in [0, 1] defined at $x = i/2^N$ for all values of i from 0 to 2^N. The figure shows a very simple case: a piecewise linear function of one variable from 0 to 16, which could be used to create a 1D texture map 16 pixels wide. The left-hand column contains the graph of the individual f_N functions for N = 4, 8, and 16, the center column is the set of functions $f_N/2^N$, and the right-hand side is the sum of the functions in the center column. Obviously this is a very simple example, and a more useful noise function—or noise texture map—would be defined over a larger interval and would involve more piecewise linear functions.

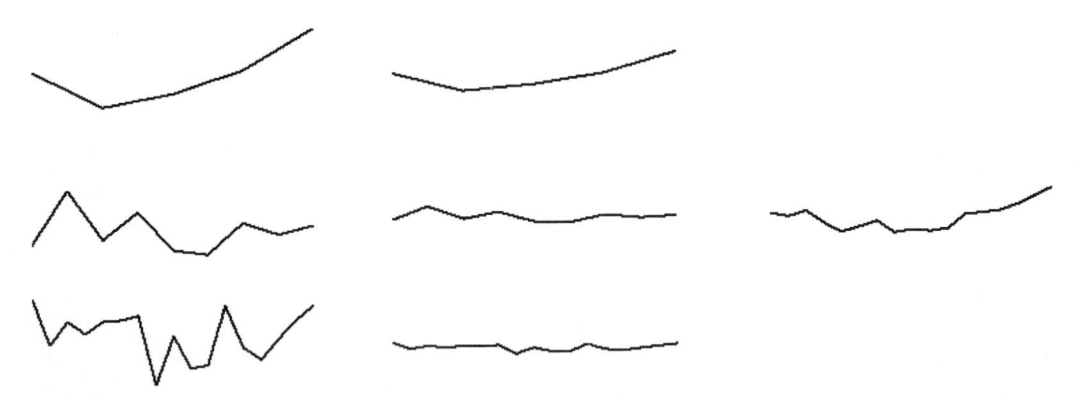

Figure 8.5 Noise functions of various frequencies (*left column*), multiplied by the reciprocals of their frequencies (*center column*), and summed to create a single noise function (*right*).

In order to create 2D or 3D noise textures, the function or texture map uses functions on 2D or 3D space instead of on 1D space. In the 2D case, you could use polygons defined by vertices with (x,y) coordinates on a regular 2D grid of size $2^N \times 2^M$ and random z-coordinates, giving a set of points on a regular grid just as we described for graphing a 2D function in Chapter 9. For each level you would interpolate points in the space between these points, giving you a surface for that level, and then you would sum these surfaces to get your noise function. In the 3D case you would need to compute values on a regular 3D grid across a cubic region of space defined by eight coordinates in 3D space and then interpolate the values at all the 3D points in this space, which is a straightforward extension of the 2D case but is much more difficult to visualize. But you will still work with functions of varying frequencies and sum them with varying weights, producing $1/f$ noise functions in 2D or 3D space.

In practice, the approach that is generally used is much more sophisticated than we have described. This approach uses gradient interpolation as discussed by Peachy in [EB]. This is also the kind of noise function used in the Renderman shader system. We will not describe this in detail, but you are encouraged to work through the sample code for such noise functions provided by Mike Bailey that is included in the supplementary materials for this book. Figure 8.6 is an example of a texture built with such a process. As an overview, let's consider this in the 3D noise case.

Figure 8.6 A texture from a 1/f noise function.

The general process for creating noise functions starts with a 3D mesh of the right frequency for a particular function f_N. We view the coordinates of each 3D mesh point as x-, y-, and z-components of a point in the noise function domain, and we compute a unit vector of three random components that represents the gradient at that point. These three components are the direction and amplitude of the gradient. We then assume a height of 0 at each grid point and use the gradients to define a smooth function as the basic noise function. The discussions in [EB] explain this process in detail, as well as some issues in using it effectively and efficiently.

Interpolation for Texture Maps

To display a 2D texture-mapped polygon, the rendering pipeline interpolates the texture coordinates for each pixel from the texture coordinates of the polygon vertices. If the scene uses a perspective projection, the highest-quality texturing is done if the interpolation takes the perspective into account by back-projecting the 2D coordinates for each pixel into the original modeling space before doing the interpolation. If this perspective correction is not done, the texture in each polygon follows a linear pattern based on the polygon boundaries, which can cause awkward artifacts at polygon boundaries. In the left-hand image of Figure 8.7, we see a quad defined as two triangles with a checkerboard texture, and we see that in the triangle at the lower left, all the lines in the texture are parallel to the left or bottom edges while all the lines in the upper right triangle are parallel to the right or top edges. But because the quad is shown with a perspective projection, the left and right sides are not parallel, leading to problems with the texture where the triangles meet. In the right-hand image of the figure, the lines of the checkerboard behave correctly with respect to perspective. This illustrates the difference that perspective-corrected interpolation can make for texture mapping. Similar problems can occur for 1D or 3D texture maps in a perspective projection situation when perspective correction is not used. This figure also shows how readily the checkerboard texture shows problems in textured images, as we suggested earlier in the chapter. The technique for doing perspective-corrected texture interpolation is simply a special case of the perspective-corrected interpolation discussed in Chapter 10.

Figure 8.7 A planar rectangular region defined by two triangles without (*left*) and with (*right*) perspective correction for the texture mapping.

Texture Mapping and Billboards

In Chapter 12 we will introduce the concept of a *billboard*—a two-dimensional polygon in three-dimensional space that is always rotated to face the viewer and that has an image texture-mapped onto it, so that the image on the polygon appears to be a three-dimensional object in the scene. This is a straightforward application of texture mapping but requires that the color of the polygon come entirely from the texture map and that some portions of the texture map have a zero alpha value so they will seem transparent when the polygon is displayed. The geometric principles behind billboards are discussed later in this chapter.

Because natural images that might be used for billboards do not come with an alpha channel, you might have to do some work to create a texture for a billboard. You start with any image and edit it to create a background color and then adjust the alpha values based on that color as you read in the image from an RGB file to an RGBA array. If a pixel is not the background color, leave the pixel's RGB alone and set the alpha to 1.0 for maximum opacity. If the pixel is the background color, set the alpha to 0.0 so that the color of the pixel will be ignored in blending. This is similar to the green-screen technique for television or film compositing.

The reason for using a billboard is to show the viewer an image of a 3D object with 2D techniques, giving the illusion of 3D objects in the scene. Billboards are generally used in situations where the eye and billboards are placed absolutely in the scene—that is, are not placed relative to other geometric objects. Another way to say this is that the eye and billboards are generally at the top level of the scene graph. This makes it easier to handle the transformations needed to orient the billboard in the scene.

Billboards are less difficult to build than might be thought. The key point for a billboard is that it must point in the direction of the viewer. This is relatively straightforward, because you can get the view direction from the definition of viewing. If your eyepoint is at (x_1, y_1, z_1) and your view reference point is at (x_2, y_2, z_2), then the direction of the view is given by the vector $d = <x_2 - x_1, y_2 - y_1, z_2 - z_1>$, suitably normalized. You can then express the direction of d in polar coordinates as $(1, \theta, \phi)$, using the computations for θ and ϕ described in Chapter 4, and rotate the billboard by an angle of θ around the vertical (if you want the vertical component of the billboard to remain fixed, as is commonly done for objects such as trees or text) or by both angles if you want the entire billboard to face in the view direction.

If you need to have billboards or the eye defined hierarchically in the scene, it is more difficult to orient the billboard to the view because of other transformations in the hierarchy. To accomplish this, we use the scene graph; there will be a set of transformations that set the position and orientation of the billboard's rectangle as it was initially placed in the scene. You must take these transformations and invert them, as discussed in Chapter 3, giving a transformation that would place them at the root of the scene graph. Then you must add any transformations that are used to orient the eyepoint. This transformation, then, is the final modeling transformation defined before the billboard is drawn, and it will always make the billboard point toward the viewer.

Including Many Textures in One Texture Map

In many graphics APIs you can have several texture maps resident in your system and switch between them to use different textures in different parts of your image. However, sometimes you may want to use more textures than you can handle individually. For example, if you are using billboarding to create labels, you might want to have a number of different labels in your scene. In this case you could create a single texture map that contains all the labels you would use and then select the individual label by choosing your texture coordinates to include only the area of the texture map with that label's content. In another example, you could create an image of a flickering flame by using a large texture map that contains several pictures of a flame. You could load the entire texture map once and by changing (in the idle callback function) the texture coordinates for the area where the flame is to be displayed get a series of images that models the flickering flame.

Selecting only a part of an image for a texture map can be useful in other contexts as well. If you have a nonrectangular part of a photo that you want to use as a texture, you can read the whole photo into texture memory and use texture coordinates to select only the part that is important to you. This lets you get around the problem of having only rectangular textures.

Antialiasing in Texturing

When you apply a texture map to a polygon, you identify the vertices in the polygon with coordinates in texture space. These coordinates may or may not be integers (i.e., actual indices in the texture map), but the interpolation process we discussed will assign a value in texture space to each pixel in the polygon. The pixel may represent only part of a texel (texture cell) if the difference between the texture-space coordinates for adjacent pixels is less than one, or it may represent many texels if the difference between the texture space coordinates for adjacent pixels is greater than one. This creates two possible kinds of aliasing—the magnification of texels if the texture is coarse relative to the object being texture mapped (handled by a *magnification filter*), or the selection of color from widely separated texels if the texture is very fine relative to the object (handled by a *minification filter*). Magnification tends to lead to blocky textures as a texel's effect is felt over many pixels. Minification tends to lead to gaps in the texture where some texels will not be included in coloring pixels. Magnification and minification filters are used to minimize these effects.

Because textures may involve aliasing, graphics APIs often have antialiasing capabilities for texturing. For magnification filtering, you will find yourself with pixel coordinates often having two adjacent points within the same texel. You can choose to use the *nearest* filter to determine the color of a pixel: The color is set to the color of the nearest texel vertex. This can alias a number of pixels to the color of a single texel vertex, giving you a blocky image. Another approach is to choose *linear* filtering, where each pixel's color is determined by a weighted average of the texel vertices around it, with the weight determined by how close the pixel is to each texel vertex. Other, more sophisticated kinds of antialiasing techniques are possible, but graphics APIs tend to keep things simple in order to achieve reasonable performance. In the OpenGL API, the only antialiasing tool available is linear filtering, but different APIs may have other tools, and certainly sophisticated, custom-built, or research graphics systems can use a number of antialiasing techniques. You may also be able to get other antialiasing with the new generation of programmable graphics cards. This needs to be considered when planning the nature of your application and choosing your API. See [EB] for more details.

MIP Mapping

We have seen that when only a single texture map is available, the graphics system must sometimes use an antialiasing process to choose the color of a pixel from the colors of pixels in the original map. If the pixel space of a polygon is larger than that of the texture map, there is no way to get individual texel information for each pixel, and techniques such as linear filtering are needed. But as a polygon gets small, the pixel space gets smaller than the texture space and you will find that pixels that are near one another in the polygon have colors that are not near one another in the texture space. As these polygons move, the colors can jump around unpredictably, causing unwanted effects.

A solution to this problem can be found by giving your system a hierarchy of texture maps of different sizes and having the system select the map that best fits the size of your polygon. One technique for doing this is MIP mapping (MIP means *multum in parvo,* or "many things in a

small place"). With this approach, you provide your texture map in many resolutions so that you can control the versions of the texture that will be seen at each level. This set of different resolution maps is all held in the same texture memory, and the proper one is selected depending on the size of the polygon to be presented. The set of maps may be held in a single array as shown in Figure 8.8, where the submaps of our penguin image are of size various powers of two. The array is read by reading each successive sub-array into a separate texture map whose dimensions are each half the size of the previous texture map. If you are using MIP mapping, you may have to create texture maps of all sizes down to the smallest when one dimension becomes 1.

Figure 8.8 An array holding several versions of a base texture for MIP mapping.

MIP maps may also be generated from an initial texture map by using functions provided by your graphics API, as is the case for OpenGL. See your API documentation for details.

MIP mapping can be seen as a level-of-detail process, as discussed in Chapter 12, but it is used less for performance reasons than for quality reasons. Thus we believe it fits best in the discussion here of providing high-quality texture mapping.

Multitexturing

Multitexturing is a rendering technique in which two or more textures are applied to a single surface in the rendering process, as shown in Figure 8.9. For example, one texture might be a wood surface and a second texture might be a light map. The combination of the two textures would produce a texture of a lighted wooden surface, as shown in Figure 8.10. This use of surface and light maps is a common technique in games programming. Other examples might include combining aerial photographs, GIS (geographic information systems) locator symbols, and elevation contour lines to produce a map that combines realistic terrain, points of interest, and elevation information.

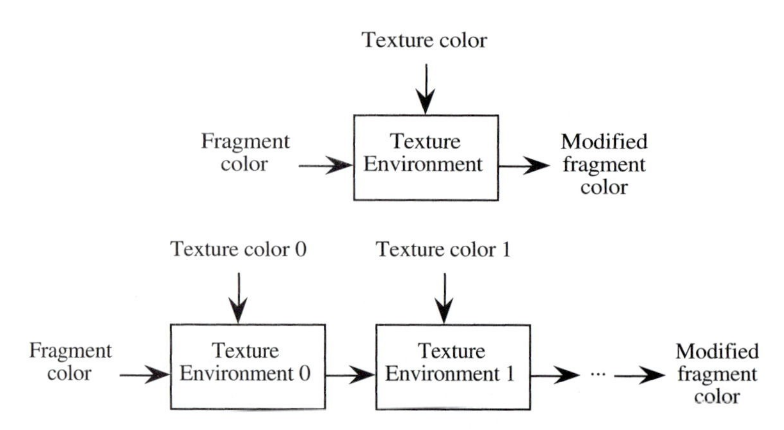

Figure 8.9 Texturing in the rendering pipeline: single texture (*above*) and multitexture (*below*).

With standard texturing capabilities you may be able to achieve similar results. It may be possible to combine separate texture maps into a single texture map if the separate maps are of the same size and share the same texture coordinates on the target to be textured. You would simply read the values in the individual texture arrays and combine them with appropriate operations into a new texture array that you could use as your single texture. However, this is not easily done in general, because texture data usually does not come in such nice packages and separate texture maps may be of different sizes and with different orientations relative to the surface to be textured. So having a multitexture capability allows you to use each texture with its own individual properties, and the combination you need will be applied in the rendering process.

In general, using multitextures is almost exactly like using several individual textures. You need to create individual texture maps from whatever sources you like, and you need to specify that you will be using a number of textures and bind the particular texture maps to each and enable them. When you specify your geometry, you will need to define the texture coordinate for each of

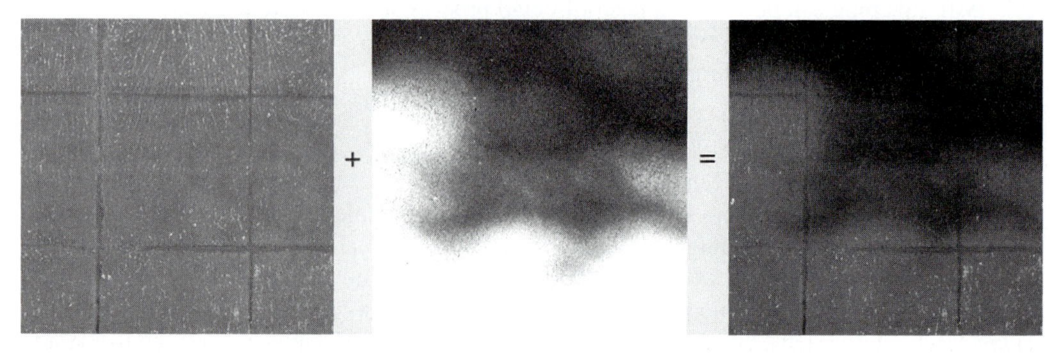

Figure 8.10 Multitexturing in use. See the figure in the color insert.

the individual textures that correspond to each vertex point. This is not especially difficult, and in the case of OpenGL multitexturing, this is discussed later in the chapter.

Texture Mapping in OpenGL

There are many details to master before you are fully skilled at using textures in your images. The full details must be left to the manuals for OpenGL or for another API, but here we will discuss many of them, certainly enough to give you a good set of skills in the subject. These details are the texture environment, texture parameters, building a texture array, defining a texture map, and generating textures. In this chapter we have examples of many of these details to help you see how they work.

One of the details you need to understand is which texture-related functions are used to define each of the different aspects of texture mapping. While there are not a large number of these functions, you must use them carefully and in an appropriate sequence in order for your textures to work properly. A list of the primary texture-related functions in OpenGL is given here, and later in the chapter you will see more details of their use. There are some simple considerations for ordering these function calls that we will describe as we discuss examples.

`glEnable(...)`	enables texture mapping as needed in your program; also `glDisable(...)` to disable texture mapping when no longer needed
`glGenTextures(...)`	generates one or more names (integers) that can be used for textures
`glBindTexture(...)`	binds a texture name (generated in `glGenTextures`) to a texture target such as `GL_TEXTURE_1D`, `GL_TEXTURE_2D`, or `GL_TEXTURE_3D`
`glTexEnv*(...)`	defines the action of the texture when it is applied to the object on a per-fragment basis
`glTexParameter*(...)`	defines how antialiasing, wrapping, and similar functions are to be applied to the texture
`glTexImage*(...)`	binds values to most of the parameters that are used to define a texture, such as the number of color coordinates and the internal format of the texture data, how the texture is to be interpreted, the size of the texture map, and the like
`glTexCoord*(...)`	associates a texture coordinate to a vertex of a graphic object
`glTexGen*(...)`	controls the automatic generation of vertex coordinates for an object
`glDeleteTextures(...)`	deletes one or more textures that had been generated by `glGenTextures`

There are four main effects of these functions. The first three functions (`glEnable, glGenTextures, glBindTextures`) set the OpenGL system so that it is prepared to use texture mapping. The next two functions (`glTexEnv, glTexParameter`) define how the texture is to be applied to a graphics object as it is rendered by the system. The next function, `glTexImage`, identifies the data array that is to be used by the texture and how it is to be interpreted as the texture is loaded into texture memory. The next function, `glTexCoord`, allows you to identify the texture coordinates that are to be associated with the geometric coordinates for your modeling. The order in which these functions are usually applied is given in later examples of texture mapping.

Associating Vertices and Texture Points

You define your geometry in OpenGL with the basic primitives as described in Chapter 3. Within a `glBegin(...) ... glEnd()` pair, you are used to using both `glVertex*()` and `glNormal*()` functions; you can also include `glTexCoord*()` functions to define the texture coordinate for each vertex. As always, these functions come in several varieties, depending on what kind of coordinates you use, and they follow familiar patterns:

```
glTexCoord1f(float)
glTexCoord2f(float, float)
glTexCoord3f(float, float, float)
glTexCoord1fv(float[1])
glTexCoord2fv(float[2])
glTexCoord3fv(float[3])
```

You must specify texture coordinates before you call the `glVertex()` function that defines the point because the state of the vertex is set at that point.

The actual texture coordinates represent the real number that represents the position of the texture point within the texture map, so coordinates in the range [0, 1] give you points within the texture space. Coordinates outside this range are interpreted according to your choice of texture wrap or clamp, as described later in this chapter.

Capturing a Texture from the Screen

A useful approach to textures is to create an image and save the color buffer (the frame buffer) as an array that can be used as a texture map. This can let you create a number of different kinds of images for texture maps. This operation is supported by many graphics APIs. For example, in OpenGL, the `glReadBuffer(mode)` function determines the color buffer from which subsequent buffer reads are to be done, usually the front buffer if you are using single buffering or the back buffer if you are using double buffering. The `glReadPixels(...)` function, used with the RGB or RGBA symbolic format, can then copy the values of the elements in that buffer into a target array. This function can do much more, however; it can save the values of any one color channel, of the depth buffer, or of the luminance, among others. This gives you the ability to retrieve a number of different kinds of information from an image. We will not go into more detail here but refer you to the manuals for the advanced use of these functions.

The array returned by the `glReadPixels(...)` function may be written to a file for later use or may be used immediately in the program as the texture array. If it is saved to a file, it will probably be most useful if it is saved in a raw format, holding nothing but the values read from the buffer, but you may want to add extra information to allow it to be used more readily. For example, if you start the file with the width and height of the image, your file will resemble the .ppm format, which can be used by many image manipulation programs. If you capture a stream of images into files with names that include sequential numbers, it may be possible to write scripts that will pick these up and make them into a digital movie to display your images as an animation. We refer you to Chapter 11 for more details.

Texture Environment

To use texture mapping with a graphics API, you must define your texture environment to specify how texture values are to be used when the texture is applied to a polygon. In OpenGL, the appropriate function call is

```
glTexEnvi(GL_TEXTURE_ENV, GL_TEXTURE_ENV_MODE, *)
```

The meaning of the texture is determined by the value of the last parameter. The options are

```
GL_BLEND, GL_DECAL, GL_MODULATE, or GL_REPLACE.
```

In this and the other behavior descriptions, we use *C*, *A*, *I*, and *L* for color, alpha, intensity, and luminance, respectively, and subscripts *f* and *t* for the fragment and texture values, respectively.

If the texture represents *RGB color,* the behavior of the texture when it is applied is defined as:

- `GL_BLEND`: the color of the pixel is $C_f(1\text{-}C_t)$
- `GL_DECAL`: the color of the pixel is C_t, simply replacing the color by the texture color
- `GL_MODULATE`: the color of the pixel is $C_f{*}C_t$, replacing the color by the product of the colors
- `GL_REPLACE`: same as `GL_DECAL` for color

If the texture represents *RGBA color*, then the behavior of the texture is defined as:

- `GL_BLEND`: the color of the pixel is $C_f(1\text{-}C_t)$, and the alpha channel in the pixel is $A_f{*}A_t$
- `GL_DECAL`: the color of the pixel is $(1-A_t)C_f + A_tC_t$, and the alpha channel in the pixel is A_f
- `GL_MODULATE`: the color of the pixel is $C_f{*}C_t$, as above, and the alpha channel in the pixel is $A_f{*}A_t$
- `GL_REPLACE`: the color of the pixel is C_t and the alpha channel in the pixel is A_t

If the texture represents the *alpha channel*, the behavior of the texture is defined as:

- `GL_BLEND`: the color of the pixel is C_f, and the alpha channel in the pixel is A_f
- `GL_DECAL`: the operation is undefined
- `GL_MODULATE`: the color of the pixel is C_f, and the alpha channel in the pixel is $A_f{*}A_t$
- `GL_REPLACE`: the color of the pixel is C_f and the alpha channel in the pixel is A_t

If the texture represents *luminance*, the behavior of the texture is defined as:

- `GL_BLEND`: the color of the pixel is $C_f(1\text{-}L_t)$, and the alpha channel in the pixel is A_f
- `GL_DECAL`: the operation is undefined
- `GL_MODULATE`: the color of the pixel is $C_f{*}L_t$, and the alpha channel in the pixel is A_f
- `GL_REPLACE`: the color of the pixel is L_t and the alpha channel in the pixel is A_f

If the texture represents *intensity,* the behavior of the texture is defined as:

`GL_BLEND:`	the color of the pixel is $C_f(1\text{-}I_t)$, and the alpha channel in the pixel is $A_f(1\text{-}I_t)$
`GL_DECAL:`	the operation is undefined
`GL_MODULATE:`	the color of the pixel is C_f*I_t, and the alpha channel in the pixel is A_f*I_t
`GL_REPLACE:`	the color of the pixel is I_t and the alpha channel in the pixel is I_t

Texture Parameters

The texture parameters define how the texture will be presented on a polygon in your scene. In OpenGL, the texture parameters define texture wrap and texture filtering. Texture wrap, defined by the `GL_TEXTURE_WRAP_*` parameter, specifies what happens when you define texture coordinates outside [0,1] in any texture dimension. The two options are *repeating* or *clamping* the texture, as shown in Figure 8.11, and these can be applied separately to the horizontal and vertical texture behaviors. Repeating the texture is done by taking only the decimal part of any texture coordinate, so when you go beyond 1 you start over at 0. This repeats the texture across the polygon to fill the texture space you have defined. Clamping the texture takes any texture coordinate outside [0,1] and translates it to the nearer of 0 or 1. This continues the color of the texture border outside the region where the texture coordinates are within [0,1]. The `glTexParameter*(...)` function repeats, or clamps, the texture. The functions are

Figure 8.11 A quad with a texture that is wrapped in the vertical direction and clamped in the horizontal direction.

```
glTexParameteri(GL_TEXTURE_2D,GL_TEXTURE_WRAP_S,GL_CLAMP);
glTexParameteri(GL_TEXTURE_2D,GL_TEXTURE_WRAP_T,GL_REPEAT);
```

If you use repeating textures you will effectively be tiling your polygons, and it is worth thinking about what makes a good tiling texture. A tiling figure needs to have the same colors and overall textures at both the left and right hand side of the figure as well as at the top and bottom side. You may find some of these as Web page backgrounds, but there are also techniques to make good tiling figures. One is to use a tool such as Photoshop and translate the figure so that the former edges of the figure are in the middle of the new image and are adjacent to each other. Using the Photoshop tools, the middle of the figure is blurred or manipulated so that the line formerly in the middle is not visible. When the picture is then translated back so that the edges are back where they started, its left and right sides will tile correctly. A similar operation can make the top and bottom of the tile match correctly, and this completes the process of making the tile figure.

Another important texture parameter controls the filtering for pixels to deal with aliasing issues. In OpenGL, these are called the minification (if there are many texture points that correspond to one pixel in the image) or magnification (if there are many pixels that correspond to one point in the texture) filters, and they control the way an individual pixel is colored based on the texture map. For any pixel in your scene, the texture coordinate for the pixel rarely corresponds exactly to an index in the texture array, so the system must create the color for the pixel with a computation in the texture space. You control this in OpenGL with the texture parameter `GL_TEXTURE_*_FILTER` that you set in the `glTexParameter*(...)` function. The filter you use depends on whether a pixel in your image maps to a space larger or smaller than one texture element. If a pixel is smaller than a texture element, then `GL_TEXTURE_MIN_FILTER` is used; if a pixel is larger than a texture element, then `GL_TEXTURE_MAG_FILTER` is used. An example of the usage is:

```
glTexParameteri(GL_TEXTURE_2D,GL_TEXTURE_MIN_FILTER,GL_NEAREST);
glTexParameteri(GL_TEXTURE_2D,GL_TEXTURE_MAG_FILTER,GL_NEAREST);
```

The symbolic values for these filters are `GL_NEAREST` and `GL_LINEAR`. This difference between the two is shown in Figure 8.12 with a close-up of the penguin image, and it is easy to see that

Figure 8.12 The penguin head texture with the GL_NEAREST (*left*) and GL_LINEAR (*right*) magnification filters.

choosing GL_NEAREST for the magnification filter gives a much coarser image than does the GL_LINEAR filter. If you choose the value GL_NEAREST for the filter, then the system chooses the single point in the texture space nearest the computed texture coordinate; if you choose GL_LINEAR, then the system averages the four nearest points to the computed texture coordinate with weights depending on the distance to each point. The former is faster but has problems with aliasing; the latter is slower but produces a much smoother image. Your choice will depend on the relative importance of speed and image quality in your work.

Getting and Defining a Texture Map

This set of definitions is managed by the glTexImage*D(...) functions. These are a complex set of functions with a number of different parameters. The functions cover 1D, 2D, and 3D textures (the dimension is the asterisk in the function name) and have the same structure for their parameters.

Before you can apply the glTexImage*D(...) function, however, you must define and fill an array that holds your texture data. This array of unsigned integers (GLuint) will have the same dimension as your texture. The data in the array can be organized in many ways, as we will see when we talk about the internal format of the texture data in a moment. You may read the values of the array from a file or you may generate the values through your own programming. The examples in this chapter illustrate both options.

The glTexImage*D(...) function has one of the more complex parameter lists of the texture definition functions. These parameters are, in order,

- The *target,* usually GL_TEXTURE_*D, where * is 1, 2, or 3. Proxy textures are also possible but are beyond the range of topics we will cover here. This target will be used in a number of places in defining texture maps.
- The *level,* an integer representing level-of-detail number. This supports multiple-level MIP mapping. Level 0 is used for an image without MIP mapping.
- The *internal format* of the texture map, one of the places where an API such as OpenGL must support a large number of options to meet the needs of a wide community. For OpenGL, this internal format is a symbolic constant and can take many values, but we will list only a set we believe will be most useful to you. Most of the other options deal with other organizations that involve a different number of bits per pixel of the component. Here we deal only with formats that have eight bits per component, and we leave the others (and information on them in manuals) to applications that need specialized formats.

  GL_ALPHA8
  GL_LUMINANCE8
  GL_INTENSITY8
  GL_RGB8
  GL_RGBA8
- The *dimensions* of the texture map, of type GLsizei, so the number of parameters here is the dimension of the texture map. If you have a 1D texture map, this parameter is the *width;* if you have a 2D texture map, the two parameters are the width and *height;* if you have a 3D texture map, the three parameters are width, height, and *depth.* Each of these must have a value of $2^N + 2*(border)$ for some integer N, where the value of *border* is either 0 or 1 as specified in the next parameter.
- The *border,* an integer that is either 0 (if no border is present) or 1 (if there is a border).

- The *format,* a symbolic constant that defines the data type of the pixel data in the texture array. This includes the following, as well as some other types that are more exotic:
  GL_ALPHA
  GL_RGB
  GL_RGBA
  GL_INTENSITY
  GL_LUMINANCE

  The format indicates how the texture is to be used in creating the image. We discussed the effects of the texture modes and the texture format in the discussion of image modes earlier.
- The *type* of the pixel data, a symbolic constant that indicates the data type stored in the texture array per pixel. This is usually pretty simple, as shown in the examples later in this chapter, which use only GL_FLOAT and GL_UNSIGNED_BYTE types.
- The *pixels,* an address of the pixel data (the texture array) in memory.

So the complete function call is

```
glTexImage*D(target, level, internal format, dimensions, border,
   format, type, pixels)
```

An example of this complete function call can be found in this chapter's examples for the 2D texture on the surface of a cube.

The glTexImage*D(...) function simply defines how the texture array is stored and what it is taken to mean. It does not say anything about the source of the image; if you want to use a compressed image format to store your image outside the file, it would have to be uncompressed in order to put the content into the *pixels* array.

You will create your textures from some set of sources and probably using the same kind of tools. When you find a particular approach that works for you, you'll most likely settle on that particular approach to textures. The number of options in structuring your texture is phenomenal, as you can tell from the number of options in some of the parameters above, but you should not be daunted by this broad set of possibilities and should focus on finding an approach you can use.

Texture Coordinate Control

As you apply a texture to a polygon, you may specify how the texture coordinates correspond to the vertices with the glTexCoord*(...) function, as we have generally assumed above, or you may direct the OpenGL system to assign the texture coordinates for you. This is done with the glTexGen*(...) function, which allows you to specify the details of the texture-generation operation.

The glTexGen*(...) function takes three parameters. The first is the texture coordinate being defined, which is one of GL_S, GL_T, GL_R, or GL_Q with S, T, R, and Q being the first, second, third, and homogeneous coordinates of the texture. The second parameter is one of three symbolic constants: GL_TEXTURE_GEN_MODE, GL_OBJECT_PLANE, or GL_EYE_PLANE. If the second parameter is GL_TEXTURE_GEN_MODE, the third parameter is a single symbolic constant with value GL_OBJECT_LINEAR, GL_EYE_LINEAR, or GL_SPHERE_MAP. If the second parameter is GL_OBJECT_PLANE, the third parameter is a vector of four values that defines the plane from which an object-linear texture is defined. If the second parameter is GL_EYE_PLANE, the third parameter is a vector of four values that defines the plane that contains the eyepoint. In both these latter cases, the object-linear or eye-linear value is computed based on the coefficients of the plane. If the second parameter is GL_TEXTURE_GEN_MODE and the third parameter is GL_SPHERE_MAP, the texture is generated based on an approximation of the reflection vector from the surface to the texture map.

Applications of this texture generation include the ChromaDepth texture, which is a 1D eye-linear texture generated with parameters that define the starting and ending points of the texture. Another example is automatic contour generation, where you use a GL_OBJECT_LINEAR mode and the GL_OBJECT_PLANE operation that defines the base plane from which contours are to be generated. Because contours are typically generated from a sea-level plane (one of the coordinates is 0), it is easy to define the coefficients for the object plane base. Finally, GL_SPHERE_MAP texture generation lets you generate environment maps.

Texture Interpolation

As we saw earlier in the chapter, if the image projection is perspective, the scanline interpolation for rendering a polynomial needs to take perspective into account to get the highest possible texture quality. The interpolation process is controlled by the quality you specify with the OpenGL hint function

```
glHint(GL_PERSPECTIVE_CORRECTION_HINT, hint).
```

Here the hint may be GL_DONT_CARE (take the system default), GL_NICEST (perform the perspective correction to get the best image), or GL_FASTEST (don't perform the perspective correction to maximize speed). These fragments are then passed to the per-fragment operations. You should not assume that the default is GL_FASTEST; many OpenGL implementations use perspective-corrected interpolation as the default.

Texture Mapping and GLU Quadrics

As we saw in chapter 3 on modeling in OpenGL, the GLU quadric objects have built-in texture mapping capabilities, and this is one of the features that make them very attractive for use in modeling. To use these, we must carry out three tasks: load the texture to the system and bind it to a name, define the quadric to have normals and a texture, and then bind the texture to the object geometry as the object is drawn. The short code fragments for these three tasks are given below, with a generic function readTextureFile(...) specified that you will probably need to write for yourself, and with a generic GLU function to specify the quadric to be drawn.

```
readTextureFile(...);
glBindTexture(GL_TEXTURE_2D, texture[i]);
glTexImage2D(GL_TEXTURE_2D,...);
glTexParameteri(GL_TEXTURE_2D,GL_TEXTURE_MIN_FILTER,GL_LINEAR);
glTexParameteri(GL_TEXTURE_2D,GL_TEXTURE_MAG_FILTER,GL_LINEAR);

myQuadric = gluNewQuadric();
gluQuadricNormals(myQuadric, GL_SMOOTH);
gluQuadricTexture(myQuadric, GL_TRUE);
gluQuadricDrawStyle(myQuadric, GLU_FILL);
glPushMatrix();

    // modeling transformations as needed
    gluXXX(myQuadric, ...);
glPopMatrix();
```

Multitextures

Multitexturing operates by defining multiple texture objects with the OpenGL function `glGenTextures(N, texNames)`. No guaranteed minimum number of textures is supported, but you may inquire that number of your system. For each of the texture objects, you define the properties of the texture through the functions `glTexImage*()` and `glTexParameteri()` in the same way you would for any texture. You then define texture units for each of your textures with the `glBindTexture()` and `glTexEnvi()` functions, giving you a set of textures that will be applied in the order of their integer names. When an object is rendered with these textures, the first texture will be applied first, the second texture to the object that is the result of the first texture mapping, and so on as shown in Figure 8.9.

In actually applying the textures to an object, you must assign the texture coordinates for each of your textures to the each of the vertices of the object with the `glMultiTexCoord*()` functions. This is illustrated in the multitexturing code example at the end in this chapter.

Some Examples

We saw earlier that textures can be applied in several different ways with the function

```
glTexEnvf(GL_TEXTURE_ENV, GL_TEXTURE_ENV_MODE, mode)
```

One way uses a decal technique, with mode `GL_DECAL`, in which the content of the texture is applied as an opaque image on the surface of the polygon, showing nothing but the texture map. Another way uses a modulation technique, with mode `GL_MODULATE`, in which the content of the texture is displayed on the surface as though it were colored plastic. This mode lets you show the shading of a lighted surface by defining a white surface and letting the shading show through the modulated texture. There is also a `GL_BLEND` mode that blends the color of the object with the color of the texture map based on the alpha values, just as other color blending is done. In the following examples, the ChromaDepth image is created with a 1D modulated texture so that the underlying surface shading is displayed, while the mapped-cube image is created with a 2D decal texture so that the face of the cube is precisely the texture map. You may use several different textures with one image, so that (for example) you could take a purely geometric white terrain model, apply a 2D texture map of an aerial photograph of the terrain with `GL_MODULATE` mode to get a realistic image of the terrain, and then apply a 1D texture map in `GL_BLEND` mode that is mostly transparent but has colors at specific levels and that is oriented to the vertical in the 3D image in order to get elevation lines on the terrain. Your only limitations are your imagination and the time needed to develop all the techniques.

Below we have three specific examples of common ways to use texture maps in an application. The first uses a 1D texture map to define colors by the distance from a point in the model. In this case, the distance is the distance from the eye in 3D eye space, and the colors are used with special viewing glasses to give depth to a scene. In the second, a 2D texture is applied to a polygon in order to add information to a rather plain scene. And in the third, a particular kind of 2D texture is applied in order to create the illusion of an object reflecting the world around it.

Using the ChromaDepth Process

The ChromaDepth process uses 1D texture maps to create the illusion of depth. If you apply a lighting model with white light to a white object, you get a pure expression of shading on the object. If you then apply a 1D texture by attaching a point near the eye to the red end of the ramp and a point far from the eye to the blue end of the ramp, you get a result like that shown in Figure 8.13 (see the color insert for the real effect). This creates a very convincing 3D image when it is viewed through ChromaDepth glasses because these glasses have a diffraction grating in the lenses that bends red light more than blue light, so the angle between red objects as seen by both eyes is larger than the angle between blue objects. The human visual system interprets objects having larger angles between them as closer than objects having smaller angles, so with these glasses, red objects are interpreted as being closer than blue objects.

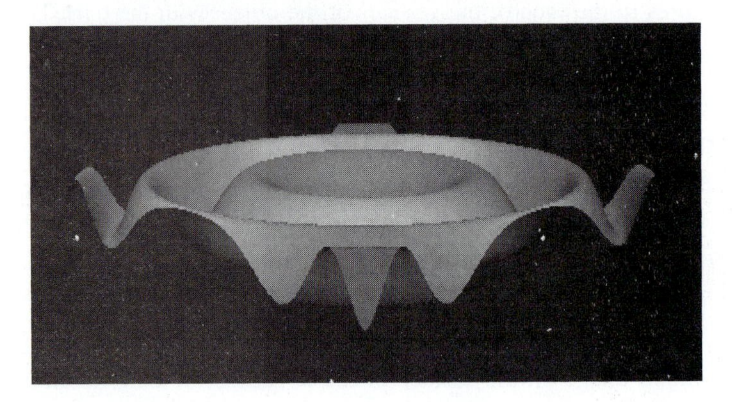

Figure 8.13 A ChromaDepth-colored image of a mathematical surface. See the figure in the color insert.

The code for this is presented in the 1D color ramp example below. We define the color ramp in much the same way we did when creating a pseudocolor ramp in Chapter 5. We associate that ramp with a 1D texture through the `glTexImage1D()` function and then set up the texture environment and parameters needed for a 1D texture. Finally we use the `glTexGen*()` functions to generate an eye-linear automatic texture that is applied to the surface as it is generated. See the 1D color ramp example later in this chapter for more details.

Using 2D Texture Maps to Add Interest to a Surface

The most common use of texture maps is to create relatively simple objects and add texture maps to make them look complex, particularly when you want to create models that mimic things in the real world. We do this by mapping images (for example, images of the real world) onto simpler objects. In Figure 8.14, the penguin image was used as the texture map on one face of a cube. This creates a cube that has more visual content than its geometry alone, and it is extremely simple to connect the square image with the square face of the cube. The complete code for this is presented in the 2D texure example below.

Environment Maps

Environment maps let us create the illusion that an object reflects images from a texture that we define. This can provide some very interesting effects, because realistic reflection of real-world

Figure 8.14 A 3D cube with the penguin texture map on one face.

objects is an important visual realism clue. With environment maps, we can use photographs or synthetic images as the things we want to reflect, and we can adapt the parameters of the texture map to give us realistic effects. One of the easy effects to get is the reflection of things in a chrome-like surface. In Figure 8.15, we see an example of this with a texture map made from a photograph of Hong Kong that has been modified in Photoshop with a spherical filter. The spherical filter makes the environment map much more convincing because the environment map uses the surface normals at a point to identify the texture points for the final image.

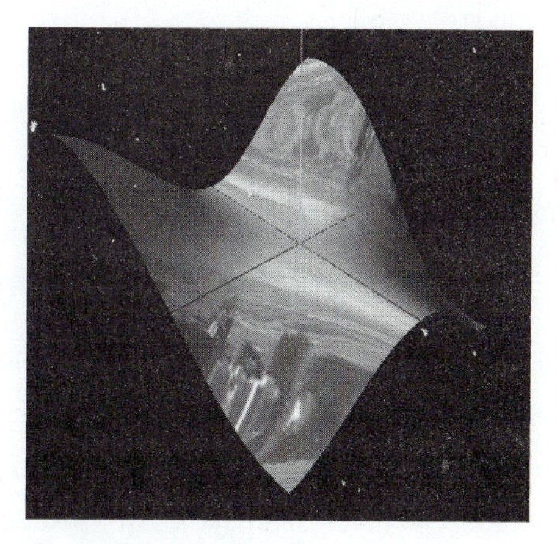

Figure 8.15 The original texture for an environment map (*left*) and the map on a surface (*right*). Courtesy of Jordan Maynard.

Many parts of this example are handled just as any other 2D texture would be, but the texture is automatically generated by the `glTexGeni()` function and the texture coordinates for the surface are generated by using the normal vectors at each vertex. As we saw with the 1D linear texture example earlier, this example uses lighting on a white surface and adds the texture in GL_MODULATE mode to preserve the shape information from lighting and the texture information from the environment map.

A Word to the Wise

Texture mapping is a much richer subject than these fairly simple examples have been able to show. You can use 1D textures to provide contour lines on a surface or to give you a color encoding for a height value we discussed in the section on visual communication in Chapter 5. You can use 2D textures in several sophisticated ways to give you the illusion of bumpy surfaces (use a texture on the luminance), to give the effect of looking through a variegated cloud (use a fractal texture on alpha), or of such a cloud on shadows (use the same kind of texture on luminance on a landscape image). This subject is a fruitful area for creative work.

There are several points you must consider to avoid problems when you use texture mapping. If you select your texture coordinates carelessly, you can create effects you might not expect because the geometry of your objects does not match the geometry of your texture map. One example of this is if you use a texture map that has a different aspect ratio from that of the space you are mapping it onto, which can change proportions in the texture that you might not have expected. More serious, perhaps, is trying to map a rectangular area into an object that isn't rectangular so that the texture is distorted nonlinearly. Imagine the effect if you were to try to map a brick texture into a nonconvex polygon, for example, or onto a cone. This is shown in Figure 8.16, where we try to create a texture a frustum of a cone with bricks. Another problem can arise if you texture map two adjacent polygons with maps that do not align at the seam between the polygons. Much like wallpaper that doesn't match at a corner, the effect can be disturbing and can ruin any attempt at creating realistic effects. Finally, if you use texture maps whose resolution is significantly

Figure 8.16 A frustum of a cone is tiled with bricks, showing significant problems with mismatched edges and inconsistent sizes.

different from the resolution of the polygon using the texture, you can run into problems of aliasing textures caused by selecting only portions of the texture map. We noted the use of magnification and minification filters earlier in this chapter, and these help you handle this situation.

In a different direction, the 1D texture-mapping process to use ChromaDepth™ glasses for 3D viewing gives excellent 3D effects but does not let you use color as a way of encoding and communicating information. It should only be used when the shape alone carries the important information in an image, but it has proved to be particularly useful for geographic and engineering images, as well as molecular models.

Code Examples

A 1D Color Ramp

Sample code to use 1D texture mapping in the ChromaDepth example is shown below. The declarations set up the color ramp, define the integer texture name, and create the array of texture parameters.

```
float D1, D2;
float texParms[4];
static GLuint texName;
float ramp[256][3];
```

In the `init()` function we find the following function calls, which define the texture map, the texture environment and parameters, and then enable the texture generation and application.

```
makeRamp();
glPixelStorei(GL_UNPACK_ALIGNMENT, 1) ;
glTexEnvf(GL_TEXTURE_ENV, GL_TEXTURE_ENV_MODE, GL_MODULATE) ;
glTexParameterf(GL_TEXTURE_1D, GL_TEXTURE_WRAP_S, GL_CLAMP) ;
glTexParameterf(GL_TEXTURE_1D,GL_TEXTURE_MAG_FILTER,GL_LINEAR) ;
glTexParameterf(GL_TEXTURE_1D,GL_TEXTURE_MIN_FILTER,GL_LINEAR) ;
glTexImage1D(GL_TEXTURE_1D,0,3,256,0,GL_RGB,GL_FLOAT,ramp) ;
glEnable(GL_TEXTURE_GEN_S) ;
glEnable(GL_TEXTURE_1D) ;
```

The `makeRamp()` function creates the global array `ramp[]` that holds the data of the texture map. This ramp does not use RGB values, as our earlier ramp examples did, but interpolates values in the HSV color model in which hues are defined through angles (in degrees) around the circle which has saturation and value each equal to 1.0. The use of the number 240 in the function comes from the structure of the HSV model: The color red is at 0 degrees and blue is at 240 degrees, with green between at 120 degrees. Thus an interpolation of fully saturated colors between red and blue, going through green, will use the angles between 0 and 240 degrees. The RGB values are calculated by the function `hsv2rgb (...)`, which is found in Chapter 5.

```
void makeRamp(void)
{
    int i;
    float h, s, v, r, g, b;
```

```
//  color ramp for 1D texture:
//  starts at 0, ends at 240, 256 steps
    for (i=0; i<256; i++) {
        h = (float)i*240.0/255.0;
        s = 1.0; v = 1.0;
        hsv2rgb(h, s, v, &r, &g, &b);
        ramp[i][0] = r; ramp[i][1] = g; ramp[i][2] = b;
    }
}
```

Finally, the `display ()` function contains the following code, where `ep` is the eyepoint parameter used in the `gluLookAt(...)` function. This controls the generation of texture coordinates and binds the texture to the integer name `texName`. Note that the values in the `texParms []` array, which define where the 1D texture is applied, are defined based on the eyepoint, so that the image will be shaded red (in front) to blue (in back) in the space whose distance from the eye is between D1 and D2.

```
glTexGeni(GL_S, GL_TEXTURE_GEN_MODE, GL_EYE_LINEAR);
D1 = ep + 1.0; D2 = ep + 10.0;
texParms[0] = texParms[1] = 0.0;
texParms[2] = -1.0/(D2-D1);
texParms[3] = -D1/(D2-D1);
glTexGenfv(GL_S, GL_EYE_PLANE, texParms);
glBindTexture(GL_TEXTURE_1D, texName);
```

The values of the `texParms []` array are a bit mysterious, but they represent the structure of 3D eye space after the perspective projection has been applied, with the x- and y-terms both zero and the z- and w-terms corrected for the depth of the space where the texture is to be applied.

A 2D Texture Example

Sample code for the 2D texture mapping on a polygon is in four parts. In the first part, we have the data declarations that establish the internal texture map `(texImage)` and the set of texture names that can be used for textures `(texName)`, and in the `init ()` function we have the `glEnable ()` that allows the use of 2D textures. In the second part, we read a file into a texture array, while in the third part we set up the OpenGL functions that define how the texture map is to be applied and in the fourth part we draw the face of the cube with the texture map applied.

```
#define TEX_WIDTH 512
#define TEX_HEIGHT 512
static GLubyte texImage[TEX_WIDTH][TEX_HEIGHT][3];
static GLuint texName[1];     // parameter is no. of textures used
void init() {
    ...
    glEnable(GL_TEXTURE_2D); // allow 2D texture maps
    ...
}

========================
```

```
void setTexture(void) // read file into RGB8 format array
{   FILE * fd;
    GLubyte ch;
    int i,j,k;

    fd = fopen("penguin.512.512.rgb", "r");
    for (i=0; i<TEX_WIDTH; i++) {
        for (j=0; j<TEX_HEIGHT; j++) {
          for (k=0; k<3; k++) {
            fread(&ch, 1, 1, fd);
            texImage[i][j][k] = (GLubyte) ch;
          }
        }
      }
    fclose(fd);
}

========================

//  enable textures for the last face
    glEnable(GL_TEXTURE_2D);
    glGenTextures(1, texName); // define texture for sixth face
    glBindTexture(GL_TEXTURE_2D,texName[0]);
    glTexEnvi(GL_TEXTURE_ENV, GL_TEXTURE_ENV_MODE, GL_DECAL);
    glTexParameteri(GL_TEXTURE_2D,GL_TEXTURE_WRAP_S,GL_CLAMP);
    glTexParameteri(GL_TEXTURE_2D,GL_TEXTURE_WRAP_T,GL_REPEAT);
    glTexParameteri(GL_TEXTURE_2D,GL_TEXTURE_MIN_FILTER,GL_LINEAR);
    glTexParameteri(GL_TEXTURE_2D,GL_TEXTURE_MAG_FILTER,GL_LINEAR);
    glTexImage2D(GL_TEXTURE_2D,0,GL_RGB8,TEX_WIDTH,TEX_HEIGHT,
      0,GL_RGB,GL_UNSIGNED_BYTE,texImage);

========================

    glBegin(GL_QUADS);            // sixth quad: negative X face
    glNormal3fv(normals[1]);      // single normal; flat shading
      glTexCoord2f(0.0, 0.0); glVertex3fv(vertices[0]);
      glTexCoord2f(0.0, 1.0); glVertex3fv(vertices[1]);
      glTexCoord2f(1.0, 1.0); glVertex3fv(vertices[3]);
      glTexCoord2f(1.0, 0.0); glVertex3fv(vertices[2]);
    glEnd();
    glDeleteTextures(1, texName);
```

This is a typical sequencing of the texture functions in OpenGL. First an array is defined and is loaded with texture data, either by reading a file or by creating a synthetic texture. Then the sequence

Enable the texture

Generate a texture for a texture name

Bind the texture to a texture type (here GL_TEXTURE_2D)

Set the texture environment

Define the texture parameters

Create the texture image

sets up the OpenGL environment for texturing. The order is important for some of these functions but not for all; setting the texture environment and defining the texture parameters can be done in any order. But it is probably easiest to find a sequence that works for you and to use that sequence consistently in your work.

An Environment Map

The environment map example uses a 2D texture map, modified in Photoshop with a spherical distortion to mimic the behavior of a very wide-angle lens. The primary key to setting up an environment map is in the texture parameter function, where we also include two uses of the `glHint (...)` function to show that you can define really nice perspective calculations and point smoothing—with a computational cost, of course. But the images in Figure 8.15 suggest that it might be well worth the cost.

```
glHint(GL_PERSPECTIVE_CORRECTION_HINT,GL_NICEST);
glHint(GL_POINT_SMOOTH_HINT,GL_NICEST);

...

//   the two lines below generate an environment map in both the
//   S and T texture coordinates
glTexGeni(GL_S, GL_TEXTURE_GEN_MODE, GL_SPHERE_MAP);
glTexGeni(GL_T, GL_TEXTURE_GEN_MODE, GL_SPHERE_MAP);
```

Using Multitextures

When we introduced the way OpenGL defines multitextures, we hinted at the kinds of changes you would need to make to use them. Here we will give that code in some detail for a case using two textures so you may see what it would look like.

The declaration of the `textures[]` array would be:

```
int textures[2];
```

In an initialization function we might find the following definitions of the texture objects:

```
//   load and bind the textures
glGenTextures(2, &textures);

//   load the first texture data into a temporary array
file.open("tex0.raw");
file.read(textureData, 256*256*3);
file.close();

//   build the first texture
glBindTexture(GL_TEXTURE_2D, texture[0]);
glTexParameteri(GL_TEXTURE_2D,GL_TEXTURE_WRAP_S,GL_REPEAT);
glTexParameteri(GL_TEXTURE_2D,GL_TEXTURE_WRAP_T,GL_REPEAT);
glTexParameteri(GL_TEXTURE_2D,GL_TEXTURE_MAG_FILTER,GL_LINEAR);
```

```
glTexParameteri(GL_TEXTURE_2D, GL_TEXTURE_MIN_FILTER,
    GL_NEAREST_MIPMAP_LINEAR);
gluBuild2DMipmaps(GL_TEXTURE_2D, GL_RGBA, 256,256, GL_RGB,
    GL_UNSIGNED_BYTE, textureData);

//  load the second texture data into a temporary array
file.open("tex1.raw");
file.read(textureData, 256*256*3);
file.close ();

//  build the second texture
glBindTexture(GL_TEXTURE_2D, texture[1]);
glTexParameteri(GL_TEXTURE_2D,GL_TEXTURE_WRAP_S,GL_REPEAT);
glTexParameteri(GL_TEXTURE_2D,GL_TEXTURE_WRAP_T,GL_REPEAT);
glTexParameteri(GL_TEXTURE_2D,GL_TEXTURE_MAG_FILTER,GL_LINEAR);
glTexParameteri(GL_TEXTURE_2D, GL_TEXTURE_MIN_FILTER,
    GL_NEAREST_MIPMAP_LINEAR);
gluBuild2DMipmaps(GL_TEXTURE_2D, GL_RGBA, 256,256, GL_RGB,
    GL_UNSIGNED_BYTE, textureData);
```

In `display()`, we might find the following definitions of the texture units:

```
//  set the texture to the first one then bind the texture
glActiveTextureARB(GL_TEXTURE0_ARB);
glEnable(GL_TEXTURE_2D);
glBindTexture(GL_TEXTURE_2D, textures[0]);
glTexEnvi(GL_TEXTURE_ENV, GL_TEXTURE_ENV_MODE, GL_REPLACE);
//  set the texture to the second one then bind the texture
glActiveTextureARB(GL_TEXTURE1_ARB);
glEnable(GL_TEXTURE_2D);
glBindTexture(GL_TEXTURE_2D, textures[1]);
glTexEnvi(GL_TEXTURE_ENV, GL_TEXTURE_ENV_MODE, GL_MODULATE);
```

And in `display ()` or another function that actually implements the geometry of your model, you might find the following code, which associates both sets of texture coordinates to each vertex:

```
glBegin(GL_TRIANGLE_STRIP);
    glMultiTexCood2fARB(GL_TEXTURE0_ARB, 0.0, 0.0);
    glMultiTexCood2fARB(GL_TEXTURE1_ARB, 0.0, 0.0);
    glVertex3f(-5.0,-5.0,0.0);
    glMultiTexCood2fARB(GL_TEXTURE0_ARB, 0.0, 1.0);
    glMultiTexCood2fARB(GL_TEXTURE1_ARB, 0.0, 1.0);
    glVertex3f(-5.0,5.0,0.0);
    glMultiTexCood2fARB(GL_TEXTURE0_ARB, 1.0, 0.0);
    glMultiTexCood2fARB(GL_TEXTURE1_ARB, 1.0, 0.0);
    glVertex3f(5.0,-5.0,0.0);
    glMultiTexCood2fARB(GL_TEXTURE0_ARB, 1.0, 1.0);
    glMultiTexCood2fARB(GL_TEXTURE1_ARB, 1.0, 1.0);
    glVertex3f(5.0,5.0,0.0);
glEnd();
```

Summary

In this chapter we saw that texture mapping is a straightforward process that lets you add a great deal of extra information to an image in several different ways. By now you should understand how to create textures from photographic and synthetic sources, and how to associate texture coordinates to geometric coordinates as you model a scene. We discussed how texture mapping is done with the OpenGL graphics API, so you should be able to write graphics programs that use texture maps and to create texture maps from both natural and synthetic sources. We did not go into any detail on how texture mapping is carried out in creating an image; this is covered in Chapter 10. Most of this work is managed by simple linear interpolation, but you should see the value of perspective adjustment for textures.

OpenGL Glossary for the Chapter

This chapter described a major feature of the OpenGL graphics API that involves managing a significant amount of detail. As such it introduced a rather large set of functions and especially parameters that are summarized here, though some of the more esoteric functions and parameters have been omitted. However, with the amount of detail involved in these functions, we strongly suggest that you not try to use this glossary as a manual; it's probably best simply as a reminder of what things' names are.

OpenGL Functions

`glBindTexture(...)`: binds a named texture to a texture target

`glDeleteTextures(...)`: deletes named textures from the active texture list

`glGenTextures(...)`: generates a set of texture names that can be used

`glHint(parm, value)`: selects an option for OpenGL operations

`glPixelStore*(parm, value)`: specifies how pixels are to be packed or unpacked in storage

`glReadBuffer(mode)`: specifies the color buffer from which to read pixels

`glReadPixels(...)`: reads a block of pixels from the color buffer

`glTexCoord*(...)`: defines the texture coordinates of the vertex currently being defined; the * identifies the number of dimensions in the texture, the type of the data for the texture coordinates, and whether the coordinates are given in scalar or vector form

`glTexEnv*(...)`: specifies the values of several texture environment parameters

`glTexGen*(...)`: controls the generation of texture coordinates; the options for * determine whether the parameter is taken as integer, float, or double, and whether the parameter is scalar or vector

`glTexImage*D(...)`: specifies a texture image of dimension determined by whether * is 1, 2, or 3; the function has a number of parameters

`glTexParameter*(...)`: defines the target texture and the property of the texture that is to be defined and specifies the value for that property

GLU Functions

`gluBuild2DMipmaps(...)`: builds a series of prefiltered 2D texture maps of decreasing resolution (mipmaps) `gluQuadricTexture(quadric, value)`: specifies if a GLU quadric object should have its texture coordinates generated

OpenGL Parameters

`GL_ALPHA`: specifies that a texture array is to be taken as holding single alpha values

`GL_ALPHA8`: specifies that the internal format of the texture is to be taken as holding alpha values that are 8-bit integers

`GL_BLEND`: specifies how a texture value is to be applied to the pixel that is being texture mapped

`GL_BLUE`: specifies that a texture array is to be taken as holding single blue components

`GL_CLAMP`: specifies that textures are to be clamped when their coordinates exceed their bounds

`GL_DECAL`: specifies how a texture value is to be applied to the pixel that is being texture mapped

`GL_DONT_CARE`: parameter to the `glHint()` function to specify that the system can use whatever level of the process it wishes

`GL_EYE_LINEAR`: specifies that a texture is to be generated relative to a reference plane in eye coordinates

`GL_EYE_PLANE`: specifies that an eye-linear texture is to be generated and that the following parameters are the coefficients of the plane containing the eye

`GL_FASTEST`: parameter to the `glHint()` function to specify that the system should use the value of the process that will work the fastest

`GL_GREEN`: specifies that a texture array is to be taken as holding single green components

`GL_INTENSITY`: specifies that a texture array is to be taken as holding single intensity values

`GL_INTENSITY8`: specifies that the internal format of the texture is to be taken as intensity values that are 8-bit integers

`GL_LINEAR`: specifies that the texture value to be used is the average of the four texture elements closest to the center of the pixel being textured

`GL_LUMINANCE`: specifies that a texture array is to be taken as holding single luminance values

`GL_LUMINANCE8`: specifies that the internal format of the texture is to be taken as holding luminance values that are 8-bit integers

`GL_MODULATE`: specifies how a texture value is to be applied to the pixel that is being texture mapped

`GL_NEAREST`: specifies that the texture element to be used is the one nearest (in $s + t$ distance) to the center of the pixel being textured

`GL_NICEST`: Parameter to the `glHint()` function to specify that the system should use the value of the process that makes the highest-quality image

`GL_OBJECT_LINEAR`: specifies that a texture is to be generated relative to the world space coordinates

`GL_OBJECT_PLANE`: specifies that an object-linear texture is to be generated and that the remaining parameters define the plane which defines the texture

GL_PERSPECTIVE_CORRECTION_HINT: specifies the hint (the direction) given to the perspective-correction process for texture mapping

GL_Q: specifies the homogeneous (fourth) dimension of a texture map

GL_R: specifies the third dimension of a texture map

GL_REPLACE: specifies how a texture value is to be applied to the pixel that is being texture mapped

GL_RED: specifies that a texture array is to be taken as holding single red components

GL_RGB: specifies that a texture array is to be taken as holding values that are RGB triples

GL_RGB8: specifies that the internal format of the texture is to be taken as holding RGB values that are 8-bit integers

GL_RGBA: specifies that a texture array is to be taken as holding values that are RGBA quadruples

GL_RGBA8: specifies that the internal format of the texture is to be taken as holding RGBA values that are 8-bit integers

GL_S: specifies the first dimension of a texture map

GL_SPHERE_MAP: specifies that a texture is to be generated as a sphere map

GL_T: specifies the second dimension of a texture map

GL_TEXTURE_*D: specifies the target texture of the glTexImage*() functions

GL_TEXTURE_ENV: the first and required parameter for the glTexEnv*() functions

GL_TEXTURE_ENV_MODE: specifies that the next parameter is to be the mode of generating textures (modulate, decal, blend, replace)

GL_TEXTURE_GEN_MODE: specifies that a texture is to be generated as defined by subsequent parameters

GL_TEXTURE_WRAP_*: identifies for each texture coordinate (specified by *) that subsequent parameters will specify whether a texture is to be clamped or repeated

GL_TEXTURE_MAG_FILTER: specifies the texture magnification function to be used when a pixel being textured maps to an area less than or equal to one texture element

GL_TEXTURE_MIN_FILTER: specifies the texture minification function to be used when a pixel being textured maps to an area greater than one texture element

GL_UNPACK_ALIGNMENT: parameter to the glPixelStore*() function that specifies the alignment requirements for each pixel row in memory

GL_REPEAT: specifies that textures are to be repeated when their coordinates exceed their bounds

Questions

1. The sequence of OpenGL function calls needed for texture mapping has some functions that need to come first, and then other functions can come later and in an arbitrary sequence. Discuss why this sequence is required.
2. What work is needed to use image files in formats such as GIF or JPEG as sources for texture maps? Does your graphics API have any texture loaders that will allow you to use any of these file formats?
3. Think about how you would achieve certain effects if you had multitexturing. Begin with some simple effects, such as distressed wood, bullet holes in metal, or water spots on a

surface, and then envision some new effects and decide how you would create them. If you have multitexturing capability with your graphics API, create the individual textures needed and then implement your ideas.

Exercises

1. Make a number of texture maps from easily available sources. Use as many of the following as possible: (a) digital photographs, (b) scanned photographs, (c) screen captures, and (d) the contents of the frame buffer from an OpenGL program, captured by saving the front buffer. In each case, be sure the texture map is saved in a format that can be read into a texture array for your programs.
2. Implement a set of labels by writing them on separate lines in one image using the text functions in an application such as Photoshop, and save this image as a file that you can use as a texture. Identify the points in the image that separate the individual words or phrases and write a small graphics program that maps these labels to different parts of an image.
3. Consider a triangle in 2D space with coordinates $V0 = (1,1)$, $V1 = (9,1)$, and $V2 = (1,3)$ counterclockwise, and take the point $P = (3,2) = \alpha * V0 + \beta * V1 + \delta * V2$ for some values of the coefficients α, β, and δ with $\alpha + \beta + \delta = 1$. If a texture has dimensions 256×256 and the texture coordinates for the triangle's vertices are $T0 = (50,20)$, $T1 = (180,70)$, and $T2 = (30,80)$ for $V0$, $V1$, and $V2$ respectively, calculate α, β, and δ and then the texture coordinates for the point P. If the texture coordinates of these points are not integers, discuss how you would calculate the actual color for point P in terms of colors for nearby points in texture space and relate these to the filtering options for textures in OpenGL.
4. As an example of a procedural synthetic texture, create a "straw thatch" texture by drawing many parallel lines within a rectangle, each having a given start point and endpoint, and

See the figure in the color insert.

each having a color that is within the general range of brown to tan that one would find in straw. This texture can also be used to simulate wood grain. An example of this texture is shown with this project. You can choose to generate the line segments with known coordinates, or you can make the overall process random. Of course, you need to draw enough of these lines to cover the space, which cannot be guaranteed with a modest number of line segments, so be sure to specify a generous number.

5. Besides scanning photos, you can paint synthetic textures as a way to create textures for your images. In this exercise we will draw on one of the world's great visual cultures, the Ndebele of South Africa. Observe the accompanying four small photographs of Ndebele homes with their extraordinary patterns. Your task is to use an image creation program or to write appropriate procedures to create patterns similar to those in these Ndebele images, and then save your work in a format that is appropriate to use in texture maps. (These figures are available as JPEG images in the resource materials for this chapter.)

See the figure in the color insert. Courtesy of Vali Lalioti.

6. Create a different synthetic texture from the one shown in Figure 8.3. For example, you could choose a set of random points in 2D integer space and a sequence of random colors, and for each point in texture space you could give that point a color that depends on the point to which it is nearest. Or you could use some sort of 2D function pseudocoloring as is discussed in Chapter 9. Then use this synthetic texture as we did the checkerboard texture and observe the visual results.

7. Define a 3D filter as a $3 \times 3 \times 3$ array of non-negative numbers that sum to 1.0, and write code to filter the values in a 3D array with this filter to achieve the kind of smoothed random texture that was described in the 2D case in the chapter.

Experiments

1. Consider the various ways texture can be applied to a surface: `GL_BLEND`, `GL_DECAL`, `GL_MODULATE`, and `GL_REPLACE`. Create a scene with a texture map and try these different kinds of texture environments. Record the results.
2. Consider the effects of texture filtering on an image by creating a simple scene (perhaps a single polygon) with texture maps that are either too large (there are too many texels per pixel) or too small (there are too few texels per pixel) and using different min or mag filters with the texturing. Discuss the relationship between the texel/pixel ratio and the effective filters.
3. Using the 1D texture map concept introduced for the ChromaDepth process, define 1D texture maps that could be used to show the elevation on a height field, as introduced in Chapter 9. Extend this to include contour mapping.
4. Use a generally available program such as POVRay and experiment with the texture options it provides. The goal is to get a sense of how these textures look, especially textures built on the noise function.
5. Make a texture map suitable for use as a billboard by taking a natural image and editing it so that the background is in a unique color, different from any color in the part of the image you want to keep. Save the edited image as a raw RGB image file. Then modify the function in this chapter that reads in a raw RGB image file so that an alpha channel is created as described in the chapter. Use this image with an RGBA texture to see how the alpha blending will work.
6. Pick a texture map that allows you to see the fine details of the texture, such as a checkerboard texture with relatively small squares, and map it onto the GLU quadric objects. Look for points where the texture map on the surface behaves unusually and see if you can identify those points with any particular geometry on the surface.
7. Take some of the example textures you created in the first exercise and apply them to the other faces of the cube in Figure 8.14, whose code was given previously.
8. Use an artificial texture such as a black-and-white checkerboard pattern to experiment with the use of texture mapping on intensity, luminance, or blending. The results should show the checkerboard pattern, but the pattern should be visible only in the effects on the polygon color—that is, the checkerboard itself should not be visible.
9. Take an image and create a second image by doing a "fisheye" conversion of the first using a tool such as Photoshop. Apply both images to some smooth geometry using environment map techniques and discuss the results.
10. Use interactive techniques to experiment with the way a 2D texture fits onto a polygon. Define a simple shape (such as a single quad) and choose texture coordinates from its vertices from a texture map you know well. Using keyboard or mouse techniques, move the shape around on the texture (or move the texture around behind the shape; either point of view works). Use the interactive techniques to change all the texture coordinates equally (add the

same amount to each component of each texture coordinate) so that you have a "texture inspector" tool.

11. Consider the situation shown in Figure 8.16, where we mapped a brick texture onto the frustum of a cone. This figure was not very successful because there was no way to map the bricks onto the cone and keep the size consistent. Experiment with the synthetic brick texture to see if you can distort it in a way that makes the bricks look consistent in size when they are used on the frustum.
12. As in the previous exercise, take a simple shape and a well-known texture and use interactive techniques to distort the texture behind the shape. For example, move the texture coordinates of only one of the vertices so that more (or less) of the texture is mapped onto the shape. Look at the way the texture is distorted and discuss the way the patterns change. Do this with different aliasing filters and discuss how the filters affect the distorted texture pattern.
13. Many institutions will have a library of image handling programs available, or perhaps you can find one as source code online. Find a program or function that reads a file containing an image in compressed format and displays the image, and adapt it to be a function that reads the file and creates an image array. Use this function to read files in this compressed format into your programs as texture maps.
14. Write a function that will read an image array in RGB format and create an array in RGBA format by creating the alpha value from the RGB values. You may copy one of the primary colors to the alpha channel, take the largest of the three values as the alpha channel, or do other such operations. Use this to modify a simple RGB image array and create an RGBA array, and then use that array as a texture map to experiment with the nature of texture mapping an alpha value.

Projects

1. (The small house) Take the texture maps you created from the Ndebele houses and apply them to the exterior and interior walls of the small house you designed in the earlier chapter, and see what you get when you walk through the resulting house. Do not be surprised if your have a much slower refresh rate for the walkthrough than you did earlier, because the computer is working much harder to rebuild all the texture maps as you reuse them.
2. (A scene graph parser) Add texture mapping to your scene graph parser as described in this chapter, and have the parser write appropriate OpenGL code to include this feature in the `display()` function it writes.

9 Graphical Problem Solving in Science

This chapter describes how computer graphics is used as a problem-solving tool in the sciences, giving a focus to the visual communication we have seen so far throughout the book. We do this by example; as we discuss various graphical techniques for presenting different kinds of information, we include examples of graphics modeling and images for science. These images are produced by programs that use techniques we have seen so far, applied to an actual, though usually fairly simple, scientific problem. Several of the examples in this chapter have their source code included with the resources for the book. These techniques range rather widely, and it is not easy to define a natural sequence for them, so the presentations are organized according to the author's interests. When you have finished this chapter, you should have a good grasp of several techniques for graphical modeling and simulation that are used in the sciences, and you should understand how these techniques create images that convey information in various scientific fields.

To benefit from this chapter, you need to know computer graphics concepts and practice through modeling, viewing, and color, and have enough programming experience to implement the various programming techniques that will be discussed in this chapter to produce the images. It will also help if you have some understanding of the science topics we discuss.

Introduction

In the past twenty years, the growing complexity of scientific theory and the volume of scientific data have led to a wide use of images to represent a number of concepts and experiments. The general name for this representation is *scientific visualization,* and it is a critical part of a great deal of scientific work today. The important thing about scientific visualization is not the images that are created to describe scientific principles or processes; it is the graphical problem solving that must be done in order to create the images, the visual communication that must be done to present the images in an effective way, and the understanding of the science that is created by the images for the science community. This understanding can be used to help students learn the science, to help the public or funding sources appreciate the developments in the science and support further development, or to help the researchers in the science grasp the implications of their work as they see it more fully. It is not an accident that the general expression of understanding is "Now I see it!" because our mental processes for understanding images are among the most highly developed of all our abilities.

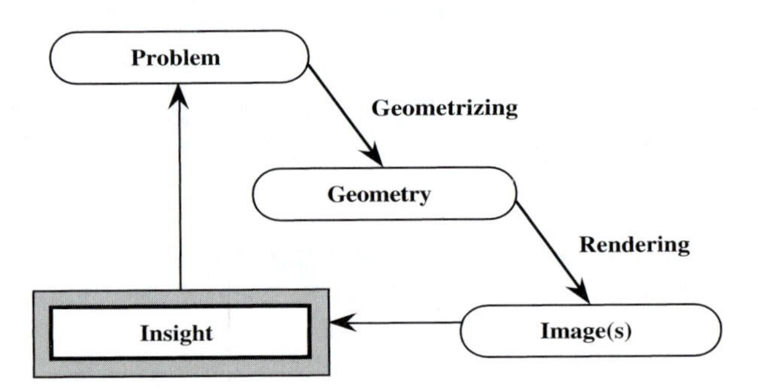

Figure 9.1 The graphical problem-solving cycle.

The role of computer graphics in problem solving—both within and outside of science—is to provide a better understanding of the problem. We express the problem in visual or geometric terms, take that expression and make it concrete by developing an actual image or set of images, and finally use that image as a source of reflection on and insight into the problem that can lead to better understanding. This is described by the closed cycle in Figure 9.1. The initial problem solving task is captured in the *Problem* → *Geometry* link below. Here is where we must understand the science and find a way to model the science and represent that model by geometric means. The concrete expression of that model in computer graphics terms is shown in the *Problem* → *Geometry* and *Geometry* → *Image(s)* links, which capture the modeling of the science in terms of modeling the graphics (geometrizing) as well as the graphical presentation of the model (rendering) and the user's interaction with the model. If the modeling of the science and the visual communication of the graphics and interaction are done well, they give the user an informed reflection on the problem that can lead to better understanding, as shown in the *Image(s)* → *Insight* link. With this approach, supported by the use of computer graphics, we are able to reach the *Insight* → *Problem* link, where the real advancement of our understanding is provided. Together these components describe a powerful way to address any kind of problem by engaging a combination of analytic and visual capabilities.

As we consider our problems and how we can view them graphically or geometrically, we find that we have some basic questions to answer. Can our problem naturally be expressed in terms of objects that have a natural image (automobiles, houses, machines, animals, . . .) or have a familiar representation (bar, sphere, pyramid, surface, . . .)? If so, then you can start with these natural or familiar objects and see how you can represent your problem in their terms. If not, then you need to try to find or create such a representation of the problem, because you cannot display a solution without geometry. As Galileo said.

> Philosophy is written in this grand book the universe, which stands continually open to our gaze. But the book cannot be understood unless one first learns to comprehend the language and to read the alphabet in which it is composed. It is written in the language of mathematics, and its characters are triangles, circles, and other geometric figures, without which it is humanly impossible to understand a single word of it; without these, one wanders about in a dark labyrinth. [SOV, p. 16]

The overall process we are describing here is what we call *graphical problem solving*. The key point of this process is being able to identify ways to describe a problem in geometric terms that permit you to design and create images that represent part of the problem. The general process of representing a problem in ways that permit better understanding is called *modeling* the problem, and modeling scientific problems is a large topic. This modeling is deeply embedded in science, often using applied mathematics such as differential equations to build models. However, to help you understand the kind of modeling that is part of graphical problem solving, in this chapter we describe some kinds of graphical modeling that have been used for various problems in science. These will be relatively simple models because we're looking at the kind of graphical models that can be created using your beginning graphics tools; much more complex and sophisticated kinds of models have been created and are being used, and you should look at the general literature of scientific visualization to get an understanding of the greater depth that is possible.

As we look at the examples of graphical modeling, we will consider different kinds of scientific problems. For each we will describe the problem and how it can be modeled graphically, and where appropriate describe tradeoffs that we made in choosing the particular representation. We will then describe the way we can build an image based on that model. Later in the chapter we will discuss some details in the computer modeling (as distinct from the problem modeling) that go into creating the images for the models; these will sometimes include discussions of the graphics techniques and will sometimes focus on other programming issues. The end product of this work will be a description of the problem-solving process that you should be able to apply to your own projects or problems. Together with the set of examples illustrating this process, this should give you the tools to use graphical problem solving to accomplish your own goals.

Data and Visual Communication

Before we discuss the examples of scientific applications, we should say a word about the kinds of data you may encounter when you're working with scientific information because you must be careful to use models that are appropriate to your data. There are different kinds of data, called interval, ordinal, and nominal data, that must be treated differently when you represent them graphically. *Interval data* can be represented by real numbers, *ordinal data* are data that have a natural ordering but no meaningful numerical representation, and *nominal data* are data that are in different categories but have no ordering. There are few challenges in dealing with interval data, such as temperatures, forces, cost, or counts. We are familiar with the numerical nature of this data and can represent it in traditional ways, such as values in dimensions or even as color ramps. With ordinal data, we are dealing with concepts of more/less or larger/smaller; an example might be the amount of education someone has, where this is broken into categories such as elementary school, middle school, high school, college, or postgraduate levels. Here we can use positioning, relative sizes, a discrete set of colors of increasing brightness, or some other way to see relative sizes. With nominal data, we simply have a set of different properties to consider, such as male/female, country or continent of location, or religious affiliation; there is no way to order such data. For such data we can use different shapes or distinct colors, but we probably need to use some sort of legend to identify which representation we use for each value because likely no natural identification will be available. But remember that there may be unconscious hierarchies in your audience (or yourself) and that source representations may imply hierarchies, so be conscious of your devices.

Most scientific work tends to use measured—and hence interval—data. Certainly there will be nominal data associated with studies or theories that involve different environments or different test groups; an example might be responses to medical treatments for male or female patients, where the patient class would be a nominal value. However, the responses would probably be interval data and the presentation might be a pair of line or surface graphs, one for each interval value. Comparing these graphs would let you compare the values for the nominal groups. Thus we will not see any formal treatments of nominal data in this chapter.

One characteristic of many scientific studies or theories is that they are high-dimensional; they involve a number of samples at a point or a number of related variables. When we work with interval data of high dimension and the dimension of the data (or the dimensions of the domain and range of a function together) exceeds the three dimensions we can directly plot, we may need to allow the user some options in viewing the data space. This has been discussed in Chapter 2, but exploring scientific data may involve giving the user more control over how the higher-dimensional viewing is done. Data exploration can be supported by providing various projections and controls for moving around the data to see the different projections. We are used to thinking of 2D screen projections of 3D space, but we will need to consider projections into 3D space from higher-dimension spaces as well. With the growth of genuine immersive viewing devices for 3D viewing, in the future it may not be necessary to project below 3D space at all.

Examples

As noted previously, in this chapter, we describe a number of techniques you can use to work on problems in the sciences. In a sense, presenting a set of techniques may tend to make you focus on the graphical technique rather than on the problem you are examining, so you may miss the point of starting with the problem first and finding a graphical or visual representation later. However, our goal is to give you a set of arrows from which you can choose when you aim at a problem. Learning to analyze the problem and find an appropriate technique will come only with practice.

Our techniques are taken from several years of observing presentations and discussions of visual approaches to the sciences. The examples we will share are usually not the most sophisticated kinds of images in these presentations because we want to show work that you can do, based on your own programming with a simple graphics API such as OpenGL, rather than with sophisticated scientific visualization tools. When you master these simpler techniques, however, you will have a very good background to understand the way the more complex tools work and to take advantage of them when they are available.

Diffusion

Diffusion is a widely observed process in which a property that is present at one point in space is spread throughout the space by migrating from its original point to adjacent points over time. A number of different processes might cause this migration, but we are not interested in them; we are interested only in the fact of the migration. When diffusion is modeled for computational purposes, the space is usually divided into a grid of "points" that are usually a unit of area or volume, and the amount of the property at each grid point in the space is assumed to have some initial numeric value. The property might be a quantity of salt dissolved in a unit volume of water, a quantity of heat in a unit volume of a material, or the number of events in a unit area. The process is modeled by assuming that quantities of the property transfer from a given grid point to neighboring grid points proportionately to the difference between the amount of property present at each point, either determinately or with some randomness included in the process. This is a very general kind of process that can be applied to a wide range of problems, and in this section we will look at two models built from it.

Temperatures in a Bar

Here we make a more formal examination of the example we saw in Chapter 0, and it will serve as a bridge between the informal kind of visualization we did then and a more scientific kind of modeling. Let us start with a rectangular bar of some material that is embedded in an insulating medium and has points at which fixed-temperature connectors may be attached. Our goal is to consider the distribution of temperatures throughout the bar over time. We assume that the bar has constant thickness and that the material in the bar is homogeneous throughout its thickness at any point, so we may treat the bar as a 2D entity. The bar may be homogeneous or heterogeneous; the material the bar is made of may have varying thermal conductivity properties; the connectors may be active or inactive and may have time-varying temperatures (but their temperatures are directed by an outside agent and have no relation to the temperatures of the bar). The basic property of the distribution of heat is described by the *heat equation* $\frac{\partial F}{\partial t} = k \frac{\partial^2 F}{\partial x^2}$, the partial differential equation for heat transfer, with the value of k determined by the material in the bar. If the material is homogeneous, then k is a constant; if it is heterogeneous, then k may be a function of position in the bar. This latter condition leads to very difficult differential equations and is not used in our simple example, but it can be useful for models that include different materials such as insulators.

This equation says, basically, that at a given point, the rate of change of heat with time is proportional to the gradient (the second derivative) of the heat with space—that is, that the change in heat with time is associated with changes in the heat transfer over space. If the distribution of heat in space is constant, whatever that distribution is, then the rate of change dF/dt is zero and there is no change in heat over time. Differences in the spatial distribution of heat are necessary to have changes over time. Our goal is to determine at any given time approximately the distribution of heat in the bar, given initial conditions and boundary conditions.

We have three basic sets of decisions to make in modeling the distribution of heat in the bar: how to represent the distribution of heat for computational purposes, how to define and model the thermal properties of the bar, and how to display our results in order to communicate the behavior of temperatures in the bar.

For the first decision, we could solve the differential equation directly, or we could model the heat transfer process by modeling the bar as a grid—a 2D array of cells—and model the heat transferred from one cell to another adjacent cell as being proportional to the heat in the original cell. If two adjacent cells have the same heat, then the effect will be that they exchange the same amount of heat and end up with the same heat with which each started.

For the second decision, we will choose to model the thermal behavior by a simple diffusion process in which we consider the flow of heat between cells. In the standard case of a cell that is adjacent to four other cells of similar properties, if the proportion of heat energy retained by a cell is α, then the proportion to be transferred to each of the adjoining cells is

$(1-\alpha)/4$. We start with an initial condition and update all the cells' heat from that condition, replace the computed values with any values that are assumed to be constant (e.g., the cells at the positions of fixed-heat points), display the values in the cells at the end of this update, and take the resulting condition as the initial condition for the next round of the simulation. We may make the value of α a constant for all the cells, or we may set different values of α for different cells if we want to model a heterogeneous material. For an actual implementation of this problem, we must decide whether the bar itself is homogeneous or heterogeneous, where the connectors will be attached, and what the heat properties of the connectors will be. In the simplest case we would have a homogeneous bar with connectors at fixed points and fixed temperatures, and this case will be discussed below. We could also consider the case of heterogeneous materials and will suggest how a student might address the case of varying temperatures or connections from the connectors.

For the third decision, we need to go back to the discussion of visual communication in Chapter 2, where this kind of problem was discussed. There we saw that we could represent the temperature at points in the bar either through color or through height, and we discussed how each of these can affect what the viewer sees in the image. We will use both color and height to show how the temperature varies in the bar, as this seems to be the strongest visual presentation of the information. The results are shown in Figure 9.2, and the code for this solution is given in the initial chapter of the book.

Figure 9.2 A simple representation of the temperatures in a bar with fixed-temperature connections. See the figure in the color insert.

For the simplest case we saw above, the results are pretty simple to understand; the bar is hottest next to the points where the hot points are attached and is coldest next to the points where the colder points are attached. We do not show a legend that correlates the temperature with the color, and we should do that to make the figure more informative. We also do not show any change in the position or temperature of the attachment points, although there might be changes in the setup of this problem over time. These changes in temperature or position of the attachments could be controlled by user interaction to achieve various effects in the bar, and we invite the student to try some possibilities and see what happens. Specifically, we suggest that you look at a bar with the attached points at one end and with the constant temperatures at those attached points alternating periodically between hot and cold. You should be able to see waves of heat and cold moving down the bar from the attachment points, and you should then try to explain why you see the behavior the display shows.

For the more complex case of a heterogeneous material, suppose that we are concerned that some region of the bar not get too hot, at least not get hot very quickly, no matter how much heat is input into it at some fixed hot spots. We know that we can create a composite bar that includes segments with different thermal qualities. Let us assume that the node connections are on one end and let us define a bar that contains an insulating section between the two ends. For the cells that have this material, we will use a much lower constant for thermal transfer so that the heat will come into, and go through, that material much more slowly. In this case we will have much less heat transmitted by the insulating material than we would in a bar that had no insulator, and we would see a much slower heating of the material on the side away from the connections. We can model this kind of heterogeneous material more generally and store information on the heat properties of the material in each cell of the bar, adjusting the way we model the spread of heat and getting a good understanding of the way heat moves in such an object.

These examples show the qualitative behavior of the temperature distributions in the bar fairly well, but how accurate are they, and how could we have made them more accurate? We have used a discrete approximation to a continuous process, and we have approximated the physical nature of the heat transfer with a diffusion model, so we know that we do not have an exact solution to the problem. We can compare the results of our model with the results of experimental measurements, however, to let us make better approximations of the diffusion values, we can increase the number of mesh points to reduce the error from the discrete approximation, and we can decrease the time step and adjust the parameters of the model to represent these smaller steps. This will usually let us draw good inferences from the model so that we can understand the nature of the heat distribution, and in many cases this can let us improve designs for heat-sensitive environments by helping us choose satisfactory materials. We can even do more sophisticated modeling by creating a heterogeneous model that includes insulating materials.

Spread of Disease

As another application of a problem based on a diffusion model, let's consider the behavior of a communicable disease in a region made up of a number of different communities. We need not try to be specific about the illness, because many illnesses have this kind of behavior, nor will we try to be too specific about the behavior of the communities being modeled. However, we will find that we need to make a number of assumptions to model this application in a way that lets us create simple displays.

The general assumption for this diffusion model is that the basic mechanism of disease spread is for an infected person and a susceptible (uninfected and not immune) person to come in contact with each other. When that happens, there is a certain probability that the susceptible person will become infected. Because we cannot model every possible meeting of individuals, we assume that the number of meetings between two populations is proportional to the product of the numbers of persons in the two populations. We further assume that we have a gridlike distribution where the region is divided into a set of rectangles with one community per rectangle, and that meetings happen only between members of adjoining communities only, where adjoining is assumed to mean communities in the same row or column, differing in position by only one index.

As for the disease itself, we begin by assuming that the entire initial population in each community is susceptible to the disease. We further assume that the disease is not fatal, and once an individual has recovered from the disease (s)he is permanently immune to it. We assume that an infected person recovers with a probability of β in a unit of time (this also controls the duration of the illness) and that a susceptible person becomes ill with a probability of α times the number of possible meetings between that person and an infected person. We will assume that the number of possible meetings is defined in the previous paragraph.

With these assumptions, we derive a model that contains an array `pop[][3]` of susceptible, infected, and immune persons that represents the number of persons in each community in the 2D grid. Each now of the array represents a community. For each time step in the simulation, we are able to calculate the number of meetings between infected persons and susceptible persons for each grid point by using the product of susceptible persons at that point and the numbers of infected persons at each neighboring point (including the point itself). We update the number of immune persons by calculating the number recovering and subtracting that number from the infected group, and then we add in the number of new infections from the group itself and from each of the neighboring groups. Finally, we subtract the number of newly infected persons from the number of susceptible persons. These computations are done with a diffusion-like model for new infections based on a 2D filter `m[3][3]` that defines the likelihood of meeting someone from each neighboring cell:

```
infected[i][j] = α *pop[i][j]*(m[1][1]*pop[i][j] +
                     m[0][1]*pop[i - 1][j] + m[2][1]*pop[i + 1][j] +
                     m[1][0]*pop[i][j - 1] + m[1][2]*pop[i][j + 1])
```

and with appropriate updates for the immune and recovering populations in cell `[i][j]` as needed.

The simulation starts with an initial value, which we have defined as an infection in a single cell. This is computed with discrete time steps, and the diffusion model tells us how the number of infected persons changes in each cell. Once we have computed the new numbers for the new time step, the display is updated and redrawn; Figure 9.3 shows a frame from the animation produced for a simulation built on this model. The simulation introduces one additional feature

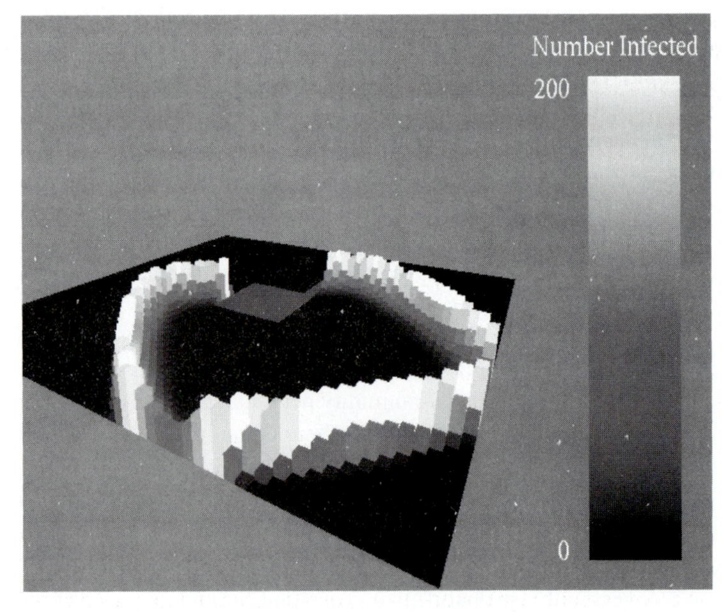

Figure 9.3 The disease spread model showing the behavior around the barrier region.

by including a region for which there is no population; this changes the shape of the spread but does not change the fact that the infection spreads to the entire region. The code for this simulation is included with the materials for the book.

Note that the model predicts that everyone in each community will eventually become immune to the disease, and thus the disease will spontaneously disappear from the region permanently after it has run its course. This is evidently not a reasonable conclusion, but if we examine the weaknesses in the model we can see how its inaccuracies arise. We assume no births, because a newborn person has not yet acquired an immunity to the disease, and we assume no travel except between neighboring communities, so a new case of the disease would have to arise spontaneously somewhere in the region. We also assume no mutations in the disease organism that would make formerly immune people susceptible to the mutated disease. So this model is very simplistic, and yet it helps present the nature of communicable diseases at a simple level that can be refined by making appropriate additions to the model.

Function Graphing and Applications

We are used to seeing many functions graphed with curves and surfaces in mathematics, science, and engineering textbooks, so it is not surprising to find that curves and surfaces are considered to be effective tools in understanding problems and finding solutions. In fact, we are so used to seeing problems phrased in terms of their graphs, curves, or surfaces that we may find it difficult to see that standard drawings of curves and surfaces can be a problem. But we will try to help you see this and to see how you can make them more effective.

Drawing a graph of a real function of a single variable is very simple. The graph of the function f is defined to be the set of points $(x, f(x))$ for values of x in the domain of the function. The graph is usually drawn as you learned to draw graphs in school: by choosing sample values in the domain, calculating the function's value for each value in the domain, and drawing a straight line from one pair to the next. We are familiar with this kind of 2D graphing from elementary mathematics and will not describe it further, but you should make sure you see how you could draw such a graph with a program.

Drawing a graph of a real function of two variables is a little more complex, but we described the basis for this in Chapter 2. An example of a straightforward surface graphed in this manner is the "ripple" function that shows rings proceeding outward from a central point, as shown in Figure 9.4. We saw this image in Chapter 6, where we focused on the way the image is presented. We call this function "ripple" because it looks like the ripples produced when a stone lands in water. This is calculated as described above, and the function being graphed is $z = \cos(x^2 + y^2 + t)$. Over the square domain $-5 = x = 5$ and $-5 = y = 5$, a double loop iterates both x and y and calculates the value of z for each pair (x, y). The values can be calculated and stored in a 2D array of z-values, or we can calculate the values in the domain as we go. We iterate over the domain and draw the triangles needed for the surface. Note that the function in this example contains a parameter t (think of time), and as this parameter is increased, the value of the argument to the cosine function is also increased. With this parameter increased linearly by adding a constant amount to t in the `idle()` function each time the image is redrawn, the figure is animated and the waves move continually away from the center. This parametric coding models the actual motion of waves over time and is a good example of a time-based presentation. The image here is made very smooth by the use of a large number of triangles and the use of lighting and material techniques, as we discussed in Chapter 6.

Figure 9.4 An example of a function surface display.

The code for this kind of graphing is pretty straightforward. Assuming that our domain is from X_0 to X_1 and from Y_0 to Y_1, and that we are taking N steps in each direction, we have:

```
Xstep = (X1-X0)/N; Ystep = (Y1-Y0)/N;
    for (x = X0; x += Xstep; x < X1)
        for (y = Y0; y += Ystep; y < Y1) {
            xx = x + Xstep; yy = y + Ystep;
                glBegin(GL_TRIANGLE_STRIP);
                    glVertex3f(x,  y,  f(x,y));
                    glVertex3f(x,  yy,  f(x,yy));
                    glVertex3f(xx, y,  f(xx,y));
                    glVertex3f(xx, yy,  f(xx,yy))
                glEnd();
}
```

Of course there are many ways to make this programming more efficient, but this simple code will compute and display the basic triangles that make up the surface.

Many problems can be understood in terms of a mathematical function, and this function can often be understood better with the help of its graph. For example, let's consider a set of electrostatic charges on a plane, and we want to understand the distribution of electrostatic potential at points in the plane. We could start by noting that the scalar electrostatic potential P at a point (x, y) in the plane, when there are charges Q_i at points (x_i, y_i) in the plane, is given by Coulomb's law:

$$P(x, y) = \sum \frac{Q_i}{\sqrt{(x - x_i)^2 + (y - y_i)^2}}$$

For any set of fixed charges at fixed points, this defines a function of two variables that can be graphed as noted above. This function is fairly simple, but it's not at all clear from just the equation

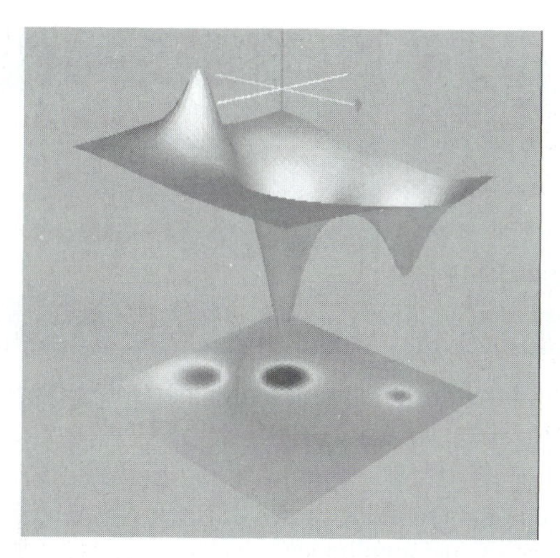

Figure 9.5 The Coulombic surface from three point charges (one positive, two negative) in a plane, with both a 3D surface and a planar pseudocolor presentation.

what the nature of the electrostatic potential is. For a particular configuration with one positive charge and two negative charges at given points, the graph in Figure 9.5 describes the electrostatic potential in a rectangle, as described earlier in the Chapter 5 description of color issues in visual communication. From this graph we see clearly that the potential looks like an elastic sheet with spikes directed upward or downward depending on the sign of the charge. The actual values of the potential at a point could be estimated from the 2D pseudocolor plane if we were to include a scale in the image.

If you want to create a specific electrostatic potential at a given point with a set of moveable charges, each with fixed potential, you can start with this kind of graph and define a way to select one of the point charges to move in the plane using the mouse or keyboard. If you want to create a specific potential with variable-potential charges at fixed points, you can select the point and change the amount of charge at that point. Both of these techniques will change the graph, letting you see the changing potential at your particular point. With a little experimentation, you will be able to get the appropriate potential at your point of interest, and you can even experiment more to see whether there are other ways you could achieve the same potential in easier ways. Thus the image provides an interactive tool for creating the potentials you want at the places you want them.

Another example of function surfaces that can show different behaviors is the phenomenon of interacting waves. In our example we have two wave functions (we could have more, but we will restrict ourselves to two to keep this discussion simpler), and the overall displacement at any point is the sum of the two functions. There are two kinds of waves we may want to consider: wave trains and waves from a given point. A wave train is a set of parallel waves moving in a single direction. It is described by a function such as $f(x, y) = a \sin(bx + cy + d)$ that contains an amplitude a, a frequency and direction determined by b and c, and a displacement given by d. By incrementing the displacement with each successive redrawing of the image, we can animate the wave behavior. The behavior of two wave trains is thus given by a function that is the sum of two such equations. In the left-hand side of Figure 9.6 we see the effect of one wave train of relatively high frequency meeting a wave train of about the same amplitude but a lower frequency at an

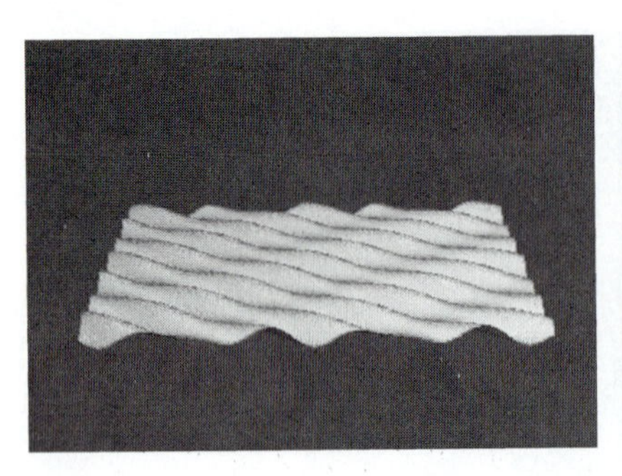
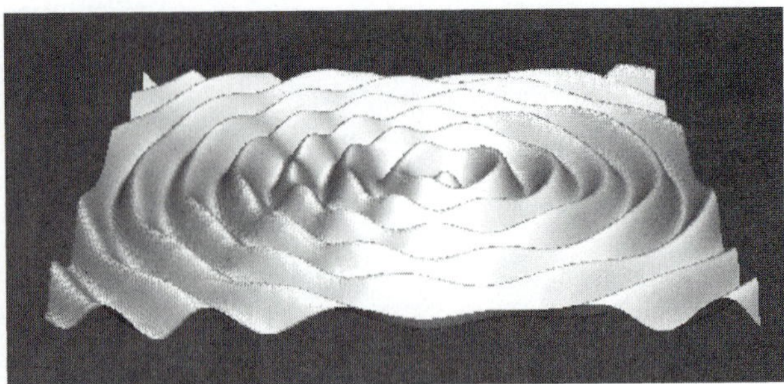

Figure 9.6 Two wave trains intersecting at a shallow angle (*left*) and two circular waves whose origins are offset by 3π/2 (*right*).

angle of about 120°. It is common to model water waves as a sum of many different wave trains of different angles, frequencies, and amplitudes.

A second kind of wave function is given by waves from a given point, which behave much as the example shown in Figure 9.5. This kind of wave is given by a function whose general form is extended from the "ripple" example earlier as $f(x,y) = a\cos(b((x - x_0)^2 + (y - y_0)^2)$. Thus each such wave function is defined by an initial point (x_0,y_0), an amplitude a, and a frequency b. A set of two waves with their own initial points, amplitudes, and frequencies is given by a sum of two of these functions. When two (or more) of these wave functions are added together, they create a complex pattern of interference and reinforcement, as shown in the right-hand side of Figure 9.6, where two wave functions with slightly offset centers and the same amplitudes and frequencies are added to form a complex surface. Of course, in the same way that you get ripples when you throw a stone into a lake, you can look at the interaction of a wave train and a circular wave as well.

Parametric Curves and Surfaces

A parametric curve is given by a function from a line or line segment into 2D or 3D space. This function might be analytic (given by a formula or set of formulas) or it might be an interpolation of data values. It is probably easier to work with analytic curves for now, but we will see examples of interpolation curves in Chapter 8.

As a first example of an analytic curve in 3D space, let's consider what we would have if we drew circles with two variables and used the third to move the circles in space. In a first version, let's use the parameter to define the radius of the circles and as the offset from a given plane. If we name our parameter t and use the parametric equations

```
x = a*t*sin(c*t)+b
y = a*t*sin(c*t)+b
z = c*t
```

for real constants a, b, and c, we see a curve that looks like an inverted incense cone, with very tight circles at the bottom that increase in radius as the curve moves upward. This is shown in the left-hand image in Figure 9.7.

In another version of this kind of example, let's give the circles a fixed radius but move them around a torus by using the third variable as the angle around a central line. We will increase

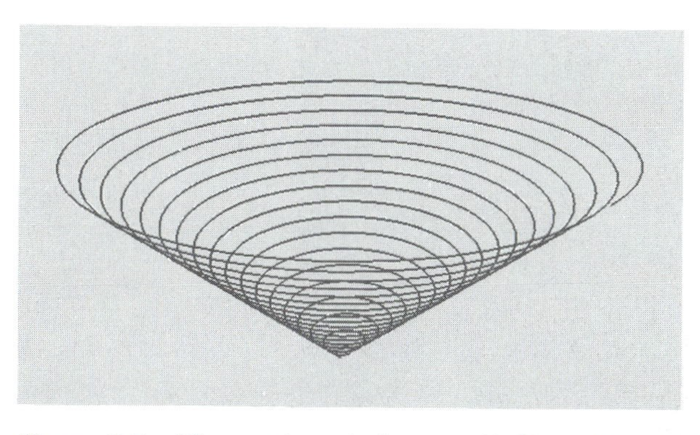
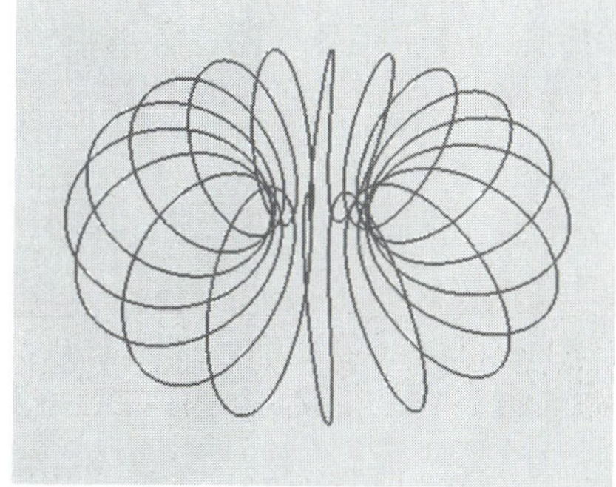

Figure 9.7 The conic spiral curve (*left*) and toroidal spiral curve (*right*).

the angle at a slow rate and the effect should be much like a coil (such as a Slinky) with its ends joined. If we use the parametric equations

```
x = (a*sin(c*t)+b)*cos(t)
y = (a*sin(c*t)+b)*sin(t)
z = a*cos(c*t)
```

for real constants a, b, and c, we see that the part `(a*sin(c*t)+b)` is the parametric form for a circle, and the rest of the equation moves that circle around in another circle. The first part, then, defines a spiral, and the second part moves the spiral around in a circle. The example in the right-hand image of Figure 9.7 shows us this spiral with $a = 2.0$, $b = 3.0$, and $c = 18.0$. The parametric spiral shown moves around a torus as t takes on the values between 0 and 2π. The parametric equations are evaluated at very small steps in the parameter t, giving a sequence of points that are joined by straight lines, yielding the rather smooth display of the curve. This spiral goes around the torus eighteen times (c = 18) while describing a circle with radius 2 and center three units from the origin, as you can see fairly readily from the figure.

Parametric surfaces can be a little more challenging. For such a surface we take a 2D region in the plane and map it into 3D space in various ways. This kind of modeling may need some work to lay out, but you can achieve some very interesting results. Let's consider *Boy's Surface,* whose domain is a rectangle with dimensions $[0, \pi]$ in both parameters s and t. This surface is shown in Figure 9.8, and the full code for the example is included in the resources for the book.

We created the code for this figure by adapting the parametric functions from the Maple algebra system that are given at the Web site `http://www.geom.uiuc.edu/zoo/toptype/pplane/boy/`.

```
x := cos(t)*sin(s);
y := sin(t)*sin(s);
z := cos(s);
f := 1/2*((2*x^2-y^2-z^2)+2*y*z*(y^2-z^2)+z*x*(x^2-z^2)+x*y*(y^2-x^2));
g := sqrt(3)/2*((y^2-z^2) + z*x*(z^2-x^2) + x*y*(y^2-x^2));
h := (x+y+z)*((x+y+z)^3 + 4*(y-x)*(z-y)*(x-z));
plot3d([h/8,f,g], s=0..Pi, t=0..Pi)
```

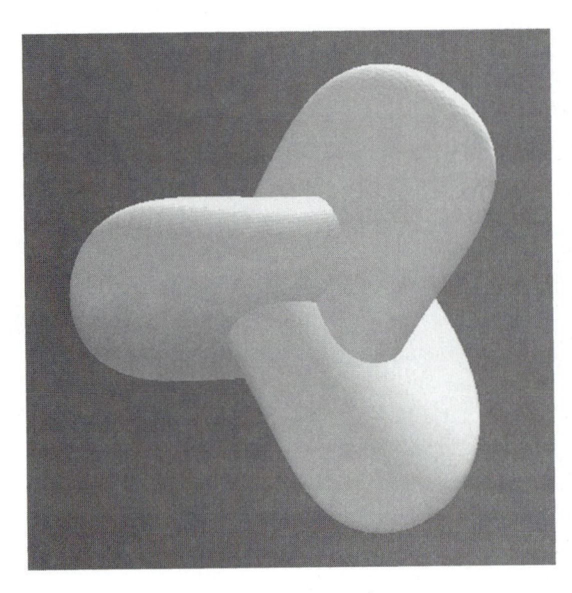

Figure 9.8 The *boy's surface* graph of the example.

This Maple code translates into code that loops across both s and t from 0 to π and calculates u, v, and w coordinates for each pair (s, t) as in that code, with $u = h/8$, $v = f$, and $w = g$. The resulting surface is plotted by making two triangles from the four points you get from a quad in the domain:

```
(u(s_i, t_j), v(s_i, t_j), w(s_i, t_j))
(u(s_i, t_j+1), v(s_i, t_j+1), w(s_i, t_j+1))
(u(s_i+1, t_j+1), v(s_i+1, t_j+1), w(s_i+1, t_j+1))
(u(s_i+1, t_j), v(s_i+1, t_j), w(s_i+1, t_j))
```

In Figure 9.9 we show a more complex example of a parametric surface, called a (4,3)-torus. Here we took a planar rectangle and divided it into three parts, folding the cross-section into an equilateral triangle. Then we twisted that triangle around 4/3 times and stretched it around a torus, putting the two ends of the triangular tube back together. The resulting surface is one-sided (you can trace all the surface without crossing any of the triangle edges) and is interesting to hold and manipulate; in Chapter 15 on hardcopy you can see photographs of the surface that have been created with various 3D hardcopy technologies.

To look at this surface in more detail, the domain is the rectangle in parameters u and v defined for $-2\pi \leq u \leq 2\pi$ and $-2\pi \leq v \leq 2\pi$, and given by the equations

```
x(u,v) = (4+2cos(4u/3+v))cos(u)
y(u,v) = (4+2cos(4u/3+v))sin(u)
z(u,v) = 2*sin(4u/3+v)
```

This should look fairly familiar, because it is much the same as the toroidal spiral curve above. The difference is that for the spiral we stepped the single parameter t in small steps, while here we step the parameter v in small steps (e.g., one hundred steps around the torus) while stepping

Figure 9.9 A 3D parametric surface of two variables.

the parameter u only three times, giving us large spaces between steps and making the cross-section of the surface triangular. This is shown in the layout of the parameter space shown in Figure 9.10; in general, laying out the parameter space in this way before going on to define the surface in more detail can be very helpful. In particular, you can see from the parameter space layout that the u-space is used to create the triangles and the v-space to create the steps around the torus. You

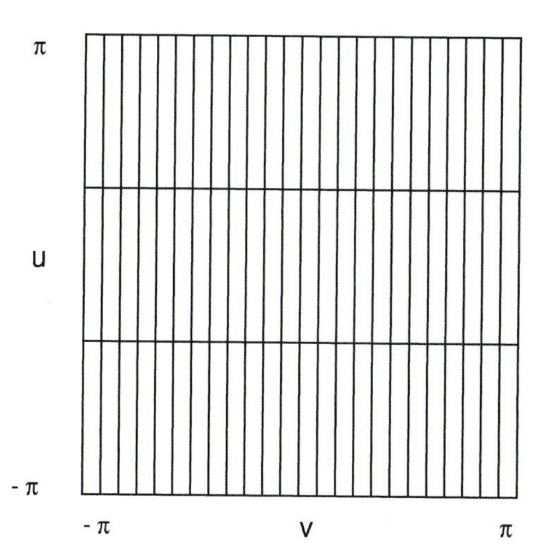

Figure 9.10 The fundamental parameter space for the surface shown in Figure 9.9, simplified by reducing the number of steps in the v parameter.

might conjecture what could be produced if you used four steps instead of three in u-space (did you see a square cross-section?) or another number, but if you do this, you must be careful to change the constant 4/3 in the equations so that you will still get a closed surface.

For the actual display of the surface, we found that the long, narrow triangles we got from the simple parameter space gave us very strange shading. We solved the problem by breaking each of the long rectangles into a series of smaller rectangles so that we had much more equal-sided triangles.

If you find that these parametric surfaces are fairly simple, you can test your geometric intuition by mapping your 2D domain into 4D space and seeing what you can produce there. Of course, you probably cannot display the 4D surface directly, so you will want to use various projections of the result into 3D space. There are some classic surfaces of this kind, such as the Klein bottle. A set of parametric equations (in 3-space only) for the Klein bottle is given by

```
bx = 6*cos(u)*(1 + sin(u));
by = 16*sin(u);
rad = 4*(1 - cos(u)/2);
if (Pi < u <= 2*Pi) X = bx + rad*cos(v + Pi);
   else X = bx + rad*cos(u)*cos(v);
if (Pi < u <= 2*Pi) Y = by;
   else Y = by + rad*sin(u)*cos(v);
Z = rad*sin(v);
```

as translated from a Mathematica function. The left-hand image in Figure 9.11 was obtained by replacing the functions for the torus in Figure 9.9 with the functions given here and changing the domain to $[0,2\pi]$ instead of $[-\pi,\pi]$. In fact, once you have a good program for parametric surfaces, adapting to different kinds of surfaces should be easy.

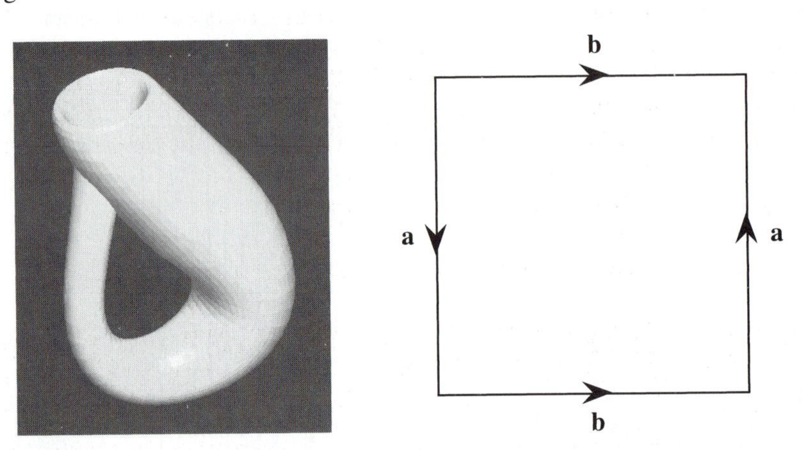

Figure 9.11 A 4D parametric surface, the Klein bottle (*left*), and the structure of the parametric region that defines it (*right*).

The actual construction for the Klein bottle is a little more complicated than shown here. The domain for the Klein bottle is a rectangle in 2D space, similar to the domain for the twisted torus above, but the function has one very different treatment for the domain: As shown in the right-hand image of Figure 9.11, with the sides identified as shown, the two sides labeled b are matched as they were when we created the cylinder above, but the two sides labeled a are matched in reverse order. This cannot be done in 3D space, but it can in 4D space, and the result has properties much like those of a cylinder but with an embedding that can only be suggested by any 3D projection. The parametric approach is one construction of the Klein bottle, but there are many others that are of interest and that illustrate other properties of the surface; for example, the Klein bottle may be created by gluing two 3D Möbius bands together in 4-space.

Graphical Objects That Are the Results of Limit Processes

Sometimes curves and surfaces arise through processes that are different from the closed-form function graphing we described previously. Some of these graphical objects are, in fact, quite surprising, such as some that arise from limit processes. We will look at some of these in Chapter 14 because some limit processes are related to fractals and iterated function systems. Here we look at an example that defines a surface to be graphed.

One of these limit-process objects might be of particular interest. In calculus, it is shown that while any function that is differentiable at a point must be continuous at that point, the converse is not true: a function can have continuity without differentiability. Some examples of continuous but nowhere differentiable functions are given in most calculus texts, but it can be difficult to see the actual results of the process. One of these functions is called the *blancmange function* because its graph—the surface defined by the function—looks somewhat like the very lumpy blancmange pudding often served in England at holidays. This surface is defined recursively as the sum of an increasing number of piecewise bilinear functions that connect the points $(i/2^k, j/2^k, z)$ at level k, where z is 0 if i or j is even and $1/2^k$ if i and j are both odd. Because the sum at any point is not larger than $\sum_k 1/2^k$, which is a converging geometric sequence, this sum converges and the surface is well defined. However, within any neighborhood of any point $(x,y,f(x,y))$ in the surface there will lie many points $(i/2^k, j/2^k)$ for even values of i and j, and at each of these points there is a sharp corner (a non-differentiable point) in one of the summands. Because there are corners of the summands within any neighborhood of any point, the function cannot be differentiable anywhere. An approximation of the graph of this function is shown in Figure 9.12, and you can increase the iterations of the function as much as you like by increasing the number of points in the domain. Be warned, though, that the computation—and thus the time it takes—increases geometrically with the number of iterations. This makes any interactive exploration of the surface difficult. For more on the mathematics of the blancmange function, see [TAL].

Figure 9.12 The blancmange surface (*left*) and zoomed in with more iterations (*right*).

A very similar surface can be constructed with replacing a quad with a set of four triangles, constructed by displacing the point at the center of the quad upward by a distance proportional to the width of the quad and using this point and the four vertices of the quad to create a triangle fan. This is called the Takagi fractal surface and is described in [PIE]. A more general approach uses a random displacement to create a surface with a variety of topographies. See the discussion of fractals in Chapter 14 for more details.

Scalar Fields

A *scalar field* is a real function of a variable on a domain, which is a very general principle. If the domain is a region in a 1D real space, it is called a 1D scalar field and defines an ordinary function of one variable. A 2D scalar field is a scalar field on a 2D domain, or a real function of two real variables, but this concept is much more general than the kind of graph of a closed-form or iterative function we discussed above. Many kinds of processes can give rise to such a function, and those processes can produce functions that are far from the continuous surface we were working with. An example is a data-derived function produced by scanning or by radar altimetry. These processes can easily give us functions that cannot be expressed in a closed form (that is, in terms of equations). 3D scalar fields, or real-valued functions of three variables, are discussed below when we talk about volume data, because they are usually thought of in volume terms.

An interesting example of a 2D scalar field is the digital elevation map (DEM). These maps, available from the USGS and other sources (see, for example, geogdata.csun.edu), are 2D grayscale images whose grayscale value represents the elevation of each point in a map space. They are actually examples of images colored with pseudocolor data that represents elevations. If you know the base and top of the elevation scale for a map, you can read the pixels and calculate elevations for each point, giving you a surface grid that is a good representation of the topography of the area. In addition you may be able to get an aerial photograph, radar scan, or other image of the same area. Google Earth is an excellent way to get earth images. In Figure 9.13 we

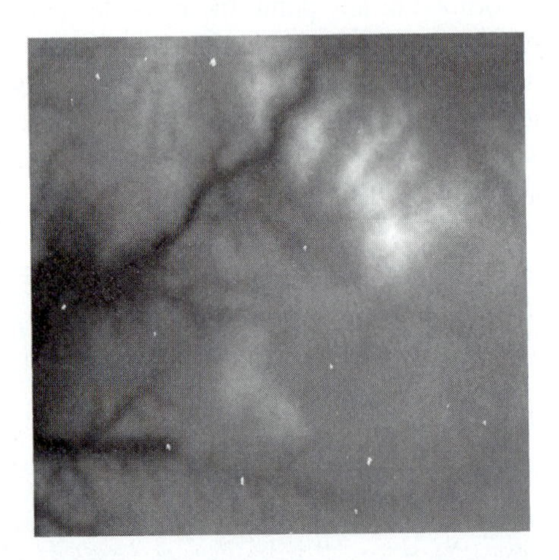

Figure 9.13 Height field from USGS digital elevation map (*left*) and texture map of a portion of the same space from aerial photographs. Courtesy of Jeff Sale, San Diego Supercomputer Center.

see the image of a digital elevation map (an example of a grayscale height field as we discussed in Chapter 6) and of an aerial photograph of a portion of the same space, specifically of the San Diego State University campus area. You will find the campus at the lower left of the right-hand image of Figure 9.13 and toward the lower right of Figure 9.14.

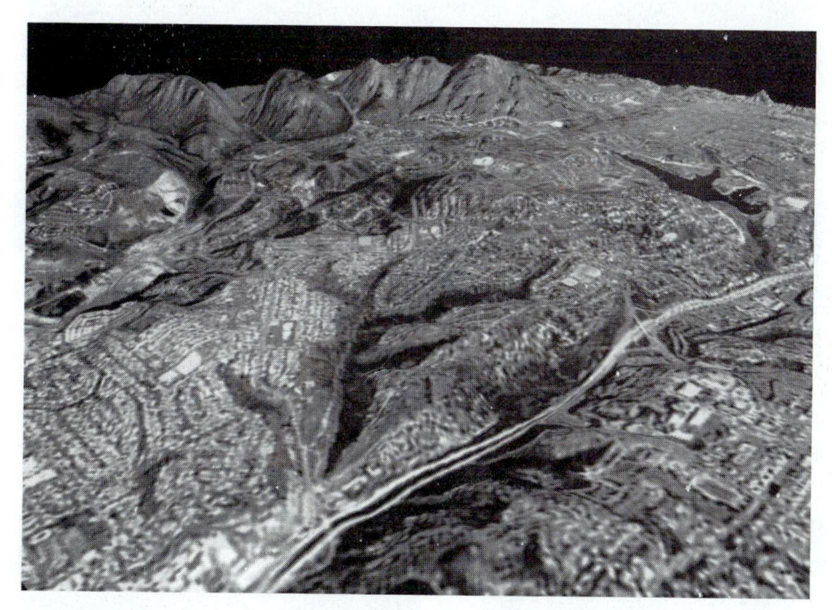

Figure 9.14 Height field and texture map made into a terrain visualization.

When the height data is turned into polygons and they are texture mapped with the photographs, the results can be strikingly realistic. In Figure 9.14 we see an example of the San Diego area east of downtown, courtesy of Jordan Maynard; the San Diego State University campus can be seen near the lower right of the image. You may notice that because the image is texture mapped from a photograph, the actual buildings are not seen as they would be in a photograph from this angle; only the shapes of the buildings are shown.

There are a number of other places where values are sampled on a domain, and we can think of these as samples of a scalar field. For example, laser range scanning produces a scalar field for distances from a sampling point; as in the terrain map case, the sample points may be converted into geometric vertices of polygons of the space being scanned. As an example of this approach, the research into the paleolithic cave art of Cap Blanc used both photographs of the cave, as shown in Figure 9.15, and laser range scans of the cave. This is all courtesy of Alan Chalmers of the University of Bristol.

The cave's geometry is computed from the results of a laser scan carried out in the cave. The scanner captures the vertical and horizontal offset from the original scanner position at each of many hundred systematically scanned points. This produces a height field shown as both raw laser scans (left), calculated from the offsets and distance. This is further

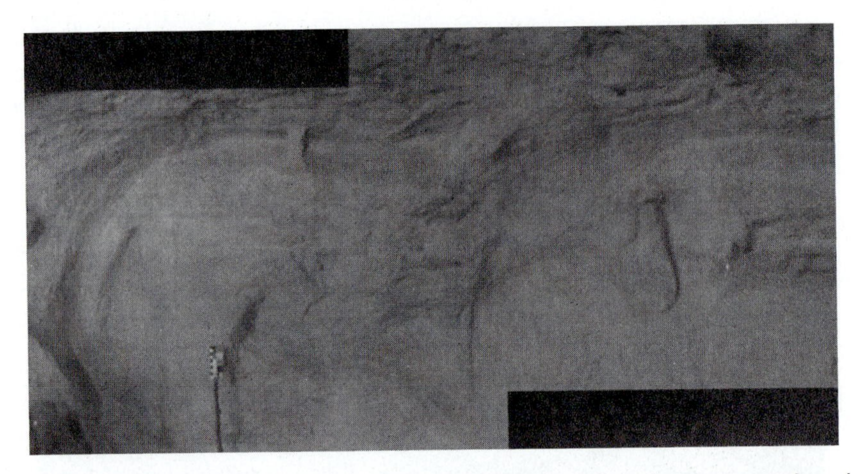

Figure 9.15 Photograph of cave site with photogrammetric reference card and laser scan point. See the figure in the color insert. Courtesy of Alan Chalmers.

developed into a mesh (right), both shown in Figure 9.16. The position of each point on the mesh is then matched with a position on the photograph that acts as a texture map for the cave wall, letting the researcher create an accurate model of both the geometry and color of the cave wall.

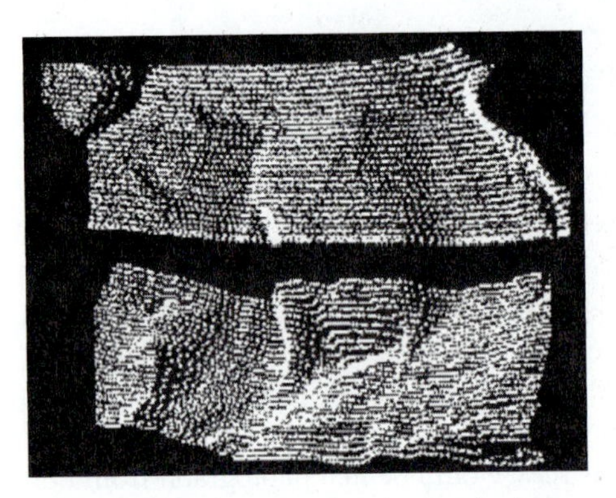

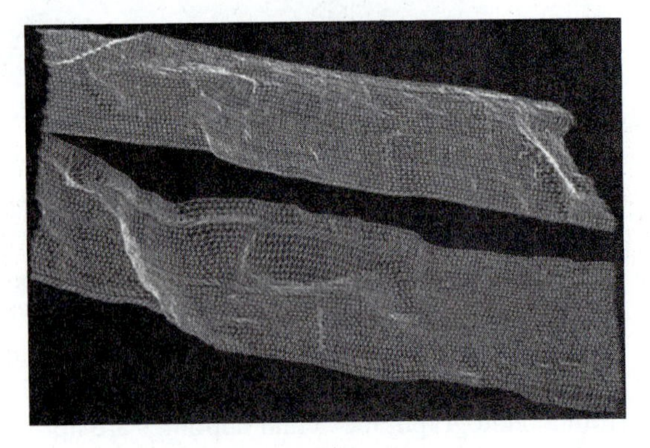

Figure 9.16 Original laser scan data (*left*) and the geometric mesh computed from that data (*right*).

This model is then used in studies of the cave itself. For example, to understand how the cave might have looked under different lighting conditions, researchers can generate synthetic images of the cave as defined above to study the effect of different kinds of firelight in various positions. An example of this is shown in Figure 9.17, and you will see how the shape of a horse stands out from the light of a lamp. Initially the lamp is shown at the center bottom of the space. As this lamp is moved from left to right the horse seems to move, showing that the original cave inhabitants may have been able to carve the wall in order to present the idea of a living horse from the carving.

Another kind of surface is the artificial landscapes, called *fractal forgeries*. The techniques for creating them have some of the same properties associated with fractals: They are self-

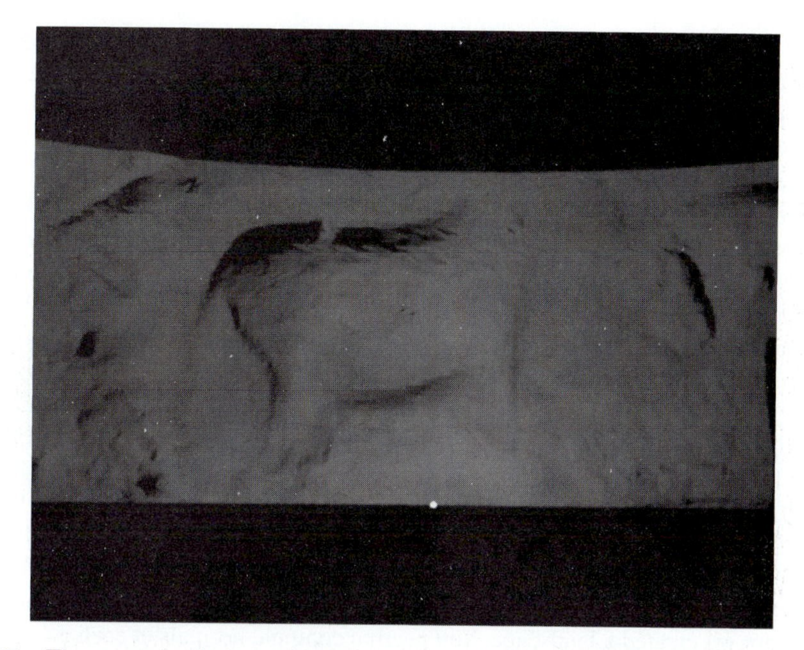

Figure 9.17 The cave wall shown with a simulated animal-oil lamp. See the figure in the color insert. Courtesy of Alan Chalmers.

similar, with small regions having a resemblance to larger regions. These landscapes use polygon-based modeling. Figure 9.18 shows an example of such an image courtesy of Ben Eadington, a student of the author's.

Figure 9.18 A "fractal forgery" landscape with shading and transparent water. See the figure in the color insert. Courtesy of Ben Eadington.

The process of creating such a landscape is fairly simple, but there are a few details to master. This is a traditional function surface image, but the function is not analytically defined; rather, it is defined procedurally as a program is run. There is a degree of randomness in the process, so you can get a number of different kinds of landscapes.

We start with a grid in the domain of the function. We will be subdividing an initial set of values, so we need the grid to have dimension 2^N+1 for some integer N. We want that integer to be large enough to offer a number of subdivisions, but not so large that it will take too long to create and draw the surface. The image in Figure 9.18 is built on a 257×257 grid, so the grid indices are each 0 to 256. We map these grid points into a domain space that we will call points (x, y).

We initialize the values on a small set of grid points where indices are small powers of 2. For example, you might initialize the values on grid points with indices 0, 128, and 256, a total of nine grid points. You can choose initial values to give you some general control of the shape of the final landscape, so for each of these points we have an initial value of z to start defining the surface. We then iterate through larger and larger powers of 2 and define a z-value for each new grid point by taking the average of the z-values for adjacent grid points and offsetting that by a random number that is scaled to be no more than a proportion of the distance between these adjacent points. We continue this until we have defined z-values for each grid point in the domain.

We now graph a complete surface by creating a pair of triangles for each quad in the grid, but we have not yet created a landscape. You need to compute normals at each grid point so you can add lighting to the scene. You need to use a coloring technique for each triangle in the landscape, and you can either use a height-based technique or could texture map a scene onto the landscape. The height-based technique in Figure 9.18 adds some randomness to the height of a triangle before determining the color, so we get a ragged tree line and snow line. You can add other features such as the water in the figure to make it more interesting. To add water, define a height as the water level and test each triangle against that height. If the triangle is lower than the water level, define a new triangle that represents the water surface and color it a blue with a modest alpha value. If the triangle meets the water level, define a new polygon that is at the water level and use the same blue color. Then draw the triangles along the grid, always drawing the landscape surface before the water surface, and you get the image in the figure.

Simulation of Objects and Behaviors

In some cases it is possible to represent an object of interest and to create a simulation of the object or its behavior so it can be studied and so the simulation can be compared with the actual object. This kind of simulation can help us understand an object or a phenomenon. In these cases our images help us to visualize the behavior as expressed in the simulation.

This is actually a very broad topic, and we cannot go into much detail on simulations here. We will present two simulations of the behavior of an ideal gas and will show how we can not only visualize the behavior but also get data from the simulation to test hypotheses on the behavior. This allows us to get both numerical and visual results, allowing us to verify that the simulation has the right analytic properties while we look at its visual properties. We will also present a simulation of a scientific instrument so that we can understand its operation and be better able to interpret its output.

Gas Laws and Diffusion Principles

The behavior of ideal gases under various conditions is a standard part of chemistry and physics studies. Our first simulation will put a number of objects (points, actually, but they represent molecules) into a closed space. Each will be given a random motion by generating a random direction (a vector with random coordinates, normalized to make it a direction) and moving the object a given distance in that direction. This simulates the behavior of a gas under constant temperature. We test for collisions of objects with the walls, and when these are detected, the object direction is changed to simulate the object's bouncing off the wall. However, we do not detect and account for internal collisions between objects. The behavior of molecules in the space and the numerical output of the simulation are displayed in Figure 9.19, with the pressure (the number of objects

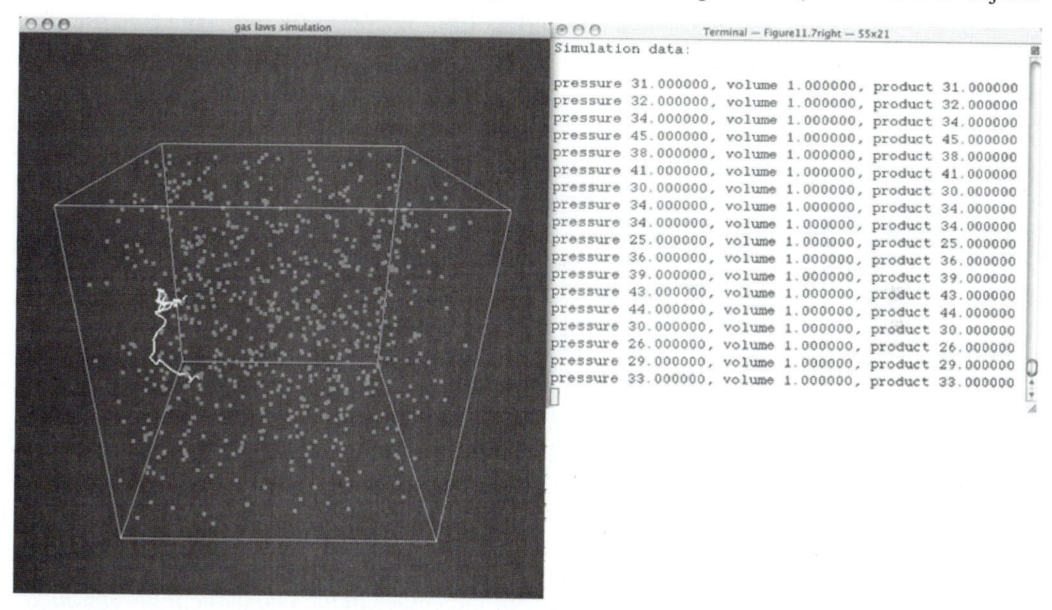

Figure 9.19 Displaying the gas as particles in the fixed space, including simulation printouts. See the figure in the color insert.

hitting a wall is counted at each step) and volume (the product of the dimensions of the box) being displayed, as well as their product. The user can test the simulation by pressing a key and getting the pressure P, volume of the box V, and the product. This product should be a constant for an ideal gas because of the gas law, $PV = nRT$: Pressure times volume is a constant times the gas temperature, with the constant being the product of the number of moles of the gas, n, and the universal gas constant R. There is a statistical element to this, and the gas law expresses the results when the numbers are so large that the randomness essentially vanishes, but in our simple (and very small) simulation the numbers are large so the randomness is important. We also show the path of a single molecule to create interest and to show that the simulation works as described.

This simulation would be of minimal interest if it did only what we've described above, but we also let the user increase or decrease the volume of the box. If this is an accurate simulation of the behavior of an ideal gas, we should have the same product of pressure and volume (within statistical limits) as we change the volume of the box, although we need to wait for the gas to expand or contract before we test the model. A user should be able to take the data from several samples at different volumes and perform a statistical test of the hypothesis that the product of the pressure and volume is a constant. The display in Figure 9.19 shows the objects in the box (with one traced through several steps to show the random walk behavior of the gas) as well as the results of several tests. Code for this simulation is included in the materials for the book, and it may be worth modifying the code to write results to a file so that you can do statistical analysis on the results.

Another simulation we could create, building on the one above, examines the behavior of gas in a box that is divided by a semipermeable membrane. Such a simulation is shown in Figure 9.20. If a gas molecule hits the membrane from one side, there is a different probability of its passing through the membrane than if it hits from the opposite side, concentrating that

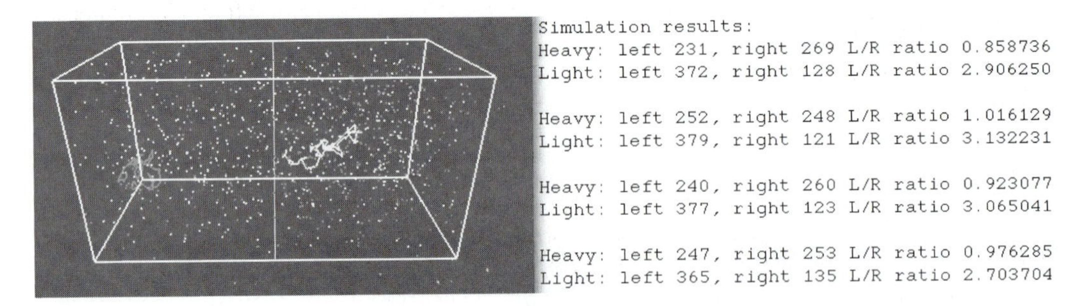

Figure 9.20 Display of the diffusion simulation, directly across the membrane (including data output from the simulation). See the figure in the color insert.

gas somewhat more on the side to which transmission is easier. If there are two different kinds of molecules in the gas and if the objects are treated differently by the membrane, we should expect to see some separation of the two kinds of molecules in the two parts of the space. We simulate this with particles simulating the gas molecules, as above, and using the same kind of code to detect particles hitting either a wall or the membrane. Again, we show the motion of one particle of each type. If a particle hits the membrane, a random number function determines whether the particle passes through the membrane or is reflected back. We are again able to tabulate the state of the particles in the system at any time, but in this case we count the number of particles on each side and calculate the ratio of particles on the left and right sides of the membrane. In the initial state, all the particles are on one side of the membrane; as the simulation runs, we expect to see a steady state reached with different left/right ratios for the two kinds of gas. In the figure we see a snapshot of the space, and we show the display of the tabulation at several times before the screen capture image. Again, the code for this simulation is included with the book.

Molecular Display

Sometimes we don't have functions or processes to deal with; we simply want to see some kind of invisible objects or structures in order to understand a problem better. This has long been the case in chemistry, where the ability to identify and display the structure of molecules has been an important part of chemistry students' education and where molecular visualization has led to great developments in drug design and other developments. Molecular visualization is a large topic, however, and many of the visualizations are very complex and require a deep understanding of molecular-level physics. We cannot hope to create this kind of complex work in a beginning computer graphics course, but we can show the beginning of the process.

The traditional start to understanding molecular structure (at least in the author's student days!) was the spring-and-ball display of a molecule. In this display, each atom is represented by a ball whose color represented a particular kind of atom, and each bond was represented by a spring that connected two balls. This lets you assemble fairly simple molecules and manipulate them by moving the assembled structure around and seeing it from various angles. We can do at least this much fairly readily, and perhaps we can suggest some ways this could be extended.

To begin, we need to know the basic geometry of molecules. To a large extent, this geometry has been determined and is readily available to the public. One of the major information sources is the *Protein Data Bank* at `http://www.rcsb.org` (and at several mirror sites), and another is MDL Information Systems (`http://www.mdli.com`). Molecular descriptions are stored at these (and many more) sites in standard formats, and you can go to these sources, find and download descriptions of the molecules you want to examine, and use them to create displays of these molecules. The descriptions are usually in one of two major formats: .pdb (protein data base) format or .mol (CT files) format. An appendix to the book gives you the details of the formats, and the source code resources for the book include some very simple functions to read the basic geometry from them. Check out the "Molecule of the Month" listing from the University of Bristol for some interesting examples: `http://www.bris.ac.uk/Depts/Chemistry/MOTM/motm.htm`.

Creating a display from the molecule description is quite straightforward. Once you have decoded the description file, you will have a list of atom names and positions in the molecule, as well as a list of atomic bonds in the molecule. You can then draw the atoms at the positions indicated and draw in the links that represent the bonds. It is common to draw the atoms as spheres with colors and sizes that are traditional for each kind of atom; the spheres may be drawn as opaque or partially transparent, and the colors and sizes can be provided in the file reading function. Links are usually drawn as some kind of line. Figure 9.21 shows a couple of examples

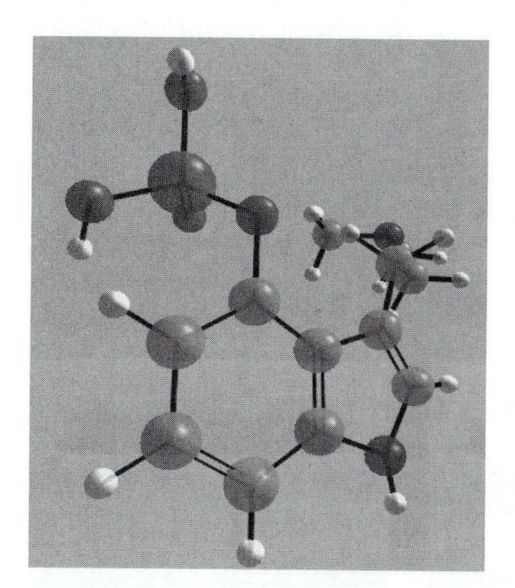

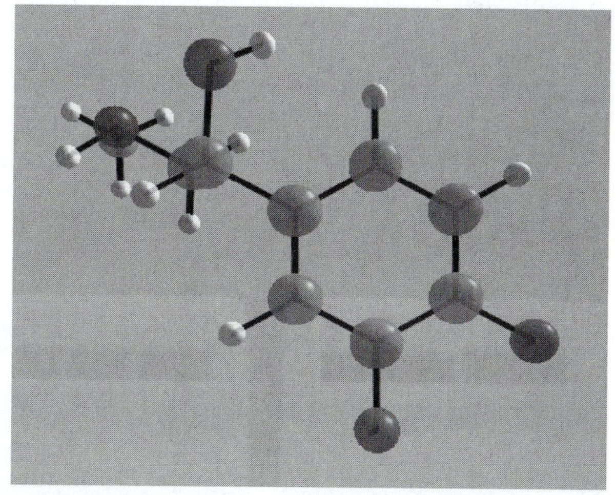

Figure 9.21 Displays from psilocybin.mol (*left*) and adrenaline.pdb (*right*). See the figure in the color insert.

of simple molecules from the molecule reader provided with the resources for the book and a display function written by the author. The colors of the atoms are included in the source code resources and can be changed if you want. Note that the atoms are drawn with a fairly small alpha value so that the bonds and other atoms can be seen; note also that in the example from the .mol file, double bonds are shown where they are known (these are included in the .mol file format but not in the .pdb format). It is straightforward to include various kinds of interaction with these displays, as described in Chapter 7.

In more advanced work, it is common to use displays that include additional information, such as displaying the molecule as a smoothed surface around the spheres with colorings that illustrate the electrostatic forces at various places on the surface. This kind of display helps to demonstrate how molecular docking would happen by showing the surface shapes as well as the forces that would guide the docking process.

A Scientific Instrument

Besides visualizing scientific processes and structures, we can think of visualizing how scientific instruments work. One of these is the gas chromatograph, which measures the quantity of different kinds of molecules in a substance as the substance is vaporized and the vapor is driven down a tube. As the molecules pass down the tube, the more massive molecules move more slowly than lighter molecules, and as molecules pass a detector at the end of the tube, the numbers of molecules are recorded in a strip chart. This process produces different profiles for different substances and so is used to identify the components of a material.

In order to understand how the gas chromatograph works, a simulation written by a student, Mike Dibley, shows a group of molecules starting at the left-hand end of a tube. The molecules are of three different types, indicated by single-point objects of different colors. They all start at the same time at the left-hand end of the tube, and they move down the tube at different (and slightly randomized) rates depending on the weights of the molecules. When they pass the right-hand end of the tube, they are counted and the number of particles that reach the end at any time is recorded in a strip chart that is presented at the bottom of the screen. Thus the presentation includes both a 3D component, the tube that contains the particles, and a 2D component, the strip chart. Three stages of the simulation are shown in Figure 9.22. In this figure, the image at left shows the simulation when the first set of particles (red) are leaving the tube; the center image when the second set (green) is leaving; and the third when the last set of particles (black) is leaving. Notice that the slower particles have more time for their motion to be randomized and so are more scattered at the end of the tube; the strip chart reflects this by being broader and less higher with the later readings.

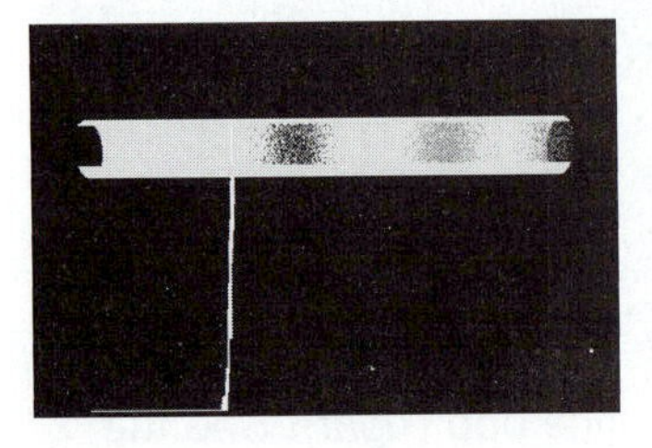
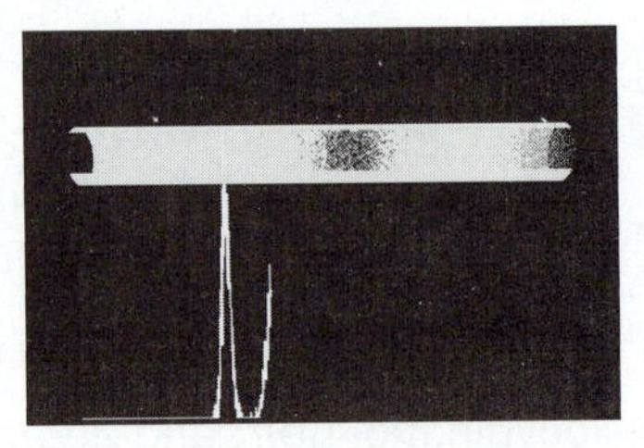
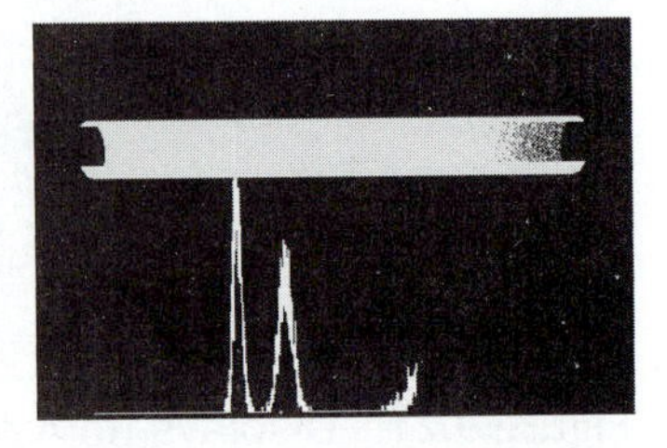

Figure 9.22 Three stages in the gas chromatograph simulation. Courtesy of Mike Dibley.

Monte Carlo Modeling Process

We have seen some simulations based on random motions of molecules, but there are many more kinds of simulations in the sciences. A number of interesting simulations are built by generating large numbers of random occurrences and looking at the long-term behavior of the system. Because random numbers have long been associated with gambling, and because the casino at Monte Carlo is known worldwide, such processes are often called *Monte Carlo processes*. Monte Carlo processes can range from very simple to quite complex. We have already seen the gas law and diffusion simulations that are an example, but there are many other kinds of Monte Carlo simulations.

Let's look at a very simple example: estimating volumes. Consider a 2D region that is bounded by a complex curve that makes it very difficult to measure the area of the region. If you can determine quickly whether a given point is inside or outside the region, then a Monte Carlo approximation of the region's area could be made by generating a large number of random points in a known (probably rectangular) area containing the region. You can then count the total number of points generated and the number that lie within the region and calculate the ratio of these numbers. This ratio, times the known area of the region, is an estimate of the region's area. A very similar process operating in 3D space lets you estimate volumes, and this is illustrated in Figure 9.23. Here we have 10,000 points in a cube that is two units on a side and contains a number of randomly placed (and overlapping) spheres. The goal is to estimate the volume of the region inside one or more spheres. In the figure, the spheres are rendered in yellow with a low blending value, points lying inside the spheres are colored red, and points lying outside are colored green.

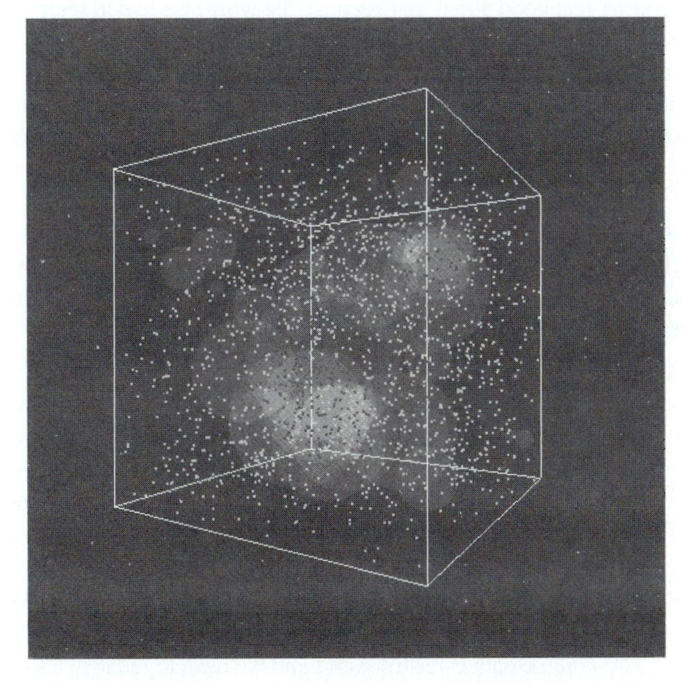

Figure 9.23 A Monte Carlo estimate of a complex volume. See the figure in the color insert.

This gives you a general idea of the relative proportions of the points. This Monte Carlo process is not oriented toward getting an exact solution, but it gives you a reasonable estimate that could be very helpful if you were trying to explain the concept and process to a lay person (or, perhaps, a judge or jury). It is presented by a program, included with the book's resources, that lets the user rotate the volume in arbitrary directions to see how the highlighted points lie in the volume.

More complex and interesting kinds of Monte Carlo simulations can be found in other areas. For example, in queuing theory and transportation engineering, arrivals are defined to be random with certain parameters (mean, standard deviation, probability distribution) and service or transit times are also defined randomly. The system being studied is driven by these events, and the nature of the system is then studied through its reaction to these simulations. Visualizations of the system help the user understand how the system behaves over time and whether the system will eventually reach an equilibrium. For example, in a traffic simulation, you could use colors to display the traffic flow in the transportation system, with high-attention colors used to show problem areas and low-attention colors used to show smooth flow. If you set these colors to be red and green, respectively, this could be a nice link to a traffic study! These simulations are probably beyond the scope of this discussion, but they provide interesting examples of the power of a simple technique. And, of course, statistical simulations can be made more and more complex, so that war games, business simulations, and large-scale economic simulations are all in some sense Monte Carlo models.

4D Graphing

Dimensions present an interesting question in computer graphics. We now say that graphics is natively 3D and we feel good about that because the world we live in seems 3D to us. Of course, we're talking about computer graphics APIs and standard presentations. But graphics and visualization really aren't only three-dimensional; they really have many more dimensions that we don't often think about. We think about driving as a 2D process because our streets are laid out in a 2D pattern, but when we drive we also have velocity vectors, fuel levels, temperatures, and a number of other quantities besides our position that we must constantly balance while driving. When we start doing computer graphics to solve problems, we often find that our ability to define and view things in three-dimensions is too limited to express everything we need. So as we discussed when we talked about higher dimensions in modeling and in visual communication, we also find that we must create models having more than three dimensions for many of our problems. We will discuss some examples of these techniques in the science context here.

Volume Data

Volume data is data that has one dimension, one real value, at each point in a volume. We saw that we could extend the notion of a two-dimensional scalar field to think of this of as a scalar field on a three-dimensional space. We will think of scalar volume data as coming from a real-valued function of three variables. Because we cannot really see the four-dimensional space this gives us, we will take two approaches to the display of the field: We will find implicit surfaces in the volume, or we will display the values in a cross-section of the field.

The implicit surfaces we will consider are surfaces made up of the points where the function has a constant value; these are also called *isosurfaces* of the function in the volume. Finding them can be hard, because volume data is unstructured and we have to identify a structure in the data to create displays of these surfaces. This is done in several ways, but the most common is the *marching cubes* process, where the volume is divided into a number of small cubes and each cube is analyzed to see whether the surface passes through the cube. If it does, then a detailed analysis of the cube is done to see for which edges the volume crosses the edge; this allows us to see what kind of structure the surface would have on that cube, and the surface within the cube is displayed. For a good reference on this process, see [WA2]; the detailed programming it needs is beyond the scope of our discussion, but the graphics itself is simply straightforward polygon drawing.

Instead of the marching cube process for implicit surfaces, we will simply identify those cubes that contain a point whose value defines the surface, and we will display those cubes in a way that implies the surface. The simplest kind of display for this is simply to place a small lighted sphere in the cube, as shown in the left-hand image of Figure 9.24. This gives us the general shape

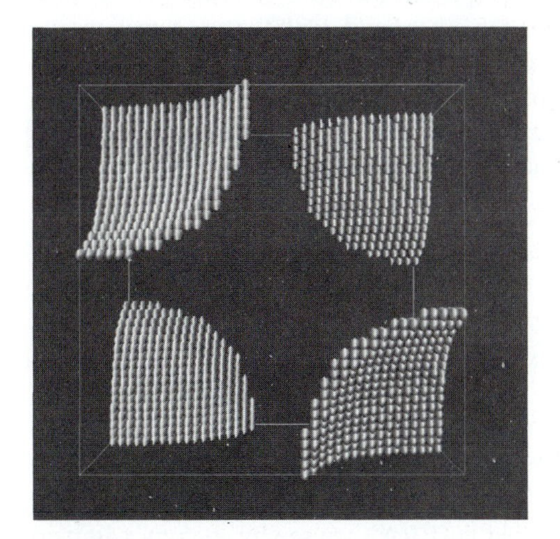

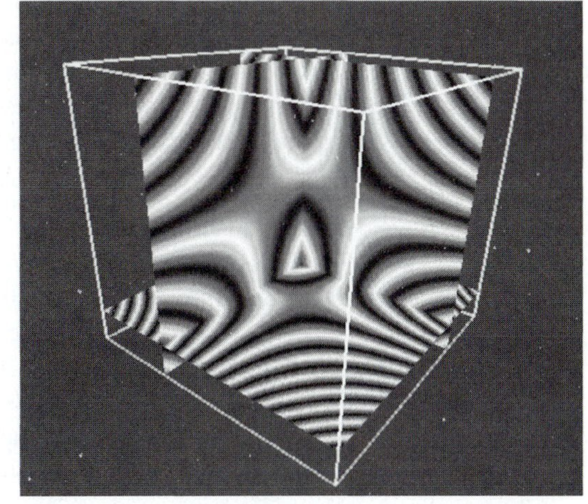

Figure 9.24 An implicit surface approximation that uses spheres to locate a surface (*left*) and cross-sections of a function's values (*right*). See the figure in the color insert.

of the surface (though with very little detail) with a modest amount of shape from the way the spheres are lighted and is a way to start the analysis of the scalar field in the cube. The display is smoother if the number of cubes—and thus spheres—is increased, but this slows down computation, so you need to trade off smoothness for speed. This kind of display can lead to an exploration of the space by using an interactive technique to change the value that defines the surface. By sweeping the value through a range that covers the volume being studied, we can see the overall shape of the scalar field and get a better understanding of the problem that generates the field.

Another way to understand the nature of the scalar field in the space is to slice the space and see the scalar field as a 2D display on the slicing plane, or cross-section of the volume, as shown in the right-hand image of Figure 9.24. This lets us think of the function as a set of 2D scalar fields and to use whatever kind of mesh and pseudocolor we want on the slicing planes in order to see the field, so in some ways this is a more precise approach to the problem than the implicit surface. It also gives us an understanding of the relationships of the values throughout the space, in contrast to the shape of the level values, so it complements the implicit surface process well. Again, the display can be interactive so that the user can explore the space at his or her leisure, and sweeping the planes through the space can give us an overall idea of the nature of the scalar field.

Both of the images in Figure 9.24 come from interactive programs that allow the user to sweep the space by increasing or decreasing the value defining the implicit surface, or by moving any of the three cutting planes parallel to the axes in order to see the entire shape of the scalar field. These interactive explorations are critical to understanding the data fully and are quite easy to implement; sample code is included in the resources for the book. See Chapter 7 on interaction for more details and examples.

The two images in this figure actually represent the same function: the three-variable hyperbolic function $f(x, y, z) = xyz$. The implicit surface describes the geometry of the subspace where $f(x, y, z)$ is constant, which is a set of hyperbolas in four of the eight octants of 3D space. The four octants are those in which the signs of the variables are right for the sign of the constant, and the shape in each octant is determined by the constant. On the other hand, with the cross-sections we are looking for ways to use a color ramp to represent the values in the 2D spaces that slice through a cube in 3D space. We have used a rapidly repeating color ramp to show the contours of the scalar field, but a single color ramp across all the values in the cube would have been better if we had wanted to be able to read off actual values from the image. Chapter 5 has more details on this topic.

Vector Fields

We can extend the notion of function from scalar fields to include vector-valued functions on 2D or 3D space. These functions are called *vector fields,* and they arise in a number of situations. Not all vector fields are necessarily presented as vectors; any function whose range lies in 2D or 3D space (or higher dimension) can have its values considered as vectors, even if that might not be the intent when the function is initially defined. For example, a complex function of a complex variable has a 2D domain and a 2D range because of the identification of complex numbers as pairs of real numbers. Let's consider some examples of functions that give rise to vector fields.

We've already mentioned complex functions of a complex variable, so let's start there. If we consider the function $w(z) = z^3 + 12z + 2$ described in [BRA], we see by analogy with real functions that as a cubic function, we should expect to have three "roots" of the equation—that is, three points where $w(z) = 0$. In the left-hand image of Figure 9.25, we take advantage of the

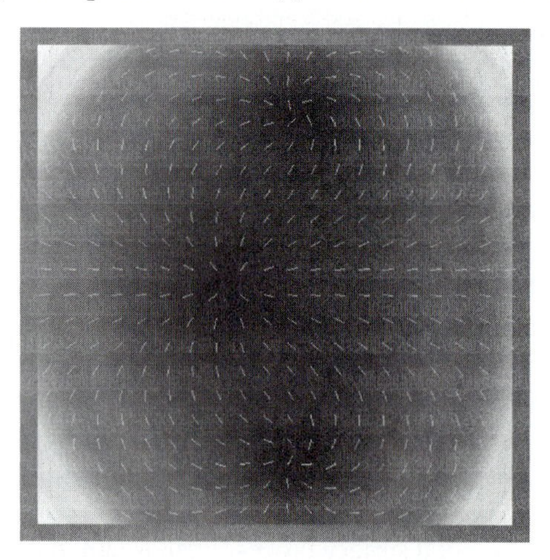

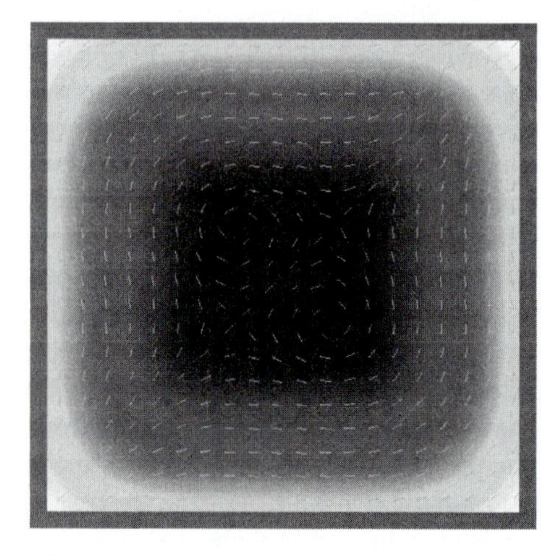

Figure 9.25 Two visualizations with a constant theme: a complex-valued function of a complex variable (*left*) and the direction vectors for a differential equation (*right*). See the figure in the color insert.

alternate representation of complex numbers as $re^{i\theta}$ to display the graph of the equation by showing the magnitude of r as a color (in the uniform luminance color ramp defined in Chapter 5) and by showing the direction θ as a direction vector. The three blackest points in the image correspond to the three roots we would expect, and we see that we have a smooth vector field across the space. This shows that the complex function is smooth (indeed, infinitely differentiable) across its domain. With this display we can get a better understanding of the nature of the function and its behavior.

Another kind of problem generates differential equations that describe the nature of the change in a value across a domain, and we can use a very similar kind of display for it. For example, if we think of fluid flowing across a plane, we see that the fluid has a velocity at each point of the plane; the plane is a 2D domain and the velocity at each point is a 2D value. The point is a position, and the fluid flow at that point can be seen as a 2D derivative of the position; to solve the differential equation is to determine the function that describes the fluid flow. In the right-hand image of Figure 9.25, we see the pair of differential equations $\partial x/\partial y = y^2 - 1$ and $\partial y/\partial x = x^2 - 1$ [BUC] that describe such a situation, and the image shows the nature of the flow: low speed (magnitude of the velocity) at the four points $(\pm 1, \pm 1)$, vortex flow at the two of these points where the signs differ, and source/sink flow at the two points whose signs are the same. As above, we use the color value to indicate the speed of the flow and the vector to show the direction.

Graphing in Higher Dimensions

We can go further and consider functions on 3D space whose values are also in 3D space. This can challenge our imaginations because we are actually working in six dimensions, but such problems are everywhere around us. So standard examples include electromagnetic and electrostatic forces, gravitational fields, and fluid flow functions, especially when we consider fluid flow to include air as well as more usual fluids. Because we are considering examples of graphical thinking in such problems we must be careful about taking on examples that are too challenging computationally, so we will not pursue the fluid flow problems; instead we will consider electromagnetic and electrostatic forces.

Consider electromagnetic fields generated by a current moving in a wire. These fields have vector values at every point in space and so are represented by a function from 3D space to 3D space, and it takes six dimensions to represent this function fully. The function can be shown by sampling the domain on a regular grid and showing the field vector at each point, as shown in Figure 9.26, taken from a student project by Jordan Maynard, whose code is included with the materials for the book. This kind of vector field is commonly used for many higher-dimensional problems, but it can be difficult for a novice user to understand.

Another approach to a problem with 3D values in 3D space is to use a set of vectors to see the effects of the function at a selected set of points in the domain. We used vectors to visualize a 2D problem in 2D space earlier, so this is a familiar technique. For the 3D problem let's return to Coulomb's law of electrostatic force that we saw in scalar form earlier in this chapter. This law states that the electrostatic force between two particles is given by $F = kQq/r^2$, where q and Q are the charges on the two particles, r is the distance between the particles, and k is an appropriate constant. This force is directed along a vector from one particle to the other, and the value computed above may be taken as the length of that vector.

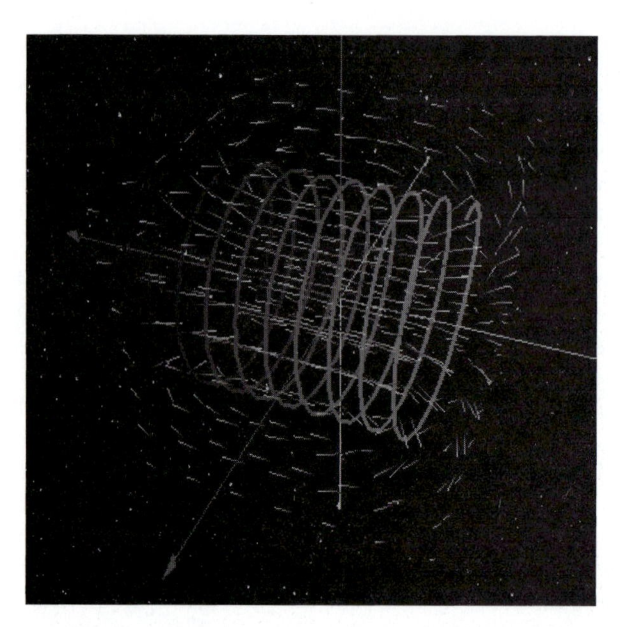

Figure 9.26 A magnetic field around a coil with a moving current. See the figure in the color insert. Courtesy of Jordan Maynard.

If we look at this in three dimensions, we start with a unit positive charge Q for one particle at an arbitrary point in space and calculate the force between that particle and a set of particles with charges q_i in space. We get the equation

$$F(x,y,z) = \sum_i kq_iV_i/r_i(x,y,z)^2$$

for the force vector $F(x,y,z)$ at any point in 3D space, where V_i is the vector from the arbitrary point to the ith particle and $r_i(x,y,z)$ is the distance between the point (x,y,z) and the ith particle. In Figure 9.27, we show the way this force is distributed in 3D space containing a set of particles with charges of +2 (green) or −1 (red) and a collection of cyan-to-orange vectors in that space. In addition to the static force vectors, the figure also shows the path traced by a particle of charge +1 that is released at zero velocity at a point within the space. You can trace the paths of single particles or multiple particles in this way, and it can be useful to track a set of points that are initially very close so that you can see the shape of the forces on a region rather than a single point.

You can choose many different kinds of displays in these higher-dimensional cases. For example, just above we saw an example of displays of a 2D vector field on a 2D domain that separated magnitude and direction; we could examine a 3D vector field on a 3D domain by using 2D slices of the domain and on each slice displaying the 3D direction and the 1D magnitude of each vector. There is a lot of opportunity to be creative here.

An example of a field that has a long history of multidimensional data is statistics. Here it is rare for a data set to have as few as three variables, so there has been a lot of work with adding extra information to 3D scatterplots and other displays to try to see more information and with allowing user exploration of data by selecting which variables or combinations of variables to use. One of the key features of this kind of display is that the viewer needs to be able to move around

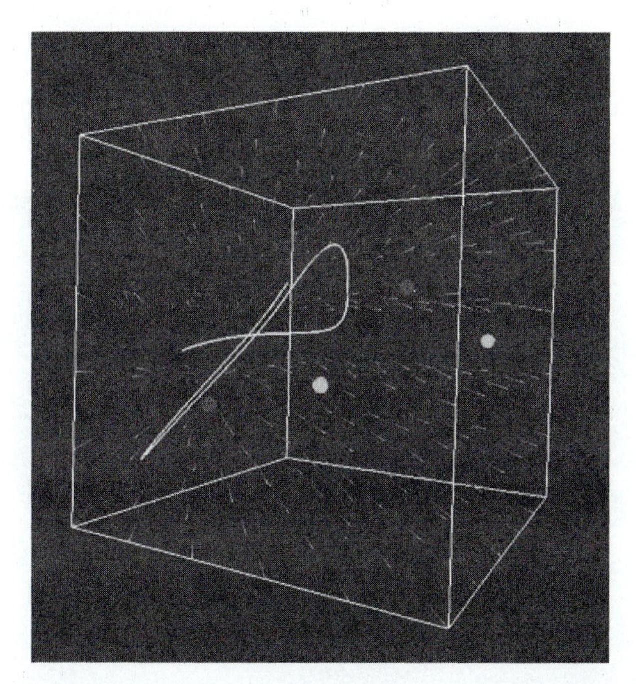

Figure 9.27 The 3D Coulomb's law simulation with a 3D vector field. See the figure in the color insert.

the space to see the scatterplots from various angles in order to see any structure that might be present. Our emphasis on interactive graphics will help you find ways to let your viewer choose and manipulate the data and space where viewing happens.

Data-Driven Graphics

When we develop graphics based on data rather than on theory or principles, we have some new issues to consider. Data are not always accurate, are not always directly comparable within a data set (for example, data may be gathered at different times of day or under different conditions), may not be collected at points that make it easy to graph, or may not measure exactly what we would like to present. But these are issues for the science to deal with; for visualization, we need to deal with the data as it is given to us as we develop images that represent the data. One of the results of our visualization, however, might be to understand that there are flawed data that needs to be addressed.

The visual representation of the data in data-driven displays need not be sophisticated. For data with a few dimensions, a scatterplot can be an excellent way to visualize the data. Patterns may be efficiently unveiled by simply drawing each data point as a geometric object in the space determined by one, two, or three numeric variables of the data, while its size, shape, color, and texture can be determined by other variables of the data. We must realize that it is very important to make both the position and the representation of the data communicate the meaning of the data to the viewer. As we discussed when we thought about representing different types of data, nominal data can be represented by shape or texture, ordinal data by discrete colors, and interval data by position and continuous color.

A very classical kind of graphing is the line graph. This is very familiar, but we usually see it in its two-dimensional form, plotting one independent variable against one dependent variable. With the tools of computer graphics, this kind of graph can present much more information. Figure 9.28 illustrates the effectiveness of this kind of graph in plotting the state of the economy (the moving line)

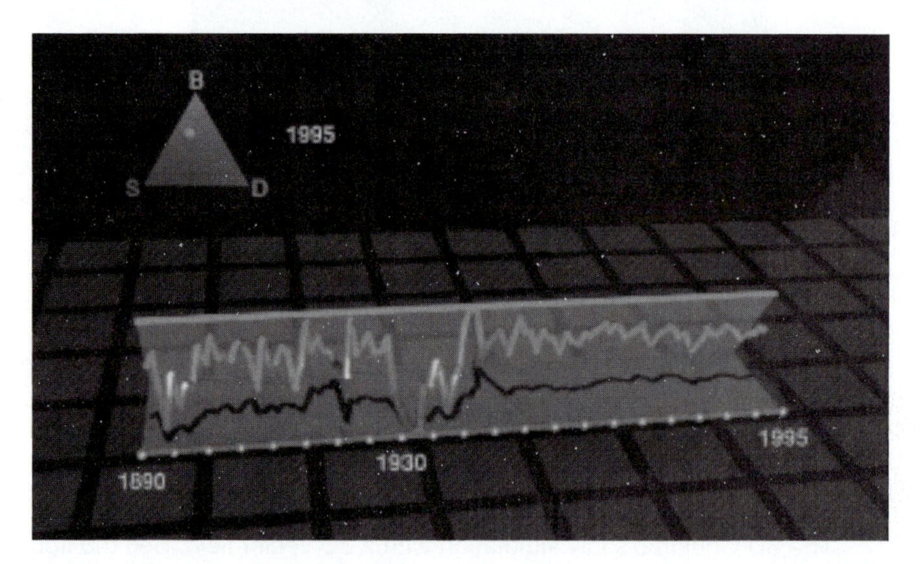

Figure 9.28 The economic data presentation. See the figure in the color insert. Courtesy of the San Diego Supercomputer Center.

against time (the red axis with years marked). The description of this graph by its author, Bernard Pailthorpe [PAI], is "The state of the economy in any given year is plotted according to its similarity to three characteristics, or archetypes: boom (green), stagflation (blue), and depression (red). The colors help indicate the position relative to the three axes; the shadow line represents the economy's position relative to the depression and stagflation axes." Notice the triangle in the upper left of the figure; it shows you the exact data for each year and acts as a legend for the meaning of the colors.

If the data are known to come from a pattern with two independent variables and one dependent variable, we can present it as an approximation of a surface. If we have no idea whether the data comes from a continuous process, we may be able to present only a scatterplot that suggests a surface. If we believe the data to be continuous, we can create a more traditional surface to represent the data. We may not have a regular distribution of the independent variables on a two-dimensional domain, so we may need to subdivide the domain into triangles and create a flat-shaded polygonal surface to represent the actual data distribution. On the other hand, we may have reason to know that the data come from sampling a known class of surfaces, so we may want to use the data to define the parameters of the actual surface (for example, using a technique such as least-squares parameter fitting) and then draw the computed surface along with the data, shown as points. There is again a lot of opportunity for creative thinking about how you communicate this kind of information to the viewer.

As we noted when we talked about visual communication, it is important that you tell the truth with your images. It is very easy to create smooth surfaces that contain or fit your data and that seem to say that the actual data varies smoothly, but sometimes the data actually contains jumps and other artifacts that simply aren't smooth, and making a smooth surface implies a continuity of values that is not true. Simplicity and truth are more important than attracting the eye with an attractive but incorrectly defined image.

Code Examples

We did not want to slow down the general discussion of the kinds of modeling and visualizations above by discussing implementation and code questions, but we believe it is useful to discuss implementation and show some sample code that was used to implement the models for the figures and examples in this chapter. The discussion and the code will focus not on the graphics itself but on the modeling and the processing to support that modeling. When we want to point out something about the graphics, we may use generic API calls from which it should be relatively easy to infer the equivalent OpenGL calls. However, sometimes we may need to use the exact OpenGL to make the point we want you to see in the discussion.

Diffusion

Our model for diffusion processes is the heat flow example we first saw at the beginning of the book. Diffusion processes work on a grid, so the first task is to define an appropriate grid on some 2D rectangle. This grid needs to be mirrored by an array of real numbers that will hold the values of the variable on the grid, so we could use declarations such as the following to implement these:

```
#define LENGTH 50
#define WIDTH 30
float grid[LENGTH][WIDTH]
```

Once these are defined and the grid is initialized, we can think about the code that defines how the value diffuses in the material. When we do, however, we realize that we will have to use the values in the grid to calculate new values in the grid, which would instantly lead to errors if we used the newly calculated values instead of the original values. So we will need to use a mirror of the grid to hold the values we are creating, and this must also be defined

```
float mirror[LENGTH][WIDTH]
```

In general, the processing on the grids will look like calculating weighted sums. While the actual working of heat depends on the difference between the temperatures of each pair of adjacent cells, we will calculate the heat based on only the heat in the cells; the working of the processing for the two cells will take care of the difference. The general calculation for the heat at a given cell in a grid is

$$heatKept + \sum_{adjCells} heatAvail(cell)^{*} weight$$

where *heatKept* is the heat retained in a cell, *heatAvail* is the heat available (not retained) in a cell to be shared with adjacent cells, and *weight* depends on the diffusion model we are using. Conservation of energy requires that the heat retained and heat available be the same as the original heat in the cell, and the heat we do not keep is assumed to be shared equally between the four nearest cells. We assume that for any material, a fixed proportion of the heat in a cell is kept by that cell. The weight is the proportion of the heat given up that is shared with neighboring cells, or .25 if we are sharing the heat equally with all four neighbors. Thus the equation of heat for any cell says that the heat in a cell is the proportion kept by the cell, plus the amounts from the adjacent cells. This value is calculated and stored in the mirror array, and at the end of the computation, the mirror array is copied back into the grid array. In terms of rough coding, this is given by

```
#define KEPT prop // the proportion of the property kept in a cell
#define SHARED .25*(1.-KEPT) // the proportion shared with others
for i
    for j {
        mirror[i][j]  = KEPT*grid[i][j];
        mirror[i][j] += SHARED*grid[i+1][j];
        mirror[i][j] += SHARED*grid[i][j+1];
        mirror[i][j] += SHARED*grid[i-1][j];
        mirror[i][j] += SHARED*grid[i1][j-1];
    }
for i
    for j
        grid[i][j] = mirror[i][j]
```

An alternate, and more flexible, approach would be to define a 3×3 filter (or a different size if you wish), or array of non-negative values that sums to 1.0, and multiply the `grid[ ][ ]` cells around the `[i][j]` position by the values of that filter. This was the approach of the code for the heat flow example. You then calculate the heat in the cell with a small double loop as follows:

```
 float filter[3][3] = {{.05,.1,.05},{.1,.4,.1},{.05,.1,.05}};
 mirror[m][n] = 0.0;
   for i
       for j
           mirror[m][n] += filter[i][j]*grid[m+i-1][n+j-1];
```

The shift in the coordinates in the last line is because the filter has indices i and j with values 0 to 2, while the grid indices must run from $m - 1$ to $m + 1$ and from $n - 1$ to $n + 1$. This is a classical process for many kinds of computation and should be in your bag of tricks, if it isn't already.

Of course, this does not take into account the behavior at boundary cells, where you will have to change your logic so that heat is not received from the out-of-bounds cells (and where less heat is given away, presumably). This is left as a logic exercise for the reader. Finally, in case any of the grid points are being held at a fixed temperature (for example, if a hot source or cold sink is present), these points need to have their fixed values restored after the diffusion operation to maintain their fixed values.

Above we had assumed that the material is homogeneous, but if it is not we must take into account the different coefficients of heat of the materials. If two adjacent grid cells are different, we must use an appropriate coefficient for the heat transfer. This needs to be symmetric—the value used by one cell with its neighbor must be the same, no matter which individual cell has the higher or lower heat coefficient—and we suggest that the minimum of the two coefficients would be used. This change could be applied to both homogeneous and nonhomogeneous materials without affecting the homogeneous case, of course, so we recommend it to the reader. This would require the addition of an array of these proportions of retained heat (which we can view as values between 0 and 1), so we need to have declared

```
float prop[LENGTH][WIDTH]
```

and instead of working with a fixed value of `prop` in the computations, we would use the minimum of the proportions of the original point and the new point. So for the first of the adjacent points we might define the shared heat by

```
.25*(1-min(prop[i][j],prop[i+1][j])*grid[i+1][j];
```

But in any case, your computation must conserve the overall heat in the model.

When we finish each step of the simulation, we need to display the results of the computation. We can use a generic cube as the basis for a cell and can scale, translate, and color the cube to represent each grid cell as we draw it. If we have a cube of unit side that is defined in the first octant and has a vertex at the origin, and define the grid to be in the first quadrant and starting at the origin, we can create a grid with each grid element having length L by

```
 for i
   for j
      set color to colorRamp(grid[i][j]);
      set translation(i*L, j*L);
      set scaling(L, L, L*grid[i][j]);
      draw cube;
```

If you have defined a reasonable view and set things such as depth buffering so the sequence in which you draw the grid cells doesn't matter, this should give you a good image. You can then enhance the display by adding the user interaction you might want so that the viewer can examine the situation flexibly. You should probably use the idle event to keep updating the image as the simulation runs, because you will probably want the viewer to see how the temperatures change over time as the heat diffuses through the space.

Function Graphing

This graphing process was introduced briefly above. It is based on building a uniform grid in the domain space, somewhat like the grid used for the diffusion simulation above, and calculating the function values at each point in the grid. We then use the grid coordinates and the function value as the vertices for the quads and triangles that make up the surface. We give a little more detailed description of this process in the following code. This is such a fundamental operation that you must be absolutely sure you understand all the details. This code is written assuming that all the setup and declarations have been done, and using some meta-API statements to draw triangles and the like:

```
//   assume a function calcValue(x,y) that calculates a function for each
//   point in the domain; assume further that we are using the same number
//   of points in each direction in the domain, and save the calculated
//   values in a 2D real array values. Assume functions calcXValue and
```

```
//  calcYValue that compute the x- and y- values of the grid points in the
//  domain. Note that we use one more point in each of the directions than
//  the number of rectangular regions we will create.

for (i=0; i<=NPTS; i++)
    for (j=0; j<=NPTS; j++) {
        x = calcXValue(i); // calculate i-th point in x-direction
        y = calcYValue(j); // calculate j-th point in y-direction
        values[i][j] = calcValue(x,y);
    }
//  with the values now calculated, create the surface mesh by creating
//  two triangles for each rectangular piece of the grid. We work in
//  the counterclockwise direction based on looking down on the grid.
for (i=0; i<NPTS; i++)
    for (j=0; j<NPTS; j++) {
    //  calculate the x and y coordinates of the corners of the rectangle
        x0 = calcXValue(i);
        x1 = calcXValue(i+1);
        y0 = calcYValue(j);
        y1 = calcYValue(j+1);
        // draw first triangle
        beginTriangle();
            // calculate properties of the triangle such as its normal;
            // this is omitted here
            setPoint(x0,y0,values[i][j]);
            setPoint(x1,y0,values[i+1][j]);
            setPoint(x1,y1,values[i+1][j+1]);
        endTriangle();
        beginTriangle();
            // calculate properties of the triangle
            setPoint(x0,y0,values[i][j]);
            setPoint(x1,y1,values[i+1][j+1]);
            setPoint(x0,y1,values[i][j+1]);
        endTriangle();
        }
```

Parametric Curves and Surfaces

For parametric curves, it is straightforward to divide the domain, which will be an interval [a,b] on the real line, by defining a number of points along it at which to evaluate the parametric functions. If you use the parametric equation $ta+(1-t)b$ to define the interval, the domain consists of all points for all values of t in [0,1]. To divide the interval into N equal pieces (it's probably easiest to use equal subdivisions, but it's not required), for values of i between 0 and N, the ith point is simply $f(ta+(1-t)b)$ where $t = i/N$ and we assume that the function f produces points instead of single values. The curve is then drawn by simply drawing line segments between points determined in this way. The process will be the same if the parametric curve lies in either 2D or 3D space. If you want to use unequal subdivisions along the domain interval, the computation of each point in the interval will be different, but drawing the curve by connecting the function values for each point will be the same.

Code to carry this out is quite straightforward, assuming that we have parametric functions *fx*(t), *fy*(t), and *fz*(t) that determine the x, y, and z coordinates of a point on the curve:

```
#define START 0.0
#define END 1.0    // could be any values to start, end interval
beginLines();
  x = fx(START); y = fy(START); z = fz(START);
  setPoint(x,y);
  for i from 1 to N, inclusive
    t = START*(N-i)/N + END*i/N;
    x = fx(t); y = fy(t); z = fz(t);
    setPoint(x,y,z);
endLines();
```

For parametric surfaces the process is a little more complicated, but not much. The domain of the curve will be a rectangle in u,v-space, with $a = u = b$ and $c = v = d$, and we probably want equal spacing on each of the intervals for the surface. The spacing may be different for each variable, of course, as we saw in the discussion of the triangular cross-section for the torus. We then compute the points (u_i,v_j) in the rectangle that represent the ith point in the u direction and the jth point in the v direction, compute the surface coordinates from these points with the parametric equation, and create quads (or pairs of triangles) from the four points in the surface that are computed from the four vertices of a grid unit in the domain. These triangles or quads may be drawn with any of the properties available from your graphics API. The code for this operation is very much like the code for the triangles in the function surface above, except that all three coordinates of every point on the surface are determined by the function, not just the single coordinate.

Limit Processes

Limit processes are something of a contradiction for computation, because computation is always finite while limit processes are essentially infinite. However, once we realize that converging limit processes will become arbitrarily close to their final state in a finite amount of time, we see that we can compute very good approximations to the final results and show these approximations to the viewer.

For the idea of a limit curve or surface, then, we simply take the process out to as many steps as we wish, realizing that more steps give us more accuracy but can take more time and perhaps require more memory. Once we have done the finite calculations, we simply have a function value (or perhaps several functions for a parametric operation), and we can use that result in making our image as above.

Scalar Fields

A 1D or 2D scalar field is essentially the same as a function graph or surface except that possibly there is another way to determine the scalar value at each point of the domain. Thus displaying a 1D or 2D scalar field is covered by our discussions above. 3D scalar fields are covered under 4D graphing below.

Representation of Objects and Behaviors

Sometimes, as in the previous example of the gas chromatograph, computer graphics is used in the sciences to display objects and their behavior in simulations. The examples we have given in this chapter are fairly simple graphically, and our main challenge is to handle the details of the display. When we present the simulations of gas behavior, for example, we choose to display a relatively small number of points in the volume because we don't want to clutter it up and lose track of the fact that individual particles are being tracked in the simulation. We generate the random motion of the particles by adding a small random number to each of the coordinates of each particle in the system, and we show the behavior of a typical particle by tracking it through time by maintaining a trail of its positions.

Probably the most interesting feature of these two simulations is noting and responding when a particle hits the boundary of a region. In the gas law example we have the particle bounce back into the volume; in the semipermeable membrane example we do the same for the walls, but for the membrane boundary we generate a random number and let that determine whether the particle penetrates or bounces off the membrane. In this sense the simulation has some Monte Carlo aspects.

We are able to detect a situation when a particle would leave the volume under its normal random motion. In that case, we register a hit by incrementing an accumulator, which is simple. We also calculate the point to which the particle would bounce by generating a pure reflection, assuming that particles obey the usual "bounce" rules. The reflection is straightforward and is described in Chapter 4. You may want to look at that chapter or at the geometry of a perfect rebound before you read the brief code that follows, which assumes that the region is bounded by walls that are a constant distance from the origin and that the array `p[i][j]` contains each of the coordinates of each point, in turn:

```
typedef GLfloat point3 [3];
point3 p [NPTS];
if (p[i][j] > bound)
      {p[i][j] = 2.0*bound - p[i][j]; bounce++;}
if (p[i][j] <-bound)
      {p[i][j] = 2.0*(-bound) - p[i][j]; bounce++;}
```

Drawing the trails for an individual point is straightforward; we simply maintain an array of the last *N* positions the particle has had, and every time we generate a new display we move each position back one in the array, put the new position at the front, and draw a set of connected line segments between points in the array. This is very helpful in showing the behavior of an individual point and helps make the simulation display much more understandable to the viewer.

Finally, we gather the various statistics (how many particles are in each part of the space, how many hit the walls of the volume in the last time step, etc.) and display them either with the graphics system or by printing them to the text console or to a file. Printing to the console slows the simulation, so you may want to trigger it by an event; we usually use a simple keystroke.

Molecular Display

Our displays of molecules are driven from arrays created by the functions that read the .pdb and .mol file formats, as noted earlier. These arrays are of the form

```
typedef struct atomdata {
    float x, y, z;
    char name[5];
    int colindex;
    } atomdata;
atomdata atoms[AMAX];
    typedef struct bonddata {
    int first, second, bondtype;
    } bonddata;
bonddata bonds[BMAX];
```

Here the program will find this field colindex in the atom structure by looking up the name in the lookup tables described below. This index will then be used to find the color and size that match the appropriate atom for the display.

The functions read the files and store the results in arrays of these structures, as indicated in the declarations. At the next step, the arrays are traversed and additional data is retrieved from lookup tables that hold information such as size and color for individual atoms. The first stage is to look up the atom by its name and return the index of the atom in the tables. After this information is stored in the array, the images are created when the program traverses the arrays and draws the molecules with size and color from the tables with this index; a partial sample of these lookup tables follows, with the first table being used to match the name and the others used to get the color and size associated with the atoms.

```
char atomNames[ATSIZE][4] = { // lookup name to get index
    {"H "},  // Hydrogen
    {"He "}, // Helium
    {"Li "}, // Lithium
    {"Be "}, // Beryllium
    {"B "},  // Boron
    {"C "},  // Carbon
    {"N "},  // Nitrogen
    {"O "},  // Oxygen
    ...
    };

float atomColors[ATSIZE][4] = { // colors are arbitrary
    {1.0, 1.0, 1.0, 0.8}, // Hydrogen
    {1.0, 1.0, 1.0, 0.8}, // Helium
    {1.0, 1.0, 1.0, 0.8}, // Lithium
    {1.0, 1.0, 1.0, 0.8}, // Beryllium
    {1.0, 1.0, 1.0, 0.8}, // Boron
    {0.0, 1.0, 0.0, 0.8}, // Carbon
    {0.0, 0.0, 1.0, 0.8}, // Nitrogen
    {1.0, 0.0, 0.0, 0.8}, // Oxygen
    ...
    };
```

```
float atomSizes[ATSIZE] = { // sizes are in angstroms
     {0.37},  // Hydrogen
     {0.50},  // Helium
     {1.52},  // Lithium
     {1.11},  // Beryllium
     {0.88},  // Boron
     {0.77},  // Carbon
     {0.70},  // Nitrogen
     {0.66},  // Oxygen
     ...
     };
```

Once you have each atom's position and the properties from looking up its name, it is pretty straightforward to draw the atoms, and the bonds are simply drawn as wide lines between the locations of the atoms whose index is defined for each bond. In case a double bond is indicated, two lines can be drawn, each slightly offset from the atom center. Because your viewer will want to look at the structure of the molecule from all viewpoints, you will probably want to allow arbitrary rotations. It can also be useful to let the viewer choose alternate descriptions of the atoms, such as more or less transparency, a larger size (to get the space-filling kind of representation), or other options by letting the user select options through a control panel, menu, or keystroke.

Monte Carlo Modeling

We use the term *Monte Carlo* rather loosely to refer to any kind of process based on random values. In that sense, the gas law and semipermeable membrane simulations were Monte Carlo models, and that was noted when we talked about them. Sometimes, however, Monte Carlo simulations are taken to mean simulations wherein events are directly set up by random numbers, and the volume estimation example we give is of this type where the events are placing individual points. It is no trick to figure out whether a given point `(p.x, p.y, p.z)` lies within a radius `sphere.r` of a point `(sphere.x, sphere.y, sphere.x)`, so generating a large number of randomly placed points and counting those that lie within the sphere's radius from the sphere's center for one or more spheres is not difficult.

Other kinds of Monte Carlo modeling might be a little more challenging. A famous experiment estimates the value of π, for example; called the Bouffon needle experiment, it consists of drawing a number of parallel lines on a sheet of paper exactly as far apart as the length of a needle, and then dropping a large number of these needles on the sheet. The proportion of needles that cross one of the lines is an approximation of $2/\pi$. Simulating this with computer graphics is straightforward: You generate one random point as one end of the needle, generate a random angle (number between 0 and 2π) and place a second point one unit distant from the first along that angle, and compare the values of the endpoints to see whether the "needle" crossed the "line." And, of course, you can draw the needles and the lines as you go so that the viewer can watch the experiment proceed.

4D Graphing

A 3D scalar field can be a difficult object to display because it has a 3D domain and a 1D range, so we are working at the 4D level. We have seen two different ways of presenting this kind of information, and of course there are always many more besides these. The code for these two approaches is fairly straightforward. For the isosurface approach, we divide the volume into a number of cubes and evaluate the scalar field function at each of the eight vertices of the cube. If the function passes through the fixed value that defines the isosurface, we will see that some of the vertices' values will be larger than the fixed value and some smaller, so that cube contains part of the surface and we present that by drawing a sphere at that location. We identify whether the function passes through the fixed value by a simple trick: subtracting that value from the value of the function at each vertex and then multiplying these differences. If the sign of that product is negative for any of the edges, the fixed value is crossed. So the code consists of a triple-nested loop with a number of tests, and if the test is positive, we draw a sphere, as follows:

```
for (i=0; i<XSIZE; i++)
    for (j=0; j<YSIZE; j++)
        for  (k=0; k<ZSIZE; k++) {
             x = XX(i); x1 = XX(i+1);
             y = YY(j); y1 = YY(j+1);
             z = ZZ(k); z1 = ZZ(k+1);
             p1 = f(x, y, z);  p2 = f(x, y,z1);
             p3 = f(x1, y,z1); p4 = f(x1, y, z);
             p5 = f(x,y1, z);  p6 = f(x,y1,z1);
             p7 = f(x1,y1,z1); p8 - f(x1,y1, z);
        if (((p1-C)*(p2-C)<0.0)      || ((p2-C)*(p3-C)<0.0) ||
            ((p3-C)*(p4-C)<0.0)      || ((p1-C)*(p4-C)<0.0) ||
            ((p1-C)*(p5-C)<0.0)      || ((p2-C)*(p6-C)<0.0) ||
            ((p3-C)*(p7-C)<0.0)      || ((p4-C)*(p8-C)<0.0) ||
            ((p5-C)*(p6-C)<0.0)      || ((p6-C)*(p7-C)<0.0) ||
            ((p7-C)*(p8-C)<0.0)      || ((p5-C)*(p8-C)<0.0))  {
               drawSphere (x, y, z, rad);
    }
}
```

For the cutting plane display, we simply define a plane in the space and treat the plane as the domain of a function, iterating across it in the same way we would for a 2D scalar field. That is, we use the 3D grid in the space to put a 2D mesh on the two remaining variables, calculate the value of the function at the midpoint of each rectangle in the mesh, and draw the mesh rectangles in 3D space in a color determined by the function value. Because this is so much like the 2D scalar field technique, we will not include code for it here. It is straightforward to use interaction techniques to change the coordinate axis across which we are cutting or to change the value on the axis that defines the cut. It would be possible, though a little more complicated, to define other planes to cut the space, but we have not done that.

When we consider 2D vector fields on a 2D domain, we again have four dimensions and we have a choice of how we want to organize our display. We obviously cannot display an actual 2D vector at each point of the domain, because that would make it impossible to find any single vector. However, if we know that the vector field is relatively smooth, we can display the result vector at selected points in the domain, giving the viewer an image with vectors of various lengths and directions. When we do this, we ask the viewer to understand the results and integrate an image that could have (or could not have, depending on the vector field) overlapping result vectors. This is not a bad approach, but it would take some care to make it work. It does have a potential flaw, though, because if there is a gap between your selected points and you miss an essential feature of the vector field, such as a sudden singularity, then the image is misleading.

We have chosen to take a slightly different approach and show the magnitude and direction of the result vectors separately. The magnitude is simply a scalar field, and we have seen how we can display a scalar field with techniques such as pseudocolor ramps. With the magnitude shown separately, we can display the vector's direction with a unit vector in that direction, which shows how the directions are distributed across the domain. Together these two parts give a fairly simple and informative display. However, we should understand that a user might not immediately understand what the display is saying because the color and direction are not related concepts. Some sort of user familiarity (or education) is probably needed.

The vectors in our display are drawn at the middle point in each 10×10 block of the domain grid after the scalar field itself has been drawn. We draw each of the vectors in cyan because it contrasts with the black-to-yellow colors of the scalar field. The following code assumes that we have calculated the boundary x and y values for each of the grid rectangles in the domain and have calculated the vector value for the midpoint of the rectangle. This code sketches only how we could create the vector portion displays shown for this section.

```
if ((i%10==5) && (j%10==5)) { // middle of every 10th cell
x = 0.5*(XX(i)+XX(i+1));
y = 0.5*(YY(j)+YY(j+1));
len = 5.0 * sqrt(vector[0]*vector[0]+vector[1]*vector[1]);
glBegin(GL_LINES);
   glColor4f(0.0, 1.0, 1.0, 1.0);
   glVertex3f(x,y,EPSILON); //so the vector is above the surface
   glVertex3f(x+vector[0]/len, y+vector[1]/len, EPSILON);
glEnd();
}
```

Higher-Dimensional Graphing

When we get into any higher-dimensional graphics, we must be very careful to keep the image clear and focused, because it can easily become confused if we try to include too much information. With more information in the other dimensions that we cannot readily show, you need to plan what data to present and how to present it, or you need to plan how you can give your viewer these choices.

When we talk about vector fields on domains where the dimension is larger than two, we have the problems described above about showing too much information, as well as problems caused by projections hiding some of the information. It is extremely important to let the viewer move around the data (or, alternately, to let the viewer move the data volume around) so that it can be seen from all angles. It is also important to show only selected information so that the viewer can get the sense of the data instead of having to see everything at once. Instead of trying to show all the vectors for each point in the 3D grid space, we can use a technique similar to the vector display above and show only a relatively few vectors in the space. By placing these in a regular pattern in the space, we can show the shape of the vector field rather than the complete field. Code for this is straightforward, as in this pseudocode:

```
set the color for the vectors
for i
   for j
     for k {
       calculate coordinates of the i,j,k-th point
       calculate vector from magnetic field function for point
       begin lines
         set the point
         set the offset from that point by the vector
       end lines
     }
```

We will not try to pursue more choices in higher-dimensional graphing here, because there are simply too many to deal with. Instead, keep your eyes open for good examples of high-dimensional graphing in the sciences by reading sources such as *Science* or *Scientific American*, both of which are known for the quality of their visuals—only some of which are computer generated. As we saw in the earlier discussions on visual communication, there are ways to use color, shape, and other clues to indicate higher-dimensional information. Some of these work better for nominal data (e.g., shapes), and some for ordinal data (e.g., colors), but considerable creativity can be called for when you need to go very far in this direction.

Summary

In this chapter you saw techniques for modeling and presenting scientific problems, ranging from surface graphing to tracing the motion of a particle in a force field. This should give you a good set of examples to extend the way you can think about scientific problem solving with computer graphics, and indeed to think about graphical problem solving in general. The ultimate goal of this book is to help you learn to use computer graphics to extend your problem-solving skills, and this chapter plays a particularly key role in moving toward that goal.

Questions

1. In many problems in modeling scientific phenomena, we find continuous operations such as derivatives or integrals. However, in many cases we do not have simple equations to represent these operations and must use discrete versions of the operations. Unless we are able to use complex numerical techniques, we must often use simple difference equations to model these operations, but these can introduce errors. Describe some errors that can be caused by using difference equations, and describe ways to reduce such errors.
2. In Chapter 5, we focused quite a bit on the creation and use of color ramps in giving a visual expression of numeric data. Are there any additional issues in the color ramps you might want to use for scientific data graphing? Are there any scientific phenomena that have expressions in colors that could help you choose a color ramp?
3. Get an issue of *Science* or *Scientific American* and look through it carefully to identify all the articles that include high-quality images. Pick at least one and write a short paper on the kind of modeling, graphics techniques, and visual communication it uses to create its images. Create an approximation of one of the images using your graphics API and the tools you have learned so far.

Exercises

1. Find an example of a function of two continuous variables that comes from a problem in the sciences and create a surface representation of that function.
2. Find a parametric surface representation from a source such as the one given for Boy's Surface in the chapter and create an image of that surface.
3. Find an example of forces acting within a space, such as gravitational or electrostatic forces, and create a representation of the trajectories of objects that move in the space based on these forces. Use simple piecewise linear trajectories with very small time steps, if you don't have a good numerical integrator available.
4. Find a height field image and create a surface based on the heights you are able to interpret by the grayscale values from the image.
5. The diffusion model described in the heat transfer example or the disease spread model is quite common in a number of areas of science. For example, there is a model for population growth in a region in which population diffuses outward from the completion of freeways in the region. Find a diffusion-based problem and model it, showing the growth modeled by the diffusion.
6. For the heat diffusion program, consider each cell as a point and create a surface that represents the temperatures in the bar. (To do this, create x and y values for the cell index and let z be the temperature in the cell. Let the color of the vertex be the color of the cell.) Use smooth shading for the triangles or quads you produce. Does the surface image represent a better or worse model for the temperature in the cell?
7. Using relatively simple standard .pdb or .mol molecular descriptions and the functions from the book's resources to read in the molecular data, create representations of the molecules, and allow the user to manipulate them with simple controls.
8. Find an example of a function of three continuous variables that comes from a problem in the sciences and create a volume representation of that function.
9. Implement the Bouffon needle experiment by generating a number of unit-length line segments and drawing them in a window that also includes a set of parallel lines, one unit apart. Count the number of line segments that cross a line and calculate the proportion of all the needles that do so. Is this ratio a good estimate of $2/\pi$? How can you tell? Does the estimate get better if you generate more needles?

Experiments

1. Modify the heat diffusion example so that instead of having a constant temperature at fixed points, the temperature at those points changes over time. Can you create a varying temperature in this model that will drive heat through the space in repeating waves?
2. Modify the heat diffusion example of the chapter to make the diffusion process more interesting. To begin, make the heat transfer asymmetric (directional) by changing the diffusion filter to allow heat to transfer to diagonally adjacent squares as well as directly adjacent squares. Then change the diffusion filter so that heat transfers more easily on one diagonal than in any other direction. (This could model a material that is fibrous, for example, and that transfers heat along the fibers more than between them.) Run the program to see how heat moves in that case.

3. In the discussion of the (4,3)-torus, we suggested that you might be able to make other surfaces of interest in a similar way. One of these interesting surfaces is the Möbius band, a simple plane rectangle whose ends are joined in opposite directions. Using the (4,3)-torus template, create a Möbius band.
4. In the discussion of volume data we showed both an implicit surface and cross-sections as ways to understand the nature of the information in the volume. See if you can find another way to represent this information and ask yourself if this gives you a better understanding of the volume.
5. In the section on function graphing we discussed a particular function that was everywhere smooth (had continuous derivatives of any degree). Graph a function that has a discontinuity of some sort and examine the nature of the surface that is produced. Can you find a way to deal with the discontinuity that does not look as though the surface is continuous?
6. A good source of problems in the sciences comes from forces acting on objects. These can be modeled by choosing initial positions and velocities for the objects and then using the classic equation $f = m*a$ to calculate the accelerations at a given time and then updating the velocities with the acceleration and the positions with the velocities. Do this for the *n-body problem,* the problem of determining the behavior of a system of n objects, each of which has a gravitational attraction for each other object based on the classic gravitation equations. See if your results are realistic, or if they suffer because of their being based on difference equations instead of on differential equations.

Projects

1. Simulate the behavior of a set of mobile charged particles on the surface of an insulating sphere to find the lowest energy state of the system. Assume that all the particles have an equal charge so that the actual charges factor out of the system. You may use any approach you like, but the following $O(N^2)$ algorithm is a place to start:
   a. Assign N points randomly on the surface of a unit sphere.
   b. Plot the points on the sphere surface, using a semitransparent or wireframe sphere. If you use a large number of points, you may not even need to display the sphere.
   c. For each point,
      - Compute a vector from each point to each of the other points.
      - Weight each of these vectors by the inverse square of its length (Coulomb's law).
      - Add the weighted vectors to get the force vector at the point.
   d. Normalize the system by dividing all the force vectors by the magnitude of the largest.
   e. Take the force vector for each point and subtract its radial component (the unit radius vector dotted with the force vector) to get the force vector tangent to the sphere. You may want to scale all these vectors by a small constant (you might try .05) to make the movement of the points easier to see.
   f. For each point, add the vector to the position of the point and divide the new point's coordinates by the distance from the point to the center to restore the point to the surface of the sphere.

   Repeat steps b–f until the points have converged to whatever accuracy you want. At convergence, all of the "force" is radially outward, so the points do not move. This algorithm will always converge to an optimal solution. The solution is coordinate system–independent; any simultaneous rotation of all the points about the center of the sphere is equally valid.

If you want to experiment with this problem, allow the points to have varying charges (but all of the same sign) and adapt the second point in step c to account for that.

2. Use the "fractal forgery" method to create landscapes, using all the tools you now have at your disposal. For example, create a landscape with a very small variation and texture map an aerial photograph of farmland onto it, or create a landscape with extreme variation and use colors that model the Grand Canyon in Arizona. This is a good place to let your creativity come out!
3. (Examine a scientific problem of your choice) Find a problem in the sciences that interests you and develop a question about that problem that should be explained or understood. Create a model for the problem that examines this problem and write up the problem and why this model is a good representation of it. Write code to implement the model in OpenGL or another graphics API to create an image that communicates information about the problem and write up how the image does so and how it provides an understanding of the problem.

10

Rendering and the Rendering Pipeline

This chapter describes how a polygon-based graphics system implements image rendering based on the geometry and appearance information discussed in the earlier chapters of the book. We introduced the geometry pipeline at the beginning of the book, and the rendering pipeline picks up the geometry produced by the geometry pipeline and produces the actual image specified by your graphics program. This involves computation of appearance information at each vertex produced by the geometry computation, decomposition of each geometric object into fragments that correspond to scanlines in the output raster, and several computations including color, depth, and texturing that place the fragment on the actual color buffer. We describe some techniques for breaking a line segment into points on separate scanlines that determine the ends of the fragments and discuss both linear and perspective-corrected interpolations of properties on these scanlines. In order to get the most from this chapter, you should understand graphics primitives and the geometry pipeline so you can see how the primitives are handled by the rendering operations the chapter discusses. This chapter is not necessary to do graphics programming, but after finishing this chapter you should understand the processes that graphics systems use to create images, and that should help you create more efficient graphics programs.

Introduction

In earlier chapters you saw the outline of the geometry pipeline, and we described how graphics API operations transform geometry from 3D model coordinates to 2D screen coordinates. With these screen coordinates, it is still necessary to carry out a number of operations to render the actual image you see on your screen or other output device. These operations can be carried out in several ways, depending on the graphics system used, but in general they also have a pipeline structure that we will call the *rendering pipeline* because it creates the rendered image from the output of the geometry pipeline.

We should point out that the rendering pipeline we describe applies to polygon-based graphics systems that render a scene by processing each polygon through operations that develop its appearance as it is rendered. Not all graphics systems work this way. A ray-tracing system will generate a ray (or a set of rays) for each pixel in the display system and will calculate the intersection of the ray with the nearest object in the scene, and it will then calculate the visible appearance of that intersection from properties of the object or from operations based on optical properties of the object. We describe this further in Chapter 14 when we discuss per-pixel operations. The rendering process here is simply the appearance calculation for each pixel of each polygon. Thus ray tracing has no rendering pipeline in the sense we describe in this chapter.

This chapter looks at the rendering pipeline for polygon-based graphics systems in some detail, describing the various operations that must be performed in rendering an image and eventually focusing on the implementation of the pipeline in the OpenGL system.

The Pipeline

When we begin to render an actual scene, we have only a few pieces of information to work with. We have the fundamental structure of the various pieces of the scene (such as triangles, quads, polygons, bitmaps, texture maps, lights, or clipping planes). We have the 2D screen coordinates of each vertex that describes the geometry along with additional information for each point such as the depth of the pixel, the color of the point, the normal at the point, the texture name and texture coordinates for the point, and the like. We also have the basic information that describes the scene, such as whether or not we have enabled depth buffering, smooth shading, lighting, fog, or other operations. The rendering task is to take all of this data, some of which will change from object to object in the scene, and create the image it describes.

This process goes through several stages. In one, the vertex data for each polygon in your scene is interpolated to raster information to define the endpoints of each scanline in each polygon so that the properties of the pixels in the polygon may then be interpolated. In another, the color of each pixel is defined as the scanline is interpolated, using color data, lighting data, or texture data that is applied to the pixels as they are processed. In yet another, the data for each pixel is modified to apply effects such as depth testing, clipping, fog, or color blending. Overall, these processes provide the computations that make high-quality visual representations of the model you have defined with the image properties you have specified.

We have already seen how the computations of the geometry pipeline are applied, as shown in the first parts of Figure 10.1. These are the transformation operations on the vertices of the models that take the vertices from model space to 2D screen space. From screen space the

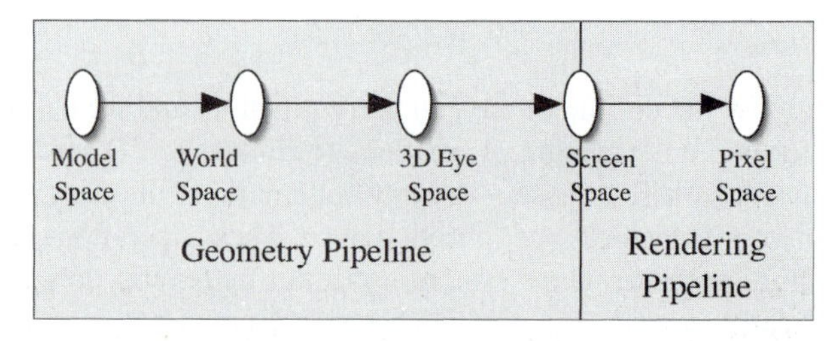

Figure 10.1 The geometry pipeline leading into the rendering pipeline.

process moves to the rendering pipeline, shown in the later part of Figure 10.1, where the vertices in screen space (along with other information held on each vertex) are translated into the eventual pixels that are displayed on the screen or other display. The vertex data structure holds a complete description of the vertex and is much richer than just the 2D X- and Y-coordinates of a screen point. It also holds the depth of the pixel in the original model space, which is needed for accurate polygon interpolation; color information from simple color definition or a lighting computation, needed to determine the color for a polygon or for simple color interpolation; texture coordinates of the vertex, needed for texture mapping; and other information that depends on the graphics API used. For example, you would want to include the vertex normal in world space if you were using Phong shading for your lighting model.

The rendering pipeline starts with the transformed modeling data (the 2D screen vertex and data defined for that vertex). That screen vertex is part of the definition of a polygon, but the pipeline must gather the information on all the polygon's vertices. Once all the vertices of the polygon are present, the polygon can begin to be rendered, which involves defining the properties of each pixel in the polygon and writing the visible pixels to the graphics output buffer.

We will assume that the graphics hardware you will use is scanline-oriented—that is, it creates its image a line at a time as shown in Figure 10.2. A *scanline* is the set of pixels on your display device that have the same value of y; it is one horizontal row on the display. The set of pixels in one polygon on one scanline is called a *fragment*. Rendering the polygon requires that you define all the fragments that make up the polygon and determine the properties of all the pixels in each fragment. On a convex polygon, each scanline will meet the polygon in a single fragment, while on a nonconvex polygon there may be more than one line segment on a scanline. This is one reason why most graphics APIs work only with convex polygons and require you to break up a nonconvex polygon into convex parts before it can be displayed. In OpenGL, for example, any polygon you define with the `GL_POLYGON` statement will be treated as if it were convex. If it is not, the image that is built will likely look quite strange.

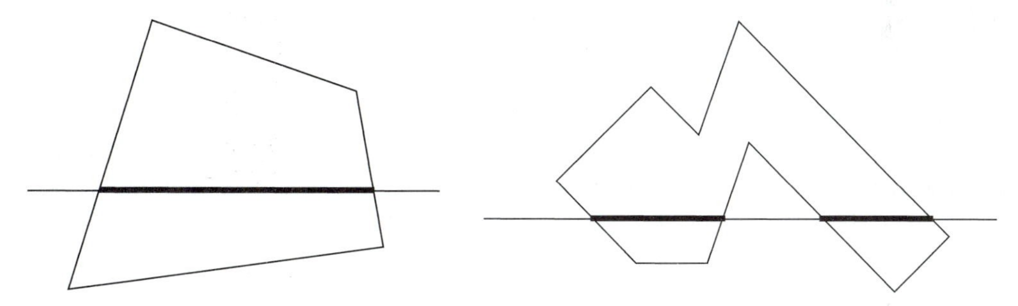

Figure 10.2 A scanline on a convex polygon (*left*) and nonconvex polygon (*right*).

Once you have the vertices of the polygon in screen space from the geometry pipeline, the first step in the rendering pipeline is interpolating the polygon vertices to define the points on the edges of the polygon that are the endpoints of the scanline segments so you can process these segments and write them to the frame buffer. Here you will interpolate the coordinates of the endpoints of each line segment bounding the polygon to calculate the coordinates of the original point on the polygon that would be projected to the screen point that lies on the desired scan line. This same interpolation is also applied to other properties that are defined for each vertex, such as z-depth and texture coordinates. The interpolation can be linear or perspective-corrected, and this choice affects the computations for the depth, texture coordinates, and possibly other data for the interpolated vertices. This was mentioned in Chapter 8 and is discussed in detail in the next section, on rasterization.

When the scanline endpoints (and their data) have been calculated, you can create the pixels on the scanline between the endpoints, filling this fragment. Again, you must interpolate the data between the endpoints, and again, some perspective correction may be applied. Now you have actual colors or actual texture coordinates of each individual pixel, so you can determine the color of each pixel. However, not all pixels are actually written to the output buffer because there may be depth testing or clipping applied to the scene, so several tests must be applied to each pixel before it is finally written. If depth testing is being done, then the pixel will be written only if its depth is less than the depth at this pixel in the depth buffer, and in that case the depth buffer will be modified to show this pixel's depth. If other clipping planes have been enabled, the original coordinates of the pixel will be recalculated and compared with the clipping plane, and the pixel will or will not be written, depending on the result. If there is an alpha channel with the pixel's color and the pixel is visible, color blending will be applied to the pixel color and the color in the image buffer before the pixel is written. If there is a fog effect, then the fog calculations will be done, depending on the pixel depth and the fog parameters, before the pixel is written. This set of pixel-by-pixel operations can take time to execute, so most of it can be enabled or disabled, depending on your needs.

Besides these operations for displaying pixels, you may also need operations to create the texture information to be applied to the pixels. Your texture map may come from a file, a computation, or a saved piece of screen memory, but it must be translated into the internal format needed by your API. This will usually be an array of color values in any of several internal formats. The indices in the array will be the texture coordinates used by your model, and because the texture coordinates for individual pixels may not be integers, there will be some computation to get the appropriate color from the texture map for each pixel.

The Rasterization Process

The rasterization process plays a key role in the rendering pipeline. Polygons come into the process as sets of screen space vertices, and the vertex geometry is translated into scanline-oriented fragments for further detailed processing by per-fragment operations. This process is called doing a *scan conversion* of the polygon. The result is the polygon as a set of pixels that can be displayed by your program. Scan conversion is carried out within the OpenGL system, so it isn't necessary to understand it in order to do basic graphics programming, but certain details of the process will help you understand some of the fundamental concepts of computer graphics. In this section we describe the rasterization process in some detail.

First, let's recall the information that is present at each vertex in the geometry as it gets to the rendering pipeline. We have the 2D screen coordinates of the vertex, calculated by projecting the vertex from 3D eye space to 2D eye space and then mapping that space to screen space. We have the z-value of the vertex in 3D eye space, because we do not need to change it for the screen display but we do need it for some computations; this z-value may have been converted to a more convenient form such as an integer with 0 at the front of the view volume and the largest system integer at the back of the view volume, as OpenGL stores it. We have the color of the vertex, usually as an RGB triple, either given by the model or calculated from the lighting model. We may have the normal at the vertex if we are using smooth shading or other shading computations. And we may have the texture coordinates of the vertex. So each vertex carries a great deal more information than just its screen geometry.

As we go through the rasterization process, we must take the vertices from the geometry and scan-convert the line segments they define—interpolate the endpoints of the segments to get the fragments and find the pixels the polygon will use for each fragment—to determine the total set of pixels to be displayed for the polygon. Scan conversion operates first on each edge of the polygon to get the set of pixels which represents that edge. When this is done for all the edges, you have all the pixels that bound the polygon. For a convex polygon only two edges intersect any one scanline, so you can organize the pixels into a set of pairs, one for each scanline. Each pair then determines a fragment that contains the pixels between them.

There are many algorithms for rasterizing a line segment, and we will begin with the one that is probably the simplest: the DDA (Digital Differential Analyzer) algorithm. This algorithm takes the screen space coordinates of the two endpoints of a line segment and uses the usual line equation and roundoff to calculate the pixel(s) of the line segment on each scanline. Because each pixel's coordinates are integers and a line segment is continuous, we must realize that any rasterization will create only an aliased approximation of the line segment, not the exact segment. The DDA will make this a best approximation by calculating the pixel on each scanline that is the closest to the real-valued point on that scanline.

To begin, let's assume that our line segment has endpoint vertices (X_1, Y_1) and (X_2, Y_2), and let's label $\Delta X = X_2 - X_1$ and $\Delta Y = Y_2 - Y_1$. so the slope of the line segment is $m = \Delta Y/\Delta X$. For convenience, we assume that ΔX and ΔY are both positive; if they aren't, you can adjust the algebraic sign in the code and discussions that follow. Notice also that we can translate our line segment however we want, because once we calculate all the pixels for the line we can translate the entire line segment by translating each pixel of the segment. So we can assume that our line segment lies in the first quadrant.

Now the nature of the pixels for the line segment differs if $\Delta Y > \Delta X$ or $\Delta X > \Delta Y$. If $\Delta Y > \Delta X$, then there will be only one pixel on each scanline, while if $\Delta X > \Delta Y$, there will be only one pixel lying on any vertical line in screen space. We will describe the algorithm for the case $\Delta Y > \Delta X$ and note that this case can be seen as expressing X as a function of Y, but you can easily exchange the X and Y terms in the algorithm to deal with the other case.

For each scanline between Y_1 and Y_2, we want to compute the pixel on the scanline that best represents the exact point on the line segment. We begin with the equation of a line that expresses X as a function of Y:

$$X = X_1 + ((Y - Y_1)/(Y_2 - Y_1)) * (X_2 - X_1)$$

Here the term $(X_2 - X_1)/(Y_2 - Y_1)$ represents the slope of the line in terms of $\Delta X/\Delta Y$ instead of the more usual $\Delta Y/\Delta X$ because we are calculating how much X changes between scanlines in Y. Once we have calculated the value of X for each (integer) scanline Y, we simply round that value of X to the nearest integer to calculate the pixel nearest the actual line. In pseudocode, this becomes the algorithm

```
Input:   two screen points (X1,Y1) and (X2,Y2) with Y2 > Y1 and
         with (Y2-Y1)/(X2-X1) > 1
Output:  set of pixels that represents the line segment between
         these points in screen space
for (int Y = Y1; Y < Y2; Y++) {
    // we do not include Y2 as discussed below
    float P = (Y-Y1)/(Y2-Y1);
    float X0 = X1 + P*(X2-X1);
    int X = round(X0);
    setpixel (X,Y);
}
```

Another scan-conversion process for a line segment is the *Bresenham algorithm*. This depends on managing an error value and deciding what pixels to choose based on that value. For the following discussion we consider only the simplest case, with the line we are interpolating having a slope no larger than 1.0 and having as its left-hand vertex the (0, 0) pixel. These lines are said to lie in the *first octant* of the plane in standard position. For this line, we set only a single pixel for each value of X in screen coordinates, and the question for any other pixel is simply whether the new pixel will be alongside the previous pixel (have the same Y value) or one unit higher than the previous pixel, and this is what the Bresenham algorithm decides.

The algorithm takes as input two vertices, (X_0,Y_0) and (X_1,Y_1), and assumes $X_0 < X_1$ and $Y_0 < Y_1$, and we compute the two total distance terms $DX = (X_1 - X_0)$ and $DY = (Y_1\ Y_0)$. We want to set up a simple way to decide for any value of X whether the value of Y for that X is the same as the value of Y for X–1 or one larger than the value of Y at X–1.

We begin with the first vertex X_0, which is at the lower left of the line segment, and we ask where the pixel will be for X_0+1. In the leftmost part of Figure 10.3 we see the setup for this question, which really asks whether the actual line will have a Y-value larger than $Y_0 + .5$ for $X = X_0 + 1$. This can be rephrased as asking whether $(DY/DX) > 1/2$, or whether $2*DY > DX$. This gives us an initial decision term $P = 2*DY - DX$, along with the decision logic that says that Y increases by one if $P > 0$ and does not increase if $P < 0$.

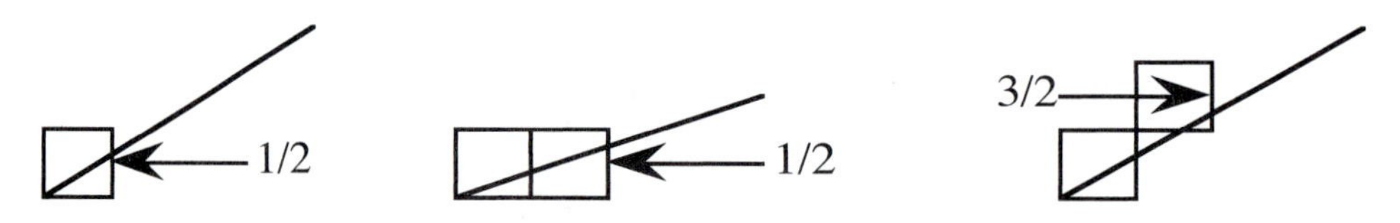

Figure 10.3 Moving from one pixel to the next and considering the decision term.

With the first new vertex of the line settled, let's now look at the second vertex. If we did not change Y for the first vertex, we find ourselves in the situation of the middle part of Figure 10.3. In this case, the decision for the second vertex is whether $2*(DY/DX) > 1/2$. We calculate this out quickly as $4*DY > DX$, or $4*DY - DX > 0$. But this decision term can be written in terms of the previous decision term P as $P + 2*DY > 0$. This case is, in fact, general, and so we name the update term $C_1 = 2*DY$ and write the general operation: If $P < 0$, then we create a new value of the decision variable P by $P = P + C_1$.

But if we do change Y for the first vertex, we find ourselves in the situation of the right-hand part of Figure 10.3. Here the decision for the second vertex is whether $2*(DY/DX) - 1 > 1/2$. We again calculate this and get $2*DY > 3*DX/2$, or $4*DY - 3*DX > 0$. But again using the previous value of the decision term, we see that we now have $P + 2*(DY - DX) > 0$. Again, this case is general and we name the update term $C_2 = 2*(DY - DX)$ and write the general operation: If $P > 0$, then we create a new value of the decision variable by $P = P + C_2$.

The process of defining an initial value of the decision variable, making a decision about the next pixel, and then updating the decision variable depending on the last decision, is then carried out from the first pixel in the line to the last. It is not difficult to take care of the general cases of the algorithm so that we can interpolate lines of any slope in any direction. The full Bresenham algorithm implements the discussion above and looks like this:

```
BresLine(x1, y1, x2, y2)
int x1, y1, x2, y2;
{   int dx, dy, bx, by, xsign, ysign, p, const1, const2;
    int sign;

    bx = x1;
    by = y1;
    dx = (x2 - x1);
    dy = (y2 - y1);
    if (dy == 0)  /* have a horizontal line */
    { xsign = dx / abs(dx);
        setpixel(bx, by, COLOR);
        while(bx != x2)
            { bx += xsign;
              setpixel(bx, by, COLOR);
            }
        }
else if (dx == 0) /* have vertical line */
{ ysign = dy / abs(dy);
    setpixel(bx, by, COLOR);
    while(by != y2)
    { by += ysign;
      setpixel(bx, by, COLOR);
    }
}
else                        /* use Bresenham algorithm */
{ xsign = dx / abs(dx);
    ysign = dy / abs(dy);
    dx = abs(dx);
    dy = abs(dy);
    setpixel(bx, by, COLOR); /* set initial point on line */
    if(dx < dy)      /* line more vertical than horizontal */
    { p = 2 * dx - dy;
      const1 = 2 * dx;
      const2 = 2 * (dx - dy);
      while (by != y2)
```

```
        { by = by + ysign;
          if(p < 0) p = p + const1;
          else
            { p = p + const2;
              bx = bx + xsign;
            }
            setpixel(bx, by, COLOR);
        }
    }
    else                    /* line more horizontal than vertical */
    { p = 2 * dy - dx;
        const2 = 2 * (dy - dx);
        const1 = 2 * dy;
        while (bx != x2)
        { bx = bx + xsign;
          if (p < 0) p = p + const1;
          else
          { p = p + const2;
            by = by + ysign;
          }
          setpixel(bx, by, COLOR);
        }
      }
    }
}
```

This algorithm can readily be adapted to interpolate any property that is not depth dependent by creating a step value for the property and adding it to the property value each time you generate a new pixel. But if you choose the property to be the reciprocal of the depth, this algorithm can interpolate these value so that you can approximate the actual depth of the pixel, and you can use that depth to do perspective-corrected texture interpolation.

The work of these algorithms is illustrated in Figure 10.4, where the left-hand side shows a raster with two endpoints of a line segment as well as the analog segment. Each pixel is assumed to have the coordinates of its lower left corner, the usual convention. The right-hand side then shows how a scan-conversion algorithm populates the scanlines between the endpoints. Note that a roundoff that rounds an X-value upward will give you a pixel to the right of the actual line, which is consistent with the relation between the pixels and the line given by the endpoints.

When you scan-convert a complete polygon, you begin by scan-converting all the line segments that make up its boundaries. The boundary pixels are not written immediately to the frame buffer but are saved in a pixel array so that you can get them later for further processing into the fragments that make up the polygon. A good mental model is a 2D array, with one index being the scanline and the other representing the two pixels you might have for each scanline (recalling that for a convex polygon, each scanline meets the polygon in either zero or two points). You will write each pixel to the appropriate array, and as you do so you will sort each scanline's 2D array by the X-value of the pixels. Each of these 2D arrays, then, represents a fragment—a line segment within the polygon having a constant scanline value—for the polygon.

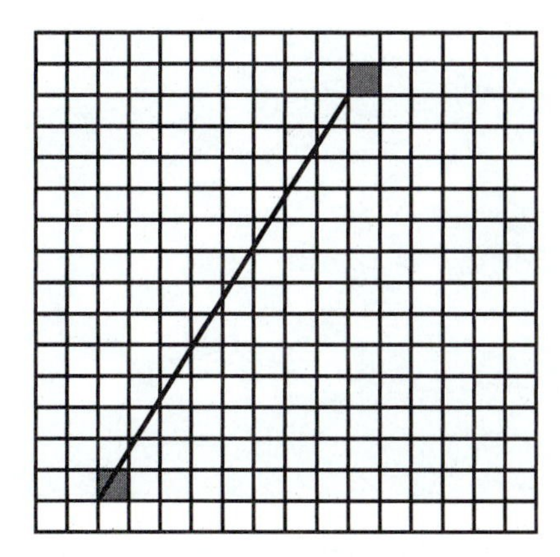

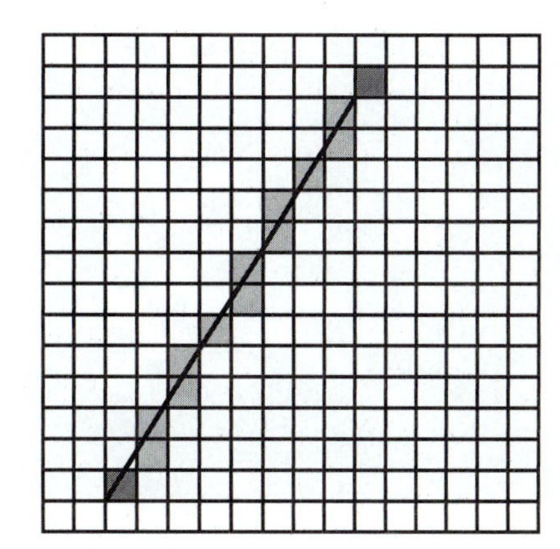

Figure 10.4 Scan-converting an edge.

You need to understand some details of handling these scanline fragments, because the process as we have defined it so far includes some ambiguous points. For example, we have not talked about the "fragment" you would get at the highest or lowest vertex in the polygon, where you would include the same pixel twice, or vertices that are shared between two edges, where we have a similar problem. We have also not talked about the relation between this polygon and others with which it might share an edge; that edge should be part of one, but not both, of the polygons. If we included it in both polygons, then the image we get would depend on the order in which the polygons were drawn, which would be a problem. To address these problems we introduce a couple of conventions to creating fragments. First, we assume that we include a horizontal boundary fragment only if it represents the bottom of the polygon instead of the top. This is easily handled by including every pixel except the topmost pixel for any nonhorizontal boundary segment. Second, we will include any left-hand boundary in a polygon but no right-hand boundary. This is also easily handled by defining the fragment for each scanline to include all pixels from, and including, the left-hand pixel up to, but not including, the right-hand pixel. Finally, we handle all scanlines as fragments, so we do not process any horizontal edge for any polygon.

With the algorithm and conventions above, we can take any convex polygon and produce the set of fragments that present that polygon in the frame buffer. As we interpolate the vertices across scanlines, however, other things must also be interpolated for each pixel, including color, depth, and texture coordinates. Some of these properties, such as color, are independent of the pixel depth, but others, such as texture coordinates and depth itself, are not. Any depth-independent property can be treated simply by linearly interpolating it along each edge to get values for the endpoints of each fragment and then interpolating it along the fragment when that is processed. This interpolation works in exactly the same way the DDA or Bresenham algorithm interpolates geometry. But for depth-dependent properties, we do not have a linear relationship between the property and the pixel in the plane and ordinary linear interpolation can fail, as shown in Figure 10.5, taken from Chapter 8.

As we interpolate linearly across the pixel coordinates in screen space, the actual points on the line segment that correspond to these pixels are not themselves distributed linearly, as we see

Figure 10.5 Texture on a rectangle defined by two triangles without (*left*) and with (*right*) perspective correction for the texture mapping.

in Figure 10.6, where the space between points at the top of the actual line segment is much larger than the space between points at the bottom. We must use a perspective correction to reconstruct the actual point in 3D eye space. Recalling from Chapter 2 that the perspective projection gets the 2D eye space coordinates of a vertex by dividing by the vertex's z-value, we need the actual depth value z to compute the original vertex coordinates. Once we calculate—or estimate, which is all we can do because of the aliased nature of pixel coordinates—the original depth, we can estimate the original vertex coordinates and then use simple geometric principles to estimate the actual texture coordinates.

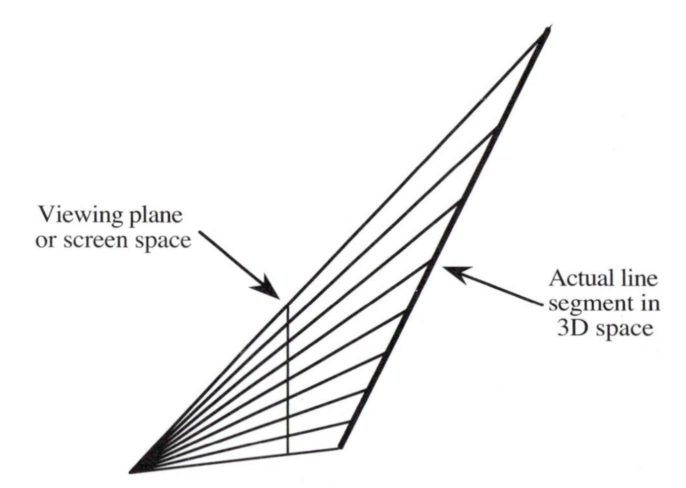

Figure 10.6 The distribution of points on the original edge that correspond to a linear sequence of pixels.

To interpolate the z-values, we must recognize that we are interpolating points that have been transformed by a perspective transformation. If the original point in 3D eye space is (x,y,z) and the point in 2D eye space is (X,Y), the perspective transformation is given by $X = x/z$ and

$Y = y/z$. Now if we are interpolating, say, x_1 and x_2, then we are interpolating x_1/z_1 and x_2/z_2. To do this we must interpolate $1/z_1$ and $1/z_2$ to get our estimate of $1/z$ and thus z for our interpolated point. If we consider the X-coordinate of the point, $x = (1-t)*x_1+t*x_2$, then the corresponding value of z would be $(1-t)/z_1 + t/z_2 = ((1-t)*z_2 + t*z_1)/(z_1*z_2)$. We can then reconstruct the original point in 3D eye space by multiplying the x and y values of the interpolated point by this estimated z value.

The Rendering Pipeline for OpenGL

The OpenGL system is defined in terms of the processing described by the overall system structure shown in Figure 10.7. System input comes from the CPU through the OpenGL functions in the program, and the output is finished pixels in the frame buffer. The input information consists of geometric vertex information, transformation information that goes to the evaluator, and texture information that goes through pixel operations into the texture memory. The details of many of these operations are controlled by system parameters that you set with the `glEnable` function and are retained as state in the system. We will outline the various stages of the system's operations so that you will understand how your geometry specification is turned into the image in the frame buffer. Much of this comes from the OpenGL specifications.

Let us begin with a simple polygon in immediate-mode operation. The model-space vertex geometry that you specify is passed from the CPU and is sent to the polynomial evaluator for the full set of transformations and for the clipping operations. This part is essentially the geometry pipeline. The resulting 2D vertex information is then forwarded to the per-vertex operations. At this point lighting operations are applied and the color data for each vertex is calculated. The result is the transformed vertex (along with the other information on the vertex that has been retained through this process), ready for primitive assembly and rasterization.

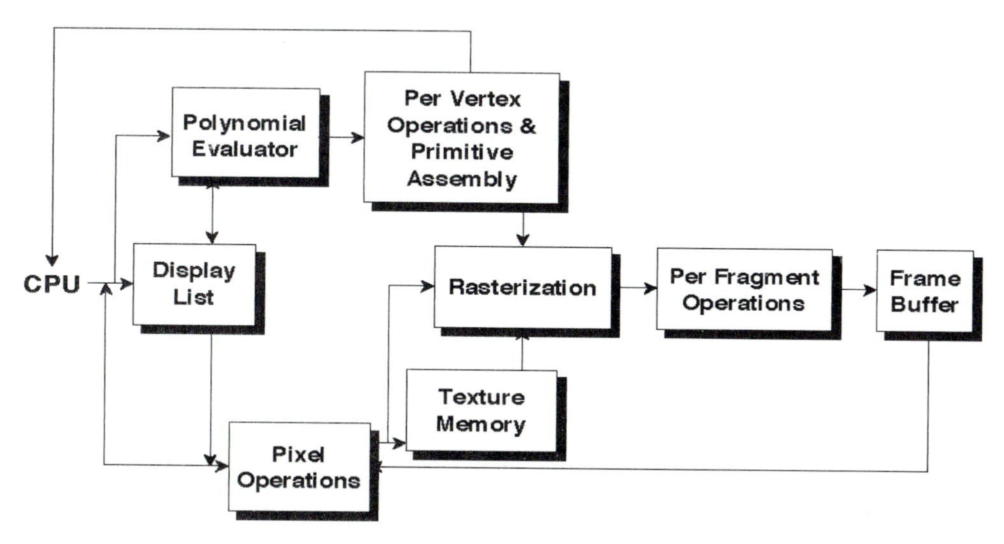

Figure 10.7 The OpenGL system model.

If you are compiling display lists instead of working in immediate mode, then the vertex and transformation operation data are sent to the polygon evaluator, but when the computations are finished the results do not go to the vertex operations for rasterization. Instead, the vertex and operation information goes into display list memory for later use. When the display list is executed, the operations are passed into the rendering process just as if they been passed in immediate mode, except that there is no computational overhead to apply the transformations and there may be some optimization done on the data as it is put into the display list.

At this point the vertices of the completed primitives go into the rasterization stage. This applies the interpolation and scanline processing described previously. Some aspects of this process, such as whether a perspective-corrected interpolation is performed as described in Chapter 8, may be defined at this point. As the visibility and colors of the individual pixels are computed, color or texture data is computed for each, depending on your specifications, and the resulting scanline data is ready to go on the per-fragment operations.

You may not have noticed the feedback line from the per-pixel operations to the CPU, but it is very important. This mechanism supports pick and selection operations that we discussed in Chapter 7. This connection lets the system note that a given pixel is involved in creating a graphics primitive object, and that fact is noted in the selection buffer that is returned to the application.

While we have discussed the actions on vertex points, the OpenGL system includes other operations. For example, the polynomial evaluator is used when we are working with splines and use evaluators based on a set of control points. These evaluators may be used for geometry or for a number of other graphic components, and here is where the polynomial produced by the evaluator is handled and its results are made available to the system for use.

Texture Mapping in the Rendering Pipeline

Texture mapping involves texture memory and other parts of the rendering system. A texture map can be created by reading a file or by applying pixel operations to data from the frame buffer or other sources. This texture map is the source of the texture data for rasterization. The contents of the texture map are transferred into texture memory so they can be used for texture mapping. The arrow from the frame buffer back to the pixel operations in Figure 10.7 tells us that we can take information from the frame buffer and write it into another part of the frame buffer; the arrow from the frame buffer to texture memory indicates that we can even make it into a texture map itself. The details for this are shown in Figure 10.8.

In the figure we see that the contents of texture memory can come from the CPU, where they are translated into array form after being read from a file. Because OpenGL does not know about file formats, you may need to decode data from the usual graphics file formats (see [MUR], for example) to make it useable. And, as we saw in the texture-mapping chapter (Chapter 8), we can also fill the array as a result of computations. However, the texture memory can also be filled by copying contents from the frame buffer with the `glCopyTexImage*D(...)` function or by performing other pixel-level operations. This can let you create interesting textures, even if your version of OpenGL does not support multitexturing.

It is rare for an individual pixel to have a texture coordinate that exactly matches the indices of a texture point. Instead of integer texture coordinates, the pixel will probably have real-valued texture coordinates, and the texture data for the pixel will need to be computed. This can involve choosing the nearest texture point or creating a linear combination of the adjoining points, as described in the texture-mapping chapter (Chapter 8).

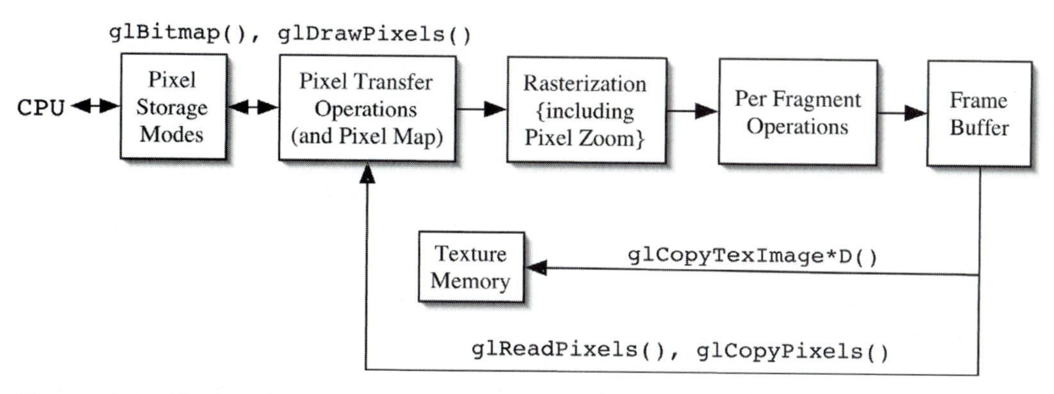

Figure 10.8 Processing for texture maps.

Per-fragment Operations

Much of the power of OpenGL lies in its treatment of the fragments, or small sets of scanline data, that are computed by the rasterization process. The fragment operations follow a subpipeline shown in Figure 10.9. Some of the possible fragment operations fall under the heading of advanced OpenGL programming and we will not cover them in depth. Most of these operations must be enabled (for example, with `glEnable(GL_SCISSOR_TEST)`, `glEnable(GL_STENCIL_TEST)`, or the like), and some require particular capabilities of your graphics system that you may not have. If you are interested in any details that aren't covered adequately here, consult the OpenGL manuals or an advanced tutorial for more information.

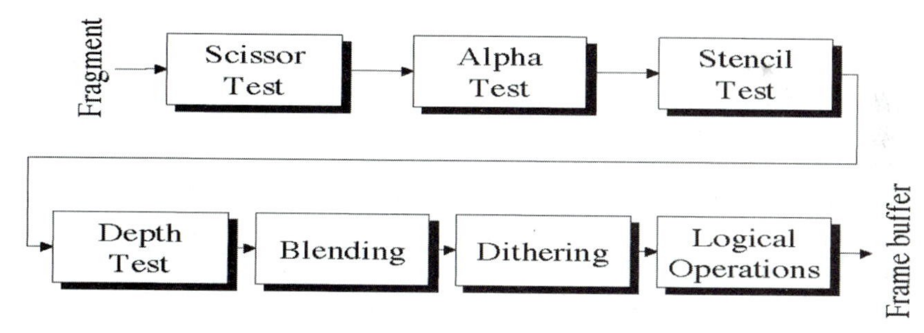

Figure 10.9 Details of fragment processing.

The first fragment operation is a scissor test that lets you apply additional clipping to a rectangular bounding box defined by `glScissor(...)`, and the second operation allows you to use a test against a pixel's alpha value to create a mask for textures, defined by `glAlphaFunc(...)`. The next operation applies a stencil test, which is much like the alpha test except that it creates a mask based on values in a stencil buffer. The stencil operations are based on a stencil mask you can draw to with normal OpenGL operations, and it is used to choose whether to eliminate a pixel from a fragment when it is drawn. The stencil test is based on a comparison of the value in the stencil buffer and a reference value, and each pixel in the fragment is either kept or replaced by a value that you can set. The key functions for stencil testing are `glStencilFunc( ... )` to set the test function, `glStencilMask( ... )` to control writing to the stencil buffer, and `glStencilOp( ... )` to specify the actions for the stencil test.

The next set of operations is more familiar. These operations begin with the depth test that compares the depth of a pixel with the depth of the corresponding point in the depth buffer and accepts or rejects the pixel, updating the depth buffer if the pixel is accepted. Following this is the blending operation, which blends the color of the pixel with the color of the frame buffer as specified by the blending function and as determined by the alpha value of the pixel. This operation also supports fog, because fog is primarily a blending of the pixel color with the fog color (which is calculated from the depth of the pixel). The dithering operation allows you to create the appearance of more colors than your graphics system has by using a combination of nearby pixels of different colors that average out to the desired color. Finally, the logical operations allow you to specify how the pixels in the fragment are combined with pixels in the frame buffer. This series of tests determines whether a fragment will be visible and, if it is, how it will be treated as it moves to determine a pixel in the frame buffer.

OpenGL and Programmable Shaders

In this section we briefly discuss programmable vertex and fragment operations and the idea of a shading language, with the goal of giving you some background on these ideas. Emerging versions of OpenGL, or at least generally accepted extensions, will allow this kind of programmable operations.

In standard OpenGL, when a vertex comes into the rendering pipeline we know much more about it than just its coordinates. We also know its color (whether determined by a lighting model or by simply setting the color), and perhaps its texture coordinate. There is no reason why we could not define much more than this about a vertex, however. We could also store displacement vectors, up to eight multitexture coordinates, and particular transformations. Vertices could even store addresses of programs that could compute shape, color, anisotropic shading by computing lighting-oriented normals instead of geometric normals, or bump maps. Graphics cards are beginning to include a great deal of per-vertex programmability with sixteen or more 4D real vectors per vertex to hold additional data, although each card will have a distinct instruction set that is oriented to its particular architecture.

Besides having a program that can be attached to each vertex, however, we can apply other techniques to per-fragment operations than are available with the fragment processing described above. There are programmable operations in some graphics cards, modeled on the idea of texture-combining operations, that will let you apply additional kinds of operations for processing fragments. The result can be thought of as a programmable rendering pipeline, with three programmable stages: group processing, vertex processing, and fragment processing. Two of these are familiar from the OpenGL rendering pipeline in Figure 10.7, with group processing representing operations on collections of vertices instead of individual vertices for efficiency. This programmable pipeline is shown in Figure 10.10.

These give us a good idea of the developments we should see in advanced versions (or extensions) of OpenGL or other graphics APIs. We can provide a program with each vertex to compute vertex properties such as we described above. For compatibility with a wide range of hardware, the language of such a program can be independent of the particular graphics card, and the graphics API provides a way to either compile or interpret the language into the specific operations needed for the card. It will be interesting to see what this does for advanced programming with graphics APIs.

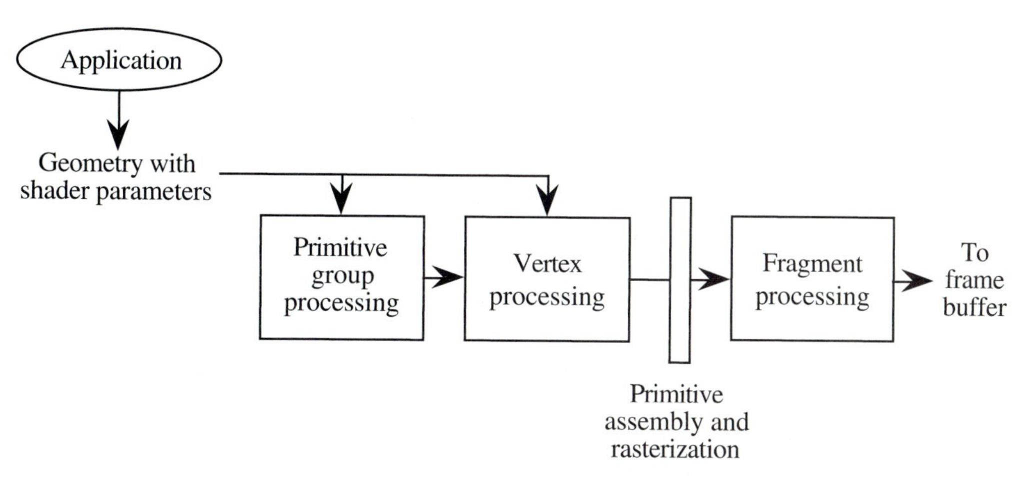

Figure 10.10 Programmable pipeline with three programmable stages.

An Implementation of the Rendering Pipeline in a Graphics Card

The system shown in Figures 10.7 to 10.9 is very general and describes the behavior required to implement OpenGL processes. In practice, the system can be implemented in many ways, and the diagram in Figure 10.11 shows the implementation in a typical fairly simple OpenGL-compatible graphics card.

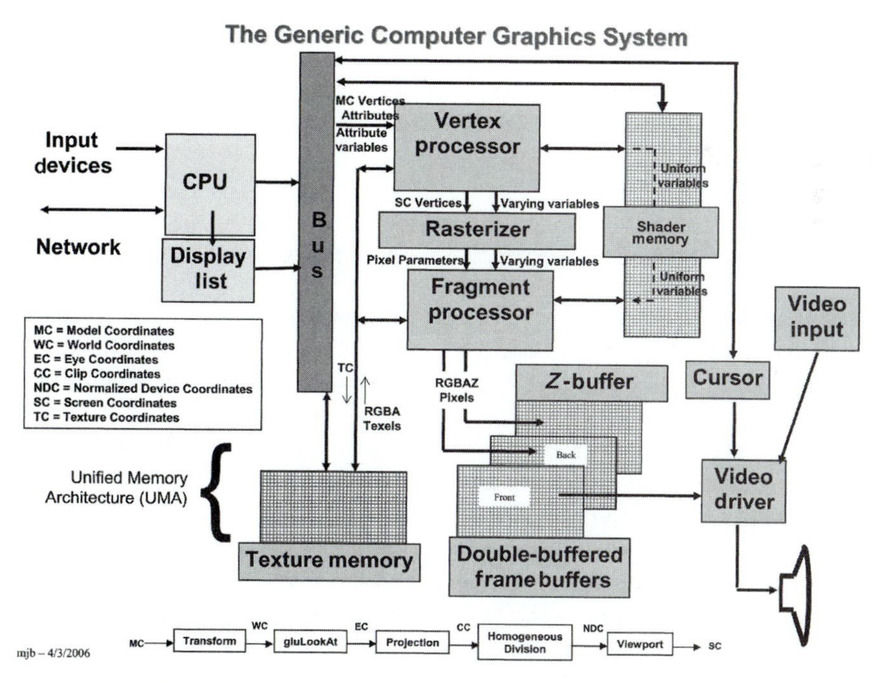

Figure 10.11 An implementation of the OpenGL system in a typical graphics card. Courtesy of Mike Bailey.

The pipeline processor carries out the geometry processing and produces the fully developed 2D screen pixels from the original 3D modeling space vertices as described above. The texture memory is self-describing and holds the texture map after it has been decoded by the CPU. The rasterizer handles both rasterization operations and the per-fragment operations, and the Z-buffer and double-buffered frame buffer hold the input and output data for some of these operations. The cursor is handled separately because it needs to move independently of the frame buffer contents, and the video driver converts both the frame buffer content and the other inputs (cursor, video) to drive the monitor display mechanism. This kind of mapping of API functionality to hardware functionality is one of the reasons that OpenGL has become an important part of current graphics applications—it provides good performance and good price points to the marketplace.

Some 3D Viewing Operations with Graphics Cards

Besides the techniques for creating 3D views presented earlier, there is a technique that involves preparing images so that they can be picked up and displayed by special hardware such as the CrystalEyes glasses from StereoGraphics Corp. This technology takes content from the frame buffer to present images alternately to the left and right eyes so the viewer sees the two images as though they were two views of the same scene. There are a variety of ways that a left-eye image and a right-eye image can be picked up by special display hardware; these include side-by-side images, above-and-below images, and interlaced images. These combinations may require some distortion of the images that will have to be handled by the display hardware, as suggested by the distortions in the images in Figure 10.12, and the video stream may have to be manipulated in other ways to accommodate these approaches. If the left- and right-eye images are to be seen on the same screen, the display hardware must separate the stream into two images that are displayed in synchronization with alternating polarized blanking of one eye, allowing the two eyes to see two distinct images and thus see the stereo pair naturally.

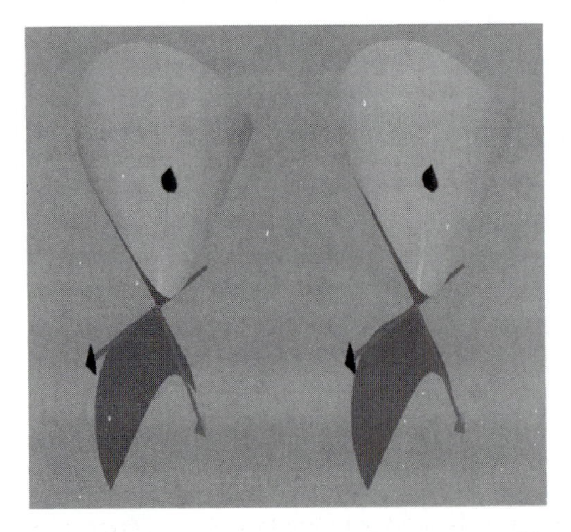

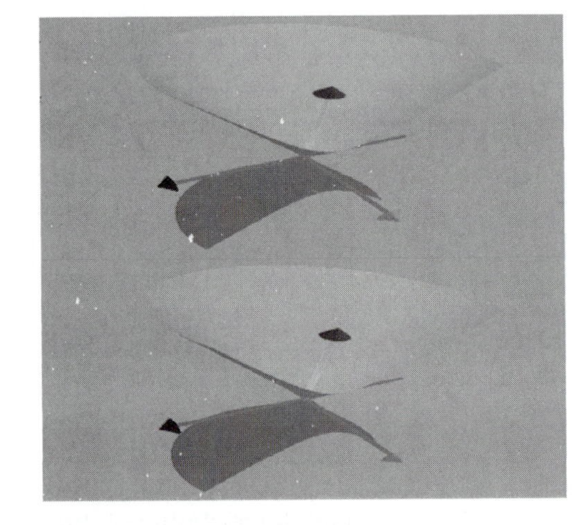

Figure 10.12 Side-by-side images (*left*) and above-below images (*right*).

These images are rasterized differently than the usual process described above. Each of the two images is sent to a different display buffer by doubling each pixel. In the case of the side-by-side images, the pixels are doubled horizontally and the buffers are switched when the middle band is reached. In the case of the above-below images, the pixels are doubled vertically and the buffers are again switched when the middle band is reached. This lets the system maintain two separate images from one original, creating the dual images needed by the alternating presentation hardware.

Summary

This chapter described the processing needed to create an image in an output color buffer, a raster of pixels, from the geometry and appearance information you have in an ordinary graphics program with most graphics APIs. Based on this you can understand the amount and kind of processing needed to create a graphics image, so you will understand why some kinds of images take longer to create than others, and will be prepared to consider some of the techniques described in Chapter 12 to create higher-performance graphics programs. You will also have some background in case you want to undertake a more detailed study of computer graphics later in your studies.

OpenGL Glossary for the Chapter

This chapter introduced a few OpenGL functions that are quite specific to operations in the polygon rasterization pipeline. These have limited use for simple programs but can be important to many advanced operations.

OpenGL Functions

`glAlphaFunc(parm, value)`: lets you set the function (from a list of available symbolic options) that will be used for alpha testing

`glCopyTexImage*D( ... )`: copies pixels into a texture image whose dimension is given by the value of * (1, 2, or 3); a number of parameters specify the format, size, and location of the pixels

`glScissor()`: defines a rectangle within the graphics window; when the scissor test is enabled, only pixels within that rectangle may be modified

`glStencilFunc()`: sets the stencil function and reference value for stencil testing

`glStencilMask()`: specifies a bit mask to control the writing of specific bits in the stencil planes

`glStencilOp()`: specifies actions to be taken if the stencil test fails or passes

OpenGL Parameters

`GL_SCISSOR_TEST`: parameter to `glEnable()` which specifies that a scissor test is to be applied

`GL_STENCIL_TEST`: parameter to `glEnable()` which specifies that a stencil test is to be applied

Questions

1. Draw an image containing only a small triangle with different colors at each vertex and smooth shading. Use a screen capture utility to grab the computer screen with this image

showing, and open the captured image with a program such as Photoshop that allows you to greatly enlarge an image. Enlarge the image and look at the triangle; identify the scanlines on the triangle and note the fragments that make up the triangle across the scanlines. How do the fragments change as you move from the top to the bottom of the triangle?

2. Manually create a short fragment (perhaps 10 pixels long) with depth and color (including alpha) information for each pixel, and manually create a scanline with its own set of depth and color information. Manually walk through the operation of placing the fragment on the scanline, using both the depth and color buffers. Show how the depth buffer is used to choose whether a fragment pixel will be used, and if it is, show how the color buffer and the pixel's alpha value determine the color the scanline pixel will become. Assume whatever blending function you like.
3. Show that if a polygon is convex, each scanline meets the polygon in only one fragment, but the converse is not true: There are polygons for which each scanline meets the polygon in only one fragment, but the polygon is not convex.

Exercises

1. Create a small pseudoscreen which consists of a grid of squares that can each be made any color you want—kind of a "fat pixels" screen. Adapt the Bresenham algorithm to interpolate a vertex property (such as color) that is not depth-dependent, and see how this works by plotting colored squares as the interpolated color indicates. See if you can interpolate depth or perspective-corrected texture coordinates as suggested in the chapter.

Experiments

1. In the discussion of how fragments are processed, we talked about different operations that need to be carried out to support different kinds of graphics processes. In an experiment, define some simple geometry, render it with different techniques, and see how long it takes. Because graphics systems are now quite fast, you will need to draw several thousand (or maybe even tens of thousands) of simple objects in order to get a measurable difference. Do this with the following kinds of triangles: flat-shaded triangles, smooth-shaded triangles, and texture-mapped triangles.

11

Dynamics and Animation

In this chapter we cover some topics about creating animated images, or images that move over time without the intervention of the user or viewer. This involves understanding how things move from both the physical principles embodied in the scene as well as the way we can communicate particular information to the viewer. We need to take a broader view of our work than just the technical issues required in making moving images. We will talk about the topics in animations by presenting and discussing a set of examples, but these only begin to illustrate the animation process. You need to make an effort to understand motion for your particular subject in ways that go beyond the technology of computer graphics to make fully effective animations.

Computer animation is a very large topic, and there are a number of books and courses on the subject. We cannot hope to cover the topic in any depth in a first course in computer graphics, and indeed the toolkits needed for a great deal of computer animation are major objects of study and skill development in themselves. Instead we focus on relatively simple animations that illustrate something about the kind of models and images we have been creating in this book, with a continuing emphasis on topics from the sciences.

We think of animation as presenting a sequence of individual images, or *frames,* rapidly enough that the viewer perceives the objects in the frames as moving smoothly. There are two kinds of animation—real-time animation, or animation in which each frame is presented by the program while it is running, and frame-at-a-time animation, or animation that is assembled by rendering the individual frames and assembling them into a viewable format (possibly through film or video in a separate production process, as we discuss in Chapter 15). Both share the problems of defining how models, lighting, and viewing change over time, but frame-at-a-time animation tends to create more sophisticated frames that take very detailed modeling and sophisticated rendering, while real-time animation accepts simpler modeling and rendering in order to get screen refresh rates that are high enough to be effective. Real-time animation may not be as realistic as frame-at-a-time animation because simpler modeling and rendering are used or images may be provided at a slower rate, but it can be very effective in conveying an idea and can be especially effective if the user can interact with the animation program as it is running. Real-time animation is becoming more and more useable as graphics systems and computer speeds improve, and animations that needed frame-at-a-time techniques a few years ago now run well in real time.

This chapter does not take sides in the question of real-time versus frame-at-a-time animation. Both use the same principles, and we focus on those principles here. As with everything in this book, we believe that the reason for doing animation is visual communication, and there are some special vocabularies and techniques found in using animation for communication. This chapter browses these topics rather than trying to cover them in depth, but we suggest that you spend some time looking at successful animations and trying to discover for yourself what makes them succeed. To start, we suggest that you focus your thoughts on clarity and simplicity and work hard to create a focus on the particular ideas you want to communicate.

No matter what kind of animation you do, the key is to create a scene that changes over time and to display a sequence of images that corresponds to these changes. So animation is tied closely to scene design but requires that you master the additional concept of changing the scene as time passes.

This is an unusual chapter, because it includes few figures that really illustrate its topic. The topic is motion, and we cannot readily capture motion in a printed document. It would be possible to include movie files in the materials that come with the book, but we have chosen to include code rather than movies because this book is about creating graphics and graphical communication, not about looking at images. Work with the examples and code segments that we provide to create the animations yourself and see them execute on your own systems. Be aware that with many of these programs, the system speed will affect the animation speed, so you may see something that moves more quickly (or slowly) than you would expect.

In order to get the most out of this chapter, you need to understand how to define a view in terms of parameters that define the size, shape, position, orientation, appearance, or other aspects of a scene. This is probably best done through the scene graph. You also need to understand how to change these parameters from frame to frame in order to change the view over time. Actually generating new frames is usually done by using a time-based event such as idle or timer, or using the system clock, to update the parameters and call for a new frame.

An Example

When we introduced graphics programming in Chapter 0 ("Getting Started"), we used an example of heat flowing in a bar. We used animation to rotate the bar, letting the viewer see it from all sides, showing how the temperatures across the bar changed over time, so the viewer could understand the (invisible) flow of heat. This is an example of using animation in the sciences, but there are others, particularly looking at the actual motions of objects in space. So to start this chapter we will introduce a useful modeling technique, *particle systems,* and will show how we can animate particle systems to show motion over time.

A particle system is a collection of points, or object, such as very small spheres that represent points, where each sphere represents some kind of object or process. For example, we could model a fluid as a particle system by regarding each point as a small element of the fluid and look at how the fluid flows by animating the particles through the forces that act on the fluid. A simple example might be a fountain; another example that seems to be a common exercise is a piece of fireworks. The basic approach is to define a large array of positions and velocities, one for each particle, and then apply the physics of the environment to model accelerations for each particle. For a defined time step, the new position and velocity for each particle are computed, and all the active particles are displayed. Active particles are those that are displayed and acted on by the process being shown; inactive particles are in a data reserve from which particles are drawn and made active, and to which particles are returned when they are no longer displayed. The computation for each active particle can use any appropriate technique, but some standard ones are standard equations of motion from physics (when closed-form solutions are known), difference equations (new velocity is old velocity plus a scaled acceleration at the original position, and then new position is old position moved by this new velocity), or numerical integration to calculate the new position and velocity.

As an example, let's model a waterfall using a particle system such as the one shown in Figure 11.1. We start with water flowing along a fixed-width stream at constant velocity until it comes to a sharp edge. It then falls with gravitational acceleration until it encounters a ledge, at which point it splashes up and then continues to fall. Without thinking about code, we see that there are four essential areas of the model: particles moving in the stream, particles falling, particles hitting the ledge and bouncing, and particles falling again. With some simplifications (we show nothing but the particles, and we show the particles as simple spheres with three light sources and shading), the result is an animation with one frame as shown.

A few particles are generated at each time step from a large set of particles that we model as an array. They flow horizontally along a simulated stream bed at a slightly random velocity (with the stream bed not shown), begin to fall when they reach a point where the stream bed ends, and continue to fall until they hit a ledge. There they get a new vertical velocity that is determined by a bouncing process and then fall again until they get to a second lower level, when they are destroyed and returned to the set of available particles.

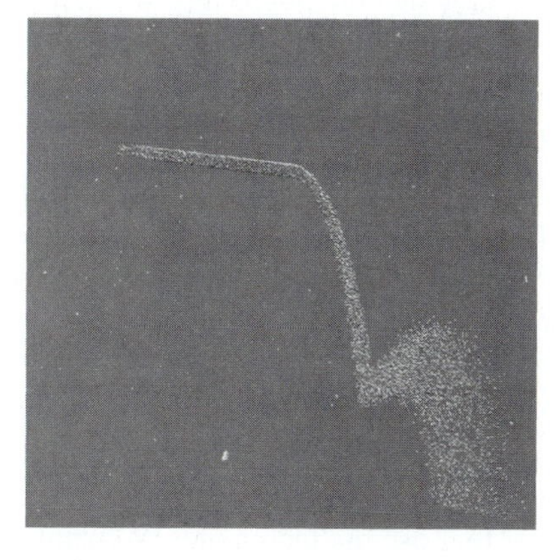

Figure 11.1 One frame from the particle system animation.

The motion of each particle can be modeled in different ways. An approach one might take based on elementary physics could use an equation for the horizontal motion of the particles, such as:

$$x = x_0 + v_x \Delta t$$

with a constant horizontal velocity v_x, ignoring friction and gravity. For the vertical component, once the particle passes the end of the stream bed one could use the equation of vertical motion under gravity:

$$y = y_0 + v_y \Delta t + 0.5 g \Delta t^2$$

where y_0 is the height of the stream bed and v_y is the initial y-velocity, or 0, because we assume that the stream bed is horizontal. The horizontal velocity v_x continues as before. After the particle hits the ledge, with the logic that the ledge is at a given y-value, new values of y_0 (now the height of the ledge) and v_0 are generated. The velocity at the ledge is calculated by taking the difference in values of y between the previous and current point. The particle then gets that value as its new velocity, with the sign changed and some random variation added to both x- and y-velocity to model splashing behavior. The process then continues for each particle until it gets to a "bottom" y-value, when it is destroyed and returned to the particle pool.

Our approach to the animation shown in the figure is different. It saves data for both position and velocity, and it models the vertical acceleration of the particle at each point using a zero acceleration as long as the particle is in the stream bed and the standard 32 m/sec^2 gravitational acceleration after the particle goes over the edge of the falls. This acceleration (scaled for the time step) is then added to the vertical velocity in a difference equation, and the position of the particle is updated for the next drawing. The velocity is handled as above when the particle hits the ledge, and the particle is also destroyed as above. We model the particles with a seven-dimensional array that contains the position and velocity for each particle, as well as a logic value that tells whether the particle is active. The active logic lets us select inactive particles from the array to add to the particle system at each step and lets us return particles to inactive status when the particle falls off the bottom of the animation. This cycle of creating, flowing, falling, bouncing, falling, and destroying each particle is repeated continually. We do not include the code for this in this chapter, but it is available with the resources for the book.

Types of Animations

Animation is the process of creating a sequence of images and presenting them so that the viewer's eye perceives them as occurring in a smooth motion sequence. The motion sequence can illustrate the relationship between things, can show processes for assembling objects, can allow you to design a sequence of ways to present information, or can allow a user to see a scene from a variety of viewpoints that you can design.

There are many ways to design an animation sequence, basically limited only by your imagination as you design the animated scenes. A few common techniques are simple to use and understand, though, and we'll describe these briefly and either give examples or refer to examples we have seen earlier that use the techniques. We should note that our techniques and examples are much simpler than those used in many games and most entertainment animations and are focused on animating concepts in the sciences.

Procedural Animation

Because we have often talked about using parameters to define a model, a good place to start with animation is to talk about modeling your scene using parameters to control features of the model. These parameters—variables that you can manipulate in your program—control positions of objects, positions or properties of lights, shapes or relationships or objects, colors, texture coordinates, or other key points in your model, and you can change the values of the parameters with time to change the audience's view as the program runs. This lets you emphasize special features of any of these facets of your model and to communicate those features to your audience. Because this kind of animation is driven by computational procedures, it is called *procedural animation*. You can explicitly control the parameters through time-based computations using the basic science or other principles for your model. This is easy to use for animating simple models where you may have only a few parameters that define the sequence (although what defines "a few" may depend on your system and your goals in the sequence).

Most of the animation we have seen in the science applications earlier in this book is procedural, where we compute the positions or behaviors of objects over time from scientific principles and display them as they vary. The waterfall example that started this chapter is also a procedural animation. This direct computation of the properties of each frame of the animation is what characterizes procedural animation. More complex models can also be animated with procedural techniques if you can write computations for all the parameters.

Animation in the Scene Graph

As you model your scene and design your animation, recall that each of the four parts of a scene, as described by a scene graph, has its own way of varying over time. Many of these involve parameters and are basically procedural, though any of these could involve user input or could have triggers that change the scene based on time or specific actions. The scene graph components and some of the ways they can be used include:

- The geometry of the scene: we can use parameters to define the geometry of the scene itself. An example of this is the parametric function surface $z = \cos(x^2 + y^2 + t)$ we saw in Chapter 9, where the parameter t might represent time. As the value of t changes, the geometry of the scene will change.
- The set of transformations in the scene: we can use parameters to define the rotation, translation, or scaling of objects in the scene. An example of this is the rotation of the bar in the heat transfer example. As the parameter is changed, the position or orientation of the object changes.
- The appearance of objects in the scene, such as color or texture: we can change the color, texture, or other appearance components as we wish. For example, a surface might have an alpha color component of $(1-t)$ to change it from opaque at time 0 to transparent at time 1. As the parameter is changed, the surface will change between opaque and transparent, allowing the user to see through the surface at a variable amount at whatever lies below it.
- The view for the scene: we can change the eyepoint, view direction, up direction, or view parameters, either by using parameters or with other techniques. Changing these over time can let you view a scene in different ways, illustrating different parts of the scene as you wish.

These are straightforward applications of modeling, and your experience with modeling by this point should make it straightforward for you to set up a model with time variation.

Interpolation Animation

If we step back from computing parameters and simply think in terms of modeling with parameters, we can think of a "parametric animation" as defining a scene in terms of a set of parameters for the model, defined as a vector $\boldsymbol{P} = <a, b, c, ..., n>$. We can denote the vector of parameters at any given frame M as $\boldsymbol{P}_M = <a_M, b_M, c_M, ..., n_M>$. In computing the frames of a segment of an animation sequence starting with frame number K and going to frame number L, then, we must calculate the parameter vectors between the parameters at these two points

$\boldsymbol{P}_K = <a_K, b_K, c_K, ..., n_K>$ and $\boldsymbol{P}_L = <a_L, b_L, c_L, ..., n_L>$.

The values of the parameter vectors at these two frames can be calculated with any kind of interpolation that makes sense for your modeling and communication. This interpolation can be either linear or nonlinear, and both kinds are described later in this chapter. This might be called *interpolation animation*. For this approach you need to define two models and interpolate the geometry of the first model into the geometry of the second model. We have an example of this later in the chapter, but it is not as common as procedural animation in the sciences.

One example of interpolation animation is *morphing*, where you start with one object (a face, an animal, an automobile) and you end with another; the goal is to emphasize the change from one thing to another. This involves creating a sequence of images by defining key points in each of two images, moving the key points of the first image to those of the second image with some form of interpolation, creating a series of "merges" of the first image to the second, and texture mapping each set of interpolated points with the corresponding merged texture map. This change from one texture to another is complicated by the fact that points which correspond in the two images should have corresponding texture points, and you need to be careful to define the starting and ending textures appropriately. For example, if you are morphing one face to another, the key features such as eyes, nose, and corners of the mouth must correspond. If you are mapping one automobile into another, features such as the headlights, wheels, windshield, and tail lights must correspond. This may require you to warp one or both of the textures to make the geometries and textures correspond, as described in [WOL]. Because you usually see morphing as an animated change from one thing to another it can be seen as an animation, but it is a very specialized operation and we will not discuss it further here.

In general, interpolations can be linear or can be more sophisticated. The entire chapter on evaluators and splines (Chapter 13) is really about interpolation, and you can use any of the techniques we introduce there. A first approach to interpolation might be to interpolate the parameter values linearly. So if we let K and L be the first and last frame numbers in the interpolation, the number of frames between these key frames, including the two end frames, is $C = L-K$ and we would have $p_i = (ip_k + (C-i)p_L)/C$ for each parameter p and each integer i between K and L. If we let $t = i/C$, we can rephrase this as $p_i = (tp_k + (1-t)p_L)$, a familiar linear interpolation. This calculation is straightforward and would produce smoothly changing parameter values that should translate into smooth motion between the key frames.

Frame-to-frame motion can be more complex than a simple linear interpolation approach like this, however. In fact, we may not want only smooth motion between two specific frames, but we may want the motion from before a frame to blend smoothly with the motion after that frame. The linear interpolation discussed above will not accomplish that but will probably produce motion that is jerky at each specified frame. Instead, we need to use a more general interpolation approach, called *easing into* and *easing out* of the motion. One approach to easing in and easing out is to start the motion from the first frame more slowly, move more quickly in the middle, and slow down the ending part of the interpolation so that we stop changing the parameter (and hence stop any motion in the image) just as we reach the second frame. In Figure 11.2, we see a comparison of simple linear interpolation on the left with a gradual startup/slowdown interpolation on the right. The right-hand figure shows a sinusoidal curve that we could readily describe by $s(t) = 0.5(1 - \cos(t/\pi))$, where t is the unit parameter for the interpolation. You can think of t as time or as frame number, for example. Then rather than a linear interpolation $p_i = (tp_K + (1 - t)p_L)$, you can use the nonlinear relationship $p_i = (s(t)p_K + (1 - s(t))p_L)$ with uniform spacing on t as in the previous paragraph. This changes very little in the programming but can be noticeable in practice. In fact it can change nothing in the programming if you always use a $s(t)$ function and simply let $s(t)$ 5 $= t$ for linear work.

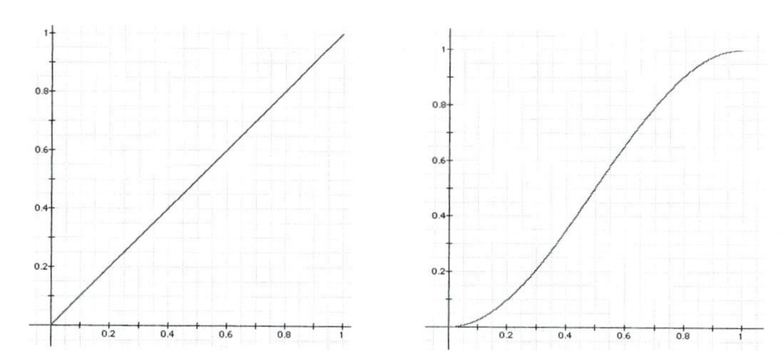

Figure 11.2 Two interpolation curves: linear (*left*) and sinusoidal (*right*).

In fact, this easing into and easing out of the motion may not be enough, because in order to emphasize the motion, you may want to have the object you are moving actually back up slightly from its original before it moves forward, and go slightly beyond its final position before it comes to rest. You can adapt the ideas above to do this by having the interpolation curve go slightly negative as it begins and go slightly above 1 just before it ends. This kind of motion subtlety is where animation becomes art, and we cannot offer sound guidelines on when to use it—except that you should use it when it works, and you should try enough examples of linear and eased interpolation so that you can build an understanding of *when* it works.

While the sinusoidal interpolation lets us move through the specified parameters slowly, we still have the problem that a parameter can provide motion (or another effect) in one direction up to a specified frame, and then that motion or effect can go off in an entirely different direction when it leaves the specified frame and goes to another one. That is, our motion is not yet smooth as it goes through a specified frame. To achieve smooth motion through key frames, we need the more sophisticated kind of interpolation we will see in Chapter 13. Just as we interpolate control points there to create a curve, we can use a Catmull-Rom spline to interpolate a sequence of points in a way that creates a smooth interpolating line that meets the original points.

Frame-Based Animation

Probably the simplest approach to animation is to define your entire scene in terms of a single parameter and to update that parameter each time you generate a new frame. You could think of the parameter as time and think of your animation in terms of a model changing over time. This is probably a natural approach when you are working with scientific problems, where time plays an active role in much of the modeling; think of how much of science deals with the amount of change per unit time. This kind of modeling might need some ideas from calculus to represent this change. If you know how long it will take to generate your scene, you can even change a time parameter by that amount for each frame so that the viewer will see the frames at a rate that approximates the real-time behavior of the system you are modeling.

Another meaning for the parameter could be frame number, the sequence number of the particular image you are computing in the set of frames that will make up the animation sequence. If you are dealing with animation that you will record in analog or digital hardcopy and play back at a known rate, you can translate the frame number into a time parameter. The difference in names for the parameter reflects a difference in thinking, however, because you will not be concerned about how long it takes to generate a frame, simply where the frame is in the sequence you are building.

Using the frame concept, you can design an animation by creating *key frames,* or particular images that you want to appear at particular times in the animation display. Animation done in this way is called *keyframe* animation. When you create a keyframe animation, you specify certain frames as key frames that the animation must produce and you create the rest of the frames so that they move smoothly from one key frame to another. The key frames are specified by frame numbers, so these are away the parameters you use, as described previously.

In cartoon-type animation, it is common for the key frames to be fully developed drawings and for the rest of the frames to be generated by a process often called "*tweening*"—generating the frames between the keys. In traditional animation, artists generate the in-between frames by redrawing the elements of the scene as they would appear in the motion between key frames. However, we are creating images by programming so we must start with models instead of drawings. If we take a keyframe approach, our key frames will have whatever parameters are needed to define the images, and we will create our in-between frames based on those parameters. If you simply interpolate the parameters from the keyframes, keyframe animation is really the same as interpolation animation.

An Interpolation Example

We are generally focusing on simpler kinds of images than those found in animations for entertainment, however, so we will use interpolation to tell simpler stories. As an example of this kind of story, consider a pair of models that represent similar objects, defined in similar ways that include both geometry and texture maps, and let's tell a story of transforming one into another smoothly. Our example will be two walls with different geometries and different surface textures. We will start by considering an interpolation of two textures and will then go on to interpolating two geometries. In the end, we will leave the combining of these two techniques as an exercise for you.

As we move from the first scene to the second and create an interpolation animation between them, we start by interpolating the texture maps we will use in the scenes. To do this, we create new texture maps for the interpolated scenes by interpolating the texture maps for the first and second walls. We create the interpolated texture maps by using a simple linear blend of the colors of each pixel in the texture arrays, using a linear combination of the colors for each pixel in the arrays. This is quite straightforward, though it may take time to create each of the intermediate texture arrays and load it into the texture map. We can use this simple approach to interpolating textures because we have been careful to make the geometries of the interpolated steps correspond. This is shown in an example in Figure 11.3.

Figure 11.3 Three interpolations of the tile texture map (*left*) and the brick texture map (*right*), corresponding to proportions 25 percent (*top*), 50 percent (*middle*), and 75 percent (*bottom*) of the rightmost texture.

Now we must think about the geometries of the walls and about how to interpolate them. The first wall will be a simple rectangle, while the second wall will be curved and will have a curved top. For this example, both walls are simple surfaces; we do not include a thickness. The geometry for the first wall is based on a set of vertical rectangles, each one texture unit wide and several texture units high. This is easy to program, and it is easy to determine texture coordinates for the geometry. The geometry of the second wall is similar and is based on vertical quadrilaterals, each one texture unit wide. The curved top makes it a little more difficult to determine the texture coordinates for the top edge, but if we continue to use texture units as our basis we should be able to take the fractional part of the height as texture vertices for the top edge. In both cases we will break up the vertical sections into squares for the actual drawing, with ease of texture coordinate computation in mind. The geometry for the original and interpolated walls is shown in Figure 11.4.

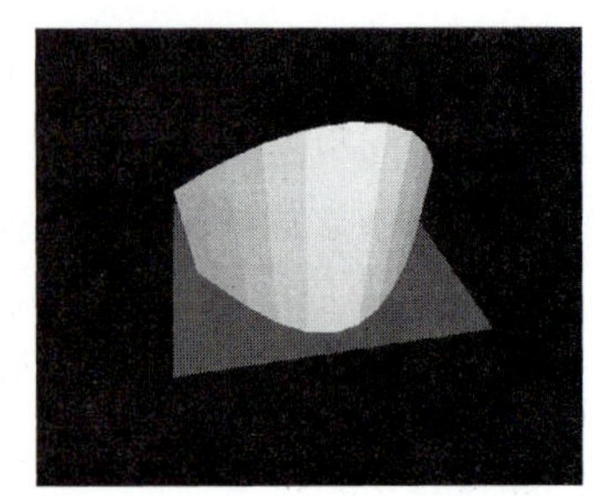

Figure 11.4 The walls we will interpolate (*left, right*) and their 50 percent interpolation (*center*).

To put these two pieces together, let's assume that the rectangular wall is made of tiles with the texture of the left-hand side of Figure 11.3, and that the curving wall is made of bricks with the texture of the right-hand side of Figure 11.3. Let's make our task easier by letting both textures go to the very edges of their respective walls. You should be able to visualize the shape and textures for the interpolated walls, so instead of giving another figure here we'll leave it to you in Exercise 2 to combine the texture and geometry interpolations.

Some Issues in Animation

When you create an animation you need to consider some things that are different from anything you would meet in a static (or even interactive) presentation. They include the frame rate and temporal aliasing, and we describe these here.

Frame Rates

A key concept in generating animations in real time is the *frame rate*—the rate at which you are able to generate new images in the animation sequence. Usually twenty-four to thirty frames per second are needed in order to make the motion smooth, though you can get reasonably good results at lower rates. As we noted above, the frame rate will be lower for highly detailed generated frames than it will be for similar frames that were pre-computed and saved in digital or analog video, but there's one other difference: Frame rates may not be constant for real-time generated images. This points out the challenge of doing your own animations and the need to be sure your animations carry the communication you want.

The frame rate of your animations can be highly variable; most of us have seen programs (and their animated output) that ran much faster when they were run on a new, faster machine. This will certainly happen if you use the idle event to drive an animation. You can get more consistent results with the timer event, but that is still uncertain. For the best results, access your system clock and always be sure that frames are generated no faster than a desired frame rate. This can be a problem if you are working on different systems, but we describe a GLUT-based solution in the set of OpenGL discussions later in the chapter. However, there is a solution for pre-created animations: The frame rate can be controlled exactly, no matter how complex the images in the individual frames, if you create your own video hardcopy of your animation. See the hardcopy discussion in Chapter 15 for more details on this.

Temporal Aliasing

In creating an animation, you are creating a sequence of images that represent the state of your model at specific points in time. When these sequences are viewed in order, however, you may find that the results show some surprising effects that you did not intend. Some of these problems may be due to problems with the graphics system; for example, if you have a very small object, it may seem to vary in size over time as more or fewer pixels get chosen for the object. This is a screen aliasing problem and can be addressed by using antialiasing techniques to include partly covered pixels in the image. But other problems are fundamental in the animation process and cannot be readily eliminated; you must recognize the possibility that your images in sequence may show some effects that can cause them to be interpreted differently from the way you intended.

Let's consider an example. Suppose you have an object like that shown in Figure 11.5 (for example, this figure might represent the spokes of a wheel that are separated by 45 degrees) and rotate the object over time. If you rotate the object slowly, the eye will naturally follow each spoke as it changes position because the position of the spoke in the next frame will be the one nearest that spoke in the previous frame. This will happen, for example, if you want to show the spokes moving clockwise and you rotate the object clockwise by an angle less than half the angle between the spokes, or 22.5°, particularly if the angle is much less than that value. But if you rotate the object a bit more quickly, say by 40 degrees, then the position of the spoke in the next frame will be only 5 degrees from the position of the next clockwise spoke in the previous frame (read that phrase over again to be sure what we're saying!) and your eye will associate each spoke with the previous image of the next spoke—so the spokes will seem to rotate counterclockwise. You may have seen this

Figure 11.5 An object that might be rotated.

happen in films or when a rotating object is lit by a strobe light, but it is important to realize that it is possible and to plan to manage it in your work. Code for this animation is included with the supporting materials for the book. As presented, the animation moves the spokes only slowly at first, but every time you press a key the movement is increased. You can see the effect described above if you compile the source code that is included with the book's resources, where the increment grows to almost the angle between the spokes and the spokes begin to move backward.

These problems are caused by *temporal aliasing,* or sampling a time sequence at discrete points in time. This is analogous to geometric aliasing, caused by sampling an image at discrete points in space, and we have seen that geometric aliasing creates problems with stairstepped lines and similar situations. Temporal aliasing causes phenomena such as the backward or apparently frozen motion of wheel spokes in movies or the same apparent motion of an airplane propeller blade at night when it is lit by the strobe light under the body of the plane.

The temporal aliasing phenomenon is seen in the real world, so you may want to keep it if you want to expose this behavior. However, if you do not, you can use techniques called *temporal antialiasing.* One is to blur the scene as described later in this chapter under motion blurring. Others involve avoiding aliasing by using smaller time slices (in the example above, this would reduce the angle between spoke positions in adjacent frames) or by using models that do not have noticeable time-aliased features.

Building an Animation

The communication you are developing with your animation is very similar to the communication that a director might want to use in a film. Film has developed a rich vocabulary of techniques that will give particular kinds of information, and animations for scientific communication can benefit from thinking about issues in cinematic terms. If you plan to do this kind of work extensively, you should study the techniques of professional animators (see, for example, [POC]). Books on animations will show you many, many more things you can do to improve your planning and execution. Initially, you may want to keep your animations simple and hold a fixed eyepoint and fixed lights, allowing only the parts of the model that move with time to move in your frames. However, just as the cinema discovered the value of a moving camera in a moving scene when directors invented the traveling shot, the camera boom, and the handheld walking camera, you may find that you get the best effects by combining a moving viewpoint with moving objects. Experiment with your model and try out different combinations to see what tells your story best.

Animation and Visual Communication

The ability of a modern graphics API to support motion is a powerful communication tool. Whether the motion is created through animation or through interaction, it lets you tell a story about your subject that can change through time or can be explored by each member of your audience individually. Presenting a time-changing display is particularly appropriate if you are considering a dynamic situation, which is a common theme in the sciences and in other areas of study. Some phenomena are simply invisible without motion—for example, detecting a planet among the night stars, where only the different motion of the planet sets it apart to the unassisted eye. Motion itself also contains information. A classic example created by Dan Sandin of the Electronic Visualization Laboratory of the University of Illinois, Chicago, shows a screen with two kinds of motion, and you can identify a region by differentiating between the motion inside and outside the region. It is not possible to show you the moving example here, but the code for an example is included with the book and is the basis for some exercises in this chapter. In Figure 11.6 we show a single frame from the animation (*left*), but without motion you cannot tell where the region's boundary is. We add an indication of the boundary that is not in the original by showing points from the boundary (*right*).

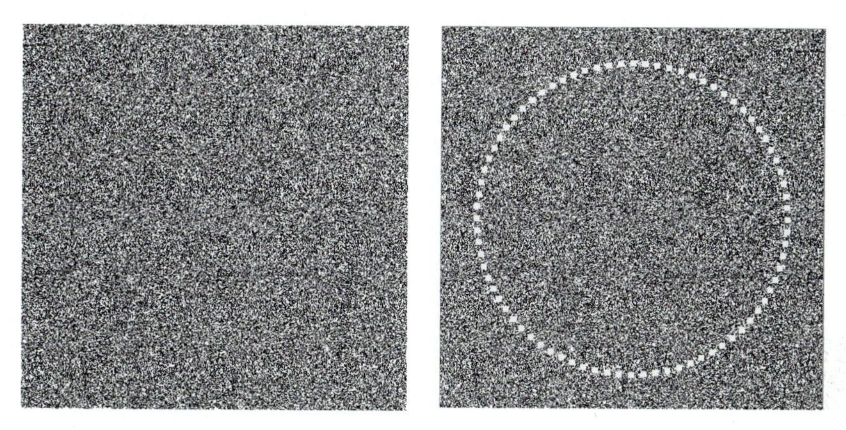

Figure 11.6 A random-noise square (*left*) that includes a region defined by motion, highlighted (*right*) by the circle.

When you create motion, you need to consider exactly what is going to move and the pace at which it is to move. Sometimes you will want to hold most of your scene fixed and have only part of it in motion, which could emphasize the way the moving part changes in relation to the rest of the scene; sometimes you will want to have everything moving so you can describe the overall motion present in the scene. If you are using animation to create this motion, it may be appropriate to use a time parameter in your modeling so that you may simply update the time and redisplay the model. In this case, of course, you will want to be sure that all the parts of your model use time the same way so that the motion is equally paced throughout your scene. If you are using interaction to create the motion, this could get more complicated because you may want to allow your viewer to move some parts of the model rather than others, but you again need to create a consistent model of the behavior you will be showing.

The nature of today's computing makes animation an interesting challenge. With faster systems and a growing hardware support for graphics, the time to render a scene keeps decreasing so you get faster and faster frame rates for pure animation. While we wouldn't want to stop or slow this trend, it does mean that we run the risk of creating a real-time online animation for our system that can come to run so fast when it's run on a newer system that it's difficult to understand. Most operating systems have a timed pause function that can be called from your program. You may want to design your animation to have a specific frame rate and use system-sensitive tools to help you maintain the frame rate you want the viewer to see. This could be a system function `pause(N)` that would idle your program for a given number of milliseconds or a similar system or API utility; we provide an example later in this chapter. Of course, this isn't an issue with interactive motion, because the human is always the slowest part of the system and the viewer will be able to control his or her own frame rate.

Because sometimes you may want to produce particularly high-quality presentations for the general public or for an audience such as a funding agency, you may need to think about other aspects of a presentation. One of these is certainly sound; in the public presentation world, you will never see an animation without a soundtrack. Current graphics APIs, do not often include sound capability, but we expect that this capability will be available soon in some auxiliary APIs, and you should think about the sound that could be used with your work. This could be a recorded voiceover, sound effects that emphasize the motion that is being displayed, or a music track—or all three. If you're going to use video hardcopy for your presentation, you need to consider this now because you can add sound in the hardcopy process; if you're going to be doing only online work, you should think about this for the future.

Showing Motion in Still Frames

When you convey information about a moving geometry to your audience, you are likely to use an animation. However, in order for your viewer to see not only the moving parts but also how these parts have moved, you might want to leave something in the frame to show where the parts were in previous frames. Two common ways to do this are through motion traces or motion blurring.

Motion Traces

A common way to show motion traces is to show your objects along with some sort of trail of previous positions of the objects. This can be handled rather easily by creating a set of lines or similar geometric objects that show previous positions for each object that is being traced. This trace should have limited length (unless you want to show a global history, which is really a different visualization) and can use techniques such as reduced alpha values to show the history of the object's position. Figure 11.7 shows two examples of such traces; the left-hand image uses a

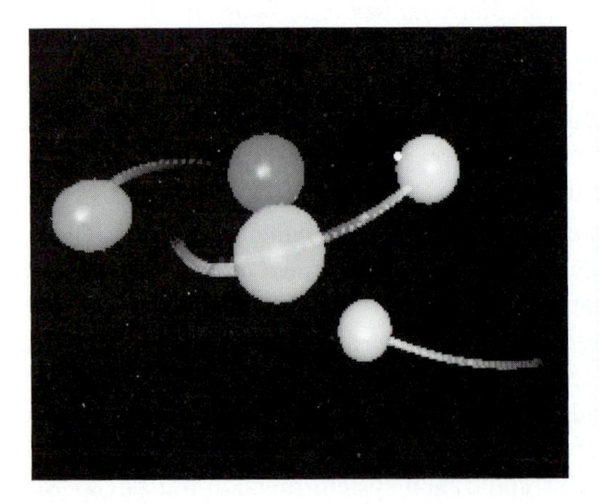

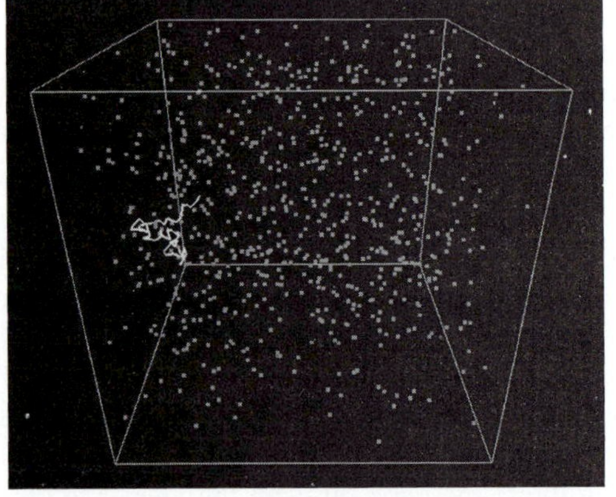

Figure 11.7 Two kinds of traces of moving objects. See the figure in the color insert. Figure on the left is courtesy of Ben Eadington.

sequence of cylinders connecting the previous positions with the cylinders colored by the object color with reducing alpha values, while the right-hand image shows a simple line trace of a single particle illustrating a random walk behavior.

Motion Blurring

In many contexts such as sports and high-speed action photography, we are accustomed to seeing moving objects blurred in a frame. One way to show motion, then, is to create images that have a blurred image of those things that are moving, and a crisp image of those things that are in fixed positions. The faster the motion, the more the blur you will want to show. In Figure 11.8 we see a plate (green) with two arms attached (red and blue) and a fixed bar between the arms (white). As one of the arms is moved, the plate and other arm are moved but the bar stays fixed. The figure shows the motion through blurring.

Figure 11.8 A moving mechanism shown with one part fixed and the rest blurred from motion. See the figure in the color insert. Courtesy of Mike Bailey.

This motion blur shown in Figure 11.8 can be created in several ways, but a standard approach is to composite images computed at slightly different times using an *accumulation buffer*. This compositing technique lets you view several images of a scene simultaneously, each taken at a slightly different time. Those objects that are moving will be seen in different positions, so they will seem blurred; those objects that are fixed will be shown in the same position, so they will be seen as crisp. Many graphics APIs provide an accumulation buffer tool, and in the OpenGL section later in the chapter we will describe how that API implements this technique.

Interesting Animation Viewing Devices

As the world began to learn about making moving images through a series of stills, a variety of devices were created to help people see motion. The devices operated manually and used preprepared sequences of animations, usually photographs or drawings, of a number of different kinds of subjects. It can be fascinating to see historical examples of these devices in museums or antique shops, as it is fascinating to see the stereopticons we described in Chapter 1. These animation viewing devices include the *zoetrope* and the *flip book*. A zoetrope is a drum having several viewing slots and containing a strip of images, as illustrated in Figure 11.9. A zoetrope can also have images on a circle that fits on the floor of the drum.

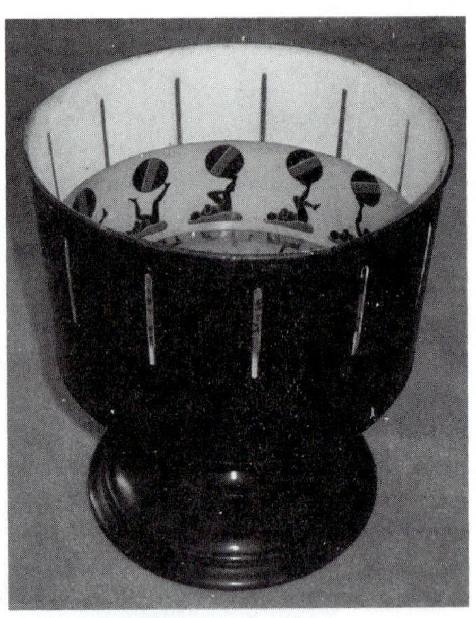

Figure 11.9 Two photographs of an antique zoetrope showing (*left*) the device mounting and (*right*) the relation between the viewing slots and the figures. Courtesy of Judy Brown.

The principle of the zoetrope is that your eye will see a certain breadth of field as you look through the slots, and when a complete figure is visible in the field your eye will grasp the figure. When that figure moves on, your eye will grasp the next figure, and so on. As your eye focuses on the sequence, then, it fuses them into a single moving figure. A strip of images for a zoetrope is shown in Figure 11.10 and in more detail in Figure 11.11. The geometry of the zoetrope and the spacing and number of images are important in making your eye fuse the separate images into a moving image.

Figure 11.10 A paper strip holding a set of very simple images for the antique zoetrope.

Figure 11.11 Three images from the whole strip, showing how adjacent images are handled.

Building a zoetrope is a bit more complex. The one shown in Figure 11.9 has 13 slots, each 3/16″ wide, in a metal drum that has a 36″ inside circumference. The strip of images is 36″ long and has 13 individual images, each just under 3″ wide including a small white space between them. The drum is rotated manually on a simple spindle as the viewer looks through the slots, and the viewer can see only a single image on the strip at a time. As the drum is rotated at an appropriate speed, the images fuse in the viewer's vision and form an animation. This is most effective if the animation cycles, so that the image at the end of the strip is adjacent in time to the image at the start of the strip, but as you can see this is not necessary—and in fact, with many of the early hand-drawn animations, as in Figure 11.10 with more detail in Figure 11.11, a sequence simply starts at one end and stops at the other.

The slits in the drum in the antique device shown are cut into the side of the metal drum, but we have seen other zoetropes where the slits are actually slots cut into the drum from the top. This looks like a simpler construction but might not have the strength of a side cut, and if the drum is made of metal the corners of the slots might be dangerous. We suggest that if you make a zoetrope this way, you use some sort of strip on the top of the drum that protects fingers from the edge of the drum and the corners of the slots.

It would seem that you could create a zoetrope with a different number of images on a drum and a different radius, but there are questions about the size of the image to be seen by the viewer and the diameter of the drum. If you want to include more images on the zoetrope strip, you probably want to make the drum larger. However, if you do, you see a wider area of the drum through the viewing slit. We have seen different sizes of zoetropes that all have twelve, thirteen, or fourteen images per strip, so we recommend using those numbers, but you are welcome to experiment with the number. However, to do so you will need to build different drums, and that could be a lot of work!

A flip book is a simpler kind of animation construction that does not have most of the physical limitations of the zoetrope. A flip book is made from a stack of sheets of paper, each containing a single image, usually bound or stapled into a booklike shape. Creating a flip book is simple. You print the sequence of images for your animation on separate sheets of paper and leave a margin on one side (usually the left or top) that is large enough to fasten the sheets together. Assemble the sheets in the order in which they are to be viewed, and fasten (for example, using one or more staples) the sheets in the margin. The animation can be viewed by holding the sheets at the fastened margin and placing a finger opposite the margin, and letting the sheets slip through your finger slowly enough to glimpse each image. If the images go by at a reasonable rate, the animation is seen. An animation seen in a flip book could have any number of images, unlike a zoetrope, but with heavier paper it would probably have twenty-five to one hundred pages. The biggest trick to making a flip book seems to be to get a fairly stiff paper for the images, so there is some resistance to letting an image slip past the viewer's finger, and getting the images on the right size of paper. Flipbooks have an early place in the history of animation; some early animation machines were just flipbooks held in viewers, and you flipped the pages by rotating a dial at the side of the viewer.

A Word to the Wise

Designing the communication in an animation is quite different from the same task for a single scene, and it takes some extra experience to get it really right. Among the techniques used in professional animation is the storyboard—a layout of the overall animation that says what will happen when the program executes, and what each of your shots is intended to communicate to the viewer.

Animation Examples in OpenGL

Following are several examples of animations that use some of the ideas above, including code fragments as appropriate. As the code examples show, animation is often controlled by changing parameters of the model in your scene in the callback for the `idle` event. These examples use this callback to control several aspects of the model, the scene, and the display. Expand on these examples and experiment as widely as you can to see what kind of things you can control and how you can control them in order to become fluent in using animation as a communication tool.

Moving Objects in Your Model

Because animation involves motion, one approach to animation is to move individual things in your model. We may take a mathematical approach to defining the position of a cube, for example, to move it around in space; in this very simple example, a cube is translated from its original position at the origin by the amounts `cubex`, `cubey`, and `cubez`. These are set by simple trigonometric functions of a time variable, `aTime`, that is updated by the amount `deltaTime`. Because the positions are set by computations, this is a procedural animation. The effect of this is that the cube moves in each direction in ways that look quite different, so the motion looks random—but is not. This motion control is created in the idle event callback function `animate()` that we show here:

```
void animate(void)
{
    #define deltaTime 0.05
//  define position for the cube by modeling time-based behavior
    aTime += deltaTime; if (aTime > 2.0*PI) aTime -= 2.0*PI;
    cubex = sin(2.0*aTime);
    cubey = cos(3.0*aTime);
    cubez = cos(aTime);
    glutPostRedisplay();
}
```

This function sets the values of the three variables `cubex`, `cubey`, and `cubez` that are later used in the `display()` function as the parameters for the translation that positions the cube in space. You could similarly use other transformations with parameters to set variable orientation, size, or other properties of your objects as well.

Controlling Time for Your Animation

In most of the examples of animated programs we've seen so far, we've use the idle event to call a function (often called `animate()`, if you want to search for this in the source examples) that updates the model and posts a redisplay event. The idle event, however, occurs whenever the program has finished generating a frame, and so the faster the computer is, or the faster the program creates the frame, the sooner the next frame is generated. So if your animation is a mix of simple and complex frames, the idle event can create uneven images. When you run the program on a faster (or slower) computer, its animations run at a different speed from the original speed so the viewer can be confused by or bored with the animation. It is important to manage the speed of your animation.

One approach to this is to use the `timer` event rather than the `idle` event. As we saw in Chapter 7, the timer event will occur when a given number of milliseconds has elapsed since the callback was last registered. It has a fairly high system overhead because it involves continually re-registering the callback (in our example in the earlier chapter, the timer callback function registers the event as it executes) and does not give you as good a control as you might like—but it is clearly better than using the idle event.

There is another way to control frame rates, based on accessing the system clock directly. GLUT includes a function `glutGet(state)` that returns a value of a system state variable; one of the system states that can be returned is the system clock if you use the `GLUT_ELAPSED_TIME` state. So `glutGet(GLUT_ELAPSED_TIME)` returns the number of milliseconds since either `glutInit()` was called or since the first call to `glutGet(GLUT_ELAPSED_TIME)`. You can then call this function to get the time when you generate a frame (when you call `glutPostRedisplay()`) and check the time when you have finished computing the next frame and are ready to generate it. If enough time has passed, you can generate the redisplay; if not, you can wait (spin or make some kind of system sleep call) until enough time has passed and then generate the redisplay. This lets you ensure that your animations will not run too quickly, no matter how fast your computer is.

Moving Parts of Objects in Your Model

Just as we moved whole objects above, you could move individual parts of a hierarchical model. You could change the relative positions, relative angles, or relative sizes by using variables when you define your model, and then changing the values of those variables in the appropriate event callback. You can even get more sophisticated and change colors or transparency when those help you tell the story you are trying to get across with your images. In the discussion of hierarchical modeling in the modeling chapter (Chapter 2) we developed the scene graph for a rabbit's head, shown in Figure 11.12. The scene graph includes transformation nodes that include a parameter t to control the rabbit's ears. The following code increments the parameter t and then uses that parameter to set a rotation angle to wiggle the ears. Here we note that there are transformations that place the ears on the head, but we do not yet define them in detail; this is done in the code.

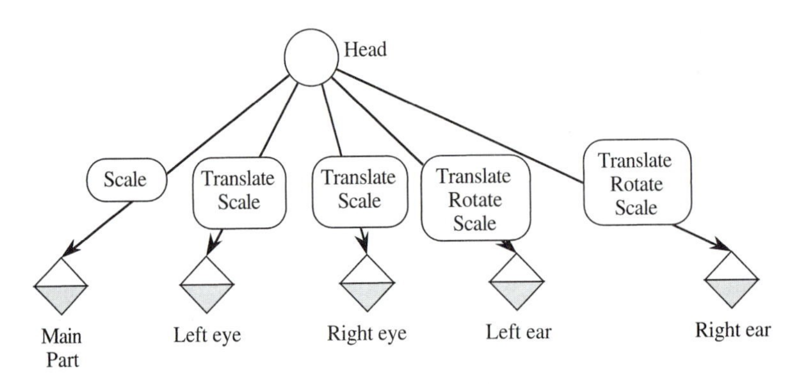

Figure 11.12 The scene graph for the rabbit's head.

The code that defines one of the rabbit's ears is as follows. Note that a number of transformations are involved in this process, but only the two transformations that rotate the two ears from frame to frame involve the parameter *wiggle;* the others are fixed transformations are that do not change between images.

```
glPushMatrix();
    // model the left ear
    glColor3f(1.0, 0.6, 0.6);              // pink ears
    glRotatef(-10.0*wiggle, 0.0, 0.0, 1.0);
    glTranslatef(-1.0, -1.0, 1.0);
    glRotatef(-45.0, 1.0, 0.0, 0.0);
    glTranslatef( 0.5, 0.0, 0.0);          // begin
    glRotatef(-10.0*wiggle, 0.0, 0.0, 1.0);
    glTranslatef(-0.5, 0.0, 0.0);          // end
    glScalef(0.5, 2.0, 0.5);
    myQuad = gluNewQuadric();
    gluSphere(myQuad, 1.0, 10, 10);
glPopMatrix();
```

The idle callback `animate()` shown below manipulates the parameter *wiggle* by uniformly increasing the angle of rotation for the ears.

```
void animate(void)
{
#define twopi 6.28318

    t += 0.1;
    if (t > twopi) t -= twopi;
    wiggle = cos(t);
    glutPostRedisplay();
}
```

Moving the Eyepoint or the View Frame in Your Model

Another kind of animation is provided by defining a controlled motion around a scene to give the viewer a sense of all the parts of the model and to examine particular parts from particular locations that you might want to present. This motion can be fully scripted or it can be under user control, though of course the latter is more difficult. In a first example of this technique, the eye moves from in front of a cube to behind a cube, always looking at the center of the cube, but a more complex (and interesting) effect would have been achieved if the eyepath were defined through an evaluator with specified control points. The *z*-coordinate of the eyepoint is moved between two endpoints by the `animate()` function, and this eyepoint is used in the `gluLookAt(...)` function. The question of moving the eye position using spline interpolation is visited in an experiment at the end of the chapter.

```
void display(void)
{
//   Use a variable for the viewpoint, and move it around ...
     glMatrixMode(GL_MODELVIEW);
     glLoadIdentity();
     gluLookAt(ep.x, ep.y, ep.z, 0.0, 0.0, 0.0, 0.0, 1.0, 0.0);
...
}

void animate(void)
{
     GLfloat numsteps = 100.0, direction[3] = {0.0, 0.0, -20.0};

     if (ep.z < -10.0) whichway = 1.0;
     if (ep.z > 10.0) whichway = -1.0;
     ep.z += whichway*direction[2]/numsteps;
     glutPostRedisplay();
}
```

A more complex example could use the interpolation techniques described in Chapter 13 to determine the eyepoint as the eye moves through the scene. You can define several points where you want the eye to go and add extra control points to define the way the eye is to go through those points. These extra points should be chosen to allow smooth changes from one part of the path to another, as described in the splines chapter. For this technique the Catmull-Rom spline could be a good choice of interpolation technique, because it defines a curve that goes through appropriate control points. The discussion of spline curves in Chapter 13 will fill in the details.

In order to move the eye through the space, you will evaluate the functions $x(t)$, $y(t)$, and $z(t)$ for an interpolating parameter t to determine the eye position. You need to determine the view direction, and you can use the previous and current points on the curve to determine that direction because this is a good approximation of the direction in which you are going. You also need the up direction, but it is reasonable to use a constant up direction, determined by the logic of your scene. Figure 11.13 shows a view of a simple model space (four high-rise buildings, perhaps) with control points and with the resulting eyepoint curve displayed; you are invited to complete the moving eyepoint process in exercise 4 at the end of this chapter.

As your eyepoint travels through a space, you need to control not only the position of the eyepoint but also the entire viewing environment—in OpenGL terms, the entire parameter list for the `gluLookAt(...)` function. So not only the eyepoint but also the view reference point

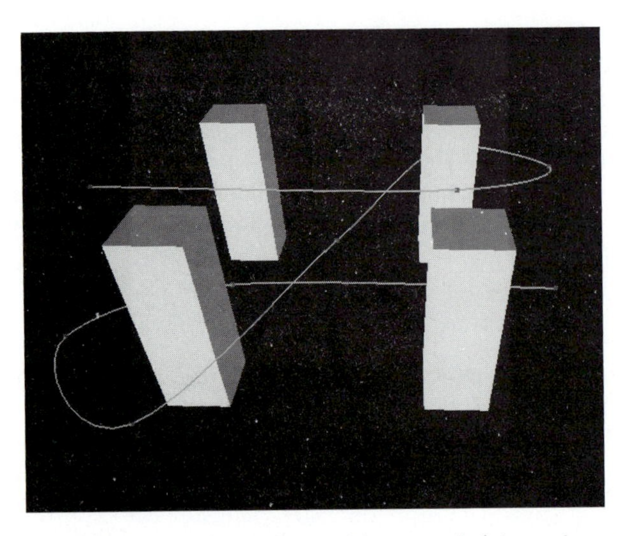

Figure 11.13 An eye path through a space, with control points shown.

and the up vector must be considered in creating an effective moving viewpoint. Further, as you move around you will sometimes find yourself moving nearer to objects or farther from them. This means you will have the opportunity to use level-of-detail techniques from Chapter 12 to control how those objects are presented to the viewer while you keep the frame rate as high as possible. A lot of work is required to do everything right, but you can make a good start much more easily.

Another approach to defining motion could be to define an initial position and a set of velocities that are to be applied at given times. Each velocity is a 3D vector, so we could see the velocities as points, and we could create a spline curve that interpolates these points, creating a set of velocities. Then a motion could be defined by starting at the initial point and applying the sequence of velocities defined by the curve.

Interpolating Textures in Your Scene

As we discussed the texture interpolation shown in Figure 11.3, we said that we simply created a linear combination of the colors in the two basic texture arrays to create the interpolated texture. This is shown in the following code fragment, where `tex1` and `tex2` are assumed to be texture arrays created by whatever process you like, and `texImage` is a texture array of the same size that is to be used by the texture mapping process.

```
for (i = 0; i < TEX_WIDTH; i++)
    for (j = 0; j < TEX_HEIGHT; j++)
        for (k = 0; k < 3; k++)
            texImage[i][j][k] = alpha*tex1[i][j][k]+(1.-alpha)
                                *tex2[i][j][k];
```

For each frame of the animation, you will need to destroy the old interpolated texture, create the new interpolated texture, and link the new texture as the active texture. When you do this, the textures will change smoothly as the geometry changes between frames.

Changing Features of Your Model

There are many other special features of your models and displays that you can change with time to create the particular communication you want. Among them, you can change colors, properties of your lights, transparency, clipping planes, fog, texture maps, granularity of your model, and so on. Almost anything that can be defined with a variable instead of a constant can be changed by changing the model.

In the particular example for this technique, we will change the size and transparency of the display of one kind of atom in a molecule, as we show in Figure 11.14. The change in the image is driven by a parameter *t* that is changed in the `idle` callback, and the parameter in turn gives a sinusoidal change in the size and transparency parameters for the image. This will allow us to put a visual emphasis on this kind of atom so that a user can see where that kind of atom fits into the molecule. This is just a small start on the overall kinds of things you could choose to animate to put an emphasis on a part of your model.

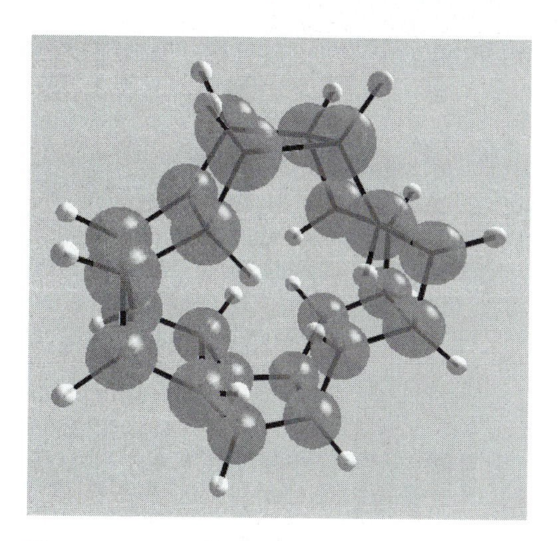
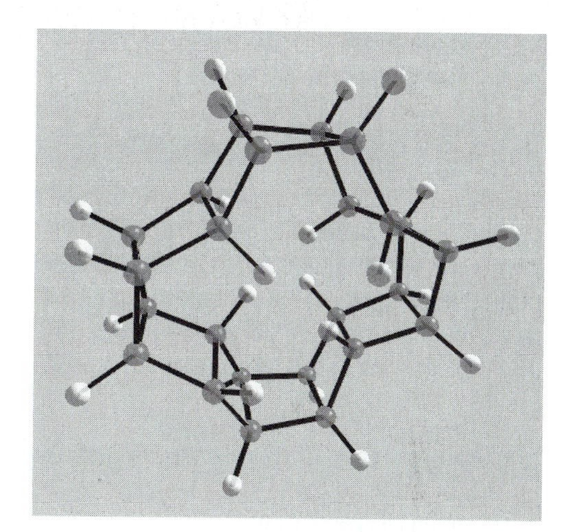

Figure 11.14 Molecule with carbon atoms shown expanded (*left*) and contracted (*right*).

Code to carry out this operation is shown below, based on the molecular viewing examples in Chapter 9. The `animate()` function below simply changes the values of the `sizeMult` and `alphaAdd` parameters, and these in turn are used to set the alpha value of the molecule's color and the size of the `gluSphere` that represents the atom.

```
void molecule(void)
{
...
    j = atoms[i].colindex;      // index of color for atom i
    for (k=0; k < 4; k++)
    {   // copy atomColors[j], adjust alpha by alphaMult
        myColor[k] = atomColors[j][k];

    }
    if (j==CARBON) myColor[3] += alphaAdd;
    glMaterialfv(..., myColor);
```

```
    glPushMatrix();
        glTranslatef(...);
        if (j==CARBON)
            gluSphere(atomSphere,sizeMult*ANGTOAU(atomSizes[j]),GRAIN,
            GRAIN);
        else
            gluSphere(atomSphere,ANGTOAU(atomSizes[j]),GRAIN,GRAIN);
    glPopMatrix();
...
}
...
void animate(void)
{
    t += 0.1; if (t > 2.0*M_PI) t -= 2.0*M_PI;
    sizeMult = (1.0+0.5*sin(t));
    alphaAdd = 0.2*cos(t);
    glutPostRedisplay();
}
```

Creating Traces

One way to create the trace of an object, as shown in Figure 11.7, is to create a sequence of cylinders that connect a certain number of previous positions of an object and fade out as the points get older. The following code does that, based on a global variable, `tails`, that maintains the last several positions of the object in an array `list`. Elements of the list describe the previous positions and directions of the object, as well as the color and length of each segment. The variable `valid` is used as the trace is initialized and not all segments of the trace are yet created.

```
typedef struct { // hold properties of individual tail cylinders for bodies
    point4 color;
    point3 position;
    point3 direction;
    float length;
    int valid;
} tailstruct;

void draw_tail()
{
    int j;
    float angle;
    point3 rot_vect;
    point3 origin={0.0,0.0,0.0};
    point3 y_point={0.0,1.0,0.0};

    for(j=0; j < T_LENGTH; j++)
    if(tails.list[j].valid) {
        glMaterialfv(GL_FRONT,GL_AMBIENT_AND_DIFFUSE,tails.list[j].color);
        // calculate angle to rotate cylinder so it points in right
           direction
```

```
            angle = asin(tails.list[j].direction[1]
                /sqrt(tails.list[j].direction[0]*tails.list[j].direction[0]
                +tails.list[j].direction[1]*tails.list[j].direction[1]
                +tails.list[j].direction[2]*tails.list[j].direction[2]));
            angle = angle*180/PI+90;
            // calculate vector perpendicular to direction vector and y axis
            // for the line to rotate around.
            normal(tails.list[j].direction, origin, y_point, rot_vect);
            glPushMatrix();
            // move tail segment to right location, rotate, and set length.
            glTranslatef(tails.list[j].position[0],
                tails.list[j].position[1], tails.list[j].position[2]);
            glRotatef(angle, rot_vect[0], rot_vect[1], rot_vect[2]);
            glScalef(1.0, tails.list[j].length, 1.0);
            // draw tail segment as cylinder with 12 slices
            cylinder(radius/30., 12);
            glPopMatrix();
        }
}
```

In the other example of Figure 11.7, showing a random walk of a certain number of steps of a single particle, a similar but simpler kind of process is used because we do not try to fade out the individual steps of the trace. Instead, we merely retain a certain number of previous positions and draw a polyline that connects them in a contrasting color.

Using the Accumulation Buffer

The accumulation buffer is one of the buffers available in OpenGL to use with your rendering and was the main tool used to create Figure 11.8. This buffer holds floating-point values for RGBA colors and corresponds pixel-for-pixel with the frame buffer. The accumulation buffer holds values in the range $[-1.0, 1.0]$, and if any operation on the buffer results in a value outside this range, its results are undefined (that is, the result may differ from system to system and is not reliable) so you should be careful when you define your operations. It is intended to be used to accumulate the weighted results of a number of display operations and has many applications that are beyond the scope of this chapter; anyone interested in advanced applications should consult the manuals and the literature on advanced OpenGL techniques.

As is the case with other buffers, the accumulation buffer must be chosen when the OpenGL system is initialized, as in

```
glutInitDisplayMode(GLUT_RGB|GLUT_DOUBLE|GLUT_ACCUM|GLUT_DEPTH);
```

The accumulation buffer is used with the function `glAccum(mode, value)`, which takes one of several possible symbolic constants for its mode, and with a floating-point number as its value. The available modes are:

`GL_ACCUM` Gets RGBA values from the current read buffer (by default the `FRONT` buffer if you are using single buffering or the `BACK` buffer if double buffering, so you will probably not need to choose which buffer to use), converts them from integer to floating-point values, multiplies them by

	the value parameter, and adds the values to the content of the accumulation buffer. If the buffer has bit depth n, then the integer conversion is accomplished by dividing each value from the read buffer by 2^n-1.
GL_LOAD	Operates similarly to GL_ACCUM, except that after the values are obtained from the read buffer, converted to floating point, and multiplied by value, they are written to the accumulation buffer, replacing any values already present.
GL_ADD	Adds the value of value to each of the R, G, B, and A components of each pixel in the accumulation buffer and returns the result to its original location.
GL_MULT	Multiplies each of the R, G, B, and A components of each pixel in the buffer by the value of value and returns the result to its original location.
GL_RETURN	Returns the contents of the accumulation buffer to the read buffer after multiplying each of the RGBA components by value and scaling the result back to the appropriate integer value for the read buffer. If the buffer has bit depth n, then the scaling is accomplished by multiplying the result by 2^n-1 and clamped to the range $[0, 2^n-1]$.

You will probably not need to use some of these operations to show the motion trace. If we want to accumulate the images of (say) 10 positions, we can draw the scene 10 times and accumulate the results of these multiple renderings with weights 2^{-i} for scene i, where scene 1 corresponds to the most recent position shown and scene 10 to the oldest position. This takes advantage of the fact that the sum

$$\sum_{i=1}^{10} 2^{-i}$$

is very close to 1.0, so we keep the maximum value of the accumulated results below 1.0. This technique works even if the objects are not moving, because the multiple weighted copies of the objects create almost exactly the original single-frame image. (You can remove the "very close" condition if you use 2^{-9} for the step $i=10$.) An example of code that accomplishes this is:

```
//  we assume that we have a time parameter t for the
//  drawObjects(t) function and that we have defined an array
//  times[10] that holds the times for which the objects are to
//  be drawn. This is an example of what the manuals call time
//  jittering; another example might be to choose a set of random
//  times, but this would not give us the time trail we want for
//  this example.
    drawObjects(times[9]);
    glAccum(GL_LOAD, 0.5)
    for (i = 9; i > 0; i-) {
        glAccum(GL_MULT, 0.5);
        drawObjects(times[i-1]);
        glAccum(GL_ACCUM, 0.5);
    }
    glAccum(GL_RETURN, 1.0);
```

The array `times[]` is then updated in the `idle()` function so that each call to the `display()` function shows the object sequence after the next motion step.

A few things to note here are that we save a little time by loading the oldest image into the accumulation buffer instead of clearing the buffer before we draw it, we draw from the oldest to the newest image, we multiply the value of the accumulation buffer by 0.5 before we draw the next image, and we multiply the value of the new image by 0.5 as we accumulate it into the buffer. This accomplishes the successive reduction of the older images automatically.

There are other techniques one could find here, of course. One would be simply to take whatever image you had computed to date, bring it into the accumulation buffer with value 0.5, draw the new scene and accumulate it with weight 0.5, and return the scene with weight 1.0. This would be faster and would likely not show much difference from the approach above, but it does not show the possibilities of drawing a scene with various kinds of jittering, a useful advanced technique.

Creating a Digital Video

Creating a digital animation can be relatively simple, especially when you consider the complexity of digital movie standards. Because this book is about graphics, not about digital video formats, we can use simple tools to create digital videos that capture our animations. A digital video starts out like any animation by designing a model that includes time-varying behavior and implementing that model in programming. A real-time animation creates a sequence of frames that are presented by the program using a technique such as the idle callback or clock-based redisplay. Use the same sequence of frames to create a digital video, but instead of displaying the frames (or at the same time you display them) you save each frame to an array using the OpenGL tools such as the function

```
glReadPixels(0,0,width,height,GL_RGB,GL_UNSIGNED_BYTE,the_view)
```

which reads the color buffer into an array named `the_view`. You can then write each array to a file and use the sequence of files in an animation tool. You will probably need to use some programming to give the files names that are alike except for a sequence number that can be used by the animation tool. These animation tools combine a sequence of image files into an animation using one or your choice of digital video file formats (QuickTime, MPEG, etc.) so you can share the animation, perhaps by posting it online. Among the options these tools will give you is the frame rate for playing back the animation.

The big advantage of digital video (or any other video format) is that you can use as complex a model as you want, and your playback will not be slowed down by the extra computing time it would take to build images from your model. You are also independent of whether your audience has the programming capability to compile and run your original program. Digital videos are probably the medium of choice for presenting your animations to a wide audience.

Some Points to Consider When Doing Animations with OpenGL

You need to understand some things about OpenGL more fully when you move your eyepoint than you when you simply create a single image. The viewing transformation is part of the overall modeling transformation, and it needs to be done at the right place if you are going to use parameters to define your view. In the `display()` function in the `viewcube.c` example, you will note that the modeling transformation is set to the identity, the `gluLookAt(...)` function is called, the resulting transformation is saved for future use, and then the rotation processes are called. This keeps the viewing transformation from changing the position of objects in the model and thus keeps the animation looking right.

Finally, be careful when you use texture maps in animations. There is always the possibility of aliasing with texture maps, and when they are animated the aliasing can cause strange-looking behavior in the texture rendering. Some effort in antialiasing textures is particularly important in animating them.

A Word to the Wise

Look at videos of computer graphics work to get a fuller understanding of what you can do with this tool. In general, though, you want to avoid high-end entertainment-focused animations and look at informational animations—presentations of scientific or technical work are ideal. But remember that when you look at video animations on television or commercial video, you are looking at *presentation-level* animations, or work that is done to impress others with the concepts being presented. Such work is usually very highly designed and involves a great deal of sophisticated thinking and high-end graphics systems and tools. The work you will do in a beginning computer graphics course is much more likely to be *personal-level* or *peer-level* animation: work that is done to explore an idea yourself or to share with a friend or colleague. Our experience is that even these animations can be very valuable; a number of people in the sciences have asked for copies of student animations that have been very effective at illustrating concepts in the sciences. So don't try to match the quality of the videos you watch; try to find the key communication ideas in the videos and learn from them, and your work will be valuable.

OpenGL Glossary for the Chapter

This chapter did not introduce much new OpenGL or GLUT functionality, and those it did introduce are less common than those we have seen earlier. They are interesting, however, and offer some abilities that are very useful in the right context.

OpenGL and GLUT Functions

`glAccum(param, value)`: operates on the accumulation buffer in ways specified by the parameter

`int glutGet(state)`: retrieves the value of the OpenGL state indicated by the parameter

OpenGL and GLUT Parameters

`GL_ACCUM`: specifies that `glAccum()` is to get RGBA components from the currently selected read buffer, multiply them by the value, and add them to the accumulation buffer

`GL_ADD`: specifies that the value is to be added to each element in the accumulation buffer

`GL_LOAD`: has the same effect as `GL_ACCUM` except that the scaled values from the read buffer are loaded into the accumulation buffer

`GL_MULT`: specifies that each element in the accumulation buffer is to be multiplied by the value

`GL_RETURN:` specifies that the values in the accumulation buffer are to be transferred to the color buffer selected for writing

`GLUT_ELAPSED_TIME:` parameter to `glutGet()` that defines the number of milliseconds since `glutInit` called (or first call to `glutGet(GLUT_ELAPSED_TIME)`)

Questions

1. One of the problems with older computer games and computer animations is that the speed at which they are presented can vary depending on the speed of the processor and graphics card, as well as other system properties. Discuss how, or if, you can use the `timer` event to create a more uniform speed for an animated image. Do the same for the `glutGet(...)` approach. Can these techniques make a slow animation move more quickly? Can they make a fast animation move more slowly? Support your answers.
2. Discuss the process of creating a procedural animation by modeling a physical system with motion determined by forces; see Chapter 9 for examples, but you could use the motion of a single object such as a pendulum, an object rolling down a ramp, or an object thrown into space, or you could use the motion of two objects in space that orbit around each other based on gravitational forces.

Exercises

1. Model a fireworks burn with a particle system and display the result as an animation that shows the effects of the fireworks you model. This can be simple, with a single explosion that distributes small particles in all directions and the particles burn with a single color for a fixed time. Or you can model this with particles having changing colors at different times, or secondary explosions, or explosions that are in a limited direction only; the variations (like the real fireworks) are unending. You might want to use traces for each particle.
2. Use the ideas of interpolating shape and interpolating texture to create a short animation that starts with one textured shape and ends with another. If you are not careful, the figure may look clumsy in the middle of the interpolation, so you may want to think about relating the shapes and textures to make all the steps look reasonable.
3. Create an animation by using a set of parameters that vary with time and seeing their effect on a physical system. For example, create a simple surface showing the electrostatic force in 2D space caused by a small number of point charges, using Coulomb's law as discussed in Chapter 9. Then let the amount of one of the charges vary with time, and see the effect on the forces in space as represented by the shape of the surface. Let the charge vary not only in strength but in sign.
4. Carry out the operation of creating a moving view through a space that was described in the discussion of a moving eyepoint above. Define a simple space that can include anything else you want, and in that space place appropriate control points for the eye position; the intent is that you will create a simpler space than a house, because the house walkthrough is covered in a project in this chapter. Compute a path by interpolating cubic basis functions with these points—probably using the Catmull-Rom spline, but you are welcome to choose another. Write an idle event callback function that computes

points on that path and uses them for the eye position and direction in displaying the space.

Experiments

1. Experiment with the code for the temporal aliasing example to see what kind of effects you can make. Can you make the spokes seem to be fixed and not moving? What are the conditions to make this happen? Can you simulate an acceleration similar to that of an automobile, with the spokes modeling the spokes of a wheel? What do you observe about the visual motion of the spokes as the wheel is accelerated and then decelerated? Can you relate this to any observations of wheels in movies (especially older movies)?

2. Create an interpolation from one scene to another by defining two cubic surfaces by functions $f_1(x) = a_1x^3 + b_1x^2 + c_1x + d_1$ and $f_2(x) = a_2x^3 + b_2x^2 + c_2x + d_2$ for your choice of parameter sets. Create intermediate surfaces that interpolate from the first surface to the second by interpolating the coefficients linearly over one hundred time steps and presenting the results by standard surface displays as we saw in the earlier chapters. Do the same operation but use a smooth interpolation, and see if you can sense a qualitative difference in the motion.

3. Extend the interpolation from two scenes to several scenes by creating sets of parameters $\{a_i\}$, $\{b_i\}$, $\{c_i\}$, and $\{d_i\}$ for cubic surfaces and creating a smooth interpolation for each set of parameters to move from the first scene through the others to the last one.

4. Implement the concept of creating a motion path by defining a single starting point and a set of velocities and interpolating the velocities with splines to create a sequence of velocities to be applied to the path. What kind of path do you get with such an approach?

5. To see the power of motion in seeing things that are invisible in static images, this experiment asks you to re-create the classic piece of work from Dan Sandin of the Electronic Visualization Laboratory at the University of Illinois, Chicago, that we showed in Figure 11.6. Generate a window with two viewports, one of which is the whole window and the other occupying the middle third of the window horizontally and vertically. In each window, generate a random set of points with the same density by generating one-third as many points in the smaller viewport as in the larger window. Have each point in the larger viewport move slowly to the right, while each point in the smaller viewport is to move slowly to the left. Have the motion start or stop on a keypress so you can turn the motion on or off. Can you tell from the static images that these are two separate populations of points? Can you tell from the moving images? What does this say?

6. Expand the previous project to experiment with the concept of seeing a region by different motion inside and outside the region. You can use different backgrounds from the random-noise background shown, you can use different regions from the circle shown, you can use a different logic to determine if pixels are inside or outside the region than in the original, and you can use different motions from the simple sliding motion in the original. Some interesting options are to use scanned images as the background and use complex regions made by creating bicolor versions of photographs with one of the colors defining the region. Can you draw any conclusions about human perception of regions based on motion from this experiment?

7. Take any image you have created that shows motion and use the accumulation buffer to make that motion show blurs. Try several different weights on the images you composite into the accumulation buffer, including uniform weight and weights that are centrally distributed around the time that represents the instantaneous time when the image was "captured." Which weighting method works best?
8. (The scene graph) In Chapter 7, an experiment suggested adding an event node to the scene graph to account for event-driven changes in the model or viewing environments. Do this specifically for the idle event so that you can model time-driven changes.
9. We suggested that the `idle` event, on its own, creates animations of unpredictable speed. Earlier, in Chapter 7, we noted the `timer()` callback as a way to control the speed of animations, but in this chapter we discussed the `glutGet(GLUT_ELAPSED_TIME)` function and described how you could use it to control frame rates more effectively. Create an animation and use the `idle`, `timer`, and `glutGet()` techniques to manage timing the animation. Write up your results.

Projects

1. Make a flip book that uses images from any of your previous interactive or animated projects and communicates the essential ideas of the project. Try out various sheets of various sizes and stiffness so that you find a comfortable way to flip through the book. Does this flip book communicate the ideas as well as the on-screen display does? Can you identify the features of the display that make the on-screen version better or the flip book better?
2. Build a zoetrope as a class project, and as a class create a set of short animations that use it to present a scientific topic. You can use images from an animation you created with the `idle` event callback in an earlier chapter, or you can create something that is designed to work with a small number of images in a cycle. If someone in the class has access to a zoetrope, of course, you need not build one yourselves.
3. Build a digital video from any of your previous projects by saving each frame (or saving set of frames at regular intervals) as a digital image file, converting each file as needed to a format your video editor can work with and assembling the individual files into a digital video file.
4. (The small house) In Chapter 7 on events, a project suggested adding a walkthrough to the house project. Now automate the walkthrough, choosing specific points in the house that are to be visited with specific views and use a spline curve or other technique to give the position of the eyepoints that will be visited automatically as the user walks through the house.
5. (A scene graph parser) Implement the experiment on adding an event node to the scene graph and use it to specify and generate time-driven changes in the model or the view for the image defined by the scene graph.

12 High-Performance Graphics Techniques

In this chapter we consider some computational and graphics techniques that can help you write graphics programs that run faster. This lets you increase frame rates for animations or provide faster interaction feedback to your users. This chapter is not an in-depth look at this issue, however; the large and growing literature in games programming has many techniques for making the graphics part of games programming run very quickly, and advances in graphics accelerators and graphics APIs will always be ahead of any book. Some of the techniques we consider are system-dependent, some involve modeling tricks, some take advantage of very advanced or esoteric features of graphics APIs, and some involve going outside the graphics API completely to use other kinds of graphics capabilities. For these we suggest you consult the games references in this book or the advanced games literature from game developer associations or the like.

The ultimate in high-performance graphics is real-time graphics, graphics that presents a simulation with the speed of the original system being simulated. This area includes computer graphics for immersive virtual realities, where the viewer needs to see the world being simulated in real time. This is an additional challenge that has been studied by the simulation, visualization, and virtual-reality communities, and the literature in those areas should be examined.

To benefit fully from this chapter you should have a solid understanding of computer graphics basics and know the details of the OpenGL graphics API sufficiently to consider alternatives to standard approaches to creating high-quality images.

Definitions

The speed with which we can generate an image is always of interest because we want to be able to see our results quickly, whether we're doing a single scene or an animation. Waiting for an image to be produced can be frustrating and can even get in the way of the image's effectiveness. This is evident in many kinds of graphics applications, but it is probably most evident in computer games, so this is the context that will frame much of the discussion in this chapter. However, performance is always an issue in graphical computations, so the techniques we discuss here are also important to many other graphics applications.

Making effective computer games involves many things, including storytelling, creating characters, maintaining databases of game features, and many general programming techniques to deliver maximum speed of operation to the player. One of the critical performance areas is the graphics that presents the game play to the user, because it's one of the most computational-intensive bottlenecks in presenting the game to the player. This is a different question than we've been dealing with in computer graphics to this point. So far in the book we have focused on the quality of the images while maintaining as much performance as we can, but in this chapter we reverse this emphasis: We focus on the performance of the programs while maintaining as much quality as we can. This change makes a major difference in the kind of processes and techniques we use.

In a sense, this is not a new issue in computer graphics. For more than twenty years, the computer field has included the area of "real-time graphics." This originally focused on areas such as flight simulators, real-time monitoring of safety-critical system processes, and real-time simulations, often using the most powerful computers available at the time. Additional real-time work has come from the virtual-reality environment that presents interactive worlds to the viewer. Some of the real-time graphics processes also have been used in educational applications that are essentially simulations. Most recently, the main force behind real-time graphics has been games. The demands that high-performance graphics applications place on graphics can be extreme and are focused on personal computers with widely varying configurations, making it important to bring a look at some real-time techniques into a graphics text.

Techniques

Fundamentally, high-performance computer graphics, especially as applied to games, takes advantage of a few simple principles:

- Use hardware acceleration when you can, but don't assume that everyone has it and be ready to work around it when you need to.
- Do some work to determine what you don't need to display.
  - Look for techniques that support easy ways to cull objects or pieces of objects from the set of things to be displayed.
- Take advantage of capabilities of texture mapping.
  - Create objects as texture maps instead of as fully rendered objects.
  - Use multitextures and textures with both low and high resolution.
- Use any techniques available to support the fastest display techniques you can.
  - Vertex arrays
  - Display lists
  - Level of detail
- Avoid unnecessary lighting calculations.
  - When you draw any object, enable lights near the object.
  - Use fog when appropriate to disguise lower-quality rendering.
- Approximate collision detection instead of computing it exactly.

This list includes both modeling techniques and rendering techniques, but it can be useful to separate these when we discuss them in detail. We will show you as many techniques as we can to help you improve the performance of your graphics, but there are many more that may depend on your individual system or that go beyond the scope of this text. If you find that your graphics performance is limited and you need more speed, you might need to profile your programs and see just where the time is used; this can help you decide where you might get the best return on your investment for adding techniques such as those in this chapter to your program.

There are some unique problems in some gaming situations that are not found in most other areas of graphics. The main one we will discuss is collision detection, because this is an area that requires some simple computation that we can streamline in straightforward ways.

Modeling Techniques

Modeling techniques involve changing your model in ways that simplify the scene by reducing the number of polygons that need to be rendered, or that add features to the model that make it simpler or faster to render. There are a modest number of these, but they can be important if you are pushing the limits of your graphics system.

Reducing the Number of Visible Polygons

As you lay out the overall design of your image, you can ensure that there is only limited visibility of the overall scene from any viewpoint. This is part of the reason why one sees many walls in games. We see large polygons with texture mapping for detail, and only a very few polygons are visible from any point. The sense of visual richness is maintained by moving quickly between places with different and clearly understood environments, so that when players make the transition from one place to another, they see a very different world, and even though the world is simple, the constant changing makes the game seem constantly fresh.

Other techniques involve pre-computing what objects will be visible to the player from what positions. As a very simple example, when players move out of one space into another, nothing in the space being vacated can be seen, so all the polygons in that space can be ignored. This kind of pre-computed design can involve maintaining lists of visible polygons from each point with each direction the player is facing, a classical tradeoff of space for speed.

Clever Use of Textures

We have already seen that textures can make simple scenes seem complex and can give an audience a sense of seeing realistic objects. When we take advantage of some of the capabilities of texture mapping we can also deal with graphic operations in precisely the sense that we started this chapter with: reducing the accuracy in hard-to-see ways while increasing the efficiency of the graphics. These techniques were introduced in Chapter 8 but are included here because of their value in increasing graphics performance.

One technique is *billboarding,* creating texture-mapped versions of complex objects that will be displayed as texture maps on 2D objects. By taking a snapshot—a photograph, a once-computed image, or a synthetic image—and using the alpha channel in the texture map to make everything invisible outside the object we want to present, we can put the texture onto a rectangle oriented toward the eyepoint and get the effect of a tree, or a building, or a vehicle on each rectangle. If we repeat this process many times we can build complex objects such as forests, cities, or parking lots without doing the complex computation needed to actually compute them. Orienting each billboard to the eye involves computing the positions of the billboard and the eye (which can be readily done from the scene graph by looking for translations that affect both) and computing the cylindrical or spherical coordinates of the eyepoint if the billboard is regarded as the origin. The latitude and longitude of the eyepoint from the billboard will tell you how to rotate the billboard so that it faces the eye. Note that there are two ways to view a billboard—if it represents an object with a fixed base (tree, building, person, or similar objects), then you want to rotate it only around its fixed vertical axis; if it represents an object with no fixed point (such as a label or snowflake), then you probably want to rotate it around two axes so that it faces the eye directly. In Chapter 8 we discussed how you calculate these rotations.

Another technique is to use textures at several levels of resolution through mipmaps, a set of texture maps at many resolutions. If you start with the highest-resolution (and largest) texture map, you can automatically create texture maps with lower resolution. In OpenGL, each dimension of any texture map must be a power of two, so you can create maps with dimensions half the original, one-fourth the original, and so on, yielding a sequence of texture maps that you can use to achieve your textures without the aliasing you would get if you used the larger texture.

You may also layer textures to achieve your effects. This multitexturing capability was discussed in Chapter 8. It lets you apply multiple textures to a polygon in any order you want, so you can create a brick wall as a color texture map, for example, and then apply a luminance texture map to make certain parts brighter, simulating the effect of light through a window or the brightness of a torch without doing any lighting computations whatsoever.

Reducing Lighting Computation

While we may include eight (or more) lights in a scene, each light we add takes a toll on the time it takes to render the scene. You will recall that for lighting computations we calculate the ambient, diffuse, and specular lighting for each light and add these values to compute the light for any polygon or vertex. However, if you are using positional lights with attenuation, the amount of light a particular light adds to a vertex is rather small when that vertex is not near the light. You may choose to simplify the light computation by disabling lights when they are not near the polygon you are working on. Again, the principle is to spend a little time on computation when it can offer the possibility of saving more time on the graphics calculation. The tradeoff is that if you are making an animation and eliminate a light too soon, you may have noticeable jumps in lighting.

Level of Detail

Level of detail (usually just called *LOD*) is a set of techniques for changing the display depending on the view the user needs in a scene. It can involve creating multiple versions of a graphical element and displaying a particular one based on the distance the element is from the viewer. It can also involve choosing not to display an object if it is so far from the user that it is too small to display effectively, or displaying a blurred or hazy version of an object if it is not near the eye. LOD techniques allow you to create very detailed models that will be seen when the element is near the viewer, as well as more simple models that will be seen when the element is far from the viewer. This saves rendering time and allows you to control the way things will be seen, or even whether the element will be seen at all.

Level of detail is not supported directly by OpenGL except through mipmaps, so there are few definitions to be given for it. However, it is becoming an important issue in graphics systems because ever more complex models and environments are being created and it is ever more important to display them in real time. Even with ever-faster computer systems, these two goals are at odds, and techniques must sometimes be found to display scenes as efficiently as possible.

The key concept is to be that the image of the object you're dealing with should have as nearly as possible the same appearance at any distance. This means that the farther away something is, the fewer details you need to provide or the coarser the approximation you can use. Certainly one key consideration is that one would not want to display any graphical element that is smaller than one pixel, or perhaps smaller than a few pixels. Making the decision on what to suppress at large distance, or what to enhance at close distance, is probably still a heuristic process, ongoing research work on coarsening meshes automatically could eventually make this better.

LOD is a bit more difficult to illustrate than fog, because it requires us to provide multiple models of the elements we are displaying. The standard technique for this is to identify the point in your graphical element (*ObjX*, *ObjY*, *ObjZ*) that you want to use to determine the element's distance from the eye. OpenGL will let you determine the distance of any object from the eye, and you can determine the distance through code similar to the following in the function that displayed the element:

```
glRasterPos3f(ObjX, ObjY, ObjZ);
glGetFloatv(GL_CURRENT_RASTER_DISTANCE, &dist);
if (farDist(dist)) { ... // farther element definition
}
                else { ... // nearer element definition
}
```

This allows you to display one version of the element if it is far from your viewpoint (determined by the function `float farDist(float)` that you can define), and other versions as desired as the element moves nearer to your viewpoint. You may have more than two versions of your element, and you may use the distance that

```
glGetFloatv(GL_CURRENT_RASTER_DISTANCE, &dist)
```

returns in any way you wish to modify your modeling statements for the element.

To illustrate the general LOD concept, let's display a GLU sphere with different resolutions at different distances. Recall from the modeling discussion in Chapter 3 that the GLU sphere is defined by the function

```
void gluSphere(GLUquadricObj *qobj, GLdouble radius, GLint slices,
               GLint stacks);
```

as a sphere centered at the origin with the radius specified. The two integer `slices` and `stacks` determine the granularity of the object; small values of these will create a coarse sphere and large values will create a smoother sphere, but small values create a sphere with fewer polygons that's faster to render. The LOD approach to a problem such as this is to define the distances at which you want the resolution to change, and to determine the number of slices and stacks that you want to display at each of these distances. Ideally you will analyze the number of pixels you want to see in each polygon in the sphere and will choose the number of slices and stacks that provides that number.

Our modeling approach is to create a function `mySphere()` whose parameters are the center and radius of the desired sphere. In the function, the depth of the sphere is determined by identifying the position of the center of the sphere, asking how far this position is from the eye, and using simple logic to define the values of slices and stacks that are passed to the `gluSphere` function in order to select a relatively constant granularity for these values. The essential code follows, and some levels of the sphere are shown in Figure 12.1.

```
     myQuad=gluNewQuadric();
     glRasterPos3fv(origin);
//   howFar = distance from eye to center of sphere
     glGetFloatv(GL_CURRENT_RASTER_DISTANCE, &howFar);
     resolution = (GLint) (200.0/howFar);
     slices = stacks = resolution;
     gluSphere(myQuad , radius , slices , stacks);
```

Figure 12.1 Levels of detail in the sphere, from high detail level (*left*) to lower (*right*).

As you use LOD techniques in creating animated or dynamic scenes, you must avoid having the techniques cause the sudden appearance or disappearance of objects (as they are clipped or unclipped by a distant plane, for example) as well as sudden changes in objects' appearance. These artifacts cause a break in perception that detracts from the believability of the action. It can be useful to create a fog zone deep in a scene and have things appear through the fog instead of simply jumping into place.

Fog

Fog is a technique that offers some possibility of using simpler models in a scene while hiding some of the details by reducing the visibility of the models. The tradeoff may or may not be worth it, because using simpler models may not save as much time as it takes to calculate the effect of the fog. We include it here more because of its conceptual similarity to level-of-detail questions than for pure efficiency reasons.

When you use fog, the color of the display is modified by blending it with the fog color as the display is finally rendered from the OpenGL color buffer. Details of the blending are controlled by the contents of the depth buffer. You may specify the distance at which this blending starts, the distance at which no more blending occurs and the color is always the fog color, and the way the fog color is increased through the region between these two distances. Thus elements closer than the near distance are seen with no change, elements between the two distances are seen with a color that fades toward the fog color as the distance increases, and elements farther than the far distance are seen only with the full effect of the fog as determined by the fog density. This provides a method of depth cueing that can be very useful in some circumstances.

A small number of fundamental concepts are needed to manage fog in OpenGL. They are all supplied through the `glFog*(param, value)` functions as follows, similarly to other system parameter settings, with all the capitalized terms being the specific values used for param. In this discussion we assume that color is specified in terms of RGB or RGBA.

Start and End

Fog is applied between the starting value GL_FOG_START and the ending value GL_FOG_END, with no fog applied before the starting value and no changes made in the fog after the end value. Note that these values are applied with the usual convention that the center of view is at the origin and the viewpoint is at a negative distance from the origin. The usual convention is to have fog start at 0 and end at 1.

Mode

OpenGL provides three built-in fog modes: linear, exponential, and exponential-squared. These affect the blending of element and fog color by computing the fog factor *ff* as follows:

- GL_LINEAR: $ff = density*z'$ for $z' = (end-z)/(end-start)$ and any z between *start* and *end*
- GL_EXP: $ff = \exp(-density*z')$ for z' as above
- GL_EXP2: $ff = \exp(-density*z')^2$ for z' as above

The fog factor is then clamped to the range [0,1] after it is computed. For all three modes, once the fog factor *ff* is computed, the final displayed color *Cd* is interpolated by the factor of *ff* between the element color *Ce* and the fog color *Cf* by

$$Cd = ff*Ce + (1 - ff)*Cf.$$

Density

You can think of density as determining the maximum attenuation of the color of a graphical element by the fog, though the way that maximum is reached will depend on which fog mode you use. The larger the density, the more quickly things will fade out in the fog and the more opaque the fog will seem. The density must be between 0 and 1.

Color

While we may think of fog as gray, it doesn't have to be—in a graphics system, fog can take on any color at all. This color can be defined as a four-element vector or as four individual parameters, and the elements or parameters may be integers or floats; there are variations on the glFog*() function for each of these choices. The details of the individual versions of glFog*() are very similar to glColor*() and glMaterial*() and we refer you to your manuals for the details. Because fog is applied to graphic elements but not to the background, it is a very good idea to make the fog and background colors the same, as we did in Figure 12.2

There are two additional options for fog that we will skim over lightly, but that should be mentioned at least in passing. First, you can use fog when you are using indexed color in place of RGB or RGBA color; in that case the color indices are interpolated instead of the color specification. (We did not cover indexed color when we talked about color models, but some older graphics systems used only this color technology.) Second, fog is hintable—you can use glHint(...) with parameter GL_FOG_HINT and any of the hint levels to speed up rendering of the image with fog.

Fog is easy to illustrate. All of fog's effects can be defined in the initialization function, where the fog mode, color, density, and starting and ending points are defined. The actual imaging effect happens when the image is rendered, when the colors of graphical elements are determined by

blending the color of the element with the color of fog as determined by the fog mode. This was discussed in Chapter 10. The various fog-related functions are shown in the following code fragment.

```
void myinit(void)
{   ...
    static GLfloat fogColor[4] = {0.5,0.5,0.5,1.0}; // 50% gray
    ...
//  define the fog parameters
    glFogi(GL_FOG_MODE, GL_EXP);          // exponential fog increase
    glFogfv(GL_FOG_COLOR, fogColor);      // set the fog color
    glFogf(GL_FOG_START, 0.0);            // standard start
    glFogf(GL_FOG_END, 1.0);              // standard end
    glFogf(GL_FOG_DENSITY, 0.50);         // how dense is the fog?
    ...
    glEnable(GL_FOG);                     // enable the fog
    ...
}
```

An example illustrates our ubiquitous cube with a texture map in a foggy space, shown in Figure 12.2. You are encouraged to experiment with the fog mode, color, density, and starting and ending values to examine the effect of these parameters' changes on your images. This example has three different kinds of sides (red, yellow, and texture-mapped), and a fog density of only 0.15.

Figure 12.2 A foggy cube (including a texture map on one surface). See the figure in the color insert.

Fog is a tempting technique because it looks cool to have objects that aren't as brightly colored and "finished" looking as most objects seem to be in computer graphics. This is similar to the urge to use texture mapping to create objects that don't seem to be made of smooth plastic, and the urge to use smooth-shaded objects so they don't seem to be crudely faceted. In all these cases, though, using the extra techniques has a cost in additional rendering time and programming effort, and unless the technique is merited by the communication needed in the scene, it can detract from the real meaning of the graphics.

Rendering Techniques

As some performance-improving modeling techniques involve reducing the amount of rendering that needed to be done, performance-improving rendering techniques involve making the rendering of a scene more efficient. Some of these are done by working on the geometry before it is sent to the graphics system, and others set up the geometry so that the graphics system can work more effectively.

Hardware Avoidance

The computer graphics pipeline includes a number of places where there are opportunities to put hardware into the process to get more performance, and graphics cards have usually been quick to take advantage of these. When you use OpenGL on a system with such a card, the graphics system will probably use the hardware features automatically. Paradoxical as it may seem, however, relying on this approach to speed may not be the best route to high performance. Parts of your audience might not have the kind of acceleration you are programming for, for example, and even hardware has its cost. But more fundamentally, sometimes using standard techniques and relying on the hardware to get you speed will be slower than looking for alternative techniques that can avoid the processing that the card accelerates.

As an example, consider the depth buffer that is supported on almost every graphics card. When you use the depth buffer to handle depth testing, you must apply reading, comparing, and writing operations to each pixel you draw. If you have a fast graphics card, this is higher-speed reading, comparing, and writing, of course, but avoiding these operations is faster than optimizing them. There are techniques that allow you to do some modest computation to avoid entire polygons or, even better, to avoid making depth tests altogether.

Hardware Use

Just as you may not want to take advantage of the automatic features of a graphics accelerator, you may want to design your code in ways that do take advantage of the accelerator. Some of these general techniques are noted later in this chapter, such as geometry compression, display lists, and vertex arrays. In general, the more of your problem you can load onto your accelerator so you can use its onboard processor to speed up your rendering, the faster your image(s) can be created. As graphics APIs start to include features such as vertex or fragment processing, you can create more and more sophisticated images while keeping your image creation speed at an acceptable level.

Culling Polygons

One of the traditional techniques for avoiding drawing is to design only objects that are made up of polyhedra (or that can be made from collections of polyhedra) and then to identify those polygons in the polyhedra that are back faces from the eyepoint. In any polyhedron whose faces are opaque, any polygon that faces away from the eyepoint is invisible to the viewer, so if we draw these and use the depth buffer to manage hidden surfaces, we are doing work that cannot result in any visible effects. Thus it is more effective to decide when to avoid drawing these at all.

The test of whether a polygon faces toward or away from the eyepoint is straightforward. Remember that the normal vector for the polygon points in the direction of the front (or outside) face, so that the polygon will be a front face if the normal vector points toward the eye and will be a back face if the normal vector points away from the eye. Front faces are potentially visible; while in a closed object, back faces are never visible. In terms of the diagram in Figure 12.3, with the orientation of the normal vector N and the eye vector E as shown, a front face will have an acute angle between the normal and eye vectors, so $N \bullet E$ will be positive. If E points in the opposite direction, it is a back face and makes an obtuse angle, so $N \bullet E$ will be negative. Thus a visibility test is simply the algebraic sign of the term $N \bullet E$. Choosing not to display any face that does not pass the visibility test is called *backface culling*.

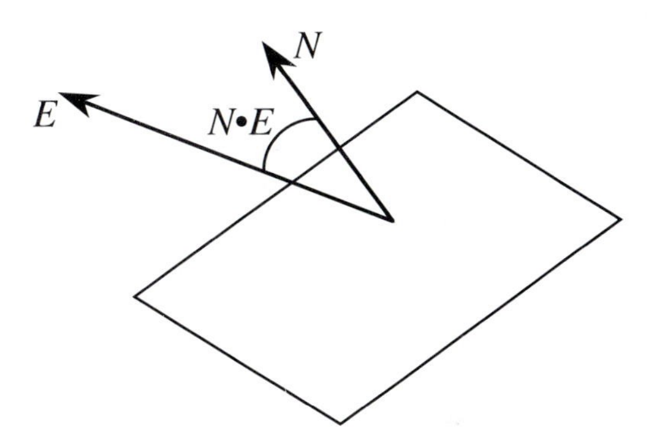

Figure 12.3 The front face test.

This kind of culling can readily be done in your graphics program before any calls to the graphics API functions, but many graphics APIs support backface culling directly. In OpenGL, culling is supported by enabling an operational procedure, `GL_CULL_FACE`. Deciding what makes up a front face is done with the function

```
void glFrontFace(Glenum mode)
```

where `mode` takes on the values `GL_CCW` or `GL_CW` (counterclockwise or clockwise orientation, respectively), depending on the orientation of the vertices of a front face as seen from the eyepoint. You can then choose which kind of face to cull with the function

```
void glCullFace(Glenum mode)
```

In this case, `mode` takes on the values `GL_FRONT`, `GL_BACK`, or `GL_FRONT_AND_BACK`. If culling is enabled, polygons are not drawn if they are the kind of face selected in `glCullFace`, where the concept of a front face is defined in `glFrontFace`.

Another kind of culling can take place on the viewing volume. Here you can compare each vertex of your polyhedron or polygon with the bounding planes on your view volume; if all of the vertices lie outside of the viewing volume based on comparisons with the same bounding plane, then the polyhedron or polygon cannot be seen in the defined view and need not be drawn. This calculation should be done after the viewing transformation so that the boundaries of the view volume are easy to use, but before the polygons are actually rendered. Recall that the viewing volume is a rectangular pyramid with apex at the origin and expanding in the negative Z-direction. The actual comparison calculations are given by the following:

$y > T*Z/ZNEAR$ or $y < B*Z/ZNEAR$

$x > R*Z/ZNEAR$ or $x < L*Z/ZNEAR$

$z > ZNEAR$ or $z < ZFAR$

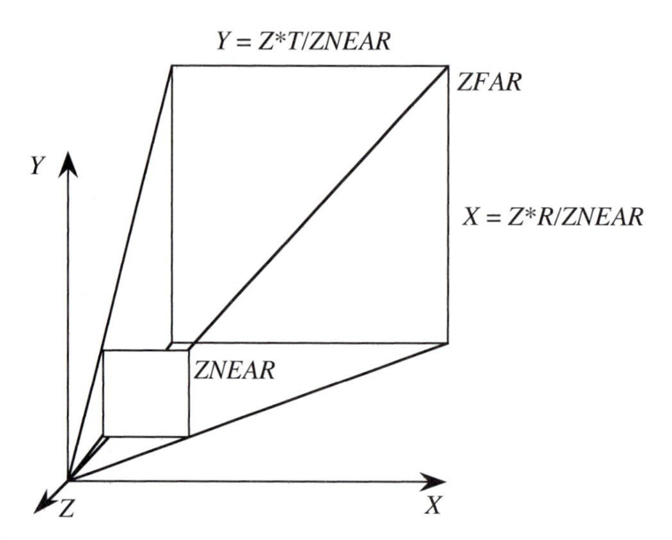

Figure 12.4 The comparisons for the bounding volume computation.

where *T*, *B*, *R*, and *L* are the top, bottom, right, and left coordinates of the near plane *Z* = *ZNEAR* as indicated by the layout in the diagram in Figure 12.4.

Avoiding Depth Comparisons

A classic computer graphics technique is to order your objects by depth and draw them from back to front, mimicking the way light would progress from objects to your eye. This is called the *painter's algorithm,* and it was most popular when the Z-buffer was beyond the scope of most graphics programming. Now we find ourselves with Z-buffer capabilities in almost all graphics systems, but it takes time to do the depth comparisons the Z-buffer requires, so we may want to avoid depth comparisons in order to increase a program's performance.

The painter's algorithm technique can be relatively simple if your model is static, has no interlocking polygons, and is intended to be seen from a single viewpoint, because these make it easy to figure out what "back" and "front" mean and which of any two polygons is in front of the other. This is not the usual design philosophy for interactive graphics, however, and particularly for games, because moving geometry and moving eyepoints are constantly changing which things are in front of what others. So if we were to use this approach, we would find ourselves having to calculate distances from a moving eyepoint in varying directions, which could be very costly to do.

It may be possible to define your scene in ways which can ensure that you will view it only from points where the depth is known, or you may need to define more complex kinds of computation to give you that capability. A relatively common approach to this problem is given by binary space partitioning.

Front-to-Back Drawing

Sometimes a good idea is also a good idea when it is thought of backward. As an alternative to the painter's algorithm approach, sometimes you can arrange to draw objects only from the front to the back. This still requires a test, but you need test only whether a pixel has been written before you write it for a new polygon. When you are working with polygons that have expensive calculations per pixel, such as complex texture maps, you want to avoid calculating a pixel only to find it overwritten later. So by drawing from the front to back you use the Z-buffer to eliminate the pixels you don't draw and calculate only those pixels you will actually draw. You can use BSP tree techniques to select the nearest objects, rather than the farthest, to draw first, or you can use pre-designed scenes or other approaches to know what objects are nearest.

Binary Space Partitioning

There are other approaches to avoiding depth comparisons. It is possible to use techniques such as binary space partitioning to determine what is visible, or to determine the order of the objects as seen from the eyepoint. In binary space partitioning we design the scene so that it can be subdivided into convex subregions by planes through the scene space and we can easily compute which of the subregions is nearer and which is farther. This subdivision can be recursive: Find a plane that does not intersect any of the objects in the scene and for which half the objects are in one half-space relative to the plane and the other half are in the other half-space, and regard each of these half-spaces as a separate scene to subdivide each recursively. The planes are usually kept as simple as possible by techniques such as choosing the planes to be parallel to the coordinate planes in your space, but if your modeling will not permit this, you can use any plane at all. This technique will fail, however, if you cannot place a plane between two objects, and in this case more complex modeling may be needed. This kind of subdivision is illustrated in Figure 12.5 for the simpler 2D case that is easier to see.

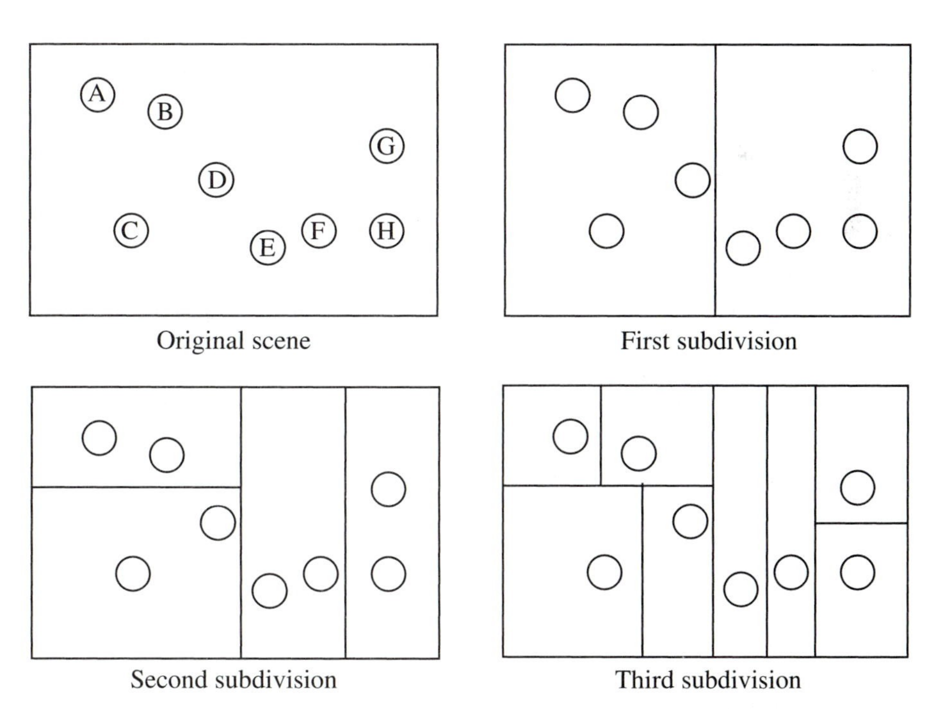

Figure 12.5 A collection of objects in a subdivided space.

This partitioning allows us to view the image space in terms of a binary space partitioning tree (or *BSP tree*). This tree has the division planes as the interior nodes and the actual drawn objects as its leaves, and it is constructed as the space is partitioned. With each interior note you can store the equation of the plane that divides the space, and with each branch of the tree you can store a sign that says whether that side is positive or negative when its coordinates are put into the plane equation. This tree is shown in Figure 12.6, with each interior node indicated by the letters of the objects at that point in the space. These support the computation of which side is nearer the eye. From any eyepoint, even as the eyepoint moves, you can determine which parts of the space are in front of which other parts by making one test for each interior node and readjusting the tree so that (for example) the farther part is on the left-hand branch and the nearer part is on the right-hand branch. This convention is used for the tree in Figure 12.6 with the eyepoint being to the lower right and outside the space. The actual drawing then can be done by traversing the tree left-to-right and drawing the objects as you come to them.

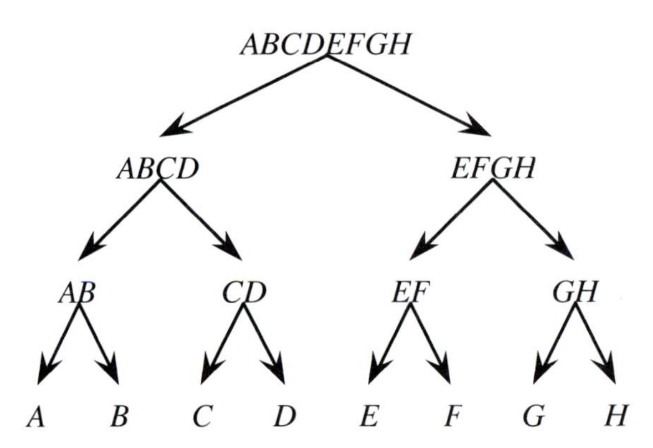

Figure 12.6 A binary space partitioning tree.

The actual test for which part is nearer can be done by considering the relation of the eyepoint to each plane that divides the space. If you put the eye coordinates into the plane equation, you will get either a positive or negative value, and objects on the side of the plane nearer the eye will have the same relation to the plane as the eye. Further, as your eye moves, you will need to recompute the orientation of the BSP tree only when your eyepoint crosses one of the partitioning planes, and you may be able to conclude that some of the orientations do not need to be recomputed at all.

If you have any moving objects in your scene, you must determine their relation to the other objects and account for them in relation to the BSP tree. It is common to have moving objects show up only in front of other things, and if this is the case then you can draw the scene with the BSP tree and simply draw the moving object last. However, if the moving object is placed among the other drawn objects, you can add it into the BSP tree in particular spaces as it moves, with much the same computation of its location as you did to determine the eye location, and with the object moved from one region to another when it crosses one of the dividing planes.

System Speedups

The simplest kind of system speedup in any graphics API is provided by the geometry compression of triangle strips, triangle fans, and quad strips. If you can ensure that you can draw your geometry using these compression techniques, even after you have done the culling and thresholding and have worked out the sequence you want to use for your polygons, these can provide performance increases by reducing the number of vertices that are transmitted to the graphics system.

Another kind of system speedup available from OpenGL is to compile geometry into a display list. As we noted in Chapter 3, you can assemble a rich collection of graphics operations into a display list that executes much more quickly than the original operations. This is because the computations are done at the time the display list is created, and only the final results are sent to the final output stage of the display. If you pre-organize chunks of your image into display lists, you can execute the lists and gain time. Because you cannot change the geometry once you have entered it into the display list, however, you cannot include things like polygon culling or changed display order in such a list.

A more general system speedup that is faster than geometry compression but not as fast as display lists is offered by using vertex arrays and normal arrays. (You can also use arrays for colors and textures.) These let you store all your geometry at once—vertices, colors, normals, textures, and more—and to use them by index. You must define the arrays, populate them with your data and then enable the arrays you want to use. Once a set of arrays is enabled, a single function, `glArrayElement(int)`, will let you access all the geometry for the vertex at that integer at once. You can go beyond that to access groups of indices within a vertex array with the functions `glDrawElements(...)` and `glDrawRangeElements(...)` for increased efficiency.

As an example of this approach, let's modify the standard cube function we saw in earlier examples so that it uses vertex arrays. This is shown in the following code. We use two arrays—one for the vertex geometry, and one for the vertex normals. The geometry will be the same as for the standard cube, and the normals will be a copy of the geometry so that the cube has the same property as a sphere: Its normals are the vectors from the center of the object to the vertices. Once the arrays are defined, you must enable the use of vertex and normal arrays with the `glEnableClientState(...)` function, and then bind the actual arrays to the array operations with the `glVertexPointer()` and `glNormalPointer()` functions. You can then use the `glDrawElements(...)` function to create the actual image. See Figure 12.7 for the results of this code.

```
void cube(float r, float g, float b)
{
//  define point and color data types
    color cubecolor;
    point3 vertices[8]=   {{-1.0, -1.0, -1.0},
                           {-1.0, -1.0,  1.0},
                           {-1.0,  1.0, -1.0},
                           {-1.0,  1.0,  1.0},
                           { 1.0, -1.0, -1.0},
                           { 1.0, -1.0,  1.0},
                           { 1.0,  1.0, -1.0},
                           { 1.0,  1.0,  1.0} };
```

```
    point3 normals[8]=   {{-1.0, -1.0, -1.0},
                          {-1.0, -1.0,  1.0},
                          {-1.0,  1.0, -1.0},
                          {-1.0,  1.0,  1.0},
                          { 1.0, -1.0, -1.0},
                          { 1.0, -1.0,  1.0},
                          { 1.0,  1.0, -1.0},
                          { 1.0,  1.0,  1.0} };
GLubyte face1[4] = {1, 5, 7, 3};
GLubyte face2[4] = {7, 6, 2, 3};
GLubyte face3[4] = {2, 6, 4, 0};
GLubyte face4[4] = {5, 4, 6, 7};
GLubyte face5[4] = {4, 5, 1, 0};
GLubyte face6[4] = {0, 1, 3, 2};
... // material and similar definitions omitted
glEnableClientState(GL_VERTEX_ARRAY);
glEnableClientState(GL_NORMAL_ARRAY);
glVertexPointer(3, GL_FLOAT, 0, vertices);
glNormalPointer(3, 0, normals);
glDrawElements(GL_QUADS, 4, GL_UNSIGNED_BYTE, face1);
glDrawElements(GL_QUADS, 4, GL_UNSIGNED_BYTE, face2);
glDrawElements(GL_QUADS, 4, GL_UNSIGNED_BYTE, face3);
glDrawElements(GL_QUADS, 4, GL_UNSIGNED_BYTE, face4);
glDrawElements(GL_QUADS, 4, GL_UNSIGNED_BYTE, face5);
glDrawElements(GL_QUADS, 4, GL_UNSIGNED_BYTE, face6);
}
```

Figure 12.7 The cube drawn with both vertex and normal arrays. See the figure in the color insert.

Notice how much more compressed this drawing code is than the earlier `cube()` function: You call one function to pass each of the vertex and normal arrays into the graphics system, and then you call one function for each face of the cube. This compares with forty-eight function calls for the standard cube function, including three separate vertex and normal function calls for each vertex of the cube. This saves the overhead of function calls and of passing vector data into the graphics system, and allows a graphics accelerator to use all its vector processing capability to achieve the highest performance.

There are a number of syntactic details of the OpenGL functions we used that we cannot really cover without this book's becoming more of a manual than we want it to be. Notice, for example, that the `glVertexPointer()` and `glNormalPointer()` functions have similar, but not identical, sets of parameters. There are also a number of different ways you can draw the geometry, as we saw previously. So you should consult a manual for more details of this technique.

Collision Detection

We introduced collision detection techniques in Chapter 4. When you do polygon-based graphics, the question of collisions between objects reduces to the question of collisions between polygons, and that can be reduced to the question of collisions between triangles. That was the basis of the Chapter 4 discussion, but here we want to look at improving performance in detecting collisions. Perhaps the best approach for performance improvement in collision detection and handling is to use low-computation approximations instead of exact computations when you can. If you can approximate your objects closely by their bounding objects, when you check the bounding object for possible collisions you can use the results to assume a real collision.

Of the bounding objects you might use, the simplest are bounding spheres. The direction for any post-collision motion can be approximated by the position of the spheres, or you can use the contact point for the spheres to calculate the normal to the nearest surface point to the collision point and use that for direction. But if your objects are moving quickly, and if it is not important to have exact collision behavior, you can probably use the sphere collisions without further refinement; the difference may not be very noticeable to the viewer.

The first steps are to avoid doing any unnecessary work by testing first for situations where collisions are impossible. You can set up bounding volumes, for example, and determine that two bounding volumes cannot intersect. If an intersection is possible, however, then move to working with the actual objects, and usually work with the triangles that most commonly make up your objects. Reducing the general polygon to a triangle reduces further to collisions between an edge and a triangle. We introduced this concept in Chapter 4 by extending the edge to a complete parametric line, intersecting the line with the plane of the polygon, and then noting that the edge meets the polygon if it meets a sequence of successively more focused criteria:

- The parameter of the line where it intersects the plane must lie between 0 and 1.
- The point where the line intersects the plane must lie within the smallest circle containing the triangle.
- The point where the line intersects the plane must lie within the body of the triangle.

This comparison process is illustrated in Figure 12.8.

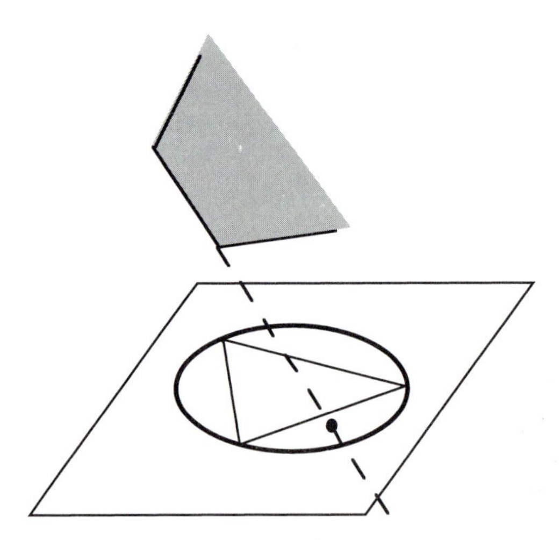

Figure 12.8 The collision detection computation.

If you detect a collision between moving polyhedra, an intersection might need more processing if you want to find the exact moment when the polyhedra met. To find this time, you must do computations in the time interval between the previous step (before the intersection) and the current step (when the intersection exists). You might want to apply a bisection process on the time, for example, to determine whether the intersection existed halfway between the previous and current step, continuing that process until you get a sufficiently good estimate of the actual time the objects met. Alternatively, you might want to do some analytical computation to calculate the intersection time given the positions and velocities of the objects at the previous and current times so you can recompute the positions of the objects to reflect a bounce or other kind of interaction between them.

Summary

This chapter included a modest number of straightforward techniques you can use to write graphics programs that present images more quickly than the standard techniques described elsewhere in the book. These techniques are only the beginning of the question of high-performance graphics but they give you a good idea of the issues involved, and if you use them as appropriate, you should be able to write programs whose images appear more quickly, that have higher frame rates, or that support faster interaction than programs that use only simpler API programming.

OpenGL Glossary for the Chapter

This chapter introduced a number of specialized operations for vertex arrays, fog, and sequencing of polygons for drawing. They may not be very useful for routine graphics programming, but they have important value for programs that present large, predefined geometry information or that use fog as image enhancers. As always, we are including only new OpenGL terms in this glossary.

OpenGL Functions

`glArrayElement(value)`: indicates which vertex of the enabled vertex array is to be rendered

`glCullFace(param)`: specifies whether front or back faces of polygons are to be culled glDrawElements(...): renders geometric primitives using array data

glDrawRangeElements(...): a restricted firm of glDrawElements() that uses only the elements in a specified range of values

glEnableClientState(...): enables client-side capabilities such as vertex arrays or normal arrays

glFog*(param, value): specifies and gives a value to fog parameters

glFrontFace(param): defines the orientation of front- and back-facing polygons, the default is GL_CCW, the counterclockwise direction

glGetFloatv(...): returns the value or values of a particular system parameter

glNormalPointer(...): defines an array of normals

glVertexPointer(...): defines an array of vertices

OpenGL Parameters

GL_BACK: indicates that glCullFace() is to cull back faces

GL_CURRENT_RASTER_DISTANCE: indicates that glGetFloat*() is to return the distance from the eye to the current raster position

GL_EXP: indicates that the fog mode is exponential

GL_EXP2: indicates that the fog mode is exponential-squared

GL_FOG: parameter to glEnable() that begins the use of fog in rendering

GL_FOG_COLOR: parameter to glFog*() indicating that the color of fog is being set

GL_FOG_DENSITY: parameter to glFog*() indicating that the density of fog is being set

GL_FOG_END: parameter to glFog*() indicating that the far distance of the fog equation is being set

GL_FOG_HINT: parameter to glHint() indicating that the hint's value is to be applied to rendering using fog

GL_FOG_MODE: indicates that the fog mode is being set; the values are linear, exponential, and exponential-squared

GL_FOG_START: parameter to glFog*() indicating that the near distance of the fog equation is being set

GL_FRONT: indicates that glCullFace() is to cull front faces

GL_FRONT_AND_BACK: indicates that glCullFace() is to cull all faces—so polygons are not drawn, though lines and points still are drawn

GL_LINEAR: indicates that the fog mode is linear

Questions

1. Why is back face culling considered a high-performance technique rather than simply a way to simplify depth testing? Compare the number of operations necessary to check for a back face with the number of operations needed to put the face into the graphics pipeline and do the pixel operations of depth testing.
2. A level-of-detail (LOD) technique is to keep something invisible unless it achieves some level where it is noticeable to the user. This is often defined in terms of the size of the object,

so that when the object becomes a certain number of pixels in some dimension of the view, it suddenly becomes visible. Discuss some variations on this policy
   a. if the object background is a solid, neutral color
   b. if the object background is a texture-mapped wall with a natural scene
   c. if the object is first presented with a very low alpha value for all its colors and that value is increased to its final value as the object gets closer to the viewer
3. We include fog as an LOD technique because we assume that the fog will shroud an object until it comes within a given range of the viewer, usually the far distance for the fog. We keep the object invisible (by not drawing it) as long as we are beyond that distance, then draw the object when it gets to that distance. Discuss whether this does a good job of keeping objects from appearing suddenly to the viewer.
4. Design a 3D scene using a scene graph, using several geometric primitives at different locations in your modeling space. Be sure that some of these primitives will overlap when viewed from the intended eyepoint. Create a BSP tree for the scene manually and code the program that implements the scene graph in the order of primitives set by the BSP tree with depth testing disabled. The scene should appear as if depth testing were done—primitives in front should not be covered by things behind.

Exercises

1. Create a geometric object that looks similar in two (or more) models, one with a large number of polygons and another with a small number of polygons. Create a scene that presents this object in some kind of context, such that when the object is far from the eye the model with a small number of polygons is used, but when the object is near, the version with a large number of polygons is used. Is the change from one model to the other smooth enough that you could use this object in a working scene? Why or why not?
2. Do as in question 4, but create the BSP computationally and use it computationally to create and control a painter's algorithm rendering the scene. Then modify the code to test the BSP tree and set the order of the primitives as part of the display operation so you can automatically respond to a changing eyepoint.

Experiments

1. Build a scene in two ways: as traditional polygons with vertices, normals, and texture coordinates, and with these same values stored as vertex arrays (`GL_VERTEX_ARRAY`, `GL_NORMAL_ARRAY`, and `GL_TEXTURE_COORD_ARRAY`, respectively) as in the example in the chapter. See if you can measure any difference in the execution time for drawing the scene with this difference. You will probably need to create a very large scene to do this, so you will want to create the geometry algorithmically. A good example might be the "fractal forgery" landscape scene discussed in Chapter 14.
2. Build a scene that is organized as a list of polygons, systematically check the distance to each polygon with the OpenGL tools in this chapter, sort the polygon list by distance from the eye, and draw them in that order with depth testing turned off. Compare the result with the same scene drawn without ordering the polygons and with depth testing on. Which is faster? Which produces the better-looking result? Add back face culling to the distance

testing to eliminate those polygons in the polygon list that are facing away from the eye, and compare the times again. Is there a difference? Is it significant?

3. Create a simple scene that uses GLU and GLUT objects in space and structure the scene with spatial partitioning so that you can always draw it from back to front. How difficult is this in comparison with the full polygon list created previously?

Projects

1. Implement a model of a pool table that uses collision detection to deal with the case when two pool balls meet or when a ball meets a table bumper. Include the physics of energy transfer between the balls and bumpers and the direction that each will take after an intersection, as well as friction so that the balls will slow down over time. Assume that collisions are not affected by spin. Note that spheres are particularly easy objects for collision detection.

13

Interpolation and Spline Modeling

This chapter introduces a new kind of graphical modeling that lets you create complex curves and surfaces by defining geometry with just a few control points. These curves and surfaces are created by interpolating the control points using linear combinations of a particular set of interpolating functions. This is both straightforward (after a little programming is done, or a graphics API capability is mastered) and flexible. We saw this interpolation in the chapter on animation (Chapter 11), where we used it to create a smooth path for the eyepoint in a flythrough kind of application. One of the most important applications of this modeling is in creating curves and surfaces by interactively manipulating the control points, making this the first fundamentally interactive kind of modeling we have seen.

Along with the modeling capabilities of this interpolation, we have straightforward ways to generate normals and texture maps for the geometry the interpolation defines based on the parameters of the interpolating functions. This lets us create sophisticated curves and surfaces and add full lighting and textures to them, making these interpolations some of the most powerful tools for creating complex geometry that you will see in a first graphics course.

In order to understand this chapter, you should have a modest understanding of parametric functions, especially functions of two parameters, together with an understanding of simple modeling with techniques such as triangle strips.

Introduction

In Chapter 4, we talked about line segments as linear interpolations of the two endpoints, though we did not phrase it exactly that way. Here we introduce other kinds of interpolations of points involving techniques called *spline curves* and *spline surfaces*. The specific spline techniques we will discuss are the Catmull-Rom and Bézier splines; these techniques are straightforward, but we will limit them mostly to one-dimensional spline curves. Extending these to two dimensions to model surfaces is a bit more complex, and we will mainly cover this idea in terms of the evaluator functions that are built into the OpenGL graphics API. Splines and other interpolating curves and surfaces are a rich study that we will not explore deeply in this book.

Spline techniques provide a very broad approach to creating smooth curves that approximate a number of points in a one-dimensional domain (1D interpolation) or smooth surfaces that approximate a number of points in a two-dimensional domain (2D interpolation). This interpolation is typically used to develop geometric models, but we will mention a number of other uses of splines later in the chapter. Graphics APIs such as OpenGL usually provide tools that allow a graphics programmer to create spline interpolations given only the original set of points, called *control points,* that are to be interpolated.

In general, we think of an entire spline curve or spline surface as a single piece of geometry in the scene graph. These curves and surfaces are defined in a single modeling space and usually have a single set of appearance parameters, so in spite of their complexity they are naturally represented by a single shape node that is a leaf in the scene graph.

Interpolations

When we talked about the parametric form for a line segment in Chapter 4, we created a correspondence between the parameter t in the unit line segment [0,1] and the points in an arbitrary line segment between P_0 and P_1. We were really interpolating the two points by creating a line segment between them. This interpolating line segment can be expressed in terms of the parametric form of the segment:

$$(1 - t)P_0 + tP_1 \text{ for } t \text{ in } [0., 1.]$$

This form is trivial to use but it is quite suggestive, because it hints that there may be a very general way to calculate a set of points that interpolate the two given points by creating a function such as

$$f_0(t)P_0 + f_1(t)P_1$$

for two fixed functions f_0 and f_1 that are somehow related. This suggests that we might think about the relationship between points and the functions that interpolate them and examine the interpolations they provide. Interpolating functions generally have some particular properties:

- They are defined on the unit interval to give us a standard domain for the parameter t.
- They generally have only non-negative values on that interval.
- The sum of the values of the functions at any value of the parameter t is usually 1, so the interpolating points are a convex sum of the original points.

We also often see that the interpolating functions have values at 0 and 1 so that the overall function gives P_0 at $t = 0$ and P_1 at $t = 1$.

If we look at the functions for the original line segment, we see that the functions $f_0(t) = (1 - t)$ and $f_1(t) = t$ have the properties that we suggested above. We see that $f_0(0) = 1$ and $f_1(0) = 0$, so at $t = 0$ the interpolant value is P_0, while $f_0(1) = 0$ and $f_1(1) = 1$ so at $t = 1$, the interpolant value is P_1. This tells us that the interpolation starts at P_0 and ends at P_1. We also see that

$$f_0(t) + f_1(t) = (1 - t) + t = 1$$

for any value of t in the interval. Further, each of f_0 and f_1 is always non-negative on [0., 1.]. Finally, because each of the interpolating functions is linear in the parameter t, the set of interpolating points forms a line.

As we move beyond a line segment interpolating two points, we will use the term *interpolation* to mean determining a set of points that approximate the space between a set of given control points in the order the points are given. This set of points can include three points, four points, or even more. We assume throughout this discussion that the points are in 3-space, so we will be creating interpolating curves (and interpolating surfaces) in three dimensions. If you want to do two-dimensional interpolations, simply ignore one of the three coordinates.

Finding a way to interpolate three points P_0, P_1, and P_2 is more interesting than interpolating only two points, because one can imagine many ways to do so. For example, any three points lie on a circle, so under some circumstances you could probably see that circle as an interpolation. But if we extend the concept of interpolating with the parametric line, we could consider a quadratic interpolation in t as:

$$(1 - t)^2 P_0 + 2t(1 - t)P_1 + t^2 P_2 \text{ for } t \text{ in } [0., 1.]$$

Here we have three functions f_0, f_1, and f_2 that participate in the interpolation, with

$$f_0(t) = (1 - t)^2$$
$$f_1(t) = 2t(1 - t), \text{ and}$$
$$f_2(t) = t^2.$$

By now, these functions have achieved enough importance in our thinking that we will give them a name; we call them the *basis functions* for the interpolation. We will call the points P_0, P_1, and P_2 the *control points* for the interpolation (although the formal literature on spline curves calls them *knots* and calls the endpoints of an interpolation *joints*). These particular functions have a similar property to the linear basis functions above, with $f_0(0) = 1, f_1(0) = 0$, and $f_2(0) = 0$, as well as $f_0(1) = 0, f_1(1) = 0$, and $f_2(1) = 1$, giving us a smooth, quadratic interpolating function in t that has value P_0 if $t = 0$ and value P_1 if $t = 1$, and that is a linear combination of the three points if t takes any value between 0 and 1. Three points and their interpolating curve are shown in Figure 13.1.

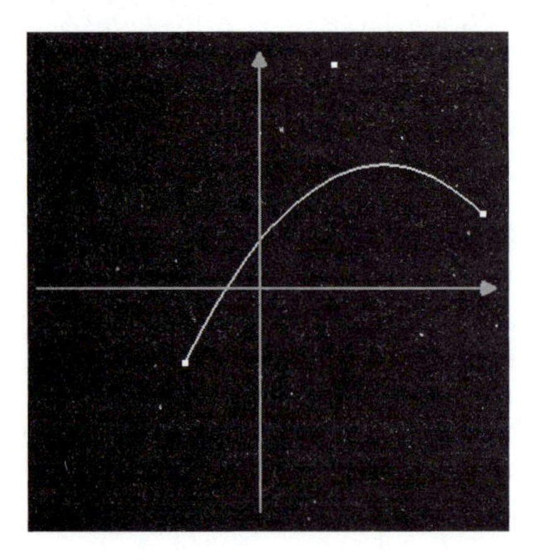

Figure 13.1 A quadratic interpolating curve for three points.

The basis functions for these two cases are also of interest because they have a common source. For linear interpolation, the functions $f_0(t)$ and $f_1(t)$ are the two terms when we expand

$$((1 - t) + t)^1,$$

and for quadratic interpolation, the functions $f_0(t)$, $f_1(t)$, and $f_2(t)$ are the terms when we expand

$$((1 - t) + t)^2.$$

In both cases, the functions add to a value of 1 for any value of t, so we have an interpolation that gives a total weight of 1 for all the coefficients of the geometric points we are using.

This observation for linear and quadratic interpolation suggests a general approach for interpolating polynomials of degree N. We could interpolate the terms of the polynomial

$$((1 - t) + t)^N$$

and take their coefficients from the geometry we want to interpolate. If we follow this pattern for the case of cubic interpolations ($N = 3$), an equation interpolating four points P_0, P_1, P_2, and P_3 could look like:

$$(1 - t)^3 P_0 + 3t(1 - t)^2 P_1 + 3t^2(1 - t)P_2 + t^3 P_3 \text{ for } t \text{ in } [0., 1.]$$

The shape of the curve this determines is shown in Figure 13.2 for a sample of four points. (To make it easier to compare the shapes of the curves, the first three of these points are the same as the three points in the quadratic spline above.) In fact, this curve is an expression of the standard *Bézier spline* function to interpolate four control points, and the four polynomials

$$f_0(t) = (1 - t)^3$$
$$f_1(t) = 3t(1 - t)^2$$
$$f_2(t) = 3t^2(1 - t)$$
$$f_3(t) = t^3$$

are called the *cubic Bernstein basis* for this spline curve. (Code for this and many other figures in this chapter is included in the resources for the text.)

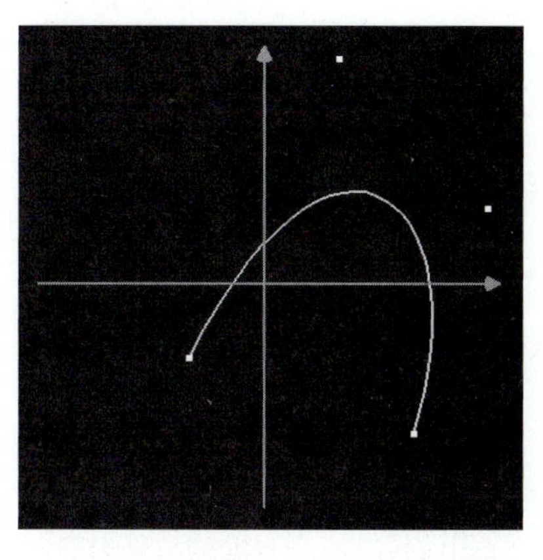

Figure 13.2 Interpolating four points with the Bézier spline based on the Bernstein basis functions.

The interpolating Bézier spline curve goes through the first and last of the four control points (P_0 and P_3) but does not go through the two middle control points (P_1 and P_2). This is because the set of basis functions for this curve behaves the same at the points where $t = 0$ and and $t = 1$, as we saw in the quadratic spline: $f_0(0) = 1, f_1(0) = 0, f_2(0) = 0$, and $f_3(0) = 0$, while $f_0(1) = 0, f_1(1) = 0, f_2(1) = 0$, and $f_3(1) = 1$. If we calculate the derivative of the Bézier spline function with respect to t, we see that at $t = 0$ the derivative is $3(P_1 - P_0)$ and at $t = 1$ the derivative is $3(P_3 - P_2)$. So as the curve goes through the first control point it is moving in the direction from the first to the second control point, and as it goes through the fourth control point it is moving from the third to the fourth control point. Thus the shape of the curve is determined by the two middle control points; these points determine the initial and the ending directions of the curve, and the rest of the shape is determined by the weights given by the basis functions. The smoothness of the basis functions gives us the smoothness of the curve.

This approach to defining the basis functions for our interpolations is not the only way to derive appropriate sets of functions. In general, curves that interpolate a given set of points need not go through those points, but the points influence and determine the nature of the curve in other ways. If you need to have the curve actually go through the control points, however, there are spline formulations for which this does happen. The Catmull-Rom cubic spline has the form

$$f_0(t)P_0 + f_1(t)P_1 + f_2(t)P_2 + f_3(t)P_3 \text{ for } t \text{ in } [0., 1.]$$

for basis functions

$$f_0(t) = (-t^3 + 2t^2 - t)/2$$
$$f_1(t) = (3t^3 - 5t^2 + 2)/2$$
$$f_2(t) = (-3t^3 + 4t^2 + t)/2$$
$$f_3(t) = (t^3 - t^2)/2$$

This interpolating curve has a very different behavior from that of the Bézier curve above, because it interpolates only the second and third control points, as shown in Figure 13.3. This is a different kind of interpolating behavior, because the basis functions have $f_0(0) = 0$, $f_1(0) = 1$, $f_2(0) = 0$, and $f_3(0) = 0$, as well as $f_0(1) = 0, f_1(1) = 0, f_2(1) = 1$, and $f_3(1) = 0$. This means that

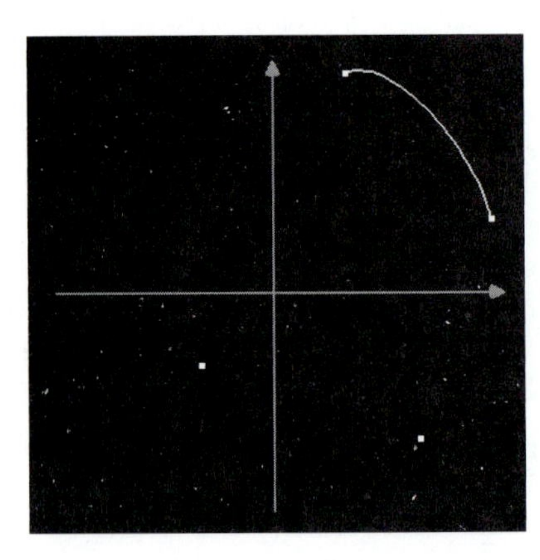

Figure 13.3 Interpolating four points with the Catmull-Rom cubic spline.

the curve interpolates only the points P_1 and P_2 and actually goes through those two points, instead of through P_0 and P_3. As you will see shortly, you can extend this spline curve across many control points and interpolate each pair. Thus the Catmull-Rom spline curve is useful when you want your interpolated curve to include all the control points, not just some of them.

We will not carry the idea of spline curves beyond cubic interpolations, though any degree of polynomial is possible. Cubic splines are the most widely used of the simple splines and are very useful tools. While our examples here are 2D curves, examples we will see later in this chapter show that if the points we are interpolating lie in 3D space, each of these techniques provides a 3D curve—that is, a function from a line segment to 3D space. We will see these 3D curves later in this chapter.

Alternate Conceptual Basis for a Bézier Spline

There are many ways to formulate spline curves, and the theory of such curves is rich with ideas. There is another way to think of Bézier splines besides the Bernstein basis, however, that has meaning for interpreting a single segment with four control points. In a very precise way, this can let you sketch a good approximation of a Bézier curve from four points.

If we think of how a single segment of a Bézier spline curve joins the end control points, we see that it leaves the first control point in the direction of the second control point and comes into the last control point from the direction of the third control point. In fact, the slopes of the curve leaving the first control point and coming into the last control point are precisely the slopes of the lines joining the first and second points and joining the third and fourth points. The actual velocities of the spline function at these endpoints are one-third of the vectors from first to second and from third to fourth. And these four facts are enough to completely determine the four coefficients of the cubic curve equation. The details are left to an exercise.

Alternate Computational Basis for a Bézier Spline

If we begin with an expression for the Bézier spline curve in terms of its basis functions and control points,

$$(1 - t)^3 P_0 + 3t(1 - t)^2 P_1 + 3t^2(1 - t)P_2 + t^3 P_3$$

we see that this is not exactly in familiar polynomial form. If we multiply this out, we get the expression

$$(-P_0 + 3P_1 - 3P_2 + P_3)t^3 + (3P_0 - 6P_1 + 3P_2)t^2 + (-3P_0 + 3P_1)t + P_0$$

This is a traditional polynomial that must be interpreted as three simultaneous equations, one each for x, y, and z, because each of the control points is a three-dimensional value. This may be more easily programmed than the basis function approach.

This polynomial approach, however, suggests yet another way to look at the expression for the spline function. If we think of this in terms of matrices, we can see that this expression can be written as

$$[P_0 \quad P_1 \quad P_2 \quad P_3]*\begin{bmatrix} -1 & 3 & -3 & 1 \\ 3 & -6 & 3 & 0 \\ -3 & 3 & 0 & 0 \\ 1 & 0 & 0 & 0 \end{bmatrix}*\begin{bmatrix} t^3 \\ t^2 \\ t^1 \\ t^0 \end{bmatrix}$$

This matrix operation clearly has the right dimensions $(1 \times 4) - (4 \times 4) - (4 \times 1)$ to yield a point, and it is quite interesting that it reduces the basis functions to a matrix representation. In fact, for any cubic spline function whose basis functions are known, you can go through an operation such as this and get a similar matrix representation for the spline.

Extending Interpolations To More Control Points

So far we have looked only at the effect of these interpolations in the smallest possible set of points, but it is straightforward to extend the interpolations to more control points. The way we do this depends on the kind of interpolation done by the particular interpolation we are working with.

For the Bézier curve, we see that the curve meets the first and last control points but not the two intermediate control points. If we simply use the first four control points, then the next three (the last point of the original set plus the next three control points), and so on, then we will have a curve that is continuous, goes through every third control point (first, fourth, seventh, and so on), but changes direction abruptly at each control point it meets. This nonsmooth curve along with its control points is shown in Figure 13.4.

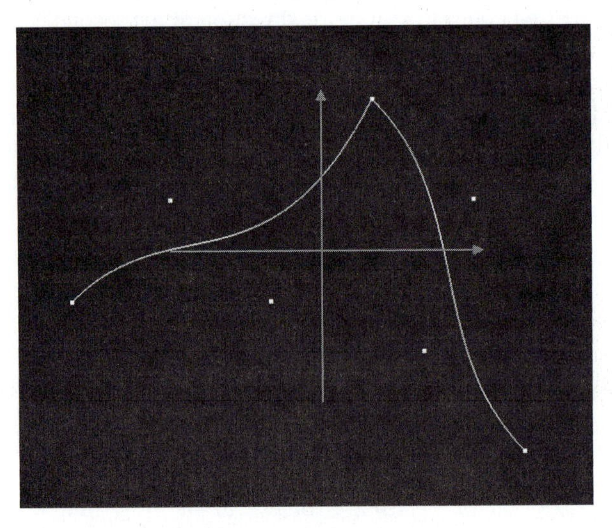

Figure 13.4 Two-segment curve without transitions.

To extend these curves so that they progress smoothly along their entire length, we need to add new control points that are defined so that the direction into the last control point of a set is the same as the direction out of the first control point of the next set. Specifically, we need to define new control points between each pair of points whose index is $2N$ and $2N + 1$ for $N \geq 1$ up to, but not including the last pair of control points. We can define these new control points as the midpoint between these points, or $Q_{N-1} = (P_{2N} + P_{2N+1})/2$. When we create these new points, we get the following relation between the new and the original control point set:

original:	P_0	P_1	P_2		P_3	P_4		P_5	P_6	P_7
new:	P_0	P_1	P_2	Q_0	P_3	P_4	Q_1	P_5	P_6	P_7

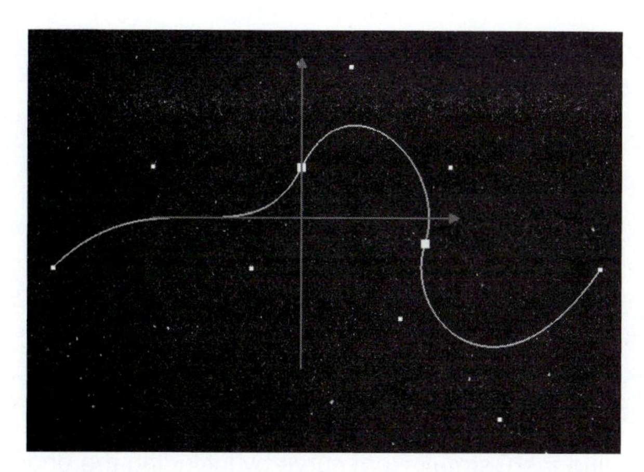

Figure 13.5 Extending the Bézier curve by adding intermediate control points, which are larger.

where each point Q represents a new point calculated as an average of the two on each side of it, as above. Then the computations would use the following sequences of points: $P_0 - P_1 - P_2 - Q_0$; $Q_0 - P_3 - P_4 - Q_1$; and $Q_1 - P_5 - P_6 - P_7$. Note that we must have an even number of control points for a Bézier curve, that we need to extend the original control points only if we have at least six control points, and that we have three of the original points participating in each of the first and last segments of the curve but only two of the original points in each of the other segments. An example of this continuation is shown in Figure 13.5, where the curve is not only continuous but also differentiable throughout.

For the Catmull-Rom cubic spline, the fact that the interpolating curve connects only the control points P_1 and P_2 gives us a different kind of approach to extending the curve. However, it also gives us a challenge in starting the curve, because neither the starting control point P_0 nor the ending control point P_3 is included in the curve that interpolates $P_0 - P_3$. Hence we need to think of the overall interpolation problem in three parts—the first segment, the intermediate segments, and the last segment.

For the first segment, the answer is simple: Repeat the starting point twice. This gives us a first set of control points consisting of P_0, P_0, P_1, and P_2, and the first piece of the curve will then interpolate P_0 and P_1 as the middle points of these four. In the same way, to end the curve we repeat the final point, giving us the four control points P_1, P_2, P_3, and P_3, so the curve interpolates the middle points, P_2 and P_3. If we consider only the four control points of the original example and add this technique, we see the three-segment interpolation of the points shown in the left-hand image of Figure 13.6.

If we have a larger set of control points and want to extend the curve to cover the total set of points, we can consider a "sliding set" of control points that starts with P_0, P_1, P_2, and P_3 and, as we move along, includes the last three control points from the previous segment as the first three of the next set and adds the next control point as the last point of the set of four points. That is, the second set of points would be P_1, P_2, P_3, and P_4, and the one after that P_2, P_3, P_4, and P_5, and so on. This kind of sliding set is simple to implement (just take an array of

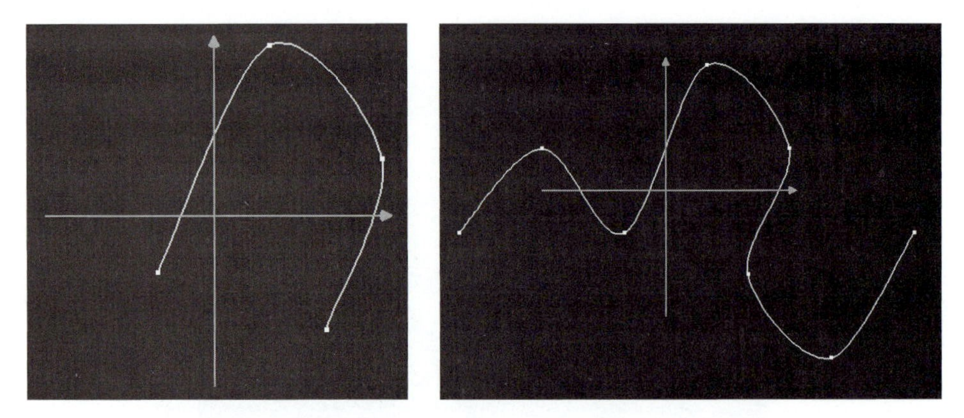

Figure 13.6 Extending the Catmull-Rom curve by including the endpoints of the set (*left*) and by stepping along the extended set of control points (*right*).

four points, move each one down by one index so $P[1]$ becomes $P[0]$, $P[2]$ becomes $P[1]$, $P[3]$ becomes $P[2]$, and the new point becomes $P[3]$). The sequence of points $P_0 - P_8$ used for the individual segments of the curve, including the end segments, are then $P_0 - P_0 - P_1 - P_2$; $P_0 - P_1 - P_2 - P_3$; $P_1 - P_2 - P_3 - P_4$; $P_2 - P_3 - P_4 - P_5$; $P_3 - P_4 - P_5 - P_6$; $P_4 - P_5 - P_6 - P_7$; $P_5 - P_6 - P_7 - P_8$; and $P_6 - P_7 - P_8 - P_8$. The curve that results when we extend the computation across all the control points is shown in the right-hand image of Figure 13.6, where we have taken the same set of control points that we used for the extended Bézier spline examples shown in Figure 13.5.

Spline Surfaces

The techniques just described for spline curves can easily be extended to generate interpolated surfaces. The same benefits for spline curves are also given by spline surfaces: They can be specified by a small number of control points, you can control their shape predictably by moving the control points, and if done properly they are smooth and can take on a wide range of forms. In fact, spline modeling usually means modeling spline surfaces, not spline curves, but starting with curves makes it easier to see what is happening with surfaces.

If you consider functions $f_0(t)$, $f_1(t)$, $f_2(t)$, and $f_3(t)$ as the basis for your cubic spline, you can apply them for two parameters u and v with $0 \leq u, v \leq 1$, and a set of sixteen control points P_{ij} for i and j between 0 and 3, to give you a function of two variables:

$$f(u, v) = \sum_{i=0}^{3} \sum_{j=0}^{3} f_i(u) f_j(v) P_{ij}$$

where the sum is taken over the sixteen possible values of i and j. You can then step along the two variables u and v in any way you like and draw the surface in exactly the same way you would graph a function of two variables, as we discussed in Chapter 9. Some code to do this follows;

here, the interpolating functions F0, F1, F2, and F3 are the cubic Bernstein basis functions seen earlier in the discussion of Bézier curves.

```
float u, u1, v, v1, ustep, vstep, x, y, z;
float cp[4][4][3];    // 4x4 array of 3D control points

for (u=0.; u<1.; u+=ustep)
    for (v=0.; v<1.; v+=vstep) {
        u1 = u+ustep; v1 = v+vstep;
        beginQuad();
            vertex3(eval(u,v,0),eval(u,v,1),eval(u,v,2));
            vertex3(eval(u,v1,0),eval(u,v1,1),eval(u,v1,2));
            vertex3(eval(u1,v1,0),eval(u1,v1,1),eval(u1,v1,2));
            vertex3(eval(u1,v,0),eval(u1,v,1),eval(u1,v,2));
        endQuad();
    }

float eval(float u, float v, int i)
{
    float result = 0.;
    result += F0(u)*F0(v)*cp[0][0][i]+F1(u)*F0(v)*cp[1][0][i];
    result += F2(u)*F0(v)*cp[2][0][i]+F3(u)*F0(v)*cp[2][0][i];
    result += F0(u)*F1(v)*cp[0][1][i]+F1(u)*F1(v)*cp[1][1][i];
    result += F2(u)*F1(v)*cp[2][1][i]+F3(u)*F1(v)*cp[3][1][i];
    result += F0(u)*F2(v)*cp[0][2][i]+F1(u)*F2(v)*cp[1][2][i];
    result += F2(u)*F2(v)*cp[2][2][i]+F3(u)*F2(v)*cp[3][2][i];
    result += F0(u)*F3(v)*cp[0][3][i]+F1(u)*F3(v)*cp[1][3][i];
    result += F2(u)*F3(v)*cp[2][3][i]+F3(u)*F3(v)*cp[3][3][i];
    return result;
}
```

We see that the function `eval(...)` computes the ith coordinate of the interpolated point for the parameters u and v, while the first piece of code steps across the coordinate space and generates the quads that are to be drawn. The visual properties of the quads are not determined, but would be worked out through the coloring, lighting, or shading operations we have seen in previous chapter. Examples of 3D spline surfaces are given later in this chapter.

Extending a Patch to a Surface

We saw earlier in this chapter that to extend a Bézier spline curve from four control points to any even number of control points and have a smooth result, we needed to add extra control points that bisected the line segment between some of the original control points. There is a similar situation for Bézier spline surfaces. In order to extend the surface from a single patch to any 2D array of control points (with an even number of points in each direction in the array) and have a smooth result, we need to add extra control points. These need to be added at the same places they were for curves: after the third point and again after each second point up to the point where there are three control points after the new one. Further, this addition must happen in both directions, creating rows and columns of new control points. But there is one new condition: A control point must be added at the "corner" where each new row and each new column of control points meet. This new point must be the average of all four of the original control points adjacent to the corner. With these points added, you can take 4×4 sets of control points and create patches for each, and you will create a surface that is differentiable in all directions. This is necessary in order to generate normals analytically for the patch for lighting the surface.

Generating Normals for a Patch

As we see, any patch can be written as a bilinear combination of the basis functions, giving us an analytic expression for any point on the patch. In particular, for each vertex in the grid that we will use to draw the patch, we can calculate the two directional derivatives for the surface's analytic function. These are given below and are simplified because each of f_i and f_j is a function of only one variable:

$$\partial f(u, v)/\partial u = \sum_{i=0}^{3}\sum_{j=0}^{3} df_i(u)/du^* f_j(v)^* P_{ij}$$

$$\partial f(u, v)/\partial v = \sum_{i=0}^{3}\sum_{j=0}^{3} f_i(u)^* df_j(v)/dv^* P_{ij}$$

These derivatives are relative not to the coordinates of world space but to the parameter space, but the derivatives will determine tangent lines and a tangent plane. With these derivatives, we can calculate two vectors tangent to the surface at any point $f(u, v)$, and we can then compute the cross product of these vectors and normalize the result, giving us a unit normal to the surface at the vertex. This lets us add normals to whatever vertex list we use for our programming, so we can apply a full lighting model to the surface.

Generating Texture Coordinates for a Patch

As we generate a patch on a spline surface, we create a grid of points in the two-dimensional unit parameter space that is used for the surface as noted above. Because this is already a grid in a two-dimensional space, it can readily be associated with any grid in any other two-dimensional space, such as a 2D texture. This gives you texture coordinates to add to your specification of vertices (and, as we just saw, of normals) for your patch. In the simplest case, for each vertex determined by a function $f(u, v)$ from 2-dimensional (u, v)-space to 3-dimensional space, you could use mappings from the parameters u, v to corresponding texture coordinates U, V and then have the texture function that associates texture coordinates (U, V) to that point on the surface. Of course, you must be careful to use adjacent texture regions for adjacent control regions on the surface in order to get a good fit of the texture to the surface.

Alternate Computational Basis for a Patch

We have seen a matrix approach to representing a cubic spline curve, and it is not difficult to extend this approach to a matrix representation for a bicubic spline surface for a patch. The details are fairly easy to extend from the earlier discussion. If we represent the 4×4 matrix that comes from the basis functions as M:

$$M = \begin{bmatrix} -1 & 3 & -3 & 1 \\ 3 & -6 & 6 & 0 \\ -3 & 3 & 0 & 0 \\ 1 & 0 & 0 & 0 \end{bmatrix}$$

and if we look at the 4×4 set of control points P_{ij} as an array G (for Geometry) and at the 4×1 array of powers of a parameter w as $E(w)$ (for Exponents):

$$G = \begin{bmatrix} P_{00} & P_{01} & P_{02} & P_{03} \\ P_{10} & P_{11} & P_{12} & P_{13} \\ P_{20} & P_{21} & P_{22} & P_{23} \\ P_{30} & P_{31} & P_{32} & P_{33} \end{bmatrix} \quad \text{and} \quad E(w) = \begin{bmatrix} w^3 \\ w^2 \\ w^1 \\ w^0 \end{bmatrix}$$

then we can define the entire patch with the expression

$$E(u)^t\, M^t\, G\, M\, E(v)$$

where the superscripts $E(u)^t$ and M^t indicate matrix transpose. This is a very compact but powerful way to express the surface and yields a relatively straightforward way to develop the code for it.

Other Kinds of Interpolating Functions

While the Bézier and Catmull-Rom splines we have seen are widely used and simple to use, many other kinds of splines are used in creating curves and surfaces professionally. The *B-spline* functions are more general than Bézier splines (that is, Bézier splines are special cases of B-splines) that have even more beneficial properties. They are not as easily computed as Bézier splines, however, and are supported only by OpenGL as special cases of NURBS.

A more general class of interpolating function than polynomials is given by *rational functions,* or quotients of two polynomials. If both polynomials are parametric, then the rational parametric functions can be used to accomplish things that are not possible with B-spline curves, such as the creation of perfect circles and other quadratic functions. Among these are the non-uniform rational B-splines, or *NURBS,* whose blending functions are rational functions with B-spline numerators and denominators. These are powerful and are the tools of choice in the professional design world, but we will not cover them in this introductory text; they are supported by GLU tools that are complex and that need a good understanding of NURBS design to use. If curve and surface design are particularly important to you, this is a good direction for additional study.

Interpolations in OpenGL

In OpenGL, the spline capability is provided by functions called *evaluators* that take a set of control points and produce another set of points that interpolate the control points. This lets you model curves and surfaces by doing only the work to set the control points and set up the evaluator, and get detailed curves and surfaces as a result.

There are two kinds of evaluators in OpenGL: one-dimensional and two-dimensional evaluators. If you want to interpolate points to produce one-parameter information (that is, curves or any other data with only one degree of freedom; think of 1D textures as well as geometric curves), you can use 1D evaluators. If you want to interpolate points in a 2D array to produce two-parameter information (that is, surfaces or any other data with two degrees of freedom; think of 2D textures as well as geometric surfaces) you can use 2D evaluators. The OpenGL evaluators implement the Bézier cubic spline we discussed above. Both are straightforward and let you choose how much detail you want in the actual display of the information.

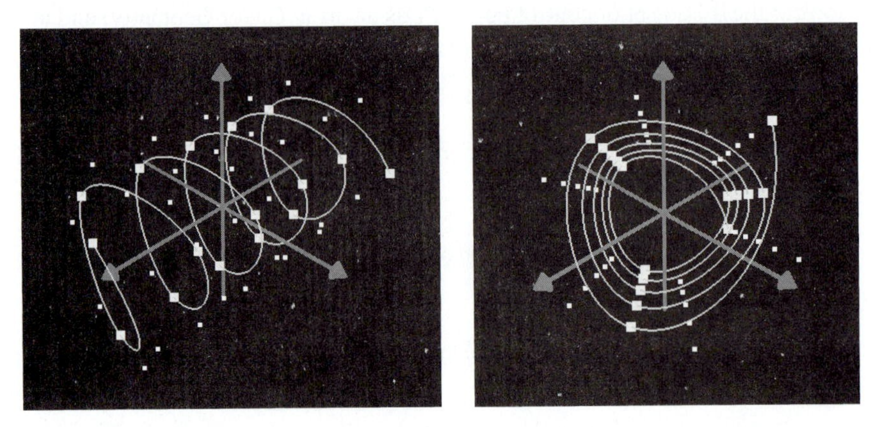

Figure 13.7 A spline curve defined via a 1D evaluator, from a point of view with $x = y = z$ (*left*) and rotated to show the relationship between control points and the curve shape (*right*). The smaller control points are the originals; the larger control control points are added as discussed when we extended simple Bézier curves.

In Figures 13.7 through 13.9 we see several images that illustrate geometry defined by evaluators in OpenGL. Figure 13.7 shows two views of a 1D evaluator that defines a curve in space showing the set of thirty control points as well as additional computed control points for smoothness; Figure 13.8 shows a 2D evaluator used to define a single surface patch based on a 4×4 set of control points; and Figure 13.9 shows a surface defined by a 16×16 set of control points with additional intermediate control points not shown. Some of the code that creates these figures is given in the Examples section.

The spline surface in Figure 13.8 has only a 0.7 alpha value, so the control points and other parts of the surface can be seen behind the primary surface of the patch. In this example, note the relation between the control points and the actual surface; only the four corner points actually meet the surface, while all the others lie off the surface and act only to influence the shape of the

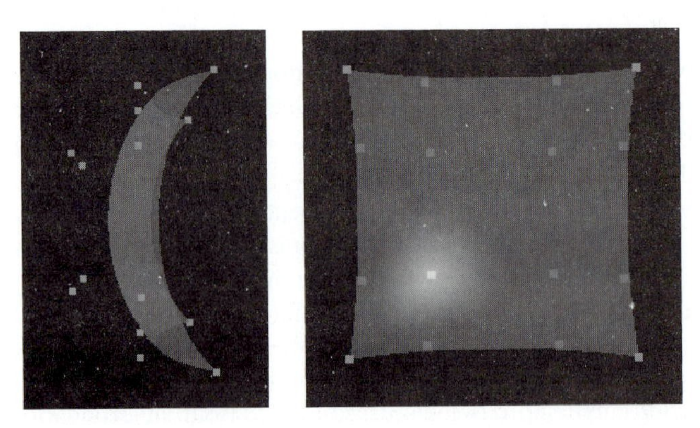

Figure 13.8 A spline patch defined by four control points using a 2D evaluator.

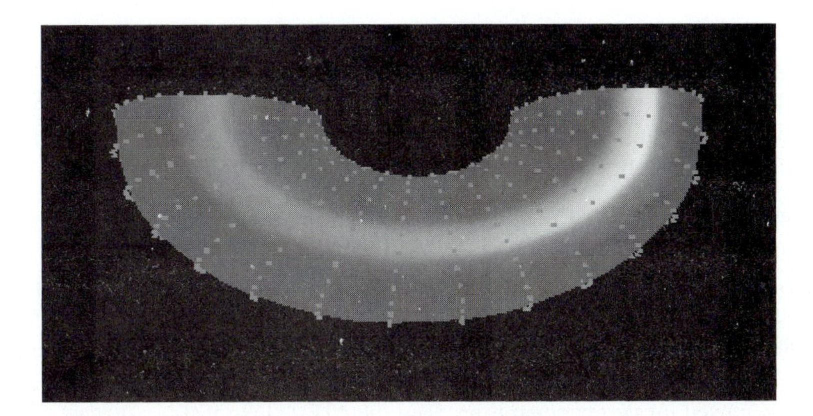

Figure 13.9 A spline surface defined by a 2D evaluator using a 16 × 16 set of control points. The original set of control points is extended with interpolated points.

patch. Note also that the entire patch lies within the convex hull of the control points. We saw this behavior for the Bézier spline earlier. The specular highlight on the patch should also help you see the shape of the patch from the lighting. In the larger surface of Figure 13.9, note that the surface extends smoothly between the different sets of control points.

These examples have used the full curve or surface generation capabilities of evaluators that generate the entire mesh based on the control points. However, there are times when you might want to generate only a single point on a curve or a surface that corresponds to particular values of the parameter or parameters. For example, if you have developed a model and you want to show a "fly-over" or "fly-through" of the model, you may want to position the eye along a curve that you define with control points. Then to generate images with eyepoints along this curve, you will want to define the eye position with particular values of the parameter that defines the curve. For each of these eye positions, you will want to evaluate the curve at the corresponding parameter value, getting the coordinates of that point to use with the `gluLookAt(...)` function.

Automatic Normal and Texture Generation with Evaluators

The images in Figure 13.8 and 13.9 include the full standard lighting model and show specular highlighting. As you will see from the code example for spline surfaces later in this chapter, neither explicit vertex definitions nor explicit normal definitions are used in the code to accomplish this. Instead, 2D evaluators are used to generate the vertices, and vertex normals are generated automatically. Basically, the key elements are as follows:

- Specify an array of 16 control points.
- Enable `GL_MAP2_VERTEX_3` to specify that you will generate points in 3D space with a 2D map.
- Enable `GL_AUTO_NORMAL` to specify that normals are to be generated analytically from the evaluator.
- Use `glMap2f(...)` to specify the details of the 2D mapping and to identify that the control point array above is to be used.

- Use `glMapGrid2f(...)` to specify how the 2D domain space is to be used in creating the vertex grid to be displayed.
- Use `glEvalMesh2(...)` to carry out the evaluation and display the surface or, if you want only to calculate a point on the surface that corresponds to a single parameter pair (u, v), use `glEvalCoord2f(u,v)` to get the coordinates of that point.

There are, in fact, a number of similar functions that you can use for similar operations in different dimensions. Look these up in an OpenGL manual for more details.

Besides generating automatic normals, OpenGL evaluators have other capabilities for generating information for your surface such as generating automatic texture coordinates for your evaluator surfaces. If you enable `GL_MAP2_TEXTURE_COORD_2`, for example, and use `glMap2f(...)` with the first parameter `GL_MAP2_TEXTURE_COORD_2` and with similar parameters to those you used for vertex generation, then the `glEvalMesh2(...)` function will generate s and t coordinates for the texture on your 2D patch. This can look daunting—see the example of spline surfaces that follows—but when you work through an example it is not hard. As above, there are many variations to generate 1D through 4D textures from 1D or 2D meshes; see the OpenGL manuals for details. The image from Figure 13.8 is extended to that of Figure 13.10 by changing the surface color to white and applying a texture with modulation using automatic texture coordinates. Sample code for Figures 13.8 and 13.10 that includes automatic normal and texture coordinate generation is provided later in this chapter.

Figure 13.10 Texture map on the patch of Figure 13.8 created with automatic texture coordinates.

You can also generate the normals from your surface from the `glMap2f(...)` function if you use the `GL_MAP2_NORMAL` parameter, or the colors from your surface if you use the `GL_MAP2_COLOR_4` parameter.

Additional Techniques

Spline techniques may be used for much more than simply modeling. You can use them to generate smoothly changing sets of colors, or of normals, or of texture coordinates—or probably just about any other kind of data that you could interpolate. There aren't built-in functions that let you apply these points automatically like those for creating curves and surfaces, however; you need to manage the parametric functions yourself. To do this, you need to define each point in the (u, v) parameter space for which you need a value and get the actual interpolated points from the evaluator using the functions `glEvalCoord1f(u)` or `glEvalCoord2f(u, v)`. You then use these points in the same way you would use any points you had defined in another way. These points may represent colors, or normals, or texture coordinates, depending on what you need to create your image.

To be more concrete, suppose you have a surface defined by two parameters, each having values in [0, 1]. If you want to determine a set of normals on the surface that will achieve a given lighting effect, you can define a set of control points that approximate the normals you want. (Recall that a normal is simply a 3D vector, just as is a point.) You can define an evaluator for the new surface defined by these new control points and a mapping from the parameters of the original surface to the parameters on the new surface. To define a normal at a point with parametric coordinates (u, v), then, you would determine the corresponding parameters (u', v') on the new surface, get the value (x, y, z) of the original surface as $f(u, v)$ for whatever parametric function you are using, and get the value (r, s, t) of the new surface with the `glEvalCoord2f(u', v')` function. You can then use these values for the vertex in the function calls

```
glNormal3f(r,s,t); glVertex3f(x,y,z);
```

that would be used to define the geometry for your image.

Another common application of splines is in animation, where you can get a smooth curve for your eyepoint to follow as we saw in the animation chapter (Chapter 11). As your eyepoint moves, however, you also need to deal with the other issues in defining a view. The up vector is fairly straightforward; for simple animations, it is probably enough to keep the up vector constant. The center of view is more of a challenge, however, because it has to move to keep the motion realistic. The suggested approach is to keep three points from the spline curve—the previous point, the current point, and the next point—and to use the previous and next points to set the direction of view; the viewpoint is then a point at a fixed distance from the current point in this direction. This should provide a reasonably good motion and viewing setup. Other applications of splines in animation include moving different parts of a model smoothly to get believable motion.

Definitions

As you saw in Figures 13.7 and 13.8, an OpenGL evaluator working on an array of four control points (1D) or 4×4 control points (2D) actually fits the extreme points of the control point set but does not go through any of the other points. As the evaluator comes up to these extreme control points, the tangent to the curve becomes parallel to the line segment from the extreme point to the adjacent control point, as shown in Figure 13.11, and the speed with which this happens is determined by the distance between the extreme and adjacent control points.

To control the shape of an extended spline curve, you need to arrange the control points so that the direction and distance from a control point to the adjacent control points are the same. You can do this by adding new control points between appropriate pairs of the original control points as described above. This will move the curve from the first extreme point to the first added

Figure 13.11 Two spline curves showing the curves with different control point layouts.

point, from the first added point smoothly to the second added point, from the second added point smoothly to the third added point, and so on to moving smoothly through the last added point to the last extreme point.

This construction and relationship is indicated by the added larger control points in Figure 13.7. Review that figure and note again that there is one added point after each two original points, excepting the first and last points; that the added points bisect the line segment between the two points they interpolate; and that the curve actually meets only the added points, not the original points; again excepting the two endpoints. To create an interactive program to let a user manipulate control points, you would give the user access to only the original control points; the added points are not part of the definition but only of the implementation of a smooth surface. The surface can be recomputed and displayed continually as the control points change.

Similarly, you can define added control points in the control mesh for a 2D evaluator and create a richer set of patches as you add the transitions from one patch to another. These should follow the same principle of equal length and same direction in the line segments coming to the edge of one patch and going from the edge of the other. This lets you achieve a surface that moves smoothly from one patch to the next. Key points of this code are included in the Example section below, but it does take some effort to manage all the cases that depend on the location of a particular patch in the surface. The example code that follows will show you these details.

So how do spline curves and surfaces work? A cubic spline curve is determined by a cubic polynomial in a parametric variable u as indicated by the equation in one parameter below, with the single parameter u taking values between 0 and 1.

$$\sum_{i=0}^{3} a_i u^i$$

The four coefficients a_i can be determined by knowing four constraints on the curve. These are provided by the four control points needed to determine a single segment of a cubic spline curve. We saw how these four values could be computed from the four basis polynomials and the coefficients determined by the control points; an OpenGL 1D evaluator computes those four coefficients based on the Bézier curve definition and, as needed, evaluates the resulting polynomial to generate a point on the curve or the curve itself.

A bicubic spline surface is determined by a bicubic polynomial in parametric variables u and v as indicated by the equation in two parameters below, with both parameters u and v taking values between 0 and 1. This requires computing the sixteen coefficients a_{ij}, which can be done by using the sixteen control points that define a single bicubic spline patch.

$$\sum_{i=0}^{3}\sum_{j=0}^{3} a_{ij}u^i v^j$$

Again, an OpenGL 2D evaluator takes the control points as its input, determines those sixteen coefficients based on the Bernstein basis functions, and evaluates the function the control points determine to create your surface model.

Some Examples

Spline Curves

The program setup to generate spline curves is given in some detail in this section. This involves defining a set of control points for the evaluator to use, enabling the evaluator for your target data type, defining overall control points for the curve, stepping through the overall control points to build four-tuples of segment control points, and then invoking the evaluator to draw the actual curve. This code produced Figures 13.2 and 13.5 showing Bézier spline curves. A few details are omitted in the following code, but the essential parts of setting up the control points are included in full. The full example is included in the resources for the book. This code returns the points on the curve using the `glEvalCoord1f(...)` function instead of the `glVertex*(...)` function within a `glBegin(...) ... glEnd()` pair; this is different from the more automatic approach of the 2D patch example that follows it.

Probably the key point in this sample code is the way thc four-tuples of segment control points have been managed. The original points would not have given smooth curves, so as discussed above, new points were defined that interpolated some of the original points to make the transition from one segment to the other continuous and smooth.

```
glEnable(GL_MAP1_VERTEX_3)
#define LAST_STEP (CURVE_SIZE/2)-1
#define NPTS 30

void makeCurve(void)
{   ...
    for (i=0; i<CURVE_SIZE; i++) {
        ctrlpts[i][0]= RAD*cos(INITANGLE + i*STEPANGLE);
        ctrlpts[i][1]= RAD*sin(INITANGLE + i*STEPANGLE);
        ctrlpts[i][2]= -4.0 + i * 0.25;
    }
}

void curve(void) {
    int step, i, j;
    makeCurve(); // calculate the control points for the entire curve.
    // Copy/compute points from ctrlpts to segpts to define each
    // segment of the curve. First and last cases are different
    // from middle cases...
```

```
    for (step = 0; step < LAST_STEP; step++) {
        if (step==0) { // first case
            for (j=0; j<3; j++) {
                segpts[0][j]=ctrlpts[0][j];
                segpts[1][j]=ctrlpts[1][j];
                segpts[2][j]=ctrlpts[2][j];
                segpts[3][j]=(ctrlpts[2][j]+ctrlpts[3][j])/2.0;
            }
        }
        else if (step==LAST_STEP-1) { // last case
            for (j=0; j<3; j++) {
                segpts[0][j]=(ctrlpts[CURVE_SIZE-4][j]
                           +ctrlpts[CURVE_SIZE-3][j])/2.0;
                segpts[1][j]=ctrlpts[CURVE_SIZE-3][j];
                segpts[2][j]=ctrlpts[CURVE_SIZE-2][j];
                segpts[3][j]=ctrlpts[CURVE_SIZE-1][j];
            }
        }
        else for (j=0; j<3; j++) { // general case
            segpts[0][j]=(ctrlpts[2*step][j]+ctrlpts[2*step+1][j])/2.0;
            segpts[1][j]=ctrlpts[2*step+1][j];
            segpts[2][j]=ctrlpts[2*step+2][j];
            segpts[3][j]=(ctrlpts[2*step+2][j]
                      +ctrlpts[2*step+3][j])/2.0;
        }

        // define the evaluator
        glMap1f(GL_MAP1_VERTEX_3, 0.0, 1.0, 3, 4, &segpts[0][0]);
        glBegin(GL_LINE_STRIP);
            for (i=0; i<=NPTS; i++)
                glEvalCoord1f((GLfloat)i/(GLfloat)NPTS);
        glEnd ();
        ...
    }
}
```

We used the OpenGL evaluator to give us points on the curve manually using the `glEvalCoord1f(...)` function. We could have taken a more automatic approach using the function `glMapGrid1f(...)` to generate a series of evenly spaced points along the curve and the function `glEvalMesh1(...)` to create the curve. This is done for spline surfaces in the following example.

Spline Surfaces

We have two examples of spline surfaces code in the materials that accompany the book. The first shows drawing a simple patch (a surface based on a single 4×4 grid of control points), and the second shows the drawing of a larger surface with more control points. Following is some simple code from the first example that generates a surface given a 4×4 array of points for a single patch, as shown in Figure 13.8. This code initializes a 4×4 array of points, enables auto normals (available because we use the `glEvalMesh(...)` function) and identifies the target of the evaluator, and carries out the evaluator operations. The data for the patch control points is deliberately over-simplified so that you can see this easily, but in general the patch points act in a parametric way that is quite distinct from the indices, as is shown a little later in the general surface code. This code also uses

`glEnable(...)` and
`glMapGrid2f(GL_MAP2_TEXTURE_COORD_2,...)`

to generate automatic texture coordinates for Figure 13.10 but does not include the details of the texture mapping code. Note that the third parameter of the `glMapGrid2f(...)` function that specifies the texture coordinate generation is 4.0; this corresponds to mapping the texture coordinates over four grid points.

```
point3 patch[4][4] =
        {{{-2.,-2.,0.},{-2.,-1.,1.},{-2.,1.,1.},{-2.,2.,0.}},
         {{-1.,-2.,1.},{-1.,-1.,2.},{-1.,1.,2.},{-1.,2.,1.}},
         {{1.,-2.,1.},{1.,-1.,2.},{1.,1.,2.},{1.,2.,1.}},
         {{2.,-2.,0.},{2.,-1.,1.},{2.,1.,1.},{2.,2.,0.}}};

void myinit(void) {  ...
    glEnable(GL_AUTO_NORMAL);
    glEnable(GL_MAP2_TEXTURE_COORD_2);
    glEnable(GL_MAP2_VERTEX_3);
}

void doPatch(void) {
// draws a patch defined by a 4 x 4 array of points
#define NUM 20    //

    glMaterialfv(...);  // whatever material definitions are needed
    glMap2f(GL_MAP2_VERTEX_3,0.0,1.0,3,4,0.0,1.0,12,4,&patch[0][0][0]);
    glMap2f(GL_MAP2_TEXTURE_COORD_2,0.0,4.0,3,4,0.0,4.0,12,4,,
        &patch[0][0][0]);
    glMapGrid2f(NUM, 0.0, 1.0, NUM, 0.0, 1.0);
    glEvalMesh2(GL_FILL, 0, NUM, 0, NUM);
}
```

As in the previous example, we could have drawn the patch manually by following the `glMap2f(...)` function with a `glBegin(GL_QUADS) ... glEnd()` pair that encloses a double loop in which we use `glEvalCoord2f(...)` to generate the actual vertices. This would not have given automatic normals and texture coordinates, however. You might want to think about which of these is preferable for a particular image based on the tradeoff between automatic operation and manual control.

The considerations for extending a single patch to create a complete surface with a 2D evaluator are similar to those for creating an extended curve with a 1D evaluator. You need to create a set of control points, define and enable an appropriate 2D evaluator, generate patches from the control points, and draw the individual patches. These are covered in the sample code that follows.

This sample code has two parts. The first part is a function that generates a set of 2D control points procedurally; this differs from the manual definition of the points in the patch example above or in the pool example of Chapter 7. Procedural control point generation is a useful tool that gives us procedural surface generation. The second part is a fragment from the section of code that generates a patch from the control points, illustrating how the new intermediate points between control points are built. Note that these intermediate points all have indices 0 or 3 for their locations in the patch array because they are the boundary points in the patch; the interior points are always the original control points. Drawing the actual patch is handled by the function `doPatch(...)` above in just the same way as it is handled for the patch example, so it is omitted here.

```
point3 ctrlpts[GRIDSIZE][GRIDSIZE];

void genPoints(void)
{
#define PI 3.14159
#define R1 6.0
#define R2 3.0
    int i, j;
    GLfloat alpha, beta, step;

    alpha = -PI;
    step = PI/(GLfloat)(GRIDSIZE-1);
    for (i=0; i<GRIDSIZE; i++) {
        beta = -PI;
        for (j=0; j<GRIDSIZE; j++) {
            ctrlpts[i][j][0] = (R1 + R2*cos(beta))*cos(alpha);
            ctrlpts[i][j][1] = (R1 + R2*cos(beta))*sin(alpha);
            ctrlpts[i][j][2] = R2*sin(beta);
            beta -= step;
        }
        alpha += step;
    }
}

void surface(point3 ctrlpts[GRIDSIZE][GRIDSIZE])
{...
    ...{ // general case (internal patch)
        for(i=1; i<3; i++)
            for(j=1; j<3; j++)
                for(k=0; k<3; k++)
                    patch[i][j][k]=ctrlpts[2*xstep+i][2*ystep+j][k];
        for(i=1; i<3; i++)
            for(k=0; k<3; k++) {
                patch[i][0][k]=(ctrlpts[2*xstep+i][2*ystep][k]
                    +ctrlpts[2*xstep+i][2*ystep+1][k])/2.0;
                patch[i][3][k]=(ctrlpts[2*xstep+i][2*ystep+2][k]
                    +ctrlpts[2*xstep+i][2*ystep+3][k])/2.0;
                patch[0][i][k]=(ctrlpts[2*xstep][2*ystep+i][k]
                    +ctrlpts[2*xstep+1][2*ystep+i][k])/2.0;
                patch[3][i][k]=(ctrlpts[2*xstep+2][2*ystep+i][k]
                    +ctrlpts[2*xstep+3][2*ystep+i][k])/2.0;
            }
```

```
            for(k=0; k<3; k++) {
                patch[0][0][k]=(ctrlpts[2*xstep][2*ystep][k]
                              +ctrlpts[2*xstep+1][2*ystep][k]
                              +ctrlpts[2*xstep][2*ystep+1][k]
                              +ctrlpts[2*xstep+1][2*ystep+1][k])/4.0;
                patch[3][0][k]=(ctrlpts[2*xstep+2][2*ystep][k]
                              +ctrlpts[2*xstep+3][2*ystep][k]
                              +ctrlpts[2*xstep+2][2*ystep+1][k]
                              +ctrlpts[2*xstep+3][2*ystep+1][k])/4.0;
                patch[0][3][k]=(ctrlpts[2*xstep][2*ystep+2][k]
                              +ctrlpts[2*xstep+1][2*ystep+2][k]
                              +ctrlpts[2*xstep][2*ystep+3][k]
                              +ctrlpts[2*xstep+1][2*ystep+3][k])/4.0;
                patch[3][3][k]=(ctrlpts[2*xstep+2][2*ystep+2][k]
                              +ctrlpts[2*xstep+3][2*ystep+2][k]
                              +ctrlpts[2*xstep+2][2*ystep+3][k]
                              +ctrlpts[2*xstep+3][2*ystep+3][k])/4.0;
            }
        }
    ...
}
```

Summary

In this chapter we saw how to interpolate geometric points based on various kinds of basis functions, giving us powerful tools for creating complex curves and surfaces with relatively few control points. The result is a new kind of modeling that extends the simple primitives we saw early in this book and lets you create much more sophisticated geometries for your models. This interpolation also lets you add shading and texture mapping to your surfaces, adding to their value to the user.

OpenGL Glossary for the Chapter

This chapter introduced the spline capabilities of OpenGL, and a number of functions and their associated parameters go with splines. The functions in this section often take a very large number of parameters that define the curve or surface being defined, and their parameters are not listed here; refer to the OpenGL manuals if you need more details than you will find in this chapter's examples. As always, the functions and parameters that we have seen before are not included here.

OpenGL Functions

`glEvalCoord*(...)`: family of functions to evaluate one- or two-dimensional enabled maps at float or double coordinates

`glEvalCoord*f(...)`: evaluates one- or two-dimensional enabled maps defined by `glMap*f()`

`glEvalMesh*(...)`: computes a one- or two-dimensional grid of points or lines

`glMap*f(...)`: defines a one- or two-dimensional evaluator based on a number of parameters

`glMapGrid*(...)`: defines a one- or two-dimensional mesh of float or double values

OpenGL Parameters

GL_AUTO_NORMAL: identifies a property that can be enabled to have glMap2() automatically generate normals when GL_MAP2_VERTEX_* is used

GL_MAP*_COLOR_4: parameter to glMap*f() to specify that the control points for the evaluator are to be RGBA components of a color; the * specifies whether the evaluator is to define a curve or surface

GL_MAP*_NORMAL: parameter to glMap*f() to specify that the control points for the evaluator are to be the components of a normal vector; the * specifies whether the evaluator is to define a curve or surface

GL_MAP*_TEXTURE_COORD*: parameter to glMap*f() to specify that the control points for the evaluator are to be texture coordinates; the * specifies whether the evaluator is to define a curve or surface, and the texture dimension is determined by the second *

GL_MAP*_VERTEX_*: parameter to glMap*f() to specify what kind of evaluator is to be defined; the first * can be 1 or 2, depending on whether a curve or surface evaluator is defined, and the second * can be 3 or 4, depending on the dimension of the control points

Questions

1. Each of the sets of basis functions in this chapter has the property that at any value in [0., 1.], each of the functions is non-negative, and the sum of their values is 1. Verify this for the Catmull-Rom spline basis functions. In addition, all the basis functions but one have a zero value at one endpoint, and that one has a value of 1. Could you use any set of functions with these properties as the basis functions for an interpolation? Would the results be similar to, or different from, the results of using the standard basis functions? Why?
2. Take some pairs of functions with the properties of the previous exercise and interpolate two points with them. These need not be linear; for example, take $f_0(t) = 1 - t^2$ and $f_1(t) = t^2$. See if you can think of other examples as well. Can the interpolating points ever have any shape but a straight line? How would you interpret this?
3. Find a set of functions that interpolate a set of three or four points and that have the properties of the standard basis functions in this chapter, but that are different from the sets of basis functions we have seen so far. Write the interpolating function in closed form and use any technique to draw the resulting curve. How much is it like (or different from) the standard interpolating curves we have seen in this chapter? Can you create an interpolating curve that is very different from these?
4. Take the statements about the Bézier spline curves with endpoints P_0, P_1, P_2, and P_3 made earlier in this chapter, starting with the general parametric equation $f(t) = at^3 + bt^2 + ct + d$ and using simple calculus to take derivatives and solve them for $t = 0$ (P_0) and $t = 1$ (P_3)
   a. the slope of the curve at P_0 is the same as that of the line from P_0 to P_1
   b. the slope of the curve at P_3 is the same as that of the line from P_2 to P_3
   c. the derivative of $f(t)$ at P_0 is one-third of the vector from P_0 to P_1
   d. the derivative of $f(t)$ at P_3 is one-third of the vector from P_2 to P_3

   Derive the equations of a single Bézier spline segment from these facts.

Exercises

1. Choose an object with a shape you find pleasing and try to design a set of points that might determine that shape, or a shape close to it, when used as control points for a spline curve or surface. Use the evaluator approach in the code examples in this chapter to draw the curve or surface from your points to check this out.
2. Given a set of six or more control points for a cubic curve, remembering that you will need to have an even number of points, hand-build the set of additional control points you will need to extend a smooth piecewise-cubic curve across all these control points. Do a similar exercise for control points for a surface, using a 2D array of control points that is larger than 4×4.
3. Adapt the derivation process of the matrix representation for the Bézier cubic spline to build a matrix representation for the Catmull-Rom cubic spline.

Experiments

1. The code examples in this chapter set up the control points for a spline curve and then call the OpenGL evaluator functions to create the actual curves or patches. However, early in the chapter we discussed how to calculate the curve or surface points for any parameter or parameter pair. Program these calculations and generate your own curve or surface points for an interpolation.
2. Take the same control points of the previous exercise and set up control point arrays for the OpenGL evaluator functions that we saw in this chapter. Again, generate the curve or surface determined by these control points, using the evaluators. Compare the programming effort needed to generate these curves or surfaces both from first principles, as in the previous experiment, and with evaluators.

Projects

1. (The small house) In the original modeling for the small house, you probably used a very simple shape for the house's roof. Update this and design a roof that is built as a spline surface in order to get a more sophisticated look to the house. Then comment out your access to the original roof function and add the new roof design to the house scene.
2. (A scene graph parser) How would you represent the geometry of an evaluator in the geometry node of a scene graph? How would you generate the code for the evaluator when you parsed the scene graph? What would you do in these two cases if you used an interpolator instead of an evaluator?

14 Nonpolygon Graphics

In the previous chapters we focused on strongly polygon-oriented graphics APIs and learned how to use this kind of tool to make effective images. However, this is not the only kind of computer graphics that you can do, and it is also not the only kind of computer graphics that can be effective.

Another kind of computer graphics works with a geometric model to determine the color of each pixel in a scene independently. We call this *per-pixel* graphics, and it covers several different approaches to making images. There is *ray casting,* a straightforward approach to generating an image in which rays are generated from the eyepoint through each pixel of a virtual screen, and the first intersection of each ray with the geometry of the scene defines the color of that pixel. There is *ray tracing,* a more sophisticated approach that begins in the same way as ray casting, but you may generate more than one ray for each pixel and when the rays intersect with the geometry they may define secondary rays by reflection or refraction that will help define the color that the pixel will eventually be given. There are also several uses of pixels to record some kind of computational value, such as one might find in a study of iterated functions or of fractals. With a wide variety of ways to take advantage of this kind of graphics, we believe it can be valuable in a beginning graphics course.

In this chapter you will see examples of different per-pixel operations that can be used to create several kinds of computer graphics images. We will not go into some of these operations in great depth, but we introduce them so you can understand their capabilities and decide whether you want to study them in more depth with other reading. To get the best from this chapter, you should be familiar with geometric operations in an algebraic setting, such as were described in Chapter 4.

Definitions

The terms *ray tracing* and *ray casting* are not always well-defined in computer graphics. We will define *ray casting* as the process of generating an image from a geometric model by sending out one ray per pixel and computing the color of that pixel by considering its intersection with the model with no computation of shadow, reflection, or refraction properties. We will define *ray tracing* as an extension of ray casting without limitations: multiple rays may be cast for each pixel as needed, and you may use any kind of shadow, refraction, and/or reflection computation that you wish. We will discuss both these processes, although we will not go into much depth on either. Refer to a resource such as the Glassner text [GL] or a public domain ray tracer such as POVRay to get more experience.

Ray Casting

In the standard viewing setup and viewing volume we defined for the perspective transformation in Chapter 1, the front of the viewing frustum can be an effective equivalent of the actual display screen. We can make this more concrete by mapping the actual screen to this space with a reverse window-to-viewport operation, in effect creating a screen-to-viewplane operation that gives us a virtual screen at the front of the frustum.

To do this, we use the idea of the perspective view volume from viewing and projection. We can create the viewing transformation as we illustrated in Chapter 4, which lets us place the eyepoint at the origin and the front of the viewing volume in the plane $z = -1$. Just as the perspective projection in OpenGL is defined in terms of the field of view α and the aspect ratio ρ, we can determine the coordinates of the upper-right corner of the front of the view volume as $x = tan(\alpha)$ and $y = \rho * x$. This space is centered on the Z-axis, has dimensions $2x$ and $2y$, and is the virtual screen we will "draw" on. You can divide this virtual screen into virtual pixels with a step size of $2*x/N$, where N is the number of pixels across the horizontal screen. A virtual screen in world space, along with the eyepoint and a sample ray, is shown in Figure 14.1. In order to manage the aspect ratio you have set, you should use the same step size for the vertical screen as well. The final parameters of the OpenGL perspective projection are the front and back clipping planes for the view; you may use these parameters to limit the range where you will check for intersections or you may choose to use your model with no limits.

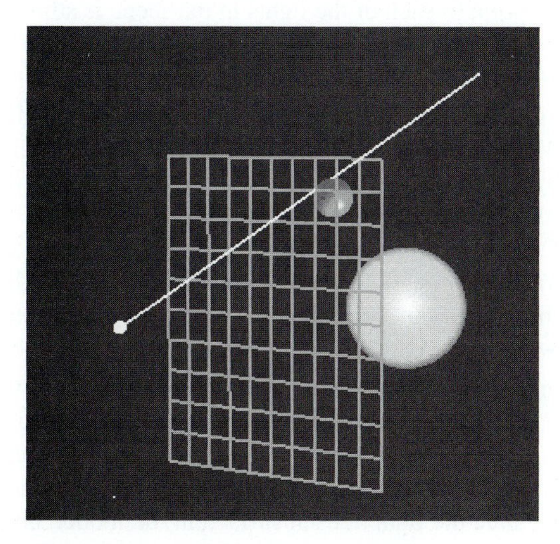

Figure 14.1 The eyepoint and virtual screen in 3D space.

The key point of ray casting is to generate a ray, which you can model as a parametric line segment with only positive parameter values, from the eyepoint through each pixel in the virtual screen. You may choose what point you want to use in the pixel because each pixel actually corresponds to a small quad determined by adjacent horizontal and vertical lines in the virtual grid. In the general discussion it doesn't matter which point you choose, but you might start with the middle point in the quad. The ray you generate will start at the origin and will go through a point $(x, y, 1)$, so the parametric equations for the ray are (xt, yt, t).

Once you have the parametric equation for the ray, you must determine the point in your model where the ray intersects some object. If there is no such point, you simply get the background color; if there is at least one intersection, you must determine the nearest intersection point. The pixel is then given the color of your model at that point of intersection. The ray–object intersection problem is the heart of the ray casting problem, and a great deal of time is spent in calculating intersections. We discussed collision testing in Chapter 4, and the ray–object intersection is just a special case of collision testing. The easiest intersection test is made with a sphere, where you can use the formula for the distance between a point and a line to see how close the line comes to the center of the sphere; if that distance is less than the radius of the sphere, there is an intersection and a simple quadratic equation will give you the intersection points.

Determining the color depends a great deal on the model you are viewing. If your model does not use a lighting model, then each object will have its own color, and the color of the pixel will simply be the color of the object the virtual pixel's ray intersects. If you do have lighting, however, the local lighting model is not provided by the system; you must develop it yourself. This means that at the point where a ray meets an object, you must do the computations for ambient, diffuse, and specular lighting that we described in Chapter 6. This will require computing the four vectors involved in local lighting: the normal vector, eye vector, reflection vector, and light vector. The eye vector is simple because this is just the ray we are using; the normal vector is calculated using analytic techniques or geometric computations just as it was for the OpenGL `glNormal*(...)` function; the reflection vector is calculated as in the discussion on mathematics for modeling; and creating a vector from the point to each of the lights in the scene is straightforward. Details of the lighting computations were presented in Chapter 6, so we will not go into them in more detail here.

Because you can create your own lighting, you have the opportunity to use more sophisticated shading models than are provided by OpenGL. These shading models generally use the standard ambient and diffuse light, but they can change the way specular highlights appear on an object by modifying the way light reflects from a surface. We saw these techniques, called *anisotropic shading* and involving creating a different reflection vector through a *bidirectional reflection distribution function* or *BRDF,* in Chapter 6. This kind of function takes the x-, y-, and z-components of the light vector and determines a direction in which light will be reflected, and a standard specular lighting computation is then done with that reflection direction vector. Details are much more complex than are appropriate here, but you can consult advanced references for more information.

Where the colors are pre-computed, ray casting can also be used to view models by any technique you want. Where each ray intersects the model, the color of that point is returned to the pixel in the image. This technique, or a more sophisticated ray-tracing equivalent, can be used to view a model that is lighted with a global lighting model such as radiosity or photon mapping. The lighting process is used to calculate the light at each surface in the model, and other visual properties such as texture mapping are applied. Then for each ray defined by a pixel in the virtual screen, the color of the intersection point is read from the model or is computed from information in the model, and the corresponding actual screen pixel is given that color. The resulting image carries all the sophistication of the model, even though it is created by a simple ray-casting process.

Ray casting has aliasing problems because we sample with only one ray per pixel, and the screen coordinates can be quite coarse when compared with the real-valued fine detail of the real world. We have seen this in our images created with OpenGL and noted that OpenGL has some antialiasing capabilities. These aliasing problems are inherent in our definition of ray casting and cannot be addressed in the original image, but you can do some post-processing of the image to smooth it out. This can lose detail, and you must decide whether the smoothness is worth it. The fundamental principle is to generate the image in the frame buffer and then save the buffer as a color array. This array may then be processed by techniques such as filtering to smooth out any aliasing. Of course, you can also use a multiple-ray-per-pixel technique as described later in this chapter to supersample the virtual pixel, even without using reflections and refractions, and then average the colors of all the samples to set the pixel's color.

Ray Tracing

As we define it, the difference between ray casting and ray tracing is that ray tracing includes any or all of the techniques of reflection, refraction, shadows, and multiple rays per pixel. Ray tracing is a common technique that is widely discussed online; the classic reference is by Andrew Glassner [GL].

Let's begin by discussing how you might handle shadows in ray tracing. When you calculate the lighting model and include a light in the model, you create a vector from the intersection point to that light. However, that light participates in the diffuse and specular lighting calculations only if the light actually reaches the surface; otherwise, the point is in shadow for that light. So you simply cast a ray from the point in the direction of the light and see if it intersects anything between the point and the light. If it does, then the point is not illuminated by that light and there is no diffuse or specular contribution from the light; the point is in shadow from that light. If that ray does not intersect anything, then that light contributes to the diffuse and specular light at the point. This requires you to generate a new ray from an arbitrary point in the scene in an arbitrary direction and will require an extra set of ray–object intersection computations, so it is not fast.

Ray tracing is often used for images with shiny or transparent surfaces because it works very well with reflective and transmissive light: light that is reflected directly from a surface and light that passes through surfaces. The behavior of reflected and refracted light are illustrated in Figure 14.2.

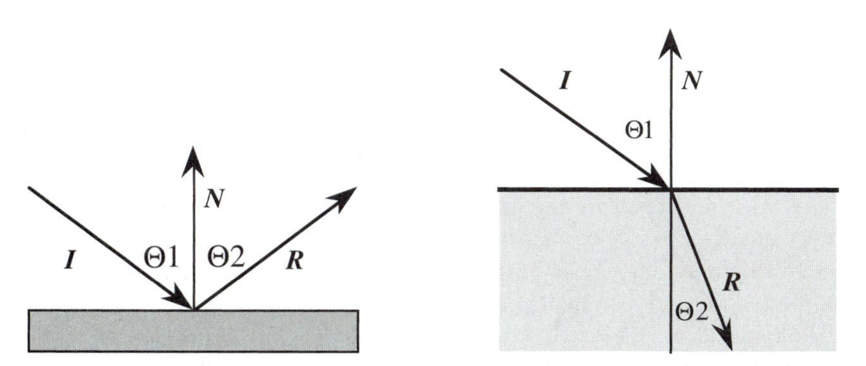

Figure 14.2 Reflected (*left*) and refracted (*right*) rays where a ray intersects an object.

Reflection is relatively easy to deal with because we have already met the concept of the reflection vector: if the incoming vector is P and the normal vector is N, then the reflection vector is $R = P - 2(N{\bullet}P)N$ as we saw in Chapter 4. The process of a light's going through a surface and continuing on the other side is called *refraction*. The ray continues in the same plane, but its direction is affected by the difference between the speed of light in the medium outside the surface and the medium inside the surface. The index of refraction η of each material measures this difference in speed. The key formula for the direction of refracted light is given by Snell's law: If Θ_1 and Θ_2 are the angles between the ray and the normal for the incoming ray and outgoing ray, respectively, and η_1 and η_2 are the indices of refraction, then $\sin(\Theta_1)/\sin(\Theta_2) = \eta_1/\eta_2$. From this you can compute the vector for the outgoing light.

Once you have the vectors for reflected and refracted light, you must generate new rays from the point where the ray meets the object. One ray is in the direction of the reflection vector and the other is in the direction of the refraction vector, and both are in the plane determined by the incoming ray and the surface normal. These are treated recursively in the same way as is the original ray, and eventually each will return a color value. These two values are combined with whatever color the object itself has, in the proportions by which the light was reflected, refracted, or simply returned diffusively.

The recursive generation of reflection, refraction, and light rays is shown in the ray tree, as depicted in Figure 14.3, which includes reflected rays R, refracted rays T, and light rays L. You cannot, of course, allow new reflection or refraction rays to be generated indefinitely; you must define a mechanism to stop generating them eventually. This can be done by keeping track of the attenuation of light, because only a part of the light is reflected or refracted, and stopping the recursion when only a very small amount of light is actually being handled. Another approach is simply not to allow any recursion past a certain level. But the recursive ray generation, with its need for a new set of ray–object intersection computations for rays that are generated from an arbitrary point, is certainly one of the reasons that ray tracing has a reputation for being quite slow. As reflection is computed, you can use simple reflection or you can use a BRDF if you want to treat anisotropic reflection in your image.

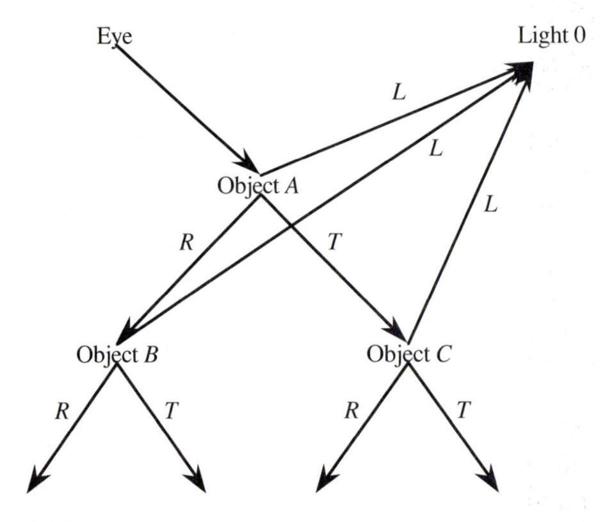

Figure 14.3 A ray tree.

With the single ray per pixel of ray casting, we could not avoid aliasing problems, so you could use a post-processing approach and compute a filter for each pixel to reduce the effects of aliasing. This approach costs you some resolution in the final image, however, and we would like to avoid that. In ray tracing, you can generate multiple rays per pixel to do a better job of determining the color that best represents that pixel's contribution to the scene. You can generate these rays systematically, dividing the pixel into regular subpieces and generating a ray for each, or you can generate them stochastically, selecting random points in the pixel through which you generate rays. There are, of course, many variations on these themes, and you need to look at the literature such as the papers in [GL] or [SHI] for more details. However, as you get the color value for each of these rays, you must reconstruct the color for the pixel from the colors of the individual rays. You may simply average these colors, or you may weight the colors across the pixel and compute the weighted average, probably with colors near the center having a larger weight than colors near the pixel edges.

Simple ray-tracing programs are only moderately difficult to write, and in some kinds of computer graphics courses, one of the student projects is to write a ray tracer. There are also several ray tracing programs that are available at no cost. Of these, the POVRay program (`http://www.povray.org`) is probably the best known; it is available for most computer systems. In fact, POVRay also qualifies as a graphics API because it has its own way to express geometry and to control rendering, and you can write scene descriptions in its language that create excellent images. Another ray tracer, Rayshade (`http://graphics.stanford.edu/~cek/rayshade/`) is available from Stanford for many platforms from Stanford. The source code for ray tracers is often available, and this is the case for both POVRay and Rayshade so you can look into all the details of these system. Figure 14.4 shows the output of the POVRay tracer on one of the benchmark scene definitions that comes with the system; notice the many reflections and shadows in the scene.

Figure 14.4 A ray-traced image created with POVRay. See the figure in the color insert.

Volume Rendering

An important application of the ideas of ray casting can be found in rendering volume data. As you will recall from Chapter 9, a function of three variables may be thought of as a volume with the function associating every point in 3D space with a value. This function may be analytic, it may be defined by a formula or process, or it may be data-derived, or defined by some experimental or constructed work. The value of the function may be a single real value, a color, a density, or any combination of these.

In Chapter 9 we discussed some simple techniques for examining a real-valued function on a volume to display an isosurface, the surface where the function has a given fixed value, but a more satisfactory approach may be to cast a set of rays into the volume and compute the points where each intersects the given isosurface. With each intersection, you determine the voxel in which the intersection occurs and you may compute a normal by examining how the level surface meets the boundary of the voxel so the usual lighting model can be applied. The resulting image is a much better presentation of a level surface in the volume.

We can use a ray-casting technique to do more than this simple isosurface study, however. Instead of dealing with a simple real function in the volume and building an image of an isosurface, you can create a much more complex model with a rich environment in the volume, and you can apply whatever techniques are appropriate for the model along each ray to create an image of the volume. For example, data from the Hubble space telescope was used to build a model of the Orion nebula, as seen in the wonderful image of Figure 14.5. At each point in

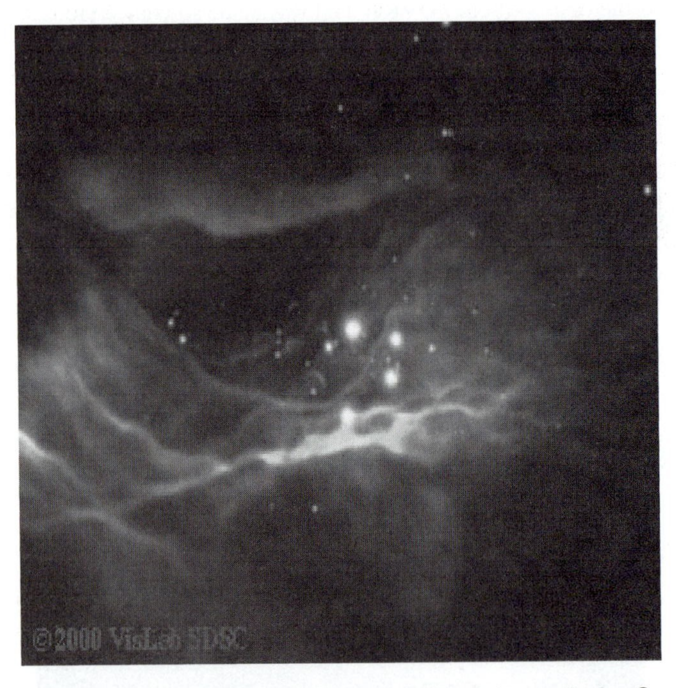

Figure 14.5 A volume visualization of a model of the Orion nebula. See the figure in the color insert. Courtesy of David R. Nadeau. Image credits: David R. Nadeau, Jon Genetti, San Diego Supercomputer Center, University of California, San Diego; Carter Emmart, Erik Wesselak, Dennis Davidson, American Museum of Natural History; C.R. O'Dell, Zheng Wen, Rice University.

the volume, the model defined both color and opacity based on the nature of the space within the nebula. As each ray is cast into this space, it accumulates color from the objects it meets, blending the colors along the path in an approach that generalizes the blending operations we saw for simple colors. As objects are met by the ray, processed from front to back, the ray develops its color as

object color +(1-opacity)*(color from remaining ray)

and the opacity is of the new object is added to the opacity value until the accumulated opacity is essentially 1. This work was described in [NAD].

Iterated Function Systems

Contraction Mappings

The concept of an iterated function system (IFS) includes a number of kinds of operations, but we will focus our discussion on only two of these. One is the *contraction mapping* operation. A contraction mapping is a function from a closed, bounded region to a closed bounded region with smaller area. Any contraction mapping has the property that if it is applied often enough, the original region will be mapped into a region of arbitrarily small area. Now if we start with a point $q = q_0$ and a set of contraction mappings $\{f_i\}$, and define $q_i = f_i(q_{i-1})$ where each function f_i is applied with probability p_i, there will be a well-defined set of points called the *attractor* of the IFS, and for any point q and for sufficiently large values of i, the point q_i will be arbitrarily close to a point in the attractor. Iterated function system images can be created by recursively drawing the image of the full domain as defined by the contraction mapping, but they are usually presented by generating a large number of random points and applying the contraction mapping repeatedly to each. After many iterations, the point is displayed and the shape of the attractor is seen.

An interesting object created by a contraction mapping is called the *Sierpinski gasket.* It can be defined in many different ways, but a definition that implements the contraction mapping is to have four functions that map the tetrahedron into four tetrahedra with equal probability, each half the height of the original tetrahedron and occupying one of the corners of the original. The linear contraction functions, written in vector form, are $f_i(p) = (p + p_i)/2$, for $\{p_i\}$ the four vertices of the tetrahedron. This process repeats without limit, giving tetrahedra whose volumes approach zero and occupy positions along the edges of all the possible subtetrahedra in the space. Each of the four contraction mappings moves every point in the tetrahedron to one that is half the distance to the corresponding vertex. These are easy to compute, and adding the random function choice gives us the following process: Choose one vertex at random and move the point one-half of the way toward the vertex. Do this many times, and the limiting positions of the points will lie on the Sierpinski gasket. For more details of this process, see [PIE] for the 2D case; the 3D case is a straightforward extension. In Figure 14.6 we see the four vertex points of a tetrahedron in red, and points in cyan that have been calculated by starting with 50,000 random points and applying this process.

Another type of contraction mapping IFS that could be of interest is the 2D mapping that models a fern leaf. Because this is a 2D mapping that involves presenting the points of attraction of the IFS, we can visualize its effects using the per-pixel operations in this chapter. The mapping for the fern is defined by the following linear functions, with the associated probability for each:

$$\mathrm{f}_0(x, y) = (0, .16y) \qquad p = .01$$

$$\mathrm{f}_1(x, y) = (.85x + .04y, -.04x + .85y + 1.6) \qquad p = .85$$

$$\mathrm{f}_2(x, y) = (.20x - 26y, .23x + .22y + 1.6) \qquad p = .07$$

$$\mathrm{f}_3(x, y) = (-.15x + .28y, .26x + .24y + .44) \qquad p = .07$$

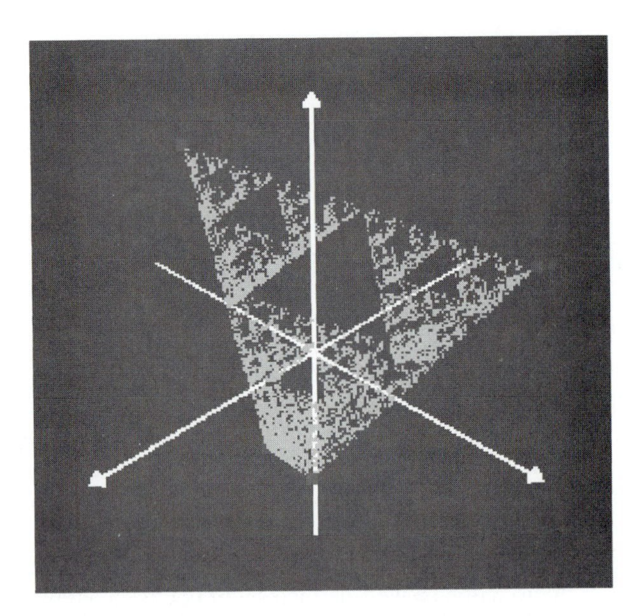

Figure 14.6 The Sierpinski gasket.

The contraction mappings take the square domain into the four regions that are shown in different colors in Figure 14.7, and the resulting figure after many iterations is seen in Figure 14.8.

Generating Functions

Another kind of IFS is created by *generating functions*. This defines a geometric structure recursively, applying a recursive generating function to each component of the geometry. The 2D

Figure 14.7 The four contraction regions for the fern leaf (black, cyan, orange, and gray, respectively).

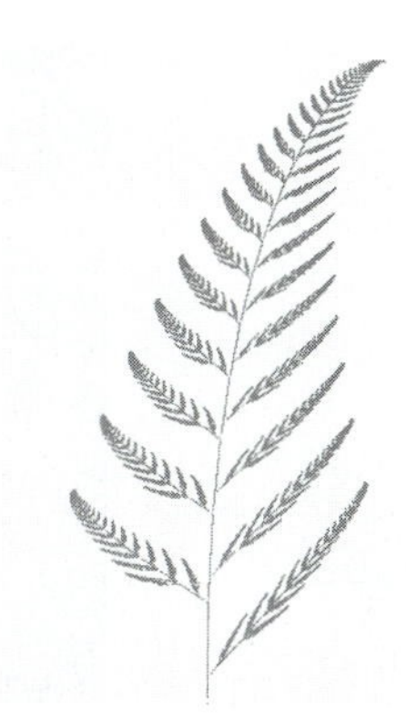

Figure 14.8 The fern image generated by accompanying the iterated function system.

version of the 3D blancmange function of Chapter 9 may be defined in this way, starting with a single line segment and replacing each segment by a pair of lines as shown in Figure 14.9, where the center of the pair is offset by one-quarter the length of the line. The "everywhere continuous" property of the resulting limit function is because the final function is the limit of a converging sequence of uniformly continuous functions; the "nowhere differentiable" property is because if you choose any pair of values, no matter how close, there will be a line segment between them for some iteration of this process, and the next iteration will have a sharp angle in the interval.

Figure 14.9 The generating process for the 2D blancmange function.

This kind of function is not presented by this chapter's per-pixel operations but by the polynomial modeling we have discussed throughout this book. We include it here because of its similarity to the contraction mapping operation.

As another example, let us consider a "dragon curve" defined by replacing a simple line segment by two segments, as was the case with the blancmange curve, but differing from that curve by putting the two segments offset to alternating sides of the line. This generating operation is shown in Figure 14.10, with the dashed lines showing the segments that are replaced with the solid segments.

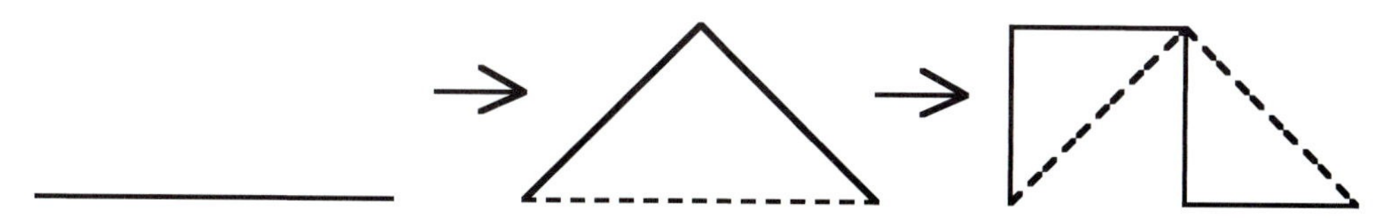

Figure 14.10 The dragon curve generator.

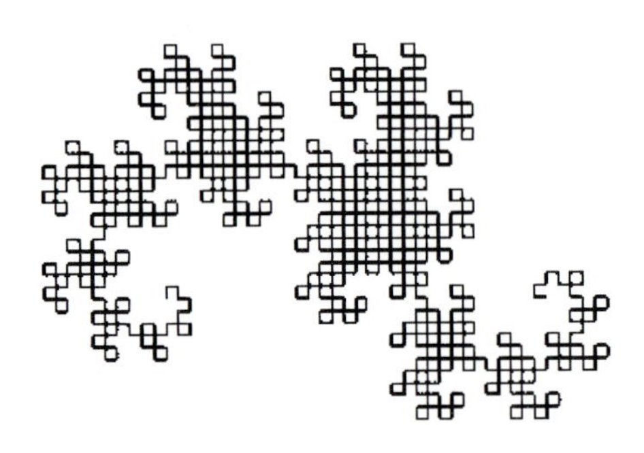

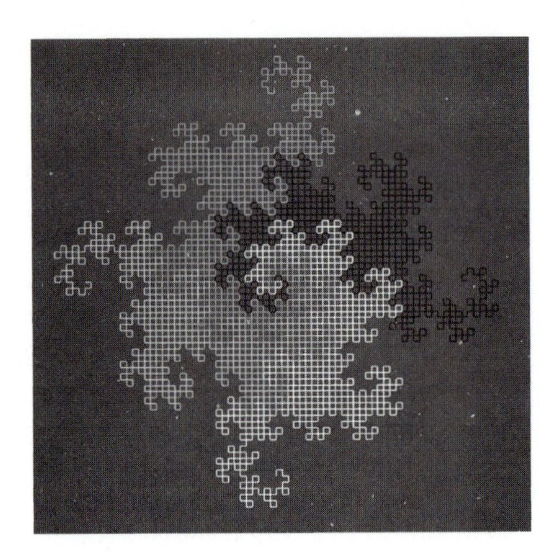

Figure 14.11 A simple dragon curve, and the set of four curves around a fixed point.

The resulting curve continues with as many iterations as you want, but when stopped at the tenth iteration the single dragon curve appears as shown as the left-hand image in Figure 14.11. A fascinating property of the dragon curve is the way these curves fill the space around a given point. This is shown in the right-hand image of the figure, where four curves of different colors meet at a point.

Mandelbrot and Julia Sets

A number of kinds of processes go under the name of fractals. We will focus on two distinctive types that produce characteristic images of dynamical systems. Many interesting issues in dynamical systems can be explored with computer graphics. References for this work include [PIE], as well as the extensive popular literature on fractals.

Consider a sequence of complex quadratic functions $\{f_k(z)\}$ defined as $f_0(z) = z^2 + c$ and $f_{n+1}(z) = f_n(z)^2 + c$. The behavior of interest is whether this sequence will converge or diverge as n increases. There is a straightforward test for this; the functions will converge if there is a bound on $|f_k(z)|$ as k increases, while they will diverge if there is no such bound. Remember that complex numbers are given by pairs of real numbers (a, b) and are usually written $z = a + b\mathrm{i}$, where $\mathrm{i}^2 = -1$. So our arithmetic is defined by

$$(a + b\mathrm{i})^2 = (a^2 - b^2) + 2ab\mathrm{i}$$

$$(a + b\mathrm{i}) + (c + d\mathrm{i}) = (a+c) + (b+d)\mathrm{i}$$

$$|a + b\mathrm{i}| = \mathrm{sqrt}(a^2+b^2)$$

Now if we take the sequence $\{f_k(z)\}$ for different complex numbers c, always starting with the initial value $z = 0$, we can investigate the behavior of the parameter space $\{c\}$. The *Mandelbrot set* is the set of complex numbers c so that this sequence converges with this initial value. If $|f_k(z)| > 2$ for any value of k, then the sequence will diverge, so we simply ask ourselves whether $|f_k(z)| < 2$ for all values of k up to a fairly large value such as, say, 500. If we find a value of k for which $|f_k(z)| > 2$ before we terminate the sequence, then the first such k is returned for the complex number c; if not, then the value of 0 is returned, and the Mandelbrot set is approximated by those complex numbers c that return the value of 0.

To display this situation graphically, we identify a complex number $(a + bi)$ with the 2D point (a, b), and we color the point based on an integer color ramp according to the value we record as above for the complex number. This identification can also go the other way: Each point defines a complex number and we apply the process above to that number to determine a color. We can then take a 2D domain and create a grid on the domain that matches the dimensions of our window as we describe in the code example, apply the process above for each grid point, and color the corresponding pixel as above. An image of the Mandelbrot set, which is probably familiar to you, is shown in Figure 14.12, along with a detail showing some of the fantastic behavior of the convergence process when we examine a very small region. The full Mandelbrot set is shown for the complex numbers $(a + bi)$ for a in $[-1.5, 0.5]$ and b in $[-1, 1]$, while the detail is the region with a in $[.30, .32]$ and b in $[.48, .50]$.

Figure 14.12 The full mandelbrot set (*left*) and a detail (*right*). See the figure in the color insert.

We can ask a very similar question about this sequence of functions $\{f_k(z)\}$ if we change the rules for what is fixed and what varies: Choose a fixed value of c, compute the sequence for different values of z, and use the same coloring technique as above. The set of complex numbers z for which the sequence converges is called a *Julia set*. Julia sets are related to the Mandelbrot set because if you create a Julia set with any complex number in the Mandelbrot set, the Julia set is connected; if you do so with a complex number outside the Mandelbrot set, the Julia set is completely disconnected. Complex numbers inside the Mandelbrot set but very near the edge create very interesting and unusual Julia sets. Figure 14.13 shows the particular Julia set computed for the fixed point $(-.74543, 11301)$, and as we did with the Mandelbrot set, you can

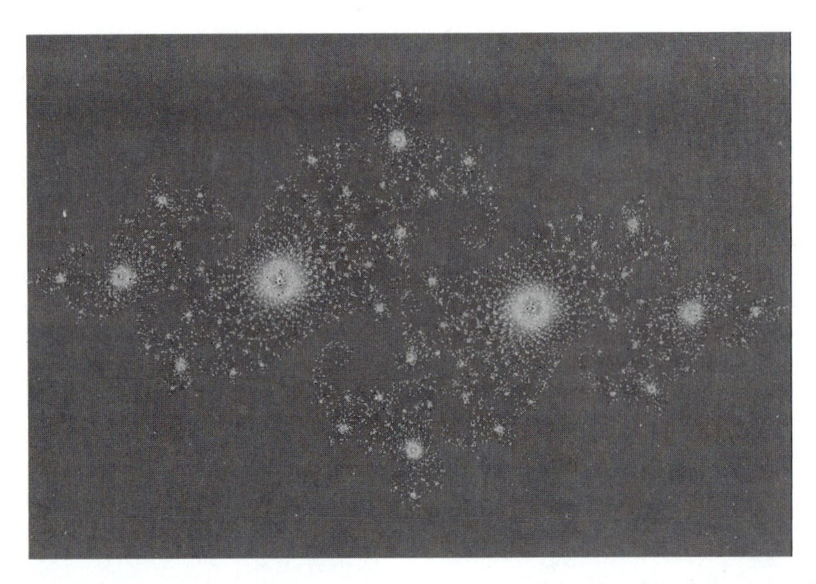

Figure 14.13 A Julia set for a particular fixed value *c*. See the figure in the color insert.

choose to display only a small part of the set and get even more detailed and fascinating images. The relation between the Julia set and Mandelbrot set will be explored in some of the experiments at the end of this chapter.

Per-Pixel Operations Supported by OpenGL

There are two ways you can use OpenGL to display an image that is the result of per-pixel operations. The first is to use the GL_POINTS rendering mode, with a color determined for each point. This would involve a looping operation something like the following:

```
glBegin(GL_POINTS)
    for row = 0 to N-1
        for column = 0 to M-1
            calculate point (x,y) for pixel (M,N)
            calculate color for point (x,y); return color
            glColor(color)
            glVertex2*(x,y)
glEnd()
```

This operation requires us to define a window that is *M* pixels wide and *N* pixels high and to set a 2D orthogonal projection with dimensions that match the window, but that is straightforward: In `main()` we have

```
glutInitWindowSize(M,N)
```

and in `init()` we have

```
gluOrtho2D(0.,(float)M,0.,(float)N).
```

This operation does not support any window reshapes that change the size of the window because it is totally tied to the original window dimensions, unless you calculate the size of the screen space and redefine the size of the display space on the fly. The image in Figure 14.12 was created with this kind of operation, and the actual detailed code for this inner computation in the Mandelbrot set follows.

```
xstep = (XMAX - XMIN)/(float)(WS-1); //WS=window size in pixels
ystep = (YMAX - YMIN)/(float)(WS-1);
glBegin(GL_POINTS);
for (i = 0; i < WS; i++) {
     x = XMIN + (float)i * xstep;
     for (j = 0; j < WS; j++) {
          y = YMIN + (float)j * ystep;
          test = testConvergence(x,y);
          // ITERMAX = maximum no. of iterations
          // colorRamp function behaves as color ramps in Chapter 6
          colorRamp((float)test/(float)ITERMAX);
          glColor3fv(myColor);
          glVertex2f((float)i,(float)j);
     }
}
glEnd();
```

There are a couple of other approaches to displaying the results of this kind of calculation. One is to create a domain with a grid having enough points to give you the desired detail and set a color value for each point in the domain as you did in the per-pixel operations. You then create a set of polygons whose vertices are determined by the grid and graph the function as a set of polygons as we did for function surfaces. If you use smooth shading, you can get an image that shows the behavior more smoothly than per-pixel operations would, although you must be careful not to disguise essential discontinuities with the smooth shading. This is a rather poor approach to presenting Mandelbrot and Julia sets, for example, because of the incredible detail on the boundary between the converging and diverging regions.

Another way to present your results is to define a height at each point in the domain using the same kind of technique that you used to define a color, and create a 3D surface with these heights. This is also not a per-pixel operation, of course, but it opens many opportunities for creating interesting presentations of fractals and similar things as shown in Figure 14.14. Here we have taken the value k of the complex dynamic systems problem and have computed a height as 1 if the value of k is 0, or $1 - 1/k$ if k is nonzero. This figure shows the Mandelbrot set from Figure 14.12 as a plateau whose sides drop off as the dynamic system diverges. The stepwise nature of the sides comes from the fact that the number of iterations to divergence is an integer, and so the height of the surface is discontinuous.

Limit processes such as the Sierpinski attractor involve other operations that we cannot describe generally because each adapts the definition of the process. For the Sierpinski attractor, the process determines the positions for individual points, and we simply draw them where they occur. The update for each step is done by an operation like the `idle()` callback discussed earlier in more detail in Chapter 7. This callback simply needs to include the operations to change

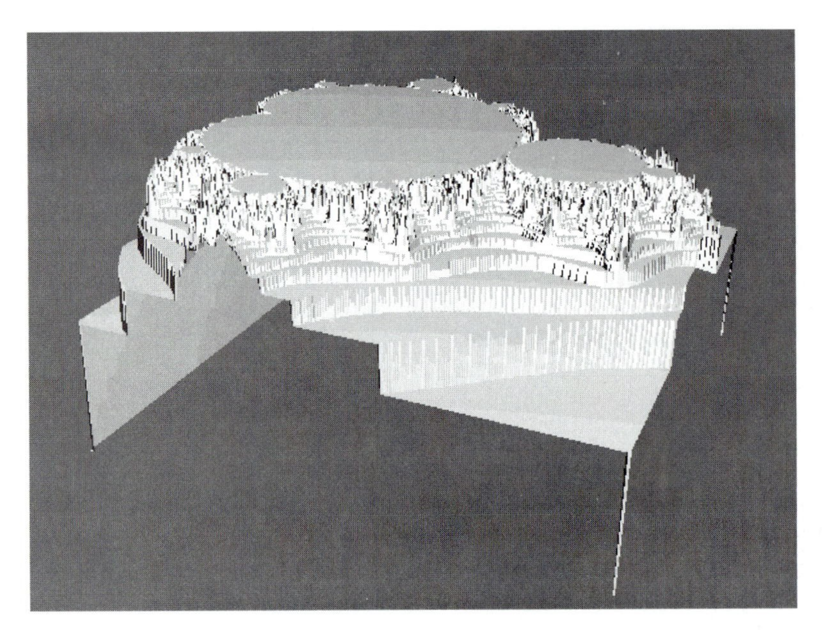

Figure 14.14 A simple surface presentation of the Mandelbrot set and its surrounding region.

each point's position and then call a redisplay operation to put it on the screen. As a code sketch, we have the following, where `vertices` is the array of vertices of the tetrahedron:

```
float points[3][N], vertices[3][4];
// in the display function, we find
beginPoints();
     for i = 0 to N
          setPoint(points[0][i], points[1][i], points[2][i]);
endPoints();
// in the idle() function, we find
for i = 0 to N {
     j = (int)random()%4;
     for k = 0 to 2 {
          points[0][k] = (points[0][k] + vertices[0][j])/2.0;
          points[1][k] = (points[1][k] + vertices[1][j])/2.0;
          points[2][k] = (points[2][k] + vertices[2][j])/2.0;
     }
}
post a redisplay event
```

Summary

This chapter introduced ray casting, ray tracing, volume rendering via ray casting, fractals, and iterated function systems, which can all be represented with per-pixel operations—operations that create an image by computing a pixel at a time instead of computing polygon-based geometry. These can give you a new way to think about graphics that can create interesting and useful images, but they require different kinds of modeling and viewing. You will need to examine these in more detail than this chapter provides if you want to use them, but they can be quite rewarding.

Questions

1. Download from `http://www.povray.org` the POVRay system for your computer and read the manuals for it. What are the geometric primitives for the system? Is there a relation between the kind of primitives it uses and the kind of geometric objects that have simple intersections with rays (for example, spheres or planes)?

Exercise

1. Consider some other generating functions and see what kind of images you can create for them. You can create a generating function by replacing any line segment with a set of line segments that are based on the endpoints of the original segment. Consider the *Koch curve* whose generating function is given by

and apply it to an initial figure that is an equilateral triangle. The resulting figure is sometimes called a Koch snowflake.

Experiments

1. With the POVRay system, read some of the sample models that are included with the system and work out how they are organized. Execute the system with some of these models to see how the resulting image looks, and then modify them to change graphics primitives, texture maps, lighting, or other features, and see how the changes affect the images.
2. Examine the relationship between the Mandelbrot and Julia sets by creating a display with two windows. In one, present the Mandelbrot set and include a mouse callback that identifies the complex number c that corresponds to a mouse click point. In the other, take that complex number and create the Julia set that corresponds to the number, with the Julia set displayed in the other window. Let this program be completely interactive so that any time there is a mouse click in the Mandelbrot set a new Julia set is generated.

Projects

1. Use the concept of experiment 2 and create an animation of the different Julia sets you get as you move the point c along a line segment that crosses the Mandelbrot set. Draw the Julia set for each value of c and save the color buffer in an array that you write to a file, and organize the files into a movie as described in Chapter 4, the animation chapter. Once you have done this, you may want to try describing a curve in the space containing the

Mandelbrot curve and follow that curve with the point c. It might be a research question to understand the nature of the Julia sets if you follow the boundary of the Mandelbrot set.

2. For any of the Mandelbrot or Julia set figures, write an interactive program that draws an initial image as described in the chapter, allows the user to select two points in the figure that are opposite corners of a rectangle, and then redraws the figure using that rectangle as the domain. The rectangle should use the same aspect ratio as the rectangle the user selects. Let the user continue to do this to explore as deeply into the image as desired. The key here is to convert selected points in screen space back into points in the domain of the image.

Hardcopy

You have worked hard to analyze a problem and have developed really good models and great images or animations that communicate your solution to that problem, but those images and animations cannot be shared with a broad audience; they only run on your computer and are presented on your screen. Now you need to take that work and present it to others, but you don't want to lose control over the quality of your work when you take it to a medium beyond the screen. Or perhaps you don't yet need to share it, but you may want to keep a record of the work in an archive you can save for future use.

In this chapter we talk about some of the issues you will face when you create a record of your work. We discuss different technologies for different kinds of computer graphics work, including digital and print images, film and video, and 3D object prototyping for creating physical images of computer models. When you have worked through this chapter, you should have a good idea of the appropriate kind of hardcopy for your work and the application for which it will be used, and you should understand some of the techniques for creating this hardcopy. To make the best use of this chapter, you need to understand the nature of color and visual communication, to appreciate what makes an effective image, and to have an idea of the wide range of ways in which people can use the results of computer graphics work.

Definitions

Computer graphics *hardcopy* is an output of your graphics computation in a fixed medium that can be physically removed from the context in which it was created and communicated to your audience without the original context. There are several ways this can be done, but the fundamental idea is that any kind of medium that can carry an image is a candidate for hardcopy. Hardcopy can use physical media (paper, sculpture) or digital media (images, video). Each medium has its own issues in terms of its capability and how you prepare your images for the medium. In this chapter we discuss some of the more common hardcopy media and give you an idea of what you must do to use each effectively.

Creating hardcopy can mean creating a digital record of the work that can be sent to some sort of output device. That device may be actually attached to the computer, such as a printer or a film recorder, or it may be a device to which we communicate data by network, disk, or CD-ROM. Some hardcopy media involve direct use of digital output, but some involve production processes. So part of the discussion of graphics hardcopy will include a description of the way data must be organized in order to use these external production processes.

Choosing an Output Medium

It is one thing to create images that are effective on the computer screen; it can be quite different to create images that are effective when presented to your audience in other media. As part of developing your graphical communication, you need to understand what media will be used to get your images to your audience and work toward those media. Print, online content, video, digital video, or physical objects created with rapid prototyping tools all have different properties that need to be considered in making your hardcopy presentation effective. You need a good understanding of media issues, usually by doing a lot of work in different media and studying the properties of the media and how they are used by your audience, before you can be comfortable that you can adjust your work to various media and retain its effectiveness.

Digital Images

If your work creates static images or you want to present single images from an interactive program, one way to save these images is by writing them to a file that is organized by some generally readable graphics file format. We have seen in earlier chapters that we can save the contents of our color buffer into an internal color array, and this array can be processed to create an image file in any of the alphabet soup of standard formats—GIF, TIFF, JPEG, PNG, or others. If you simply write the array to a file where you store each byte of the RGB format as an unsigned character, you will create what is sometimes called a *raw RGB* file. You may not want to make the effort to create your own tools to write such files in a standard format, or you may not have a library of file format conversions around. In this case, you can open a raw RGB file with a tool such as Photoshop and save it in any of the standard formats; in essence you are using Photoshop as a file format conversion utility. This use of tools has been used for many of the figures in this book and is highly recommended.

If you are not familiar with these file formats, perhaps a quick description is in order. *GIF* stands for Graphics Image Format, and it stores images in 8-bit indexed color with lossless compression. However, the GIF file format uses Lempel-Ziv-Welch (LZW) file compression, and this is a patented process so you must license it if you create any commercial software that implements this algorithm. *TIFF* is the Tagged Image File Format, a very general format that stores images with whatever color depth you need. Generally there is little file compression with TIFF files and consequently they can be very large, but the format is generally lossless and so it is a good archival format (especially given that disk or CD-R/DVD-R space is quite inexpensive). *JPEG* is a file format that often uses a lossy compression based on the discrete cosine transformation, but it can be lossless if you choose to use a very high-quality compression. JPEG does an excellent job on natural images but can be weak on images that have lines or sharp edges because the discrete cosine transformation operates on 64×64 blocks of pixels and can distribute the edge information around a pixel block. It is particularly poor for images that contain text. Its name is based on its developers: the Joint Photographic Experts Group. *PNG* stands for Portable

Network Graphics, a file format that was created in an effort to replace GIF as a widely used format for images on the networks. One of the main aspects of PNG is that it does not use any legally encumbered data compression. It includes the capabilities of GIF but adds full-color support, including alpha values, as well as 16-bit grayscale support. Very complete descriptions of these and many other graphics file formats may be found in [MUR].

Print

One version of printed hardcopy is created by a standard color printer that you can use with your computer system. Because these printers put color on paper, they are usually CMYK devices, as we talked about in Chapter 5, but the printer driver will usually handle the conversion from RGB to CMYK for you. There are color-calibration issues in going to a printer, based on the inks the printer uses, but a professional image converting program such as Photoshop can adjust images based on printer profiles that are included in the program. This is strongly recommended if you need a faithful copy of an image. In order of increasing print quality, the technologies for direct color output are

- inkjet, where small dots of colored ink are shot onto paper and you have to deal with dot spread and overwetting paper as the ink is absorbed into the paper
- wax transfer, where wax sticks of the appropriate colors are melted and a thin film of wax is put onto the paper
- dye sublimation, where sheets of dye-saturated material are used to transfer dyes to the paper

The quality of the paper used for printing is also a major factor in print quality. Inexpensive paper is usually quite porous and inkjet printing spreads out. Photo quality paper works much better.

These devices are pixel-based and have various levels of resolution, but in general each has resolution somewhat greater than that of a computer screen. All these technologies can also be used to produce overhead foils for those times when you have only an overhead projector to present your work to your audience.

Print can also mean producing documents by standard printing presses. This kind of print has some remarkably complex issues in reproducing color images. Because print is a transmissive or subtractive medium, you must convert your original RGB work to CMYK color before beginning to develop printed materials. You will also need to work with printing processes, so someone must make plates of your work for the press, and this involves creating separations as we saw in Figure 5.7, which is shown only in the color insert. In the most widely used color reproduction technology, plate separations are created by creating individual C, M, Y, and K color rasters with a screen that is laid across the image at a different angle for each color. The resulting four prints are written to a photographic film and then to printing plates that allow each of the color inks to lie on the paper with minimal interference with the other colors. A screen is shown, greatly enlarged, in Figure 15.1, where the enlargement is so great that you can see the angles of the screens for the C, M, Y, and K components. Notice that the dots in the screens are placed at fixed positions and vary only in size; sometimes this is called "AM color" for "amplitude modulation" as in the radio technology of the same name. (You should look very closely at a color image in print to see the telltale rosettes of standard separations.) Creating separations for color- critical images is something of an art form and is usually left to separation specialists in the print industry. If high-quality color is critical in your work, we strongly suggest that you insist on having high-quality color proofs of your work. You must also plan for a lower resolution in print than in your original image because the technologies of platemaking and presses do not allow presses to provide a very high resolution on paper.

Figure 15.1 C, M, Y, and K screens in a color image, greatly enlarged. See the figure in the color insert.

There are other technologies for creating color print images, including one called *stochastic screening* that uses color dots sizing and placement that determines the amount and placement of the color algorithmically to produce higher color resolutions and better color saturation than the standard screen techniques described above. This is sometimes called "FM color," after the radio technology, because the dots tend to be the same size but their placement, or frequency, changes. This technology has been available since the early 1990s in selected print shops and has been used for a wide variety of printing. It seems to have the best success when used with images that have a lot of detail that isn't picked up well by fixed-angle screens. However, it is not as commonly used as standard screening and you may have difficulty finding examples of this kind of separation. In Figure 15.2 you can see the variable dot size and placement characteristic of stochastic screening compared with the typical screening pattern.

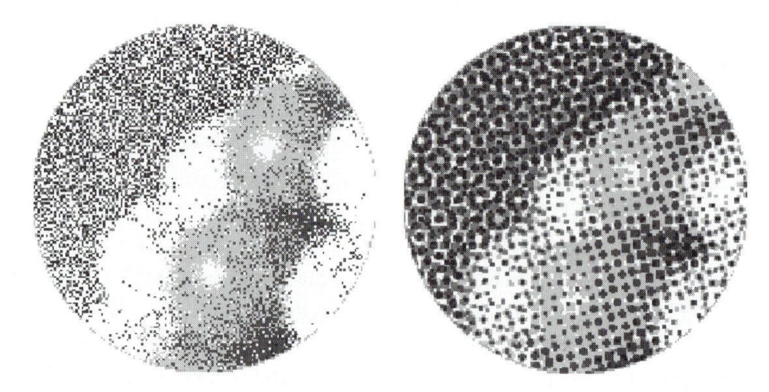

Figure 15.2 A comparison of a stochastic screen (*left*) with a fixed-angle screen (*right*). See the figure in the color insert. Courtesy of Weiser Litho, Inc.

Film

Sometimes you want to present the highest-quality images you can to an audience—the most saturated colors and the highest resolution. Sometimes you want to be sure you can present your work without relying on computer projection technology. In both cases, you want to consider standard photographic images from digital film recorders. These are devices that generate images using a very high-quality grayscale monitor, a color wheel, and a camera body and that work with whatever kind of film you want (usually slide film: Kodachrome, Ektachrome, or the like). But because of the color differences in films, be sure to use the kind of film the recorder specifies.

A film recorder is organized as shown in Figure 15.3. The grayscale monitor generates the images for each color separately, and that image is photographed through a color wheel that provides the color for the image. Because a grayscale monitor does not need to have a shadow mask to separate the phosphors for different colors, and because the monitor can be designed to have a long neck and a small screen to allow for extremely tight control of the electron beam, it can have extraordinary resolution; 8K line resolution is pretty standard and you can get film recorders with up to 32K lines. This allows you to generate your image at resolutions that would be impossible on the screen.

Film is much less of a problem than print, because you can work directly with the image and do not need to deal with separations and you work with the usual RGB color model. Because slides produce their image by having light projected through them, they behave as if slide projection were an emissive medium like the screen. Your only issue is to deal with the resolution of the camera or to accept the interpolations the film recorder will use if you don't have enough resolution.

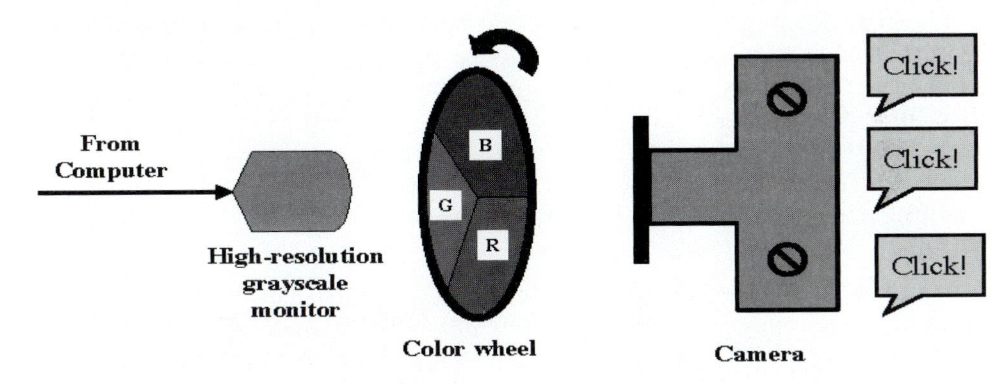

Figure 15.3 Schematic of digital film recorder.

3D Image Techniques

In Chapter 1 we saw a stereo viewing technique that created two views from different points and required the viewer to converge the images to create the stereo effect. There are other ways to make the eye see two images that it will converge into a single 3D view. In this section we talk about three techniques that can be used to store information in a single image that (for most people) can be seen as separate images by the eyes and can be converged into a single 3D image. All require the use of glasses that separate the single image into different images.

The first technique requires special technology to display images. With a pair of projectors that have orthogonal polarizing filters, you can superimpose two images that will be seen separately by a person who is wearing glasses that also have orthogonal polarization in the lenses. This is the technique behind the Geowall technology (http://geowall.geo.lsa.umich.edu/) shared by the Geowall consortium. A Geowall system can be assembled from off-the-shelf hardware and software and requires nothing more than careful alignment. We refer you to the Geowall site for more information.

A second technique for 3D viewing is based on an interesting way to manipulate the color in an image. When we discussed texture maps in Chapter 8, we described some 1D texture map techniques. One of these uses a map based on distance from the eye that colors the closer points of 3D images red and the more distant parts blue. An example of this is shown in Figure 15.4. The colors makes the images self-converge when you view them through a pair of ChromaDepth glasses, so more people can see the spatial properties of the image. This is an ordinary color image that can be stored or printed in any of the ways described previously, though the image is more effective in print if it uses bright colors and high-quality printing such as that provided by a very high-quality printer.

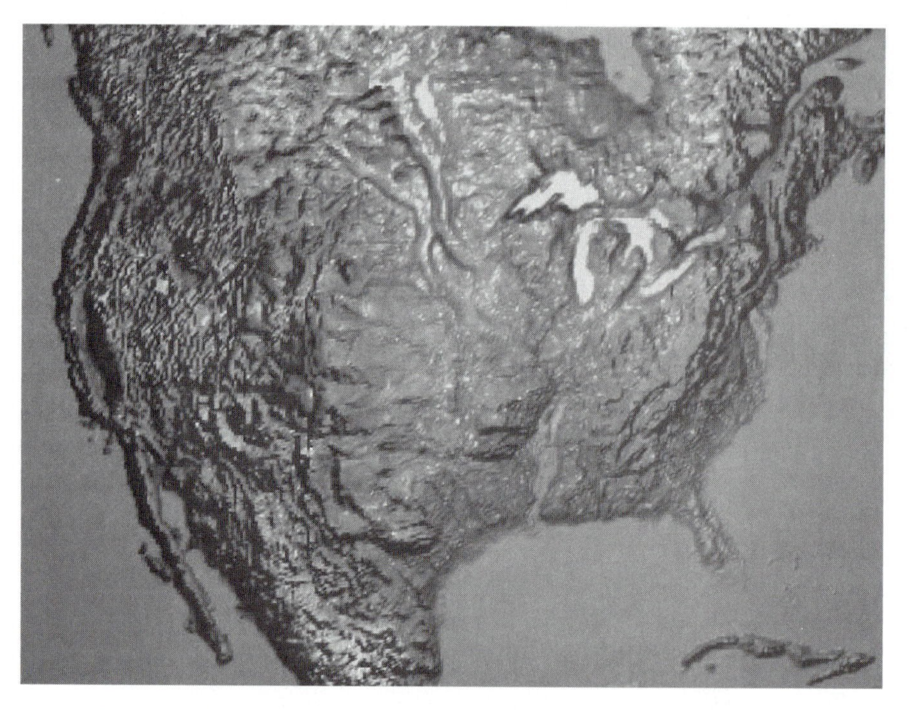

Figure 15.4 A ChromaDepth display. See the figure in the color insert. Courtesy of Mike Barley.

Another interesting technique for creating full-color images that your user can view in 3D uses the red/blue glasses from the 3D movies in the 1950s or from 3D comic books. These images are called *anaglyphs*. You can generate images for both left and right eyes, and combine the

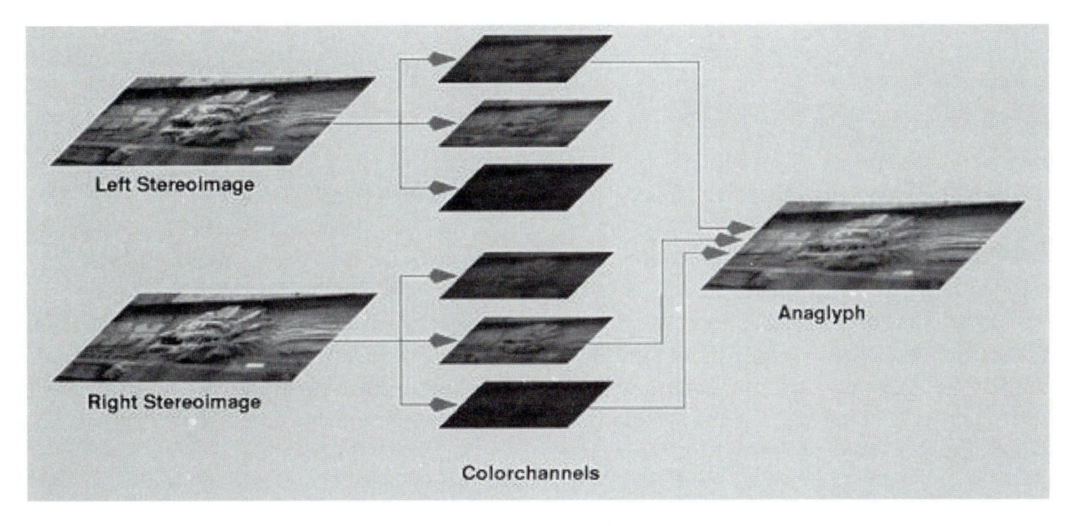

Figure 15.5 Creating a blended image from two images.

two images by using the red information for the left-eye image and the blue and green information for the right-eye image as shown in Figure 15.5. The resulting image will look similar to that shown in Figure 15.6, but when the image is viewed through red/blue (or red/green) glasses with the red filter over the left eye, you see both the 3D content and the colors from the original image. This is a straightforward effect and is relatively simple to generate; we describe how to do that in OpenGL at the end of this chapter. As above, the image can be stored in any standard file format or in print, but JPEG is probably not a good choice for a file format because it can blur the content of the red and blue/green channels. Some examples of commercial anaglyphs can be seen at `http://www.studio3D.com/pages/anaglyph.html`.

Figure 15.6 An example of a color anaglyph; when the color image in the color plates is viewed with red/blue or red/green glasses, a 3D color image is seen. See the figure in the color insert. Courtesy of Rolf Henkel.

3D Object Prototyping

There are times when having an image of an object simply isn't enough. You may need to be able to run your fingers over the object to understand its shape, you may need to hold two objects together to see how they fit, or you may need to see how something is shaped so you can see how it could be manufactured. Creating 3D objects from computer models is sometimes called *3D printing* or *3D prototyping* and is done by special tools. You can think of the objects built this way as prototypes of later manufactured objects, or you can view them as solid representations of your graphic models and images. Figures 15.7 through 15.10 show some photographs of copies of the (3,4)-torus, introduced in the chapter on graphics for the sciences, as created by several of these 3D printing techniques as noted in the figure caption. The contact information for each of the companies whose products were used for these hardcopies is given at the end of the chapter. There are, of course, other older technologies for 3D hardcopy that involve creating a tool path for a cutting tool in a numerical milling machine and similar techniques, but these go beyond the prototyping level.

There are several kinds of technologies for creating these prototype objects, but most work by building up a solid model in layers, with each layer controlled by a computation of the boundary of the solid at each horizontal cutting plane. These boundaries are computed from information on the faces that bound the object as represented in information presented to the production device. The current technologies for doing such production include those shown in Figures 15.7 through 15.10.

The Laminated Object Manufacturing (LOM) technique, available from Cubic Technologies (`http://www.cubictechnologies.com/`), lays out single sheets of adhesive-backed paper and cuts the outline of each layer with a laser. The portion of the sheets that is outside the object is scored so the scrap can be removed (carefully!) with simple tools. It is not possible to build objects that have thin openings to the outside because the scrap cannot be removed from the internal volumes. LOM objects are vulnerable to damage on sharp edges, especially those at the very top or bottom of the layers, but in general they are quite sturdy. Figure 15.7 shows the torus created with the LOM system; note the rectangular grid on the surface made by the edges of the scrap scoring, the moiré pattern formed by the burned edges of the individual layers of paper in the object, and the shiny surface in this figure made when the object is lacquered to preserve it from damage by handling, shipping, or other use.

The Z-Corp (`http://www.zcorp.com/`) 3D printers lay down a thin layer of starch powder and put a liquid binder (in recent releases, the binder can have several different colors) on the part of the powder that is to be retained by the layer. The resulting object is quite fragile but is treated with a penetrating liquid such as liquid wax or a super glue to stabilize it. Objects built with a wax treatment are somewhat fragile, but objects built with super glue are very strong. Because the parts of the original object that are not treated with binder are a simple powder, it is possible to create objects with small openings and internal voids with this technology. Figure 15.8 shows the torus created with a Z-Corp printer; note the very matte surface characteristic of objects created by powder composition of the object. Newer Z-Corp printers have higher-resolution results. The colored binder system lets an object be created with colors on the surface. This adds a color as well as shape-visualization capability to this system, an important advance.

The 3D Systems (`http://www.3dsystems.com/`) ThermaJet system builds a part by injecting a layer of varying materials for each layer of the object. The torus shown is built from wax, but much more robust materials are avilable. Such parts must include a support structure for any regions that overhang the object's base or another part of the object, and this support can either be

Figure 15.7 The torus created by the LOM system.

Figure 15.8 The torus created by the *Z*-Corp system.

designed when the object is designed or provided automatically by the ThermaJet system. The strength of the object depends on the material chosen for construction. The need for a support structure makes it difficult to include voids with small openings to the outside. Also because of the support structure, the bottom part of an object needs to be finished by removing the structure and smoothing the surface from which it was removed. Figure 15.9 shows the torus as created by the ThermaJet system; note the slightly shiny surface of the wax in the object. The color and surface properties depend on the material used.

Figure 15.9 The torus created by the 3D Systems ThermaJet system.

The 3D Systems stereolithography system creates an object by building up thin layers of a polymer liquid and hardening the part of that layer that is to be retained by scanning it with a laser beam. As with the ThermaJet system, this requires a very solid support structure for parts of the object, particularly because there is a small contraction of the polymer material when it is treated with the laser. The support structure must be removed from the object after it is completed, so some finishing work is needed to get fully developed surfaces. The polymer liquid can readily be drained from any interior spaces if there is an opening to the outside, so this technology handles nonconvex objects well. The polymer is very strong after it is hardened after the shaping is complete, so objects created with this technology are very sturdy. Figure 15.10 shows the torus as created by the stereolithography system.

One common issue for 3D prototyping systems is the durability of the objects they create. Some of the technologies produce very durable objects; the polymer material for stereolithography is very strong, and a powder-based object stabilized with a liquid super glue can survive even someone's standing on it. Other technologies, such as wax deposition or powder buildup with wax stabilization, are quite fragile. All of the technologies have some vulnerability to breakage

Figure 15.10 The torus created by the 3D Systems stereolithography system.

of small parts or sharp images. Your choice of technology will depend on just how much strength you need your objects to have.

The STL File

One thing all these 3D prototyping technologies have in common is that they all take data files in the STL (stereolithographic) file format in order to control their operations. This is a very simple file format that is easy to generate from your graphics program. The STL file for the (3.4)-torus is 2,459,957 bytes long and the first and last portions of the file are shown below. The file is organized by facets, and with each facet you have an optional normal and a list of the vertices of the facet; if you create your model in a way that will let you generate the explicit coordinates of your vertices, you can simply write the contents of the STL file instead of calling the graphics output functions. The only critical detail is that vertices on two triangles that are expected to align, such as vertices for boundary triangles, must have exactly the same values; most 3D prototyping systems are extremely fussy about small gaps. You should probably retain boundary values to be used for these vertices instead of relying on computations that can have very slight roundoff errors. The details of the STL file format are included in Appendix C.

```
solid
    facet normal -0.055466 0.024069 0.000000
        outer loop
            vertex -5.000010 -0.000013 -1.732045
            vertex -5.069491 -0.160129 -1.688424
            vertex -5.000009 -0.000013 -1.385635
        endloop
    endfacet
```

```
    facet normal -0.055277 0.019635 0.002301
        outer loop
            vertex -5.069491 -0.160129 -1.688424
            vertex -5.000009 -0.000013 -1.385635
            vertex -5.054917 -0.159669 -1.342321
        endloop
    endfacet
    ...
    facet normal -0.055466 -0.024069 0.000000
        outer loop
            vertex -5.000009 0.000014 1.385635
            vertex -5.069491 0.160130 1.688424
            vertex -5.000010 0.000014 1.732045
        endloop
    endfacet
endsolid
```

Video

Video can be a very important medium for your animated computer graphics work, because it is the only one available to show the motion that can be so important to communicate many of your ideas. At the same time, it can be one of the most limited media available to you, at least until video leaves the early twentieth century and really comes into the twenty-first century. We will focus on NTSC video here, but there are similar issues for PAL or SECAM video, and if you are reading this in one of the geographic areas where PAL or SECAM is the standard, you should check to see how much the comments here apply to you.

There are some important issues in dealing with video. The first is resolution: The resolution of NTSC video is much lower than even a minimal computer resolution. NTSC standards call for 525 interlaced horizontal scan lines, of which 480 are visible, so your planned resolution should be about 640×480. However, many television sets have adjustment issues, so never work right against the edge of this space. The interlaced scan means that only half of the horizontal lines will be displayed every 1/30 second, so you should avoid using single-pixel horizontal elements to avoid flicker; many television sets have poorly converged color, so you should also avoid using single-pixel vertical elements so they will not bleed into each other. In fact, you will have the best results for video if you design your work assuming that you have only half the resolution noted above.

A second issue in video is the color gamut. Instead of being composed of RGB components, the NTSC television standard includes significant compromises to account for limited broadcasting bandwidth and the need to be compatible with black-and-white television (the NTSC standard dates from the late 1930s, well before the widespread advent of color television or the advent of modern electronics and other technology). The NTSC color standard is a three-component model called the YIQ standard, but the three components are entirely focused on video issues. The Y component is the luminance (or brightness), and it gets most of the bandwidth of the signal. The I component is an orange-to-blue component, and it gets a little more than 1/3 of bandwidth of the Y component. The Q component is a purple-to-green component, and it gets a little more than 1/3 of the I component. The best color you can get in video always seems to be undersaturated, because that is part of the compromise of dealing with the technology available. To be more precise, the following table shows the bandwidth and the horizontal resolution for each of the components of the video image.

Component	*Bandwidth*	*Resolution/scanline*
Y	4.0 Mhz	267
I	1.5 Mhz	96
Q	0.6 Mhz	35

In order to get the best possible horizontal resolution from your image, then, you need to be sure that the elements that vary across the line have differing luminance, and you should focus more on the orange-to-blue component than on the purple-to-green component. If you want to understand how your colors vary in YIQ, the following conversion matrix should help you evaluate your image for video:

```
|Y|     | 0.299  0.587  0.114 |   |R|
|I|  =  | 0.596 -0.275 -0.321 |   |G|
|Q|     | 0.212 -0.528  0.311 |   |B|
```

The question of video is much broader than this, however. Besides NTSC (or PAL or SECAON), there are various digital video formats, such as QuickTime, AVI, or MPEG, that require computer mediation to be played back. Digital video is RGB, so it does not have many of the problems of NTSC until it is actually played on a television screen, and news television sets that handle increasingly high-quality video. In fact, MPEG II is a video standard for DVD, so this provides one alternative to doing your own conversion to NTSC.

In the longer term, television will be moving to computer-compatible native digital formats, and the high-definition television (HDTV) standards will support direct RGB color and higher-resolution, non-interlaced images, so we look forward to this discussion becoming antiquated. For the time being, however, you may need to put up with creating images that will make your graphics colleagues ask, "That looks terrible! Why are you doing that?" If they know that you're going to video, however, they'll understand.

Digital Video

Creating a digital video from an animation is straightforward with the right tools. We described this process in the chapter on animation (Chapter 11), but there are some issues you need to consider if you are thinking of using this hardcopy technique. Digital video can be system-specific because some digital video file formats run on only one platform, but we strongly suggest that you focus on platform-independent formats in order to reach the broadest possible audience. There are several levels of MPEG format, with each level having a higher compression than its predecessor. Many of the creation tools for digital animations will let you add a soundtrack to a digital video, do transitions from one animation sequence to another, or add subtitles or other text information to the movie. When you finish developing the video, you can write it to CD-R or DVD-R media to share with others, or you can share it by making it available online for download or streaming viewing. There is an extensive technology for online video, and we will not go into this further here.

OpenGL Techniques to Support Hardcopy

Capturing an Output Window in a File

OpenGL has tools to capture a color buffer that you can use to do a "screen dump" of your work at any time. The key OpenGL functions are `glReadBuffer(BUFNAME)`, which specifies the buffer to be read, and `glReadPixels(...)`, which specifies how the buffer being read is to be written into an array that is specified by the parameters. Once the buffer is read into the array, the array can be written to a file using straightforward file techniques. If you have utility functions, that will let you save the array in a standard format (e.g., JPG) either in your OpenGL implementation or in another toolkit, you might want to use them.

A straightforward function that implements these operations and saves the file as a raw RGB file is included here. Note the ordering in the outermost loop; we scan from the high-row index to the low-row index because the buffer indexing starts at the lower left, not the upper left. It's unlikely that your implementation of OpenGL will be different, but be aware that this might need to be changed.

```
#define BUF_WIDTH 512
#define BUF_HEIGHT 512
static GLubyte bufImage[WIDTH][HEIGHT][3];

//  function to read the contents of the front screen buffer into an
    array
//  whose name and dimensions are passed to the function. The resulting
//  file will be a raw RGB file that can be opened and manipulated by any
//  application that can work with that format (e.g. Photoshop).

void saveWindow(char *outfile, int BUF_WIDTH, int BUF_HEIGHT)
{
    FILE * fd;
    GLubyte ch;
    int i,j,k;

    fd = fopen(outfile, "w");
    glReadBuffer(GL_FRONT);            // set up to read the front buffer
    glReadPixels(0, 0, WIDTH, HEIGHT, GL_RGB, GL_UNSIGNED_BYTE,
                 bufImage);
    for (i=WIDTH; i>0; i--)              // for each row
        {
            for (j=0; j<HEIGHT; j++) // for each column
            {
                for (k=0; k<3; k++)  // read RGB components of the pixel
                    {
                        ch = bufImage[i][j][k];
                        fwrite(&ch, 1, 1, fd);
                    }
            }
        }
    fclose(fd);
}
```

Creating Anaglyphs in OpenGL

The techniques for creating anaglyphs use more advanced OpenGL color features. As we saw in the stereo viewing in Figure 1.12 of the earlier viewing chapter, we need both left-eye and right-eye versions of the image, and we assume that both are full RGB color images. We can use color information from the separate eye images to create a single image that your eyes can fuse to make a 3D image. We first generate both the left-eye and right-eye images of the scene and save them from the color buffer to separate color arrays. We then read each pixel of the two images and assemble them into a single image by using the red information from the pixel of the left-eye image and the blue and green information of the pixel from the right-eye image. Finally, we display the merged image and view the results through red/blue or red/cyan glasses.

To get the color arrays to assemble into the image, you use some techniques we just saw for capturing the color buffer in a file. First you generate the left-eye image in the back buffer and save that buffer into an array. Create or load the image as usual but do not call `glutSwapBuffers()` so the image is left in the back buffer. Specify the buffer for reading with the function `glReadBuffer(GL_BACK)`. Then read the contents of the buffer into an array `left_view` with the function

```
glReadPixels(0,0,width,height,GL_RGB,GL_UNSIGNED_BYTE,left_view)
```

We assume that you are reading the entire window (the lower left corner is (0,0)), that your window is `width` pixels wide and `height` pixels high, that you are drawing in RGB mode, and that your data is to be stored in an array `left_view` that contains `3*width*height` unsigned bytes (of type `GLUByte`). The array needs to be passed by being cast as a `(GLvoid*)` parameter. You could use another format for the pixel data, but the `GL_UNSIGNED_BYTE` seems simplest here. If you are using a scanned image, read the image into an array with these same properties.

After you have stored the left-eye image, do the same with the right-eye image, computating it into the back buffer and then storing it in an array `right_view`. You now have two arrays of RGB values in memory. Create a third array `merge_view` of the same type, and loop through the pixels, copying the red value from the `left-view` pixel array and the green and blue values from the `right-view` pixel array.

You now have an array that merges the colors as in Figure 15.7. You write that array to the back buffer with the function

```
glDrawPixels(width,height,GL_RGB,GL_UNSIGNED_BYTE,merge_view)
```

with the parameters as above. This can then be displayed by swapping the buffers. Alternately, you can write the anaglyph image to a file as described above.

The example image shown in Figure 15.7 is built from grayscale left and right views. This means that all the parts of the image will have red, green, and blue color information, so all of them will be distinguishable in the merged anaglyph. If the image has a region where the red channel or both of the green and blue channels are zero (more likely for a synthetic images than a scanned image), the anaglyph could have no information in that region for both eyes and could fail to work well.

Summary

This chapter discussed a number of different hardcopy techniques in electronic images, print, film, video, and 3D prototyping. With this range of opportunities to create archival versions of your computer graphics work, you should be able to consider the audience for your work or the reason for creating the archive, and select an appropriate way to present the work to that audience or save it for your archive. The examples given here will be supplemented by more techniques as time goes by, because creating permanent records of our work is a perpetual theme; you should be aware of this so you can keep your eyes out for new technologies and techniques. And you should be aware that as new techniques come in, old ones go out, so you may need to convert images stored in one way to new ways so they may continue to be useful.

The main point of this chapter is to know what your eventual medium will be and to design for that medium when you plan your image or visualization. And be prepared to experiment as you work on your design, because some of these hardcopy media simply take experience that no text can give you.

OpenGL Glossary for the Chapter

There was very little new OpenGL in this chapter, and what there was is concerned with the ability to read and draw pixels in specific image buffers.

OpenGL Functions

`glDrawPixels(...)`: writes a block of pixels into the frame buffer; a large set of parameters is needed to fully specify how the pixels are to be written

`glReadBuffer(...)`: specifies a color buffer as the source for pixels to be read

`glReadPixels(...)`: reads a block of pixels from the frame buffer into an array; a large set of parameters is needed to fully specify how the pixels are to be read and stored

Questions

1. Take an image you have created with an earlier project (particularly one with a texture map that includes a lot of detail, or one with some sharp lines) and save it with a screen capture utility or another tool that will let you save the exact screen image. Open the image with Photoshop or another image manipulation program that lets you open and save images in many different formats. Save the image in at least GIF, TIFF, and JPEG formats and compare the size and quality of the saved images.
2. Get a loupe or other powerful magnifying glass and use it to look at several kinds of color hardcopy images to see how these images are formed. Look at film negatives or prints from a film camera (not a digital camera or film recorder), color prints in high-quality art books and magazines, color prints in more general-circulation magazines, color prints in newspapers, and black-and-white prints in newspapers. Consider the resolution of the lines in the separation and the way the colors are distributed. Can you see any pattern of color dots in the print? Can you tell if the colors are AM or FM? Can you determine the angles of the separations if the print uses AM color?
3. If you can get access to a digital film recorder, create a slide from a graphics project and compare the slide with a photographic slide and with the screen image of the project. Does the slide image have a higher resolution than the screen image? Does the slide image have any image artifacts such as visible scanlines that the photographic slide does not have?
4. Look at the Web sites of the companies listed in this chapter that provide 3D rapid prototyping tools; from the information on the sites, evaluate the tools in terms of the

durability, the fineness of their details, and the difficulty of dealing with support structures for the objects.

5. There are a number of companies in many cities that use 3D rapid prototyping systems in their work. See if your instructor can arrange a visit to one of these companies for the class and look at the kind of prototypes they make. Look at their prototypes and evaluate them in the terms described above. Find out how the company uses the prototypes in its work.

Experiments

1. Create a digital image any way you like, but perhaps the best way would be with a screen capture of one of your images that has some significant shading or that uses a texture map. It is useful to have as much color variation in the image as possible. Read this image into a full-function image handling program such as Photoshop; it will doubtless be an RGB image. Now convert the image into CMYK format and print out four-color separations of the image. These will be four grayscale images that, together, will form a printed image if the right inks were used with each. Examine the four separations and see if you can determine how the RGB primaries are formed by combining the CMYK inks. If you have gotten experience at HLS or HSV images, see if you can identify how the black (K) separation relates to the lightness values of your colors.
2. Returning to the theme of local companies that do 3D rapid prototyping, see if you or your instructor can find such a company that would be willing to work on a prototype of a student-generated model, and prepare a model and its STL file that you can take to the company to prepare when its production cycle has some free time.
3. (Anaglyph) If your instructor can get red/blue or red/cyan glasses, find a stereo pair of images that you can work with. This can be a pair of computed images or a pair of digital photographs. A good choice could be a slide from a stereopticon (an old-fashioned stereo viewer), with two grayscale images with views from two viewpoints. Scan the pair of images and create an anaglyph for them by combining the channels for the two images, as described in the chapter, and view it through the glasses to see both the color and depth information the anaglyph contains.

References and Resources

[AMES] Ames, Andrea L., David R. Nadeau, and John L. Moreland, *VRML 2.0 Sourcebook*. Wiley, 1997.

[AN02] Angel, Ed, *Interactive Computer Graphics with OpenGL,* third edition. Addison-Wesley, 2002.

[BAK] Baker, Steve, A Brief MUI User Guide, distributed with the MUI release.

[BAN] Banchoff, Tom, et al., "Student-Generated Software for Differential Geometry," in Zimmermann and Cunningham, eds., *Visualization in Teaching and Learning Mathematics,* MAA Notes Number 19, Mathematical Association of America, 1991, pp. 165–171.

[BRA] Braden, Bart, "A Vector Field Approach in Complex Analysis," in Zimmermann and Cunningham, eds., *Visualization in Teaching and Learning Mathematics,* MAA Notes Number 19, Mathematical Association of America, 1991, pp. 191–196.

[BR95] Brown, Judith R., et al., *Visualization: Using Computer Graphics to Explore Data and Present Information*. Wiley, 1995.

[BR99] Robson Brown, K. A., A. Chalmers, T. Saigol, C. Green, and F. d'Errico, "An automated laser scan survey of the Upper Palaeolithic rock shelter of Cap Blanc." *Journal of Archeological Science,* 1999.

[BUC] Buchanan, J. L., et al., "Geometric Interpretation of Solutions in Differential Equations," in Zimmermann and Cunningham, eds., *Visualization in Teaching and Learning Mathematics,* MAA Notes Number 19, Mathematical Association of America, 1991, pp. 139–147.

[CO93] Cohen, Michael, and John Wallace, *Radiosity and Realistic Image Synthesis.* Morgan Kaufmann, 1993.

[CU90] Cunningham, Steve, "3D Viewing and Rotation Using Orthonormal Bases," in Glassner, ed., *Graphics Gems,* Academic Press, 1990, 516–521.

[CU92] Cunningham, S., and R. J. Hubbold, eds., *Interactive Learning Through Visualization*. Springer-Verlag, 1992.

[CU01] Cunningham, Steve, and Michael J. Bailey, "Lessons from Scene Graphs: Using Scene Graphs to Teach Heirarchical Modeling," *Computers & Graphics* 25 (2001), pp. 703–711.

[DE] Devaney, Robert L., and Linda Keene, eds., "Chaos and Fractals, The Mathematics Behind the Computer Graphics," Proceedings of Symposia in Applied Mathematics, vol. 39, American Mathematical Society, 1988.

[DU] Durett, H. John, ed., *Color and the Computer*. Academic Press, 1987.

[EB] Ebert, David, et al., *Texturing and Modeling*, third edition. Morgan Kaufmann, 2003.

[ELL] Ellson, Rich, et al., "Plastic Injection Molding," in http://archive.ncsa.uiuc.edu/SCMS/Metascience/Articles/MS_Plastic-Injection-Molding-Ellson.html

[FO] Foley, James D., et al., *Computer Graphics Principles and Practice*, second edition. Addison-Wesley, 1990.

[GG1] Glassner, Andrew S., ed., *Graphics Gems*. Morgan Kaufmann, 1990.

[GG2] Arvo, James, *Graphics Gems II*. Academic Press, 1991.

[GG3] Kirk, David, *Graphics Gems III*. Academic Press, 1992.

[GG4] Heckbert, Paul S., *Graphics Gems IV*. Academic Press, 1994.

[GG5] Paeth, Alan, *Graphics Gems V*. Academic Press, 1995.

[GL] Glassner, Andrew S., ed., *An Introduction to Ray Tracing*. Academic Press, 1989.

[GR] Green, Phil, and Lindsay MacDonald, *Colour Engineering: Achieving Device Independent Colour*. Wiley, 2002.

[HA] Hall, Roy, *Illumination and Color in Computer Generated Imagery*. Springer-Verlag, 1988.

[HE] Hearn, Donald, and M. Pauline Baker, *Computer Graphics,* second edition, C version. Prentice-Hall, 1997.

[HIL] Hill, F. S., Jr., *Computer Graphics Using OpenGL*, second edition. Prentice-Hall, 2001.

[JEN] Jensen, Henrik Wann, *Realistic Image Synthesis Using Photon Mapping*. A K Peters, 2001.

[JO] Joy, Kenneth I., et al., eds., *Tutorial: Computer Graphics: Image Synthesis*. IEEE Computer Society Press, 1988.

[LA] Landau, Rubin H., and Manuel J. Páez, *Computational Physics: Problem Solving with Computers*. Wiley, 1997.

[LE] Levkowitz, Haim, *Color Theory and Modeling for Computer Graphics, Visualization, and Multimedia Applications*. Kluwer Academic, 1997.

[LI] Lischinski, Dani, "Combining Hierarchical Radiosity and Discontinuity Meshing," SIGGRAPH 94 Course Notes, Course 28.

[LU] Luebke, David, et al., *Level of Detail for 3D Graphics*. Morgan Kaufmann, 2004.

[MAC] MacDonald, Lindsay W., and M. Ronnier Luo, eds., *Colour Image Science: Exploiting Digital Media*. Wiley, 2002.

[MCC] McCullen, Dave, "Using Infrared for Residential Energy Surveys," InfraMation 2004 Proceedings.

[MUR] Murray, James D., and William vanRyper, *Encyclopedia of Graphics File Formats*, second edition. O'Reilly & Associates, 1996.

[NAD] Nadeau, D. R., J. D. Genetti, S. Napear, B. Pailthorpe, C. Emmart, E. Wesselak, and D. Davidson, "Visualizing Stars and Emission Nebulas," *Computer Graphics Forum*, March 2001.

[PAI] Pailthorpe, Bernard, and Richard Carson, "Economics Gets a New Look at the History of the U.S. Economy," Gather/Scatter online, 1997; http://www.sdsc.edu/GatherScatter/GSspring97/pailthorpe.html

[PER] Perlin, Ken, "An Image Synthesizer," *Computer Graphics* 19(3), Proceedings of SIGGRAPH 85, July 1985, 287–296.

[PIE] Pietgen, Heinz-Otto, and Dietmar Saupe, eds., *The Science of Fractal Images*. Springer-Verlag, 1988.

[POC] Pocock, Lynn, and Judson Rosebush, *The Computer Animator's Technical Handbook.* Morgan Kaufmann, 2002.

[POR] Porter, Thomas and Tom Duff, "Compositing Digital Images," *Computer Graphics* 18(4), SIGGRAPH 84, July 1984.

[ROG] Rogers, David F., and J. Alan Adams, *Mathematical Elements for Computer Graphics,* second edition. McGraw-Hill, 1990.

[ROS] Rost, Randi, *The OpenGL Shading Language,* second edition. Addison-Wesley, 2006.

[SHI] Shirley, Peter, and R. Keith Morley, *Realistic Ray Tracing,* second edition. A K Peters, 2003.

[SHR] Shreiner, Dave, ed., *OpenGL Reference Manual,* third edition. Addison-Wesley, 2000.

[SIL] Sillion, François, and Claude Puech, *Radiosity and Global Illumination.* Morgan Kaufmann, 1994.

[SOV] Sova, Davel, *Galileo's Daughter.* Walker & Co., 1999.

[SOW1] Sowrizal, Henry, Kevin Rushforth, and Michael Deering, *The Java3D 3D API Specification.* Addison-Wesley, 1995.

[SOW2] Sowizral, Henry A., and David R. Nadeau, *Introduction to Programming with Java 3D*, SIGGRAPH 99 Course Notes, Course 40.

[SPE] Spence, Robert, *Information Visualization.* Addison-Wesley/ACM Press Books, 2001.

[SVR] The SIGGRAPH Video Review (SVR), an excellent source of animations for anyone wanting to see how images can communicate scientific and cultural information through computer graphics, as well as how computer graphics can be used for other purposes. See `http://www.siggraph.org/SVR/` for information.

[TAL] Tall, David, "Intuition and Rigour: The Role of Visualization in the Calculus," in Zimmermann and Cunningham, eds., *Visualization in Teaching and Learning Mathematics,* MAA Notes Number 19, Mathematical Association of America, 1991, pp. 105–119.

[THO] Thorell, R. G., and W. J. Smith, *Using Computer Color Effectively: An Illustrated Reference.* Prentice-Hall, 1990.

[UP] Upstill, Steve, *The RenderMan Companion.* Addison-Wesley, 1990.

[ViSC] McCormick, Bruce H., Thomas A. DeFanti, and Maxine D. Brown, eds., *Visualization in Scientific Computing*, *Computer Graphics* 21(6), November 1987.

[VDB] van den Bergen, Gino, *Collision Detection in Interactive 3D Environments.* Morgan Kaufmann, 2003.

[vSEG] von Seggern, David, *CRC Standard Curves and Surfaces.* CRC Press, 1993.

[WAT] Watt, Alan, and Fabio Policarpo, *3D Games: Real-time Rendering and Software Technology.* Addison-Wesley/ACM SIGGRAPH Series, 2001.

[WA2] Watt, Alan, and Mark Watt, *Advanced Animation and Rendering Techniques: Theory and Practice.* Addison-Wesley, 1992.

[WOL] Wolberg, George, *Digital Image Warping.* IEEE Computer Society Press, 1990.

[WO98] Wolfe, Rosalee, ed., *Seminal Graphics: Pioneering Efforts That Shaped the Field.* ACM SIGGRAPH, 1998.

[WO00] Wolfe, R. J., *3D Graphics: A Visual Approach.* Oxford University Press, 2000.

[WOO] Woo, Mason, et al., *OpenGL Programming Guide,* third edition (version 1.2). Addison-Wesley, 1999.

[WY] Wyszecki, G., and W. S. Styles, *Color Science*, second ed. Wiley, 1982.

[ZIM] Zimmermann, Walter, and Steve Cunningham, *Visualization in Teaching and Learning Mathematics*, MAA Notes Number 19, Mathematical Association of America, 1991.

PDB File Format

The national Protein Data Bank (PDB) file format comes from the Worldwide Protein Data Bank (wwPDB, at `http://www.wwpdb.org/`). This is extremely complex and contains much more information than we can ever hope to use for student projects. We will extract the information we need for simple molecular display from the reference document on this file format to present here. From the chemistry point of view, the student might be encouraged to look at the longer file description to see how much information is recorded in creating a full record of a molecule.

There are two kinds of records in a PDB file that are critical to us: atom location records and bond description records. These specify the atoms in the molecule and the bonds between these atoms. By reading these records we can fill in the information in the internal data structures that hold the information needed to generate the display. The information given here on the atom location (ATOM) and bond description (CONECT) records is from the reference. There is another kind of record that describes atoms, with the keyword HETATM, but we leave this description to the full PDB format manual that may be found at the US member, the RCSB PDB: (at `http://www.rcsb.org/`). The actual URL for the version of the PDB format on which this appendix is based, the 1992 standard, is `http://www.rcsb.org/pdb/file_formats/pdb/pdbguide2.2/PDB_format_1992.pdf` (URL current as of publication). Newer, more complex, standards extend this version.

ATOM Records

The ATOM records present the atomic coordinates for standard residues, in angstroms. They also present the occupancy and temperature factor for each atom. The element symbol is always present on each ATOM record.

Record Format

COLUMNS	DATA TYPE	FIELD	DEFINITION
1-6	Record name	"ATOM"	
7-11	Integer	serial	Atom serial number.
13-16	Atom	name	Atom name.
17	Character	altLoc	Alternate location indicator.
18-20	Residue name	resName	Residue name.
22	Character	chainID	Chain identifier.
23-26	Integer	resSeq	Residue sequence number.
27	AChar	iCode	Code for insertion of residues.
31-38	Real(8.3)	x	Orthogonal coordinates for X in Angstroms.
39-46	Real(8.3)	y	Orthogonal coordinates for Y in Angstroms.
47-54	Real(8.3)	z	Orthogonal coordinates for Z in Angstroms.
55-60	Real(6.2)	occupancy	Occupancy.
61-66	Real(6.2)	tempFactor	Temperature factor.
73-76	LString(4)	segID	Segment identifier, left-justified.
77-78	LString(2)	element	Element symbol, right-justified.
79-80	LString(2)	charge	Charge on the atom.

The "Atom name" field can be complex, because there are other ways to give names than the standard atomic names. In the PDB file examples provided with this set of projects, we have been careful to avoid names that differ from the standard names in the periodic table, but that means we have not been able to use all the PDB files from, say, the chemical data bank. If your chemistry program wants you to use a particular molecule as an example, but that example's data file uses other formats for atom names in its file, you will need to modify the `readPDBfile()` function of these examples.

Example

```
         1         2         3         4         5         6         7         8
12345678901234567890123456789012345678901234567890123456789012345678901234567890
ATOM      1  C          1      -2.053     2.955     3.329   1.00      0.00
ATOM      2  C          1      -1.206     3.293     2.266   1.00      0.00
ATOM      3  C          1      -0.945     2.371     1.249   1.00      0.00
ATOM      4  C          1      -1.540     1.127     1.395   1.00      0.00
ATOM      5  C          1      -2.680     1.705     3.426   1.00      0.00
ATOM      6  C          1      -2.381     0.773     2.433   1.00      0.00
ATOM      7  O          1      -3.560     1.422     4.419   1.00      0.00
ATOM      8  O          1      -2.963    -0.435     2.208   1.00      0.00
ATOM      9  C          1      -1.455    -0.012     0.432   1.00      0.00
```

```
ATOM     10  C     1     -1.293      0.575     -0.967    1.00     0.00
ATOM     11  C     1     -0.022      1.456     -0.953    1.00     0.00
ATOM     12  C     1     -0.156      2.668      0.002    1.00     0.00
ATOM     13  C     1     -2.790     -0.688      0.814    1.00     0.00
ATOM     14  C     1     -4.014     -0.102      0.081    1.00     0.00
ATOM     15  C     1     -2.532      1.317     -1.376    1.00     0.00
ATOM     16  C     1     -3.744      1.008     -0.897    1.00     0.00
ATOM     17  O     1     -4.929      0.387      1.031    1.00     0.00
ATOM     18  C     1     -0.232     -0.877      0.763    1.00     0.00
ATOM     19  C     1      1.068     -0.077      0.599    1.00     0.00
ATOM     20  N     1      1.127      0.599     -0.684    1.00     0.00
ATOM     21  C     1      2.414      1.228     -0.914    1.00     0.00
ATOM     22  H     1      2.664      1.980     -0.132    1.00     0.00
ATOM     23  H     1      3.214      0.453     -0.915    1.00     0.00
ATOM     24  H     1      2.440      1.715     -1.915    1.00     0.00
ATOM     25  H     1     -0.719      3.474     -0.525    1.00     0.00
ATOM     26  H     1      0.827      3.106      0.281    1.00     0.00
ATOM     27  H     1     -2.264      3.702      4.086    1.00     0.00
ATOM     28  H     1     -0.781      4.288      2.207    1.00     0.00
ATOM     29  H     1     -0.301     -1.274      1.804    1.00     0.00
ATOM     30  H     1     -0.218     -1.756      0.076    1.00     0.00
ATOM     31  H     1     -4.617      1.581     -1.255    1.00     0.00
ATOM     32  H     1     -2.429      2.128     -2.117    1.00     0.00
ATOM     33  H     1     -4.464      1.058      1.509    1.00     0.00
ATOM     34  H     1     -2.749     -1.794      0.681    1.00     0.00
ATOM     35  H     1      1.170      0.665      1.425    1.00     0.00
ATOM     36  H     1      1.928     -0.783      0.687    1.00     0.00
ATOM     37  H     1     -3.640      2.223      4.961    1.00     0.00
ATOM     38  H     1      0.111      1.848     -1.991    1.00     0.00
ATOM     39  H     1     -1.166     -0.251     -1.707    1.00     0.00
ATOM     40  H     1     -4.560     -0.908     -0.462    1.00     0.00
```

Conect Records

The CONECT records specify connectivity between atoms for which coordinates are supplied. The connectivity is described using the atom serial number as found in the entry.

Record Format

COLUMNS	DATA TYPE	FIELD	DEFINITION
1-6	Record name	"CONECT"	
7-11	Integer	serial	Atom serial number
12-16	Integer	serial	Serial number of bonded atom
17-21	Integer	serial	Serial number of bonded atom
22-26	Integer	serial	Serial number of bonded atom
27-31	Integer	serial	Serial number of bonded atom

```
32-36     Integer      serial     Serial number of hydrogen bonded atom
37-41     Integer      serial     Serial number of hydrogen bonded atom
42-46     Integer      serial     Serial number of salt bridged atom
47-51     Integer      serial     Serial number of hydrogen bonded atom
52-56     Integer      serial     Serial number of hydrogen bonded atom
57-61     Integer      serial     Serial number of salt bridged atom
```

Example

```
         1         2         3         4         5         6         7
1234567890123456789012345678901234567890123456789012345678901234567890
CONECT    1179     746    1184    1195    1203
CONECT    1179    1211    1222
CONECT    1021     544    1017    1020    1022        1211    1222    1311
```

As we noted at the beginning of this appendix, PDB files can be extremely complex, and most of the examples we have found have been fairly large. The file shown in Figure A.1 is among the simplest PDB files we've seen, and it describes the adrenalin molecule. This is among the materials provided as `adrenaline.pdb`.

```
HEADER    NONAME 08-Apr-99                                           NONE 1
TITLE                                                                NONE 2
AUTHOR    Frank Oellien                                              NONE 3
REVDAT    1  08-Apr-99   0                                           NONE 4
ATOM      1  C           0   -0.017    1.378    0.010  0.00  0.00      C+0
ATOM      2  C           0    0.002   -0.004    0.002  0.00  0.00      C+0
ATOM      3  C           0    1.211   -0.680   -0.013  0.00  0.00      C+0
ATOM      4  C           0    2.405    0.035   -0.021  0.00  0.00      C+0
ATOM      5  C           0    2.379    1.420   -0.013  0.00  0.00      C+0
ATOM      6  C           0    1.169    2.089    0.002  0.00  0.00      C+0
ATOM      7  O           0    3.594   -0.625   -0.035  0.00  0.00      O+0
ATOM      8  O           0    1.232   -2.040   -0.020  0.00  0.00      O+0
ATOM      9  C           0   -1.333    2.112    0.020  0.00  0.00      C+0
ATOM     10  O           0   -1.177    3.360    0.700  0.00  0.00      O+0
ATOM     11  C           0   -1.785    2.368   -1.419  0.00  0.00      C+0
ATOM     12  N           0   -3.068    3.084   -1.409  0.00  0.00      N+0
ATOM     13  C           0   -3.443    3.297   -2.813  0.00  0.00      C+0
ATOM     14  H           0   -0.926   -0.557    0.008  0.00  0.00      H+0
ATOM     15  H           0    3.304    1.978   -0.019  0.00  0.00      H+0
ATOM     16  H           0    1.150    3.169    0.008  0.00  0.00      H+0
ATOM     17  H           0    3.830   -0.755   -0.964  0.00  0.00      H+0
ATOM     18  H           0    1.227   -2.315   -0.947  0.00  0.00      H+0
ATOM     19  H           0   -2.081    1.509    0.534  0.00  0.00      H+0
ATOM     20  H           0   -0.508    3.861    0.214  0.00  0.00      H+0
```

Figure A.1 Example of a simple molecule file in PDB format.

```
ATOM     21  H          0   -1.037    2.972   -1.933  0.00  0.00          H+0
ATOM     22  H          0   -1.904    1.417   -1.938  0.00  0.00          H+0
ATOM     23  H          0   -3.750    2.451   -1.020  0.00  0.00          H+0
ATOM     24  H          0   -3.541    2.334   -3.314  0.00  0.00          H+0
ATOM     25  H          0   -4.394    3.828   -2.859  0.00  0.00          H+0
ATOM     26  H          0   -2.674    3.888   -3.309  0.00  0.00          H+0
CONECT    1    2    6    9    0                                     NONE 31
CONECT    2    1    3   14    0                                     NONE 32
CONECT    3    2    4    8    0                                     NONE 33
CONECT    4    3    5    7    0                                     NONE 34
CONECT    5    4    6   15    0                                     NONE 35
CONECT    6    5    1   16    0                                     NONE 36
CONECT    7    4   17    0    0                                     NONE 37
CONECT    8    3   18    0    0                                     NONE 38
CONECT    9    1   10   11   19                                     NONE 39
CONECT   10    9   20    0    0                                     NONE 40
CONECT   11    9   12   21   22                                     NONE 41
CONECT   12   11   13   23    0                                     NONE 42
CONECT   13   12   24   25   26                                     NONE 43
END                                                                 NONE 44
```

Figure A.1 (*Continued*)

CT File Format

The structure of the CT file is straightforward. The file is segmented into several parts, including a header block, the counts line, the atom block, the bond block, and other information. The header block is the first three lines of the file and includes the name of the molecule (line 1); the user's name, program, date, and other information (line 2); and comments (line 3). The next line of the file is the counts line and contains the number of molecules and the number of bonds as the first two entries. The next set of lines is the atom block that describes the properties of individual atoms in the molecule; each contains the *X*-, *Y*-, and *Z*-coordinate and the chemical symbol for an individual atom. The next set of lines is the bonds block that describes the properties of individual bonds in the molecule; each line contains the number (starting with 1) of the two atoms making up the bond and an indication of whether the bond is single, double, triple, etc. After these lines are more lines with additional descriptions of the molecule that we will not use for our discussion. An example of a simple CT file format file for a molecule is given in Figure B.1. The full description of the file format used is dated June 2005 and may be found in the CTfile format document available from Elsevier MDL (`http://www.mdl.com`) at `http://www.mdl.com/downloads/public/ctfile/ctfile.pdf` as of this book's publication.

Obviously there are many pieces of information in the file that are of interest to the chemist, and in fact this is an extremely simple example of a file. But for our project we are interested only in the geometry of the molecule, so the additional information in the file must be skipped when the file is read.

```
L-Alanine (13C)

GSMACCS-II10169115362D 1 0.00366 0.00000 0

6 5 0 0 1 0 3 V2000

-0.6622   0.5342  0.0000 C    0 0 2 0 0 0
 0.6220  -0.3000  0.0000 C    0 0 0 0 0 0
-0.7207   2.0817  0.0000 C    1 0 0 0 0 0
-1.8622  -0.3695  0.0000 N    0 3 0 0 0 0
 0.6220  -1.8037  0.0000 O    0 0 0 0 0 0
 1.9464   0.4244  0.0000 O    0 5 0 0 0 0
1 2 1 0 0 0
1 3 1 1 0 0
1 4 1 0 0 0
2 5 2 0 0 0
2 6 1 0 0 0
M CHG 2 4 1 6 -1
M ISO 1 3 13
M END
```

Figure B.1 Example of a simple molecule file in CT file format.

STL File Format

The STL (sometimes called StL) file format was developed by 3D Systems of Valencia, California. It is used to describe a file that contains information for 3D hardcopy systems. The name *STL* comes from stereo lithography, one of the technologies for 3D hardcopy, but the format is used in several other hardcopy technologies as described in Chapter 15. The information here is adapted from the description from the telemanufacturing facility at Oregon State Center for 3D Hardcopy (C3H).

The .stl or stereolithography format describes an ASCII or binary file used in manufacturing. It is a list of the triangular surfaces that describe a computer-generated solid model. This is the standard input for most rapid prototyping machines as described in Chapter 15 on hardcopy. The binary format for the file is the most compact, but here we describe only the ASCII format because it is easier to understand and easier to generate as the output of student projects.

The ASCII .stl file must start with the lowercase keyword `solid` and end with `endsolid`. Within these keywords are listings of individual triangles that define the faces of the solid model. Each individual triangle description defines a single normal vector directed away from the solid's surface followed by the *x-y-z* components for all three of the vertices. These values are all in Cartesian coordinates and are floating-point values. The triangle values should all be positive and be contained within the building volume. The maximum building volume will vary from machine to machine, but a typical size is 0 to 14 inches in *x,* 0 to 10 in *y*, and 0 to 12 in *z*. You should consider scaling or rotating your model to optimize construction time, strength, and scrap removal. The normal vector is a unit vector of length 1 based at the origin. If the normals are not included then most software will generate them using the right-hand rule. If the normal information is not included then the normal line should still be used and the three values for the normal should be set to 0.0. Following is a sample ASCII description of a single triangle within an STL file.

```
solid
...
facet normal 0.00 0.00 1.00
    outer loop
        vertex 2.00 2.00 0.00
        vertex -1.00 1.00 0.00
        vertex 0.00 -1.00 0.00
    endloop
endfacet
...
endsolid
```

When the triangle coordinates are generated by a computer program, it is not unknown for roundoff errors to accumulate to the case where points that should be the same have slightly different coordinates. For example, if you were to calculate the points on a circle by incrementing the angle as you move around the circle, you might well end up with a final point that is slightly different from the initial point. This will leave a gap in your object definition that can cause problems in any actual manufacture from your file. File-checking software will note any difference between points and may well tell you that your object is not closed, but that same software will often "heal" small gaps in objects automatically, so you need to be sure that you did not intend the gap to be present.

Vertex-to-Vertex Rule

The most common error in an STL file is noncompliance with the vertex-to-vertex rule. The STL specifications require that all adjacent triangles have two common vertices. This is illustrated in Figure C.1. The image on the left shows a top triangle containing a total of four vertex points. The outer vertices of the top triangle are not shared with one and only one other single triangle. The lower two triangles each contain one of the points as well as the fourth invalid vertex point. To make this valid under the vertex to vertex rule, the top triangle must be subdivided as in the example on the right.

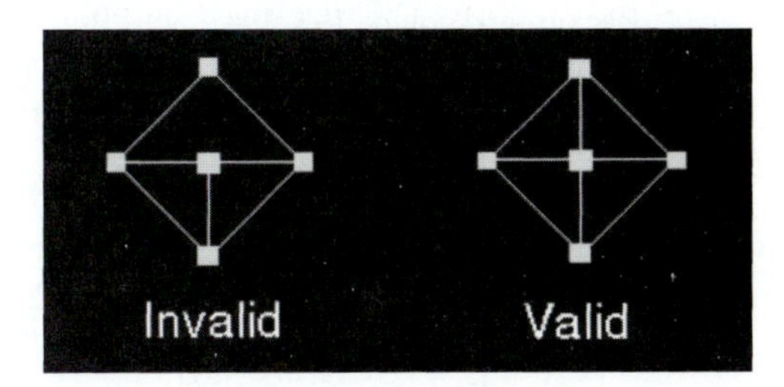

Figure C.1 Invalid vertex (*left*) with adjacent triangles that do not share the vertex in the center; valid vertex (*right*).

Index

A

B

C

D

N

O

P

Q

R

T

U

V

W

Z